THE BEACH BOYS

THE DEFINITIVE DIARY OF AMERICA'S GREATEST BAND: ON STAGE AND IN THE STUDIO

KEITH BADMAN

A BACKBEAT BOOK
First edition 2004
Published by Backbeat Books
600 Harrison Street
San Francisco
CA 94107, US
www.backbeatbooks.com

An imprint of The Music Player Network, United Entertainment Media Inc.

Devised and published for Backbeat books by Outline Press Ltd, 2A Union Court,
20-22 Union Road, London SW4 6JP, England
www.backbeatuk.com

ISBN 0-87930-818-4

EDITOR Tony Bacon
ART DIRECTOR Nigel Osborne
DESIGN Paul Cooper Design
PICTURE RESEARCH Andy Neill, Peter Symes, Keith Badman

Origination and print by Colorprint (Kong Kong)

04 05 06 07 08 5 4 3 2 1

The
Beach

THE DEFINITIVE DIARY OF AMERICA'S GREATEST BAND
ON STAGE AND IN THE STUDIO

Boys

KEITH BADMAN

Contents

1961

In Hawthorne, California, Al Jardine and Brian Wilson start to play music with Mike Love, Carl Wilson and Dennis Wilson as The Pendletones ... the group records demos and then masters, including 'Surfin', at music-publisher Hite Morgan's studio in Los Angeles ... 'Surfin' single released on Candix label and credited to The Beach Boys ... the newly-named group begins playing concerts.

page 8

1962

Al Jardine leaves The Beach Boys and David Marks replaces him ... Capitol Records signs the group ... first Capitol single 'Surfin' Safari' released ... first major tour is a 40-date Midwest jaunt ... first Capitol album Surfin' Safari recorded and released ... Capitol agrees to Brian's bold suggestion that he should produce the group and record them in non-Capitol studios.

page 18

Special Christmas Bonus from The Beach Boys
Little Saint Nick #5096

1963

First serious sessions at Western Recorders, Hollywood, and Gold Star, Los Angeles, which become the group's favourite studios from now ... second album Surfin' USA recorded and released, hitting number 2 in the charts ... US television debut ... 'Surfin' USA' peaks at number 3, the group's first Top Ten single ... Brian begins to miss some live performances, and embarks on sole production of Beach Boys sessions, often using session musicians ... Surfer Girl album recorded and released ... David Marks leaves the group ... Brian plays more live shows until Al Jardine rejoins the group ... Little Deuce Coupe album recorded and released.

page 30

1964

Shut Down Volume 2 album recorded and released ... first overseas tour, to Australia and New Zealand, supporting Roy Orbison ... 'Fun Fun Fun' single hits US number 5 ... Brian detects worrying competition as Beatlemania hits America ... All Summer Long album recorded and released, with Brian determined to demonstrate the group's musical strengths ... Murry Wilson is fired as manager ... 'I Get Around' is the group's first number 1 single ... Christmas Album recorded and released ... Concert album recorded and released, their first number 1 LP ... 'When I Grow Up (To Be A Man)' and 'Dance Dance Dance' singles recorded and released ... sessions begin for Today! album ... promotional tour of the UK and live dates in Europe ... Brian shows strain as the group's success demands ever-busier schedules; he suffers a nervous breakdown and withdraws from live shows ... Glen Campbell steps in at short notice as Brian's replacement on stage.

page 46

1965

Recording sessions for Today! album continue ... Brian announces he will cease to appear on stage with the group and intends to focus on composition and studio production ... Glen Campbell plays more dates as Brian's stage replacement ... Today! album released, with a whole side of Brian's 'new music' ... Summer Days (And Summer Nights!!) album recorded and released ... 'Help Me Rhonda' is the group's second number 1 single ... Bruce Johnston takes over as a permanent replacement for Brian on live shows and also starts contributing to recording sessions ... 'California Girls' is a US number 3 single ... unplugged Party! album recorded and released ... Brian installs his piano in a sandbox at his new Beverly Hills home ... 'The Girl I Once Knew' single recorded and released ... recordings are begun that will end up on next year's Pet Sounds album ... Brian hears The Beatles' new Rubber Soul album, considers it a challenge, and starts writing songs with lyricist Tony Asher ... 'Barbara Ann' is a US number 2 and UK number 3 single.

page 80

GOOD VIBRATIONS

NUMBER 1 IN THE USA

NUMBER 1 IN ENGLAND

Coming—With the Good Vibrations Sound!

SMILE · THE BEACH BOYS

DT 2580

Capitol RECORDS

1966

The group makes their first tour of Japan ... meanwhile in California, Brian officially starts work in the studio with the regular session team for the new album, which becomes *Pet Sounds* ... between tours and one-off dates the rest of the group gathers for vocal recordings ... sessions begin for 'Good Vibrations' ... 'Caroline No' single released, credited to Brian Wilson ... 'Sloop John B' single and *Pet Sounds* album released ... Brian begins writing songs with Van Dyke Parks, and sessions start to record their 'Heroes And Villains' ... 'Good Vibrations' sessions continue ... *Best Of* album released less than two months after *Pet Sounds* ... sessions begin for a new album, *Smile*, which Capitol schedules for Christmas release ... 'Good Vibrations' is at last completed and released, and goes to number 1 ... plans begin to create group's own

Brother Records ... the touring band plays in Europe as 'Heroes & Villains' and *Smile* sessions continue in California ... the group expresses unease with Brian's musical direction and he becomes uncertain about the *Smile* album; Capitol postpones its release until next year.

page 106

1967

Sessions for *Smile* and 'Heroes And Villains' continue ... Beach Boys file a lawsuit against Capitol for 'missing' royalties ... Brian plans a studio in his new Bel Air home ... Brian and songwriting partner Van Dyke Parks part company ... *Inside Pop* CBS TV documentary airs with Brian performing 'Surf's Up' ... European tour ... *Smile* album is abandoned ... work on *Smiley Smile* album starts, mostly at Brian's new home studio ... 'Heroes And Villains' is finally completed ... Beach Boys do not make their scheduled appearance at Monterey Pop festival ... Capitol dispute is settled and Brother Records is announced ... 'Heroes And Villains' single makes US number 12 and UK number 8 ... 'Gettin' Hungry' single, credited to Brian & Mike, fails to chart ... *Smiley*

Smile album released, baffling fans and critics and charting at a disappointing US number 41 ... *Wild Honey* album is recorded, once more largely at Brian's home studio and with the group now playing their own instruments again ... *Wild Honey* album is released … the group's critical hipness and record sales are in decline.

page 170

1968

The group, and especially Mike, become enthralled by the Maharishi and Transcendental Meditation ... recording sessions are held for the *Friends* album ... Mike flies to India to study alongside The Beatles with the Maharishi ... the group's Southern US tour is largely cancelled or re-scheduled following the murder of Martin Luther King ... Dennis meets Charles Manson ... a mostly ill-attended Beach Boys US tour with the Maharishi is halted after just seven dates ... sessions take place for *20/20* album ... *Friends* album released, but its chart peak at 126 marks the group's worst sales performance to date ... 'Do It Again' single makes US number 20 and a UK number 1 ... in a bizarre attempt to boost the group's flagging US sales, Capitol releases the *Stack-o-Tracks* backing-tracks-only album ... European tour takes place, with London performances recorded for a future live album.

page 210

1969

Recording sessions begin for a new album, to become next year's *Sunflower* ... *20/20* album released ... 'I Can Hear Music' single makes US number 24 and UK number 10 ... The Beach Boys' record label Brother Records is again launched ... Brian announces that the group has severe financial problems, soon denied by Bruce ... European tour takes place, including dates in Czechoslovakia ... on tour in London, Carl spots South African group The Flames that includes future Beach Boys Blondie Chaplin and Ricky Fataar ... 'Break Away' single makes US number 63 and UK number 6 ... Capitol contract

expires with one album still due ... deal with German label Deutsche Grammophon fails ... sessions for the album that becomes *Sunflower* continue ... The Beach Boys sign a new recording contract with Warner/Reprise ... Murry Wilson sells entire publishing rights to the group's original songs.

page 238

1970

Sessions conclude for *Sunflower* album, the first version of which is rejected by new label Warner/Reprise ... re-recordings and new work follow in the studio ... tour of New Zealand and Australia ... 'Cotton Fields' single fails to chart in the US but goes to number 2 in the UK and number 1 in Australia ... last Capitol album *Live In London* released in UK ... Warner/Reprise rejects a further version of the new album ... pressure builds as US-only single 'Slip On Through' fails to chart ... Warner/Reprise finally accepts the group's revised master tape and the *Sunflower* album is subsequently released to good reviews but poor sales ... Jack Rieley becomes The Beach Boys' new manager ... Dennis is filmed for his appearances in the *Two-Lane Blacktop* movie ... sessions start for next album, to become *Surf's Up* ... the group plays two acclaimed sets at the Big Sur festival in California that mark a return to critical hipness ... European tour, with support from Blondie and Ricky's group, subtly renamed as The Flame.

page**260**

1971

Recordings continue for *Surf's Up* album ... Dennis injures his hand badly in an accident and will not play drums again until 1974 ... Ricky Fataar takes Dennis's place on the drum stool for live dates ... *Surf's Up* album released ... the hip-again Beach Boys make the cover of *Rolling Stone* ... sessions begin for the next album, to become *Carl And The Passions – "So Tough"*.

page**286**

1972

The group decides to shift their recording base from Los Angeles to The Netherlands ... drummer Ricky Fataar and guitarist Blondie Chaplin officially join The Beach Boys ... sessions continue in California for the new album *Carl And The Passions – "So Tough"* ... Bruce Johnston leaves the group ... *Carl And The Passions* album released ... sessions start in The Netherlands for a new album, which becomes *Holland* ... Warner/Reprise rejects the first version of *Holland* and so the group replaces 'We Got Love' with the more commercial 'Sail On Sailor'.

page**300**

1973

Holland album released, including Brian's *Mount Vernon And Fairway* EP ... 'Sail On Sailor' single released ... Murry Wilson dies of a heart attack at 56 ... Brian withdraws further from the world while the live band continues to tour ... *In Concert* double-album released, becoming the group's first gold record for Warner/Reprise ... Blondie Chaplin leaves The Beach Boys.

page**324**

1974

Chicago's producer/manager James Guercio joins the group as occasional stage bassist and part-time manager ... *Endless Summer* compilation double-album released by Capitol, becoming a great success ... support tour with Crosby Stills Nash & Young ... attempts to record a new album abandoned ... Ricky Fataar leaves the group and Dennis returns to the drums ... 'Child Of Winter' single released, the first new Beach Boys material on record for nearly two years.

page**334**

1975

'Sail On Sailor' single re-released in the US, making number 49 ... Capitol releases another successful compilation album, *Spirit Of America* ... 'Beachago' US tour sees The Beach Boys and Chicago joining forces ... brief visit to the UK for a show at Wembley Stadium with Elton John ... Warner/Reprise also releases a compilation album, *Good Vibrations* ... psychiatrist Dr Eugene Landy is hired to treat Brian's continuing insecurity.

page**344**

1976

Recording sessions begin for a new album, to become *15 Big Ones* ... 'Rock And Roll Music', the first Beach Boys single for 16 months, makes number 5 in the US ... *15 Big Ones* marks Brian's 'comeback' and is the group's first studio album since 1973 ... in the US an NBC TV special and a *People* magazine

Introduction

cover-story mark the group's 15th anniversary ... Dennis works on solo-album recordings, to become *Pacific Ocean Blue* ... Brian begins essentially solo sessions for a new album, which becomes 1977's *The Beach Boys Love You* ... LA Forum show marks 15th anniversary of the first concert by The Beach Boys.

page356

POST-'76 ROUND-UP

... *The Beach Boys Love You* album ... Dennis's solo album, *Pacific Ocean Blue* ... first Caribou-label LP, *L.A. (Light Album)* ... Carl Wilson solo album ... 'Beach Boys Medley' single makes number 12 ... Mike's solo album, *Looking Back With Love* ... Dennis Wilson dies ... Beach Boys/Fat Boys single 'Wipe Out' makes number 12 ... 'Kokomo' single goes to number 1 ... *Good Vibrations* boxed set ... *Pet Sounds Sessions* boxed set ... Carl Wilson dies ... Brian's solo album, *Imagination*, and first solo tour ... Hawthorne, CA CD ... Brian tours, playing *Pet Sounds* and, later, *Smile*.

page371

Brian Wilson solo concerts 1995-2004 page379
Selected US/UK discography page380
Song recording index page382
Smile recording index page390
Session musicians page391
TV listings page393
Concert location index 1961–1976 page394
Special thanks page398

While researching a new article for *Record Collector* in June 2001 I emailed Joel McIver, a friend and colleague at the magazine, asking if he could check out a Beach Boys concert date. This long-running monthly music magazine regularly receives all the latest music books for review and has naturally built up an impressive library. So I was certain that a definitive day-by-day book on America's greatest band would reside on their shelves.

Fifteen minutes after my original request, Joel replied saying he couldn't find the information, nor a book in which my question could be answered. Surprised there was nothing at the magazine's offices, I started to search for a Beach Boys day-by-day book at all the relevant internet sites. Several hours later, I discovered that no such book had ever been published. I was aghast. Tomes dissecting the activities of the other great artists from the 1960s and 1970s – The Beatles, The Rolling Stones, Elvis Presley, Bob Dylan – have been appearing with varying degrees of success for many years but, strangely, not one exists that definitively documents America's Beach Boys. So, as the saying goes, if you can't find a book that you're after, then you should do it yourself.

The Beach Boys have always been among my four all-time favourite music groups. (For the record, the others are The Monkees, The Byrds and, of course, The Beatles.) As a child, I heard The Beach Boys' recording of 'Country Air' and was knocked out by the superb vocals and beautiful melody. I fondly remember being swept away by the marvellously intricate arrangements and optimism of 'Wouldn't It Be Nice', and I shall always recall with great affection my reaction when I first heard the opening notes of 'Good Vibrations'. That rush of excitement still surrounds me whenever I listen to the track today.

The group's 1970 *Greatest Hits* compilation was a fixture on my turntable for years and would often share space alongside the work of The Beatles. I soon realised that The Beach Boys were more than just a hits band when I listened to *Pet Sounds* – still one of my favourite albums. My realisation was confirmed when their 1970 album *Sunflower* found its way to my record player – and I continue today to tell the world just how great is that largely forgotten and underrated album.

By the middle of 2001 I had completed three well-received books on The Beatles. I knew that a day-by-day examination and analysis on the boys from California would be a brand new kind of rock book, and so I emailed my then publisher with the idea. A rejection soon followed, so I turned my attentions to a friend, Tony Bacon at Backbeat UK. I loved their stupendous book *Beatles Gear* and felt that Backbeat UK could do justice to my Beach Boys idea. Five minutes after I had sent a proposal to Tony outlining my plan I had a reply from him with a resounding "Yes". I was in business, and work on my Beach Boys book was about to begin. Three hectic and action-packed years later, here it is ... a near definitive book on America's greatest band, released exactly 40 years since they first hit the American number 1 position with 'I Get Around'.

I sincerely hope that you enjoy reading this book as much I've enjoyed researching it. I hope that it will help you appreciate the immense amount of work that went into creating the music that Brian Wilson and The Beach Boys gave us over the years. On behalf of myself and the legions of music fans around the world, thank you, boys, so very, very much.

Keith Badman,
Berkshire, England
May 2004

1961

In Hawthorne, California, Al Jardine and Brian Wilson start to play music with Mike Love, Carl Wilson and Dennis Wilson as The Pendletones ... the group records demos and then masters, including 'Surfin'', at music-publisher Hite Morgan's studio in Los Angeles ... 'Surfin'' single released on Candix label and credited to The Beach Boys ... the newly-named group begins playing concerts.

The Rendezvous Ballroom, scene of The Beach Boys' first public appearance on December 23rd 1961.

In The Beginning...

Murry and Audree Wilson, the parents of Brian, Carl and Dennis, moved to Hawthorne, California, in the 1940s. Hawthorne is situated in rural south-eastern Alachua County, very close to the boundary with Putnam County. Observers often comment on two features about Hawthorne: it has been a crossroads, and it is located in an area of natural beauty where sportsmen have found abundant fish and wildlife.

Hawthorne is named for James Madison Hawthorn, a veteran of the Second Seminole War against American Indians. He received a land grant on the north-west side of Lake Johnson and donated some of his property to encourage development of the Peninsular Railroad line that was completed from Waldo to Ocala in 1879. Hawthorne – a 30-mile car ride from the heart of Los Angeles – had grown to a thriving little town of over 100 homes by 1907. In its early days there was just one grocery store, and meat was brought by wagon from Inglewood three times a week. There was a furniture factory, an overalls factory, a glove factory, and an art leather firm. A small building served as both church and school. The school had 16 pupils ranging from kindergarten age to late teens.

Mail service began in the area in October 1908. In 1921, the city's population had reached 2,000, and by July the following year it had become a legal corporation. Many emigrants from the Oklahoma and Texas dust bowl settled there, and the first census, taken in 1930, noted 6,595 residents. Nine years later, Northrop Aircraft Inc moved to Hawthorne with 50 people on the payroll. (Later the company became Northrop Corporation and then Northrop Grumman Corporation.) Dozens of firms moved to Hawthorne to acquire Northrop subcontracts. From that time, industrial and commercial development in Hawthorne proceeded at a steady pace. Northrop and Hawthorne enjoyed a long period of prosperity and co-operation. With the growth of the aviation industry and the subsequent aerospace industry, the area became known as the Cradle Of Aviation and for many years enjoyed a boom in both jobs and real estate. The City of Hawthorne had within a relatively short space of time grown from a small, largely rural community to a well-rounded mixture of business, industries and homes.

It was into this typically suburban, post-World War II stucco community that the Wilsons moved. Murry Gage Wilson had been born July 2nd 1917 in Hutchison, Kansas; his wife Audree Neva Korthof on September 28th 1918 in Minneapolis, Minnesota. Five-year-old Murry Wilson, his sister Emily and their parents had migrated to Los Angeles in 1922 during the great flight from the dust bowl. They couldn't afford to buy a house and so were forced to take up residence in a tent on the beach alongside thousands of other Depression-hit families. The Korthof family, including ten-year-old Audree, came to Los Angeles in 1928. To all of them, California is the dream world, the so-called promised land.

They had met while studying at the Washington High School and married in Los Angeles on March 26th 1938. Both wanted a better life than their parents and to help fulfil their dreams put down $2,300 on a small, two-bedroom house at 3701, West 119th Street, Hawthorne, shortly after the birth of their second son, Dennis, on December 4th 1944. Their first child was Brian Douglas Wilson, born June 20th 1942; their third and last was Carl Dean Wilson, born December 21st 1946.

By day, pipe-smoking Murry was running ABLE (Always Better Lasting Equipment), a small company importing lathes and drills from England, essential items for Hawthorne's aviation industry. Self-made Murry had started his company with money borrowed against his Hawthorne home. Before, he'd worked on an assembly line at Goodyear, and it was there in the spring of 1945 that he had lost his right eye in an industrial accident. Murry would brag to his three sons that losing an eye was the best thing that ever happened to him because it taught him to fight. In the summer, shortly after his return to work, he moved to Garrett Air Research, and went on to set up ABLE in 1950.

Murry's greatest passion was music, though he was becoming increasingly frustrated in his futile attempts to become a famously successful songwriter. Some of his songs had been recorded – for instance 'Fiesta Day Polka', 'Hide My Tears' and 'His Little Darling' – and once he had even written English lyrics to the B-side of a Gordon MacRae single. It was a job for which he claimed he was never paid. His greatest triumph was probably 'Two Step Side Step' which Lawrence Welk's orchestra played regularly as part of their weekly live radio broadcasts in 1952.

The Wilson's home in Hawthorne would often reverberate to the sounds of the family and their cousin, Mike Love, as they sang and played music. Michael Edward Love was born to Murry's sister Emily (known as Glee) and her husband Milton on March 15th 1941 in Baldwin Hills, Los Angeles, California.

"There was a lot of music in the house, always," said Carl in *Tiger Beat*, "from when we were very, very young. We had two jukeboxes and two pianos." Audree would play the Hammond organ and Murry would plonk on a piano in the den, a converted garage. "My dad scratched tunes on the piano," Dennis remembered later in *Disc & Music Echo*, "and my mum, she played the organ: not very good, but she had a good sense of chords." Murry reminisced in *Rolling Stone*: "We'd play duets, my wife and I, and then Brian would get in the act and sing. All they ever heard was music in the house. And, on occasions, family arguments."

Murry may have loved music, but he was also a very strict father. If Brian, Dennis or Carl misbehaved, however tamely, it would often be met with a heavy blow or a humiliating punishment. Dennis's hands were often scalded with boiling water. In another incident, Murry forced Dennis to eat tomatoes until he was physically sick, a punishment for his son's refusal to eat the vegetable when it was served up on his dinner plate. Murry's tyranny stretched to tying Brian to a tree as punishment for a petty misdemeanour. He also enjoyed torturing his sons by removing his glass replacement eye and forcing them to look inside the empty, mangled socket.

Some believe that Brian's deafness in his right ear originated in a sharp blow dealt to his head by Murry when Brian was just three years old. "My dad was a very inspirational person in my life," Brian admitted on US TV in 1999, "but he was also the worst person I ever met in my life. He yelled so loud, you could have sworn that the devil was in the room. He was the loudest yeller I ever heard in my life. He was such a terrorist. He beat us up so badly that we had no choice but to lay on our beds and cry after we got beat. He'd punish us over things like the lawn, or over the dishes we didn't do … the simple chores around the house. Our dad was like the devil on our neighbourhood. The worst person. He hit me with a two by four, right to the side of my head. He totally put my right ear out. He made me so deaf."

But Murry was quick to dispel this story. "He was injured in some football game or maybe it just happened," he recalled in *Rolling Stone*. "Who knows? I never hit my kid on the ear. I spanked his bottom, you know, like any father would do to a kid.

But I never hit my son Brian on the ear. Never. When he was 11, Audree, his mother, discovered that he kept turning his head. She found out that he couldn't hear very well out of that ear." Audree, also talking to *Rolling Stone* later, said: "Brian thinks his deafness happened when he was ten. Some kids down the street whacked him in the ear. It's a damaged nerve so he could have been born that way."

Brian, Dennis and Carl soon realised that a quick way to their father's affection was through music. As a child, Brian loved the music of George Gershwin and fell in love with his 'Rhapsody In Blue'. As a teenager, encouraged by his mother, Brian would grow to love the singing group The Four Freshmen, passionately studying their intricate, close-knit harmonies. He said on US radio in 1964: "I used to sit by my mum and dad's hi-fi and I would play a little bit of the Four Freshmen's music, take the needle off the record and go to the piano and try and figure out the music. It took me about a year of hard work trying to work out their harmonies." In turn, Brian would teach these harmonies to Murry, Audree and Carl. "The four of us would just harmonise," Brian remembered in the 1998 *Endless Harmony* documentary. "We'd love it. But Dennis wasn't good enough. He was too stupid to learn."

Murry realised very soon that Brian had a gift for music and made sure that he could have any musical instrument and any tuition he wanted. Despite this wide-open opportunity, Brian chose a six-week lesson on the accordion. At school in his teenage years Brian was a good student and, for a short time, a competitive athlete. Later, he enjoyed cruising the six-lane Hawthorne Boulevard with his cousin Mike Love in a car given to Brian by Murry as a present.

Carl Wilson: "The Beach Boys grew up in the Golden State Of Plenty. We always got what we wanted. I can't remember ever wanting anything that I couldn't have."

1950: a special Christmas concert

Dennis Wilson enters York Elementary School in Hawthorne, California and regularly attends Inglewood Covenant Church with the rest of his family. Dennis recalls later in *Disc*: "I went to church because there was this outasight chick there and they made me get on my hands and knees and beg for forgiveness. I didn't know for what. I didn't know for why. What did I do? I used to try and play boogie woogie on the church piano on Friday nights when all the kids went there to play volleyball."

On Christmas Day, Murry Wilson's sister Emily – Mike Love's mother – arranges a private Christmas-night concert showcasing Murry's songs. The highlight comes with eight-year-old Brian singing a song of Mike's entitled 'The Old Soldier'.

Murry Wilson says that his sister Emily – Mike's mother – loved music. "She didn't play music or anything but she loved music and she gave this concert in my honour as a songwriter. She even hired a trio, a musical group, to play my songs for the concert. It was for school friends and teachers and friends of hers. For the concert, I bought Brian his first suit with long pants and he brought the house down. Brian showed early promise."

Mike Love will tell *Rolling Stone*: "There was one time a year when the Wilson family and the Love family would get together, and that was at Christmas time. We would do Christmas carols and get together, musically. It was a very loose structure. It was all very innocent. It was a natural expression of joyful happiness."

The following year, Murry Wilson becomes friendly with Hite and Dorinda Morgan, a husband and wife team who own Guild Music publishers in Los Angeles and run their own recording studio. They will later publish some of his songs.

1953: "the most messed-up person I know"

Dennis Wilson: "The Beach Boys were born in the back of a car, musically at any rate. My dad worked for $15,000 a year in aviation and on Fridays he'd get his pay cheque and we'd pick him up in the car. We used to sing 'Smokey Joe's Cafe' in the back seat. That's how it started."

Murry Wilson tells *Rolling Stone*: "The Wilson boys always heard music in their home from my writing songs and the friends who came over. We were so poor we'd just sit around singing and on occasions drinking a glass of beer. Not the children, but the adults."

Dennis Wilson tells *New Musical Express* later: "If my dad hadn't given me a BB gun when I was nine years old, my life would have been completely different. With that gun I had something I could take my anger out on. Hunting, fishing, racing have been my preoccupations ever since. After I got that gun, I built a fort in a tree in our back yard. Whenever my parents got me upset, I'd go and sit in the fort and start shooting, at birds, windows, trees, fences … anything. I was in a completely different world out there: my own. I was like that in school, too: in my own world. And I always made trouble, or it made me. If anything wrong happened within a 20-mile radius some people would say, 'Dennis Wilson did it,' and lots of times I did. I must be the only guy in Hawthorne ever to knock down two trees and a lamp post on the front lawn of the police station."

Carl Wilson tells *Rolling Stone*: "[Dennis] has the most nervous energy. I've witnessed energy like that. There was a big drain ditch near where we used to live. It was really dark down there and you could take it from right by our house all the way to the beach. We'd ride our bikes down it and the trip was to see how far you could go without getting scared out of your mind. It was a daredevil thing. I believe Dennis probably did go in the furthest." Brian Wilson says in *Melody Maker*: "Dennis had to keep moving all the time. If you wanted him to sit still for one second, he's yelling and screaming and ranting and raving. He's the most messed-up person I know."

1954: the Four Freshmen effect

Twelve-year-old Brian is taken by Murry to a Sunday-night concert by The Four Freshmen at the Coconut Grove in Los Angeles. The family finances restrict Murry to taking only his eldest son. After the show, Brian nervously meets the group backstage. The evening is a monumental event in Brian's life; back home he begins to explore as many records by the group as he can find, writing down every note so that the Wilson family can faithfully sing the tunes around the piano.

Brian Wilson says in the *Endless Harmony* film: "I got so into The Four Freshmen. I could identify with Bob Flanagan's high voice. He taught me how to sing high. I worked for a year on The Four Freshmen with my hi-fi set. I eventually learned every song they did." Carl Wilson will tell *Tiger Beat*: "I remember when I was eight years old [Brian] used to say, 'Mum, make Carl sing arrangements.' "

FOLLOWING PAGES American singing group The Four Freshmen pictured in the mid 1950s, when Brian sees them for the first time. Their vocal harmonies will have a great influence on his musical development.

1955: Disney boys

The Jardine family, with son Alan – born Alan Charles Jardine on September 3rd 1942 in Lima, Ohio – moves to California from Lima. Also this year, the Disneyland amusement park opens in Anaheim, California, and the Wilson family visit twice a year. Dennis particularly likes Tom Sawyer Island.

1956: Brian sees stars

Brian Wilson will tell a US TV interviewer: "My dad had me stick my hand under a boat that was held up by some bricks. He said, 'Hey, put your hands right there.' I did it, he knocked the bricks away, and the boat came down on my hands. He was laughing at me while I cried. I was 14 then. It really screwed my head up." Those close to the Wilson family believe that as Murry becomes more aware of his son's flourishing musical abilities he is also becoming increasingly jealous.

1957: football vs. music

In the spring, following an introduction by Murry's publishing friend Dorinda Morgan, Brian unsuccessfully auditions for Art Laboe's Original Sound label in Los Angeles.

On November 7th Al Jardine breaks his leg at Hawthorne High School in Culver City in a playing-field collision with Hawthorne High Cougar quarterback Brian Wilson, who calls one play and executes another. Al, a singer in folk group The Islanders and another big fan of The Four Freshmen, becomes Brian's friend. Brian is a good student but is more interested in music than sport. In his senior year he quits the football team to concentrate on music. This upsets the school's football coach who refuses to speak to Brian for the rest of the year.

1958: go-carts and tape recorders

The Marks family moves from Pennsylvania to Hawthorne. They take up residence in a motel across the street from MGM Studios and, a year later, move to 11901 Almertens Place, on the border between Inglewood and Hawthorne, close to the Wilsons. David Lee Marks (born August 22nd 1948 in Pennsylvania) will ride his skateboard right opposite the Wilson family home. Marks recalls later in an interview with Scott Keller: "Carl and Dennis were across the street, throwing trash over and doing that kind of thing. Dennis was called Dennis The Menace by his friends because of his raucous behaviour. Dennis and I got really tight and we did all sorts of creepy kid things together. There was a long drainage ditch with a quarter-mile of dead grass in it that we set on fire with alcohol from my chemistry set, then watched while three companies of firemen raced over to put it out. We chopped trees down in the park, then lied our way out of it when the cops came to our houses. Murry ran a machine shop and had a few bucks, so he was always buying them go-carts, spoiling them. I would be over there, playing with their go-carts and telescopes, hanging out. Dennis was a real bully then, punching kids in the mouth, and I was always glad to be on his side."

Carl remembers: "None of us had childhood dreams of growing up and singing for a living. Dennis wanted to be a racing-car driver, Mike didn't know what he wanted to do, and Brian never had any other dream than writing and composing. Leading a pop-song group never entered his head. My big interest then was a tree fort in two eucalyptus trees in the back yard of our house in Hawthorne. Dennis and I also used to play with kids down the street who had an even better fort in a bigger tree. One day, Dennis took the ladder away when I was up there so I couldn't get down. All the kids thought it was hilarious. My older brother, Brian, even when he was a senior, was always great to me. His girlfriends would talk to me and say, 'Ah, ain't he cute?'"

For Brian's 16th birthday – Friday June 20th – his parents give him a Wollensak tape recorder. Working with Carl, Murry and Audree, Brian makes his first four-part harmony recordings. Dennis tells *Disc*: "Brian was the freak. He used to stay in his room all day listening to records rather than play baseball. If you could get me to sing a song, yeah, I'd get into it. But I'd much rather play doctor with the girl next door or muck around with cars. My friend's dad had a 1950 Henry J, the ugliest car in the world. We were about 14. We'd get up around midnight, climb out the window, push the car about three or four blocks, hot wire it, and drive around."

This autumn Carl begins to take guitar lessons from a neighbour, 16 year-old John Maus, later to become a member of The Walker Brothers. Carl remembers later in *Tiger Beat*: "I was 10 or 11 before I held a guitar in my hands and plucked my first string. A friend of my parents, a fantastic guitarist, often dropped by to play and visit. Whenever he put down the guitar I'd grab it and start messing around, looking for chords and melodies. My folks bought me a guitar when I was 12.

"I took a few lessons from a teacher but soon got bored and quit because he had me playing simple things like 'Yankee Doodle' whereas I was already more advanced than that. Later I had lessons from John Maus. He only asked for $5 an hour. I was very enthusiastic and he was very kind. John was five years older than I was. We spent much time together, not only on lessons but we also hung out in bands and we went surfing together. He was a great teacher."

Maus also teaches guitar to the Wilsons' neighbour David Marks. Marks recalls later in *Trouser Press*: "I got a guitar for Christmas and took a few lessons from John. Carl had taken up guitar in high school and sat in with John's band for a few bar gigs, so he and I started doing Ventures tunes, sitting around the living room, learning them off the records for our own amusement."

Meanwhile, future Beach Boy Bruce Johnston is beginning his affection for music. He will recall on US radio in 1965: "After I discovered music at a very young age, and [was] getting punished for singing harmony when I was about nine years old in school, rock'n'roll came to life with Elvis. By 1958, I was in a house band where, every Saturday night, we would back up whoever was on the charts and whoever came through our town. I spent a lot of time backing up Richie Valens. I even backed up Eddie Cochran once and The Everly Brothers."

1959: the other Beach Boys' debut

Mike Love graduates from Dorsey High in Los Angeles in June and begins working for his father's sheet-metal business. In the evenings he works the night shift at a nearby gas station. It's at this time that Brian and Carl join Mike in a performance at a high school talent show. Arwin Records release the Bruce & Jerry single 'Take This Pearl' / 'I Saw Her First' featuring future Beach Boy Bruce Johnston. In November drummer Sandy Nelson has a US and UK Top Ten hit with his 'Teen Beat' single, an instrumental that Johnston later claims he wrote with Nelson, although the song's writing credits suggest it is by Nelson and Arthur Egnoian, also known as Los Angeles DJ Art Laboe.

Two years before Mike, Al and the Wilson brothers, the 'Beach Boys' name first appears on record. A Coral 7-inch single, 'Island Melody', features a group of musicians using that name as they provide vocals on a recording by The Charles 'Bud' Dant Orchestra. Shortly afterwards, the same 'Beach Boys' will reiterate their roles on the single 'Bathing Beauty' coupled with 'The Beach At Sunset' on Kapp Records.

1960: Carl & The Passions

At a track meet at Hawthorne High the school coach catches Dennis smoking and makes him run the track daily until he promises to quit. He refuses. Dennis takes drum lessons at school; teacher Fred Morgan later refers to Dennis as "a beater, not a drummer" and "a fast learner when he wanted to learn".

That spring Brian Wilson, Carol Hess and some friends perform a campaign song for the benefit of a student-body presidential candidate at Hawthorne High. The song is Brian's reworking of 'Hully Gully'. It leads to further appearances for which Brian uses Mike Love and brother Carl alongside a friend from the earlier group. But Carl is hesitant about this new venture, and in order to appease him Brian calls the group Carl & The Passions.

Later line-ups will feature Bob Barrow, Bruce Griffin and Keith Lent. The group will open for another local singing group, The Four Preps, at a school assembly.

Al Jardine recalls later in *Rolling Stone*: "I saw Brian in concert with his brother, Carl. I was quite impressed by what I heard. I persuaded Brian to start thinking about doing some singing. We had no basis or anything. We were just pals on the football field." According to music teacher Fred Morgan, Brian flunks part of his senior-year music course because instead of handing in the sonata required he delivers a melody that will later become 'Surfin'.

In June, Al Jardine and Brian Wilson graduate from Hawthorne High School. Two months later, at Audree Wilson's suggestion, young songwriters Alan and Gary Winfrey approach publisher Hite Morgan with a tape that they've made which includes the Longfellow poem 'The Wreck Of The Hesperus' set to their own music. But the Morgans are in the process of building their studio and say they will call them back (see July 15th 1961).

Brian begins his freshman year at El Camino Community College in Los Angeles in September, majoring in psychology with additional music classes, and on the 16th Al Jardine starts at Ferris University in Big Rapids, Michigan, having followed his parents back to the Midwest. At the end of the year Mike Love's mother Emily is told that his girlfriend, Frances, is pregnant and throws Mike out of the house.

January

■ Wednesday 4th

Mike Love marries Frances St. Martin in Los Angeles. At present Mike spends much of his time with Dennis at Malibu or Redondo beach. It is during one such visit that an excited Mike tries to persuade Dennis to talk to Brian about starting a group.

June

"Dennis, listening to a group on his transistor radio, swore that we could sing better than they could and tossed out the idea of forming our own group," recalls Carl in *Rolling Stone*. "He promptly forgot the suggestion. The rest of us thought that he had a good idea but we didn't follow through."

■ Friday 9th

Al Jardine completes his freshman year at Ferris University in Big Rapids, Michigan, and returns to Los Angeles. He enrols at El Camino Community College where he meets Brian again and suggests they form a group. Brian suggests including Carl and Mike. Al also reforms his old folk group, The Islanders.

Murry Wilson will tell *Rolling Stone*: "It was 1961 when Mike Love and Al Jardine were coming over to the house and Brian was teaching them songs. They sang Four Freshmen songs almost like The Four Freshmen, except they had a sweeter, younger sound." The boys' friend David Marks recalls in *Trouser Press* magazine that Brian attends El Camino Junior College, studying music. "He was 18 and really into Chuck Berry and The Four Freshmen. He and his cousin Mike, plus Al Jardine from the junior college, had a little group, Kenny & The Kadets. They weren't into surf music; they just played for parties and bar mitzvahs. Brian and Carl were on separate trips at the time. Brian with his group, Carl jamming with me and with another guy up the street who had an accordion." Carl tells *Tiger Beat* that he didn't know Al until he was almost 15. "He began coming to the house with Brian's friends. Al didn't treat me like a little kid at all. So I thought he was the greatest guy in town."

David Marks: "But then Brian started taking advantage of the family situation. He was the big brother, and began to incorporate us all into his group. 'Hey, Carl, why don't you come over here and play this guitar part? I just made up this lick on the piano.' Dennis didn't play an instrument but started learning drums. I wasn't really in the group then, though. I was practising with them, but Al Jardine was playing upright bass with them. I was just their kid friend from across the street, going: 'Hey guys, can I play too? Can I, huh, huh?'"

July

Carl recalls later that Mike and Dennis return from a fishing trip where they have talked themselves into a state of high excitement about a group plan. "They were so jazzed up … they rushed home to tell us about it. Their excitement sparked a fire in Brian's brain and soon he was pounding his piano and working on lyrics and tunes with a frenzy."

1961

■ Saturday 15th

Also this summer, young songwriters Alan and Gary Winfrey are called back by Murry's music publisher friend Hite Morgan (see also 1960). Bob Barrow is away at college so Keith Lent takes his place for the performance, and Alan, Gary and Keith perform 'Rio Grande', written by Morgan's son Bruce. After the session, Brian Wilson is approached to help out with the group.

August

In Hawthorne, Al Jardine and Brian begin to play together with Mike Love, Mike's sister Maureen, and Carl Wilson. Maureen soon drops out. The group takes the name The Pendletones, hinting at the Pendleton plaid wool shirt worn jacket-style by surfers and others. "Brian thought that would be a real cool name," says David Marks, "since all the surfers wore Pendleton shirts."

Carl recalls later in *Tiger Beat* that all five begin practising vocal harmonies at every opportunity. "Mostly we sang Coasters songs and Freshmen arrangements as Brian was high on their style of vocalising."

■ Saturday 2nd – Wednesday 6th

Over the Labor Day holiday weekend the group rents instruments using $300 food money left by Murry, plus a little extra from Al's mother. They practice throughout the five days during Murry and Audree Wilson's absence on a vacation in Mexico City. Dennis recalls in *Disc*: "Our parents gave us $100 each for food, but we decided to form a band with the money. First of all I was going to play bass, and then I decided to play drums. I spent my $100 on a set of drums: one bass drum, a snare and a cymbal. Drums seemed to be more exciting. I could always play bass if I wanted to. I was 16 at the time. We played in the house but the neighbours phoned the police. We were in the south [of Los Angeles], a real white Anglo-Saxon Protestant area – that bullshit."

Carl: "My dad said, 'Here's $100 for each of you for food and drinks, and take care … and remember, no rock'n'roll.' 'Yes, dad,' we said. We bought a secondhand drum kit instead of food and drinks. The bass drum only had one skin. I already had a guitar, Al had a bass, and Mike came along to sing. We rehearsed the whole day long. When our parents came home five days later, they found us starving from hunger and thirst. Dad was so mad. We had to keep him away from the bass drum because he wanted to break down the only skin."

Murry's anger relents when he is played a tape of the group's rehearsal. Audree Wilson tells *Rolling Stone*: "They said, 'We want to play something for you.' They were very excited about it and I thought the songs were darling. But I never thought anything would happen." Impressed with the sound, Murry calls his friends in the recording business, the husband and wife team Hite and Dorinda Morgan who run their own recording studio and a music publishing business, and tells them about The Pendletones.

September

■ Thursday 7th

The Pendletones – Brian Wilson, Dennis Wilson, Carl Wilson, Mike Love and Al Jardine – rehearse again in the Wilson family home in Hawthorne. Soon after, Al follows up Murry's phone call and fixes an appointment for the group with Hite and Dorinda Morgan, for whom he had already auditioned as part of a folk group.

Days later, The Pendletones perform 'Sloop John B' for the Morgans along with several recent chart numbers. The Morgans are not satisfied and Hite asks Brian if he can write something original. To everyone's surprise, Dennis says that they have their own song called 'Surfin'. In fact the song is not fully written yet. Brian tells the Morgans so, and promises to give them a call as soon as it is finished. Excitedly, Brian and Mike complete a rough draft of 'Surfin' before they leave the Morgans' office.

Murry Wilson will recall in *Rolling Stone*: "Dennis told them, 'Write a song about surfing.' He bugged them. Dennis was an avid surfer. He would disappear every Saturday and Sunday he could, without cutting the lawn. He loved the sport." And Carl: "Dennis was the only one who could really surf. We all tried, even Brian, but we were terrible. We just wanted to have a good time and play some music."

Surfing is the popular water-sports pastime for the country's teenagers, especially in California, and it's trumpeted by musicians and enthusiastic surfers like Dick Dale & The Del Tones. Each weekend over 30,000 surfers pack the beaches of Southern California. Surfing is more than a sport to them; it celebrates youth, sun and sex, subjects with which Dennis immediately identifies. Tracks like 'Surfin' Drums' and 'Surf Beat' are already big hits among the surfers and the Surfer's Stomp dance is a big craze among local teenagers. Brian has no inclination to share his brother's passion, but understands the craze perfectly and how it fits in with the freedom of the times.

■ Friday 15th

RECORDING Hite Morgan's home studio *Los Angeles, CA*. In Morgan's living-room on Mayberry Street, LA, The Pendletones rehearse and then record demos of the now completed **'Surfin'** (in one 'take', or attempt at a recording), **'Luau'**, a song written by Morgan's son Bruce (three takes), and **'Lavender'**, written by Dorinda Morgan (four takes). Hite Morgan is impressed with the progress at the session, and today Brian and Mike sign a songwriting contract with the Morgans' publishing company, Guild Music. The agreement deems that Brian and Mike are to receive 28.5 percent of the wholesale price on sheet music. The publishing of songs and printing of them for sale is standard record industry practice, even though the sale of compositions in recorded form long ago eclipsed that of printed music. They also are set to receive 50 percent of publishing income, as well as six cents per copy of sheet-music sold. The Morgans book The Pendletones' first proper recording session for October 3rd, and arrange for the group to join the AFM, or American Federation of Musicians, the national musicians' union.

October

■ Tuesday 3rd

RECORDING World Pacific studio *Los Angeles, CA*. In a session paid for by Hite Morgan, The Pendletones record studio-quality versions of **'Surfin'** (eight takes, with the last marked as master), **'Luau'** (12 takes; last marked as master) and **'Lavender'** (three takes). Al plays upright bass, Brian plays a drum (the bottom of a garbage can with his shirt lying across it), Carl plays guitar, and Mike, suffering from a heavy cold, adds vocals. Dennis, after prompting from his mother Audree, joins in on the session, also adding vocals. But he gets angry when Murry, who oversees the proceedings, will not let him play the drum on the session and takes off. Murry feels that Dennis isn't a good enough drummer and urges Brian to find another. After eight takes of 'Surfin'' at the studio on West 3rd Street, Hite Morgan decides to turn the demo into a record.

Carl recalls later: "Our first recording session was held in a movie dubbing studio. Not one of us knew an instrument well. Mike had been learning the saxophone but we wouldn't let him play it on the record because it didn't fit into our sound. At the session Al thumped bass, Brian took off his shirt, laid it across a drum and beat it with his hand, while we all sang into one microphone. That's how 'Surfin'' was born."

Guild Music sends a tape of the completed 'Surfin'' / 'Luau' master to Candix Records, a small independent Los Angeles-based record company that agrees to release the two tracks immediately as a single. The label also announces that they hate The Pendletones' name.

December

■ Thursday 7th
Copyright in the song 'Surfin'' is assigned to Guild Music.

■ Friday 8th
'Surfin'' / 'Luau' single released in the US. The 45 appears as Candix 331 and is credited, without the group's knowledge, to The Beach Boys. The name comes from a conversation between Candix record distributor Russ Regan and the company's A&R man, Joe Saraceno, who at first considered the name The Surfers. Days later the single is issued again, first on Morgan's own label, X Records, bearing the catalogue number 301. RCA objects to the use of the name because X has been one of the company's subsidiary labels, primarily issuing old jazz and country material and evolving into the Vik label. In January 1962 the 'Surfin'' single will appear as Candix 301.

■ Saturday 9th
'Surfin'' receives its first airing on the group's local radio station KFWB. The boys were driving in the rain down Hawthorne Boulevard in Brian's 1957 Ford. Dennis recalls in *Disc*: "We made a record that was number two in Los Angeles. We got so excited hearing it on the radio that Carl threw up. Nothing will ever top the expression on Brian's face, ever ... that was the all-time moment. I ran down the street screaming, 'Listen, we're on the radio!' It was really funky. That started it, the minute you're on the radio." Brian will tell the BBC: "It was such a thrill. I was out of my mind because it was such a thrill."

Murry remembers that it was played on three stations in Los Angeles every hour, 24 hours a day. "Russ Regan got it on KFWB and KRLA and it went to number 76 on the Top 100 chart." Carl also tells *Rolling Stone*: "The local disc jockeys liked it enough to whirl it on their turntables and soon it became the number 3 hit tune in the Los Angeles area."

The song is entered into the local radio station's phone-in contest where the first prize is a week of regular airtime for the song. Brian: "There were six songs in the contest. People would call in and say 'I vote for this' or 'I vote for that' over the phone. So what we'd do was call in and say, 'I vote for "Surfin",' in ten or fifteen different voices, just the three of us, my brothers. Then, at the end of the week, the announcer said, 'And the winner this week is "Surfin"'", and we'd scream, 'We won, we won.' It was quite an experience."

'Surfin'' will sell more than 40,000 copies in America in the dying weeks of 1961. Dennis: "But then we were cheated. The publishing company turned out to be Dishonest John. They gave us $200 – but it should have been more like $2,000!"

■ Saturday 23rd
Rendezvous Ballroom Balboa, *Newport Beach, CA* with Dick Dale & The Del Tones, The Surfaris, The Challengers
Through a booking made by Dorinda Morgan, The Beach Boys make their first public appearance. They play two songs during the intermission at a Dick Dale Christmas high-school show. The group appears wearing cheap gold jackets obtained from the Gene Ronald tailor shop on North Main Street in nearby Santa Ana. The group is poorly received and Brian feels humiliated.

Dennis will recall on US radio that the show "was really something. Our hair was blond, we wore Pendleton shirts and tennis shoes. Alan played [an upright] bass, which was bigger than him. It went down all right. When you're playing, you think it's fantastic. I don't know whether the people liked it because they'd never seen anything like it before. They all walked out. But we kept on playing and we got $10 between us. I was already professional because I wasn't doing anything else."

■ Friday 29th
'Surfin'' (Candix 331) debuts at number 33 on the KFWB Fabulous Top Forty survey. The single will remain on the chart for 14 weeks, until March 30th 1962.

■ Sunday 31st
The Ritchie Valens Memorial Dance, Municipal Auditorium *Long Beach, CA* with Ike & Tina Turner
In a booking by local radio station KFWB, The Beach Boys make their second live appearance, on New Year's Eve. They play just three numbers, including 'Surfin'', in a 20-minute set. The evening is a tribute concert held in honour of local boy Ritchie Valens, killed in a plane crash in America's Midwest on February 3rd 1959 with Buddy Holly and The Big Bopper. The Beach Boys appear immediately after Ike & Tina Turner and are so excited about their improved, more polished performance that they forget to take their drums with them when they leave. They are paid $300 for their appearance. Carl tells *Tiger Beat*: "We knew we were beginning to happen when a radio station hired us to play a show on New Year's Eve. Three days before the show my dad bought Brian an amplifier and a bass, which he learned to play in those three days. Al gave up the bass and bought an electric guitar like mine. Although we were still raw recruits in the music business, the producer of the show dug our performance enough to book us for more shows. Our first trip took us to San Diego, where we played during the intermission of a surfing movie. We were paid $500. We were on our way!"

Surfin' single

A 'Surfin'' (B. WILSON / M. LOVE)
B 'Luau' (B. MORGAN / H. MORGAN)

US release December 8th 1961 (Candix 331); December 1961 (X X-301); January 1962 (Candix 301).
Chart high US number 75.

1962

Al Jardine leaves The Beach Boys and David Marks replaces him ... Capitol Records signs the group ... first Capitol single 'Surfin' Safari' released ... first major tour is a 40-date Midwest jaunt ... first Capitol album *Surfin' Safari* recorded and released ... Capitol agrees to Brian's bold suggestion that he should produce the group and record them in non-Capitol studios.

Capitol Records Tower, the company's HQ in Hollywood, California, where the group signs recording contracts this year.

1962

January

Brian Wilson meets Gary Usher (born December 14th 1938 in San Gabriel, California) for the first time and begins a songwriting partnership with him. (See April 16th.)

■ Wednesday 17th
'Surfin'' single (Candix label) bubbles under the US *Billboard* Top 100 chart at number 118.

■ Thursday 25th
Presbyterian Church *Hawthorne, CA*
The Beach Boys perform as part of a *Surf Music Night* concert.

■ Monday 29th
'Heartbreak Lane' written by Brian and Murry Wilson is copyrighted by Mills Music. Also today Brian signs a publishing contract with Guild Music for his tunes 'Surfer Girl' and 'Surfin' Safari'. 'Surfer Girl' is allegedly written about Brian's girlfriend Judy Bowles, to whom he is engaged.

February

■ Thursday 8th
RECORDING World Pacific studio *Los Angeles, CA* 7:00-10:00pm. Given the relative success of the 'Surfin'' single, Hite Morgan books another recording session for the group, today consisting of Brian, Al and Dennis. This three-hour session produces master versions of 'Surfin' Safari' (ten 'takes', or attempts at a recording; the final one of which is marked as master), **'Surfer Girl'** (six takes; take 4 marked as master), **'Judy'** (two takes; take 2 marked as master) and **'Karate'** aka 'Beach Boys Stomp' (two takes; take 2 marked as master). Some mistakes are made on the musicians' union session log: 'Karate' is written as 'Karote' and 'Surfer Girl' as 'Little Surfin' Girl'.

In addition, two takes of guitar overdubs and one take of vocal overdubbing are added to 'Surfin' Safari', one take of vocal overdubbing is required on 'Surfer Girl', two takes of vocal overdubbing are done for 'Judy', and two takes of vocal overdubbing are recorded for 'Karate'. ('Overdubbing' is the recording of additional vocals or instruments onto an existing recorded performance on tape.)

Following Murry's suggestion that brother Dennis isn't good enough, Brian brings along a drummer to the session but he is not used. Val Polluto, a singer from vocal quartet The Jaguars, is present and used.

Within a few days of this session Al resigns from the group, deciding instead to continue his studies at El Camino College and to revive his folk group, The Islanders, for a second time. He had voiced his distaste at The Beach Boys' decision to add some Chubby Checker tunes to their current repertoire and is discouraged by the relatively small amount – $200 – that each group member has made from the success of 'Surfin''.

■ Friday 16th – Saturday 17th
The Rainbow Gardens *Los Angeles, CA*
A two-night performance by the four-piece Al-less Beach Boys line-up: Brian, Carl, Mike and Dennis.
• 'Surfin'' single (Candix label) enters US *Billboard* Top 100 chart at 93 on the 17th.

2/8/62   DECK RECORD CO
(Employer's name)

Phonograph Recording Contract Blank
AMERICAN FEDERATION OF MUSICIANS
OF THE UNITED STATES AND CANADA

000255
52060

Local Union No. 47

THIS CONTRACT for the personal services of musicians, made this 8th day of February 1962, between the undersigned employer (hereinafter called the "employer") and THREE musicians (including the leader) (hereinafter called "employees").

WITNESSETH, That the employer hires the employees as musicians severally on the terms and conditions below, and as further specified on reverse side. The leader represents that the employees already designated have agreed to be bound by said terms and conditions. Each employee yet to be chosen shall be so bound by said terms and conditions upon agreeing to accept his employment. Each employee may enforce this agreement. The employees severally agree to render collectively to the employer services as musicians in the orchestra under the leadership of BRIAN DOUGLAS WILSON as follows:

Name and Address of Place of Engagement 3713 WEST THIRD STREET LOS ANGELES CALIF.

Date(s) and Hours of Employment FEB 8th 1962 7 TO 10

Type of Engagement: Recording for phonograph records only

WAGE AGREED UPON $ SCALE
(Terms and amount)

Plus pension contributions as specified on reverse side hereof.

This wage includes expenses agreed to be reimbursed by the employer in accordance with the attached schedule, or a schedule to be furnished the employer on or before the date of engagement.

To be paid WITHIN FOURTEEN DAYS
(Specify when payments are to be made)

Upon request by the American Federation of Musicians of the United States and Canada (herein called the "Federation") or the local in whose jurisdiction the employees shall perform hereunder, the employer either shall make advance payment hereunder or shall post an appropriate bond.

Employer's name and authorized signature: DECK RECORD CO   Hite B. Morgan
Street address: 2511 MAYBERRY ST.
City LOS ANGELES   State CALIF   Phone DU-3-5463

Leader's name: BRIAN D. WILSON   Local No. 47
Leader's signature: Brian Wilson (Murry D. Wilson)
Street address: 3701-W. 119 STREET
City HAWTHORNE   State CALIF

(1) Label name DECK RECORD COMPANY   Session no.

Master no.	No. of minutes	TITLES OF TUNES	Master no.	No. of minutes	TITLES OF TUNES
	1:22	KAROTE		2:43	LITTLE SURFIN GIRL
	2:12	SURFIN SAFARI		1:56	LUAU
	2:03	SURFIN		1:58	JUDY

(2) Employee's name (As on Social Security card) Last First Initial	(3) Home address (Give street, city and state)	(4) Local Union no.	(5) Social Security number	(6) Scale wages	(7) Pension contribution
WILSON, BRIAN D (Leader)	3701-W-119 ST HAWTHORNE CAL	47	568-62-7150	107.00	8.56
WILSON, DENNIS C	3701-W-119 ST. HAWTHORNE CAL	47	562-60-0076	53.50	4.28
~~JARDINE, BRIAN~~	~~16636 YUKON TORRANCE CAL~~	~~47~~	~~545-82-8285~~	~~53.50~~	~~4.28~~
POLIUTO, VAL A.	2325 SO CONNER COMMERCE, CALIF	47	365-36-0560	53.50	4.28
				214°°	
Approved by: G. Wilson Murry Wilson Guardians					14 ??

MUSICIANS MUTUAL PROTECTIVE ASSN.
Local 47, A. F. of M.

CONTRACT RECEIVED
FEB 13 1962
WARD ARCHER
ASST. TO PRESIDENT

PAID FEB 13 1962

FEB 13 1962

(8) Total Pension Contributions (Sum of Column (7)) $ 17.12
Make check payable in this amount to "AFM & EPW Fund"

$214.00

1962

■ Friday 23rd – Saturday 24th
The Cinnamon Cinder *Los Angeles, CA*
A two-night residency in LA for the second weekend in a row.

Spring

Brian drops out of El Camino College. Dennis is expelled from Hawthorne High for fighting. He recalls in *Disc*: "It was only because of a fight with another boy. Not over a girl but over a lollipop! There was this tall guy, six foot three inches, who had ten all-day-suckers. I didn't have a nickel to buy one so I took one of his. So he said, 'Meet me in the boys' bathroom.' We had this fight and I didn't mean to hit him in the head, but I did, and I got [thrown out of school] for two weeks. I went back with my dad and told them how I felt and they said, 'Well, we don't know if we want you here.' So I left. Dad said, 'I'll educate you.' He used to take me to his office and I swept the floor. I made a dollar a day."
• Early in the month, The Beach Boys perform in a Deb-Teen fashion show concert at the Harris department store in San Bernardino, California.

March

■ Thursday 8th
RECORDING Stereo Masters Office *Los Angeles, CA*. As a favour to the Morgans, Kenny & The Cadets – Brian, Carl, Audree Wilson and Jaguars' vocalist Val Polluto – add vocals to the existing tracks **'Barbie'** (seven takes required; take 6 marked as master) and **'What Is A Young Girl Made Of'** (seven takes required; take 5 marked as master). Returning to the fold to help out is erstwhile Beach Boy Al Jardine. The recordings will be released as a Kenny & The Cadets single on April 19th, as Randy Records 422.

■ Friday 16th – Sunday 18th
Monica Hotel *Santa Monica, CA* 8:00-12:00pm
Three consecutive nights of Beach Boys performances.

■ Saturday 24th
Newport High School *Los Angeles, CA*
• 'Surfin' single peaks in US *Billboard* Top 100 chart at number 75.

■ Thursday 29th
Murry Wilson types up a contractual letter of intent and agreement with Hite and Dorinda Morgan for the purpose of recording The Beach Boys to produce music that can be used to acquire a recording deal with a major label. Murry is ecstatic about the deal.

■ Saturday 31st
Ontario National Guard Armory, John Gavin Park *Los Angeles, CA* 8:00pm-12 midnight, with The Vibrants

April

'Soupy Shuffle Stomp' / 'Moon Shot' single by Bruce Johnston released in the US. The future Beach Boy's 45 comes out on the Donna label.

• As a replacement for Al, David Marks joins The Beach Boys as the group's full-time rhythm guitarist. Brian, who's owned a bass guitar since December, now switches permanently to that instrument. David is not the first-choice replacement for Al: Paul Johnson of the local Belairs group has declined their offer. David's first concert with The Beach Boys takes place at The Bel Aire Bay Club in Los Angeles.
   David recalls in *Trouser Press*: "I was 12 years old, sitting at home with Mommy and Daddy, watching TV and getting ready for school the next day when the Wilsons came over and said, 'Do you want to be in the group? We have something going on here.' They'd been gigging around town, doing crummy gigs. We all begged my Mom and Dad to let me join. They finally said yeah, and then we all sat down to get all the details about money and everything. I couldn't have cared less about money. I just rode around on my bike wishing I could be in the group. For my first gig with them we wore ugly mustard-coloured coats that were way too big for us. Especially mine. Real nerdy."

■ Wednesday 4th
Inglewood Women's Club *Inglewood, CA* 8:00-12 midnight
This Beach Boys performance features the new five-man line-up: Brian, David, Carl, Dennis and Mike. But with no follow-up single in the works and with live bookings beginning to slow, it looks like their time in the spotlight may be short. "'Surfin'' was a smash all over the States," Murry recalls for *Rolling Stone* in 1972, "but three and a half months later The Beach Boys, as far as the music business was concerned, were through. The boys were off the air and they couldn't get back on it. No one wanted them. They thought they were a one-shot record. They were crestfallen."

■ Monday 16th
RECORDING Western Recorders studio *Hollywood, CA*. Gary Usher, who met Brian three months ago, invites Brian and the other Beach Boys to do some recordings at Western Recorders in Hollywood in an attempt to re-launch their already flagging career. Usher began his recording career in 1960 and has become known as a leading composer in the surfing and hot-rod genres.
   Today's session marks the first occasion that the group records at Western Recorders, 6000 Sunset Boulevard, which will become a familiar location in the following years. Charles Dean, better known as Chuck Britz, is the engineer at the session. He too will become a regular, remaining with the group as their chief Western engineer until 1967.
   The group makes demo recordings today of the Wilson/Usher originals **'The One Way Road To Love'**, **'Beginning Of The End'**, **'Visions'** aka **'Number One'**, and **'My Only Alibi'** aka 'Human'. Usher provides the lead vocals while Brian handles backing vocals and the full Beach Boys line-up provides instrumentation. The results of this session will go unreleased.

■ Thursday 19th
RECORDING Western Recorders studio *Hollywood, CA*. Three days after their first collaboration, The Beach Boys again team up with Gary Usher for further recordings at Western. The session today produces **'Surfin' Safari'**, a re-recording of **'Judy'**, two new Wilson/Usher compositions, **'Lonely Sea'** and **'409'**, as well as **'Their Hearts Were Full Of Spring'**. (See May 10th.)
   "We recorded at Western," David Marks will recall later, "on Sunset Boulevard, a little … soundstage that was used for radio shows. There was a little studio in the back, Studio 3, where we did all our stuff. Western told it like it was, real funky sounding. The sound and the success of the group came out of that dinky little

studio." Number 3 is the smallest, narrowest and cheapest studio in the Western Recorders building.

'Barbie' / **'What Is A Young Girl Made Of'** single by Kenny & The Cadets released in the US. The group consists of Brian Wilson, Carl Wilson, Audree Wilson, Jaguars' singer Val Polluto, and Al Jardine.

■ Saturday 21st
Redondo High School Auditorium *Redondo Beach, CA* with The Belairs (headliners), The Vibrants
The Beach Boys perform at an *Easter Week Stomp* gig.

May

As Murry had feared, Candix Records folds and with it goes any chance of a follow-up single for The Beach Boys on that label. Eager to place the group with another label, Murry takes the demo they taped on April 19th to several record companies, including Dot, Decca and Liberty. He is unsuccessful. "They asked me to manage them and I went off to see the companies," Murry says later in *Rolling Stone*. "Hite Morgan and I went to Dot Records and cooled our heels in the foyer. Nobody would talk to us. We then went to Liberty and the big shots were too busy to see us. Finally I said to Hite, 'What'll we do?' He said, 'I don't know, Murry. You're their dad and manager. Rots of ruck to you,' and he said goodbye. I was on my own."

■ Friday 4th
Inglewood Women's Club *Inglewood, CA* 8:00-12 midnight
The group is naturally despondent, feeling rejected by the music industry. They will be seen idly chatting to the audience while eating hamburgers during one of their infrequent stage performances.

■ Thursday 10th
Murry makes an important breakthrough at a meeting today that he'd booked two weeks earlier with Capitol Records at the company's Tower headquarters at 1750 North Vine Street in Hollywood. He plays The Beach Boys' April 19th demo tape to Nick Venet, Capitol's 23-year-old A&R man. Against the advice of his superiors, Venet buys the masters of 'Surfin' Safari', 'Lonely Sea' and '409' for $300. Murry and Venet negotiate a 2.5 percent royalty rate for the group.

Nick Venet will remember later that Murry comes into his office with three masters, including 'Surfin' Safari', a ready-made single for Capitol. "They'd had a minor release on an independent label, a local chart record, 'Surfin'. [Murry] wanted to make a new deal. He wanted to sell the master[s] and was asking $100 per track and a small royalty. He didn't want much. He was a very humble man.

"Murry played me the record and it was really good, probably the best record that I had heard that year. He played it to me and, every once in a while, as a producer, before the second eight bars have finished, you know that the record is a number 1. I wasn't one for hiding my feelings and I started jumping around the room. I said, 'We have to make a deal.' Of course, he got all excited because he wasn't one to hide his feelings as well. The kids were sitting outside.

"I ran down the hall and knocked on the door of Capitol's vice-president, Voyle Gilmore, and I said, 'Voyle, I have to see you for two minutes.' He said, 'I'm really busy.' I said, 'I've got to see you. We've got a hit record here and if they walk out of the office, I don't know where to call them.' So he said, 'Well, all right. Put it on.' So I put it

on the turntable and even though Voyle was in his fifties, he heard what I had heard right away. He said, 'Go back and ask them what they want for it. But for God's sake, quit dancing.'

"So I went back to my office and I asked Murry what he wanted for it. He asked for $300. I told him to stay put. I went back to Voyle's office and told them they wanted $300 and he said that was too much money. I said, 'We can't argue with the man. It would cost more than that to make it here.' Voyle insisted that I offer them $100. I was despondent and I didn't want to bargain … so I came back to my office and I said to Murry, 'I'll give you $100 but I don't think that is fair. I'll give you $300 right here.' So I went right back up to Voyle's office again and said to the vice-president, 'I'm going to resign, buy this record, and start my own company.' After minutes of telling me to stay, Voyle finally said $300 was all right. I still felt that $300 was awfully cheap. Murry wanted to give us the publishing but I advised him to open a small company with the boys, with the group, split it between them, and keep the publishing."

Carl Wilson tells *Rolling Stone* later: "The people at Capitol didn't like my dad at all because he really gave them a hard time if he thought that something was unfair. A lot of the executives didn't like him at all, which is perfectly understandable, but we were his kids, you know?"

"Murry once told me that his son Brian was the next Elvis Presley," says Venet. "I told him, 'Mr Wilson, I think Brian one day might be as big as Elvis Presley but I don't think he wants to be Presley. Brian's doing a different kind of music, which is really Brian Wilson music.' Murry kind of shook his head, looked at me and walked away."

Murry's later recollection is that Venet "started out OK. He called me up one day, after I had just handed him the tapes of 'Surfin' Safari', and said, 'Now, we can't have two producers. You're a bit over the hill, old boy. I'm young, and I know the tempo and I sold $50million worth of records for Capitol last year. So move over and let me take your kids and make big stars out of them.' That's what he told me. I said, 'OK, well, do a good job with them, Nick, they're your babies.' I was kind of glad because it was a lot of pressure. You can work a lot easier with strangers than you can with your own kids, you know. I worked out that it cost $7,600 to launch The Beach Boys in the States."

Upon signing the Capitol Records contract Mike quits his job at a metal-working firm and Brian puts down a deposit on an apartment.

■ Friday 11th
'409' and 'Lonely Sea' are copyrighted by Brian Wilson and Gary Usher.

June

■ Friday 1st
'Surfin' Safari' (written by Brian Wilson & Mike Love) and 'Judy' (solely by Brian) are copyrighted by Guild Music in Los Angeles. Soon after, following the advice he'd been given by Nick Venet at Capitol, Murry creates the Sea Of Tunes publishing company to safeguard Brian's compositions. It is an organisation co-owned by father and son.

■ Monday 4th
'409' / **'Surfin' Safari'** single released in the US. This is the first Capitol Records single by The Beach Boys and employs the

1962

---

409 single

A '409' (B. WILSON / M. LOVE / G. USHER)
B 'Surfin' Safari' (B. WILSON / M. LOVE)

US release June 4th 1962 (Capitol 4777).
Chart high US number 14 ('Surfin' Safari').

---

recordings that the company purchased on May 10th. "When Brian sat down at the piano and played 'Surfin' Safari' and said this is our next hit, I got chills," David Marks recalls later in *Trouser Press*. "Got goosebumps, man. We jumped around and pounded him on the back, 'God, you're a genius, man!'"

Nick Venet, Capitol A&R man, tells BBC radio: "Some of the people in California had put [the record] down. But [it] broke all kinds of records in New York City … for us that year, it was selling so fast."

Murry Wilson: "We told Nick Venet right at the outset we thought 'Surfin' Safari' was the A-side. But he said, 'No, "409".' So Capitol put all the push behind '409' and had to turn the damn record over in about three weeks. 'Surfin" Safari' was the song that made them surfing kings, vocally and lyrically, around the United States."

"I used to get locked up in the office with [Murry]," Venet will recall later. "I would come into work at 9 o'clock after being up all night making great music and I would walk into the office and Murry Wilson would be there. That motherfucker would sit there till 5 or 6 o'clock and tell me about his songs and play me his melodies. I had to listen to him because, somewhere in the conversation, he would always drop to me what Brian's next record was going to be. Everyone in the building avoided him. But I was stuck with him.

"One day I looked out of the window and he had cornered the president of Capitol in the parking lot. I was sent down there. I had to bump into him and say, 'Oh. Murry. I've been looking for you all day. I have some new pictures of the boys I have to show you,' just to get [him] away from the owner of the company.

"I used to hide under my desk. Murry used to look in my office to see if I was in there. So I ordered a new desk because it had a front on it. The chick downstairs would say, 'Here he comes,' and I would hide myself under my desk because there was no exit but the front door. He would come in, wouldn't take my secretary's 'He's not in', would walk right into the office, would take a look and if I wasn't there, he would split. One day he came in and used my fuckin' phone. I sat under my desk for five hours! When I came out, I couldn't use my left leg for two days."

Tuesday 12th

RECORDING *Surfin' Safari* **session 1** Capitol studio *Hollywood, CA*. The Beach Boys' first Capitol Records recording session, at the company's Tower HQ studio at 1750 North Vine Street, where today they re-record **'Surfin' Safari'**.

July

Roger Christian (born July 3rd 1934 in Buffalo, New York) supplants Gary Usher as Brian's songwriting partner. They meet after Murry hears the KFWB radio DJ discussing '409' on the air one night.

Saturday 14th

RADIO Oxnard's Plaza Park *Oxnard, CA*. KOXR and KAAR Radio live performance 'Mr. Moto', 'Surfin'', 'Surfin' Safari', broadcast 10:30am-2:30pm. The group's radio debut takes place today as they appear at Downtown Oxnard's first annual *Big Diaper Derby* and participate in a live remote broadcast from Oxnard's Plaza Park. The *Big Diaper Derby* is a race where diaper-wearing babies crawl across a 12-foot rug to reach their mothers on the other side. After several heats, the winner is one-year-old Vincent Ortega. Contrary to popular belief, the live radio show is not hosted by famous Hollywood singing star Nelson Eddy but by the chairman of the *Derby*, Richard Laubacher. He engages in a conversation with The Beach Boys just after they perform 'Mr. Moto' in front of a crowd of 150. Brian tells him that "six songs are in the can for our next album" and that The Beach Boys' next single will be 'Chug-A-Lug'. (Also on the bill today are The Surfmen.)

Monday 16th

At Capitol's Tower HQ in Hollywood, The Beach Boys – namely Brian, Dennis and Carl Wilson, Mike Love, and David Marks – sign a recording contract with Capitol Records. Murry Wilson recalls later in *Rolling Stone* that Capitol A&R man Nick Venet "acted real cool. He said, 'You come back in an hour and we'll let you know if we want you to become Capitol recording artists.' He didn't act like he was too excited. So [Brian and I] walked out of there and I said, 'Brian, let's make them wait five minutes, you know? Let's not act too eager.' We went back to Capitol in one hour and five minutes. We knew we were good."

• 'Surfer Girl' is copyrighted as a song by Guild Music.

Saturday 28th

Azuza Canteen, Azuza Teen Club *Azuza, CA*

The Beach Boys' ride to prominence continues as they make their film debut singing 'Surfin' Safari' in *One Man's Challenge*, a rarely-seen 24-minute black-and-white documentary produced and directed by Dave Smallin. The challenge of the title is to open a teen club in California. The Beach Boys' appearance in the movie is a happy accident as the group, near the start of their Midwest tour, just happen to be booked to perform at the club on the day the filming is being done. Asked if they would like to participate in the shoot, the group duly oblige. Other music in the film comes from The Surfaris and The Genteels.

TOUR STARTS US Midwest (late July-mid September) As a contracted up-and-coming Capitol recording act, The Beach Boys undertake a 40-date tour, crisscrossing the Midwest. The boys and their musical instruments are packed tightly into the back of a wagon. The group will even play the part of roadies on the tour, setting up and dismantling all their instruments at the start and finish of every show. "We used to go out in a station wagon," Mike recalls later on BBC radio. "There were five of us and a driver. We lugged our own instruments. We'd drive sometimes 500 miles to the next date. After the first tour I said, 'Never again.' It was just crazy. It was five guys crawling over each other in the back of a station wagon."

Murry is unable to go along on the tour and hires John Hamilton, former Ventures road manager, but soon fires him. After a week, Murry hires Elmer Marks, David's father, to take over, accompanied by the Wilsons' mother, Audree.

"Murry used to go on tours with us and so did my dad sometimes," David will tell Scott Keller in 1974, "but finally Murray hired this guy named John Hamilton, who had been with The

---

Gathered around the music stand at their second Capitol recording session in Hollywood on August 5th are (left to right) Mike Love, Brian Wilson, Carl Wilson, Dennis Wilson and David Marks.

Ventures. He was an old guy, but basically just a big rowdy kid. He was one of us. We really loved him. He used to take us to these whorehouses. ... I wasn't into that, you know, but I had to go through with it, to be a man, right? But I was shaking in my boots. Murray flew out to a tour date and saw us carrying on. He fired Hamilton on the spot."

August

Three months after putting down a deposit, Brian moves out of his parent's home in Hawthorne and into a small apartment on nearby Crenshaw Boulevard. He shares the $150-a-month property with Bob Norberg, a semi-professional musician whom Brian had met during a Beach Boys concert at the University of Southern California in the summer.

◼ Sunday 5th
RECORDING *Surfin' Safari* **session 2** Capitol studio *Hollywood, CA* three-hour session. During a break from concerts The Beach Boys start a monster three-day recording session and produce songs that will grace their first Capitol album, *Surfin' Safari*. Sessions today produce **'County Fair'**, **'Moon Dawg'** (instrumental), **'Cuckoo Clock'** and **'Heads You Win Tails I Lose'**. The recordings are simple affairs: the group lays down a backing track of drums, guitar and bass, and then vocals are overdubbed. Nick Venet appears on two of the tracks, howling on 'Moon Dawg' and impersonating a carnival barker on 'County Fair'. His brother Steve's girlfriend

provides the female voice on the latter track. The union log for the date indicates that songwriter/guitarist Derry Weaver is present at the session. Murry Wilson again oversees the proceedings – a father looking after his sons.

Murry exaggerates a little when he says later that the group stands and sings "for 13 straight hours to get an album out. Sometimes they were so exhausted I had to make them mad at me to get the best out of them. So I'd insult their musical integrity. I'd say, 'That's lousy. You guys can do better than that!' I'd make them so damn mad that they'd be hitting me over the head, practically. But then they'd give that extra burst of energy and do it beautifully. When they were exhausted, I drove them harder because they asked for it."

David Marks remembers: "Brian would [make] all the settings on the control board and go out into the studio, and Murray would change everything. Then Brian would come back in and go, 'What the fuck happened? It sounds different!' They were fighting all the time. I guess Murray was trying to live through his sons. It was finally agreed that Murray wouldn't try to produce any more.

"Brian did everything," Marks continues. "Played, did the arrangements, screwed up the lead sheets himself. He didn't need any help to do that. You listen to those first albums and they sound campy and corny but Brian was dead serious. Like 'Cuckoo Clock', 'Chug-A-Lug,' and 'Ten Little Indians': he was dead serious about them all and that's what made them work.

"It wasn't like Brian was trying to put something over. [He wasn't saying:] 'Is this commercial? How are we gonna trick these turkeys into buying this?' There was no formulating, no plotting or planning. He was just doing what he loved. He told me he wrote

BELOW Two shots from a photo session at Paradise Cove for the first Capitol album, with obligatory surfboard.

about things that turned him on, like girls, cars, high school. It's hard to believe that anyone could be that naive and honest, but he was. That's what made those records successful," says Marks. "You can feel the sincerity in them."

■ Monday 6th

RECORDING *Surfin' Safari* **session 3** Capitol studio *Hollywood, CA* three-hour session. A further Beach Boys recording session, with the group providing full instrumentation.

Work takes place on: **'Little Girl (You're My Miss America)'** (mis-titled 'Little Miss America' on the subsequent album; take 15 marked as best) which features Dennis's first vocal on a Beach Boys recording; **'Land Ahoy'** (which will remain unreleased until 1983, but is reworked as 'Cherry Cherry Coupe' on the group's 1963 album *Little Deuce Coupe*); and **'Summertime Blues'** (tracking take 4 and vocal take 12 marked as best; 'tracking' is the term for the initial recording of backing instruments only).

The union log again indicates that songwriter/guitarist Derry Weaver is present at today's session.

■ Wednesday 8th

RECORDING *Surfin' Safari* **session 4** Capitol studio *Hollywood, CA* 6:00-9:00pm. Concluding their three-day session – again with songwriter/guitarist Derry Weaver probably present – the group today records **'Ten Little Indians'**, **'Chug A Lug'** and **'The Shift'**.

Mike Love is not happy with the way the group's debut album is being recorded. Nick Venet rushes through the session so he can get to New York to record with Capitol artist Bobby Darin.

Brian is also unhappy. He dislikes the acoustics of Capitol's studios, designed to accommodate the large orchestras that performed and recorded there in the previous decade. He immediately suggests to Capitol executives that The Beach Boys record at another studio and, most importantly, that he should be put in charge of the recordings. It is a bold move but, amazingly, one that Capitol agrees to.

The label is reluctant to let their new up-and-coming group record anywhere other than in their own studio, but Brian is determined to move and so a compromise is reached. The group themselves will pay for all external studio costs – in exchange for a higher royalty rate.

Also as part of the new arrangement, Capitol will retain the rights to all the music that is recorded at these independent studios. Brian is pleased with the deal. The first studio he will use once ensconced in his new role as record producer is Harmony (see September 4th).

September

■ Tuesday 4th

RECORDING Harmony Recorders studio *Los Angeles, CA* 11:30am-2:30pm. Brian Wilson conducts his first session as a record producer, recording two Wilson/Usher songs, **'The Revo-lution'** and **'Number One'**, with Rachel & The Revolvers. They will be released as a single next month on Dot Records, the first record to bear the credit "Produced by Brian Wilson".

Also today, Brian produces **'Humpty Dumpty'** by Bob & Sheri (Bob Norberg, Brian's roommate in the Crenshaw Apartments, and his girlfriend, Cheryl Pomeroy). A fourth song, **'Recreation'**, is recorded today; it will remain unreleased. Dennis Wilson and saxophonist Larry Lennear are also present at the session.

■ Thursday 13th

RECORDING Western Recorders studio (3) *Hollywood, CA*. Today sees a Beach Boys tracking and vocal session for **'Cindy Oh Cindy'**

(eight instrumental takes required). The session also focuses on **'The Surfer Moon'** by Bob & Sheri, another Brian production. The 'Surfer Moon' single backed with 'Humpty Dumpty' (see 4th) will be released next month on Safari Records, a one-off label bearing the Wilsons' home address in Hawthorne. It does not chart.

■ Saturday 15th
'Surfin' Safari' single enters US trade magazine *Billboard*'s Top 40 chart at number 30.

October

■ Monday 1st
Surfin' Safari album released in the US. The Beach Boys' debut LP is issued on Capitol Records and features a photograph of them on the front taken at Paradise Cove. The group's image changes now as a set of striped shirts becomes a regular part of their costume for both stage and TV appearances. The style is inspired by the clean-cut American singing group The Kingston Trio.

■ Friday 5th
'Surfin' Safari' / '409' single released in the UK. Capitol Records issues the group's first British 45.

"The Beach Boys sound like a very ordinary vocal group to me," writes the reviewer in Britain's *Disc & Music Echo* music newspaper, "and although they've got a fairly useful chanter in 'Surfin' Safari', which is doing well in the States, I can't see it reaching very high places. Routine material and presentation, which hardly seems worth the Atlantic crossing. '409' is either a motorbike or a hot-rod car. I'm not sure which, despite the sound effects gimmicks of the twister on this B-side."

■ Saturday 13th
'409' single (Capitol's A-side) peaks on US *Billboard* chart at number 76, but 'Surfin' Safari' (B-side) peaks at number 14. (Some charts are

---

Surfin' Safari album

A1 'Surfin' Safari' (B. WILSON / M. LOVE)
A2 'County Fair' (B. WILSON / G. USHER)
A3 'Ten Little Indians' (B. WILSON / G. USHER)
A4 'Chug-A-Lug' (B. WILSON / M. LOVE)
A5 'Little Miss America' (V. CATALANO / H. ALPERT)
A6 '409' (B. WILSON / M. LOVE / G. USHER)
B1 'Surfin'' (B. WILSON / M. LOVE)
B2 'Heads You Win Tails I Lose' (B. WILSON / G. USHER)
B3 'Summertime Blues' (E. COCHRAN / J. CAPEHART)
B4 'Cuckoo Clock' (B. WILSON / G. USHER)
B5 'Moon Dawg' (D. WEAVER)
B6 'The Shift' (B. WILSON / M. LOVE)

US release October 1st 1962 (Capitol T1808).
UK release April 1963 (Capitol T1808).
Chart high US number 32; UK none.

---

still based on radio plays as well as sales, so B-sides can chart separately from their As.)

■ Sunday 28th
Pandora's Box *Los Angeles, CA*
While playing a short residence at this extremely small coffee house at the intersection of Sunset Boulevard and Crescent Heights, Brian meets Marilyn Rovell (born February 6th 1948 in Chicago, Illinois) through Gary Usher. Marilyn has a sister, Diane, and is a cousin of Usher's girlfriend Ginger Blake (real name Sandra Glantz). The three sing together in the all-girl group The Honeys.

The evening sees an incident involving hot chocolate that will later become famous. Brian recalls in his 1990 autobiography

Wouldn't It Be Nice: "At the intermission, I set down my bass, hopped off the stage and approached their table. Nervously, I wanted to make a good first impression. Gary stood up, prepared to make introductions, but before he said anything, I stumbled over my feet and knocked into Marilyn, spilling her hot chocolate on her leg. I thought, 'I've blown it.' But Marilyn took hold of my arm and laughed, 'It's OK. Don't worry about it. I'm all right.'"

Marilyn remembers in *Rolling Stone*: "Brian was on stage singing and was just finishing his set. I was drinking some hot chocolate and he said, 'Can I have a sip?' I said, 'Sure.' He gives it back to me and he spills it all over me. I thought, 'Who's this guy?' But I liked him. He was like a teddy bear. From the day I met him, I couldn't stop laughing. Just everything he did was funny. Even the way he lifted a fork was funny." Brian and Marilyn immediately begin dating.

November

'Surfin' Safari' single reaches the top spot on Sweden's Radio 3 chart. It is The Beach Boys' first number 1 record.

■ Sunday 4th
Pandora's Box *Los Angeles, CA*
The group continues the short Sunday-night residency at this tiny coffee house in Los Angeles.

■ Thursday 8th
Dennis and Carl Wilson and David Marks appear at the Los Angeles Court with their parents for approval of their Capitol Records contracts. This is essential in US law as they are 'minors', meaning they are under full legal age.

■ Sunday 11th
Pandora's Box *Los Angeles, CA*
The final night of The Beach Boys' short three-Sunday residency at the coffee bar.

■ Monday 12th
Hollywood Palladium *Los Angeles, CA* with Dick Dale & The Del Tones, Jan & Dean (headliners) and others
The Beach Boys perform on the bill of the second *Hollywood Swings* concert (the first was on the 4th).

■ Tuesday 13th
After gaining permission from the judge in the Los Angeles Court on the 8th, Dennis, Carl and David join Brian and Mike in signing a new seven-year contact with Capitol Records.

This new improved contract is offered because the label is pleased with the group's sales so far and replaces the one signed on July 16th.

Capitol president Alan Livingstone: "They hit very fast. Murry Wilson said to me, 'We want a new deal. We want more royalties.'

Thursday 20th
Civic Auditorium *Bakersfield, CA*

Saturday 22nd
Exhibition Hall *Fresno, CA*

Thursday 27th – Friday 28th
Santa Monica Civic Auditorium *Santa Monica, CA*
The group performs on both days of a two-day *Surf Fair* with an early evening show on Friday.

Friday 28th
County Fairgrounds Auditorium *Merced, CA* late-night concert

Monday 31st
Gold Rush Festival Auditorium *Stockton, CA*
This evening's performance marks the last night of this short tour. In a relatively short space of time the group has provided a minor shot in the arm for the American music industry – and next year will see steady progress.

Ten Little Indians single

A 'Ten Little Indians' (B. WILSON / G. USHER)
B 'County Fair' (B. WILSON / G. USHER)

US release November 26th 1962 (Capitol 4880).
UK release January 1963 (Capitol CL 15285).
Chart high US number 49; UK none.

I said, 'Well, I don't usually do that. I take the risk and I want to benefit by it.' But he pushed and pushed and finally I said, 'OK.' We worked out a new contract, shook hands and then, within a week, Murry came back and said, 'The boys are not satisfied. We want more.' So we had to negotiate again and I gave them a little more. We agreed but then he came back again and said, 'No, the deal's no good.' Eventually we did agree on a new contract."

Wednesday 21st
Hermosa Biltmore *Hermosa Beach, CA* with The Journeymen
This event is promoted as an *Alpha Omega Fraternity Party* and a *Thanksgiving Eve Dance & Stomp*.

Saturday 24th
Surfin' Safari album hits US charts. The LP will go on to peak at number 32.

Monday 26th
'Ten Little Indians' / 'County Fair' single released in the US.

December

Saturday 1st
'Ten Little Indians' single hits US charts. It will stall at number 49, the lowest position for a Beach Boys single until 1968 and the lowest ever apart from 'Surfin''.

Wednesday 12th
At Western Recorders studio in Hollywood, Gary Usher invites Dennis to play drums on a session for his tracks 'RPM', 'Barefoot Adventure' and 'My Sting Ray'. 'RPM' and 'My Sting Ray' are later issued as a single by Challenge Records under the group name The Four Speeds.

TOUR STARTS US California (Dec 17th-31st)

Monday 17th
Earl Warren Showgrounds *Santa Barbara, CA*
The Beach Boys begin another tour, albeit a brief one, playing seven shows in 15 days.

Murry Wilson will recall for *Rolling Stone* in 1971: "I was told by a 22-year-old man that The Beach Boys would never make more money than the group Ruby & The Romantics, who were grossing $3,500 for seven days a week. I got so mad. ... I called from my home to key places and we worked between Christmas Eve and New Year's Eve and we grossed $26,684."

Celebrating their signing of a new, improved contract with Capitol Records, The Beach Boys pose in front of the company's distinctive Tower headquarters in Hollywood.

1963

First serious sessions at Western Recorders, Hollywood, and Gold Star, Los Angeles, which become the group's favourite studios from now ... second album *Surfin' USA* recorded and released, hitting number 2 in the charts ... US television debut ... 'Surfin' USA' peaks at number 3, the group's first Top Ten single ... Brian begins to miss some live performances, and embarks on sole production of Beach Boys sessions, often using session musicians ... *Surfer Girl* album recorded and released ... David Marks leaves the group ... Brian plays more live shows until Al Jardine rejoins the group ... *Little Deuce Coupe* album recorded and released.

Promotional shot taken early this year shortly after signing to the William Morris entertainment agency.

THE BEACH BOYS

Direction: 𝕏𝕏𝕏 **WILLIAM MORRIS AGENCY, INC.**
ARTISTS' MANAGER
NEW YORK • BEVERLY HILLS • CHICAGO
LONDON • PARIS • ROME • MADRID

1963

January

'**Ten Little Indians**' / '**County Fair**' single released in the UK. This is Capitol's second Beach Boys 45 in Britain; it fails to chart.
• 'Ten Little Indians' single peaks in US *Billboard* chart at the number 49 position.

■ Wednesday 2nd
RECORDING Western Recorders studio *Hollywood, CA* three-hour session. Following Brian's request and Capitol's approval, the group begins their first serious recordings at Western studio at 6000 Sunset Boulevard. This is where the vast majority of future Beach Boys sessions will be held, because Brian likes the sound of the studio. They kick off the New Year and their time at the studio by taping '**Punchline**', a bizarre surf instrumental featuring Hammond organ and loud laughing. Written by Brian Wilson and produced by Murry, the 1:53 recording will remain unreleased until its appearance in 1993 as part of the Capitol Records boxed set *Good Vibrations*.

■ Saturday 5th
RECORDING *Surfin' USA* **session 1** Western Recorders studio *Hollywood, CA* three-hour session. Using the studio's 3-track recording facilities – meaning a tape machine that will record three individual sound tracks onto tape – work begins on The Beach Boys' second Capitol album, *Surfin' USA*. Songs recorded include '**Surfin' USA**' and '**Shut Down**' as well as early versions of '**Lana**' and '**Farmer's Daughter**' (work will resume on the latter two pieces on January 16th). Although Capitol's Nick Venet is again listed as the official producer, Brian and Murry have even more say now about how the resulting album should sound. During the sessions Brian decides that the group should double-track their vocals, and this subsequently adds more power to their performances. The ever-improving Beach Boys, with Brian at the helm, are now gaining confidence in the studio.

Brian recalls the genesis of 'Surfin' USA' on US radio: "I was going with a girl called Judy Bowles, and her brother Jimmy was a surfer. He knew all the [surfing] spots. I started humming the melody to 'Sweet Little Sixteen' and I got fascinated with the fact of doing it, and I thought to myself, 'God! What about trying to put surf lyrics to 'Sweet Little Sixteen''s melody? The concept was about, 'They are doing this in this city, and they're doing that in that city.' So I said to Jimmy, 'Hey, Jimmy, I want to do a song mentioning all the surf spots.' So he gave me a list."

TOUR STARTS US East (Jan 10th-17th) David Marks will recall in *Trouser Press* in 1981: "We didn't have roadies. We had to carry our own amps and suitcases. We had a road manager who stood at the door and counted tickets, because we got half the take plus a straight salary. We played four-hour gigs, a lot of dances and things. Then we'd pack up and drive 500 miles to the next city, where we'd sleep in a motel all day until the next night's gig. Just one-nighters, one after another. We'd be playing one-lane bowling alleys and outdoor fairs in Pennsylvania, in the rain, getting [electric shocks from] our instruments. Out of two or three months' touring, there would be maybe two or three days off. I used to get sick backstage. I wasn't drinking or taking dope then but I'd get sick anyway, from the hours and not eating right. I was a trooper. We had to do it. There was a lot at stake.

"The William Morris Agency – Marshall Berle, Milton Berle's nephew – was our agent," David continues. "Usually we'd be following somebody from city to city, like The Everly Brothers, who

were terrors. They'd be somewhere the night before, leave the place in shambles, destroy the motel, and when we got there the city council would be waiting for us. 'Behave yourselves, or leave right now,' they used to say. We had to be careful. We did our share of destroying motels, though. We'd get home from a tour and there'd be a $700 bill waiting for us for a room we'd had a water fight in."

■ Saturday 12th
Surfin' Safari album peaks on US *Billboard* chart at number 32.

■ Wednesday 16th
RECORDING *Surfin' USA* **session 2** Fine studio *New York, NY* three-hour session. The group breaks from the East Coast tour to record further versions of '**Farmer's Daughter**' and '**Lana**'. These attempts are later discarded; new versions will be tried on January 31st. The session today in New York City is notable in Beach Boys recording history because it marks one of the very few occasions that the group will record outside of Los Angeles.

■ Friday 18th
RECORDING Radio Recorders studio *Hollywood, CA* three-hour session. With the group's latest tour completed, Brian takes charge of a demo session for '**Ride Away**' in which he is joined by musicians Steve Douglas (saxophone; real name Steve Kreisman) and Ed 'Sharky' Hall (drums) while Brian himself plays guitar, bass and keyboards. The recording will remain unreleased.

■ Thursday 31st
RECORDING *Surfin' USA* **session 3** Western Recorders studio *Hollywood, CA* 8:00-11:30pm. Tonight's session is for vocal overdubbing work on '**Surfin' USA**' and '**Shut Down**'. Satisfactory backing tracks for '**Farmer's Daughter**' and '**Lana**' are also completed, and to round off the session stereo mixes are made of 'Surfin' USA' and 'Farmer's Daughter' (the latter being a mix of tracking take 9 and vocal overdub take 2).

February

■ Monday 11th
RECORDING *Surfin' USA* **session 4** Capitol studio *Hollywood, CA* 11:00pm-2:00am. Late in the evening and back once more at the Capitol Records HQ, The Beach Boys resume work on their *Surfin' USA* album, recording backing tracks and vocals for '**Let's Go Trippin'**', '**Honky Tonk**', '**Misirlou**' and '**Noble Surfer**'. Possibly due to the group's fatigue, a total of 39 'takes', or attempts, are required to reach a satisfactory vocal recording for 'Noble Surfer'. Also tonight, vocals are added to the January 31st tracking tapes of '**Farmer's Daughter**' and '**Lana**'.

■ Tuesday 12th
RECORDING *Surfin' USA* **session 5** Capitol studio *Hollywood, CA* 10:00pm-1:00am. A further session at Capitol's HQ to provide instrumentation and vocals for '**Finders Keepers**', '**Surf Jam**' (8 takes required) and '**Stoked**' (16 takes required). With that, the new album is complete.

■ Thursday 14th
Hermosa Beach High School *Hermosa Beach, CA*
Almost a month after their last concert appearance, the group returns to the stage to perform at this *Valentine Day Dance* event at

'AFM sheet', or musicians' union log, showing details of the group's fourth session for the *Surfin' USA* album, recorded at Capitol's studio in Hollywood on February 11th.

Capitol Records, Inc.
(Employer's name)

Phonograph Recording Contract Blank
AMERICAN FEDERATION OF MUSICIANS
OF THE UNITED STATES AND CANADA

59419

Local Union No. 47

THIS CONTRACT for the personal services of musicians, made this 11th day of February, 1963, between the undersigned employer (hereinafter called the "employer") and five musicians (hereinafter called "employees"). (including the leader)

WITNESSETH, That the employer hires the employees as musicians severally on the terms and conditions below, and as further specified on reverse side. The leader represents that the employees already designated have agreed to be bound by said terms and conditions. Each employee yet to be chosen shall be so bound by said terms and conditions upon agreeing to accept his employment. Each employee may enforce this agreement. The employees severally agree to render collectively to the employer services as musicians in the orchestra under the leadership of Brian Wilson as follows:

Name and Address of Place of Engagement Capitol Records, 1750 N. Vine Street, Hollywood 28, Calif.

Date(s) and Hours of Employment 11 PM to 2 AM

Type of Engagement: **Recording for phonograph records only**   SCALE   Plus pension-contributions as specified on reverse side hereof.

WAGE AGREED UPON $_____
(Terms and amount)

This wage includes expenses agreed to be reimbursed by the employer in accordance with the attached schedule, or a schedule to be furnished the employer on or before the date of engagement.

To be paid _____
(Specify when payments are to be made)

Upon request by the American Federation of Musicians of the United States and Canada (herein called the "Federation") or the local in whose jurisdiction the employees shall perform hereunder, the employer either shall make advance payment hereunder or shall post an appropriate bond.

Employer's name and authorized signature	Capitol Records, Inc.
Leader's name	Brian Wilson
Leader's signature	Brian Wilson
Local No.	47
Street address	1750 North Vine Street
Street address	3701 W. 119th Street
City Hollywood State California Phone HO 26252	City Hawthorne State California

(1) Label name Capitol   Session no. 11044

Master no.	No. of minutes	TITLES OF TUNES	Master no.	No. of minutes	TITLES OF TUNES
39190	1:55	LET'S GO TRIPPIN	39193	2:00	NOBLE SURFER
39191	2:00	HONKY TONK			
39192		MISIRLOU			

(2) Employee's name (As on Social Security card) Last First Initial	(3) Home address (Give street, city and state)	(4) Local Union no.	(5) Social Security number	(6) Scale wages	(7) Pension contribution
WILSON, BRIAN (Leader)	3701 W. 119th St. Hawthorne, Calif.	47	568-62-7150	112.00	8.96
LOVE, MICHAEL	5642½ Aldama Los Angeles 45, Calif.	47	546-56-5698	56.00	4.48
MARKS, DAVID LEE	11901 Almertens Place Inglewood 2, Calif.	47	545-66-1928	56.00	4.48
WILSON, DENNIS	3701 W. 119th St. Hawthorne, Calif.	47	562-60-0767	56.00	4.48
WILSON, CARL	3701 W. 119th St. Hawthorne, Calif.	47	568-62-6168	56.00	4.48

1963

PAID MAR 26 1963

(8) Total Pension Contributions (Sum of Column (7)) $_____
Make check payable in this amount to "AFM & EPW Fund"

FOR FUND USE ONLY:
Date pay't rec'd _____ Amt. paid _____ Date posted _____ By _____
Form B-4 Rev. 4-59

Hermosa Beach, just a few miles from Hawthorne. Beginning tonight and for a further three shows, drummer Mark Groseclose stands in after Dennis has an accident in his Chevrolet Corvair car.

Backstage, The Beach Boys meet Liberty Records recording duo Jan & Dean for the first time. Their recent single 'Linda' has just peaked in the *Billboard* charts at number 28. Since Jan & Dean do not have a live band of their own, the promoter of the show has hired The Beach Boys to back Jan & Dean. The two acts meet in a schoolroom that serves as the dressing room. In readiness for the performance, The Beach Boys have learned Jan & Dean's biggest hits, including 'Baby Talk', 'Heart And Soul', 'Linda' and 'Louie Louie'. But of course this is not enough for a whole show, so they pick out some rock standards to play together during the hour that the two groups are scheduled to play.

The Beach Boys play an opening set, before giving way to Jan & Dean. Their set is a success, except for one thing. It still isn't long enough, with the repertoire about 10 minutes short. The promoter insists that he wants his full hour's worth of music and promptly tells everybody to get back on stage and fill out the time or they will not be receiving their $500 payment.

But they haven't rehearsed any more songs for the set. They have played all the songs they know. Mike Love quickly suggests that they can do a couple of Jan & Dean's biggest hits over again. But the duo insists that it will be a lot more fun to play The Beach Boys' two biggest hits again – after all, it is 40 or 50 minutes since they were on-stage themselves. The Beach Boys are surprised by the idea – and take it as a compliment from the experienced duo. The two groups launch into 'Surfin'' and 'Surfin' Safari' and the audience flips out. At the end of the night, high on euphoria, the groups drive home together, discussing the possibility of recording together.

Dean Torrence of Jan & Dean will tell US radio in 1974: "A couple of days later Jan called Brian and reaffirmed to him how magical the musical event on stage had been. He said that he had talked it over with our producer Lou [Adler] and me and we had decided to try our hand at making surf music, if that was OK with him. Our idea was to incorporate 'Surfin'' and 'Surfin' Safari' into our upcoming *Linda* album – and we were thinking of re-titling the album *Jan & Dean Take Linda Surfing*. Brian loved the idea. After all, he was the songwriter and publisher of the two surf songs. He would just end up making that much more money, because his versions of those surf songs had already run their course, and it was a great deal for a young songwriter. Not just because of the money issue but, more importantly, [it meant] more exposure. He not only gave Jan & Dean his blessing, but he offered to help us in the studio to record the two surf songs as well." (See March 4th.)

Sunday 17th
Los Angeles Sports Arena *Los Angeles, CA*
The Beach Boys perform at a benefit concert featuring a big all-star cast.

Thursday 28th
Al copyrights his (inevitably unreleased) instrumental 'Pink Champagne'.

March

Saturday 2nd
TV KFMB Television Studios *San Diego, CA*. Syndicated *The Steve Allen Show* lip-synch 'Surfin' USA', 'The Things We Did Last

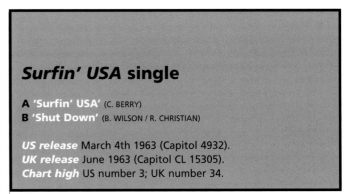

Surfin' USA single

A 'Surfin' USA' (C. BERRY)
B 'Shut Down' (B. WILSON / R. CHRISTIAN)

US release March 4th 1963 (Capitol 4932).
UK release June 1963 (Capitol CL 15305).
Chart high US number 3; UK number 34.

Summer' broadcast 11:30pm-1:00am. The group's road to prominence continues with their US television debut, appearing on *The Steve Allen Show* to plug their new Capitol single 'Surfin' USA', due for release on Monday. Wearing matching sailor outfits The Beach Boys perform on a set adorned by upright surfboards and beach-type teenagers. The two clips are telerecorded this afternoon and transmitted later this evening in black-and-white. David tells *Trouser Press*: "After a while, Brian got sick of the tour grind. He just wanted to stay home with his girlfriend. So he did the TV gigs and local appearances, but mainly stayed home to produce records and write songs. I sang Brian's part on-stage."

Monday 4th
'Surfin' USA' / 'Shut Down' single released in the US. Both sides will chart, peaking at number 3 and 23 respectively. (Some charts are still based on radio plays as well as sales, so B-sides can chart separately from their As.) The A-side features Brian's adaptation with new lyrics of Chuck Berry's 1958 hit 'Sweet Little Sixteen'. Following a lawsuit shortly afterwards from ARC Music, Berry's publisher, Brian will lose his writing credit on the song. The suit concludes with an undisclosed out-of-court settlement paid to ARC by Capitol.

• 'Surfin'' / 'Surfin' Safari' single by Jan & Dean released in the US, with The Beach Boys providing backing vocals and instrumentation. Dean Torrence tells Scott Keller in 1973: "About a week after Jan had rung Brian, he, Brian, Mike, Carl, Dennis, David and I all got together at Western studios in Hollywood and we recorded the two surf songs, and it felt like magic once again. We called Brian and told him we wanted to do 'Surfin' Safari' on our new album. He was thrilled. We asked him to bring the guys to sing on the tracks to save money, because the money was tight. Brian was thrilled with this too. So, all the guys came in the studio and played all the tracks to 'Surfin'' and 'Surfin' Safari' and we said, 'While you're here, you may as well do the vocal parts.' So they did the vocal parts and we added our parts.

"After the sessions," Torrence continues, "Brian played us their new single. It was based on a Chuck Berry tune and called 'Surfin' USA'. We were floored and Jan immediately tried to talk Brian into giving the song to us, but Brian wasn't about to give it away. But he did say that he had a similar song that was only partially completed and that he would be more than happy to give that song to Jan & Dean. He played us another tune, 'Surf City', and said, 'Here, have that one.' We loved that song too, so we gladly took it." (See May 27th.)

Tuesday 5th
RECORDING Capitol studio *Hollywood, CA* 10:00pm-1:00am. Brian produces a session for The Honeys, a female surf-music group featuring Ginger Blake, Diane Rovell and her sister, Brian's future

wife, Marilyn Rovell. They record **'Shoot The Curl'** (take 7 marked as best) and **'Surfin' Down The Swanee River'** (take 5 best). The Honeys' name comes from the Beach Boy hit 'Surfin' Safari' and its lyric: "Early in the morning, we'll be startin' out, some honeys will be comin' along...".

Musicians present David Gates (probably bass guitar), Leon Russell (piano), Billy Strange (guitar).

■ Thursday 7th

RECORDING Conway Recorders studio *Hollywood, CA* three-hour session. At this tracking and vocals session the group works on two songs, **'The Baker Man'** (six 'tracking', or backing instrumental, takes required) and **'Side Two'**.

'Baker Man' features a lead vocal by Brian on a Nick Venet production, unreleased until the Capitol *Surfin' Safari / Surfin' USA* CD in 1990. It is inspired by 'Hully Gully', later covered by The Beach Boys on their *Party!* album, and 'Peanut Butter', a song recorded by The Marathons. Sources suggest that The Beach Boys' recording of the song is nothing more than a demo for music publishers Al Nevins and Don Kirshner.

The group also makes several attempts at recording a suitable tracking tape for a song with the working title 'Side Two', but after several run-throughs it is shelved.

Following today's session, Murry Wilson insists that Brian is put in sole charge of production on future Beach Boys sessions and that Nick Venet be dropped from this role.

Murry later tells *Rolling Stone*: "Brian refused to have Nick as their producer because [Nick] didn't tell them the truth. He'd say, 'Brian, be here at 2:00pm. We're going to master your record,' and then he'd do the mastering himself, before Brian had even got there. So Brian came home one day from Capitol very upset and he broke down into tears. He said, 'Dad, will you go down there and tell Capitol we don't want him any more? He's changing our sound.' So I went down to Capitol and I talked to Voyle Gilmore, the vice-president, and I told him, 'You folks don't know how to produce a rock'n'roll hit in your studios.' Their engineers were used to good music but not rock'n'roll and we wanted to continue to use Western studios. I told him, 'Leave us alone and we'll make hits for you.' He got red in the face – but he let us do it. (See May 16th, June 12th, July 24th.)

■ Saturday 23rd

'Surfin' USA' single hits US charts, reaching number 3. The group's surfing music is breaking like a huge wave across the whole of America.

■ Monday 25th

Surfin' USA album released in the US.

April

Surfin' Safari album released in the UK.

This month Carl transfers from Hawthorne High to Hollywood Professional School for his senior year, in the company of David Marks and the Rovell sisters.

■ Monday 8th

'Shoot The Curl' / **'Surfin' Down The Swanee River'** single by The Honeys released in the US, a Capitol 45 featuring production by Brian Wilson and Nick Venet.

Surfin' USA album

A1 'Surfin' USA' (C. BERRY)
A2 'Farmer's Daughter' (B. WILSON / M. LOVE)
A3 'Misirlou' (N. ROUBANIS / F. WISE / M. LEEDS / S. RUSSELL / J. PINA)
A4 'Stoked' (B. WILSON)
A5 'Lonely Sea' (B. WILSON / G. USHER)
A6 'Shut Down' (B. WILSON / R. CHRISTIAN)
B1 'Noble Surfer' (B. WILSON / M. LOVE)
B2 'Honky Tonk' (B. DOGGETT / C. SCOTT / B. BUTLER / H. GLOVER / S. SHEPHERD)
B3 'Lana' (B. WILSON)
B4 'Surf Jam' (C. WILSON)
B5 'Let's Go Trippin'' (D. DALE)
B6 'Finders Keepers' (B. WILSON / M. LOVE)

US release March 25th 1963 (Capitol T1980).
UK release August 1965 (Capitol T1980).
Chart high US number 2; UK number 34.

■ Saturday 13th

'Surfin' USA' single enters US *Billboard* Top 40 chart at number 33.

TOUR STARTS US Midwest (Apr 27th- ends some time before May 16th)

■ Saturday 27th

The Danceland Ballroom *Cedar Rapids, IA* admission $1.50
Tonight's show is part of The Beach Boys' first Midwest tour and is the group's first concert outside California. The tour has had a shaky start as Brian refuses to partake in the two-day drive to Oklahoma City where the excursion was due to begin.

To remedy this, the agent in Oklahoma requested that extra gigs should be filled in for The Beach Boys so that they can play their way through to the City. One of the extra shows pencilled in was at the University of Arizona in Tucson. During the second show there, the ceiling caved in because of the loud vibrations that emanated from The Beach Boys' amplifiers. Large pieces of concrete cascaded down onto the group in mid performance. No one was hurt, but the college subsequently took to banning all future rock'n'roll concerts at the venue.

Brian will drop out of several engagements on this tour. He is finding it increasingly difficult to juggle time to perform in concerts, write and produce music, and compete with his father. Murry is uptight about Brian's decision to quit some of the performances and gives him a very rough time. Al Jardine is eager to rejoin his former colleagues and returns to the line-up to replace Brian on the road.

Carl will recall on the 1972 US radio show *Ten Years Of Harmony*: "Brian just said, 'I don't want to tour. I want to stay at home and make music.' I remember my dad was upset at the time. He felt that it wasn't fair for [Brian] not to go and play for the people, because they had bought the records and wanted to see him. But Brian didn't want to do it. He just wanted to stay home and write and produce. So Alan came back to the group and took his place. The loud music was hurting Brian's ears anyway. The high pressure was just too much."

• 'Shut Down' single B-side hits the US charts today.

May

■ Friday 3rd

Excelsior Amusement Park *Excelsior, MN*

According to the park's promoter, The Beach Boys receive $650 as an appearance fee and a $307 slice of the box-office takings. Approximately 1,800 attend the show.

■ Saturday 4th

Surfin' USA album hits the US charts where it will remain for 78 weeks, peaking at number 2.

■ Thursday 9th

RECORDING United Recorders studio Hollywood, CA 8:00-11:00pm. Brian holds a session this evening at which a song noted as 'Summer Moon' is recorded, but with Brian's roommate Bob Norberg again present, it is probably a further recording of **'The Surfer Moon'** (see September 13th 1962). Music publisher Nevins-Kirshner pays for this session.

Musicians present Hal Blaine (drums), Ray Pohlman (bass).

■ Thursday 16th

RECORDING Capitol studio *Hollywood, CA* 10:00am-1:00pm. Now free from any interference by A&R man Nick Venet, Brian produces two further tracks for The Honeys: **'Raindrops'** (take 19 marked as best) and **'From Jimmy With Tears'** (take 9 best). 'Jimmy' will be released as a Honeys B-side on December 2nd. Arranger is Jack Nitzsche, who last year worked with Phil Spector on The Crystals' 'He's A Rebel'. (Trumpeter Roy Caton is logged as today's 'contractor', the person who organises the various musicians to come and play on each session.)

Musicians present Hal Blaine (drums), Jimmy Bond Jr (upright bass), Russell Bridges (keyboards), Glen Campbell (guitar), Roy Caton (trumpet), Frankie Capp (percussion), Steven Douglas (saxophone), David Gates (bass guitar), Jay Migliori (saxophone), Bill Pitman (guitar), Don Randi (keyboards), Tommy Tedesco (guitar).

■ Friday 24th

Memorial Auditorium *Sacramento, CA*

The Beach Boys play one of their first headlining concerts, an *Alumni Class Of 1963* fundraising dance for a northern California high school. The show is promoted by 19-year-old Frederick Vail who books the group from the William Morris Agency. Bearing in mind the group has to travel the 400 miles or so to Sacramento from Los Angeles, Vail agrees to pay them a fee of $750.

Teenage promoter Vail remembers: "The show was a fundraiser for my high school, from where I had graduated in June 1962. The kids were raising money for this all-night Graduation Party. They graduated in the evening and then they go to this all-night party where there are buffets, movies, entertainments and door prizes.

"They had only raised $750 for the party through the year, selling candy, newspapers and doing car washes, and I told them that they didn't have enough money to do everything plus get entertainment. I suggested they take the $750, buy an act and put on a concert, sell tickets for it, and raise money that way.

"They agreed to do it but the parent advisors and school administrators didn't want them to entrust their whole budget to a kid – me – who had just graduated the year before. But they decided to let the kids have their way and if the kids lost their money, then they've learnt their lesson. And if the kids made some money, then everything is rosy. So the kids agreed to let me take their $750 and

go out and set up a concert. It then fell on me as to who we should get," Vail continues. "By pooling the kids, going and visiting the record shops and listening to the radio, I decided that The Beach Boys would be the act I wanted to book.

"I liked The Beach Boys and I liked their music. I booked them in April, and they had recently signed with the William Morris Agency. When I first called the agency, the receptionist didn't know whom I was talking about. I asked her to transfer me to the variety department and I ended up talking to the secretary there, who said, 'Oh yeah, I think we just signed that band. A surfing band, right?' I said, 'Yes, that's the one.' So she put me in touch with the junior agency and I booked the band.

"I first saw The Beach Boys six weeks later when I met them from their plane. I had borrowed my folks' Chevy station wagon and I drove out to the old Sacramento Municipal Field. I met them on the tarmac. They got off the plane and we went over to the baggage claim area to get their instruments and amplifiers, and we loaded them in the back of the wagon and drove to the gig. Here were The Beach Boys, whose ages at the time ranged from around 15 to 22.

"Brian was not with the group at this engagement; he remained home in Los Angeles. Al Jardine replaced Brian, but was not a regular member of The Beach Boys at this time. In those days, the concert promoters were older gentlemen, entrepreneurs in their 40s and 50s. So The Beach Boys presumed that, since I was a kid, I was not the promoter but the guy sent to pick them up. Carl asked, 'Who's promoting the show?' I said, 'I am.' He said, 'But you're just a kid like us.' They asked, 'Who are we opening for?' I replied, 'Didn't the William Morris Agency tell you anything? You guys are the headliners. You're the show! You are the act.'

"They were a little bit surprised and probably panicked a little bit. Before this, they were opening for Jan & Dean and for Dick Dale & The Del Tones. They did headline a few shows in '62 and '63, but it was few and far between.

"The Beach Boys and I got to the Auditorium and the boys went on and, at that time, they would do two sets," says Vail. "So they did a 45-minute performance, the curtain came down, and there was an intermission. They were pretty excited that they had gone over so well. But then it dawned on them that they still had to come back and do another 45-minute show. They had shot their wad. They didn't have enough of their own material so they were doing other people's music: Al sang the Del Shannon hit 'Runaway' and Dennis was doing one of Dion's recordings, 'The Wanderer'.

"They closed their set with Chuck Berry's 'Johnny B Goode'. So I told them to do the same songs again with slightly longer guitar solos, longer drum solos, and to put in any new songs they had. It was a captive audience so they could try them out. The second set was a smash!

"After the show was over we went back to the hotel, which was about two blocks away. A lot of kids had followed us. The Beach Boys gave a lot of autographs and hugged their fans, who told the group how great they were. Later, in one of the rooms, we all sat around a large table, talking about the concert and the crowd's reaction, which was fantastic. The group had seen success in Los Angeles, but tonight they had seen success hundreds of miles away from their home, and they weren't expecting it.

"Carl then asked Murry, 'Dad, how much did we make tonight?' Murry gets out his envelope and starts scratching down some figures, taking into account the William Morris commission, hotel bills, six airline tickets, meals, et cetera. And he figured that, after everything, the group had made about $52 apiece. They were ecstatic! $52 was a lot of money. That was more than some adults were earning in a week. They then asked how much the school and I had made, as the promoters, and I told them that I had made somewhere between $3,000 and $4,000 net. They were in shock. They couldn't believe it. Murry and the boys were amazed that a kid like myself could put together a show and make this kind of money while they, the performers, were only making a very minimal amount. I felt no reason why The Beach Boys should make thousands of dollars for the promoters when they should be making that kind of money for themselves.

"The William Morris Agency were booking the group then for between $200 and $800 a night, and I foresaw promoters getting fat and rich off The Beach Boys' popularity. So I mentioned to Murry and the boys that, if I can have this kind of success in Sacramento, California, obviously there would be other cities where The Beach Boys' popularity is just as great. So perhaps the group should think about promoting their own concert dates? Murry thought this idea was fantastic but admitted that he couldn't give it the time necessary to go out on the road and set up the shows. So I said, 'Well, I'm not doing anything, so let's enter into an agreement. I'll go out and check out the cities.' If I felt that the city warranted us putting up our money to front a show, we could do that – and we would devise a way of compensating me.

"That night in Sacramento," Vail concludes, "I earned more money than I had ever seen, and I was quite anxious to continue working with The Beach Boys. In the six or seven hours working with them that night I had become quite attached to the group. What we ended up with this night was the concept that [around the end of 1964] became American Productions. But the first year or so they were all 'Frederick Vail Productions Presents…', or we would offer 'sponsorship', so to speak, to the local rock Top 40 radio station in exchange for promoting the concert. We called that 'fronting the show'." Vail will continue to be closely associated with The Beach Boys for the next three years.

Saturday 25th
'Surfin' USA' single peaks in US *Billboard* chart at number 3. It is The Beach Boys' first Top Ten hit in America. The single's B-side, 'Shut Down', enters the US *Billboard* chart at number 38.

Monday 27th
'Surf City' / 'She's My Summer Girl' single by Jan & Dean released in the US. Both sides of this Liberty 45 are co-written by Brian, and he also contributes backing vocals to the A-side. Dean Torrence of Jan & Dean tells *Melody Maker*: "When we recorded the newly completed 'Surf City' song, Jan called Brian and invited him to the recording studio. Once in the studio, Jan and Brian sang the lead vocal together, double-tracking it.

"Then Brian and I sang some of the background parts plus the falsetto part that Brian had originally written. Brian then suggested that he and I sing the very same vocal part again, which made it four vocals, [to] see what that sounded like, so we did. The result was a very unique vocal sound. Because of the differences in the sound of our falsettos – Brian's falsetto was mainly midrange in tone but mine was mostly top-end [treble] in tone – mixing the two different voices caused a strange but very interesting [mixture]. Everybody in the studio loved the final result."
Jan & Dean Take Linda Surfin' album by Jan & Dean released in the US. It includes songs co-written by Brian and features backing vocals and instrumentation by The Beach Boys. (See March 4th.) "We worked for a long time with The Beach Boys, Brian in particular," says Dean Torrence. "He was always around. Jan would take a song to a certain point and then Brian would come into the studio and make it anything from 5 to 15 percent better. He would

take a good track and make it fantastic. We were quite free about singing on each other's records, but then the record companies started clamping down. Capitol got really uptight about The Beach Boys singing on some of our hits. It started to get stupid." (See November.)

June

'Surfin' USA' / 'Shut Down' single released in the UK. It will peak at number 34, the first time that the group dents the UK singles listings.

■ Wednesday 5th
Memorial Auditorium *Modesto, CA*

■ Wednesday 12th
RECORDING *Surfer Girl* session 1 Western Recorders studio (3) *Hollywood, CA* three-hour session. Just days before his 21st birthday, Brian enters Western to prove to Capitol Records that he is capable as his band's new producer. He takes with him engineer Chuck Britz to serve as his right-hand man, a position that Britz will keep at Western for the next four years.

Brian injects his energy into the productions and uses this time working on the new album to alleviate the strain of touring with The Beach Boys, an activity that already has caused him some distress.

Today, The Beach Boys record **'Little Deuce Coupe'** and re-record **'Surfer Girl'**, first cut to tape on February 8th 1962.

'Surfer Girl' is inspired by Jiminy Cricket's tune 'When You Wish Upon A Star' from the 1940 Walt Disney animated feature *Pinocchio*. Brian will recall on CBS radio in 1976: "I was driving to a hot-dog stand and I actually created a melody in my head without being able to hear it on a piano, and I sang it to myself. I didn't even sing it out loud in the car. When I got home that day I finished the song, wrote the bridge, put the harmonies together, and called it 'Surfer Girl'."

■ Friday 14th
RECORDING Gold Star studio *Los Angeles, CA* 11:30am-2:30pm. A further Beach Boys recording session, but this time in a new venue for the group. Gold Star, at Santa Monica Boulevard and Vine Street, is the studio famously used by Brian's musical hero, Phil Spector, and he must be thrilled to be working there. "I liked the way [Spector] sat at the piano," Brian says on the 2003 *Pet Sounds Live In London* DVD. "I liked the way he talked. I liked his voice. I liked his face. I liked the way he looked. I liked him." The musicians present at Gold Star today are all significant session players from what later came to be known as the Wrecking Crew 'band' that helped Spector create his mini-masterpieces.

(The information in this book about the musicians who appeared at particular sessions is drawn primarily from contract sheets filled in at the studio by musicians' union officials so that each player would be paid the correct union scale for their work. The union is the AFM – the American Federation of Musicians – and these historically valuable logs have thus become known as 'AFM sheets', although the official name is a 'Phonograph Recording Contract Blank'. Not every musician for every session is logged, and mistakes are evident in the listings that survive, but nonetheless they offer the most accurate account of musical contributions to Beach Boys sessions.)

Today's session produces **'Back Home'** and, according to the AFM sheets, **'Black Wednesday'**. Neither will be released now, but

CAPITOL RECORDS
(Employer's name)

Phonograph Recording Contract Blank
AMERICAN FEDERATION OF MUSICIANS
OF THE UNITED STATES AND CANADA

1484
75991

Local Union No. 47

THIS CONTRACT for the personal services of musicians, made this 12th day of June, 19 63, between the undersigned employer (hereinafter called the "employer") and five musicians (including the leader) (hereinafter called "employees").

WITNESSETH, That the employer hires the employees as musicians severally on the terms and conditions below, **and as further specified on reverse side.** The leader represents that the employees already designated have agreed to be bound by said terms and conditions. Each employee yet to be chosen shall be so bound by said terms and conditions upon agreeing to accept his employment. Each employee may enforce this agreement. The employees severally agree to render collectively to the employer services as musicians in the orchestra under the leadership of Brian Wilson as follows:

Name and Address of Place of Engagement Western Recorders, 6000 Sunset Blvd., L.A. 28, Calif.

Date(s) and Hours of Employment June 12, 1963

Type of Engagement: **Recording for phonograph records only**
WAGE AGREED UPON $ SCALE

Plus pension contributions as specified on reverse side hereof.

(Terms and amount)

This wage includes expenses agreed to be reimbursed by the employer in accordance with the attached schedule, or a schedule to be furnished the employer on or before the date of engagement.

To be paid

(Specify when payments are to be made)

Upon request by the American Federation of Musicians of the United States and Canada (herein called the "Federation") or the local in whose jurisdiction the employees shall perform hereunder, the employer either shall make advance payment hereunder or shall post an appropriate bond.

Employer's name and authorized signature: CAPITOL RECORDS, INC.

Leader's name: BRIAN WILSON Local No. 47

Leader's signature

Street address 1750 N. Vine St.

Street address 3701 W. 119th Street

Hollywood Calif. HO 26252
City   State   Phone

Hawthorne Calif.
City   State

(1) Label name Capitol Records   Session no. 11297

Master no.	No. of minutes	TITLES OF TUNES	Master no.	No. of minutes	TITLES OF TUNES
50027	1:10	LITTLE DEUCE COUPE			
50028	2:25	SURFER GIRL			

(2) Employee's name (As on Social Security card) Last First Initial	(3) Home address (Give street, city and state)	(4) Local Union no.	(5) Social Security number	(6) Scale wages	(7) Pension contribution
(Leader) WILSON, BRIAN Pd. B.	3701 W. 119th St. Hawthorne, Calif.	47	568-62-7150	112	8.96
LOVE, MICHAEL Pd. B.	5642½ Aldama Los Angeles 52, Calif.	47	546-56-5698	56	4.48
MARKS, DAVID LEE Pd. B.	11901 Almertens Place Inglewood, Calif.	47	545-66-1928	56	4.48
WILSON, DENNIS Pd. B.	3701 W. 119th St. Hawthorne, Calif.	47	562-60-0767	56	4.48
WILSON, CARL Pd. B.	3701 W. 119th St. Hawthorne, Calif.	47	568-62-6168	56	4.48

(8) Total Pension Contributions (Sum of Column (7)) $
Make check payable in this amount to "AFM & EPW Fund"

FOR FUND USE ONLY:

Date pay't rec'd _____ Amt. paid _____ Date posted _____ By _____
Form B-4 Rev. 4-59

'Back Home' – written by Brian and his roommate Bob Norberg – will be resurrected for the *15 Big Ones* album in 1976. 'Black Wednesday', a Brian and Mike composition, is the working title for 'Run-Around Lover' (see October 21st).

Musicians present Hal Blaine (drums), David Gates (probably guitar; later of the group Bread), Jay Migliori (probably saxophone), Steve Douglas (probably saxophone), Carol Kaye (bass guitar).

■ Saturday 15th
The Civic Auditorium *Honolulu, HI*

The Beach Boys perform on the second day of a three-day music festival.

■ Saturday 22nd
'Shut Down' single B-side peaks in US *Billboard* chart at number 23.

TOUR STARTS US Midwest (Jun 29th-July 5th) The group plays shows in Iowa, Minnesota, Nebraska and Illinois.

July

Surfin' USA EP released in the UK: 'Surfin' USA', 'Shut Down', 'Surfer Girl', 'Surfin' Safari'.

■ Saturday 6th
Veterans Memorial Stadium *Santa Maria, CA* with The Honeys, The Four Speeds

The Beach Boys perform at a *Surfing Spectacular* concert sponsored by radio station K-SEE.

• *Surfin' USA* album peaks in US *Billboard* chart at number 2.

■ Sunday 14th
RECORDING *Surfer Girl* session 2 Western Recorders studio *Hollywood, CA*. Session to record **'South Bay Surfer'** and **'The Surfer Moon'**, and vocals for **'Catch A Wave'**. 'Surfer Moon' becomes the first recording by the group to feature a string arrangement.

■ Tuesday 16th
RECORDING *Surfer Girl* session 3 Western Recorders studio *Hollywood, CA*. The group returns to the studio where during one lengthy, highly productive six-hour session they record vocals and instrumentation for **'Our Car Club'**, **'Your Summer Dream'**, **'Hawaii'**, **'Surfers Rule'** (tracking take 10 marked as best) and **'In My Room'** (basic vocal track take 13 marked as best).

"When Dennis, Carl and I lived in Hawthorne as kids we all slept in the same room," says Brian in a Capitol interview. "One night I sang the song 'Ivory Tower' to them and they liked it. Then a couple of weeks later I proceeded to teach them both how to sing the harmony parts to it. It took them a little while but they finally learned it. We then sang this song night after night. It brought peace to us. When we recorded 'In My Room' there was just Dennis, Carl and me on the first verse ... and we sounded just like we did in our bedroom on all those nights."

According to Gary Usher, Brian's co-writer for 'In My Room', he and Brian wrote the song in an hour after watching a baseball game. Brian says in the film *Endless Harmony* that 'In My Room' is about "somewhere where you could lock out the world, go to a secret little place, think, be, do whatever you have to do. I wrote it with a friend of mine, Gary Usher. We wrote it and then later on I said, 'Hey, these lyrics. I could use these lyrics.' After I had done

the whole song, I looked back and said, 'Oh, I know what I did. I was writing about myself.'"

Tracking sessions also take place today for **'Catch A Wave'**, **'The Rockin' Surfer'** and the energetic instrumental **'Boogie Woodie'** (seven takes required – piano and organ overdubs follow) which features a melody line based on Rimsky-Korsakov's 'The Flight Of The Bumble Bee'. Murry Wilson sits in the control booth overseeing the entire session, giving orders to The Beach Boys over the studio intercom.

• The Brian Wilson / Mike Love song 'Runaround Lover' is copyrighted today.

TOUR STARTS US Midwest (Jul 19th-28th)

The Beach Boys return to the concert stage, performing shows in Iowa, Minnesota, Nebraska, Illinois, Wisconsin, Kansas, Ohio and Indiana. Brian is absent from some of the shows and uses any excuse to return to the recording studio (see July 24th).

"It was a perfect opportunity to be rowdy and we took full advantage of it," David tells *Trouser Press* about touring. "Dennis painted his cock green once, and went down to the lobby naked for a Coke. And we got crab lice once. We were at a music store, standing behind a table, signing autographs. All these little teenage girls were there, and here are these five guys jumping around scratching their crotches. Brian said, 'Yep, we got 'em.' So we go back to the hotel and put blue ointment on our broken skin. It would burn, and there'd be five guys jumping up and down naked in front of the air-conditioner. Must have looked funny from the street."

■ Saturday 20th
'Surf City' / 'She's My Summer Girl' single by Jan & Dean becomes the first surf-music song to hit Number 1 on the US *Billboard* charts. Everyone is pleased with the success – everyone, that is, except for the group's record company, Capitol, and Murry Wilson. Murry is irate and blasts Brian for giving away a number 1 record – especially to a competitor. "'Surf City' was a song that I was never going to complete," Brian tells *Teen Beat*. "I had lost interest in it and it would have gone to waste. I tried to make the point to my dad that I was a songwriter and songwriters needed other people to sing their songs. I was proud of the fact that another group had had a number 1 song with a track that I had written and that this would give me, a young songwriter, just that much more credibility. But dad would hear none of it and he ordered me to stop working with Jan & Dean. He called Jan 'a record pirate.'"

■ Monday 22nd
'Surfer Girl' / 'Little Deuce Coupe' single released in the US. Two days after the mixed celebrations for one of Brian's compositions, this new Capitol single makes clear to the label that Brian has far

---

Surfer Girl single

A 'Surfer Girl' (B. WILSON)
B 'Little Deuce Coupe' (B. WILSON / R. CHRISTIAN)

US release July 22nd 1963 (Capitol 5009).
Chart high US number 5.

An 'AFM sheet' for the June 12th session where Brian makes a declaration of independence, taking charge at Western Recorders to prove to Capitol that he is the man to produce The Beach Boys.

exceeded anyone's expectations. Capitol promptly gives Brian its full blessing to produce the group's third album. ('Surfer Girl' will peak at number 7 in US *Billboard* chart, 'Little Deuce Coupe' at 15.)

■ Wednesday 24th
RECORDING Capitol studio *Hollywood, CA* 2:00-6:00am. During this early morning session Brian assisted by Nick Venet produces The Honeys recording **'Pray For Surf'** (28 takes required) and **'(Oly Oxen Free Free Fee) Hide Go Seek'** (take 10 marked as best). 'Seek' is written by Brian; the two tracks will appear as a Honeys single on September 2nd. The session marks the last occasion when Brian and Venet will share production duties. Brian probably also contributes musically to the session.
Musicians present Hal Blaine (drums), Steve Douglas (saxophone), Jay Migliori (saxophone), Ray Pohlman (bass).

TOUR STARTS US West (around Jul 29th)

■ Monday 29th
The Beach Boys undertake a West Coast tour with The Safaris. As usual now, Brian misses some of the performances.

August

'Little Deuce Coupe' single B-side peaks in US *Billboard* R&B chart at number 28.
'Surfin' USA' single peaks in Australian chart at number 9, and in UK *Record Retailer* chart at number 37.
• At the very start of the month Nick Venet, the man responsible for The Beach Boys' breakthrough at Capitol Records, leaves the company to set up Ben-Ven Productions, his own independent record production company.

■ Saturday 3rd – Tuesday 6th
Pandora's Box *Los Angeles, CA*
The Beach Boys play another residency at this trendy coffee house.

■ Saturday 3rd
'Surfer Girl' single hits US charts.

■ Monday 5th
RECORDING Gold Star studio *Los Angeles, CA* 1:00-4:00pm. During a break from the group's current residency, and free from any production interference by Nick Venet, Brian supervises another recording session. Three tracks are recorded this afternoon for The Survivors: **'Witch Stand'**, **'Girlie'**, and **'Hot Harp'**, the latter featuring Mike's sister Maureen on harp. The Survivors are Brian's flatmate Bob Norberg and his two friends Rich Arlarian and Dave Nowlen. Days later, the completed and mixed master tape from this session is presented to Capitol, but they reject an offer to purchase it. (See August 27th.)
Musicians present Hal Blaine (drums), Steve Douglas (saxophone), David Gates (bass guitar), Jay Migliori (saxophone).

TOUR STARTS US East (approximately Aug 7th-30th). The Beach Boys' East Coast concert tour starts with performances in Maine, Massachusetts, Pennsylvania, and New York.

■ Sunday 11th
Auditorium Theater *Chicago, IL*

■ Saturday 17th
'Surfer Girl' single enters US *Billboard* Top 40 chart at number 28.
'Little Deuce Coupe' single B-side hits US charts.
'Surfin' USA' single peaks at number 34 in UK charts.

■ Thursday 22nd
West Virginia Fair *Wheeling, WV*
David Marks tells *Trouser Press*: "Temptations came from a variety of sources. We were playing an amusement park in Wheeling … owned by an aggressive multi-millionaire named Walter Dyke. After a show he took us to a club, a former speakeasy, and after I had mentioned it was my birthday, Dyke was buying me all the Scotch I could drink, though he knew I was only just 15. He put his arm around me and said, 'Hey, see that little blonde over there sitting in a chair? Well, tell her to go upstairs and everything will be fine. Tell her it was OK with me.' She was about 20, I guess. This was his birthday gift to me. A nice guy, but I was too shy to do it, so Dennis bounced over and dragged her upstairs, taking advantage of the situation. Then he came back and said, 'I warmed her up for you, go ahead. It's your birthday!' So I went up, and she was on the bed reading a newspaper, still had her high heels on. 'Let me know when you're through, kid.' It scared the hell out of me. Boy, were my folks pissed off."

■ Tuesday 27th
RECORDING Gold Star studio *Los Angeles, CA* 1:00-4:00pm. Undisturbed by the rejection from Capitol (see August 5th) Brian produces further tracks for The Survivors, namely **'Pamela Jean'** and **'After The Game'**, with instrumental backing tracks (8 takes required), vocal overdubs (11 takes required) and saxophone solo overdubs.

■ Thursday 29th
The Avalon Ballroom *LaCrosse, WI*
Following this Coca-Cola sponsored show the group drives from Wisconsin to their next gig in Chicago.

■ Friday 30th
Unknown venue *Chicago, IL*
During the journey from Wisconsin to Chicago, 15-year-old David Marks officially leaves the group. Brian will say on US TV: "David got into an argument with my dad … and David said, 'OK. I quit the group.' And dad said, 'Right! I hold you to it,' and that was it. He quit! The other boys didn't believe he would quit and said, 'You can't quit,' but he did. I liked David as an artist but his attitude was terrible. He really could have brushed up on his attitude a little."

David tells *Trouser Press* magazine in 1981: "We were kids, and we were cocky. It was a little scary, but great, too, playing guitar and getting pressed up against chain-link fences by thousands of teenage girls. So at that young and tender age I had got arrogant. I was a star, right? I thought I had it made. So I started getting real cocky. We always had to carry our amps and suitcases, and I started refusing to carry mine. Murry would yell at me, but I didn't care.

"I didn't have any plans to quit, but Murry started pressuring me because he wanted all the money to be in the corporate family situation, and I made that difficult. My parents and Murry started having conflicts over money, which I really didn't give a shit about.

"We were in a car on the way to Chicago when I announced I was quitting the group. Murry went, 'Well, all right man. Does everybody hear that?' And all the guys went, 'Ah, that's bullshit!' It turned out I still had seven months' worth of contracts, so I could've stayed after that if I hadn't started pushing it. I started singing, 'She's real fine, my 69…' and 'Little douche kit…' on-stage, and Murry would fine me. He'd fine me for not smiling on-stage too. Finally it ended. Just more or less a mutual agreement between Murry and me.

"I don't think the guys were too happy about it, because we'd grown up together and were pretty tight. And I think Brian probably didn't want me to quit because he thought that maybe he'd have to go back out on the road or something. But Al took over rhythm guitar and they went on. I wanted to be in control. I wanted to write my own songs. I wanted to emulate Brian … . After I left the group I had $22,000 in a trust fund my folks had set up for me. Then during the 1960s I'd get $7,000 to $8,000 every six months.

"After the split I wasn't sure what to do, so I saw a buddy I'd met through Carl, a drummer who was fooling around with a garage band at Hawthorne High. I walked in and said, 'All right, guys, I'm taking over! Gonna make you stars!' So we became Dave & The Marksmen, the first rock band to be signed to A&M. We recorded, went on tours of California, got airplay on all the local stations, met a lot of boss jocks, but didn't sell any records. After a year it folded and I found myself taking a lot of LSD and laying on my back in Venice, California. But I was still ambitious."

■ Saturday 31st
Los Angeles Memorial Sports Arena *Los Angeles, CA*
The Beach Boys perform at the *Show Of Stars* concert in LA. Following Marks's departure, Brian reluctantly returns to the live group on a more permanent basis and The Beach Boys once again resume their familiar five-man line-up.

September

RECORDING Western Recorders studio *Hollywood, CA*. During this month at Western the group records the single version of **'Be True To Your School'**.
• 'Surfer Girl' single peaks in US *Billboard* R&B chart at number 18
• 'Pajama Party' / 'The Original Surfer Stomp' single by The Bruce Johnston Combo released in the UK on London Records featuring future Beach Boy Johnston.

■ Monday 2nd
RECORDING *Little Deuce Coupe* **session 1** Western Recorders studio *Hollywood, CA*. Brian is already finding the surfing theme outdated and restricting. After playing a significant part in creating Jan & Dean's monster hit 'Surf City', he feels that the time is right to move on and change The Beach Boys' music and image in time for their next album.

With that in mind, the group sets to work today recording vocals and instrumentation for some (mostly) car inspired songs: **'Ballad Of Ole' Betsy'**, **'Be True To Your School'** (alternate version), **'Car Crazy Cutie'**, **'Cherry Cherry Coupe'**, **'Spirit Of America'**, **'No-Go Showboat'**, **'A Young Man Is Gone'** and **'Custom Machine'**, all quickly written or re-worked with KFWB DJ Roger Christian or Mike Love. Accompanying Brian, Carl, Dennis and Mike at the lengthy session is returning Beach Boy Al Jardine, as well as some of Brian's growing stable of talented studio musicians.
'Pray For Surf' / **'(Oly Oxen Free Free Free) Hide Go Seek'** single by The Honeys released in the US. The group's third 45 is co-produced by Brian, who also writes the B-side.

■ Saturday 7th
The Lagoon *Farmington, UT*
During the group's time here, Brian and Mike come up with the

---

Surfer Girl album

A1 'Surfer Girl' (B. WILSON)
A2 'Catch A Wave' (B. WILSON / M. LOVE)
A3 'The Surfer Moon' (B. WILSON)
A4 'South Bay Surfer' (B. WILSON / D. WILSON / A. JARDINE)
A5 'The Rocking Surfer' (TRAD ARR B. WILSON)
A6 'Little Deuce Coupe' (B. WILSON / R .CHRISTIAN)
B1 'In My Room' (B. WILSON / G. USHER)
B2 'Hawaii' (B. WILSON / M. LOVE)
B3 'Surfers Rule' (B. WILSON / M. LOVE)
B4 'Our Car Club' (B. WILSON / M. LOVE)
B5 'Your Summer Dream' (B. WILSON / B. NORBERG)
B6 'Boogie Woodie' (N. RIMSKY-KORSAKOV ARR B. WILSON)

US release September 16th 1963 (Capitol T1981).
UK release April 1967 (Capitol T1981).
Chart high US number 7; UK number 13.

idea of a song called 'Fun Fun Fun'. Also, tonight's venue will be mentioned in their later song 'Salt Lake City', where they will tell us that "all the kids dig The Lagoon now…".
• 'Little Deuce Coupe' single B-side enters US *Billboard* Top 40 chart at number 38.

TOUR STARTS US East/South (Sep 8th-13th) The Beach Boys play shows in Maine, Alabama, Pennsylvania and New York. Mike will tell BBC Radio-1: "After our first tour in [the group] wagon, I thought 'never again', so I bought myself a Jaguar. It was my first real nifty car. I took out the right-hand seat and made a bed in it. There were three of us in that car on tour. One guy would be able to sleep, one guy would be resting, and the other guy would be driving. It worked out really well."

■ Saturday 14th
Memorial Auditorium *Sacramento, CA* 2:00 & 8:00pm
• 'Surfer Girl' single peaks in US *Billboard* chart at number 7.

■ Monday 16th
Surfer Girl album released in the US. It soon becomes a number 7 hit, and is the first Beach Boys album to bear the credit "Produced by Brian Wilson". Brian realises that he is two tracks short for the next Beach Boys album, to be released hard on the heels of this one, and so intends to pull 'Little Deuce Coupe' and 'Our Car Club' from *Surfer Girl* just prior to its release, but this never happens – and the songs appear on both LPs.

■ Tuesday 17th
RECORDING Capitol studio *Hollywood, CA*. Brian's flurry of activity continues when he produces The Honeys and **'The One You Can't Have'** (take 5 marked as best). The recording will appear as a Honeys single in the US on December 2nd.

■ Tuesday 24th
TV CBS Television City (Studio 31) *Hollywood, CA*. CBS *The Red Skelton Show* lip-synch 'Little Deuce Coupe', 'Surfer Girl', broadcast 8:00-9:00pm. The Beach Boys make their second national US TV

appearance today, guesting alongside the Hollywood child star Shirley Temple. The group lip-synch (a technical term for miming) to both sides of their latest single. Tonight's edition of *Red Skelton* is the opening show in the 11th series of this popular comedy and variety production.

■ Thursday 26th

Brian attends a recording session at Gold Star studio in Los Angeles run by his musical hero, Phil Spector. The session is for Spector's album *A Christmas Gift For You* and, at Spector's behest, Brian sits in on piano during recordings for 'Santa Claus Is Coming To Town'. Brian is in awe of Spector and feels light-headed throughout the session. It's not known if Brian's performance makes it to the released version, but he does receive a union-scale payment for his efforts.

■ Saturday 28th

The Cow Palace *San Francisco, CA*
The Beach Boys perform at a *Surf Party*.
• 'Little Deuce Coupe' single B-side peaks in US *Billboard* chart at number 5.

■ Sunday 29th

Seattle Opera House *Seattle, WA* with Freddie Cannon, Nino Tempo & April Stevens, Dee Dee Sharp, Ray Stevens, The Wailers, The Vice Roys, Gail Harris, Little Stevie Wonder
For one night only, The Beach Boys find themselves joining this *Hit Parade Of Stars* tour.

October

'Surfer Girl' single peaks on Australian chart at number 8.

■ Monday 7th

Little Deuce Coupe album released in the US. Just three weeks after the group's last LP was issued Capitol Records releases yet another

---

Little Deuce Coupe album

A1 'Little Deuce Coupe' (B. WILSON / R. CHRISTIAN)
A2 'Ballad Of Ole' Betsy' (B. WILSON / R. CHRISTIAN)
A3 'Be True To Your School' (B. WILSON / M. LOVE)
A4 'Car Crazy Cutie' (B. WILSON / R. CHRISTIAN)
A5 'Cherry Cherry Coupe' (B. WILSON / R. CHRISTIAN)
A6 '409' (B. WILSON / M. LOVE / G. USHER)
B1 'Shut Down' (B. WILSON / R. CHRISTIAN)
B2 'Spirit Of America' (B. WILSON / R. CHRISTIAN)
B3 'Our Car Club' (B. WILSON / M. LOVE)
B4 'No-Go Showboat' (B. WILSON / R. CHRISTIAN)
B5 'A Young Man Is Gone' (B. TROUP)
B6 'Custom Machine' (B. WILSON / M. LOVE)

US release October 7th 1963 (Capitol T1998).
UK release October 1965 (Capitol T1998).
Chart high US number 4; UK none.

Be True To Your School single

A 'Be True To Your School' (B. WILSON / M. LOVE)
B 'In My Room' (B. WILSON / G. USHER)

US release October 28th 1963 (Capitol 5069).
Chart high US number 6.

Beach Boys album. Erstwhile Beach Boy David Marks appears in the back cover photograph on the album, signifying his involvement in the album's recording, but Al Jardine, who *did* play on the album, is not present in the photo. To coincide with the release of this auto-themed album, Capitol supplies American DJs and record stores with a book of car-racing terms in an effort to further promote Beach Boys records.

■ Friday 11th

RECORDING Capitol studio *Hollywood, CA*. Brian is possibly singing background vocals on **'No-Go Showboat'** today for The Timers. The song is co-written by Brian and Roger Christian, and the producer at today's session is Jimmy Bowen. The single will be released on Reprise #231.

■ Saturday 12th

Surfer Girl album hits the US charts.

■ Friday 18th

RECORDING Western Recorders studio *Hollywood, CA*. Ripe and ready for a special festive release, The Beach Boys attend a tracking session for the Christmas-inspired **'Little Saint Nick'**, written by Brian, and **'Drive-In'**.

■ Sunday 20th

RECORDING Western Recorders studio *Hollywood, CA*. Vocals from the full Beach Boys line-up are added to the tracking tape of **'Little Saint Nick'** recorded two days ago.

■ Monday 21st

'Run-around Lover' / 'Summertime' single by Sharon Marie (real name Esparaza) released in the US. Brian and Mike Love wrote the A-side of this Capitol 45 and Brian produced the disc. Twenty-year-old Sharon Marie is allegedly Mike's girlfriend at the time.

■ Monday 28th

'Be True To Your School' / 'In My Room' single released in the US. Capitol issues the re-recorded album track 'Be True To Your School' as the A-side; it has a far more complex backing than the LP version, replete with marching drums as well as cheerleading courtesy of The Honeys (Marilyn Rovell, Diane Rovell and Ginger Blake). It will reach a chart peak of number 6, while the B-side, 'In My Room', will chart at number 23 in the *Billboard* singles listings. (Some charts are still based on radio plays as well as sales, so B-sides can chart separately from their As.)

■ Thursday 31st

Loyola Carnival, Loyola University *Westchester, CA* 7:00 & 10:30pm

Al Jardine (second left) returns to the line-up, replacing David Marks.

November

RECORDING Western Recorders studio *Hollywood, CA*. During this month the group tapes a version of **'The Lord's Prayer'**, a fine example of the group's a cappella singing and an early indication of their blossoming spirituality.

• As a reward for their impressive sales, The Beach Boys sign a new long-term six-year recording contract with Capitol Records.

• 'Be True To Your School' single peaks in US *Billboard* R&B chart at number 27.

• **'Drag City'** / **'Schlock Rod (Part 1)'** single by Jan & Dean released in the US. 'Drag City' is their first serious attempt at a car song and will peak at number 10 on the US *Billboard* chart, becoming Jan & Dean's third Top Ten record in a row. When it came time to record the vocals, the duo once again called upon the services of Brian Wilson, but fearing a backlash after the success with 'Surf City' they hoped that Brian could attend the session without Murry. Dean Torrence recalls on US radio: "Brian successfully ditched his dad and joined Jan and me in the studio. Brian loved being in the studio making records. He didn't care about the [other] elements of the music business, and that included being on the road. He had already practically quit touring with The Beach Boys so he could just concentrate on making great records.

"Brian realised that Jan was a good teacher and was learning a lot about studio technology from Jan, who had already been in many recording studios for the past six years. And because of Brian's high intellect, he was able to grasp the technical concepts of the quickly evolving recording equipment we were using. At the same time, Jan had experimented with different studio musicians and he had finally settled on a very talented core group of players that included two drummers – Hal Blaine and Earl Palmer – and a relatively unknown guitar player from Texas named Glen Campbell. Jan pointed out to Brian that, rather than wait for The Beach Boys to get off the road to record, he could use these studio guys instead and get his records made quicker – and that he would also save some wear-and-tear on the touring Beach Boys. After all, the Beach Boy sound came from the vocals, not necessarily from the instrumental background tracks. Brian immediately saw the advantages of using Jan's studio guys and the result was that his instrumental tracks from this point on sounded a lot more sophisticated."

■ Friday 1st
Hollywood Bowl *Hollywood, CA*
The Beach Boys are the last act on the bill for *Y-Day*, a show sponsored by the Hollywood YMCA and local radio station KFWB. The group performs 'Little Deuce Coupe', 'In My Room', 'Be True To Your School' (with The Honeys) and 'Surfer Girl', the latter an unscheduled on-the-spot performance. Their appearance ends with a short a cappella tribute to the KFWB station.

Disgruntled by the sound of the group's performance, Brian remarks to a reporter after the show, "The soundmen at the Bowl are not rock'n'roll soundmen. I would advise people who want to play there, and want to sound good, to change their plans or plan their changes."

■ Monday 4th
RECORDING Gold Star studio (B) *Los Angeles, CA*. Brian records demos of **'I Do'** and **'Ballad Of Ole Betsy'**. Four takes are made of 'Ballad', consisting of piano, guitar, bass and drums, with only the last complete and marked as master (see also September 2nd). Five takes are made of 'I Do' and again only the final take – consisting of handclaps, bass, guitar, piano and drums – is complete and marked as master, after which four takes of full group vocals are overdubbed. The final take is marked as the master, but this version of the song remains unreleased. A faster remake will be taped a few days later.

■ Thursday 7th

RECORDING RCA studio *Los Angeles, CA* 12midnight-3:00am. Back in the studio, and at a different location, The Beach Boys again attempt to record **'I Do'**, a song by Brian and Roger Christian. Seven instrumental takes and five vocal overdubs are required before a satisfactory master recording ready for mixing is achieved. The cut will remain unreleased until 1990 when it appears as a bonus track on Capitol's *Surfer Girl / Shut Down Vol 2* CD. (The song itself will see the light of day sooner, on a Warner Brothers single by The Castells released March 9th 1964.)

Musicians present Hal Blaine (drums), Jimmy Bond (upright bass), Russell Bridges (keyboards), Frankie Capp (percussion), Al de Lory (keyboards), Steve Douglas (saxophone), Plas Johnson (saxophone), Jay Migliori (saxophone), Bill Pitman (guitar), Ray Pohlman (bass guitar), Howard Roberts (guitar), Leon Russell (keyboards), Tommy Tedesco (guitar).

■ Saturday 9th

Little Deuce Coupe album hits US charts and will peak at number 4 on the *Billboard* listing.

■ Friday 22nd

Marysville Memorial Auditorium *Marysville/Yuba City, CA*
8:30pm, tickets $2

The group's Thanksgiving appearance is overshadowed by the assassination today of President John Fitzgerald Kennedy in Dallas, Texas.

Concert promoter Fred Vail: "When the day started, it was pretty much a normal day. I got up in the morning and was monitoring the radio stations to make sure they were playing our commercials for The Beach Boys concert tonight. During the morning I was out in a new car with a friend of mine from KXLA. We went downtown to drop some copy off to a client and it was on our way back that we heard the initial report saying that President Kennedy's motorcade had been fired upon in Dallas and that they were taking him to hospital. By the time we got back to the radio station, everyone there was in the station's master control room, listening to the news stories and the latest developments. Very, very shortly after, they announced that President Kennedy had died in a hospital in Dallas. When this

happened, I was concerned like everybody else. I'm an American and our president has just been killed. But I had a show to deal with.

"I had been working on setting up this concert for five weeks. It was one of my 'Fred Vail Presents' shows. So I called Murry and said, 'You're still coming, aren't you?' He said, 'Well, no. We can't come now. Our president's dead and our country is in a turmoil.' I said, 'Well, don't make a rash decision. Don't cancel the show. Let me make a few calls. You've still got a couple of hours before you drive to the airport. I'll call you back after I've made a few calls.' So I called the radio station in Yuba City. I was told that kids were calling in and they wanted to know if the concert was still on. I called the record shops where the tickets were on sale, and ticket sales had actually picked up.

"The schools had been let out and there was nothing else for the kids to do that day," Vail continues. "I called the City authorities and asked if they had a problem with the show going on. They didn't. So I called Murry back and said, 'I think we ought to do the show. The kids have been looking forward to it for weeks; we're selling tickets and they're selling briskly. There's nothing on the radio stations now except for commentary, re-hashing the story, and soft, funeral-type music. The kids want to see the band. They want to see their favourite group.' So he said OK, and he told me that Broadway, New York had gone dark and they were going to cancel all the theatre shows this evening as a mark of respect for the president. I said, 'But that's New York. This is Marysville, California. We need to do the show.' He then said, 'OK, we'll do it. Meet us at the plane.' I met them at the plane. It was the middle of winter, so it was dark at 5:30pm. We stopped at the Eldorado Hotel in Sacramento, because we had rooms there. The guys put their bags away and we drove up to Marysville.

"A local group had opened the concert. It was billed as a *Dance And Show*. The local band did their set, the curtain came down and, during the 20-minute intermission, we started setting up our gear. The kids started stomping and I asked the boys if they wanted to go on. They asked for a few more minutes so I went out front and told the crowd we should have a moment of silence for our fallen president, John Kennedy. I said, 'It was a tragedy in America today. We lost our president and before we bring out The Beach Boys, I think we should have a moment of silence in honour of the

president.' So everybody was quiet. It was dead quiet. The whole audience. I didn't know how long was a suitable silence. A minute? Half a minute? So after about 30 seconds, out of the corner of my eye, I could see the curtain open a little bit and Mike Love threw out a towel. It hit me and I knew that it was time to bring out the boys.

"The show broke the hall attendance record. There were a couple of thousand kids there. The Beach Boys did their regular set; we picked up their gear and went back to the Eldorado Hotel. And by the time we got there, it was probably about one in the morning. Everybody was real high. It had been a very emotional day. First, the tragedy with the president being assassinated – and then we had thousands of kids screaming for The Beach Boys. It had been an emotional roller-coaster.

"We had a shopping bag full of money, crumpled dollar bills, quarters, fives, and I dumped it out on one of the beds. It was about $6,000 in cash. I didn't think the guys had ever seen that much cash at any one time. They were usually paid in cheques. Then, about two in the morning, Brian and Mike started work on a song, doing little harmony things and melodies on something called 'The Warmth Of The Sun'."

Brian will recall in the 1995 film *I Just Wasn't Made For These Times* that they were naturally despondent when they heard Kennedy had been killed. "Mike said, 'Do you want to write a song in tribute to JFK tonight?' It was a spiritual night. We got going and a mood took over us. Something took us over. I can't explain it ... . Mike flipped out. He said, 'That's one of the most spiritual songs I've ever heard.' I said, 'Those lyrics are beautiful.' He wrote those lyrics. You know, stuff like that happens every 20 years. It doesn't happen every day, JFK gets shot to death and The Beach Boys go and write 'The Warmth Of The Sun'."

Mike remembers later on BBC Radio-1: "We wrote that [song] about losing someone close. I had someone in mind. 'It didn't work out but I still had the warmth of the sun' meaning the warmth of the memory within. We wrote that until three in the morning, crashed, and went to sleep."

Saturday 23rd
Memorial Auditorium *Sacramento, CA* 2:00pm
The Beach Boys, still in shock following yesterday's devastating news, manage to give another Thanksgiving performance.
• *Surfer Girl* album peaks in US *Billboard* chart at number 7.
• 'Be True To Your School' single enters US *Billboard* chart at number 19.

Saturday 30th
'In My Room' single B-side enters US *Billboard* Top 40 chart at number 38.

December

Monday 2nd
'**The One You Can't Have**' / '**From Jimmy With Tears**' single by The Honeys released in the US. The A-side is written and produced by Brian, who also produces the B-side.

Monday 9th
'**Little Saint Nick**' / '**The Lord's Prayer**' single released in the US. The A-side will peak at number 3 in US *Billboard* Christmas Chart. With its timeless quality, 'Little Saint Nick' will soon earn its status as a revered holiday classic.

Little Saint Nick single

A '**Little Saint Nick**' (B. WILSON)
B '**The Lord's Prayer**' (TRAD)

US release December 9th 1963 (Capitol 5096).
UK release November 1973 (Capitol CL 15572).
Chart high US number 3.

Thursday 19th
Memorial Auditorium *Sacramento, CA* 7:00pm

Friday 20th
Civic Memorial Auditorium *Stockton, CA* 8:00pm

Saturday 21st
'Be True To Your School' single peaks in US *Billboard* chart at number 6.
'In My Room' single B-side peaks in US *Billboard* chart at number 23.
• During the closing weeks of 1963, as the country still grieves over the senseless death of John F Kennedy – and rumours grow about an unusual British pop group whose music is beginning to reach American ears – an excited Brian is busy composing new songs with Mike Love and Roger Christian. The Beach Boys go into the Christmas and New Year holiday period knowing that a session in the studio is booked for the first day of 1964. With no real competition facing the band – or so they think – their optimism is sky-high. For now, the group's success is like a runaway train ... and a train that is about to come off the rails.

Performing at the *Y-Day* radio-sponsored show on November 1st at the Hollywood Bowl, one of the biggest venues the group has played.

1964

Shut Down Volume 2 album recorded and released ... first overseas tour to Australia and New Zealand, supporting Roy Orbison ... 'Fun Fun Fun' single hits US number 5 ... Brian detects worrying competition as Beatlemania hits America ... *All Summer Long* album recorded and released, with Brian determined to demonstrate the group's musical strengths ... Murry Wilson is fired as manager ... 'I Get Around' is the group's first number 1 single ... *Christmas Album* recorded and released ... *Concert* album recorded and released, their first number 1 LP ... 'When I Grow Up (To Be A Man)' and 'Dance Dance Dance' singles recorded and released ... sessions begin for *Today!* album ... promotional tour of the UK and live dates in Europe ... Brian shows strain as the group's success demands ever-busier schedules; he suffers a nervous breakdown and withdraws from live shows ... Glen Campbell steps in at short notice as Brian's replacement on stage.

Visiting Britain for the first time, pictured outside EMI headquarters in London on November

CAPITOL RECORDS
(Employer's name)

Phonograph Recording Contract Blank
AMERICAN FEDERATION OF MUSICIANS
OF THE UNITED STATES AND CANADA

000001
94187
64

Local Union No. **47**

THIS CONTRACT for the personal services of musicians, made this **1st** day of **January** 19**68**
between the undersigned employer (hereinafter called the "employer") and **NINE (9)** musicians
(hereinafter called "employees"). _(including the leader)_
WITNESSETH, That the employer hires the employees as musicians severally on the terms and conditions below, and as further specified on reverse side. The leader represents that the employees already designated have agreed to be bound by said terms and conditions. Each employee yet to be chosen shall be so bound by said terms and conditions upon agreeing to accept his employment. Each employee may enforce this agreement. The employees severally agree to render collectively to the employer services as musicians in the orchestra under the leadership of **Steven Douglas** as follows:

Name and Address of Place of Engagement **Western Studios**
6000 Sunset Blvd, Hollywood, Calif.

Date(s) and Hours of Employment **1-1-64**
12:30PM to 4:45PM

Type of Engagement: **Recording for phonograph records only**
WAGE AGREED UPON $ **Premium time SCALE**

PAID JAN 29 1964

Plus pension contributions as specified on reverse side hereof.
(Terms and amount)

This wage includes expenses agreed to be reimbursed by the employer in accordance with the attached schedule, or a schedule to be furnished the employer on or before the date of engagement.
To be paid **FIFTEEN DAYS**
(Specify when payments are to be made)

Upon request by the American Federation of Musicians of the United States and Canada (herein called the "Federation") or the local in whose jurisdiction the employees shall perform hereunder, the employer either shall make advance payment hereunder or shall post an appropriate bond.

Employer's name and authorized signature	Leader's name	Leader's signature	Local No. 47
CAPITOL RECORDS _Brian Wilson_	Steve Douglas _Ste Drgds_		
Street address 1750 No. Vine St.	Street address 5646 Lemona Ave		
City Hollywood 28 State Calif. Phone	City Van Nuys State Calif.		

(1) Label name _____ Session no. _____

Master no.	No. of minutes	TITLES OF TUNES	Master no.	No. of minutes	TITLES OF TUNES
	2:45	"FUN FUN FUN" (TRACK)			
	2:15	"THE WARMTH OF THE SUN (TRACK)			

(2) Employee's name (As on Social Security card) Last First Initial	(3) Home address (Give street, city and state)	(4) Local Union no.	(5) Social Security number	(6) Scale wages	(7) Pension contribution
(Leader) DOUGLAS, Steve	5646 Lemona Ave Van Nuys, Calif.	47	556-46-1005	427.08	34.17
1 dbl. BLAINE, Hal	2441 Castilian Dr. Hollywood 28, Calif.	47	047-20-5900	245.57	19.65
Pd. D. WILSON, Brian	3701 W. 119th St. Hawthorne, Calif.	47	568-62-7150	213.54	17.08
Pd. D. LOVE, Michael E.	3701 W. 119th St. Hawthorne, Calif.	47	546-56-6598	213.54	17.08
MIGLIORI, Jay	928 So. Albany Los Angeles 8, Calif.	47	208-24-6118	213.54	17.08
Pd. D. WILSON, Dennis C.	3701 W. 119th St. Hawthorne, Calif.	47	562-60-0767	213.54	17.08
POHLMAN, M.R.	2804 Westshire Dr. Hollywood 28, Calif.	47	558-34-6698	213.54	17.08
Pd D. WILSON, Carl D.	3701 W. 119th St. Hawthorne Calif.	47	568-62-6168	213.54	17.08
Pd D. JARDINE, Alan C.	3701 W. 119th St. Hawthorne A Calif.	47	566-54-3798	213.54	17.08

NO ARRANGEMENTS
Ste Drgds

~~CONTRACT RECEIVED~~

JAN 2 - 1964

~~WARD ARCHER~~
ASST. TO PRESIDENT

(8) Total Pension Contributions (Sum of Column (7)) $**173.38**
Make check payable in this amount to "AFM & EPW Fund"

FOR FUND USE ONLY:
Date pay't rec'd _____ Amt. paid _____ Date posted _____ By _____
Form B-4 Rev. 4-59

January

Rev-Up album and '**Little Ford Ragtop**' / '**Happy Hodaddy**' single by The Vettes released in the US. The group includes future Beach Boy Bruce Johnston; both records come out this month on the MGM label. Johnston is also half of Bruce & Terry, with Terry Melcher, and they release the 45 '**Custom Machine**' / '**Makaha At Midnight**' on the Columbia label.

■ Wednesday 1st
RECORDING *Shut Down Volume 2* **session 1** Western Recorders studio *Hollywood, CA* 12:30-7:00pm. With the new year just hours old, The Beach Boys assemble excitedly in the studio to begin recording *Shut Down Volume 2*, their fifth album. Recordings begin today with '**Fun Fun Fun**' and '**The Warmth Of The Sun**'.

"When I was young and really energetic, I could go in a studio and cut a record in three hours," Brian will tell *Newsweek* in 1977. "I could get a record cut and done in three fucking hours! I was a kid and I was ready for some competition. I'd run in the studio and say, 'Hey, we'll make the best record ever tonight!' I had that kind of spirit – and goddamn if it didn't work, you know?"

Before the sessions begin, The Beach Boys jam an improvised, slower, bluesier version of 'Fun Fun Fun'. The taping of Mike's lead vocal then follows a prompt recording of the song's familiar backing track. Recording of percussion and guitar inserts follow (six takes required). An 'insert' is a vocal or instrumental part, often of short duration, added usually to one tape track of the existing recorded performance.

This work is then followed by the full Beach Boys line-up making vocal overdubs onto the piece (19 takes required). Work on a subsequently unreleased alternate version of the song featuring different vocal and guitar parts completes the first part of the session. The group then moves to tracking and vocal recordings for 'The Warmth Of The Sun'. Brian's girlfriend Marilyn Rovell is present at the gathering. (Recordings for *Shut Down Volume 2* will continue on the 7th.)
Musicians present Hal Blaine (drums), Steve Douglas (saxophone), Jay Migliori (saxophone), Ray Pohlman (bass guitar).

■ Thursday 2nd
RECORDING Western Recorders studio *Hollywood CA* 8:00-11:00pm. Brian takes charge of a non-Beach Boys session with work today focusing on taping a song co-written by Brian and Roger Christian, '**She Rides With Me**', for Paul Petersen, an actor who plays Jeff Stone, son of Donna in ABC TV's *The Donna Reed Show*. It will be issued as a single by Colpix Records in the US in March.
Musicians present Hal Blaine (drums), Jimmy Bond Jr (upright bass), Al de Lory (keyboards), Steve Douglas (alto and tenor saxophone), David Gates (bass guitar), Joseph Gibbons (guitar), Plas Johnson (alto and tenor saxophone), Larry Knechtel (organ), Jay Migliori (baritone saxophone), Ray Pohlman (bass guitar), Tommy Tedesco (guitar).

■ Monday 6th
'**Pamela Jean**'/ '**After The Game**' single by The Survivors released in the US. Brian produces this Capitol disc and sings the lead vocal on the A-side, which is in fact a re-worked version of 'Car Crazy Cutie' from The Beach Boys' *Little Deuce Coupe* album. The Survivors consist of Brian, Mark Groseclose, Bob Norberg, Dave Nowlen and Rich Petersen (real name Richard Alarian).
Drag City album by Jan & Dean released in the US. The Liberty disc

features backing vocals and instrumentation on the title track by The Beach Boys. (See November 1963.)

■ Tuesday 7th
RECORDING *Shut Down Volume 2* **session 2** Gold Star studio *Hollywood, CA* 8:00-11:00pm. Recordings for the new album resume with the recording of the instrumental track for '**Why Do Fools Fall in Love**', a song originally recorded in 1956 by Frankie Lymon & The Teenagers. Besides Brian, no other Beach Boys are in attendance. The group have already begun to use Phil Spector's favoured Gold Star studio as an occasional alternative to Western, an idea that came originally from Mike.
Musicians present Hal Blaine (drums), Jimmy Bond Jr (upright bass), Russell Bridges (keyboards), Frankie Capp (percussion), Al de Lory (keyboards), Steve Douglas (saxophone), Plas Johnson (saxophone), Jay Migliori (saxophone), Bill Pitman (guitar), Ray Pohlman (bass guitar), Tommy Tedesco (guitar).

■ Wednesday 8th
RECORDING *Shut Down Volume 2* **session 3** Gold Star studio *Hollywood, CA*. The group overdubs vocals onto the previous day's tracking master of '**Why Do Fools Fall in Love**'. Immediately following the session The Beach Boys begin preparing for their first overseas trip, a three-week tour of Australia and New Zealand.

■ Friday 10th
RECORDING Unknown studio *Los Angeles, CA*. Brian produces a vocal session for The Castells' version of '**I Do**' (co-written with Roger Christian) using a backing track from November 7th 1963. The result will be issued as a Castells single A-side on March 9th 1964.

TOUR STARTS Australia & New Zealand (Jan 13th-Feb 1st)
The group, complete with Brian, make their first venture down under. They perform as one of the supports to singer Roy Orbison and appear alongside other US acts Paul & Paula and The Surfaris, plus Sydney pop group The Joy Boys. At a cost of £50,000 the tour is promoted by Pacific Promotions, run by New Zealander Harry M Miller, and is advertised as *Surfside 64* with "16 American Stars" and promising "two-and-a-half hours of non-stop excitement".

"It's a miracle that we're getting them all out together," Miller admits to the *Sun-Herald* newspaper. "It took me weeks in the States to organise it. We'd get one lot lined up and then we'd have trouble with some of the others. First they could come and then they couldn't come. Some of The Beach Boys and The Surfaris are still at school and we had to get permission from the headmasters to make the trip. You can lose so much money on these deals if you're not careful. But it looks like we've been lucky. Bookings are good." Miller will be the man responsible for bringing The Rolling Stones to Australia later this year.

Despite the fact that Roy Orbison tops the bill on all of these Australian and New Zealand dates, many teenagers attend the shows only to hear the sounds of the surf music acts. The shortlived musical craze remains popular around a country full of keen surfers, with surf music particularly popular in Sydney and Brisbane.

■ Monday 13th
This morning The Beach Boys and other members of the tour arrive in Australia on Pan-Am airlines at Mascot Airport in Sydney for a stop-over promotional visit. Channel 9 TV news reporters await their arrival. A four-minute interview by Sydney reporter John Faul with Roy Orbison, Paul & Paula and The Beach Boys is filmed

This 'AFM sheet', or musicians' union log, is for the January 1st session for 'Fun Fun Fun' and 'The Warmth Of The Sun'. It notes the presence of sax-men Steve Douglas and Jay Migliori, drummer Hal Blaine and bassist Ray Pohlman, all among the gang fast becoming Beach Boy session regulars.

for later use on an episode of long-running Australian pop music programme *Bandstand*. Also filmed are scenes of the artists exiting the plane and walking across the tarmac with screaming fans close by. Later this day and for the majority of the following, The Beach Boys spend time sightseeing and relaxing on the beach. According to the local *TV Times* magazine, "The Beach Boys are very keen and very capable surfers and surf-board riders. The boys are looking forward to catching some waves on Sydney beaches." The group also finds time to meet Sandra McBride and grants her permission to run an official Australian branch of The Beach Boys' fan club.

■ Wednesday 15th
Festival Hall *Brisbane, Queensland, Australia* 6:00pm & 8.45pm, with Roy Orbison, The Surfaris (joint headliners), Paul & Paula, The Joy Boys
At 9:35am the entourage arrives at Eagle Farm Airport, Brisbane, en route from Sydney on an Ansett aircraft. This evening the first concerts of the tour take place at the Festival Hall. The following day is spent relaxing.

■ Friday 17th
Sydney Stadium *Sydney, New South Wales, Australia* 6:00 & 8.45pm, with Roy Orbison, The Surfaris (joint headliners), Paul & Paula, The Joy Boys; compères: 2SM radio DJs Bob Rogers, Mike Walsh and Mad Mel
Performances of 'Papa Oom Mow Mow', 'Little Deuce Coupe' and 'What I'd Say' during the second show are captured on tape by Radio 2SM: 'What I'd Say', with spirited saxophone playing by Mike Love, will be issued in 1981 on the speedily withdrawn Beach Boys/Brian Wilson *Rarities* album on Australian Capitol.
• Meanwhile back in the US it is announced that The Beatles' single 'I Want To Hold Your Hand' has reached number 1. Only a handful of British acts have ever managed to crack the American charts, and as far as the country's record buyers are concerned the UK is a wasteland for popular music. But this attitude is soon to change. The Beatles will herald a tidal wave of many British acts who will visit the country and change the face of American popular music forever. The invasion is set to start in just a few weeks, on February 7th.

■ Saturday 18th
Sydney Stadium *Sydney, New South Wales, Australia* 2.30, 6:00 & 8.45pm, with Roy Orbison, The Surfaris (joint headliners), Paul & Paula, The Joy Boys; compères: 2SM radio DJs Bob Rogers, Mike Walsh and Mad Mel
Sitting in the seventh row from the front at the 6:00pm concert is blonde 19-year-old Sydneysider Sandra Rice who so captures the attention of Mike Love that he seeks her out in the crowd at the end of the show. After accepting his invitation to share a milkshake with him, the two get on so well that Sandra decides to stay to watch the 8.45 show. Afterwards, the two spend the remainder of the night seeing the sights of Sydney's Kings Cross district. "I guess it was love at first sight," Mike recalls to 2SM radio DJ Bob Rogers.
The reviewer for the Sydney *Daily Telegraph* writes: "*Surfside 64* brought the world's top surfin' music stars to the Stadium and had our local 'stompie-wompies' stomping in the aisles! The line-up was young and talented and the King of the show was the young Surfaris' drummer Ron Wilson who really swung. I thought the *Surfside* vocalists almost drowned in the loud band backings, but the teenagers didn't mind. They loved it!"

■ Monday 20th
Centennial Hall *Adelaide, South Australia, Australia* 6:00 &

8.45pm, with Roy Orbison, The Surfaris (joint headliners), Paul & Paula, The Joy Boys
The previous day 8,000 people welcomed the *Surfside 64* entourage at Adelaide Airport upon their arrival from Sydney.

■ Tuesday 21st
Festival Hall *Melbourne, Victoria, Australia* 6:00 & 8.45pm, with Roy Orbison, The Surfaris (joint headliners), Paul & Paula, The Joy Boys; compères: 3UZ radio DJs Don Lunn and John Vertigan
Footage of The Beach Boys performing 'Monster Mash' (a cover of the 1962 novelty hit for Bobby 'Boris' Pickett & The Crypt-Kickers) later appears in a nine-minute experimental 16mm film *Fun Radio* by Melbourne filmmaker Nigel Buesst. The film also includes the group's arrival at Essendon Airport today where 5,000 fans are on hand to welcome 'The Big 16'.

■ Wednesday 22nd
Festival Hall *Melbourne, Victoria, Australia* 6:00 & 8.45pm, with Roy Orbison, The Surfaris (joint headliners), Paul & Paula, The Joy Boys; compères: 3UZ radio DJs Don Lunn and John Vertigan
• Australian magazine *Women's Weekly* publicises a series of competitions currently being run in each state in which fans have the opportunity to meet the stars of *Surfside 64* in person. Winners who successfully list ten articles that they would need to bring on a surfing safari with members of the two groups have the chance either to have breakfast with The Beach Boys or supper with The Surfaris. (See January 25th.)

■ Thursday 23rd
Town Hall *Hobart, Tasmania, Australia* 6:00 & 8.45pm, with Roy Orbison, The Surfaris (joint headliners), Paul & Paula, The Joy Boys
This morning the entourage flies from Melbourne to Hobart where they perform two concerts at the Town Hall, completing the Australian live dates on the tour.

■ Friday 24th
TV ATN-7 Television Studios, Sydney, New South Wales, Australia. ATN-7 *Surf Sound* lip-synch 'Surfer Girl' broadcast February 1st 7:00-7:30pm, 'Little Deuce Coupe' broadcast February 8th 7:00-7:30pm.
The touring entourage flies back to Sydney to film an appearance on the premiere episode of this new teenage pop-music television programme. Following an interview with the programme's host – budding local pop star Rob EG, better known in later life as producer and manager Robbie Porter – The Beach Boys lip-synch (a technical term for 'mime') to two songs. Joining the group on the shows are a number of local artists, including Al Lane, Vikki Forrest, Tony Hamilton, and The Stampedes.

■ Saturday 25th
In Sydney the lucky winners of the *Meet The Stars Of Surfside 64 In Person* competition (see January 22nd) collect their prizes and win either breakfast with The Beach Boys or supper with The Surfaris. This morning the first five successful girls begin their day by meeting at radio station 2SM and are then escorted to The Beach Boys' hotel by DJs Bob Rogers and Tony Murphy. Original plans to organise the breakfast on the beach are shelved when it starts to rain. As the winners meet The Beach Boys, Mike helps to break the girls' rather nervous silence by cracking jokes. Soon the entourage is talking about everything from local politics to the 'stomp' dance. The Surfaris' supper takes place later tonight with five different girls.
The contest winners are featured in a teenage supplement in the Australian *Women's Weekly's* magazine on the 26th, with a colour

picture of The Beach Boys and the girls at the Hawaiian breakfast. Murry Wilson is interviewed and says: "For acts of disobedience, the boys must pay fines – ranging from $25 to $200 – according to the offence." Carl is asked about Australian girls. "What a change!" he reckons. "They enjoy the sun and wind and a brisk walk. American girls are the laziest creatures. They must catch a bus, or be driven, even one block. Australian girls don't wear tight clothes and their make-up isn't heavy. They're your biggest tourist attraction." After a couple more days relaxing in Australia, the entourage flies out to New Zealand on the 29th.

■ Wednesday 29th
Wellington Town Hall *Wellington, North Island, New Zealand* 6:00 & 8.30pm, with Roy Orbison, The Surfaris (joint headliners), Paul & Paula, The Joy Boys
Capacity crowds attend both shows and the concerts run without an interval. Wellington's main newspaper *The Dominion* reviews one of the shows and reveals the programme. First on are The Joy Boys, who then back the following act, Paul & Paula. The Beach Boys appear next and perform 'Surfin' Safari', 'Runaway' and 'Johnny B Goode', plus an encore that includes 'Wild City'. Then comes The Surfaris, and last Roy Orbison, also backed by The Joy Boys. Orbison performs 'Only The Lonely', 'Mean Woman Blues', 'Blue Bayou', 'Running Scared', 'Leah' and 'In Dreams'.

■ Thursday 30th
Founders Hall *Hamilton, North Island, New Zealand* 6:00 & 8.30pm, with Roy Orbison, The Surfaris (joint headliners), Paul & Paula, The Joy Boys

■ Friday 31st
Auckland Town Hall *Auckland, North Island, New Zealand* 6:00 & 8.30pm, with Roy Orbison, The Surfaris (joint headliners), Paul & Paula, The Joy Boys

February

'Be True to Your School' single peaks in Swedish chart at number 6. *Hey Little Cobra And Other Hot Rod Hits* album by The Rip Chords released in the US. The group includes future Beach Boy Bruce Johnston on this Columbia LP.

■ Saturday 1st
Auckland Town Hall *Auckland, North Island, New Zealand* 2:00, 6:00 & 8.30pm, with Roy Orbison, The Surfaris (joint headliners), Paul & Paula, The Joy Boys
Originally only the Friday night shows were planned for Auckland but due to great public demand these three extra concerts were added to the itinerary just a week earlier, and the 2:00pm matinee show was only announced in newspapers yesterday.

■ Sunday 2nd
The Beach Boys and their entourage – minus Mike – fly out of New Zealand and return home to Los Angeles. Mike in the meantime flies back to Sydney to track down Sandra Rice and continue their romance. He has not obtained her contact details and so through associations made with the 2SM presenters who compèred the Sydney shows, he broadcasts an appeal on the station for her whereabouts. Mike's message successfully reaches her and they spend a couple of days together. As Mike departs from Sydney to

rejoin the rest of the band in Los Angeles he declares that he will return to Sydney as soon as he can to ask Sandra's parents for their permission to be married. Sandra tells 2SM DJ Bob Rogers: "I'm completely overwhelmed by it all. Marrying Mike would mean a very different life in America, but I know that just being with him would be wonderful." Mike does not return – but the incident inspires Brian to write 'Help Me Rhonda'.

The Beach Boys' tour down under is a great success, but the group will not make this long journey again for another six years (see April 17th 1970). Accompanying them on the tour was prudish Murry Wilson who had spent each night of the visit camped in the hallway guarding the group's rooms to stop eager fans from breaking in. His control over the group has been almost limitless and by the end of the visit everyone is agreed that he'll have to go. For now, The Beach Boys are home for the release of their next Capitol single and to witness the first serious challenge to their American musical crown.

■ Monday 3rd
'Fun Fun Fun' / 'Why Do Fools Fall In Love' single released in the US. Just four days before the British music invasion is due to begin in America, The Beach Boys issue their seventh Capitol 45, an electrifying record. It will hit the US charts just two weeks after The Beatles touch down on American soil. The group is sure that this impressive, catchy disc will give them their first American number 1 single … but it stalls at 5 in the *Billboard* chart, behind The Four Seasons with 'Dawn (Go Away)' and The Beatles, who will occupy the top three places. (The B-side, 'Why Do Fools', features a unique single mix not used for the *Shut Down* album.)

■ Friday 7th
At 1:20pm Beatlemania arrives in America as The Beatles land at John F Kennedy International Airport in New York City. For the first time in The Beach Boys' career their position as number-one group in America is threatened. Until now, it has been plain sailing for them: alongside Motown and Phil Spector they are the best thing to have happened to American music since Elvis Presley. But now along comes The Beatles who will radically change everything – including, of course, The Beach Boys' career.

Brian is concerned. He witnesses the hysteria that The Beatles cause when they perform before an audience of 73,700,700 television viewers on Sunday February 9th's edition of CBS Television's top-rated *Ed Sullivan Show*. Murry Wilson is adamant that The Beach Boys will fight to overcome this invasion, but probably knows it will be tough, especially given the evidently exceptional talent within The Beatles. His 17-year-old son Carl is a big fan of the group. Pictures of The Beatles adorn his bedroom walls! Murry knows very well that the coming months will prove to be a big test for The Beach Boys' popularity and insists that they rise to the challenge.

Brian will tell radio station WKXJ in 1966: "'I Want To Hold Your Hand' really blew my mind. I knew we were good but it wasn't until The Beatles arrived that I knew we had to get going. The Beatles invasion shook me up a lot. They eclipsed a lot of what we'd worked for. We were naturally jealous. I just couldn't handle the fact that there were these four guys from England coming over here to America to invade our territory. When we saw how everybody was screaming for The Beatles, it was like, 'Whooa!' We couldn't believe it. I was shook up as hell.

"Michael and I went out to dinner about a week after 'I Want To Hold Your Hand' hit big and he sat there, scratching his head, saying, 'What the fuck is going on here?' And I said, 'Well, I don't think we should quit.' He was discouraged by the way that Beatlemania hit America. We were very threatened by the whole thing. The Beach Boys' supremacy as the number one vocal group in America was being challenged. So we stepped on the gas a little bit.

"After that," Brian continues, "we'd do a concert and the kids would scream at us but we'd think, 'Hey, wait a minute. You're screaming for The Beatles through us.' The Beatles beat us, in a way. Their songs were more original. I think that as a songwriting idea, The Beatles beat us. But as an overall, versatile group sound, I think we tied 'em. I think we tied."

■ Saturday 8th

Little Deuce Coupe album peaks in US *Billboard* Chart at number 4.

■ Monday 17th

RECORDING Gold Star studio (A) *Hollywood, CA* 2:00-5:00pm. A day after The Beatles make a further successful appearance on *The Ed Sullivan Show*, Brian returns to the studio to supervise a session for The Honeys' fourth single, with engineer Larry Levine. Taped are **'He's A Doll'** (eight takes required), a song written by Brian and issued as the A-side of the single on April 13th, and the ultimately unreleased **'I Can See Right Through You'** (six takes; also known as 'Go Away Boy' and 'You Brought It All On Yourself').

Musicians present Hal Blaine (drums), Jimmy Bond Jr (upright bass), Russell Bridges (keyboards), Al de Lory (keyboards), Steve Douglas (saxophone), Gene Estes (probably guitar), Gary Coleman (percussion), Joseph Gibbons (guitar), Plas Johnson (saxophone), Larry Knechtel (organ), Jay Migliori (saxophone), Bill Pitman (guitar), Ray Pohlman (bass guitar).

■ Tuesday 18th

RECORDING Gold Star studio *Hollywood, CA* 2:00-5:00pm. One day after his session for The Honeys comes another non-Beach Boys production job for Brian as he experiments for himself, updating **'Endless Sleep'**, a 1958 Top Ten hit by Jody Reynolds for Demon Records (Reynolds was once a member of LA group The Storms). Brian again uses the services of eight of the session musicians who graced the Honeys session yesterday. The recordings conclude with the overdubbing of a lead vocal by Larry Denton, an acquaintance of Brian's.

Musicians present Hal Blaine (drums), Jimmy Bond Jr (upright bass), Russell Bridges (keyboards), Frankie Capp (percussion), Al de Lory (keyboards), Steve Douglas (saxophone), Jay Migliori (saxophone), Bill Pitman (guitar), Ray Pohlman (bass guitar), Tommy Tedesco (guitar).

■ Wednesday 19th

RECORDING *Shut Down Volume 2* **session 4** Western Recorders studio *Hollywood CA*. The Beach Boys are dejected by the speed with which The Beatles seem to have become the kings of American pop, but continue work on their next album. After a six-week break, recordings for the LP focus on **'Keep An Eye On Summer'** (incorrectly listed on AFM sheets as recorded February 2nd) and **'Pom Pom Playgirl'** which features Carl's first Beach Boy solo vocal (and is incorrectly listed by AFM as taped on January 20th). According to regular Western engineer Chuck Britz, it is no accident that Beach Boys records always sound good on the radio. "Airplay was where the money was," Britz tells *Billboard*, "so to find out in the studio how a record would sound on the radio, they would listen to a potential single on a little cheap eight-inch speaker I had."

■ Thursday 20th

RECORDING *Shut Down Volume 2* **session 5** Western Recorders studio *Hollywood CA*. Sessions for the album continue today with work on **'Don't Worry Baby'**, **'In The Parkin' Lot'**, **'This Car Of Mine'**, **'Cassius Love vs. Sonny Wilson'**, **'Denny's Drums'** and **'Louie Louie'**. In addition the group cuts the instrumental **'Shut Down Part 2'** featuring saxophone playing by Mike. After just five sessions, the group's latest album is finished. With an eye on a quick release, mixing is completed within days. But Brian is unhappy that the album has been rushed and even considers scrapping the project and starting from scratch. It is an idea soon defused by Capitol, but Brian is determined to improve on his and The Beach Boys' musical output. So during the next two months Brian and Mike set off on a remarkable writing spree, determined to compose the best songs of their career. Ultimately, their aim is to show the world that The Beatles are about to meet their musical match.

■ Friday 21st

Hoquiam Hi-School *Gymnasium Seattle*, **WA** 10:00pm-1:00am, with The Beachcombers, The Capris, Gail Harris & The Chandells; tickets $2.50

The group's US concert duties resume with the first of two weekend shows in Seattle. The concert is sponsored by KHOK Radio and is the last to take place in this gym as the school board fears damage to their immaculately preserved hardwood basketball court.

■ Saturday 22nd

Seattle Center Opera House *Seattle*, **WA** with Bobby Vinton, Trini Lopez, Jimmy Gilmer & The Fireballs, The Cascades, H.B. Barnum, Mel Carter

• 'Fun Fun Fun' enters US *Billboard* Top 40 chart at number 27; it will peak at number 5.

■ Friday 28th

Santa Clara County Fairgrounds *San Jose*, **CA** 8:30pm; tickets $4.00; promoted by Jack Hayes & Larry Mitchell

March

'Fun Fun Fun' / 'Why Do Fools Fall In Love?' single released in the UK. It fails to chart. Meanwhile, following the group's touring success, 'Fun Fun Fun' single peaks in Australian chart at number 6.
'She Rides With Me' / 'Poorest Boy In Town' single by Paul Peterson released in the US. Brian co-writes and produces the A-side of this Colpix 45.

• Dennis moves out of the Wilson family home and takes up residence at an address in Hollywood.

Shut Down Volume 2 album

A1 'Fun Fun Fun' (B. WILSON / M. LOVE)
A2 'Don't Worry Baby' (B. WILSON / R. CHRISTIAN)
A3 'In The Parkin' Lot' (B. WILSON / R. CHRISTIAN)
A4 "Cassius' Love vs. 'Sonny' Wilson'
A5 'The Warmth Of The Sun' (B. WILSON / M. LOVE)
A6 'This Car Of Mine' (B. WILSON / M. LOVE)
B1 'Why Do Fools Fall In Love' ALBUM MIX (F. LYMON / M. LEVY)
B2 'Pom-Pom Play Girl' (B. WILSON / G. USHER)
B3 'Keep An Eye On Summer' (B. WILSON / B. NORMAN)
B4 'Shut Down Part II' (C. WILSON)
B5 'Louie Louie' (R. BERRY)
B6 'Denny's Drums' (D. WILSON)

US release March 2, 1964 (Capitol T2027).
UK release July 1964 (Capitol T2027).
Chart high US number 13; UK none.

Monday 2nd

Shut Down Volume 2 album released in the US. Just ten days after the group completes the recordings, Capitol issue this hastily compiled and strangely titled LP. The name is intended to echo Capitol's various-artists non-Beach Boys *Shut Down* album released in summer 1963.

The group's new album is promoted as a 'hot-rod' record – even though it includes only four car songs. It is not a massive seller now, missing the Top Ten and peaking at number 13 in the US, but does eventually go gold. It displays undeniable proof of the group's developing style and, in particular, Brian's growing talents. Brian himself nonetheless feels frustrated that his musical ambitions are not materialising: he is dissatisfied with the album's production, hearing it as rushed and uncomplicated, and recognises that the dialogue and filler tracks at the end of the record slow down the pace. He is determined to correct these flaws on the group's next LP.

Tuesday 3rd

RECORDING Western Recorders studio *Hollywood CA*. Following The Beatles' decision to record German-language versions of 'She Loves You' and 'I Want To Hold Your Hand', The Beach Boys, with Brian again on lead vocal, tape a German-language version of '**In My Room**' entitled '**Ganz Allein**', using tracking take 13 of the original recording. Unlike the Beatle recordings which are issued in Germany, this version of 'In My Room' is never issued now in Germany, or anywhere else. It subsequently appears on the 1983 album *Beach Boys Rarities* and the 1990 CD of *Surfer Girl / Shut Down Volume 2*.

Saturday 7th

'Why Do Fools Fall in Love' single B-side peaks in US *Billboard* chart at number 120.

Monday 9th

'**I Do**' / '**Teardrops**' single by The Castells released in the US. Some historians subsequently credit Brian with producing both sides, but the B-side is the work of Hank Levine. 'I Do' was recorded by The Beach Boys in 1963 (see November 7th 1963; it will remain unreleased until the 1990 Capitol CD *Surfer Girl/Shut Down Volume 2*) and this year by the Brian-produced Castells, both using the same backing track. Brian first used the melody for his song 'County Fair', recorded for the *Surfin' Safari* album in 1962.

Thursday 12th

TV KFMB Television Studios *San Diego, CA*. Syndicated *The Steve Allen Show* live performance 'Surfin' USA', 'Fun Fun Fun', broadcast March 27th 10:30pm-12:15am. Just over a year after the show had given them their first major American TV exposure, The Beach Boys videotape their second appearance on *Steve Allen*, syndicated across the US on the 27th. Following afternoon camera rehearsals and in front of a highly appreciative studio audience, the group opens the show with a live version of 'Surfin' USA' and later in the programme 'Fun Fun Fun'. Joining them on tonight's show are special guests Anthony Perkins, Ethel Ennis, and attorney Samuel G. L. King who asks, "Can marriage work?" The group will find themselves in front of television cameras again just two days later.

Saturday 14th

TV NBC Television Studios *Burbank, CA*. US media company National General Corporation has capitalised on the huge impact of The Beatles in America by arranging a short series of closed-circuit broadcasts of Beatle-headlining concerts, to be screened in selected cinemas across the country. The shows will also feature top music stars of the day, and although The Beach Boys have just been dethroned as America's top music act they happily accept a last-minute invitation to appear.

At 10:00am this morning the group videotapes a concert at NBC's TV studios in Burbank, performing live versions of 'Fun Fun Fun', 'Long Tall Texan', 'Little Deuce Coupe', 'Surfer Girl', 'Monster Mash', 'Surfin' USA', 'Shut Down', 'In My Room', 'Papa-Oom-Mow-Mow' and 'Hawaii'. This recording along with The Beatles' sequence (taped by CBS at the group's first American show at the Washington Coliseum on February 11th) and a tape of Lesley Gore are broadcast four times in the special closed-circuit broadcasts across selected US cinemas, beginning at 12 noon and then again at 3:00pm (with the broadcasts repeated at the same times the following day). Among the venues showing the unique NGC broadcasts are the Spokane Coliseum in Washington, DC, the Norva Theatre in Norfolk, VA, and the Fox Village Theatre in Westwood Village, Los Angeles, CA. (Close examination of the NBC TV footage will reveal Brian's girlfriend Marilyn sitting one seat away from Beach Boys promoter and friend Fred Vail among the packed audience.)

After these four original transmissions, The Beach Boys' taped performance will go missing until it is found 34 years later, in 1998, during research for the Delilah Films documentary on the group, *Endless Harmony*. That same year the concert is released officially as *The Beach Boys: The Lost Concert* by Image Entertainment, by which time 'Monster Mash' had been excised from the tape.

TV ABC Television Center studio *Hollywood, CA*. ABC *American Bandstand* lip-synch 'Don't Worry Baby' broadcast April 18th 12:30-1:30pm LA time. Once the taping is concluded at NBC, the group heads to the ABC television studios in Hollywood where this afternoon they lip-synch 'Don't Worry Baby' for the popular weekly music show *American Bandstand*. The Beach Boys' apparent secondary status to the 'four lads from Liverpool' is underlined today when they find themselves performing on a special *Beatles Day* edition of the 45-minute show. Aside from the one Beach Boys song, Beatles music is played and danced to throughout the programme, though the group do help to present a new dance called The Surf and are interviewed by host Dick Clark.

■ Saturday 21st

'Fun Fun Fun' single peaks in US *Billboard* chart at number 5.

■ Wednesday 25th

The Four Seasons and The Crickets perform a concert this evening at the Memorial Auditorium in Sacramento, California. Beach Boys concert promoter and friend Fred Vail says: "I turned 20 in March 1964 and Carl and Dennis flew to Sacramento to wish me a happy birthday. I went to the door at my folks' house and there were the two Beach Boys who had flown up from LA. They went with me to the concert this evening. The Crickets were opening for The Four Seasons and when the kids at the show found out that Carl and Denny were there, they went crazy!

"They started screaming for the boys during the middle of The Four Seasons' set and they wouldn't quieten down until I brought the two Beach Boys out on stage to say hi. They basically said, 'Listen, we're just here to see our buddy, Fred, and The Four Seasons and we don't want to distract from the show.' After the concert, the three of us went out for a meal where Carl and Denny presented me with a tie for my birthday."

April

'Fun Fun Fun' single peaks in German *Hit Bilanz* chart at number 49.

■ Thursday 2nd

RECORDING *All Summer Long* session 1 Western Recorders studio *Hollywood CA*. In his favourite environment, Brian begins laying down tracks for the next Beach Boys album. Carl is on lead guitar, Brian on bass, Al on rhythm guitar, and Dennis on drums. Brian needs to take the group in a new direction, and this is where it all begins. Today they record the instrumental basis for **'I Get Around'** (tracking take 15 marked as best) followed by vocal overdubbing and the taping of guitar and keyboard instrumental inserts. Tracking and vocals are also recorded for **'Little Honda'**. Session musicians are on hand to provide the saxophone and piano required on 'I Get Around'.

After the shortcomings of *Shut Down Volume 2* Brian is determined that the group's next long-player will consolidate the band's many strengths, so he initiates a few crucial changes. Notably, the production on the new disc will improve and the album will not be dragged down by many weak, filler tracks (though it will include the lightweight 'Our Favorite Recording Sessions'). In addition, unlike the group's first three albums which centred more or less on surfing or cars, this new disc will be free from the restraints of such themes. Although a couple of songs intended for it will have a car-inspired flavour, the notion of writing hot-rod songs has become thoroughly unappealing to The Beach Boys' leader. Brian tells Earl Leaf, American columnist for *Teen Beat*: "We needed to grow. Up to this point we had milked every idea dry. We milked it fucking dry. We had done every possible angle about surfing and then we did the car routine. But we needed to grow artistically."

His desire for musical nirvana will propel The Beach Boys into another realm of popular music – and one that will help change pop forever. As recordings begin today for the next LP, which becomes *All Summer Long*, Brian feels sure that he has his best collection of songs yet, with more complex arrangements than he has ever attempted. In addition, his search for musical perfection will manifest itself as he pushes his bandmates to deliver flawless vocal performances. It will be extremely hard work for everyone.

This opening session also produces the ultimate sacrifice. During the recording of 'I Get Around' and 'Little Honda' today, Murry is fired as The Beach Boys' manager. As far as the group is concerned he has long overstayed his welcome and has been consistently interrupting sessions with pointless criticisms, and generally undermining Brian. To please his father, and to make him feel that he is an integral part of the group's sessions, Brian had given Murry a fake mixing desk, the controls of which were completely useless and played no part in the recordings. Tensions have now reached boiling point and, during a heated exchange, Brian fires his father. He recalls on American TV: "We finally said, 'Look, we can't deal with you any more. We've got to let you go and get a new manager.'"

Though Brian will continue periodically to seek a musical opinion from his father over the next few years, Murry is pushed out of The Beach Boys' professional lives. Devastated, Murry retires to bed for nearly a month. The Beach Boys immediately hire Cummings & Currant, Murry's tax accountants, to handle their finances.

Murry's wife Audree Wilson remembers in *Rolling Stone*: "That was a horrible time for me. [Murry] was just destroyed by that. He already had an ulcer and it was really too much for him. He loved them so much.

"He was so overly protective. He couldn't let them go. He was angry towards me. You always take it out on the one you're closest too. He was also angry at the whole world. He stayed in bed a lot." Carl also tells *Rolling Stone*: "I remember having a conversation with my dad in his bedroom at home. I said, 'They really don't want you to manage the group any more.' When I think about it, that must have really crushed him. After all, he gave up his home and business for us. He was kind of crackers over us."

Beach Boy promoter and friend Fred Vail: "Murry was a businessman. He had grown up through the depression, lived through World War II, and was a very stern disciplinarian. I used to describe Murry as like an Army drill sergeant. He was very firm, but he was a good and honest man. The role he played in the group was one of the key reasons for their success.

"In America at this time it was an *Ozzie & Harriet* kind of existence: the dad was expected to be the breadwinner and the mum was expected to stay at home. Dad was the disciplinarian. Murry was not only the manager of The Beach Boys but he was also their father, and sometimes walking that line was very difficult. Murry wasn't in it for the money. Murry was in it to help his sons, to help make his sons a hit band. He wasn't greedy like a lot of other managers. With Murry, it was love, it was family.

"When The Beatles came on the scene, you had two of the world's biggest bands on the same label [in the US], Capitol. Who was going to fight for The Beach Boys if not Murry? I never saw him attack The Beach Boys physically. I saw him fine the boys for cussing or for doing some childish pranks. But his important role in the boys' career was overlooked."

■ Friday 3rd
Whittier High School Auditorium *Whittier, CA*
With Murry no longer in control, The Beach Boys perform a benefit show in the supposedly haunted auditorium of this school.

■ Saturday 4th
The Beatles have the entire Top Five positions to themselves in the American *Billboard* Hot 100 Singles chart. It seems as if The Beach Boys' position as the top pop group in the States is being relinquished to the four lads from Liverpool.

1964

■ **Saturday 11th**

Shut Down Volume 2 album hits the US charts.

■ **Monday 13th**

'He's A Doll' / 'The Love Of A Boy And A Girl' single by The Honeys released in the US. Brian produces this Warners 45, the fourth Honeys single, and writes the A-side.

■ **Tuesday 14th**

A tape dub of 'Lonely Sea' is made for use in the *Girls On The Beach* motion picture (see 16th/17th).

■ **Thursday 16th – Friday 17th**

Around this time the group shoots their sequences for the *Girls On The Beach* movie at Paramount studios in Hollywood; the scene with Brian singing 'Lonely Sea' on the beach will be one of the film's highlights.

■ **Wednesday 29th**

RECORDING *All Summer Long* session 2 Western Recorders studio *Hollywood CA* 10:30am-1:30pm. At this session The Beach Boys record **'Hushabye'**, **'Wendy'** (tracking and vocals), **'Drive-In'** (vocals; see also June 23rd), **'Don't Back Down'** (two very different versions; the second remains unreleased until Capitol's 1990 *Little Deuce Coupe / All Summer Long* CD) and **'We'll Run Away'** (tracking). In addition, the sessions produce the instrumental **'Carl's Big Chance'** (originally titled 'Memphis Beach', written by Chuck Berry in 1958) that features Carl playing lead guitar along with the studio musicians (13 takes required).

Musicians present Hal Blaine (drums), Ray Pohlman (bass guitar).

■ **Thursday 30th**

RECORDING *All Summer Long* session 3 Western Recorders studio *Hollywood CA*. A further tracking session for **'We'll Run Away'**.

May

'Three Window Coupe' / 'Hot Rod USA' single by The Rip Chords and **'In My 40 Ford'** / 'Clutch Rider' single by The Kustom Kings released in the US. Future Beach Boy Bruce Johnston features in both groups.

■ **Wednesday 6th**

RECORDING *All Summer Long* session 4 Western Recorders studio *Hollywood CA*. Today sees a Beach Boys tracking session for **'All Summer Long'** (instrumental track take 43, including xylophone, piccolo, saxophone, guitar, bass and drums, is marked as best) and **'Do You Remember'** (instrumental track take 10 best). The session also produces **'Our Favorite Recording Sessions'**, a series of out-takes and miscellaneous studio chatter edited into a two-minute filler.

■ **Thursday 7th**

RECORDING *All Summer Long* session 5 Western Recorders studio *Hollywood CA*. The Beach Boys add vocals to the previous day's tracking master of **'All Summer Long'**.

■ **Saturday 9th**

Sacramento Memorial *Auditorium* Sacramento, CA

After a five-week break The Beach Boys – Brian, Carl, Dennis, Mike

---

I Get Around **single**

A 'I Get Around' (B. WILSON / M. LOVE)
B 'Don't Worry Baby' (B. WILSON / R. CHRISTIAN)

US release May 11th 1964 (Capitol 5174).
UK release June 1964 (Capitol CL 15350).
Chart high US number 1; UK number 7.

and Al – return to the concert stage, performing at a charity show that has been sponsored by The Sacramento County Guild For Crippled Children.

■ **Monday 11th**

'I Get Around' / 'Don't Worry Baby' single released in the US. 'I Get Around' will become the group's first American number 1, while the flip side will make number 24 in the US charts.

■ **Tuesday 12th**

TV CBS Television City *Hollywood, CA*. CBS *The Red Skelton Show* lip-synch 'In My Room', 'I Get Around', broadcast 8:00-9:00pm. This afternoon The Beach Boys tape another American TV appearance, this time a return to the *Red Skelton* variety show. Also on is American character actor Raymond Burr. (The performances will later be seen – in black-and-white – in Malcolm Leo's *American Band* documentary.)

■ **Monday 18th**

RECORDING *All Summer Long* session 6 Western Recorders studio *Hollywood CA*. Back in the studio the group completes work on **'Do You Remember'** (six takes required) and **'We'll Run Away'**, overdubbing vocals onto the existing tracking masters. ('Overdubbing' is the recording of additional vocals or instruments onto an existing recorded performance on tape.)

■ **Tuesday 19th**

RECORDING *All Summer Long* session 7 Western Recorders studio *Hollywood CA*. In one long session The Beach Boys record and finish **'Girls On The Beach'** with a tracking session and vocal overdubs (ten takes required). Early takes are marred by infectious laughter among the group members. (The song will become the theme to the 1965 film of the same name, which also briefly stars The Beach Boys.) With that, recordings for the *All Summer Long* album are completed. Brian is much more satisfied with the results, believing that the group has finally recorded an album that can stand alongside the work of The Beatles – and anyone else for that matter. But as usual Brian still feels that improvements can be made.

■ **Saturday 23rd**

Shut Down Volume 2 album peaks in US *Billboard* chart at number 13.

June

'I Get Around' / 'Don't Worry Baby' single released in the UK. It will peak in the British charts at number 7 after a public

endorsement from Rolling Stones singer Mick Jagger on the hip TV show *Ready Steady Go!*.

'Yes Sir That's My Baby' / 'Jack's Theme' single by Hale & The Hushabyes released in the US. The A-side of this Capitol 45 features backing vocals by Brian. Hale & The Hushabyes are a fictitious group consisting of session singers; besides Brian, members include Sonny & Cher, Jack Nitzsche, The Blossoms, Jackie DeShannon, Darlene Love, Edna Wright, and Albert Stone.

Fun Fun Fun EP released in the UK: 'Fun Fun Fun', 'In My Room', 'Little Deuce Coupe', 'Why Do Fools Fall In Love'.

• Murry and Audree Wilson move 20-plus miles east from Hawthorne to Whittier, only to separate shortly after. Murry sells his ABLE Machinery business.

■ Monday 1st

'Sacramento' / 'Just The Way I Feel' single by Gary Usher released in the US. The A-side of the Capitol 45 is co-written by Brian and Usher, and Brian produces both sides of the disc.

'Thinkin' 'Bout You Baby' / 'Story Of My Life' single by Sharon Marie released in the US. Both sides of this, her second Capitol 45, are produced by Brian and co-written by Brian and Mike. The A-side is a prototype of the song that will later become 'Darlin'', a 1967 single release for The Beach Boys.

■ Wednesday 3rd

RECORDING Western Recorders studio *Hollywood CA*. Murry Wilson returns to the recording studio, producing three tracks – **'Car Party'**, **'Casanova'** and **'Leaves'** – for erstwhile Beach Boy David Marks and his new group The Marksmen (formerly The Jaguars). Leading them is drummer Mark Groseclose, who had once been a substitute Beach Boy when he replaced Dennis (see February 14th 1963). Among the musicians present at the session today are drummer Hal Blaine and guitarist Glen Campbell. ('Leaves' will be re-recorded as a piano instrumental for Murry Wilson's October 1967 album *The Many Moods Of Murry Wilson*.)

■ Saturday 6th

'I Get Around' single enters the US *Billboard* Top 40 chart at number 17.

■ Monday 8th

RECORDING Western Recorders studio *Hollywood CA*. This session sees tracking and then vocal overdubbing for Brian and Mike's **'She Knows Me Too Well'** (16 takes required for the instrumental track). The song defines the kind of music that Brian has in mind for future Beach Boys releases. At one point Capitol will seriously consider releasing this version as one side of the group's next single, but ultimately it will not appear until later in the year when a newly recorded version will grace the B-side of the 'When I Grow Up (To Be A Man)' single, and then the following year's *Beach Boys Today!* album. (See July 6th, August 5th & 8th.)

■ Tuesday 16th

RECORDING Sunset Sound studio *Los Angeles, CA*. The group has been signed to appear in the opening title sequence of Walt Disney's new teen comedy *The Monkey's Uncle*. But with that many months away, today the instrumental backing track for the title song is recorded, with no Beach Boys in attendance. Shortly afterwards the group will add their backing vocals for **'The Monkey's Uncle'** at the same studio along with the film's star Annette Funicello. This title song is written by Richard and Robert Sherman, who wrote music for Disney classics such as *Mary Poppins* and *The Jungle Book*. Besides

appearing on the film's opening sequence, the track will feature as part of *The Monkey's Uncle* soundtrack album, which will be released in the US on August 5th.

Musicians present Hal Blaine (drums), Steve Douglas (saxophone), Gene Estes (probably percussion), Jay Migliori (saxophone), Bill Pitman (guitar), Tommy Tedesco (guitar).

■ Thursday 18th

RECORDING *Christmas Album* session 1 Capitol studio *Hollywood, CA* 2:30-5:30pm. Brian begins to piece together The Beach Boys' seventh album, the one planned beyond the not-yet-released *All Summer Long*. For the new record, *The Beach Boys' Christmas Album*, he will use a 41-piece orchestra. His arranging duties are halved by his ingenious decision to compose and arrange only four new recordings for the 12-song album. He summons Dick Reynolds, arranger to The Four Freshmen, to oversee the arranging and recording of strings for the traditional songs to be included.

Recordings for the album begin today with orchestral tracking sessions for **'We Three Kings Of Orient Are'**, **'Santa Claus Is Comin' To Town'**, **'White Christmas'** and **'Blue Christmas'**. An alternative version of the group's 1963 holiday hit single **'Little Saint Nick'** is also made as Brian records new vocals and strips off the sleigh bells and glockenspiels of the original to match the sound of the newer recordings. (Sessions for the album will resume full-time on June 24th, but see June 23rd.)

■ Monday 22nd

RECORDING Western Recorders studio *Hollywood CA* 3:30-6:30pm. This afternoon Brian, Dennis, Carl and Al attend a Beach Boys instrumental tracking session for **'Don't Hurt My Little Sister'** (18 takes required plus two vocal overdubbing sessions; see also January 18th 1965). Brian originally wrote this song for The Ronettes and submitted it to their producer Phil Spector, who then altered the lyrics and called it 'Things Are Changing (For The Better)'. Brian will recall that Spector kicks him off the session because he "couldn't play the song right". Spector later cuts the revamped song with The Blossoms as a public-service announcement for equal opportunities.

Musicians present Hal Blaine (drums), John Gray (guitar, or possibly engineer), Ray Pohlman (bass guitar).

■ Tuesday 23rd

RECORDING *Christmas Album* session 2 Western Recorders studio *Hollywood CA*. A Beach Boys vocal overdubbing session for an alternative version of **'Little Honda'** (see July 6th). With an eye still on the developing *Christmas* LP, the session also produces an extremely odd recording where the group attempts to overdub a vocal of 'Little Saint Nick' onto the October 18th 1963 instrumental track of 'Drive-In'. (The result will remain unreleased until Capitol's 1998 CD of the *Christmas Album*. Since the single version of 'Little Saint Nick' was also recorded in October 1963, it is possible that Brian and Mike's original set of lyrics was meant to go with the melody from what we now know as 'Drive-In'. When the experiment failed, Brian was probably forced to write a new melody for 'Little Saint Nick', resulting in the single. Needing another song this year for *All Summer Long*, he and Mike most likely drafted the 'Drive-In' lyrics, recording vocals on April 29th 1964.)

■ Wednesday 24th

RECORDING *Christmas Album* session 3 Capitol studio *Hollywood, CA* 8:00-11:00pm. The Beach Boys return to Capitol to resume work on their *Christmas Album*. Today they focus on recording instrumental tracks for **'Frosty The Snowman'**, **'I'll Be Home For**

Christmas', 'Jingle Bells' and 'Christmas Eve'. The last two will remain unreleased.

■ Thursday 25th
RECORDING *Christmas Album* **session 4** Western Recorders studio *Hollywood, CA*. Further tracking recordings for the *Christmas Album* produce '**The Man With All The Toys**', '**Merry Christmas Baby**' (ten takes required) and '**Santa's Beard**'. Brian is on piano, Dennis on drums, Carl on rhythm and lead guitar, and Al on bass guitar; 21 instrumental rehearsals are followed by serious studio recordings. The session also produces '**Christmas Day**' (eight instrumental takes), but because Brian is unhappy with the results, a further 24 try-out takes follow, and then seven further instrumental takes. The session is rounded off as the group records an a cappella version of '**Auld Lang Syne**'. With tracking recordings for the *Christmas* songs now complete, work will start on Saturday on vocal overdubs.

■ Saturday 27th
RECORDING *Christmas Album* **session 5** Western Recorders studio *Hollywood, CA*. For the next four days the group's collective, intricate vocals are overdubbed onto the *Christmas Album* tracking masters taped between June 18th and 25th. The first session focuses on '**The Man With All The Toys**' (lead vocals by Brian and Mike), '**Santa's Beard**' (Mike) and '**Christmas Day**' (which has Al performing his first lead vocal on a Beach Boys recording; eight sets of backing vocal overdubs are recorded onto lead vocal take 7, which is marked as

best). Many attempts at recording takes are again ruined by riotous laughter among the group members.
• 'Don't Worry Baby' enters US *Billboard* Top 40 chart at number 29.

■ Sunday 28th
RECORDING *Christmas Album* **session 6** Western Recorders studio *Hollywood, CA*. The group records vocals for '**Blue Christmas**' (Brian on double-tracked vocal with no backing – eight vocal overdubs follow), '**White Christmas**' (three vocal overdubs are made onto Brian's vocal take 3, marked as best) and '**Santa Claus Is Coming To Town**' (lead vocals by Brian and Mike; five takes of a Brian-only vocal intro are followed by 24 takes of the group in unison). Mike's continual belching greatly annoys Brian during the recordings.

■ Monday 29th
RECORDING *Christmas Album* **session 7** Western Recorders studio *Hollywood, CA*. Beach Boys vocal sessions for '**Frosty The Snowman**' (Brian on lead) and '**We Three Kings Of Orient Are**' (Brian and Mike sharing lead).

■ Tuesday 30th
RECORDING *Christmas Album* **session 8** Western Recorders studio *Hollywood, CA*. Vocal sessions for '**Merry Christmas Baby**' (Mike on lead) and '**I'll Be Home For Christmas**' (Brian). Taping for *The Beach Boys' Christmas Album* is concluded. ('Merry Christmas Baby' will also be issued as a single in Germany in December 1967.)

July

Shut Down Volume 2 album released in the UK.
Three Window Coupe album by The Rip Chords released in the US, featuring future Beach Boy Bruce Johnston.

■ Wednesday 1st

'I Get Around' single reaches number 1 position in US *Variety* charts published today. It is The Beach Boys' first American chart topper.

■ Thursday 2nd

Just before they fly out to Hawaii to start their next tour, the group receives *Billboard*'s Top Single award for 'I Get Around', presented by the magazine's West Coast advertising manager Bill Wardlow.

TOUR STARTS US *Summer Safari* (Jul 3rd–Aug 8th)

■ Friday 3rd & Saturday 4th

Honolulu International Center Arena *Honolulu, HI* 7:30pm (Friday) and 2:00 & 6:30–9:00pm (Saturday), with Jan & Dean, Jimmy Clanton, Ray Peterson, The Kingsmen, The Rivingtons, Jody Miller, Bruce & Terry, Jimmy Griffin, Mary Saenz, Peter & Gordon, The K-Poi All Star Band

With their latest single 'I Get Around' sitting pretty in the number 1 position in charts across the country, The Beach Boys begin their 36-date *Summer Safari* tour by headlining both days of a two-day *Million Dollar Party* sponsored by the K-Poi radio station, billed as "The biggest show ever to play Hawaii". The K-Poi All Star Band features Hal 'drummer man' Blaine and future Beach Boy guitarist Glen Campbell.

■ Saturday 4th

'I Get Around' single peaks in US *Billboard* chart at number 1, up from the number 2 position, replacing Peter & Gordon's 'A World Without Love'. It becomes the first number 1 on the singles chart by an American group in eight months, breaking the dominance of British-based artists, and will remain in the top spot on *Billboard* for two weeks. Meanwhile its B-side, 'Don't Worry Baby', peaks in the *Billboard* chart at number 24. (Some charts are still based on radio plays as well as sales, so B-sides can chart separately from their As.)

■ Monday 6th

A Capitol acetate dated today twins alternate mono recordings of 'Little Honda' (featuring a very prominent organ, taped on June 23rd) with 'She Knows Me Too Well' (taped June 8th). The pairing of the two tracks, which carry different master numbers to those of the normal releases, suggests that Capitol may be planning a quick follow-up single to 'I Get Around'. It is an idea that ultimately will be shelved, perhaps because Brian has already written 'When I Grow Up (To Be A Man)' as the follow-up, or maybe because he has promised 'Little Honda' to Gary Usher.

University of Arizona Auditorium *Tucson, AZ* afternoon and evening performance, with Freddie Cannon, Jimmy Griffin, Lynn Easton, The Kingsmen

The Beach Boys' US *Summer Safari* tour continues. The *Arizona Daily Star* reviewer writes: "A small but appreciative audience gave a noisy welcome to The Beach Boys and other rock'n'roll recording artists. The afternoon audience of nearly 4,000, most in pre-adolescence, was a well-behaved one, making the policemen that walked around the auditorium look out of place. Reaction to the loud electric guitars and amplified voices ranged from head-shaking and foot-tapping to bouncing up and down in the seats as if they were trampolines.

"The Beach Boys sated the crowd with 15 songs, ranging from loud songs to instrumental pieces. Some of the songs sounded much like the others, but the one thing they all had in common was deafening loudness … . When the guitars and drums weren't drowning out the voices, The Beach Boys exhibited an eerie sort of harmony that is not unpleasing to the ear. Mike Love, the lead singer and saxophonist, was the clown of the group and his mugging was successful in provoking laughter from the audience."

The *Tucson Citizen* says: "Five bright-faced lads fresh from the beaches of California brought a tidal wave of entertainment to Tucson last night. The Beach Boys, America's homogenised answer to the British Beatles, rode into the University of Arizona auditorium atop the crest of a towering wave of popularity with the surfin' set and paddled out again with a beach buggy full of loot. These wailing boys are far from tone deaf but they certainly run the risk of becoming stone deaf. The decibel level in the auditorium was sky high. Only with difficulty could one catch enough of the words from amidst the amplified whanging of steel guitars [sic] even to fit a song with a title, as if that mattered.

"Beach Boys fans made [this concert] sound like a High School prep rally. Shrieks, squeals and whinnies greeted the initial chord of every number. The crowd couldn't have loved The Beach Boys more had they had Tonto on the tom-toms. Dennis Wilson, whose every toss of his blond mop brought a groundswell of sighs from the girls, drummed and tossed unremittingly throughout the evening. … Nothing living can resist that beat. And it's just one beat. It serves nicely for 'Surfin' USA', 'In My Room' and 'I Get Around', the number 1 song in the country. Taken at varying speeds, the beat still has the quiet insistence of a jackhammer."

■ Tuesday 7th

Civic Auditorium *Denver, CO* 8:00pm

■ Friday 10th

Tulsa Assembly Center *Tulsa, OK*
The audience totals 5,500 and the show grosses $11,000, from which The Beach Boys would typically take 60 percent

■ Saturday 11th

Omaha Civic Auditorium *Omaha, NE*
The audience tonight totals 7,500 and the concert grosses $15,000.

■ Sunday 12th

Municipal Auditorium *Kansas City, MO*

■ Monday 13th

Veterans Memorial Auditorium *Des Moines, IA*
Tonight's audience totals 3,400 and the show grosses $8,800.
All Summer Long album released in the US. With The Beach Boys' American popularity at a high, the LP will peak in the US charts at number 4 and spends 49 weeks on the listings. It goes a long way in fulfilling Brian's wishes to be a respected musical force in the wake of The Beatles, but with the success comes the attendant problem for Brian of how to top this achievement.

■ Tuesday 14th

RKO Orpheum Theater *Champaign, IL*

■ Wednesday 15th

Kiel Opera House *St Louis, MO* 6:30 & 9:00pm

LEFT The group with singer Annette Funicello filming the opening sequence for the new Walt Disney comedy *The Monkey's Uncle*.
FOLLOWING PAGES Little Fender amps and a great big crowd: Brian, Dennis, Carl and Mike rock out on the *Summer Safari* tour.

All Summer Long album

A1 'I Get Around' (B. WILSON / M. LOVE)
A2 'All Summer Long' (B. WILSON / M. LOVE)
A3 'Hushabye' (D. POMUS / M. SCHUMAN)
A4 'Little Honda' (B. WILSON / M. LOVE)
A5 'We'll Run Away' (B. WILSON / G. USHER)
A6 'Carl's Big Chance' (B. WILSON / C. WILSON)
B1 'Wendy' (B. WILSON / M. LOVE)
B2 'Do You Remember' (B. WILSON / M. LOVE)
B3 'Girls On The Beach' (B. WILSON)
B4 'Drive-In' (B. WILSON / M. LOVE)
B5 'Our Favorite Recording Sessions' (B. WILSON / C. WILSON / D. WILSON / M. LOVE / A. JARDINE)
B6 'Don't Back Down' * (B. WILSON / M. LOVE)
* Early copies list 'Don't Back Down' in error as 'Don't Break Down'.

US release July 13th 1964 (Capitol T2110).
UK release June 1965 (Capitol T2110).
Chart high US number 4; UK none.

■ Thursday 16th
Kentucky State Fairgrounds *Louisville, KY* 8:30pm; tickets $2.00
The audience totals 9,800 and the show grosses a total of $21,200.

■ Friday 17th
Indiana Beach Shafer Lake *Indianapolis, IN* 8:45pm & 12:45am
Today's 11,300 crowd (grossing $23,600) beats the previous attendance record at the venue jointly held by The Glenn Miller Orchestra and The Kingston Trio.

■ Saturday 18th
State Fairgrounds, The Coliseum *Indianapolis, IN*
The local WIFE radio station sponsors the concert. At this halfway point, the 36-date *Summer Safari* tour has racked up $160,000 in gross receipts. Each night's performance has been attended by an average of 4,000 patrons – and most of those are hysterical, arm-waving, screaming teenagers.

■ Sunday 19th
Milwaukee Auditorium *Milwaukee, WI* 3:00 & 8:00pm
The Milwaukee Journal's reviewer writes: "The Beach Boys, America's answer to The Beatles, brought their 'music to surf by' to the auditorium for two shows on Sunday. Houses of 2,481 in the afternoon and 3,750 in the evening passed up outdoor beach partying on a steamy hot Sunday to do their sweltering indoors. The two performances by the Californian rock'n'roll group and supporting acts were received with screams of girlish exuberance. At the end of the evening show the boys jumped off the stage to greet their admirers. Two music-loving girls grabbed drummer Dennis Wilson and a general charge to the stage seemed imminent. But ushers hurried the boys away and serious trouble was averted. ... Beach Boys songs are distinguishable from the other sounds which today's teenagers are using for music by unusual harmonising and the falsetto voices of leader Mike Love and arranger Brian Wilson.

On the ballad 'In My Room' there was even a suggestion of Four Freshmen influence."

■ Monday 20th
Veterans Auditorium *Des Moines, IA*

■ Thursday 23rd
Capitol Theater *Madison, WI* 7:00 & 9:30pm

■ Friday 24th
Arie Crown Theater *Chicago, IL* 8:30pm

■ Saturday 25th
Mary E Sawyer Auditorium *La Crosse, WI* 7:30 & 9:30pm
Audiences are not permitted to dance at either concert.

■ Tuesday 28th
Red Rocks Theater *Denver, CO* 8:15pm
First annual *Beach Party* at the venue.

■ Wednesday 29th
The Terrace Ballroom *Salt Lake City, UT* 8:00pm

■ Thursday 30th
State Building Auditorium *Reno, NV* 7:00 & 9:30pm

■ Friday 31st
Oakland Civic Auditorium *San Francisco, CA* 8:30pm

August

'I Get Around' single peaks in UK *Record Retailer* chart at number 7, and in German *Hit Bilanz* chart at number 38. The Beach Boys are now becoming a global success rather than just an American phenomenon.
'One Piece Topless Bathing Suit' / **'Wah-Wahini'** single by The Rip Chords released in the US, featuring future Beach Boy Bruce Johnston.

■ Saturday 1st
Civic Memorial Auditorium *Sacramento, CA* two shows
Since December 1963 a few Beach Boys concerts have been captured on tape for posterity, and today's shows at the Civic Memorial Auditorium in Sacramento are also taped. The following month, back in the studio and with an eye on an official release, Brian as producer will re-work today's live tapes, assisted by engineer Chuck Britz, re-recording some of the group's vocals and possibly instruments, for at least 'I Get Around' and 'Fun Fun Fun'. He submits the results to Capitol, along with yet another single. A compilation of the tapes will appear on the Capitol album *Beach Boys Concert*, released in the US on October 19th 1964 and charting on November 7th, ultimately reaching the number 1 position.
Set-list (first show) 'Little Honda', 'Papa-Oom-Mow-Mow', 'The Little Old Lady From Pasadena', 'Hushabye', 'Hawaii', 'Let's Go Trippin'', 'The Wanderer' (Dennis on lead; Brian plays drums), 'Surfer Girl', 'Monster Mash', 'Be True To Your School', 'Graduation Day', 'Surfin' USA', 'Don't Back Down', 'Don't Worry Baby', 'Wendy', 'I Get Around', 'Fun Fun Fun'.
Set-list (second show) 'Little Honda', 'Fun Fun Fun', 'Little Old Lady From Pasadena', 'Hushabye', 'Hawaii', 'Let's Go Trippin'', 'The

Wanderer', 'Wendy', 'Monster Mash', 'Surfer Girl', 'Be True To Your School', 'Graduation Day', 'Surfin' USA', 'Don't Back Down', 'Don't Worry Baby', 'I Get Around', 'Papa-Oom-Mow-Mow'.
• *All Summer Long* album hits the US charts.

■ Tuesday 4th
The Earl Warren Showgrounds *Santa Barbara*, *CA* 8:15pm, with Eddie Hodges, Lynn Easton, The Kingsmen

■ Wednesday 5th
RECORDING Western Recorders studio *Hollywood CA* 3:00-6:00pm. With another American concert tour due to kick off on August 21st and the group's first tour of Europe coming in November, Capitol Records urgently requires a new Beach Boys single. With that in mind work begins today on both sides of their new 45, with instrumental tracking (piano, bass and drums) for **'When I Grow Up (To Be A Man)'** and a new version of **'She Knows Me Too Well'** (see June 8th; 16 takes required).

The intricate arrangement of 'When I Grow Up (To Be A Man)' forces The Beach Boys to record 37 takes until they can achieve a satisfactory instrumental master to which the vocals can be overdubbed the following week. After the recording of a stunning harpsichord track, the day closes with an instrumental insert (five takes required). Recording work on 'When I Grow Up (To Be A Man)' will resume on August 10th.

Brian tells the *Birmingham Post*: "When I was younger, I used to worry about turning into an old square over the years. I don't think I will now, and that is what inspired 'When I Grow Up'."
Musicians present Carrol Lewis (trumpet).
• *Annette At Bikini Beach* album by Annette Funicello released in the US. It features The Beach Boys vocally backing Funicello on the theme tune of the Walt Disney movie *The Monkey's Uncle*.

■ Saturday 8th
RECORDING Western Recorders studio *Hollywood CA*. Using the instrumental backing tracks recorded on August 5th, work concludes at Western on **'She Knows Me Too Well'** with the overdubbing of the group's vocals.
Russ Auditorium, San Diego High School *San Diego, CA*
Meanwhile, this evening marks the last date of the *Summer Safari* tour as the group performs in San Diego.

■ Monday 10th
RECORDING Western Recorders studio *Hollywood CA* 8:00-11:00pm. Work on the group's next single is wrapped up this evening when the full Beach Boys line-up perform vocal overdubs onto the tracking master of **'When I Grow Up (To Be A Man)'**. The second of the two vocal overdubs requires 14 takes.

The recordings – which are hindered by Dennis who insists on fooling around – conclude with a further instrumental insert to the song (five takes required).

■ Monday 17th
RECORDING Western Recorders studio *Hollywood CA* 5:00-8:00pm. Brian and Bob Norberg, his former flatmate and one-time member of The Survivors, co-produce a session this evening for 'Peep And Hide', a working title for **'Baby What You Want Me To Do'**, composed by Jimmy Reed. On July 29th 1965 Norberg will issue 'Baby…' on Tower Records under the moniker Bob & Bobby ('Bobby' is his new singing partner, Jane Canada).
Musicians present Hal Blaine (drums); Tommy Morgan (harmonica), Bill Pitman (bass), Tommy Tedesco (guitar).

When I Grow Up (To Be A Man) single

A 'When I Grow Up (To Be A Man)' (B. WILSON / M. LOVE)
B 'She Knows Me Too Well' (B. WILSON / M. LOVE)

US release August 24th 1964 (Capitol 5245).
UK release October 23rd 1964 (Capitol CL 15361).
Chart high US number 9; UK number 27.

TOUR STARTS US East/South/Midwest (Aug 21st-Sep 30th)

■ Friday 21st
Public Auditorium *Cleveland, OH*
Just over two weeks after completing their last tour, the group sets off again, this time for a 30-date six-week US tour.

■ Saturday 22nd
Syria Mosque *Pittsburgh, PA* 7:30 & 9:30pm
Local radio station KQV sponsors the gig.
• *All Summer Long* album peaks in US *Billboard* chart at number 4.

■ Monday 24th
'When I Grow Up (To Be A Man)' / 'She Knows Me Too Well' single released in the US. It will peak at number 9 in the US and number 27 in the UK.

■ Friday 28th & Saturday 29th
Springlake Park *Oklahoma City, OK*

■ Saturday 29th
'I Get Around' single hits the UK *Record Retailer* chart at number 7.

September

'I Get Around' single peaks in Dutch chart at number 38.

■ Tuesday 1st
'Little Honda' single by The Hondells released in the US, the A-side featuring a lead vocal by Brian.

■ Thursday 3rd
War Memorial Auditorium *Buffalo, NY* with Jan & Dean

■ Friday 4th & Saturday 5th
Seattle Opera House *Seattle, WA*
The group performs for two nights at the Seattle *Teen-Age Fair*.
• 'When I Grow Up (To Be A Man)' single hits the US charts.

■ Sunday 6th
Boston Garden *Boston, MA*

■ Wednesday 9th
RECORDING *Today!* session 1 Western Recorders studio (3) *Hollywood CA* 4:00-6:00pm. A two-hour session this afternoon has

---

FOLLOWING PAGES Camera rehearsals on September 27th for 'Wendy' for the first of three appearances by the group on *The Ed Sullivan Show*, broadcast live from CBS TV studios in New York City.

Brian working on arrangements for '**I'm So Young**' (12 takes required). The recordings today, also attended by Al and Carl, conclude with two vocal overdubbing sessions for the song, which will appear in different form on *The Beach Boys' Today!* album. This version, with a flute and more prominent bassline, will go unreleased until Capitol's 1990 CD *Today! / Summer Days (And Summer Nights!)*. The song itself was originally released in 1958 by The Students, and Brian decides to cover it because his hero Phil Spector has issued a version by Veronica (presently a Ronette and the future Mrs Spector) as 'So Young' on the newly formed Phil Spector record label. At the end of this session, Brian and engineer Chuck Britz make a least three mono mixes of 'I'm So Young'.
Musicians present Jay Migliori (flute), Maurice Miller (probably drums).

■ Thursday 10th
Dillon Stadium *Hartford, CT*

■ Friday 11th
Lagoon *Salt Lake City, UT*

■ Saturday 12th
The Pavilion *Boise, ID*

■ Sunday 13th
Boise High School Auditorium *Boise, ID* 6:30 & 9:00pm

■ Wednesday 16th
RECORDING Western Recorders studio *Hollywood CA* 2:30-6:00pm. A Beach Boys instrumental tracking session for '**All Dressed Up For School**' (nine takes required) and, later, two vocal overdubs. Carl plays guitar, Dennis is on drums and Brian provides piano. Brian employs four bassists for the session – Al Jardine on electric, plus Jimmy Bond, Melvin Pollan and Lyle Ritz on uprights.

The song, originally titled 'What'll I Wear To School Today', is written by Brian and Roger Christian for Mike Love's discovery Sharon Marie (Esparza), and will remain unreleased for 26 years until its appearance as a bonus track on the 1990 Capitol CD *Little Deuce Coupe / All Summer Long*. Before that, Brian will use its melody for 'I Just Got My Pay', a track intended for The Beach Boys' unreleased 1970 album *Add Some Music*, and then for 'Marcella' on the group's 1972 LP *Carl And The Passions – "So Tough"*.

At the end of today's session, handclaps are added and a rough mono mix is made simultaneously. Brian berates the group's handclapping abilities and Al comments that Brian should save these for their 'clapping only' album. These handclaps are not heard on the 1990 CD because a new stereo mix is created from the multi-track by engineer Mark Linett.
Musicians present Jimmy Bond (upright bass), Steve Douglas (saxophone), Carl Fortina (accordion), Melvin Pollan (upright bass), Lyle Ritz (upright bass).

■ Thursday 17th
Cameo Theater *Miami Beach, FL*

■ Friday 18th
Alabama State Coliseum *Montgomery, AL* with Jan & Dean, Norma Jean, Bobby Wood, Ace Cannon
The Beach Boys perform at *The Big Barn Fall Show*.
Set-list 'Fun Fun Fun', 'Surfin' USA', 'Little Deuce Coupe', 'Surfer Girl', 'Shut Down', 'I Get Around', 'Johnny B Goode', 'Monster Mash', 'In My Room', 'Be True To Your School', 'Don't Worry Baby', 'Little Honda'.

■ Saturday 19th
Alabama Theater *Birmingham, AL*
• 'When I Grow Up (To Be A Man)' single enters US *Billboard* Top 40 chart at number 34, while its B-side, 'She Knows Me Too Well', peaks at number 101.

■ Sunday 20th
Atlanta Stadium *Atlanta, GA*

■ Monday 21st
Civic Auditorium *Knoxville, TN*
4 By The Beach Boys EP released in the US: 'Wendy', 'Don't Back Down', 'Little Honda', 'Hushabye'. The disc is a relative failure, charting only at number 44.

■ Tuesday 22nd
RECORDING Columbia studio *Nashville, TN* six-hour session. Taking advantage of the nearest studio, The Beach Boys break from their tour of America's Southwest to record a basic guitar-drums-bass version of Brian and Carl's '**Dance Dance Dance**' (two 'takes', or attempts at a recording, are required), followed by the taping of a guitars-and-tambourine insert and vocal overdubs. A stereo mix of the day's recording (Master No. 51509) completes the session, but Brian is dissatisfied with the result and decides to re-work the song at the first available opportunity (see October 9th). Today's version will remain unreleased until it appears on the 1990 *Today/Summer Days (And Summer Nights!!)* CD.

■ Wednesday 23rd
Alexandria Roller Rink *Alexandria, VA* 7:00pm; tickets $2.50-$3.50.
A press release hails this show as the group's first East Coast appearance.

■ Thursday 24th
Loew's State Theater *Providence, RI* 8:15pm

■ Sunday 27th
TV CBS TV (Studio 50) *New York, NY*. CBS *The Ed Sullivan Show* live performance 'I Get Around', 'Wendy', broadcast 8:00-9:00pm New York time. The penultimate leg of the tour rounds off in New York City with a live appearance on CBS Television's top-rated and prestigious variety show. The group performs live versions first of 'I Get Around', surrounded by impressive hot-rod cars, and then later in the show 'Wendy'. In his announcement of the group, host Ed Sullivan mistakenly informs viewers that The Beach Boys are Swedish, and backstage three of the group play along with Sullivan's belief. Following the broadcast – the first of three the group will make on the show – The Beach Boys return home to California where they will begin preparing for their first trip to Europe. But on the way, the group plays another show.

■ Wednesday 30th
Memorial Auditorium *Worcester, MA* with Jan & Dean
The final night of the tour, which in total has grossed $328,693. The night is marred when large and excitable crowds cause more damage to the Auditorium than at any time in the building's 31-year history. Most is put down to fans outside who are unable to get in to see the show. After 14 minutes of The Beach Boys' performance police are forced to scrap the concert due to the ensuing bedlam, and the Auditorium's fire curtain comes down on the group. (The Beach Boys will return to concerts on October 16th.)

October

'When I Grow Up (To Be A Man)' single peaks in Canadian *RPM* chart at number 1.
Little Honda EP track peaks in Canadian *RPM* Chart at number 15.
'I Get Around' single peaks in Swedish Radio 3 chart at number 10.

■ Monday 5th
NBC TV in America begins broadcasting the new situation comedy series *Karen* (7:30-8:00pm) which features a title theme performance by The Beach Boys, with Mike singing lead. The *Karen* theme is written by Jack Marshall and show producer Bob Mosher – best known as producer of US television series *Leave It To Beaver*. The programme stars Debbie Watson in the lead role as an energetic 16-year-old whose activities constantly confound her tolerant parents, played by Richard Denning and Mary LaRoche. (The series will run on NBC until August 30th 1965.)

■ Friday 9th
RECORDING RCA studio *Hollywood, CA* 2:00-5:30pm. After his dissatisfaction with the version recorded on September 22nd Brian moves to RCA, the so-called 'music center of the world', to supervise a new tracking session for **'Dance Dance Dance'** (17 takes required). Brian plays bass, Dennis drums, Carl and Al guitars. Vocal overdubbing by Mike, recorded later in the day, requires 14 takes.
Musicians present Hal Blaine (Latin percussion, 'mallets'), Glen Campbell (12-string guitar), Steve Douglas (saxophone), Carl Fortina (accordion), Jay Migliori (saxophone), Ray Pohlman (bass guitar).

■ Wednesday 14th
RECORDING *Today!* session 2 Western Recorders studio *Hollywood, CA* 10:30pm-1:30am. Continuing with work on the *Today!* album, Brian produces an instrumental tracking session for **'Guess I'm Dumb'** (23 takes required). (See March 8th 1965.)
Musicians present Arnold Belnick (violin), Hal Blaine (drums), Harry Betts (trombone), Louis Blackburn (trombone), Glen Campbell (guitar), Roy Caton (trumpet), Steve Douglas (saxophone), Jesse Ehrlich (cello), Jim Getzoff (violin), Anne Goodman (cello), Larry Knechtel (bass guitar), Leonard) Malarsky (violin), Jay Migliori (saxophone), Oliver Mitchell (trumpet), Alexander Neiman (viola), Sidney Sharp (violin), Tommy Tedesco (guitar), Darrel Terwilliger (viola),

■ Friday 16th
San Jose Civic Auditorium *San Jose, CA*
The first of three weekend shows.

■ Saturday 17th
Long Beach Arena *Long Beach, CA*
• 'When I Grow Up (To Be A Man)' single peaks in US *Billboard* chart at number 9.

■ Sunday 18th
Mountain Home *Boise, ID*
Concert promoter Fred Vail recalls: "Our American Productions Company was running now, The Beach Boys' concert production firm. For the next show we did together The Beach Boys went from a $500-to-$800 flat fee that William Morris was giving them to $3,000 or better per night.

"I remember coming back from an engagement one evening and we weren't prepared to handle all the money that had come in

---

Beach Boys Concert album

A1 'Fun Fun Fun' (B. WILSON / M. LOVE)
A2 'The Little Old Lady From Pasadena' (D. ALLFIELD / R. CHRISTIAN)
A3 'Little Deuce Coupe' (B. WILSON / R. CHRISTIAN)
A4 'Long Tall Texan' (H. STREZLECKI)
A5 'In My Room' (B. WILSON / G. USHER)
A6 'Monster Mash' (B. PICKETT / L. CAPIZZI)
A7 'Let's Go Trippin'' (D. DALE)
B1 'Papa-Oom-Mow-Mow' (A. FRAZIER / C. WHITE / J. HARRIS / T. WILSON)
B2 'The Wanderer' (E. MARESCO)
B3 'Hawaii' (B. WILSON / M. LOVE)
B4 'Graduation Day' (J. SHERMAN / N. SHERMAN)
B5 'I Get Around' (B. WILSON / M. LOVE)
B6 'Johnny B Goode' (C. BERRY)

US release October 19th 1964 (Capitol TAO2198).
UK release February 1965 (Capitol T2198).
Chart high US number 1; UK none.

---

that night at the box office. We stuffed dollar bills in our pockets and in our briefcases. We had even resorted to stuffing money in shopping bags. We came back to the hotel and we dumped all this money on the bed in the hotel room. The boys were totally in shock. They were bewildered to see three or four thousand dollars in cash, and it was theirs. It was just like Christmas in June.

"This was the beginning of their quick and rapid rise in popularity. The success of the shows Murry and I did with The Beach Boys opened the eyes of managers and agents all over the country. People began to realise the potential impact of the group and began to give consideration to The Beach Boys as a major attraction."

■ Monday 19th
Beach Boys Concert album released in the US. Issued a week before their next single 'Dance Dance Dance', *Concert* will stand as a superb document of The Beach Boys in a live setting with Brian still on-stage with the group. Much to their delight the album is a great success, spending the whole of December locked at the number 1 position in the US charts. It will be The Beach Boys' first and really their only chart-topping album: although *Endless Summer* will reach the top spot in 1974, it will simply be a collection compiled and released by Capitol while The Beach Boys are contracted to another label.

■ Friday 23rd
'When I Grow Up (To Be A Man)' / 'She Knows Me Too Well' single released in the UK. EMI Records issues the new 45 to coincide with the group's first promotional tour of the country, set to start in ten days' time (see November 2nd). The disc will rise to number 44 and then, following the group's visit, re-enter the chart to peak at 27.

■ Monday 26th
'Dance Dance Dance' / 'The Warmth Of The Sun' single released

LEFT Brian sings 'Surfer Girl' for the *TAMI Show* filmed live at the Civic Auditorium in Santa Monica, California, on October 28th. BELOW Carl, Brian, Dennis, Mike and Al on November 2nd face their first British press gathering alongside a suitably American-looking dragster outside EMI in central London.

Dance Dance Dance single

A **'Dance Dance Dance'** (B. WILSON / C. WILSON / M. LOVE)
B **'The Warmth Of The Sun'** (B. WILSON / M. LOVE)

US release October 26th 1964 (Capitol 5306).
UK release January 1965 (Capitol CL 15370).
Chart high US number 8; UK number 24.

---

in the US. The Beach Boys' 11th single will peak at number 8 in the US chart. Also today, the group records almost 40 different spoken radio-station promo spots. Brian takes time to personalise some for specific DJs.

■ Wednesday 28th
Civic Auditorium *Santa Monica, CA*

In front of a large and hysterical audience The Beach Boys record a live appearance on the music extravaganza *The TAMI Show* (*The Teen Age Music International Show* or *Teen Age Music International*). They perform 'Surfin' USA', 'I Get Around', 'Surfer Girl' and 'Dance, Dance, Dance'. The live music show – which also features unique performances by The Barbarians, Billy J Kramer & The Dakotas, Gerry & The Pacemakers, Chuck Berry, Lesley Gore, Marvin Gaye, Smokey Robinson & The Miracles, The Supremes, The Rolling Stones, and James Brown & The Fabulous Flames – is advertised as shot on 'Electronovision' (video tape). But shortly before its release to cinemas in America, the UK and Europe, The Beach Boys' segment is excised from the completed 117-minute prints upon Brian's insistence.

November

Four By The Beach Boys EP released in the UK: 'Wendy', 'Don't Back Down', 'Little Honda', 'Hushabye'.
'When I Grow Up (To Be A Man)' single peaks in UK *Record Retailer* chart at number 27, and in Australian chart at number 20.

TOUR STARTS UK and Europe (Nov 1st-18th)

■ Sunday 1st

The band makes its second overseas trip, an 18-day promotional tour of the UK and Europe, playing a few gigs and appearing on various television shows. As Brian waits to board a plane at Los Angeles airport he glances over at his girlfriend, Marilyn Rovell, who appears to be gazing at fellow Beach Boy and cousin Mike Love. The sight upsets Brian. He will recall in *Sounds*: "I was about to go on tour with The Beach Boys and before I left I said to Marilyn, 'You're in love with Mike,' and she said, 'No I am not!' I said, 'I know you are.' By the way she was looking at him, I thought she was in love with Mike. I had a nervous breakdown over it."

It does not help that Brian is already experiencing mood swings and dislikes touring and flying. Loud concert volumes hurt his good ear and subsequently cause buzzing in his bad one. Most importantly, the shows take him away from what he really wants to do: produce records.

After Brian and Marilyn have said their emotional goodbyes, The Beach Boys board a plane en route to London. During the flight Brian suffers a mild panic attack. The only thing that keeps him calm is thoughts about his girlfriend, Marilyn. Upon arrival in London, he calls her and proposes. Marilyn tells *Rolling Stone*: "I saw Brian off from the airport and then, after a 13-hour flight, he called. Two telegrams had come in the meantime. He told me that he needed me and had to have me as his wife. This was 4 o'clock in

POWERED BY
Ford

GOOD*YEAR*

6

the morning. He called me three times a day, each day, during the tour. It was $3,000-worth of phone calls."

After a three-hour hold-up at Shannon Airport in Ireland, where they meet and speak with Beatles manager Brian Epstein, The Beach Boys arrive for the first time in the UK and take up residence at the plush Hilton Hotel in London. Carl explains the reasoning behind the need for separate rooms for each group member: "However well you get on with a bunch of guys," he tells *Disc*, "there are still times when you want to get away on your own. Let's face it, we see an awful lot of each other."

During their eight-day stay in Britain, The Beach Boys meet American group Martha Reeves & The Vandellas, also in the country on a promotional visit, and run into Rolling Stones manager Andrew Loog Oldham, who unfortunately gets a punch in the mouth from Dennis. Oldham unintentionally upsets the drummer by remarking to him and the other Beach Boys that he is a great admirer of their father, Murry. On another occasion Mike and Al leave their London hotel rooms and head for a nearby eatery where they chance upon a girl who expresses her desire to dance for The Beach Boys. Almost immediately the trio jumps into a cab and heads back to The Hilton where, in their rooms, the girl proceeds to give the two Beach Boys a private show.

Monday 2nd

This morning outside the EMI Records HQ in Manchester Square, central London the group poses for pictures alongside an impressive dragster car. Afterwards, gathered inside EMI's building under a huge 'Welcome To Great Britain' banner, The Beach Boys hold their first ever British press conference. Brian begins by telling the assembled hordes: "The Beach Boys want to record here, in an English studio. Everyone comes here to record. We think we may get a better sound in one of your studios. The song I'm writing now, and one that we would like to record here, is on a personal level, about the basic love between two people."

The group is asked how they feel about being regarded as the originators of surf music. Brian replies angrily: "We don't play surfing music. We're tired of being labelled as the originators of the surfing sound. We just produce a sound that the teens dig, and that can be applied to any theme. The surfing theme has run its course. Cars are finished now, too. And even Hondas are over. We're just gonna stay on the life of the social teenager."

On the subject of cars, Dennis chips in: "I wanna buy your fastest car and race it here. And I wanna buy some of your crazy English clothes. I'm a nut on clothes and cars. I've bought about $30,000 worth of clothes in the last three years. It's fun to shop. Every time I'm at home, I find myself walking down Hollywood buying clothes, clothes and more clothes." Responding to a question from Penny Valentine of UK music paper *Disc*, Carl tells her that The Beach Boys are disappointed at not being able to play a live show in England during their visit.

Their meeting with the British press concluded, the group spends the afternoon at EMI's headquarters preparing for their UK radio debut appearance this evening. The slot is for the label's most influential *Friday Spectacular* show, a weekly Radio Luxembourg programme featuring airtime bought and paid for by EMI to promote its most important artists and new record releases. Taped at EMI's Manchester Square HQ in front of around 100 specially invited and wildly applauding teenagers, The Beach Boys mime to 'When I Grow Up (To Be A Man)' and 'I Get Around' and partake in a question-and-answer session with the show's host (and TV presenter) Muriel Young. The results are transmitted on Radio Luxembourg the following Friday, November 6th, 10:00-11:00pm.

Wednesday 4th

TV TWW Television Centre *Bristol*. TWW/ITV *Discs A Go Go* live performance 'When I Grow Up (To Be A Man)', broadcast in Westward, South West, South Wales, Ulster and Border ITV regions, November 9th, 7:00-7:30pm. The group's scheduled appearance in Manchester yesterday for BBC Television's *Top Of The Pops* was scrapped, so this is The Beach Boys' first television recording in the UK, for a Television Wales & West pop show. By the time the recording is transmitted on November 9th the group will be heading for Europe. Also on the show are The Yardbirds and Gene Pitney.

Thursday 5th

TV BBC Television Centre *west London*. BBC-2 *The Beat Room* live performance 'I Get Around', 'When I Grow Up (To Be A Man)', broadcast November 9th, 7:30-8:00pm, repeated November 14th, 6:30-7:00pm. Another day, another television appearance, this time on BBC-2's new weekly pop music show. Following rehearsals, which begin at 10:30am, the group 'telerecord' two songs for show 19 in the series. (Telerecording involves filming off the screen of a TV monitor in the studio.) The Beach Boys receive a fee of £100 for their appearance.

Brian tells Earl Leaf: "Of all the places we went, the thing that dragged me down the most was the standing around in studios in England. We waited for 12 hours just to do three minutes of lip-synch, which was worth it in the end. But it took so much out of you."

At the start of the day, shortly after their camera rehearsal, the group receives a visit from *Melody Maker* reporter Chris Welch. He later writes: "Meeting The Beach Boys is like meeting those people that kick sand in your face in those 'I-trade-new-bodies-for-old' advertisements. They are tough, cynical and very self-assured. British groups are concerned with paying tribute to influences and authenticity. The Beach Boys talk about money, women and competition."

Friday 6th

TV Television House (Studio 9) *central London*. ARTV *Ready Steady Go!* live performance 'I Get Around', 'When I Grow Up (To Be A Man)', broadcast 6:08-7:00pm on some ITV regions including Rediffusion in London.

RADIO Playhouse Theatre *central London*. BBC Light Programme *Top Gear* live performance 'I Get Around', 'Hushabye', 'Surfin' USA', 'Graduation Day', 'Wendy', 'Little Old Lady (From Pasadena)', 'When I Grow Up (To Be A Man)', broadcast November 19th, 10:00pm-12 midnight.

Around 9:00am this morning the group partakes in a photoshoot at the Tower Of London, one of the most famous and well-preserved historical buildings in the world. Later, The Beach Boys make their first (and only) personal appearance on Associated-Rediffusion's top-rated pop show *Ready Steady Go!*, which will become one of the most celebrated British music programmes of the swinging sixties.

Following afternoon rehearsals, their performance of 'I Get Around' and 'When I Grow Up (To Be A Man)' – complete with false start – is transmitted live this evening. (A recording of the programme is broadcast across the rest of the ITV regions on different days and times, including the Southern ITV region where it is screened on November 8th, 3:08-3:50pm.) The show's co-host Keith Fordyce asks Mike about surfing and Brian about his thoughts on Britain, but questions and replies are drowned out by hysterical screams from the studio audience. With the delayed transmissions of

The group plays no concerts in Britain during this visit, but makes several radio and TV appearances: here, Brian mimes in London for the EMI-sponsored Radio Luxembourg *Friday Spectacular Show* on November 2nd.

the *Discs A Go Go* and *Beat Room* appearances, this *Ready Steady Go!* slot becomes the first chance that TV viewers in the UK have to see the group in action. (Although they do not collectively appear again on the show, there will be Beach Boy involvement in *Ready Steady Go!* on May 20th and October 21st 1966.) Brian tells Earl Leaf: "*Ready Steady Go!* was a blast! But they pulled Mike into the crowd off camera, which was kind of stupid."

The group now heads across London to the BBC's Playhouse Theatre where between 7:30 and 11:15pm they tape their one and only BBC radio appearance during this visit to the UK, consisting of seven live songs recorded for later broadcast. The Beach Boys receive a fee of £63 for their performance.

During the afternoon session the group meets up again with Tony Rivers and some of his group, The Castaways. Rivers remembers: "No one else was in the place for their Playhouse Theatre recording for *Top Gear*, but we were OK because they knew us there: we recorded lots of times for the Beeb. The Beach Boys were set up casually on stage just as if it was a rehearsal, but of course miked up for recording. Because Al was so short, he had to stand on a chair to reach the microphone. I can't remember which song it was, but the boys started to get the giggles. As it does in those situations, it built up until they couldn't do anything for laughing.

"Bernie Andrews, who was in the control room, wasn't amused, and kept talking over the speakers, asking them to get back to recording. Remember, the Beeb's engineers didn't like to miss valuable pub time. Anyway, he eventually erupted in anger and let fly a volley of insults. At this, Dennis suddenly lost his cool and told him in no uncertain terms that they'd been very busy lately and were just letting off a bit of steam, and not to threaten them or he'd have Dennis to deal with.

"Eventually, the atmosphere lightened a little, and they got back to recording. Well, for us to be sitting in the front row listening to these stunning harmonies being sung just blew us all away, and sealed my future for a very long time to come. I now knew I had to get to the bottom of this sound! We all applauded when the song had finished, and Brian Wilson, who up to this point had been too shy to have a conversation with any of us, took off his bass, came over to the front of the stage, sat down, and asked if we really liked that song, 'Graduation Day'. It was the first time that we had a talk to him, and obviously we had something in common at last."

■ Saturday 7th
TV Riverside Studios *Hammersmith, west London*. BBC-2 *Open House* live performance 'When I Grow Up (To Be A Man)', broadcast 4:00-5:15pm. Following rehearsals, which begin at 10:00am, The Beach Boys make another television appearance, this time back on the BBC for a live teatime music-and-arts show. The group receives a fee of £105 for their appearance. Other musical guests on the show today are Gene Pitney, Vince Hill, and Jimmy Young.

■ Sunday 8th
TV Alpha Television Studios *Aston, Birmingham*. ABC *Thank Your Lucky Stars* live performance 'When I Grow Up (To Be A Man)', broadcast ITV regions November 14th, 5:50-6:35pm.
National Boxing Stadium *Dublin, Ireland* 8:00pm
This afternoon in Birmingham the group tapes an appearance on ABC TV's long-running weekly pop show. Backstage before their appearance, *Birmingham Planet* reporter Mary McGrane interviews the group. She reports: "Guitarist Al Jardine says his only impression of England is that it is cold. But Carl Wilson, in shirtsleeves, said Al was a cissy and the weather is bracing." Immediately following the recording the group flies from London to Shannon Airport in

Ireland, and perform a stadium show in Dublin. After that, they fly out to mainland Europe.

■ Monday 9th
The Beach Boys' Christmas Album released in the US and (around this time) in the UK.
'The Man With All The Toys' / **'Blue Christmas'** single released in the US
After the success of a number 1 album and two Top Ten hits, there is still this further album and (in the US) single before the year is out, issued just weeks after the group's live album. As expected, both will be large sellers during the holiday season. (In America, the new single makes the number 3 position in the Christmas singles chart, and the album, which eventually goes Gold, peaks at number 6 in the festive LP chart.) The *Beach Boys' Christmas Album* is, amazingly, the group's fourth new US album of the year.

Shortly after the release of the *Christmas* LP, Brian is interviewed about the record at Capitol studio by radio DJ Jack Warner. The taped interview is sandwiched between tracks from the *Christmas Album* and the result is distributed to US radio stations as part of *The Beach Boys' Christmas Special*, occupying one side of Capitol's *Silver Platter Service* promotional album. (The interview is later made available as a bonus track on the 1998 CD *Ultimate Christmas*.)

The Beach Boys' increasing success mirrors their prolific output, and while the group is basking in the glory, leader Brian Wilson, still

The Beach Boys' Christmas Album

A1 'Little Saint Nick' (B. WILSON)
A2 'The Man With All The Toys' (B. WILSON)
A3 'Santa's Beard' (B. WILSON / M. LOVE)
A4 'Merry Christmas Baby' (B. WILSON / M. LOVE)
A5 'Christmas Day' (B. WILSON)
A6 'Frosty The Snowman' (S. NELSON / J. ROLLINS)
B1 'We Three Kings Of Orient Are' (J. HOPKINS)
B2 'Blue Christmas' (B. HAYES / J. JOHNSON)
B3 'Santa Claus Is Comin' To Town' (J.F. COOTS / H.GILLESPIE)
B4 'White Christmas' (I. BERLIN)
B5 'I'll Be Home For Christmas' (W. KENT / K. GANNON)
B6 'Auld Lang Syne' (TRAD)

US release November 9th 1964 (Capitol T2164).
UK release November 1964 (Capitol T2164).
Chart high US number 6; UK none.

The Man With All The Toys single

A 'The Man With All The Toys' (B. WILSON)
B 'Blue Christmas' (B. HAYES / J. JOHNSON)

US release November 9th 1964 (Capitol 5312).
Chart high US number 3.

only 22 years old, is beginning to feel the weight of commitments bearing down hard on his shoulders. Unknown to those around him, he is beginning to crumble.

Wednesday 11th
Piper Club *Milan, Italy*
The tour moves to mainland Europe.

Thursday 12th
Festhalle *Frankfurt, West Germany*

Friday 13th
Ernst Merck Halle *Hamburg, West Germany*

Saturday 14th
KB Hallen *Copenhagen, Denmark*
Brian's emotions pour out as he writes the song 'Kiss Me Baby' in his room at The Royal Hotel, Copenhagen.
• 'Wendy' EP track peaks in US *Billboard* chart at number 44, and 'Little Honda' EP track at number 65.

Sunday 15th
Njordhallen *Oslo, Norway*

Monday 16th
Konserthuset *Stockholm, Sweden* 8:00pm, with The Mascots, Jackie De Shannon
The European jaunt continues. Swedish radio station Sverige broadcasts tonight's performance during the *Pop-O-Rama* show on December 21st (repeated January 15th 1965). Klas Burling produces the show, which runs for a total of 28:50. The Beach Boys fly on to Paris the following afternoon.
Set-list 'Fun Fun Fun', 'Long Tall Texan', 'In My Room', 'Graduation Day', 'Papa-Oom-Mow-Mow', 'Little Deuce Coupe', 'Surfer Girl', 'Monster Mash', 'Surfin' USA', 'Don't Worry Baby', 'I Get Around', 'Johnny B Goode'.

Wednesday 18th
TV TF2 TV Studios *Paris, France*. TF2 *Age Tendre Et Tête De Bois* lip-synch 'I Get Around', 'When I Grow Up to Be A Man' broadcast 8.30-9.15pm. At the start of the day The Beach Boys pose for photographs by the famous Arc De Triomphe monument in Paris. But trouble ensues when Mike and Dennis proceed to climb up a nearby lamppost, forcing some local gendarmes to speed up to the group with sirens blasting. Two policemen swear profusely (in French) at the boys, telling them to behave and not to damage French property. This afternoon the group are at the TF2 television studio to perform on Albert Raisner's teenager-aimed show *Age Tendre Et Tête De Bois* (meaning something like 'Headstrong Teens'). They appear in front of a dazzling, hi-tech graphics video screen, and the clip, screened this evening, opens with Dennis arriving on the set carrying a surfboard adorned with the title of the show.
Olympia Theatre *Paris, France* with Dick Rivers
This evening the group plays the Olympia and the last date on the tour; highlights of the show are transmitted on the French Europe 1 radio show *Musicorama* on December 14th. *Melody Maker*'s reviewer writes: "It was the first time that I have heard Beatles-type shrieks at the famous Paris theatre. And though the sons and daughters of Paris's large American colony were there in force, it was clear from the chants of 'une autre, une autre' that The Beach Boys have a big following among French teenagers. Before they were halfway through their act, the kids were dancing wildly in the aisles and rushing the stage for autographs. Of the numbers they did, the most acclaim was for 'Surfin' USA' and 'Johnny B Goode'."
• Following the concert the group pays a visit to Paris's world-famous *Folies Bergère* show. Brian is not impressed. With their duties completed in France and the European tour at an end, The Beach Boys fly to New York for more concert appearances and to promote their latest Capitol single.
• **'My Buddy Seat'** single by The Hondells released in the US. The A-side is co-written and produced by Brian.

Friday 20th
War Memorial Theater *Rochester, NY*
Immediately after returning from Europe the group performs two quick Thanksgiving one-nighters, chiefly to help promote their latest single 'Dance Dance Dance'.

Saturday 21st
Cobo Hall *Detroit, MI*
Brian tells Earl Leaf: "At the airport, around 16 cars full of people came to take our luggage back to the hotel. We get to the hotel, we take our luggage out of the cars, and we found that six of our suitcases had gone. It was funny because it was the ones with all the gifts we had brought back, like Rolex watches. Somebody had a great Christmas." The group returns home to Los Angeles, knowing that Beach Boy duties are on hold until December 16th.
• 'Dance Dance Dance' single enters US *Billboard* Top 40 chart at number 29.

December
'The Man With All The Toys' single peaks in US *Billboard* Christmas Chart at number 3.
• 'Little Saint Nick' single peaks in US *Billboard* Christmas Chart at number 6.
• 'Dance Dance Dance' single peaks in Canadian *RPM* chart at number 7.
• **'Everyday'** / **'Roger's Reef'** single by The Rouges released in the US. The group features tireless future Beach Boy Bruce Johnston.
• Murry Wilson says this month in *Melody Maker*: "My three sons are extremely generous. In fact, it seems that that Dennis can be a little too generous. Where the other boys invested or saved their money, Dennis spent $94,000. He spent $25,000 on a home but the rest just went. Dennis is like that: he picks up the tab wherever he goes. He was so upset when at the end of this year I had a long talk with them. He cried when he learned about how much he had wasted. I remember once when Audree flew back to Los Angeles. Dennis went to the airport to meet her and had to borrow 35 cents to get the car out of the parking lot."
• Also this month Brian, back from the group's recent tour, is introduced to marijuana by Loren Schwartz, an assistant at the William Morris agency. Schwartz becomes Brian's new best friend. Brian is attracted by the drug's apparent abilities to relieve stress and enhance creativity. The year has been a physically and emotionally demanding one for each of The Beach Boys, especially Brian. With his father's dismissal in April, Brian has found that the group's managerial pressures have come to rest on his already heavily laden shoulders. His brutal and punishing work schedule – with extensive amounts of writing, producing, singing, recording, concerts and television and radio appearances – causes him extreme mental and emotional exhaustion.

Phonograph Recording Contract Blank

(Employer's name)

AMERICAN FEDERATION OF MUSICIANS
OF THE UNITED STATES AND CANADA

002958
105614

Local Union No._____

THIS CONTRACT for the personal services of musicians, made this _____ 16th day of December , 19 64 ,
between the undersigned employer (hereinafter called the "employer") and TWELVE (12) musicians
(hereinafter called "employees").
(including the leader)

WITNESSETH, That the employer hires the employees as musicians severally on the terms and conditions below, and as further
specified on reverse side. The leader represents that the employees already designated have agreed to be bound by said terms and conditions. The leader agrees that the employees yet to be chosen shall be so bound by said terms and conditions upon agreeing to accept his employment. Each
employee may enforce this agreement. The employees severally agree to render collectively to the employer services as musicians in
the orchestra under the leadership of Hal Blaine as follows:

Name and Address of Place of Engagement Western Studios
6000 Sunset Blvd, Hollywood, Calif.

Date(s) and Hours of Employment Dec. 16, 1964
1:00PM to 4:00PM

Type of Engagement: **Recording for phonograph records only**
WAGE AGREED UPON $ Union Scale B (includes tracking rate)   Plus pension contributions as
specified on reverse side hereof.
(Terms and amount)

This wage includes expenses agreed to be reimbursed by the employer in accordance with the attached schedule, or a schedule
to be furnished the employer on or before the date of engagement.
To be paid within 15 days
(Specify when payments are to be made)

Upon request by the American Federation of Musicians of the United States and Canada (herein called the "Federation") or
the local in whose jurisdiction the employees shall perform hereunder, the employer either shall make advance payment hereunder
or shall post an appropriate bond.

Employer's
name and CAPITOL RECORDS
authorized
signature

Leader's
name Hal Blaine
Leader's
signature   Local
No. 47

Street
address 1750 No. Vine St.

Street
address 2441 Castilian Dr.

Hollywood, Calif.   HO. 2-6252
City   State   Phone

Hollywood 28, Calif
City   State

(1) Label name _____   Session no. _____

Master no.	No. of minutes	TITLES OF TUNES	Master no.	No. of minutes	TITLES OF TUNES
	2:25	"KISS ME BABY" *TRACK*			

(2) Employee's name (As on Social Security card) Last First Initial	(3) Home address (Give street, city and state)	(4) Local Union no.	(5) Social Security number	(6) Scale wages	(7) Pension contri- bution
(Leader) BLAINE, Hal	2441 Castilian Dr. Hollywood 28, Calif	47	047-20-5900	162.68	13.02
sax-contractor KREISMAN, Steven D.	6950 Chisholm Ave. Van Nuys, Calif.	47	556-46-1005	162.68	13.02
1 dbl.mallets-percussion WECHTER, Julius	12247 Hesby No. Hollywood, Calif.	47	557-40-3644	81.33 93.54	7.48
piano BRIDGES, Russell	7709 Skyhill Dr. Hollywood 28, Calif.	47	448-40-7735	81.34	6.51
sax MIGLIORI, Jay	538 No. Shelton Burbank, Calif.	47	208-24-6118	81.34	6.51
English Horn CHRIST, Peter	1421 So. Palm Ave Alhambra, Calif.	47	557-48-8906	81.34	6.51
French Horn DUKE, David	5501 Verdun Los Angeles 43, Calif.	47	553-58-0072	81.34	6.51
Fender Bass KAYE, Carol	4905 Forman Ave No. Hollywood, Calif.	47	555-46-5189	81.34	6.51
bass POHLMAN, M.R.	2804 Westshire Dr. Hollywood 28, Calif.	47	556-34-6698	81.34	6.51
guitar KESSEL, Barney	1727 Las Flores Dr. Glendale, Calif.	47	449-12-3334	81.34	6.51
guitar STRANGE, William E.	17312 Osborne St. Northridge, Calif.	47	547-36-6814	81.34	6.51
guitar PITMAN, William	9124 Nagle Ave. Pacoima, Calif.	47	068-16-6762	81.34	6.51

NO ARRANGING OR COPYING

CONTRACT RECEIVED

DEC 23 1964

WARD ARCHER
ASST. TO PRESIDENT

Total Pension Contributions (Sum of Column (7)) $ 92.11
Make check payable in this amount to "AFM & EPW Fund"

FOR FUND USE ONLY:
Date pay't rec'd _____ Amt paid _____ Date posted _____ By _____
Form B-4 Rev. 4-59

Saturday 5th

Beach Boys Concert album peaks in US *Billboard* chart at number 1. It is the group's first chart-topping album.

Monday 7th

In an attempt to bring emotional stability to his demanding life, Brian impulsively marries 16-year-old Marilyn Rovell (born February 6th 1948 in Chicago, Illinois) at Los Angeles City Court House. Unfortunately the good times don't last. Sixteen days later Brian will suffer his first nervous breakdown.

Friday 11th

A dub of just the backing track for 'Dance Dance Dance' is made to use in upcoming promotional appearances (see 17th/18th) where the band can provide live vocals.

• In the UK, the *New Musical Express* paper publishes the results of their annual readers' poll. In a clear indication that their popularity is growing, The Beach Boys are placed fifth in the World Vocal Group category. As expected, The Beatles are in top position.

Wednesday 16th

RECORDING *Today!* session 3 Western Recorders studio *Hollywood CA* 1:00-4:00pm. With Brian producing, The Beach Boys attend a tracking session for his recently composed **'Kiss Me Baby'** (nine instrumental takes required, followed by two vocal overdubs). 'Tracking' is the term for the initial recording of backing instruments only: here consisting of two acoustic guitars, an electric guitar, bass guitar, drums, percussion and more. At the end of the session a rough 'tracking mix' of just this backing track is made in mono. Work will resume on the recording, intended for inclusion on the next album, on January 15th 1965.

Musicians present Hal Blaine (drums), Russell Bridges (piano), Peter Christ (English horn), Steve Douglas (saxophone), David Duke (French horn), Carol Kaye (bass guitar), Barney Kessel (guitar), Jay Migliori (saxophone), Bill Pitman (guitar), Ray Pohlman (bass), Billy Strange (guitar), Julius Wechter (percussion, 'mallets')

Thursday 17th

TV ABC Television Center studio *Hollywood, CA.* ABC *Shindig!* live vocals over taped backing tracks 'Dance Dance Dance', 'Little Saint Nick', 'Monster Mash', 'Papa-Oom-Mow-Mow', 'Johnny B Goode', 'We Three Kings Of Orient Are', broadcast December 23rd, 8:30-9:00pm LA time. Having had a little over three weeks of rest, the group starts a heavy year-end round of TV and personal appearances, beginning today with the taping of their first appearance on Jack Good's popular weekly pop-music show. For this special Christmas edition The Beach Boys are the headline act, opening the show with 'Dance, Dance, Dance' and closing it with 'We Three Kings Of Orient Are'. Also on are Adam Faith, Marvin Gaye, Bobby Sherman, and The Righteous Brothers.

Brian says in *Melody Maker*: "Jack Good told us, 'You sing like eunuchs in a Sistine chapel,' which was a pretty good quote. The Beach Boys are lucky. We have a high range of voices. Mike can go from bass to the E above middle C; Dennis, Carl and Al progress upwards through G, A and B. I can take the second D in the treble clef. The harmonies we were able to produce gave us a uniqueness, which is really the only important thing you can put into records: some quality no one else has got into."

Friday 18th

TV NBC studio *Burbank, CA.* NBC *The Bob Hope Comedy Special* live vocals over taped backing tracks 'Dance Dance Dance', broadcast 8:30-9:30pm LA time. Joining them on the show are US showbiz celebrities Nancy Wilson, Martha Raye, Kathryn Crosby and, as special guest, actor James Garner.

Saturday 19th
Tulsa Assembly Center *Tulsa, OK*

Tonight's appearance is for a one-off show. Brian will tell *Rolling Stone*: "I used to be Mr Everything. I felt I had no choice. I was run down mentally and emotionally because I was running around, jumping on jets from one city to another on one-night stands, also producing, writing, arranging, singing, planning, teaching, to the point where I had no peace of mind and no chance to actually sit down and think or even rest. I was so mixed up and so overworked."

• 'Dance Dance Dance' peaks in US *Billboard* chart at number 8.

TOUR STARTS US South/Midwest (Dec 23rd 1964-Jan 7th 1965)

Wednesday 23rd
Music Hall *Houston, TX*

The start of a two-week US tour, but this latest jaunt immediately runs into trouble when Brian suffers his first nervous breakdown. Five minutes into the flight to Houston from Los Angeles he starts crying into a pillow, makes shrieking noises, and spins out of his seat. He falls sobbing to the cabin floor. Attempts by Carl and Al to comfort him are unsuccessful. Brian recalls in *Sounds*: "We were going to Houston to kick-off a two-week tour. I said goodbye to Marilyn. We weren't getting along too good. The plane had been in the air only five minutes when I told Al Jardine I was going to crack up at any minute. He told me to cool it. Then I started crying. I put a pillow over my face and began screaming and yelling."

Al tells *NME*: "We were really scared for him. We were concerned for him because he was so upset. He obviously had a breakdown. None of us had ever witnessed something like that." Dennis says in *Melody Maker*: "I was really terrified for my brother." Mike doesn't recall the incident when questioned later by *Rolling Stone*. "I don't know if it was because I wasn't there, or some other reason. I might have been in another part of the plane. I think his brothers were closer to that than I was at the time."

Brian says in *Teen Beat*: "I told the stewardesses, 'I don't want any food. Get away from me.' Then I started telling people that I'm not getting off the plane. I was getting far out, coming undone, having a breakdown, and I just let myself go completely. I dumped myself out of the seat and all over the plane. I let myself go emotionally. They took care of me well. They were as understanding as they could be. They knew what was happening and I was coming apart. The rubber band had stretched as far as it would go."

Arriving in Houston, Brian insists on returning to Los Angeles, but eventually spends time in his hotel room regaining his composure. He plays the Houston show this evening and returns to Los Angeles the following day. His performance tonight will be his last regular appearance as a member of the live Beach Boys for almost 12 years.

Brian continues in his account to Earl Leaf in *Teen Beat*: "Next morning I woke up with the biggest knot in my stomach and I felt like I was going out of my mind. I must have cried about 15 times the next day. Every half-hour I'd start crying. Carl came to my hotel room. I saw him and I just slammed the door in his face. I didn't want to see him or anybody else because I was flipping out. Nobody knew what was going on. I wouldn't talk. I just put my head down and wouldn't even look at anyone.

"That night the road manager took me back to LA and I didn't want to see anybody except my mother. She was at the airport to

LEFT An 'AFM sheet' for December 16th shows hornmen and multiple guitarists on 'Kiss Me Baby', a song that will appear on the 1965 album *Today!*.
FOLLOWING PAGES Performing 'Dance Dance Dance' at NBC TV studios in Burbank, California, for the *Bob Hope Comedy Special* on December 18th.

meet me. As soon as I saw her again, I started crying. I just needed to hear her talk to me," says Brian. "It's a kind of security to be able to talk to your mother, as I can talk to Audree. We went over to our old house and we had a three-hour talk. I told her things that I had never told anyone in my life. She sort of straightened me out. Generally I dumped out a lifelong hang-up. This was the first of a series of three breakdowns I had. The other guys didn't want to bug me but they wanted to know what was happening. There [would be] four Beach Boys plus Glen Campbell on the road. … They finished out that tour without me."

Ron Foster, a member of Houston band The Detours and later to become an 'oldies' DJ with the ABC radio network, remembers meeting Dennis backstage this evening, December 23rd. According to research by reporter Paul J MacArthur, the middle Wilson brother takes Foster to the dressing room. Although he is unaware of the day's events, Foster senses a negative aura in the room.

As the group is teaching the inquisitive Foster the chords to 'The Warmth Of The Sun' he notices Brian "staring off into space. He wasn't rude. He didn't tell us to get out or anything like that. He was just kind of like staring off into the corner like he wasn't there". Foster watches the concert from backstage and it seems to him like a regular Beach Boys concert. But Al tells MacArthur that Brian never goes on-stage tonight. "He stayed in his room and then went home," says Al.

Brian had removed himself from the road before, on several occasions in 1963. He spent that time exerting total authority over making records and became the first major rock figure with such power. But there was a downside: he was the only musician who was writing, arranging and producing his own albums at the time, as well as performing regualrly on-stage.

He is of course under tremendous pressure to produce hit material. Now, he needs time to work on records without the strains of touring as well. While no one is aware of its importance at the time, what happens on the morning of Wednesday December 23rd 1964 will come to be seen later as a pivotal moment in the history of popular music.

Thursday 24th
Sam Houston Coliseum *Houston, TX*

Tonight, Beach Boy session guitarist Glen Campbell makes his on-stage debut as a live Beach Boy, standing in for Brian. (Campbell was born on April 22nd 1936 in Delight, Arkansas.)

He will recall for Scott Keller: "I filled in for Brian for a few dates in Dallas and Houston. Mike and Carl called me on a Wednesday and said, 'Glen, can you be here tomorrow? You gotta play bass and do Brian's part.' I said, 'Sure.' I had been doing their sessions, so I could easily fill in. The only problem was I didn't know all the words to the songs. They'd be singing 'Pasadena' and I would sing something else. I didn't know what I was saying. But the screams were so loud from the girls, you'd walk on-stage and you couldn't hear a thing anyway."

Saturday 26th
Memorial Auditorium *Dallas, TX*

Glen Campbell performs as a Beach Boy for the second time, in place of Brian.

Sunday 27th
Civic Auditorium *Omaha, NE*

After the show, Glen Campbell's third with the group, The Beach Boys return to California where they will remain for four days, spending Christmas with their families.

Thursday 31st
The Coliseum *Charlotte, NC*

Glen Campbell again plays with the group, this time at a New Year's Eve concert in Charlotte. After the show the group flies home to California. Brian tells *Teen Beat*: "When they came back, I didn't want to talk to them, or anybody. I just wanted to sit and think and rest, pull myself together, check my life out and once again evaluate what I am, what I'm doing, and what I should be doing. I knew I should have stopped going on tours much earlier to do justice to our recordings and business operations. I was also under pressure from my old man. He figured that I would be a traitor if I didn't travel on one-nighters with the other guys. He always has had a problem of understanding people and their feelings. I had a lot of static from everyone outside the group as well as the members. The only way I could do it was by breaking down as I did. The boys stayed home for a long rest, about two weeks; then we started recording *The Beach Boys Today!* album."

Brian, invigorated and refreshed after his enforced break at the end of the year, is now ready to usher in a new phase in the group's career.

Glen Campbell steps in for an absent Brian Wilson on stage at the Sam Houston Coliseum in Texas on December 24th. From now on Brian will spend as much time as possible in the recording studio and very little on the live stage.

1965

Recording sessions for *Today!* album continue ... Brian announces he will cease to appear on stage with the group and intends to focus on composition and studio production ... Glen Campbell plays more dates as Brian's stage replacement ... *Today!* album released, with a whole side of Brian's 'new music' ... *Summer Days (And Summer Nights!!)* album recorded and released ... 'Help Me Rhonda' is the group's second number 1 single ... Bruce Johnston takes over as a permanent replacement for Brian on live shows and also starts contributing to recording sessions ... 'California Girls' is a US number 3 single ... unplugged *Party!* album recorded and released ... Brian installs his piano in a sandbox at his new Beverly Hills home ... 'The Girl I Once Knew' single recorded and released ... recordings are begun that will end up on next year's *Pet Sounds* album ... Brian hears The Beatles' new *Rubber Soul* album, considers it a challenge, and starts writing songs with lyricist Tony Asher ... 'Barbara Ann' is a US number 2 and UK number 3 single.

Brian (far left) meets his hero Phil Spector (in waistcoat) at Gold Star studio in Los Angeles on January 11th. Also pictured are Bobby Hatfield of The Righteous Brothers (far right) and, next to him, Mike Love.

January

'Dance Dance Dance' / 'The Warmth Of The Sun' single released in UK. It will peak at number 24.
• 'Skateboard' / 'Fun Last Summer' single by The Sidewalk Surfers released in the US. The Jubilee 45 features Bruce Johnston in the group, and both sides are written by Bruce using an alias.
• 'Dance, Dance, Dance' single peaks in Australian chart at 36.
• 'Little Honda' single peaks in German *Hit Bilanz* chart at number 44, in Swedish Radio 3 chart at number 2.
• The Wilsons' cousin Steve Korthof is hired as The Beach Boys' equipment manager, and Dick Duryea and Terry Sachen as road managers.

■ Saturday 2nd
Alan B Shepard Convention Center *Virginia Beach, VA* two shows
The live band, with Glen Campbell still in place of Brian, give their first shows of the year, in effect continuing their two-week tour that commenced in Texas back on December 23rd 1964. Campbell will recall on *Biography*, broadcast on the A&E cable/satellite channel: "It was total screaming. The crowds were crazy! Some girls jumped on me just because I had touched Dennis. I even lost my Rolex watch. It was an experience I shall never forget."

■ Sunday 3rd
The Mosque *Richmond, VA*

■ Tuesday 5th
War Memorial Auditorium *Greensboro, NC*

■ Wednesday 6th
Wilmington Armory *Wilmington, DE*
After the performance and following a request from Brian, Glen Campbell returns to Los Angeles for recording sessions with Brian and other musicians at Western Recorders tomorrow.
• *Beach Boys Concert* album certified gold by RIAA in the US.

■ Thursday 7th
RECORDING *Today!* **session 4** Western Recorders studio *Hollywood, CA* 7:00-10:30pm. After a most traumatic couple of weeks an invigorated Brian returns to the studio, from now until the 19th. He records a new range of material for the group's next album, ultimately to be titled *The Beach Boys Today!*. Several cuts that will appear on the LP were recorded last year, namely 'She Knows Me Too Well', 'Don't Hurt My Little Sister' (in June), 'When I Grow Up (To Be A Man)' (August) and 'Dance Dance Dance' (September), and the music track for 'Kiss Me, Baby' (December 16th). 'When I Grow Up' and 'Dance' have already scored as hit singles.

This evening, working with 11 of LA's finest session musicians, Brian produces the instrumental track for his co-composition with Mike titled **'Please Let Me Wonder'** (25 takes required; take 23 marked as best). Glen Campbell, fresh from Beach Boys touring duties and missing tonight's show, is present at the session playing guitar. As a sign of things to come, Brian's developing need for perfection leads him to stop several takes of this ballad after just a few bars because the musicians are off pitch or at the wrong tempo.
Musicians present Glen Campbell (guitar), Steve Douglas (saxophone), Plas Johnson (saxophone), Carol Kaye (probably bass guitar), Barney Kessel (guitar), Jack Nimitz (saxophone), Earl Palmer (drums, timbales), Don Randi (piano, organ), Billy Lee Riley (harmonica), Billy Strange (guitar), Jerry Williams (vibes, tympani).
International Ampitheater *Chicago, IL*
The Beach Boys, minus Glen Campbell, perform the last show on their two-week tour. With concert duties completed, the group heads back to Los Angeles.

■ Friday 8th
RECORDING *Today!* **session 5** Western Recorders studio *Hollywood, CA* 1:00-4:00pm. With Brian once again in charge, today sees a tracking session for **'Help Me Ronda'** (31 takes required). Glen Campbell is once again present at the session, playing guitar. (The recording of the more familiar single version of 'Rhonda' will begin on February 24th; work on this version resumes on the 19th.)
Musicians present Hal Blaine (drums, timbales), Glen Campbell (guitar), Steve Douglas (saxophone), Plas Johnson (saxophone), Jay Migliori (saxophone), Bill Pitman (guitar), Ray Pohlman (bass), Billy Lee Riley (harmonica), Leon Russell (piano), Billy Strange (guitar), Julius Wechter (percussion).

■ Saturday 9th
RECORDING *Today!* **session 6** Western Recorders studio *Hollywood, CA*. Joined at a session by his Beach Boys buddies who are now back from touring duties, probably now (though the precise date is unknown) Brian overdubs his lead vocal onto the January 7th tracking tape of **'Please Let Me Wonder'**. This is followed by Mike who also attempts to record his joint lead vocal. Brian becomes angry when Mike insists on moving away from the microphone during the taping, resulting in an uneven, less-than-perfect vocal recording.

Brian: "That's not on, Mike. You're too heavy here."
Mike: "You'd rather I was a little soft than a little loud?"
Brian: "Yeah. I'd rather a little soft than a little loud. It's gotta be right on the nose. Every word has got to be right."
Mike (mumbling): "Yeah. That's hip."
Brian: "Mike! God! The whole thing is you just don't realise how important it is to stay in the same spot for the whole fucking time."

Mike is frustrated by the number of re-takes Brian requires and heated exchanges follow. Subsequently, the full Beach Boys line-up tapes a backing vocal overdub (nine takes required). At the end of the day's work, during which the session players are again led by Glen Campbell, Brian overdubs bass guitar onto the 4-track recording.

■ Monday 11th
RECORDING *Today!* **session 7** Gold Star studio *Los Angeles, CA* 2:00-5:30pm. Today sees a surprise change of studio for tracking sessions for **'Do You Wanna Dance'** (three takes required), a cover of Bobby Freeman's Top 5 hit of 1958. Once again the cream of Los Angeles session musicians provides instrumentation, and the other Beach Boys are with Brian once more in the studio. To round off this highly productive session Dennis tapes his impressive lead vocal and the full group line-up add backing vocals.
Musicians present Hal Blaine (drums), Russell Bridges (organ), Steve Douglas (saxophone), Plas Johnson (saxophone), Larry Knechtel (bass guitar), Jay Migliori (saxophone), Bill Pitman (guitar), Jay Migliori (saxophone), Billy Strange (guitar), Tommy Tedesco (guitar), Julius Wechter (tympani, tambourine).

■ Wednesday 13th
RECORDING *Today!* **session 8** Western Recorders studio *Hollywood, CA*. Brian and Mike's composition **'In The Back Of My Mind'** is

started today (31 tracking takes required) featuring another – but still rare – lead vocal by Dennis. Lush orchestral overdubs follow. In addition, the first session is taped for **'Good To My Baby'** (17 tracking takes required) along with the bizarre piece entitled **'Bull Session With Big Daddy'**. This is a spoof interview with 'Big Daddy' (journalist Earl Leaf) amid much fooling around as the group reminisce about their European Tour late last year. The original taping session runs to 20:12, but when released on the *Today!* album it will be trimmed down to just 2:10.

Musicians present ('Good To My Baby') Hal Blaine (drums), Steve Douglas (saxophone), Plas Johnson (saxophone), Carol Kaye (bass guitar), Jay Migliori (saxophone), Bill Pitman (guitar), Don Randi (piano, organ), Billy Strange (guitar), Tommy Tedesco (guitar), Julius Wechter (percussion).

• At the end of today's recording date, as the session musicians prepare to pack up and go home, Brian informs Dennis, Carl, Mike and Al that he has retired from touring and will not accompany them on their next tour.

Brian tells Earl Leaf for a piece published in *Teenset* magazine this year: "We were about halfway through the album when I decided to tell the guys I wasn't going to perform on stage any more and that I can't travel. I wanted to sit at the piano and write songs while they were out touring.

"The night when I gave them the news of my decision they all broke down. I'd already gone through my breakdowns and now it was their turn. When I told them, they were all sitting on chairs and they were in shock. Mike had a couple of tears in his eyes; he couldn't take the reality that their big brother wasn't ever going to be on the stage with them again. He lost his cool and felt like there was no reason to go on.

"Dennis picked up a big ashtray and told some people to get out of there or he'd hit them on the head with it. He kind of blew it. In fact, the guy he threatened to hit with the ashtray was Terry Sachen, who became our road manager within two weeks. Al Jardine broke out in tears and broke out in stomach cramps. He was all goofed up and my mother, who was there, had to take care of him. Good ol' Carl was the only one who never got into a bad emotional scene. He just sat there and didn't get uptight about it. He always kept a cool head. If it weren't for Carl, it's hard to say where we'd be. He is the greatest stabilising influence in the group. He's been like that ever since he was a kid, and he's like that now, together with a lot of experience and brains. Carl has mastered his emotions. He cooled Dennis, Mike and Al down.

"I told them I foresee a beautiful future for The Beach Boys group," Brian continues, "but the only way we could achieve it was if they did their job and I did mine. They would have to get a replacement for me. I didn't say 'they'. I said 'we' because it isn't they and me, it's 'us'. I told them, 'It's gonna be well worth it because I'm gonna write you some good songs.'"

Staying off the road will have its benefits. While not touring, Brian is able to focus on composing and producing, and he will grow steadily and impressively in these areas. Throughout the remainder of the year Brian will push pop music in unforeseen directions as he comes up with catchy, radio-friendly, highly commercial songs and introspective ballads that challenge the conventions of the industry.

■ Friday 15th
RECORDING *Today!* session 9 Western Recorders studio *Hollywood, CA*. Using the instrumental backing tracks recorded on December 16th last year, The Beach Boys overdub a vocal onto **'Kiss Me Baby'**. Brian tapes his own lead vocal and then repeats it on a second tape track, as he often did.

■ Monday 18th
RECORDING *Today!* session 10 Western Recorders studio *Hollywood, CA*. Tracking session for **'I'm So Young'**, a W.H. Tyrus Jr composition originally recorded by The Students in the late 1950s but more recently heard on the Phil Spector-produced *Fabulous Ronettes* album. There is also evidence that some work is done during this session on **'Please Let Me Wonder'** and **'Don't Hurt My Little Sister'**.

■ Tuesday 19th
RECORDING *Today!* session 11 Western Recorders studio *Hollywood, CA* 1:00-4:00pm. Sessions for the next Beach Boys album are wrapped up today with guitar and vocal overdubs for **'Good To My Baby'**, **'I'm So Young'**, **'In The Back Of My Mind'** (five takes required for second vocal overdub) and **'Help Me Ronda'** (album version). Al provides the lead vocal on 'Ronda', and admits to *Teen Beat* that it gives him some difficulty. "It was the second Beach Boys song I sang lead on [and] I was only used to singing background vocals. It was a whole different thing and quite complex. It seems quite simple now but it's something called timing, meter and rhythm. It was a matter of getting your mind-body concentration together, and finally it came together real well."

TOUR STARTS North America (Jan 27th-Feb 27th)

■ Wednesday 27th
Memorial Coliseum *Portland, OR*
The opening night of the group's latest tour, a four-week excursion consisting of one-nighters, and the first concert with Brian officially not part of the on-stage group. Glen Campbell is again Brian's stage replacement. The show at the 10,000-seater Coliseum grosses $17,000, of which The Beach Boys receive 60 percent. Radio station KISM sponsors the evening.

■ Friday 29th
Empire Stadium *Vancouver, BC, Canada*

■ Saturday 30th
Seattle Center Coliseum *Seattle, WA*
Oddly, the printed show-guide for today's event features a picture of The Beatles on its cover, from the British group's August 21st 1964 appearance at the venue.

February

Beach Boys Concert album released in the UK.
Beach Boys Concert EP released in the UK: 'The Little Old Lady From Pasadena', 'Papa-Oom-Mow-Mow', 'Johnny B Goode', 'Let's Go Trippin''.
• 'Little Honda' single peaks in Norwegian chart at number 8.
• 'Dance Dance Dance' single peaks in UK *Record Retailer* chart at number 24, and in Swedish Radio 3 chart at number 6.

■ Saturday 6th
Kemper Arena *Wichita, KS*
Concert in front of a sell-out 4,200 crowd, with The Beach Boys guaranteed an appearance fee of $4,000.

■ Wednesday 10th
Memorial Auditorium *Dallas, TX*

■ Friday 12th
Convention Hall *Philadelphia, PA*
Tonight's performance in front of a sell-out 13,000 crowd grosses a remarkable $32,000.

■ Saturday 13th
The Academy Of Music *New York, NY*
Surprisingly, Brian rejoins the band on-stage in New York City tonight after Glen Campbell, hired to replace Brian at these shows, returns to Los Angeles, possibly due to commitments to the *Shindig!* TV programme. Brian's temporary return to the live group will continue until the 20th, after which Campbell returns.

■ Monday 15th
'Do You Wanna Dance' / 'Please Let Me Wonder' single released in the US. The A-side will peak in US chart at number 12, the B-side at 52.

■ Wednesday 17th
Rhodes Ballroom *Cranston, RI*

■ Thursday 18th
All Summer Long album certified gold by RIAA in the US.

■ Friday 19th
The Forum *Montreal, PQ, Canada*
A performance before a sell-out crowd of 6,000.

■ Saturday 20th
The Capital Theatre *Ottawa, ON, Canada* 7:30pm
Tonight sees another sell-out, with an audience of 7,000.

■ Sunday 21st
Maple Leaf Gardens *Toronto, ON, Canada* 7:00pm, with The Esquires, The Big Town Boys, The Girl Friends; compère: CHUM Radio DJ 'Jungle' Jay Nelson
Yet another sell-out crowd, of 8,000. For tonight and the rest of the tour Glen Campbell is free to replace Brian and rejoins the group. Today sees a photo session of The Beach Boys – including Campbell – posing by and in a meat truck; the shots are later much used.

■ Wednesday 24th
RECORDING Western Recorders studio *Hollywood, CA*. Brian hears that Terry Melcher and his band The Rip Chords are keen to record and release their own version of 'Help Me Ronda' as a single (see March 24th), and so decides to re-record the song (first taped on January 8th). He changes the spelling of 'Ronda' to 'Rhonda' and intends to release it as The Beach Boys' next single. With Al again on lead vocal, the group – with a break in the touring schedule –

Do You Wanna Dance single

A '**Do You Wanna Dance**' (B. FREEMAN)
B '**Please Let Me Wonder**' (B. WILSON / M. LOVE)

US release February 15th 1965 (Capitol 5372).
Chart high US number 12.

---

assembles at Western today to record the new live instrumental track and vocals for what will become the familiar single version of '**Help Me Rhonda**'. Glen Campbell is again on guitar. However, the excitement of the session is halted when Murry Wilson, sitting in the studio's control room with his wife Audree, takes over the session, and makes comments to the group about the rehearsals and recordings. Brian is clearly annoyed. The exchanges take place in a studio packed full of friends and hanger-ons.

Murry comes on the studio intercom: "Brian, you've got a wonderful tune here. Al, loosen up a little and say sexy 'Rhonda' more. Mike, come on in closer on the mike. Carl, 'oooh' better, and Brian, you're awfully shrill tonight, so soften it a little and we've got it. Dennis, don't flat any more."

The group resumes their attempt to overdub vocals onto the backing track recorded earlier. After another take the session breaks down, and Murry is back on the intercom: "Brian, have the guys loosen up. You've a beautiful tune here, but loosen up. You're so tight fellows, I can't believe it."

Miscellaneous jams follow until Brian calls a halt to the musical ramblings. Take 4 of 'Help Me Rhonda' follows but is halted by a heated discussion between Brian and Murry about the song's lyrics, prompting Brian to insist sarcastically that Murry sing the song.

Murry: "Do you want me to leave, Brian?"
Brian: "No, I just want you to let him sing it."
Murry: "Your mother and I can leave now if you want, for the first time in my life."
Brian: "Oh bull! The first time?"
Murry (to the crowd gathered in the studio): "Brian said, 'Come down and relax,' so I did."

Further vocal overdubbing on 'Help Me Rhonda' follows. After several more takes, the group breaks for a while and uses the opportunity to discuss Murry, out of his earshot.

Mike: "I don't really give a shit."
Brian: "I know you don't give a shit."
Mike: "Oh God, so he's the greatest thing you'll ever have in the world?"
Brian: "No, I just don't like him putting me down. There's a difference between getting shoved and a guy saying, 'Come on, you're wasting time.' I mean, you can't be that cocky about things."
Mike: "Well, sorry. Maybe I was wrong?"
Brian: "Fuck me! Just don't start, Mike, transferring all hostility onto one poor mite."
Mike: "In the first place, I was just talking, for Christ's sake."
Al: "Let's all just forget about it."
Carl: "Al, it'll be easier for you too."

Sessions for 'Help Me Rhonda' resume with more vocal rehearsals. After several more run-throughs, Murry again makes some comments. This time, Brian will snap.

Murry (still sitting in the control box): "Fellows, I have 3,000 words to say. Quit screaming and sing from your hearts. You're doing fine now. Watch your 'oooohs', come in on the low notes, and Mike, **Dennis:** you're flatting. Let's get ready to roll. You're big stars. Let's fight for success. Let's go. OK. Let's go. Loosen up. Be happy. OK fellows? If you've got any guts, let's hear it."
Brian: "That's only 82 words."
Murry: "I said 3,000. Come on, Brian, let's knock it off. If you guys think you're good, let's go. As a team, we're unbeatable. Let's go.

You're doing wonderful."
Brian (screams): "Oh shit! He's driving me nuts!"
Murry: "Forget it."
Mike: "Don't worry about it."
Brian: "God damn it."
Murry: "I'll leave, Brian, if you're going to give me a bad time."
Brian: "That really gets me."
Murry: "I don't care if it does, let's go. If you've got any guts, let's see it. I don't care how many people are here."
Brian: "One ear left, and your big bad voice is killing it."
Murry: "I'm sorry I'm yelling. Let's go. Loosen up, Al. Let's roll. Loosen it up, fellows."
Brian (to Mike): "I can't take it."
Murry: "OK, Audree and I will leave."

They stay. Strained vocal rehearsals for 'Help Me Rhonda' follow, but the next take breaks down after 19 seconds. A further attempt is halted because studio engineer Chuck Britz is still busy repairing some recording equipment. After several more ill-fated attempts at the song, feelings between Brian and Murry come to a head.

Brian: "Go ahead, say what you want to say."
Murry: "We need Al to loosen up, Dennis is flatting, and Mike is flatting the high notes. We need help."
Brian: "Who needs help?"
Murry: "We need the honest projection we used to have. When the guys get too much money, you start thinking that you're gonna make everything a hit. I'm sorry, I'll never help you guys mix another session."
Brian: "Why?"
Murry: "Because you don't appreciate the good help that Chuck and I have given you. Listen, let me tell you something. When you guys get so big that you can't sing from your hearts, you're going downhill."
Brian: "Downhill?"
Murry (screaming): "Downhill!"

Murry and Audree get up to leave. Before they do so, Murry aims another shot at his eldest son.

Murry: "Son, I'm sorry. I've protected you for 22 years. But I can't go on if you're not going to listen to an intelligent man."
Brian: "Are you going now? Are you going or staying? I want to know."
Murry: "So you think you've got it made?"
Brian: "No, I don't. We would like to record in an atmosphere of calmness."
Murry: "I love you. Your mother loves you, and first of all, you shouldn't have all these people here."
Brian: "They're not saying anything. You're the one that's talking."
Murry: "And so, remember this. You always have to fight for success, because success comes from your heart. Success never comes from phoney singing … "
Brian (interrupting): "Why don't you go and tell Johnny Rivers that?"
Murry: "I don't care who you tell. You sing from your heart … . Forget it, we'll never come to another recording session. Carl, I'm so sorry."
Audree: "I'm sorry, Carl. I'll talk to you later."
Carl: "I know."
Murry (to Audree): "The kid got a big success and he thinks he owns the business. I'm sorry, I'm so sorry dear. I'm sorry."

Murry (to Brian): "Chuck and I used to make one hit after the other in 30 minutes. You guys take five hours to do it … "
Brian (interrupting): "Times are changing."
Murry: "You know why? Because you guys think you have an image."
Brian: "Times are changing."
Murry: "Don't ever forget. Honesty is the best policy. Right Mike? You know what I'm talking about, Mike? Forget about your image. You can live for 200 years if you grow. OK, let's forget it. Let's go."

Murry and Audree depart, leaving The Beach Boys to complete the recordings for the 'Help Me Rhonda' single.

■ **Friday 26th**
San Diego Sports Arena *San Diego, CA* 8:30pm
The tour continues, with Glen Campbell in place of Brian.

■ **Saturday 27th**
Civic Auditorium *Sacramento, CA* 7:00 & 9:30pm, with Paul Revere & The Raiders, The Marauders
The last night of The Beach Boys' month-long tour, which has earned the group a net profit of $98,414 before agency commission.
• 'Do You Wanna Dance' single hits the US charts.

March

'**All Summer Long**' / '**Do You Wanna Dance**' single released in the UK. It fails to chart.
'**Don't Be Scared**' / '**Bunny Hill**' single by The Rip Chords released in the US, featuring Beach Boy part-timer Bruce Johnston.
'**Carmen**' / '**I Love You Model T**' single by Bruce & Terry released in the US, another Columbia 45 featuring Bruce Johnston (and Terry Melcher).
• 'Do You Wanna Dance' single peaks in Canadian RPM chart at number 17.

■ **Wednesday 3rd**
RECORDING Western Recorders studio *Hollywood, CA*. Today sees a further session of vocal work to develop the single version of '**Help Me Rhonda**'.

■ **Thursday 4th**
RECORDING Western Recorders studio *Hollywood, CA*. Another vocal session today for '**Help Me Rhonda**' (single version) is followed by a rough mix of the recording. Work on the song will resume on March 21st. Also today, a reel of Beach Boys ad libs is compiled for possible use in another studio-chat filler track.

All Summer Long single

A '**All Summer Long**' (B. WILSON / M. LOVE)
B '**Do You Wanna Dance**' (B. FREEMAN)

UK release March 1965 (Capitol CL 15384).
Chart high UK none.

The Beach Boys Today! album

A1 'Do You Wanna Dance' (B. FREEMAN)
A2 'Good To My Baby' (B. WILSON / M. LOVE)
A3 'Don't Hurt My Little Sister' (B. WILSON / M. LOVE)
A4 'When I Grow Up (To Be A Man)' (B. WILSON / M. LOVE)
A5 'Help Me Ronda' ALBUM VERSION (B. WILSON / M. LOVE)
A6 'Dance Dance Dance' (B. WILSON / C. WILSON / M. LOVE)
B1 'Please Let Me Wonder' (B. WILSON / M. LOVE)
B2 'I'm So Young' (W. H. TYRUS JR)
B3 'Kiss Me Baby' (B. WILSON / M. LOVE)
B4 'She Knows Me Too Well' (B. WILSON / M. LOVE)
B5 'In The Back Of My Mind' (B. WILSON / M. LOVE)
B6 'Bull Session With Big Daddy' (B. WILSON / C. WILSON / D. WILSON / M. LOVE / A. JARDINE)

US release March 8th 1965 (Capitol T2269).
UK release April 1966 (Capitol T2269).
Chart high US number 4; UK none.

■ Saturday 6th
'Please Let Me Wonder' single hits the US *Billboard* chart.

■ Monday 8th
The Beach Boys Today! album released in the US. The group's first new album of the year has the first side packed full of the group's hits, the other heaped with Brian's new-style music. It is the first time that a Beach Boys album is not named after one of their songs. The LP is a huge success in the US, peaking at number 4. Despite these significant sales, Capitol Records (along with Mike Love) question Brian about what they perceive as his less-than-commercial musical direction on the album. They tell him they want a return to simpler, happy-go-lucky themes on future Beach Boys releases, insisting that this is what the group is all about. Undeterred, Brian does not bow to their demands. He knows that his best is yet to come.
RECORDING Western Recorders studio *Hollywood, CA*. As a goodwill gesture for his playing on the recent Beach Boys concerts, Glen Campbell is rewarded with a Brian-produced recording at Western. During today's three-hour session, Campbell's vocals are overdubbed onto the resurrected, unused **'Guess I'm Dumb'** tracking tape recorded on October 14th 1964. The Honeys – Marilyn, Ginger and Diane – provide backing vocals. The recording was up for consideration for *The Beach Boys' Today!* album, but will now be used for the A-side of Campbell's next single, his tenth for Capitol, which is issued on June 7th.

■ Saturday 13th
'Do You Wanna Dance' single enters US *Billboard* Top 40 chart at number 29.

■ Tuesday 16th
RECORDING Western Recorders studio *Hollywood, CA*. Brian returns to Western where he produces the first tracking session for **'Let Him Run Wild'** (take 16 marked as best), which originally boasts a working title of 'I Hate Rock'n'Roll'. Vocal overdubs follow and a mono mix of the recordings completes the session. Work on the song will resume on the 30th.

■ Sunday 21st
RECORDING Western Recorders studio *Hollywood, CA*. The Beach Boys overdub live instrumental and vocals tracks onto the recordings for the **'Help Me Rhonda'** single tracked and compiled on March 4th. Later in the day more elements are added: castanets, a 12-string guitar, piano, and a distinctive high "wah wah wah" harmony vocal track. A mix is made and labelled "final mono master", but Brian feels that it can be improved further, and this mix will remain unreleased until its appearance on the Capitol compilation CD *Endless Harmony* in 1998.

■ Monday 22nd
RECORDING Western Recorders studio *Hollywood, CA*. The single version of **'Help Me Rhonda'** is completed. Unhappy with the mix of the previous day, Brian recalls the group to Western for another crack at the song, preparing the final mix after overdubbing a new solo and a new set of vocals. With recordings for this next Beach Boys single completed, Brian immediately turns to preparations for the group's next album. After the less than happy sound of their last long player, Mike insists that the group's next album be more upbeat and positive. At first Brian opposes this idea but ultimately relents. Recordings will begin just a week later, on the 29th.

■ Wednesday 24th
RECORDING Western Recorders studio *Hollywood, CA*. Two days after Brian completes his second version of **'Help Me Rhonda'**, Terry Melcher records his version of the song, which ultimately will remain unreleased. Among the session musicians at the studio today is keyboard player Daryl Dragon, a future member of The Beach Boys' touring line-up.

■ Friday 26th
McCormick Place *Chicago, IL* two shows
The Beach Boys – with Brian – perform two special one-off shows in Chicago for another possible live album. Why they would be recording another live album so soon is not known. However, the show and some rehearsals are captured on 3-track tape by Wally Heider's mobile unit. The level of crowd noise on the tapes is probably a major factor in the decision not to use them. In 1998, recordings from the show will be mixed and considered for release on the *Endless Harmony* soundtrack; 'Shut Down' is used later for the *Hawthorne, CA* CD.

■ Saturday 27th
The Beach Boys Today! album hits US charts.
• 'Please Let Me Wonder' single B-side peaks in US *Billboard* chart at number 52.

■ Monday 29th
RECORDING *Summer Days* session 1 Western Recorders studio *Hollywood, CA* 9:00pm-1:30am. Recordings begin this evening for what will become The Beach Boys' next album, *Summer Days (And Summer Nights!!)*.
This first session for the new record focuses on tracking (instrumental) recordings for a piece with the working title **'Sandy'** – noted on the union log as 'Sherri She Needs Me'. It features on guitar Carl and on organ Bruce Johnston (live Beach Boy, session musician, and Columbia recording artist). The backing track recorded today will remain free of any vocals until 1976 when Brian finally adds his lead vocal track, and by which time it has definitely become 'Sherri She Needs Me', co-written with Russ Titleman. In June 1998 Brian will release a revised version on *Imagination*, his

second solo album, now titled 'She Says She Needs Me' and with new lyrics by Carole Bayer Sager.

Brian will mix many of the 4-track instrumental tracking recordings for *Summer Days (And Summer Nights!!)* into mono on a single tape track of the impressive new 8-track recorder housed at the Columbia studio nearby in Los Angeles. This process allows Brian the luxury and freedom of seven empty tape tracks on which to then record Beach Boys vocals. At the time, very few studios in Los Angeles or anywhere else are equipped with a state-of-the-art 8-track machine. Even Brian's favourite studio, Western Recorders, does not have one, much to his annoyance.

Also at today's session, Brian and engineer Chuck Britz make mono mixes of 'Help Me Rhonda' featuring a different backing vocal pattern, handclaps and an alternative solo section – possibly the March 21st version. It is likely that the single version – which is days away from being issued – is not yet finalised.

Musicians present Jimmy Bond Jr (upright bass), Russell Bridges (piano), Roy Caton (trumpet), Jerry Cole (guitar), Al de Lory (piano), Steve Douglas (saxophone), Steve Dweck (vibes), Billy Green (saxophone), Carol Kaye (guitar), Jay Migliori (saxophone), Earl Palmer (drums, timbales), Jack Nimitz (saxophone), Howard Roberts (guitar), Billy Strange (guitar).

■ Tuesday 30th

RECORDING *Summer Days* **session 2** Western Recorders studio *Hollywood, CA*. Today sees a session for **'Salt Lake City'**, with Carl on guitar. The song's tracking recordings (nine takes required) follow

extensive rehearsals. Alternative versions of **'Let Him Run Wild'** are also recorded today, one of which will grace the forthcoming *Summer Days* album.

Musicians present Hal Blaine (drums), Russell Bridges (piano, organ), Frankie Capp (vibes), Roy Caton (trumpet), Jerry Cole (guitar), Al de Lory (piano), Steve Douglas (saxophone), Plas Johnson (saxophone), Carol Kaye (bass guitar), Jay Migliori (saxophone), Lyle Ritz (upright bass), Howard Roberts (guitar), Billy Strange (guitar).

April

'Come On Let's Go' / **'Roger's Reef Part 2'** single by The Rouges released in the US, yet another Columbia 45 featuring Bruce Johnston.

• 'Do You Wanna Dance' single peaks in Swedish Radio 3 chart at number 9.

• Brian is now moving in hip LA circles, and this month experiences his first LSD trip after being given the drug by his friend Loren Schwartz. He tells Marilyn that he sees God, and breaks down in tears. Brian reveals later in his book *Wouldn't It Be Nice: My Own Story*: "I took LSD and it just tore my head off. After I took acid, I came to grips with everything I could be or couldn't be. You just come to grips with what you are, what you can do [and] can't do, and learn to face it." Marilyn insists that Brian quits taking drugs. He

refuses and she moves out of their home. After a month, Brian begs her to return. She agrees.

Murry Wilson will recall in 1971 for the benefit of *Rolling Stone*: "We were driving to a recording studio and I said, 'I heard that you experimented with LSD. Did you do it?' And he said, 'Yes, dad, I did,' and I said, 'Well, tell me Brian, do you think you're strong enough in your brain that you can experiment with a chemical that might drive you crazy later?' He said, 'No dad. But it's opened a lot of things for me.' I said, 'Brian, who are trying to kid?' He said, 'Well, I had weird, weird hallucinations. It made me understand.' I said, 'Who are you trying to kid, Brian? What did you understand, except seeing a bunch of different nightmares in your brain, like colours and things like that? You know, Brian, one thing that God gives you is a brain. If you play with it and destroy it, you're dead. You're a vegetable.' He agreed that he would never do that again."

■ Monday 5th

'Help Me Rhonda' / **'Kiss Me Baby'** single released in the US. It will become the group's second American number 1 single.
Melodyland Theatre *Anaheim, CA* 5:00 & 9:00pm, with The Munsters Singing Group, Pat & Lolly, The Vegas Trio
Tonight's show is a warm-up for the group's tour set to begin on Friday. Once again Glen Campbell takes Brian's place.

■ Tuesday 6th

RECORDING *Summer Days* session 3 Western Recorders studio *Hollywood, CA.* Working again with some of LA's finest studio musicians, Brian begins recording the intricate instrumentation for what will become a Beach Boy classic, **'California Girls'**. He is unsure at this stage what to call the song, so it starts life with the apt title 'We Don't Know'. Vocals will be added to today's tracking tape on June 4th. In a later Capitol interview Brian recalls: "Everybody was up. The whole gang was there. It became my favourite session. The intro to this song is the greatest piece of music that I've ever written. I was looking for an introduction which would be totally different to the rest of the song, but would lead into it. The song was a big record for us but I never really liked anything but the intro."
Musicians present Hal Blaine (drums), Russell Bridges (piano), Frankie Capp (vibes), Roy Caton (trumpet), Jerry Cole (guitar), Al de Lory (piano), Steve Douglas (saxophone), Carol Kaye (bass guitar), Jay Migliori (saxophone), Jack Nimitz (saxophone), Lyle Ritz (upright bass), Howard Roberts (guitar), Billy Strange (guitar).

■ Wednesday 7th

Carl, Dennis, Mike and Al travel to New Orleans to prepare for the start of their latest American tour. Soon after they arrive, the group's regular stand-in Glen Campbell tells them by phone that he is unable to play with the group due to his touring commitments

with The Righteous Brothers, with dates scheduled to run until April 14th. Brian tells *Melody Maker*: "Glen got sick [sic] and couldn't tour. The Beach Boys were really in trouble now because they couldn't cancel out of the tour. So Mike, in the last minute, phones up Bruce [Johnston] back in Los Angeles to see if he can find a fill-in."

Bruce Arthur Johnston was born Benjamin Baldwin on June 27th 1944 in Chicago, Illinois. Before graduating from high school he had played bass on the Phil Spector-produced hit for The Teddy Bears, 'To Know Him Is To Love Him', and drums on 'La Bamba' with Richie Valens. In 1963 Bruce worked at Columbia Records as a record manager, right across the street from where The Beach Boys had been recording. As we've seen, Johnston has been involved in a large number of Columbia singles; see for example April 1962, September 1963, and various dates this year and in 1964.

After Mike's request to Bruce Johnston to try to find a fill-in, Johnston in turn calls Eddie Carter, whom he has known since grammar school, but Carter declines because he is studying for exams this week. So Bruce tells Mike that he can do it himself. "I was producing records at Columbia when Mike called me and said he'd like me to stand in for two weekend concerts because Brian was sick," Bruce tells Scott Keller in 1974. "They wanted someone yesterday – it was a real rush thing. I said, 'Look, Mike, I can't find anyone, so I'll come. I don't play bass, I play piano, but I suppose I could sing all the high parts if you show me what to do.'"

■ Thursday 8th

Bruce Johnston boards a plane to New Orleans where he will join up with the other Beach Boys. Once there, he gets together with Carl who attempts to teach Bruce the group's repertoire. Bruce learns enough to enable him to join the group on stage tomorrow night.

Brian tells *Teen Beat*: "We've known Bruce for a couple of years. He was making records with Terry Melcher before he joined us. Bruce and Terry discontinued their act because of the different paths they had taken. Bruce sounds somewhat like me when he sings falsetto. He sings and plays well. Bruce ended up making The Beach Boys his living. We love Bruce. He came just at the right time when we were against the wall. It was very logical for him to join us as Bruce has done surfing records very similar to The Beach Boys."

"I first heard 'Surfin'' on the way to the beach to surf back in '61," Bruce recalls in *NME*. "The record just blew my mind – and I even bought it. A couple of years later, I went to Hawaii to surf and I met Murry Wilson at the airport when I landed. He told me to look up the boys who were there in Honolulu too. I met them all except for Brian and we sort of dug each other."

TOUR STARTS US South/East (Apr 9th-May 7th)

■ Friday 9th

Municipal Auditorium *New Orleans, LA* with Bobby Goldsboro, Sam The Sham & The Pharaohs
With all the group's thoughts focused on the music they are performing rather than the clothes they are wearing, new live-band member Bruce Johnston is forced to slip into a spare set of Al Jardine's stage trousers, which are three sizes and four inches too small. For the next few nights, Al plays bass while Bruce sings Brian's high parts and plays electric piano to fill out the instrumental sound. Bruce will play six consecutive nights with the group.

"Brian was still sick the next week so they asked me to do two more [dates]," says Bruce in *Teen Beat*. "I ended up finishing the rest of the tour. I had never been on the road before in my life and I didn't know how to play bass guitar. So I locked myself in my hotel

---

Help Me Rhonda single

A 'Help Me Rhonda' (B. WILSON / M. LOVE)
B 'Kiss Me Baby' (B. WILSON / M. LOVE)

US release April 5th 1965 (Capitol 5395).
UK release May 1965 (Capitol CL 15392).
Chart high US number 1; UK number 27.

New Beach Boy Bruce Johnston (right) poses with his longtime songwriting and production partner Terry Melcher.

room for two weeks in Miami, Florida, and taught myself all the songs. I taught myself how to smile, how to relax, and how to bounce around. I was scared. On the first night I appeared on-stage the kids started yelling out, 'Where's Brian?' and I thought, 'Oh baby, they're going to stone me.'

"The audience reaction to The Beach Boys really overwhelmed me at first. My ears rang for two weeks afterwards and it inspired me to play and do things on stage. My mother couldn't believe I was playing with a successful group. When we went on those long trips she would think I was in jail or something. It was only when we appeared on coast-to-coast television that she started to believe the group really existed."

Tonight's show grosses $9,500, of which The Beach Boys receive typically 60 percent. Between dates on the forthcoming tour Bruce will learn from Carl the bass parts of the songs performed in the show. When Glen Campbell briefly returns on April 15th, Bruce will nonetheless remain on the tour, usually running the lights.

■ Saturday 10th
Ellis Auditorium Amphitheatre *Memphis, TN* 8:30pm, with Bobby Goldsboro, Sam The Sham & The Pharaohs, Bobby Woods
Bruce Johnston's second date with the group. Radio station WMPS sponsors the show, which grosses $13,900.
• 'Do You Wanna Dance' single peaks in US *Billboard* chart at number 12.

■ Sunday 11th
Municipal Auditorium *Atlanta, GA* 3:30pm, with Bobby Goldsboro, Sam The Sham & The Pharaohs, Bobby Woods.
Bruce's third show with the group grosses $12,100.

■ Wednesday 14th
RECORDING *Summer Days* **session 4** Western Recorders studio *Hollywood, CA* 1:00-4:00pm. Back in California, Brian resumes recordings for the *Summer Days (And Summer Days!!)* album with a tracking session for his and Mike's **'Amusement Parks USA'** (tracking take 9 marked as best). Vocals will be added on May 5th.
Musicians present Charles Berghofer (upright bass), Hal Blaine (drums), Russell Bridges (piano), Jerry Cole (guitar), Steve Douglas (saxophone), Carol Kaye (bass guitar), Jay Migliori (saxophone), Billy Strange (guitar), Julius Wechter (vibes).

■ Thursday 15th
Miami Convention Hall *Miami Beach, FL* 8:30pm
Glen Campbell, free from his commitments with The Righteous Brothers, rejoins The Beach Boys and plays with them for the rest of the tour. Since Campbell has already announced his intention of leaving after this tour, Bruce Johnston sticks around and continues to learn how to play the bass parts on the group's songs.

■ Friday 16th
RECORDING Western Recorders studio *Hollywood, CA* 1:30-5:00pm, 5:30-8:30pm. Tracking and sweetening sessions for what is noted on the union log as **'Untitled Ballad'**.
Musicians present Arnold Belnick (violin), Hal Blaine (drums), Jimmy Bond Jr (upright bass), Russell Bridges (piano), Frankie Capp (vibes), Roy Caton (trumpet), Jerry Cole (guitar), Steve Douglas (saxophone), Michael Henderson (saxophone), Jim Horn (saxophone), Harry Hyams (viola), Jules Jacob (oboe), Carol Kaye (bass guitar), Bernard Kundell (violin), William Kurasch (violin), Irving Lipschultz (cello), Lenny Malarsky (violin), Jay Migliori (saxophone), Alexander Neiman (viola), Jerry Reisler (violin),

Joseph Saxon (cello), Ralph Schaeffer (violin), Sidney Sharp (violin), Billy Strange (guitar), Tibor Zelig (violin).

■ Saturday 17th
'Help Me Rhonda' single hits the US charts.

■ Monday 19th
Tinker Field Stadium *Orlando, FL* 8:00pm
Hotfoot from another of his recording sessions, Campbell is again on-stage to play with the band.

■ Tuesday 20th
The Wilmington State Armory *Wilmington, DE* with The Sonics, The Nebulas
Judith M Roales reviews the show for the *Evening Journal*: "About 3,500 screaming teenagers packed the aisles, stood on chairs and frantically cheered their current Number 1 idols … . The Beach Boys dashed on-stage amid up-stretched arms, paper planes saying, 'Dennis we love you' or 'All the way boys', and a deafening roar of young voices. The roar never stopped. Fans cheered from the moment the rumour spread that the stars had entered the building until long after the last note died away. Every song was greeted with a new outburst atop the already resounding one.

"Songs ranged from 'Little Deuce Coupe' to 'Monster Mash' with Mike Love, the oldest of the group, cavorting around the stage as a 'monster', thrilling dozens of smitten girls as he reached out and touched their fingertips. 'I'll never wash it again,' a starry-eyed blonde confessed, hugging her hand to her cheek. Signs with warm greetings to the group, pictures and programs waved above the audience. Flashbulbs popped and pocket tape recorders whirred. But police kept ambitious autograph and souvenir seekers off the stage. Two officers interrupted one determined miss just as she crawled over the edge, heading for Alan Jardine at the center mike, and tossed her back to her friends in the audience.

"The Beach Boys played with drums borrowed from an earlier act and hastily-assembled costumes. Their normal gear had missed the plane in Washington DC but no one really seemed to care. As Dennis Wilson, on the borrowed drums, led into the song 'Do You Wanna Dance', tears streamed down the cheeks of infatuated females yelling 'Yes, yes.' There was one other substitute on the program. Brian Wilson, the group's songwriter and one of the performers, missed the tour because of illness and was replaced by Bruce Johnston. But no one seemed to mind that either. Hoarse and half deaf, the audience continued to clap and cheer 45 minutes later when the group escaped the stage, sheltered by a wall of unformed police."

■ Wednesday 21st
TV ABC Television Studios *New York, NY*. ABC *Shindig!* live performance 'Do You Wanna Dance', 'Fun Fun Fun', 'Long Tall Texan'; live vocals over record backing 'Please Let Me Wonder', 'Help Me Rhonda', broadcast 8:30-9:00pm. In the midst of touring dates where Brian is being replaced on stage by Glen Campbell or Bruce Johnston, The Beach Boys make a return appearance on *Shindig!* – and, surprisingly, Brian is back in the line-up. They perform live versions of 'Do You Wanna Dance' (at the start of the show), truncated takes of 'Fun Fun Fun' and 'Long Tall Texan', and deliver live vocals against pre-taped backing tracks for 'Please Let Me Wonder' (also truncated) and 'Help Me Rhonda'. Other guests on tonight's show include Rita Pavone, Cilla Black, Wayne Fontana & The Mindbenders, Ian Whitcomb, Joe & Eddie, Joey Cooper, Dick & Dee Dee, The Ikettes, and The Shangri-Las.

Following the TV session The Beach Boys (minus Brian but including Glen Campbell) travel to tonight's venue. Brian goes home to Los Angeles and will return to the studio next week.
Colonial Theatre *Keene, NH*
Following the afternoon TV session in New York City, The Beach Boys with Campbell perform this evening in New Hampshire.

■ Friday 23rd
Civic Centre *Baltimore, MD*
Bruce Johnston plays bass during tonight's concert.

■ Saturday 24th
Washington Coliseum Washington, DC 8:00pm
Glen Campbell is back to play bass during the show. Ronnie Oberman writes in the *Washington Star*: "The Beach Boys … played before more than 7,000 fans … . With their return came some interesting facts. For instance, 22-year-old Brian Wilson will not participate in tours in the immediate future. Two other singers, who will alternate, have been found to replace Brian on tours. They are Glen Campbell, who is frequently seen on *Shindig!*, and Bruce Johnston, formerly of The Rip Chords. Campbell appeared on stage with The Beach Boys in Washington and Bruce was around too. 'I've known these guys for three or four years,' 20-year-old Bruce says. 'It's groovy on the road with them. They never hassle. It's a gas and I just dig them.'"

■ Sunday 25th – Thursday 29th
The Pier *Raleigh, NC*
University of North Carolina *Greensboro, NC*
The Coliseum *Charlotte, NC*
Due to his appearances on ABC TV show *Shindig!* Campbell is forced to drop out of the concerts taking place between the 27th and 29th, and Bruce again takes over on bass.

■ Wednesday 28th
RECORDING *Summer Days* session 5 Western Recorders studio *Hollywood, CA*. Backing vocal overdubs and mono mixes are made of **'Let Him Run Wild'** with engineer Chuck Britz. It is likely that the month-old recording is completed at this session.

■ Friday 30th
RECORDING *Summer Days* session 6 Western Recorders studio *Hollywood, CA*. Album sessions continue with the taping of instrumental tracking for Brian's **'Girl Don't Tell Me'** (16 takes required). Instrumental 'inserts' (short parts added usually to one tape track of the existing recorded performance) and vocal overdubs are also recorded, and later Carl dubs on his lead vocal, his first since the group's *Shut Down Volume 2* album. From this point, Carl's voice will feature prominently in Beach Boys recordings.

May

'Help Me Rhonda' / 'Kiss Me Baby' single released in the UK. It will peak at number 27.

■ Saturday 1st
The Beach Boys Today! album peaks in US *Billboard* chart at number 4.
• 'Help Me Rhonda' single enters US *Billboard* Top 40 chart at number 35.

■ Monday 3rd
RECORDING *Summer Days* session 7 Western Recorders studio *Hollywood, CA*. Selected members of The Beach Boys begin recording another song intended for the next album, a cover version of the Phil Spector/Ellie Greenwich/Jeff Barry composition **'Then I Kissed Her'** – a hit for The Crystals in 1963 as 'Then He Kissed Me'. Before Al can overdub his lead vocal, the group – Brian on piano, Dennis on drums, Carl on electric rhythm guitar, Ron Swallow on tambourine and an unknown musician on castanets – records the song's backing track (16 takes required). The taping of instrumental inserts and further vocal overdubs rounds off the session; Brian will overdub the bass parts later. (Two years later, 'Then I Kissed Her' will surprisingly be released as a single in the UK, Australia and elsewhere, and in the UK will peak at number 4 in the charts.)

■ Wednesday 5th
RECORDING *Summer Days* session 8 Western Recorders studio *Hollywood, CA*. Working with regular Western engineer Chuck Britz, Mike and Brian overdub their vocals onto the April 14th tracking tape of **'Amusement Parks USA'**. Two further vocal overdubbing sessions follow. It may be regular Beach Boys session drummer Hal Blaine providing the spoken parts in the instrumental break.

Featuring a full group line-up, including Bruce Johnston, work today also focuses on recordings for **'Graduation Day'** (eight vocal 'takes', or attempts at a recording, are required). A single guitar provided by a session musician accompanies them. The recordings are strained and Brian becomes angry when re-takes are required. Mike begins to question why they have to record the song at all. Arguments become so intense that Chuck Britz walks out, saying, "I'll be back in ten minutes." Later, The Beach Boys minus Brian head for tonight's tour performance with Glen Campbell again replacing Brian on bass.
New Haven Arena *New Haven, CT*

■ Friday 7th
Legion Field *Birmingham, AL* 7:00pm, with The Rolling Stones, The Righteous Brothers, Cannibal & The Headhunters, Marty Robbins, Sonny James, Skeeter Davis, Del Reeves, Archie 'Rindercella' Campbell This last night of the tour sees an audience officially totalling 20,800. Bruce plays bass tonight.

■ Wednesday 12th
RECORDING *Summer Days* session 9 Capitol studio *Hollywood, CA* 11:00am-4:00pm. Intending to achieve a new sound, Brian changes studio again with a move to Capitol's studio in Hollywood. Here he supervises the first recordings of his instrumental **'Summer Means New Love'**, featuring a horn and string arrangement. Work will resume on the song on June 1st. ('Summer Means New Love' will eventually appear as the flip side of Brian's first ever solo single, released in the US on March 7th 1966.)
Musicians present Israel Baker (violin), Arnold Belnick (violin), Hal Blaine (drums), Frankie Capp (percussion), Joe Difiore (viola), Steve Douglas (saxophone), Jim Getzoff (violin), Harry Hyams (viola), Carol Kaye (bass guitar), Bernard Kundell (violin), Lenny Malarsky (violin), Jay Migliori (saxophone), Ralph Schaeffer (violin), Sidney Sharp (violin), Billy Strange (guitar), Bill Hinshaw (French horn), Tibor Zelig (violin).
• *The Girls On The Beach*, a colour Paramount Pictures movie starring Noreen Corcoran and Martin West and featuring a cameo musical appearance by The Beach Boys, is premiered in cinemas across the US. The film, also known as *Summer Of '64*, is according

Phonograph Recording Contract Blank
AMERICAN FEDERATION OF MUSICIANS
OF THE UNITED STATES AND CANADA

Local Union No. 47

N° 162322

THIS CONTRACT for the personal services of musicians, made this **12th** day of **May** , 19**65** between the undersigned employer (hereinafter called the "employer") and **17** musicians (hereinafter called "employees").

(Including the leader)

WITNESSETH, That the employer hires the employees as musicians severally on the terms and conditions below, **and as further specified on** reverse side. The leader represents that the employees already designated have agreed to be bound by said terms and conditions. Each employee yet to be chosen shall be so bound by said terms and conditions upon agreeing to accept his employment. Each employee may enforce this agreement. The employees severally agree to render collectively to the employer services as musicians in the orchestra under the leadership of

Steven Kreisman as follows:

Name and Address of Place of Engagement **Capitol Records, 1750 No. Vine Street, Hollywood, Calif.**

Date(s) and Hours of Employment **5-12-65   1 - 4 P.M.**

Type of Engagement: Recording for phonograph records only.

WAGE AGREED UPON $ **union scale**

Plus pension contributions as specified on reverse side hereof.

(Terms and amount)

This wage includes expenses agreed to be reimbursed by the employer in accordance with the attached schedule, or a schedule to be furnished the employer on or before the date of engagement.

To be paid **within 15 days**

(Specify when payments are to be made)

Upon request by the American Federation of Musicians of the United States and Canada (herein called the "Federation") or the local in whose jurisdiction the employees shall perform hereunder, the employer either shall make advance payment hereunder or shall post an appropriate bond.

Employer's name and	**Capitol Records, Inc.**
authorized signature	
Street address	**1750 North Vine Street**
	Hollywood 28, California

Leader's name	**Steven D. Kreisman**
Leader's signature	
Street address	**6950 Chisholm Avenue**
	Van Nuys, California

Local No. **47**

CONTRACT RECEIVED MAY 1 9 1965

WARD ARCHER ASST. TO PRESIDENT

PAID JUN 9 1965

(1) Label Name

Master No. / No. of Minutes / TITLES OF TUNES

Summer Means New Love (track)

Benell 12/5

Session No.

(2) Employee's Name (As on Social Security Card) Last First Initial	(3) Home Address (Give Street, City and State)	(4) Local Union No.	(5) Social Security Number	(6) Scale Wages	(7) Pension Contribution
(Leader) Kreisman, Steven D.	6950 Chisholm Avenue Van Nuys, Calif.	47	556-46-1005	162.68	13.02
Blaine, Hal (contractor)	2441 Castilian Drive Hollywood 28, Calif.	47	047-20-5900	162.68	13.02
Baker, Israel	12947 Galewood Street No. Hollywood, Calif	47	324-18-2806	81.34	6.51
Belnick, Arnold	17107 Lisette Street Granada Hills, Calif.	47	074-12-1214	81.34	6.51
Capp, Frank	23000 Bryce Street Woodland Hills, Calif.	47	013-24-7193	81.34	6.51
Di Fiore, Joseph	5943 Carlton Way Hollywood 28, Calif.	47	565-14-9535	81.34	6.51
Getzoff, James	8617 Allenwood Road Los Angeles 46, Calif.	47	568-01-2208	81.34	6.51
Hinshaw, William A.	22833 Mac Farlane Woodland Hills, Calif	47	571-01-6455	81.34	6.51
Hyams, Harry A.	6248 Booman No. Hollywood, Calif.	47	132-09-7647	81.34	6.51
Kaye, Carol	4905 Forman No. Hollywood, Calif.	47	555-46-5389	81.34	6.51
Kundell, Bernard	6706 Murietta Avenue Van Nuys, Calif.	47	115-07-1222	81.34	6.51
Malarsky, Leonard	3201 Dos Palos Drive Hollywood 28, Calif.	47	555-24-2243	81.34	6.51
Migliori, Jay	1701 No. Lincoln Burbank, Calif.	47	208-24-6118	81.34	6.51
Schaeffer, Ralph	815 Lockearn Street Los Angeles 49, Calif.	47	186-07-2346	81.34	6.51
Sharp, Sidney	1000 La Jolla Ave. Los Angeles 46, Calif.	47	198-12-0344	81.34	6.51

(8) Total Pension Contributions (Sum of Column (7)) $

Make check payable in this amount to "AFM & EPW Fund."

FOR FUND USE ONLY:

Date pay't rec'd _____ Amt. paid _____ Date posted _____ By _____

Form B-4 Rev. 4-59

to its synopsis about "sorority girls [who] have to raise $10,000 to save their Sorority House and resort to desperate measures like entering a cooking contest, a beauty contest, and trying to get The Beatles to perform at their local hot spot". During the movie The Beach Boys are seen singing 'Girls On The Beach', 'Little Honda' and 'Lonely Sea'. Other musical contributions in the movie come from Lesley Gore and The Crickets. (See also June 23rd.)

■ Sunday 16th

TV CBS TV (Studio 50) *New York, NY*. CBS *The Ed Sullivan Show* live performance 'Help Me Rhonda', broadcast 8:00-9:00pm. As a preview to the group's next American tour, scheduled to begin next Wednesday, The Beach Boys make their second appearance on CBS's *Ed Sullivan Show*. Following afternoon rehearsals, the group performs in a live (black-and-white) transmission. Joining the group on tonight's show are singers Petula Clark and Frankie Randall, ballet dancers Rudolf Nureyev and Margot Fonteyn, comedians Alan King and Sue Carson, and US group The West Point Glee Club.

TOUR STARTS US Midwest/West (May 19th-31st). Promoter is Irving Granz.

■ Wednesday 19th

Memorial Auditorium *Canton, OH* with Sam The Sham & The Pharaohs
The opening night of this tour sees a gross of $14,129, of which the group typically receives 60 percent and are then responsible for paying for the services of the support act.

■ Thursday 20th

Sports Arena *Toledo, OH* with Glen Campbell
Bruce Johnston begins playing with The Beach Boys on a regular basis, replacing Campbell – who joins this tour as a support act.

■ Friday 21st

Hara Arena *Dayton OH* 8:30pm with Sam The Sham & The Pharaohs, Glen Campbell
• The Beach Boys make the cover of America's prestigious *Time* magazine alongside other artists such as The Righteous Brothers and The Supremes to spotlight a piece inside headed "Rock'n'Roll: Everybody's Turned On".

■ Sunday 23rd

Cobo Arena *Detroit, MI*

■ Monday 24th

RECORDING *Summer Days* **session 10** Western Recorders studio *Hollywood, CA*. With a short break in touring, today sees a resumption of recordings for the next album. The group indulge in one long, highly productive session, recording 'tracking' (instrumental backing) and vocals for **'The Girl From New York City'** (17 tracking takes required), **'You're So Good To Me'** (24 tracking takes required), **'And Your Dream Comes True'**, and **'I'm Bugged At My Ol' Man'**.

'And Your Dream Comes True' is a vocals-only song constructed piece by piece on an 8-track recorder, and will remain unreleased until the 2001 CD *Hawthorne, CA*. Bruce Johnston is also present in the studio today and may play a musical role.
Musicians present ('Girl From New York City') Hal Blaine (drums), Steve Douglas (saxophone), Jack Nimitz (saxophone), Clifford Hils (upright bass), Ray Pohlman (bass guitar).

■ Wednesday 26th

San Diego Arena *San Diego, CA*

■ Friday 28th

Reno Arena *Reno, NV* with Dick & Dee Dee, Glen Campbell
The show grosses $10,200.

■ Saturday 29th

Lagoon Ballroom *Salt Lake City, UT*
• 'Help Me Rhonda' single peaks in US *Billboard* chart at number 1.

■ Sunday 30th

Denver Auditorium Arena *Denver, CO* 8:00pm with Glen Campbell, Dick & Dee Dee, The Moonrakers
Tonight's concert grosses $12,600, from which the group receives 60 percent and then has to pay the rest of tonight's line-up.

■ Monday 31st

Municipal Auditorium *Oklahoma City, OK*
Last night of the tour, with Bruce Johnston in the live band.

June

All Summer Long album released in the UK.
• 'Help Me Rhonda' single peaks in Canada at number 1.
• 'Amusement Park USA' single becomes a number 3 hit in Japan.

■ Tuesday 1st

RECORDING *Summer Days* **session 11** Capitol studio *Hollywood, CA*. Brian returns to Capitol to complete the instrumental **'Summer Means New Love'**. Session musician Tommy Tedesco provides the final 'sweetening' for the track with a guitar overdub.

■ Friday 4th

RECORDING *Summer Days* **session 12** Columbia studio *Los Angeles, CA*. Today concludes sessions for the new album. Brian revisits the instrumental track taped on April 6th and completes work on **'California Girls'**. Its existence without a proper title continues briefly today, and at one point during the session Brian refers to it as 'Yeah I Dig The Girls'.

He has shifted to Columbia to take advantage of the studio's rare, hi-tech 8-track tape machine – one that will record eight individual sound tracks onto tape, rather than the more common three or four – which enables him to record The Beach Boys' vocals using multiple tape tracks. Today he tapes three tracks of backing vocals by the group and manually triple-tracks a lead vocal by Mike.

The session is also notable for featuring Bruce Johnston's first vocals on a released Beach Boys recording. Bruce tells Capitol later: "I came home from The Beach Boys' tour [on Tuesday] and they said, 'Why don't you come and sing on our next album?' The first song I sang on was 'California Girls'. At this point I still wasn't a proper member of the group. I was still working at Columbia Records as their record manager and was reluctant to leave because I felt that Brian would come back to the [stage] group at any time."

■ Monday 7th

'Guess I'm Dumb' / 'That's All Right' single by Glen Campbell released in the US. The A-side is produced and co-written by Brian. To help promote the single, Campbell makes an appearance on the ABC TV pop show *Shivaree!* singing the topside.

An 'AFM sheet', or union contract form, showing the string and horn players present at one of Brian's earliest attempts at his 'new music', the instrumental 'Summer Means New Love' which he records at Capitol studio on May 12th.

LEFT Out on tour in the summer, Dennis prepares himself backstage. BELOW Brian rarely appears on stage now, but here he is at a soundcheck in the blazing California sunshine at the Hollywood Bowl on July 3rd, rehearsing his bandmates for their coming set.

■ Wednesday 9th

Brian receives a letter from his father in which he reminds his eldest son of a promise he made three years earlier to give Murry sole ownership of the Sea Of Tunes publishing company. Along with the typewritten note are the deeds that, once signed, will make Murry's ownership official.

■ Thursday 10th

Yankee Stadium *New York, NY* with Ray Charles, The Byrds
Following a two-week break, The Beach Boys return to the concert stage for a one-off show.

■ Wednesday 23rd

For the second time in six weeks a movie featuring a cameo and musical appearance by The Beach Boys' receives its American release. Today, Walt Disney's latest colour film *The Monkey's Uncle*, starring Tommy Kirk and Annette Funicello, goes on release across the country.

According to the movie's synopsis, "College whiz-kid Merlin Jones concocts a method for teaching advanced information to a chimpanzee, then creates a flying machine of his own design, ultimately raising havoc on the college campus."

The Beach Boys appear in the film's opening title sequence, lip-synching to the title song with Funicello at a teenage dance.

■ Friday 25th

Dillon Stadium *Hartford, CT* 11:00am & 8:00pm
A further one-off performance in readiness for the tour set to start on July 2nd.

July

'**Amusement Parks USA**' / '**Salt Lake City**' single issued in the US by Capitol as a promotional-only item courtesy of "Downtown Salt Lake City stores".
• 'Help Me Rhonda' single peaks in UK *Record Retailer* chart at number 27, in Dutch chart at number 27, and in Swedish Radio 3 chart at number 5.

TOUR STARTS US (Jul 2nd-24th) Promoter is Irving Granz.

■ Friday 2nd

Community Concourse Arena *San Diego, CA* 8:30pm, with Sam The Sham & The Pharaohs, Sonny & Cher, Ian Whitcomb
The group kicks off another tour, with tonight's show grossing $13,138 from 3,800 paying customers at a 4,100-seater stadium. Bruce replaces Brian in the live line-up.

1965

■ Saturday 3rd

Hollywood Bowl *Los Angeles, CA* 8:15pm, with The Righteous Brothers, Sam The Sham & The Pharaohs, The Byrds, Donna Loren, Sir Douglas Quintet, Sonny & Cher, Dino Desi & Billy, The Kinks, Ian Whitcomb

Tonight's Beach Boys' *Summer Spectacular* show grosses $55,135 from an audience totalling 14,327. Brian turns up around midday to coach the group through the set. Later, during the afternoon soundcheck, Billy Hinsche of Dino, Desi & Billy meets the group – now minus Brian – for the first time. Hinsche will become a Beach Boy in 1974. (The Beach Boys were at one time booked to appear at Atlantic City's Convention Hall this evening but that show was scrapped due to complaints from rival pier and amusement park managers in the area who had feared the competition.)

■ Sunday 4th

Cow Palace *San Francisco, CA*

■ Monday 5th

Summer Days (And Summer Nights!!) album released in the US. Capitol issues the second new Beach Boys LP of the year, this one with a jacket picture featuring the group aboard a boat – minus Bruce and Al.

Bruce was present at the shoot, but contractual restraints with Columbia Records, to whom he is still signed, prevent his appearance on the jacket. Al, meanwhile, explains his non-appearance with a note on the back of the album cover: "That very day the picture was taken," Al writes, "I had to spend in bed with a flu bug, instead of on a yacht with the photographer."

Ads for the impending release of *Summer Days* have appeared in *Billboard* magazine two days earlier. The album will peak at number 2 in the US charts, residing behind The Rolling Stones' *Out Of Our Heads*, and will reach number 4 in the UK next summer after its release there in June 1966.

■ Tuesday 6th

Canobie Lake Park Ballroom *Salem, NH*

Summer Days (And Summer Nights!!) album

A1 'The Girl From New York City' (B. WILSON / M. LOVE)
A2 'Amusement Parks USA' (B. WILSON / M. LOVE)
A3 'Then I Kissed Her' (P. SPECTOR / E. GREENWICH / J. BARRY)
A4 'Salt Lake City' (B. WILSON / M. LOVE)
A5 'Girl Don't Tell Me' (B. WILSON)
A6 'Help Me Rhonda' SINGLE VERSION (B. WILSON / M. LOVE)
B1 'California Girls' (B. WILSON / M. LOVE)
B2 'Let Him Run Wild' (B. WILSON / M. LOVE)
B3 'You're So Good To Me' (B. WILSON / M. LOVE)
B4 'Summer Means New Love' (B. WILSON)
B6 'I'm Bugged At My Ol' Man' (B. WILSON / M. LOVE)
B6 'And Your Dream Comes True' (B. WILSON / M. LOVE)

US release July 5th 1965 (Capitol T2354).
UK release June 1966 (Capitol T2354).
Chart high US number 2; UK none.

■ Wednesday 7th

Hampton Beach Casino *Hampton Beach, NH*

■ Thursday 8th

Balboa Stadium *San Diego, CA*
A further *Summer Spectacular* show.

■ Saturday 10th

Convention Hall *Asbury Park, NJ*

■ Sunday 11th

Selland Arena *Fresno, CA*

■ Monday 12th

RECORDING Western Recorders studio *Hollywood, CA* 12:00midnight-3:00am. With the group's latest long-playing effort doing brisk business in stores across the US, Brian is itching to produce more music and begins work on the instrumental tracking for **'Sloop John B'** (14 takes required). Engineer as usual at Western is Chuck Britz. Helping Brian to capture on tape the delightful and wondrous sounds cascading around his head for the last year are Phil Spector's regular group of musicians who go by the curious collective name of The Wrecking Crew. However, bassist Carol Kaye says later that there never was a Wrecking Crew in the 1960s. "That moniker," says Kaye, "was applied by drummer Hal Blaine long after the event. No one used it at the time. The so-called Crew was the cream of the 'you pay, we'll play' LA session pool, a crack team of 50 or 60 musicians."

The composition is a West Indian folk song from the 1920s that was first given a modern arrangement by composer and conductor George Wathall around 1927 and is named for *The John B*, a ship that lies embedded in the sand at Governor's Harbour in Nassau in the Bahamas. After several more variations on the original song, The Kingston Trio recorded it in 1958 as 'The Wreck Of The John B'. The first pop version came in 1960 with Jimmy Rogers's interpretation, 'Wreck Of The John B', which became a minor hit and was covered that same year by Britain's king of skiffle, Lonnie Donegan, renamed as 'I Wanna Go Home'.

The idea for The Beach Boys to record the song came from Al, the group's longstanding folk-music fan, who must be aware of the fusion of folk-rock that is beginning to take hold in US pop music. He played his new adaptation of the song to Brian on piano. "I told Brian if it was done in our style he might enjoy it," Al will recall in the *Endless Harmony* documentary. "I tried persuading Brian to record the track a year before we finally cut it. I sat and played these chord progressions, basically three chords done on guitar, banjo and keyboards. I knew I had to have keyboards, otherwise I knew it wouldn't get his attention."

Brian decides to record a version and today tapes his first instrumental arrangement of the song, changing just one line: "This is the worst trip since I was born" becomes "This is the worst trip I've ever been on." This is enough for a credit on the resulting records of "Traditional arr Brian Wilson", the 'arr' meaning 'arranged by'.

Although no one is aware of the fact now, today in effect marks the beginning of work on what will become The Beach Boys' greatest album, *Pet Sounds*. At the end of the day's three-hour session Brian is unsure what to do with the recording of 'Sloop John B', and it will sit untouched for five months (see December 6th). For now, he feels instinctively that The Beach Boys' next album – when he is ready to record it – will be a very special one, and the one that he's been leading up to. These exciting thoughts circle around in his head for the rest of the month as the live band continues to tour without him.

After pressure from Al, Brian finally cuts a tracking session for the traditional song 'Sloop John B' at Western Recorders, Hollywood, on July 12th, as noted on this musicians' union studio log.

THE BEACH BOYS......1 TRACK, PREMIUM DATE   CAPITOL RECORDS, INC.
                                            (Employer's name)

Phonograph Recording Contract Blank
AMERICAN FEDERATION OF MUSICIANS
OF THE UNITED STATES AND CANADA

1929
№ 196222

Local Union No. 47

THIS CONTRACT for the personal services of musicians, made this __12__ day of __July__, 19_65_ between the undersigned employer (hereinafter called the "employer") and ____ **13** musicians (including the leader) (hereinafter called "employees").

WITNESSETH, That the employer hires the employees as musicians severally on the terms and conditions below, **and as further specified on** reverse side. The leader represents that the employees already designated have agreed to be bound by said terms and conditions. Each employee yet to be chosen shall be so bound by said terms and conditions upon agreeing to accept his employment. Each employee may enforce this agreement. The employees severally agree to render collectively to the employer services as musicians in the orchestra under the leadership of

Stven D. Kreisman   as follows:

Name and Address of Place of Engagement **Western Recorders, 6000 Sunset Blvd. Los Angeles, Calif.**

Date(s) and Hours of Employment **July 12, 1965   12 Midnight to 3 A.M.**

Type of Engagement: Recording for phonograph records only.   Plus pension contributions as specified on reverse side hereof.

WAGE AGREED UPON $ ____ **Union Scale**
                                        (Terms and amount)

This wage includes expenses agreed to be reimbursed by the employer in accordance with the attached schedule, or a schedule to be furnished the employer on or before the date of engagement.

To be paid **Within 14 Days**
                                (Specify when payments are to be made)

Upon request by the American Federation of Musicians of the United States and Canada (herein called the "Federation") or the local in whose jurisdiction the employees shall perform hereunder, the employer either shall make advance payment hereunder or shall post an appropriate bond.

Employer's name and	Capitol Records, Inc.	Leader's name	Steven D. Kreisman	Local No. 47
authorized signature		Leader's signature		
Street address	1750 N. Vine St.	Street address	6950 Chisholm	
Hollywood, Calif. Ho-26252		Van Nuys, Calif.		
City State Phone		City State		

(1) Label Name **CAPITOL RECORDS**   Session No. ____

Master No.	No. of Minutes	TITLES OF TUNES	Master No.	No. of Minutes	TITLES OF TUNES
	3:06	SLOOP JOHN "B:			

(2) Employee's Name (As on Social Security Card) Last First Initial	(3) Home Address (Give Street, City and State)	(4) Local Union No.	(5) Social Security Number	(6) Scale Wages	(7) Pension Contribution
(Leader) Kreisman, Steven D.	6950 Chisholm Van Nuys, Calif.	47	556-46-1005	223.68	17.89
Blaine, Hal (contractor)	2441 Castilian Dr. Hollywood 28, Calif.	47	047-20-5900	223.68	17.89
Britz, Charles D.	4501 Wawona St. Los Angeles 65, Calif	47	567-26-4273	111.84	8.95
Capp, Frank	23000 Bryce St Woodland Hills, Calif	47	013-24-7193	111.84	8.95
Casey, Alvin W.	830 N. Van Ness Hollywood, Calif.	47	526-46-9373	111.84	8.95
Delory, Alfred V.	5524 Ruthwood Calabasas, Calif.	47	559-36-9796	111.84	8.95
Horn, James R.	3225 Oakshire Dr. Hollywood 28, Calif.	47	570-56-6753	111.84	8.95
Kaye, Carol	4905 Forman No. Hollywood, Calif.	7	555-46-5389	111.84	8.95
Kolbrak, Jerry	4605 Vineland Ave. No. Hollywood, Calif.	47	394-36-7847	111.84	8.95
Migliori, Jay	1701 N. Lincoln Burbank, Calif.	47	208-24-6118	111.84	8.95
Nimitz, Jack	12250 La Maida St. No. Hollywood, Calif.	47	578-36-4141	111.84	8.95
Ritz, Lyle	1971 N. Curson Ave. Los Angeles 46, Calif.	47	549-38-1490	111.84	8.95
Strange, William E.	17312 Osborne St. Northridge, Calif.	47	547-36-8814	111.84	8.95

NO ARRANGER OR COPYIST THIS SESSION***

(8) Total Pension Contributions (Sum of Column (7)) $ **134.23**
Make check payable in this amount to "AFM & EPW Fund."

FOR FUND USE ONLY:

Date pay't rec'd ____ Amt. paid ____ Date posted ____ By ____

Form B-4 Rev. 4-59

California Girls single

A 'California Girls' (B. WILSON / M. LOVE)
B 'Let Him Run Wild' (B. WILSON / M. LOVE)

US release July 12th 1965 (Capitol 5464).
UK release August 1965 (Capitol CL 15409).
Chart high US number 3; UK number 26.

Musicians present Hal Blaine (drums), Frankie Capp (percussion), Al Casey (guitar), Jerry Cole (guitar), Al de Lory (piano), Steve Douglas (saxophone), Jim Horn (saxophone), Carol Kaye (bass guitar), Jay Migliori (saxophone), Jack Nimitz (saxophone), Lyle Ritz (upright bass), Billy Strange (guitar).

Dorton Arena *Raleigh, NC*

'California Girls' / 'Let Him Run Wild' single released in the US. It will peak in US *Billboard* chart at number 3.

■ Tuesday 13th
Greensboro Coliseum *Greensboro, NC*

■ Wednesday 14th
Bangor Auditorium *Bangor, ME*

■ Thursday 15th
Ballpark At Old Orchard Beach *Portland, ME*

■ Saturday 17th
Memorial Auditorium *Greenville, SC*

■ Sunday 18th
City Auditorium *Atlanta, GA* 3:00pm, with Billy Joe Royal & The Rosemans

■ Monday 19th
Municipal Auditorium *Nashville, TN* 8:15pm, with The Zombies, The Searchers, Ray Lynn
Back at the hotel between shows The Zombies teach The Beach Boys to play British football.

■ Friday 23rd
The Coliseum *Montgomery, AL* with The Zombies, Del Shannon

■ Saturday 24th
The Coliseum, Civic Auditorium *Jacksonville, FL* 5:00pm & 9:00pm
Last night of the current Beach Boys tour.
• 'California Girls' single hits US charts.
• *Summer Days (And Summer Nights!!)* album hits the US charts and will reach number 2.

August

'California Girls' / 'Let Him Run Wild' single released in the UK. It will peak at number 26.

Surfin' USA album released in the UK, a belated issue of the LP that came out in the US over two years ago.
• During this month Capitol Records dashes Brian's idyllic plans for a new Beach Boys album by requesting that the next LP by the group be submitted this October, ready for the lucrative Christmas market. Brian knows that it is impossible to make the type of album he has in mind in two months. Fortunately, he comes up with a solution (see September 8th).

■ Thursday 5th & Friday 6th
Waikiki Shell *Honolulu, HI* 8:00pm with Dino Desi & Billy, Barbara Lewis

■ Sunday 22nd
Carl and Mike visit The Beatles backstage between the Liverpudlians' two performances today at the Memorial Coliseum in Portland, Oregon. During the meeting, Paul asks where Brian is. Carl replies, "Oh, he's given up touring. He just stays at home, producing and recording our records." To which Paul replies, "That's a good idea." The Beatles will cease touring next year.

TOUR STARTS North America (Aug 26th-Sep 6th)

■ Thursday 26th
Kentucky State Fairgrounds *Louisville, KY* 8:30pm, with The Shangri-Las, Sir Douglas Quintet, The Keyes

■ Friday 27th
Cincinnati Gardens *Cincinnati, OH* 8:30pm, with Johnny & The Hurricanes, Dave Osborn's Action Unlimited, Sir Douglas Quintet

■ Saturday 28th & Sunday 29th
Arie Crown Theater, McCormick Place *Chicago, IL* 8:30pm (Sat), 7:00pm (Sun), with The Shadows Of The Night, Jonathan David & Albert
A press report explains Brian's absence from both sell-out shows because he is "busy being a genius and composing more songs". The group records the performances on 2-track tape.
• 'California Girls' single peaks (28th) in the *Billboard* Top 40 chart at number 3, having entered three weeks ago at 28.

■ Monday 30th
'Ten Little Indians' / 'She Knows Me Too Well' single released in the US.
'Be True To Your School' / 'In My Room' single released in the US. Both are new couplings of old recordings.

September

'Raining In My Heart' / 'Four Strong Winds' single by Bruce & Terry released in the US, featuring Bruce Johnston and Terry Melcher.
• 'California Girls' single peaks in Dutch chart at number 28.
• 'Help Me Rhonda' single peaks in German *Hit Bilanz* chart at number 10.

■ Wednesday 1st
Civic Arena *Pittsburgh, CA*
The tour continues, with Bruce still in the line-up in place of Brian.

■ Saturday 4th

The Coliseum *Ottawa, ON, Canada* with The Esquires
• *Summer Days (And Summer Nights!!)* album peaks in US *Billboard* chart at number 2.

■ Sunday 5th

Maple Leaf Gardens *Toronto, ON, Canada* with Sonny & Cher, The Esquires

■ Monday 6th

The Forum *Montreal, PQ, Canada* with Sonny & Cher
Last night of the tour.

■ Wednesday 8th, Tuesday 14th, Wednesday 15th, Thursday 23rd

RECORDING *Party!* **sessions** Western Recorders studio (2) *Hollywood, CA* 12:00 midday-6:00pm (8th), 5:00-8:00pm, 9:00pm-12midnight (14th), 5:00-8:00pm (15th), 9:00pm-12midnight, 12:30-3:30am (23rd). In order to appease Capitol who are hounding Brian for a new Beach Boys album, the group begins a series of recordings that will ultimately result in the unplugged *Beach Boys' Party!* LP. They have already tried a Christmas album and a live concert record, and thoughts about a premature *Greatest Hits* LP are quickly dismissed. So Brian comes up with the simple *Party* concept: The Beach Boys are throwing a party for family and friends and they decide to record it. With that in mind, Brian leads the assembled cast through renditions of their favourite songs along with a couple of originals during these four days at Western, with trusty engineer Chuck Britz on hand. The party noises heard on the disc, including chatting and clinking of glasses, will be overdubbed on the 27th.

Carl will tell BBC Radio-1: "We did this album just to give us the time to do our next album. It only took us a few days. I thought it was an odd [one] at the time but we were under pressures from Capitol to deliver another record."

The recordings on the 14th are delayed when the group's assistant, Ron Swallow, forgets the keys to the studio's store closet in which their instruments are stored. Dennis is forced to miss the sessions because he is suffering from bronchitis; Hal Blaine takes over bongo duties.

On the final day, the 23rd, and within two minutes of him dropping into the studio, Dean Torrence of Jan & Dean finds himself singing the lead vocal on the group's cover of The Regents' 1961 hit 'Barbara Ann'. (Dean's singing partner Jan refuses to join in because the duo's label, Liberty Records, has threatened to withhold his royalties if he appears on a Beach Boys recording.) Everyone present realises that the joyous and memorable song will make an appropriate ending for the album.

Torrence tells *Melody Maker*: "I was recording 'You Really Know How To Hurt A Guy' with Jan in the studio next door. I stormed out of the session because I hated it so much. I told Jan I wasn't going to sing on it and I was going along to The Beach Boys session. The session was for the *Beach Boys' Party!* album, and when I got there they were all drunk. They started scratching around for another track and, because I was there, somebody suggested they should do 'Barbara Ann' and I should sing lead. When the album came out, there was my voice quite clearly singing on 'Barbara Ann'." Brian tells *Melody Maker*: "[Dean] was real charming, I guess. I think he charmed Mike Love into letting him sing. They mixed it so Dean's voice was louder than mine."

During the four sessions the group accompanies their singing with just acoustic guitars, bongos (from Hal Blaine) and hand-claps.

Songs recorded and/or jammed include: '**I Should Have Known Better**' (Beatles cover; three takes), '**Ruby Baby**' (Dion hit; six takes), '**Satisfaction**' (Stones cover; three takes), '**Hully Gully**' (Olympics hit; nine takes), '**Blowin' In The Wind**' (Dylan cover; one take), '**Little Deuce Coupe**' (three takes), medley '**I Get Around**' / '**Little Deuce Coupe**' (one take), '**Mountain Of Love**' (Johnny Rivers hit; six takes, including Carl's future brother-in-law Billy Hinsche on harmonica), '**Ticket To Ride**' (Beatles cover; one take), '**Riot In Cell Block Number 9**' (Leiber & Stoller cover; two takes), Bob Dylan Parody 1 ('**Laugh At Me**') (one take), '**One Kiss Led To Another**' (Coasters hit; one take), Bob Dylan Parody 2 ('**She Belongs To Me**' / '**I Got You Babe**') (one take), '**Alley Oop**' (Hollywood Argyles hit; three takes), '**Tell Me Why**' (Beatles cover; two takes), '**You've Got To Hide Your Love Away**' (Beatles cover; three takes), '**California Girls**' (one take), '**Papa-Oom-Mow-Mow**' (one take), '**Devoted To You**' (Everly Brothers hit; six takes), '**There's No Other (Like My Baby)**' (Crystals hit; one take), '**The Times They Are A-Changin'**' (Dylan cover; two takes), '**Heart And Soul**' (Jan & Dean cover; one take), medley '**Heart And Soul**' / '**Long Tall Sally**' (one take), '**Smokey Joe's Cafe**' (Coasters hit; two takes), and '**Barbara Ann**' (one take).

TOUR STARTS North America (Sep 17th-Oct 7th)

■ Friday 17th

Hara Arena *Dayton, OH*
The group, with Bruce in place of Brian, returns to the road to start another brief US tour.

■ Sunday 19th

National Guard Armory *Washington, DC* 8:00pm
Washington-based company Show Biz Productions runs a competition to coincide with the show offering a personal meeting with The Beach Boys as top prize, open only to local Junior High and High School students. *The Evening Star*'s reviewer writes: "To the screams of thousands of fans … the fivesome clowned and sang everything from 'California Girls' to Mike Love's version of 'Monster Mash'. The boys with the surfer sound were mobbed by teenagers who threw questions and pieces of paper at them for autographs during and after the show. Bruce Johnston, formerly of The Rip Chords, substituted for Brian Wilson, and Barbara Twombly of Bethesda won the Honda that was given away at the big show."

■ Thursday 23rd

Coliseum *Fort Wayne, IN*
• There is a further recording session today for the *Party!* album: see September 8th.

■ Friday 24th

Empire Stadium *Vancouver, BC, Canada*

■ Saturday 25th

Memorial Coliseum *Portland, OR*

■ Thursday 26th

Cleveland Stadium *Cleveland, OH*

■ Monday 27th

RECORDING *Party!* **sessions** Western Recorders studio (2) *Hollywood, CA*. Ambient sounds of partygoers chatting and chinking glasses are overdubbed onto the *Party!* album recordings. Then a mix is made of the completed LP with: 'Hully Gully' (lead vocal by

NO TRACKING

Capitol Records
(Employer's name)

Phonograph Recording Contract Blank
AMERICAN FEDERATION OF MUSICIANS
OF THE UNITED STATES AND CANADA

№ 2492
No 195438

Local Union No. 47

THIS CONTRACT for the personal services of musicians, made this **23** day of **September**, 19**65** **7** musicians
between the undersigned employer (hereinafter called the "employer") and _____ (including the leader)
(hereinafter called "employees").

WITNESSETH, That the employer hires the employees as musicians severally on the terms and conditions below, and as further specified on reverse side. The leader represents that the employees already designated have agreed to be bound by said terms and conditions. Each employee yet to be chosen shall be so bound by said terms and conditions upon agreeing to accept his employment. Each employee may enforce this agreement. The employees severally agree to render collectively to the employer services as musicians in the orchestra under the leadership of

Hal Blaine as follows:

Name and Address of Place of Engagement **Western Recorders, 6000 Sunset Blvd, Los Angeles, Calif.**

Date(s) and Hours of Employment **Sept. 23, 1965 9P.M. to 12 Midnite and 12:30 A.M. to 3:30 A.M.**

Type of Engagement: **Recording for phonograph records only.**

WAGE AGREED UPON $ _____ **Union Scale**
(Terms and amount)

Plus pension contributions as specified on reverse side hereof.

This wage includes expenses agreed to be reimbursed by the employer in accordance with the attached schedule, or a schedule to be furnished the employer on or before the date of engagement.

To be paid **Within 14 Days**
(Specify when payments are to be made)

Upon request by the American Federation of Musicians of the United States and Canada (herein called the "Federation") or the local in whose jurisdiction the employees shall perform hereunder, the employer either shall make advance payment hereunder or shall post an appropriate bond.

Employer's name and authorized signature	**Capitol Records, Inc.**
Leader's name	**Hal Blaine**
Local No. **47**
Street address	**1750 N. Vine St.**
Leader's street address	**2441 Castilian Dr.**
Hollywood 28, Calif. **HO26252**	**Hollywood 28, Calif.**
City State Phone	City State

(1) Label Name **Capitol Records, Inc.** Session No. _____

Master No.	No. of Minutes	TITLES OF TUNES	Master No.	No. of Minutes	TITLES OF TUNES
	1:55	"You Got To Hide Your Love Away"		1:10	"Smokey Joe"
	1:40	"Barbara Ann"		1:00	"Fun Tonight"
	2:12	"Times, they Are A-Changin"		40 Sec.	"Heart and Soul"

(2) Employee's Name (As on Social Security Card) Last First Initial	(3) Home Address (Give Street, City and State)	(4) Local Union No.	(5) Social Security Number	(6) Scale Wages	(7) Pension Contribution
(Leader)	2441 Castilian Dr.				
Blaine, Hal	Hollywood 28, Calif.	47	047-20-5900	305.00	24.40
Britz, Charles D.	4501 Wawona St. Los Angeles 65, Calif.	47	567-26-4273	152.50	12.20
Jardine, Alan C. POST OPEN	1212 Elm Ave. Manhattan Beach, Calif.	47	556-54-3708	152.50	12.20
Johnston, Bruce A.	11679 Montana Ave. Los Angeles 49, Calif.	47	573-54-9241	152.50	12.20
Wilson, Brian POST OPEN	1448 N. Laurel Way Beverly Hills, Calif.	47	568-62-7150	152.50	12.20
Wilson, Carl POST OPEN	9171 Wilshire Blvd. Beverly Hills, Calif.	47	568-62-6168	152.50	12.20
Wilson, Dennis POST OPEN	124 W. Hillsdale Inglewood, Calif.	47	562-60-0762	152.50	12.20
NO ARRANGER OR COPYIST THIS SESSION************************************					

(8) Total Pension Contributions (Sum of Column (7)) $ _____
Make check payable in this amount to "AFM & EPW Fund."

FOR FUND USE ONLY:

Date pay't rec'd _____ Amt. paid _____ Date posted _____ By _____

Form B-4 Rev. 4-59

Mike), 'I Should Have Known Better' / 'Tell Me Why' (Carl and Al), 'Papa-Oom-Mow-Mow' (Brian and Mike), 'Mountain Of Love' (Mike), 'You've Got To Hide Your Love Away' (Dennis), 'Devoted To You' (Brian and Mike), 'Alley Oop' (Mike), 'There's No Other (Like My Baby)' (Brian and group), medley 'I Get Around' / 'Little Deuce Coupe' (Mike), 'The Times They Are A-Changin'' (Al), and 'Barbara Ann' (lead vocal by Brian and Dean Torrence).

'Barbara Ann' is edited from the original studio tape to a 2:53 album version, while the single version will run to 2:39. The *Beach Boys' Party!* LP will be released by Capitol in the US on November 8th. With this commitment to Capitol now completed, Brian is free to return to his pet project, experimenting with new musical sounds in the studio for the next proper Beach Boys album.

Cincinnati Gardens *Cincinnati, OH* with Sir Douglas Quintet, Johnny & The Hurricanes, Actions Unlimited; compères WSAI Radio DJs Steve Kirk & Dusty Rhodes

■ Saturday 28th
Minneapolis Auditorium *St Paul, MN*

October

Little Deuce Coupe album released in the UK, a belated issue of the LP that came out in the US two years ago.
'California Girls' single peaks in UK *Record Retailer* chart at 26, in German *Hit Bilanz* chart at 30, and in Swedish chart at 6.
• Brian and Marilyn Wilson move out of their rented apartment in Gardner Street, West Hollywood, and take up residence at their new home at 1448 Laurel Way in an expensive area of Beverly Hills. Shortly after the couple moves in, Brian hires a carpenter to build a wooden box in the dining room. The boxwood construction stands several feet off the ground – some say as much as four feet. Brian places his grand piano in the box and then surrounds it with two feet of sand. With his shoes off and his feet dangling in the sand, Brian will sit happily playing the piano. Business meetings are also carried out in the sandbox.

Marilyn Wilson tells US Radio KHJ: "He wanted a sandbox, so he got a sandbox. He said, 'I want to play in the sand. I want to feel like a little kid. When I'm writing these songs, I want to feel what I'm writing.' We had this really good gardener come up to the house and, in the dining room, this guy built a gorgeous wooden sandbox, about two and a half feet tall. Then they came with a dump truck and dumped eight tons of sand into it.

"One day, our piano tuner walked into the house and said, 'OK, where's the piano?' I was quite busy so I said, 'Oh, it's over there in the sandbox,' thinking nothing about it. He looked at me and said, 'Oh.' All of a sudden, he walked over to the sandbox, sits down, and starts taking off his shoes and socks. That made me howl! He just took them off, like, 'Oh, sand. I've got to take my shoes and socks off to go into the sand.'

"Because there is no sun [in the dining room] the sand was freezing cold and the dog also used it. You know what it's like with dogs and sand. Brian lifted up the hood of the piano and he acted like he was going to have a nervous breakdown. Brian shouted, 'My God, this piano is filled with sand!' and he had to vacuum it out."

■ Friday 1st
Boutwell Auditorium *Birmingham, AL*
The tour continues.
• *The Beach Boys Today!* album certified gold by RIAA in the US.

■ Thursday 7th
Dillon Stadium *Hartford, CT*

■ Wednesday 13th
RECORDING Western Recorders studio *Hollywood, CA* 2:00-6:30pm. Just three weeks after partaking in the largely throwaway sessions for the group's forthcoming *Party!* album, Brian takes charge of a recording session for '**The Little Girl I Once Knew**', easily his most daring and intricate recording to date. He takes a fragmentary approach with the song, clearly demonstrating the progression in his style of writing. Rehearsals are followed by the taping of the song's instrumental track (15 takes required) and the taping of insert vocals by the full Beach Boys line-up follows a lead-vocal overdub by Carl, Brian and Mike. (A further vocal session will be held for 'Little Girl' on October 24th). The three-hour session concludes with the first try at '**Don't Talk (Put Your Head On My Shoulder)**' as Brian attempts eight rehearsal takes. Each subsequent recording features him overdubbing his vocal on to the last to create multiple layers of sound. Work on 'Don't Talk' will begin properly on February 11th 1966.
Musicians present Hal Blaine (drums), Frankie Capp (percussion), Roy Caton (trumpet), Al de Lory (keyboards), Jim Horn (saxophone), Larry Hulley (guitar), Plas Johnson (saxophone), Carol Kaye (bass guitar), Barney Kessel (guitar), Jay Migliori (saxophone), Don Randi (keyboards), Lyle Ritz (upright bass), Howard Roberts (guitar), Billy Strange (guitar).

■ Friday 15th
RECORDING United Recorders studio (A) *Los Angeles, CA* 1:00-4:00pm. With one eye on the ambitious orchestrations he intends for the next Beach Boys album, Brian wants to train himself to work with and arrange a large multi-piece orchestra. Today he moves studios – though only a few feet, as United is next door to his favourite Western – and once more enlists the help of arranger Dick Reynolds and a 43-piece orchestra. (Reynolds and many of the musicians at today's session worked with Brian a year earlier during the recording of the *Christmas* album; see June 18th 1964.)

During the three-hour session under the stewardship of Reynolds, complex instrumental recordings are made of '**Stella By Starlight**', a 1940s movie tune by Ned Washington and Victor Young that became something of a jazz standard, and '**How Deep Is The Ocean**', the Irving Berlin standard that Brian probably grew up hearing by Bing Crosby. Five takes are required for 'Stella' and nine for 'Ocean'. With Brian following every move, Reynolds then overdubs his own lead vocal onto the tracks. After that, Brian takes control and supervises the taping of an instrumental version of '**Three Blind Mice**'. These experimental recordings will remain unreleased.
Musicians present Robert Barene (violin), Arnold Belnick (violin), Harry Bluestone (violin), George Callender (tuba), Frankie Capp (drums), Gene Cipriano (saxophone), Eugene DiNovi (piano), David Duke (French horn), Jesse Ehrlich (cello), Virgil Evans (trumpet), Jim Getzoff (violin), Billy Green (saxophone), Urban Green (trombone), Clifford Hils (upright bass), Dayton Howe (percussion), Robert Jung (saxophone), Armand Kaproff (cello), Ray Kelley (cello), Bernard Kundell (violin), William Kurasch (violin), Henry Laubach (trumpet), Alfred Lustgarten (violin), Arthur Maebe (French horn), Lew McCreary (trombone), Oliver Mitchell (trumpet), Richard Nash (trombone), Richard Perissi (French horn), Al Porcino (trumpet), Lou Raderman (violin), Dorothy Remsen (harp), Karl Rossner (cello), Henry Roth (violin), Joseph Saxon (cello), Wilbur Schwartz (saxophone), Frederick Seykora (cello), Paul

'AFM sheet' marking the final session for the unplugged *Party!* album at Western studio, Hollywood, on September 23rd.

Shure (violin), Marshall Sossen (violin), Darrel Terwilliger (violin), Al Viola (guitar)

• Fulfilled and invigorated by the session, Brian feels confident enough to apply what he has learned today to the next Beach Boys album and within days of this session begins composing songs. Up to now his musical inspirations have come mostly from sun, cars, girls and the sea. But this time it will come from above.

Brian will tell radio station KXOJ in 1977: "Carl and I used to hold a series of prayer sessions for the world. I got into marijuana and it opened some doors for me and I got a little more committed to music than I had done before, more committed to the making of music for people on a spiritual level. Carl and I both prayed and I said, 'Let's pray. Let's pray for people. Let's pray for Jesus Christ.' Then Carl said, 'What if we make an album after these prayer sessions, an album for people? A special album.' I said, 'That's a good idea.'

"So I went into the living room, sat at my piano, started playing around," Brian continues, "and right away, without even flinching, I started coming up with ideas, creative ideas. It was a total surprise. I thought it was going to take weeks before I got something going that was on a par with the prayer sessions that Carl and I had. I sat up in the house for five months, planning every stage of our next album. I didn't mind people being around because there were visitors up there most of the time, so long as there weren't too many and provided I could cop out and sit, thinking. I had a big Spanish table and I sat there hour after hour making the tunes inside my head …. I was taking a lot of drugs, fooling around with pills, a lot of pills, and it fouled me up for a while. It got me really introspective."

■ Wednesday 20th

The Beach Boys record new backing tracks for the songs they are to be seen performing two days later on *The Andy Williams Show*. Since these are new recordings, probably without vocals, they will give the impression that the group is performing live.

■ Friday 22nd

TV NBC Television, Color City Studios *Burbank, CA*. NBC *The Andy Williams Show* live vocal over new backing tracks 'Help Me Rhonda', 'Their Hearts Were Full Of Spring', 'Little Honda', broadcast in colour NBC May 2nd 1966, 9:00-10:00pm, BBC-2 (UK) August 11th 1967, 9:05-9:55pm. On the eve of yet another US concert tour and a new Capitol album, the group – here including Brian but without Bruce – tape an appearance on this top-rated weekly NBC music and variety show hosted by the king of easy listening. Following their introduction by Williams set against 'California Girls', The Beach Boys perform 'Help Me Rhonda', an a cappella version of 'Their Hearts Were Full Of Spring' and, along with Williams, 'Little Honda' (which due to fears of TV advertisers is sung as "little cycle"). Live vocals are sung over new backing tracks recorded on the 20th, with Carl's guitar the only live instrument on the show. Mike introduces each member of the band to Williams between the first two songs.

■ Saturday 23rd

TV NBC Television, Color City Studios *Burbank, CA*. NBC *Jack Benny Hour* live vocal over existing backing track 'California Girls', live performance 'Barbara Ann', broadcast in colour November 3rd, 9:00-10:00pm. The group's second television appearance in as many days, again with Brian, is part of an hour-long show. Following a live-vocal performance of 'California Girls' the group takes part in a humorous sketch with comedian Bob Hope and host Jack Benny who pose as long-haired surfers struggling to understand surfing slang such as 'hang ten' and 'catch a tip'. During the skit, which is

concluded with a brief, reprised live-vocal version of 'California Girls', Brian describes the pair as "senior citizen drop-outs". Later in the show, which is videotaped this afternoon in front of a studio audience, the group return to their regular candy-stripe shirts and perform 'Barbara Ann'. Also on the show are actress Elke Sommer and world-famous animator Walt Disney. (This is Jack Benny's first TV special since the demise of his regular, long-running series; in order to appeal to younger viewers Benny himself has booked The Beach Boys.)

■ Sunday 24th

RECORDING Western Recorders studio (3) *Hollywood, CA*. Today sees a vocal overdub session as the group returns to **'The Little Girl I Once Knew'**, with Chuck Britz engineering. Mono mix-downs are made, and production work on this song is probably completed now.

November

RECORDING Western Recorders studio *Hollywood, CA*. This month Brian continues his explorations in the recording studio and tapes the vocal group The Honeys singing a version of the old nursery rhyme **'Row Row Row Your Boat'**. Several attempts are made, each vocal overdubbed onto the previous take, building on the idea he'd tried for the experimental recording of 'Don't Talk (Put Your Head On My Shoulder)' on October 13th. Although very low-key and relatively simple, the result of this technique today is an effectively lavish layer of recorded vocal harmonies. The experiment will remain unreleased.

After that, Brian's experimentation continues with his first foray into recordings focusing on humour and laughter. He tapes a bizarre piece entitled **'Dick'** that features a girl, Carol, asking, "What's long and thin and covered in skin and heaven knows how many holes it's been in?" Brian replies, "Dick?" "No," she responds. "What?" Brian enquires. "A worm," she replies. Laughter fills the studio but Brian insists that the laughter doesn't have to be that hard.

Just as with his music, Brian insists on perfection for 'Dick' and has The Honeys improve their laughter. Six further attempts are made by Carol to tell the joke. A rehearsal for the laughing responses follows. Then the group moves to the next joke. This one is entitled **'Fuzz'**. Again, Carol is the joker. "What's black and white and has fuzz inside?" she asks. "Erm," Brian puzzles, "I don't know. A lorry?" Carol replies with the punchline, "A police car." The bizarre recording continues as Carol says to Brian, "Do you have haemorrhoids?" He replies, "No." She responds, "Well, let me shake your hand." Brian asks, "Why?" Carol replies, "It's really great knowing a perfect asshole."

The unusual session rolls on. Brian tells the girls, "Quit laughing at me! It isn't very nice. Now stop it." His requests are met with more inane laughing. "I said quit it," Brian insists, before asking, "What's funny? Is it because one of my ears is bigger than the other one?" His remark is greeted with more hysterical laughter. "Hey, really, this is really the rudest thing I've ever seen. Cut it out. I'm going home, OK? I'm gonna stay. Now don't do that again." A playback of the recording follows. Brian's idea for a comedy album will see him taping a few more such sessions over the next two years, all of which will remain unreleased, including today's.

■ Monday 1st

RECORDING Western Recorders studio *Hollywood, CA*. As part of the continuing build-up to the recordings for the next Beach Boys album, Brian produces tracking tapes for a piece called **'Trombone Dixie'** (11 takes required), which will remain unreleased until the 1990 CD of *Pet Sounds*, and **'In My Childhood'**, which will be started properly on January 24th 1966 and later re-titled 'You Still Believe In Me' for inclusion on *Pet Sounds*.

Musicians present Hal Blaine (drums), Roy Caton (trumpet), Jerry Cole (guitar), Steve Douglas (saxophone), James Henderson (trombone), Carol Kaye (bass guitar), Barney Kessel (guitar), Lew McCreary (trombone), Jay Migliori (saxophone), Don Randi (piano), Lyle Ritz (upright bass), Billy Strange (guitar), Julius Wechter (percussion, Latin percussion, vibes), Jerry Williams (percussion).

■ Monday 8th

(Recorded "Live" At A) Beach Boys' Party! album released in the US. With a huge sigh of relief, and with an eye on the lucrative Christmas market, Capitol Records issues this new stopgap Beach Boys LP, recorded in just a handful of days.

The group's third new album of the year is released with 15 full-colour wallet-sized photographs inside, and will reach number 6 in US charts.

The songs – "Recorded live at a Beach Boys party" – include many covers such as 'I Should Have Known Better' from The Beatles' *Hard Day's Night* film and Carl's favourite by the group. Further Beatles songs include 'Tell Me Why', another from *A Hard Day's Night*, and 'You've Got To Hide Your Love Away' from their most recent film, *Help!*. Also included on the new record is a version of Bob Dylan's 'The Times They Are A Changin'' which gets the full Beach Boys 'unplugged' treatment.

■ Sunday 14th

Madison Square Garden *New York, NY* 8:00pm, with Carroll Baker, Carol Bruce, Red Buttons, Johnny Carson, Joan Crawford, Robert Culp, Sammy Davis Jr, Henry Fonda, Peter Falk, Eydie Gorme,

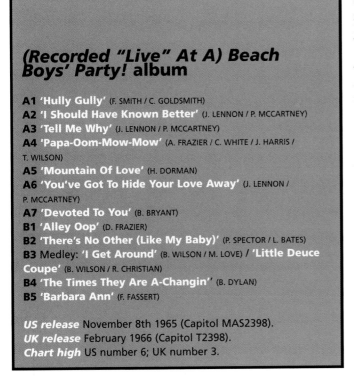

(Recorded "Live" At A) Beach Boys' Party! album

A1 'Hully Gully' (F. SMITH / C. GOLDSMITH)
A2 'I Should Have Known Better' (J. LENNON / P. MCCARTNEY)
A3 'Tell Me Why' (J. LENNON / P. MCCARTNEY)
A4 'Papa-Oom-Mow-Mow' (A. FRAZIER / C. WHITE / J. HARRIS / T. WILSON)
A5 'Mountain Of Love' (H. DORMAN)
A6 'You've Got To Hide Your Love Away' (J. LENNON / P. MCCARTNEY)
A7 'Devoted To You' (B. BRYANT)
B1 'Alley Oop' (D. FRAZIER)
B2 'There's No Other (Like My Baby)' (P. SPECTOR / L. BATES)
B3 Medley: **'I Get Around'** (B. WILSON / M. LOVE) / **'Little Deuce Coupe'** (B. WILSON / R. CHRISTIAN)
B4 'The Times They Are A-Changin'' (B. DYLAN)
B5 'Barbara Ann' (F. FASSERT)

US release November 8th 1965 (Capitol MAS2398).
UK release February 1966 (Capitol T2398).
Chart high US number 6; UK number 3.

Barry Gray, Skitch Henderson, The Hullabaloo Singers & Dancers, Alan King, Frankie Laine, Steve Lawrence, Joe E. Lewis, Shari Lewis, Anthony Newley, Blanche Thebom, Eleanor Steber, Ed Sullivan, The Supremes, Robert Vaughan, Bobby Vinton, William B. Williams, and others; tickets $5 - $100

For one night only The Beach Boys are joined on stage by a dazzling array of the biggest stars from Broadway, Hollywood, television and recording for a swinging *USO A Go Go!* concert. Proceeds from the all-star event help pay for sending entertainment to the US armed services around the world.

■ Monday 15th

Surfin' USA and *Surfer Girl* albums are certified as gold records by the RIAA in the US.

■ Wednesday 17th

RECORDING Western Recorders studio *Hollywood, CA* 2:00-6:00pm. Amid a flurry of new ideas and production techniques, Brian continues with his fresh batch of experimental recordings by taping an instrumental, the James Bond-inspired piece **'Run James Run'** (take 3 marked as best). It will later be re-titled 'Pet Sounds' (see March 3rd 1966) and become the title track of the next album. As usual, Brian begins the session with no written music or sketches, simply working from the ideas inside his head. Two empty Coca-Cola cans are used to achieve the percussion effects on the track. Work continues with the taping of two insert instrumental pieces for the song, ably supported by members of the so-called Wrecking Crew team of LA session players. A mono mix of the piece completes the session.

Carl, Al and Bruce feel that they can reach the required standards demanded by Brian in the studio, but the hyperactive Dennis is not concerned with such detail. The strict discipline of lengthy recording sessions does not fit with his rebellious lifestyle.

Musicians present Roy Caton (trumpet), Jerry Cole (guitar), Ritchie Frost (drums), Billy Green (tenor saxophone, percussion), Jim Horn (tenor saxophone), Plas Johnson (saxophone), Carol Kaye (bass guitar), Jay Migliori (baritone saxophone), Lyle Ritz (upright bass), Billy Strange (guitar), Tommy Tedesco (acoustic guitar), Brian Wilson (piano).

TOUR STARTS 3rd Annual US Thanksgiving Tour (Nov 18th-Dec 4th). Earlier Thanksgiving concerts had been individual dates rather than tours; nonetheless the group name this their third such 'tour'.

■ Thursday 18th

Mayo Civic Center *Rochester, MN*

This is the opening concert of the ten-day Thanksgiving jaunt and it 'grosses' $8,350, an industry term for the total amount received by the venue for ticket sales. Bruce is again playing on-stage in the live band to replace Brian.

■ Friday 19th

Guthrie Theater *Minneapolis, MN*

Tonight's show grosses $21,750, of which the group typically receives 60 percent.

■ Saturday 20th

Municipal Auditorium *Kansas City, MO* 8:30pm, with The Gentrys, The Strangeloves; compères: WHB Radio DJs Ron Martin and John Dolan

The performance grosses $22,250.

■ Sunday 21st

Kiel Opera House *St Louis, MO* 7:30pm
Tonight's concert grosses $13,000.

■ Tuesday 23rd

University Of Massachusetts *Amherst, MA*
The Beach Boys' first college performance on the East Coast is for a special *JFK Memorial Concert* with profits from the show helping to fund a JFK Room at the University.

The following morning the University's program advisor, Mary Hudzikiewicz, drafts a letter to Steve Leber at the group's booking agent, the William Morris Agency in New York. "Last night we had one of the best concerts this campus has ever seen," Hudzikiewicz writes. "The reception that was given to The Beach Boys by the 4,000 students in attendance was gratifying to all concerned. ... There was no hysterical screaming, mobbing or unruliness, which would have distracted from the performance. The boys seemed to feel that it was one of their better performances and I know that the students realised it also. The entire evening was a tremendous success and I feel that it was due mainly to the fact that we restricted sales as much as possible to college students with identification cards. ... Again, I want to emphasise just how pleased we were with the show."

■ Wednesday 24th

Rhode Island Auditorium *Providence, RI*

■ Friday 26th

Boston Garden *Boston, MA*

■ Saturday 27th

'The Little Girl I Once Knew' / 'There's No Other (Like My Baby)' single released in the US. Capitol issues the 45 to tie in with the new *Party!* album, drawing the B-side from that record, although the A-side is the first public sign of Brian's 'new' music. The single performs disappointingly in the US, peaking only at number 20, possibly because of a distinct lack of radio airplay: the A-side includes an unconventional and commercially suicidal few seconds of dead air.

Brian is depressed by the lack of success for 'Little Girl', his first daringly different recording. In turn, the other Beach Boys are concerned that Brian is getting too experimental. In truth, Brian's period of experimentation is only just beginning.
Beach Boys' Party! album hits the US charts.

■ Sunday 28th

Quimby Auditorium *Fort Wayne, IN*
Last night of the tour.

The Little Girl I Once Knew single

A 'The Little Girl I Once Knew' (B. WILSON)
B 'There's No Other (Like My Baby)' (P. SPECTOR / L. BATES)

US release November 27th 1965 (Capitol 5540).
UK release December 1965 (Capitol CL 15425).
Chart high US number 20; UK none.

December

'The Little Girl I Once Knew' / 'There's No Other (Like My Baby)' single released in the UK.
• 'The Little Girl I Once Knew' single peaks in Canadian *RPM* chart at number 10.

■ Saturday 4th

Civic Auditorium *Albuquerque, NM* 8:30pm, with Lindy & The Lavells, The Viscounts, The Defiants

■ Monday 6th

The Beatles' *Rubber Soul* album is released in the US by Capitol Records, and becomes a further creative stimulus for Brian. He recalls hearing the US version of the album this month. "I was sitting around a table with some friends when we heard the disc for the first time. I smoked a joint and then I listened to it. It blew me fucking out. The album blew my mind because it was a whole album with all good stuff. It was definitely a challenge for me. I saw that every cut was very artistically interesting and stimulating.

"I suddenly realised that the recording industry was getting so free and intelligent. We could go into new things – string quartets, auto-harps, and instruments from another culture. I decided right then: I'm gonna try that, where a whole album becomes a gas. I'm gonna make the greatest rock'n'roll album ever made!

"So I went to the piano thinking goddamn, I feel competitive now. So I immediately went to work on the songs for *Pet Sounds*. I said, 'Come on. We gotta beat The Beatles.' That was the spirit I had, you know? Carl and I had another prayer session and we prayed for an album that would be better than *Rubber Soul*. It was a prayer but there was also some ego there. We intertwined prayer with a competitive spirit. It worked, and the next album happened immediately. I called in a collaborator named Tony Asher and we spent two months working on and off together. He proved to have the lyrical ability to work with me."

Intent on trying something different, Brian contacts Asher (born May 2nd 1938 in London, England), at present an advertising copywriter and jingle writer for the LA-based Carson Roberts ad agency. Their mutual friend Loren Schwartz has suggested Asher to Brian. Brian is interested in Asher supplying lyrics, and so the writer immediately takes a three-week break from his job and spends time with Brian discussing and putting together songs for the next Beach Boys album. Asher later tells *US Today*: "When Brian and I first got together to write, he played the *Rubber Soul* album to me and said, 'I wanna do something that is better than this album,' which was an incredible challenge. But that's what we set out to do."

During their first working day together, Brian plays Asher the tracking tape of 'Sloop John B' recorded July 12th as well as the piece with the working title 'In My Childhood' tracked on November 1st. On most days that they work together, and before writing anything, Brian and Asher will have long, meaningful conversations about life and love, about affairs and relationships they've had. They soon discover that they have shared similar experiences. Once work starts, Brian will tape their flourishing musical ideas and, at the end of every daily session, Asher will take the recordings home, where he will add new lyrics and verses for Brian to hear the following day. "For the most part," says Asher, "all I ever heard was Brian playing, in a very simple way, tunes on a piano. I knew that he heard a lot of things in his head that I had no idea of, and when I heard what he came up with I was just blown away." Brian too will remember the process well in a later Capitol interview. "When I had thought out a theme, I would go to the piano and sit playing feels, rhythm patterns and fragments of ideas. Then the song would start to blossom and become a real thing, and all the while, in the back of my mind, I would think about the limitations and capabilities of the group."

Marilyn Wilson says she remembers Brian's enthusiasm for what will become *Pet Sounds*. "He told me one night, 'Marilyn, I'm gonna make the greatest album, the greatest rock album ever,' and he meant it. He would sit for hours at his piano in the sandbox."

■ Saturday 11th

'The Little Girl I Once Knew' single enters US *Billboard* Top 40 chart at number 32.

■ Monday 20th

'**Barbara Ann**' / '**Girl Don't Tell Me**' single released in the US. In an effort to offset the less than spectacular chart performance of 'The Little Girl I Once Knew', Capitol – apparently without the group's knowledge – quickly edits 'Barbara Ann' to 2:05 from the 2:53 *Party!* version and releases it as a single. It will reach number 2 in the US chart by January 1966, sitting behind The Beatles' 'We Can Work It Out'. In the UK 'Barbara Ann' will become a smash hit, peaking at number 2 in March 1966 amid the group's rapidly rising popularity there.

Brian insists that 'Barbara Ann' isn't a 'produced' record and doesn't represent his developing music. "We were just goofing around for a party type album. Somebody in Boston started playing ['Barbara Ann' and] started it all off. So Capitol had to put it out as a single. But that's not The Beach Boys. It's not where we're at, at all. Personally, I think the group has evolved another 800 percent in the last year. We have a more conscious, arty production now that's more polished. It's all been like an explosion for us."

The success of such an off-the-cuff cover bewilders Brian and the group. Naturally, Capitol wants more of the same. But Brian doesn't have time to consider the demands of the label or the reasons why 'Barbara Ann' is doing so well in the charts. His mind is firmly on course for creating the most important album of his career.

■ Wednesday 22nd

RECORDING Western Recorders studio *Hollywood, CA*. Following his recent preview of the tracking tapes for Tony Asher, Brian returns to the recording of '**Sloop John B**' and devises for the piece a lavish landscape of vocal arrangements. Today, using the instrumental track recorded on July 12th, Brian and Mike record their first vocal overdubs. As Brian attempts to record his solo vocal overdub, he still includes the line, "This is the worst trip since I've been born." The day ends with the recording of five instrumental

---

Barbara Ann single

A 'Barbara Ann' (F. FASSERT)
B 'Girl Don't Tell Me' (B. WILSON)

US release December 20th 1965 (Capitol 5561).
UK release February 1966 (Capitol CL 15432).
Chart high US number 2; UK number 3.

---

insert pieces for the song, ably provided by members of the so-called Wrecking Crew.

■ Wednesday 29th

RECORDING Western Recorders studio *Hollywood, CA*. Brian supervises the second vocal overdubbing session for '**Sloop John B**', including a lead vocal by Carl and a dual lead vocal by Carl and Dennis, later scrapped in favour of the released Brian-and-Mike lead. Four vocal overdubbing sessions are also completed during the day by the full Beach Boys line-up. Later, with today's session satisfactorily completed, the group travels to San Carlos for tonight's concert performance.

Session musician Billy Strange is present at Western to overdub an electric 12-string guitar onto 'Sloop John B'. Because he doesn't own a guitar of this type, a Fender instrument and suitable Fender amplifier are acquired from Wallichs Music City store. (The store is located on the northwest corner of Sunset And Vine in Los Angeles and is owned by Glenn Wallichs, one of the founder members of Capitol Records.) Strange manages to record his guitar part in one take. For his time, Brian pays the guitarist $500 in cash and gives him the instrument and amp as a present.

Circle Star Theater *San Carlos, CA* 8:30pm, with Mitch Ryder & The Detroit Wheels, Jackie Lee & The T Bones
After the 'Sloop John B' vocal session in Los Angeles, the group – as usual now without Brian – travels to San Carlos for this concert.

■ Thursday 30th

Oakland Auditorium *Oakland, CA* 8:00pm, with The Turtles
After the show the group boards a plane bound for Washington state where, on Friday morning, they check into their Hilton Inn hotel rooms in Tacoma and later face a press conference.

■ Friday 31st

UPS Field House *Tacoma, WA* 8:00pm, with Gary Lewis & The Playboys, The Yardbirds, The Beau Brummels, Vejtables, Alexys, The Mojo Men
This *1966 New Year's Eve Teen Spectacular* attracts a sell-out crowd of 4,500. Bruce tells *Record Mirror*: "I liked The Yardbirds. I was talking to Jeff Beck and we got on very well. ... Their amplifiers had blown up so we lent them our equipment. Dennis plays drums, so he doesn't understand about amps, and Mike just sings, so he doesn't understand what's going on with amps either. So Jeff turns his guitar towards the amps to get some feedback and both Dennis and Mike were going to pull the plugs out! They thought The Yardbirds were harming our equipment! I had to stop them and explain what was happening. They were getting really mad."

Reviewing tonight's show, the *Tacoma News Tribune*'s reporter writes: "For nearly four hours the Field House rocked with straining amplifiers and screaming voices. The big sounds continued until three minutes past midnight. That's when about 50 youngsters charged the stage and the performance came abruptly to a halt. The Beach Boys were rocking out at the time but they quickly lost their professional composure and leaped off the stage as if they were bailing out of a diving airplane. Tacoma police quickly controlled the melee and only about a half dozen youths managed to scramble onto the stage." Bruce adds: "At the end, they all got up and pushed the stage. I thought it was all over for me! We got out of there fast. It was really frightening."

• As the year closes, The Beach Boys are unaware that their remarkable run of success is about to reach its apex. Nineteen-sixty-six will turn out to be the group's finest and most successful year. Their dreams of worldwide success are soon to be fulfilled.

1966

The group makes their first tour of Japan ... meanwhile in California, Brian officially starts work in the studio with the regular session team for the new album, which becomes *Pet Sounds* ... between tours and one-off dates the rest of the group gathers for vocal recordings ... sessions begin for 'Good Vibrations' ... 'Caroline No' single released, credited to Brian Wilson .. 'Sloop John B' single and *Pet Sounds* album released ... Brian begins writing songs with Van Dyke Parks, and sessions start to record their 'Heroes And Villains' ... 'Good Vibrations' sessions continue ... *Best Of* album released less than two months after *Pet Sounds* ... sessions begin for a new album, *Smile*, which Capitol schedules for Christmas release ... 'Good Vibrations' is at last completed and released, and goes to number 1 ... plans begin to create group's own Brother Records ... the touring band plays in Europe as 'Heroes & Villains' and *Smile* sessions continue in California ... the group expresses unease with Brian's musical direction and he becomes uncertain about the *Smile* album; Capitol postpones its release until next year.

Brian pictured at home in Los Angeles while his bandmates are out on the road

1966

January

■ Saturday 1st
The Coliseum *Seattle, WA* 8:30pm, with Gary Lewis & The Playboys, The Yardbirds, The Beau Brummels, Vejtables, Alexys, The Mojo Men

Nineteen-sixty-six opens with this second of two New Year spectaculars promoted by Pat O'Day and Dick Curtis; yesterday's concert was in Tacoma. Today's show, featuring the same support acts, is performed on The Coliseum's revolving stage. Afterwards, the touring Beach Boys band boards a plane and returns home to California where they begin preparations for their next big tour, a visit to the Far East. Three days later, on the 4th, the group boards a plane at San Francisco's International Airport for the 15-hour flight to Japan.
• *Beach Boys' Party!* album peaks in US *Billboard* chart at number 6.
• 'The Little Girl I Once Knew' single peaks in US *Billboard* chart at number 20.
• Capitol Records Tower, Hollywood, California

■ Monday 3rd
Voyle Gilmore, vice president and A&R man at Capitol Records, presents The Beach Boys with three gold records for LPs that topped the $1million sales mark in November 1965. Gilmore makes the presentation at a special ceremony in the company's Capitol Tower HQ in Hollywood. The albums qualifying are *Surfer Girl*, *Surfin' USA*, and *The Beach Boys Today!*.

■ Thursday 6th
Newly arrived in Japan, the group attends a reception organised by Toshiba Records at the Magnolia Rooms of Tokyo's Prince Hotel.

TOUR STARTS Japan (Jan 7th-23rd)

■ Friday 7th
Shibuya Koukaido (public hall) *Tokyo, Japan*
The opening night of the group's first Japanese tour. At the conclusion of the performance each member of The Beach Boys is presented with a bouquet of flowers by a woman attired in national dress.
Set-list 'Fun Fun Fun', 'Hawaii', 'Surfin' USA', 'Surfer Girl', 'Little Honda', 'Papa-Oom-Mow-Mow', 'Monster Mash', 'Let's Go Trippin'', 'You've Got To Hide Your Love Away', 'Little Deuce Coupe', 'Shut Down', 'Barbara Ann', 'California Girls', 'I Get Around', 'Johnny B. Goode'.

■ Saturday 8th
Nagoya-shi Koukaido *Nagoya, Japan*

■ Sunday 9th
Osaka Sankei Hall *Osaka, Japan*

■ Monday 10th
Kyoto Kaikan Hall *Kyoto, Japan*
Before the show the group is given a guided tour of Kyoto's famous Samurai Studios. Later, they are outfitted in traditional Samurai costumes – and four photographs taken now will grace the rear of their next studio album.

■ Wednesday 12th
Kobe Kokusai Kaikan *Kobe, Japan*

■ Thursday 13th
Osaka Sankei Hall *Osaka, Japan*

■ Friday 14th
Fukuoka Kyuden Taikukan *Fukuoka, Japan*

■ Saturday 15th
Otemachi Sankei Hall *Tokyo, Japan*
• 'Barbara Ann' single enters US *Billboard* Top 40 chart at number 31.

■ Sunday 16th
Shinjuku Kousei Nenkin Hall *Tokyo, Japan*

■ Tuesday 18th
RECORDING *Pet Sounds* **session 1** Western Recorders studio (3) *Hollywood, CA* 9:30am-12:30pm. Back in California, Brian returns to the recording studios for the first time since the Christmas and new-year holidays, with today the official start date of sessions for The Beach Boys' next album. Recordings for *Pet Sounds* will span 27 sessions over four months using facilities at Western, Gold Star, Sunset Sound and Columbia studios. However, some work has already been done: instrumentation for 'Sloop John B' was cut back in July 1965 and vocals in December, and 'In My Childhood' – to be renamed 'You Still Believe In Me' after input from Tony Asher – was tracked in November 1965, along with an instrumental that will become the title track of *Pet Sounds*.

Brian will record the *Pet Sounds* instrumentation on a 3-track or 4-track tape machine, usually a Scully model 280 4-track, as he did for the *Summer Days…* album. (The terms 3-track, 4-track etc refer to a tape machine that will record three, four or more individual sound tracks onto tape.) "Most of the songs are cut with everyone playing live in a single take," says Mark Linett, who becomes Brian's engineer in the 1980s. "Usually drums, percussion, keyboards and so on are recorded on tape track one; horns on track two; and bass, additional percussion and occasional guitar on track three. When available, the fourth tape track is used for a rough mono reference mix of the other three tracks, for playback at the end of each session." This fourth-track reference mix will then be erased as additional instrumentation, usually strings, is added.

Soon after the initial recording, the instrumentation is mixed in mono to one track of another 4-track machine, or to an 8-track at Columbia studio in Los Angeles. "So by the time Brian comes to overdub his and/or the group's vocals," says Linett, "he already has the song's backing tracks 'locked' into mono, the sound medium favoured by his musical inspiration, Phil Spector."

(A stereo mix of *Pet Sounds* is not even considered now because for artistic reasons Brian wants the album to come out only in mono – and technically these recording methods do not allow for a stereo mix anyway. Later in 1966, however, Capitol Records will release the album in 'duophonic', an electronic process that simulates stereo. It will not be until 1996 that Linett will synchronise all of the original studio recordings to create the first true stereo mix of the album for inclusion in the *Pet Sounds Sessions* boxed set.)

Before recording begins today, Brian spends time with each of the 12 session musicians present and explains exactly what he requires. This is the first time he has brought thoroughly worked-out songs to a session, and he comes ready with prepared chord patterns and melody lines. During the three-and-a-half-hour session, work focuses on the basic instrumental tracks for **'Let's Go Away For Awhile'** (noted for now as 'Untitled Ballad'; take 18 marked as master). The song becomes Brian's tribute to Burt Bacharach, the

A historic 'AFM sheet' logging on January 18th the first official recording session for a new album, which becomes *Pet Sounds*. The 'Untitled Ballad' noted here will soon be given its real title, 'Let's Go Away For Awhile'.

Phonograph Recording Contract Blank
AMERICAN FEDERATION OF MUSICIANS
OF THE UNITED STATES AND CANADA

Local Union No. **47**

THIS CONTRACT for the personal services of musicians, made this **18th** day of **January**, 19 **66**,

between the undersigned employer (hereinafter called the "employer") and ___ **13** ___ musicians
(hereinafter called "employees"). (including the leader)

WITNESSETH, That the employer hires the employees as musicians severally on the terms and conditions below, and as further specified on reverse side. The leader represents that the employees already designated have agreed to be bound by said terms and conditions. Each employee yet to be chosen shall be so bound by said terms and conditions upon agreeing to accept his employment. Each employee may enforce this agreement. The employees severally agree to render collectively to the employer services as musicians in the orchestra under the leadership of **Steve Douglas Kreisman (Beach Boys)** as follows:

Name and Address of Place of Engagement **Western Recorders**
6000 Sunset Blvd.

Date(s) and Hours of Employment **January 18, 1966   9:30 A.M. to 12:30 P.M.**

Type of Engagement: **Recording for phonograph records only**

WAGE AGREED UPON $ **union scale (including 1 track)**   Plus pension contributions as specified on reverse side hereof.
(Terms and amount)

This wage includes expenses agreed to be reimbursed by the employer in accordance with the attached schedule, or a schedule to be furnished the employer on or before the date of engagement.

To be paid **within 15 days**
(Specify when payments are to be made)

Upon request by the American Federation of Musicians of the United States and Canada (herein called the "Federation") or the local in whose jurisdiction the employees shall perform hereunder, the employer either shall make advance payment hereunder or shall post an appropriate bond.

Employer's name and authorized signature	Capitol Records, Inc.	Leader's name	Steve Douglas Kreisman	Local No. 47
	Paul A. Emerson	Leader's signature	*St. Dyk /612*	
Street address	1750 North Vine Street	Street address	6950 Chisholm Avenue	
	Hollywood, California		Van Nuys, California	
	City State Phone		City State	

(1) Label name ___   Session no. ___

Master no.	No. of minutes	TITLES OF TUNES	Master no.	No. of minutes	TITLES OF TUNES
		Untitled Ballad			

CONTRACT RECEIVED

(2) Employee's name (As on Social Security card) Last / First / Initial	(3) Home address (Give street, city and state)	(4) Local Union No.	(5) Social Security number	(6) Scale wages	(7) Pension contribution
Kreisman, Steve D. (Leader)	6950 Chisholm Avenue Van Nuys, Calif.	47	556-46-1005	162.68	13.02
Britz, Charles D. (Contractor)	4501 Wawona Street Los Angeles 65, Calif.	47	567-26-4273	162.68	13.02
Kessel, Barney	1727 Las Flores Dr. Glendale 7, Calif.	47	447-12-3334	81.34	6.51
Migliori, Jay	1701 No. Lincoln Burbank, Calif.	47	208-24-6118	81.34	6.51
Horn, James R.	3225 Oakshire Drive Hollywood 28, Calif.	47	570-56-6753	81.34	6.51
Johnson, Plas	4120 West 59th Street Los Angeles, Calif. 90043	47	434-44-2284	81.34	6.51
Kaye, Carol	4905 Forman North Hollywood, Calif.	47	555-46-5389	81.34	6.51
Blaine, Hal	2441 Castilian Dr. Hollywood, 28, Calif.	47	047-20-5900	81.34	6.51
deLory, Alfred V.	5524 Ruthwood Calabasas, Calif.	47	559-36-9796	81.34	6.51
Ritz, Lyle	1971 No. Curson Ave. Los Angeles 46, Calif.	47	549-38-1490	81.34	6.51
Caton, Roy V.	3760 Willowcrest Ave. No. Hollywood, Calif.	47	192-20-7730	81.34	6.51
Casey, Alvin W.	6355 Primrose Ave. Hollywood, Calif.	47	526-46-9373	81.34	6.51
Wechter, Julius DOUBLE -Tymps - Vibes	12247 Hesby No. Hollywood, Calif.	47	557-40-3644	93.54	7.48

(8) Total Pension Contributions (Sum of Column (7)) $ ___
Make check payable in this amount to "AFM & EPW Fund"

FOR FUND USE ONLY:
Date pay't rec'd ___ Amt. paid ___ Date posted ___ By ___
Form B-4 Rev. 4-59

Phonograph Recording Contract Blank
AMERICAN FEDERATION OF MUSICIANS
OF THE UNITED STATES AND CANADA

Local Union No. **47**

N⁰ **195427**

1 0198

THIS CONTRACT for the personal services of musicians, made this **22** day of **January**, 19 **66**
between the undersigned employer (hereinafter called the "employer") and **16** musicians
(hereinafter called "employees").
WITNESSETH, That the employer hires the employees as musicians severally on the terms and conditions below, **and as further specified on** reverse side. The leader represents that the employees already designated have agreed to be bound by said terms and conditions. Each employee yet to be chosen shall be so bound by said terms and conditions upon agreeing to accept his employment. Each employee may enforce this agreement. The employees severally agree to render collectively to the employer services as musicians in the orchestra under the leadership of

Hal Blaine   as follows:

Name and Address of Place of Engagement **Gold Star Recorders, 6252 Santa Monica Blvd. Los Angeles, Calif.**

Date(s) and Hours of Employment **January 22, 1966 7: P.M. to 11:30 P.M.**

Type of Engagement: **Recording for phonograph records only.**
WAGE AGREED UPON $ **Union Scale**   Plus pension contributions as specified on reverse side hereof.
(Terms and amount)
This wage includes expenses agreed to be reimbursed by the employer in accordance with the attached schedule, or a schedule to be furnished the employer on or before the date of engagement.
To be paid **Within 14 Days**
(Specify when payments are to be made)
Upon request by the American Federation of Musicians of the United States and Canada (herein called the "Federation") or the local in whose jurisdiction the employees shall perform hereunder, the employer either shall make advance payment hereunder or shall post an appropriate bond.

Employer's name and **Capitol Records, Inc.**

authorized signature _____

Street address **1750 N. Vine St.**

Hollywood 28, Calif.   HO-26252
City   State   Phone

Leader's name **Hal Blaine**   Local No. **47**

Leader's signature _Hal Blaine_

Street address **2441 Castilian Dr.**

Hollywood 28, Calif.
City   State

(1) Label Name **Capitol Records, Inc.**   Session No. _____

Master No.	No. of Minutes	TITLES OF TUNES	Master No.	No. of Minutes	TITLES OF TUNES
	2:32	WOULDN'T IT BE NICE			

(2) Employee's Name (As on Social Security Card) Last First Initial	(3) Home Address (Give Street, City and State)	(4) Local Union No.	(5) Social Security Number	(6) Scale Wages	(7) Pension Contribution
(Leader)	Hollywood, 28, Calif.				
Blaine, Hal	2441 Castilian Dr.	47	047-20-5900	284.72	22.78
Kreisman, Steven Douglas	6950 Chisholm Ave. Van Nuys, Calif.	47	556-46-1005	284.72	22.78
bells, tympani, percussion					
Capp, Frank, 2-Dbls	3017 Dona nenita Pl. Studio City, Calif.	47	013-24-7193	172.87	13.83
Caton, Roy V.	3760 Willowcrest Ave. No. Hollywood, Calif.	47	192-20-7730	142.36	11.39
DeLory, Alfred V.	5524 Ruthwood Dr. Calabasas, Calif.	47	559-36-9796	142.36	11.39
Fortina, Carl	838 N. Orange Dr. Hollywood 38, Calif.	47	554-32-8082	142.36	11.39
Johnson, Plas	4120 W. 59th St. Los Angeles 43, Calif.	47	434-44-2284	142.36	11.39
Kaye, Carol	4905 Forman No. Hollywood, Calif.	47	555-46-5389	142.36	11.39
Knechtel, Lawrence W.	4847 Van Noord Sherman Oaks, Calif.	47	553-54-6386	142.36	11.39
Kessel, Barney	1727 Las Flores Dr. Glendale 7, Calif.	47	447-12-3334	142.36	11.39
Kolbrak, Jerry	4121 Oak St. Burbank, Calif.	47	394-36-7847	142.36	11.39
Marocco, Frank	7063 Whitaker Ave. Van Nuys, Calif.	47	329-22-0203	142.36	11.39
Migliori, Jay	1701 N. Lincoln Burbank, Calif.	47	208-24-6118	142.36	11.39
Pitman, William	9124 Nagle Ave. Pacoima, Calif.	47	068-16-6762	142.36	11.39

SEE ATTACHED CONTINUATION SHEET ************************************

(8) Total Pension Contributions (Sum of Column (7)) $ **207.46**
Make check payable in this amount to "AFM & EPW Fund."

FOR FUND USE ONLY:

Date pay't rec'd _____ Amt. paid _____ te posted _____ By _____

Form B-4 Rev. 4-59

legendary American composer; he has written lyrics for the song but feels it is better as an instrumental. As each take is attempted Brian listens intently and when at several points the musicians play at an incorrect tempo or miss an entrance, he orders a re-take. Chuck Britz is again the engineer at this and most of the subsequent Western Recorders sessions.

Musicians present Hal Blaine (drums), Al Casey (guitar), Roy Caton (trumpet), Al de Lory (piano), Steve Douglas (saxophone), Jim Horn (saxophone), Plas Johnson (saxophone), Carol Kaye (bass guitar), Barney Kessel (guitar), Jay Migliori (saxophone), Lyle Ritz (upright bass), Julius Wechter (timpani, vibes).

Miyagi Kenmin Kaikan *Sendai, Japan*

Meanwhile in Japan, tonight the touring group plays this tenth date of the tour there. Dennis and Carl regularly phone Brian at the studio to keep up to date with the progress of the recordings. As the sessions and phone calls continue they get to hear more and more of Brian's latest recordings as he plays them acetates down the line. Brian sends out to the boys on the road an acetate containing a rough mix of 'Sloop John B' for what he describes as their "listening pleasure".

■ Wednesday 19th

RECORDING *Pet Sounds* **session 2** Western Recorders studio (3) *Hollywood, CA* 3:00-9:00pm. Brian supervises overdubbing work on the instrumental **'Let's Go Away For Awhile'**. It's clear that he has consigned straightforward, regimented recordings to the past: today he employs 12 violins, four saxophones, piano, oboe, flute, cello, viola, vibes – and a guitar with a Coca-Cola bottle sliding across the strings. This is the first time that Brian becomes really adventurous in the studio and it marks a new era of recording for him. Perhaps this is why he later describes 'Let's Go Away' as "the most satisfying piece of music I've ever made".

Musicians present Joe Difiore (viola), Justin Ditullio (cello), Steve Douglas (flute), Jim Getzoff (violin), Harry Hyams (viola), Jules Jacob (flute), William Kurasch (violin), Lenny Malarsky (violin), Jerry Reisler (violin), Joe Saxon (cello), Ralph Schaeffer (violin), Sidney Sharp (violin), Tibor Zelig (violin).

■ Thursday 20th

Sumpu Kaikan *Shizuoka, Japan*

The Japanese tour continues.

■ Friday 21st

Yokohama Bunka Taikukan *Yokohama, Japan*

■ Saturday 22nd

RECORDING *Pet Sounds* **session 3** Gold Star studio (A) *Los Angeles, CA* 7:00-11:30pm. Three days into the new album sessions in California, and Brian shifts today to Gold Star and engineer Larry Levine, taking charge of the first session for **'Wouldn't It Be Nice'**, a song Brian will say is inspired by an infatuation with his secretary. Recordings today focus on the instrumental backing tracks (21 takes required). The first six takes break down because drummer Hal Blaine is unable to grasp Brian's wishes for the drum part. The day concludes with Brian overdubbing a vocal onto the track. Later he recalls a signature sound of the recording: "On 'Wouldn't It Be Nice' I had two accordion players playing at once, both playing the same thing and it just rang through the room, in the booth, and everyone was saying, 'What *is* that sound?'"

Musicians present Hal Blaine (drums), Frankie Capp (timpani, bells, percussion), Roy Caton (trumpet), Jerry Cole (guitar), Al de Lory (piano), Steve Douglas (saxophone), Carl Fortina (accordion), Plas

Johnson (saxophone), Carol Kaye (bass guitar), Barney Kessel (guitar), Larry Knechtel (piano), Frank Marocco (accordion), Jay Migliori (saxophone), Bill Pitman (guitar), Ray Pohlman (guitar), Lyle Ritz (upright bass).

Shinjuku Kousei Nenkin Hall *Tokyo, Japan*

■ Sunday 23rd

Ootaku Taikukan *Tokyo, Japan* (daytime concert)
Shinjuku Kousei Nenkin Hall *Tokyo, Japan* (evening concert)
After these last dates on the Japanese tour the touring group begins their journey home, stopping over in Hawaii (see 29th).

■ Monday 24th

RECORDING *Pet Sounds* **session 4** Western Recorders studio (3) *Hollywood, CA*. After several rehearsals, Brian supervises the instrumental tracking session for **'You Still Believe In Me'** (23 takes required). His co-writer Tony Asher says later that to get the song's unique opening sound "one of us had to get inside the piano to pluck the strings while the other guy had to be at the keyboard pushing the notes so that they would ring". The session is concluded with Brian overdubbing vocals for the song.

Musicians present Hal Blaine (drums), Roy Caton (trumpet), Al de Lory (harpsichord), Glen Campbell (guitar), Steve Douglas (tenor saxophone), Billy Green (alto saxophone), Jim Horn (alto saxophone), Plas Johnson (tenor saxophone), Carol Kaye (bass guitar), Barney Kessel (guitar), Jay Migliori (baritone saxophone), Lyle Ritz (upright bass), Julius Wechter (bicycle bell, finger cymbals).

■ Saturday 29th

HIC Arena *Honolulu, HI* 8:30pm with Jackie Lee, Lou Christie, The Mop Tops, The Undertakers, Frankie Samuels & The Kinfolks
The Far East tour is over, but The Beach Boys take a short break and it is not until February 9th that they will participate in their first sessions for the new album that Brian has been working on back in Los Angeles.

• 'Barbara Ann' single peaks in US *Billboard* chart at number 2.

■ Monday 31st

RECORDING *Pet Sounds* **session 5** Western Recorders studio (3) *Hollywood, CA* 2:00-6:00pm. Brian works on at the studio without the rest of the band. Today sees a basic instrumental tracking session for **'Caroline No'** (17 takes required) after which he tapes his lead vocal and an instrumental insert for the song.

'Caroline No' is one of the few songs that Brian has written under the influence of marijuana. It was composed in just 20 minutes. His wife Marilyn thinks it is about her and takes the song personally, but according to Brian: "Tony Asher must have known a girl who had cut her hair off. She hardened and she lost the glow she once had, and it made the guy go to pieces. Made him real sad because she didn't love him any more." After Brian reminisces about his high-school crush, Carol Mountain, Tony Asher originally sets the title as 'Carol I Know' but Brian mishears this as 'Caroline No' and the new title sticks.

During today's session, drummer Hal Blaine plays an empty plastic Sparkletts spring-water bottle upside down to achieve the unusual 'hollow' percussion hit in the song's opening. Brian makes two early mixes of the song (one in mono) to complete the session.

Musicians present Hal Blaine (drums), Glen Campbell (guitar), Frankie Capp (percussion), Al de Lory (harpsichord), Steve Douglas (saxophone), Billy Green (flute, bass flute), Jim Horn (saxophone), Plas Johnson (saxophone), Carol Kaye (bass guitar), Barney Kessel (guitar), Jay Migliori (saxophone), Lyle Ritz (ukulele).

LEFT The third session for *Pet Sounds* sees instrumental recording for 'Wouldn't It Be Nice', as detailed on this union log for January 22nd.
FOLLOWING PAGES Impromptu stage craft as Mike holds the microphone for Dennis to sing 'Do You Wanna Dance' to a packed auditorium.

February

'**Barbara Ann**' / '**Girl Don't Tell Me**' single released in the UK. It will peak in the *Record Retailer/Music Weekly* chart at number 3.
(*Recorded "Live" At A*) *Beach Boys' Party!* album released in the UK.
• 'Barbara Ann' single peaks in Canadian *RPM* chart at number 2.
• During one of the frequent breaks in the recordings of *Pet Sounds* this month, Brian meets professional songwriter, arranger and session musician Van Dyke Parks (born January 3rd 1943 in Hattiesburg, Mississippi) at a party at Terry Melcher's house. Melcher is the son of screen actress Doris Day and a long-time musical associate of Beach Boy Bruce Johnston.

Parks was a classical music student and came to Hollywood, California, when he was 13. He was also a child actor – he once played opposite legendary screen actress Bette Davis. He attended the Carnegie Institute, studying classical music and composition, and after graduating went to MGM, hoping to compose soundtracks for Walt Disney films but instead providing songs, arrangements or keyboards for American pop groups The Mojo Men and Harpers Bizarre. He provided similar assistance to The Beau Brummels and The Byrds during this period, and with his own group released two singles on MGM as The Van Dyke Parks.

It was in September 1965 that Parks auditioned unsuccessfully for Columbia Pictures' new musical television series *The Monkees*, and during this period he met other MGM hopefuls Danny Hutton and David Anderle (of whom more later). By a strange twist of coincidence, Parks has collaborated on songwriting with Tony Asher. The friendship between Brian and Parks develops quickly, probably fuelled by mutual admiration, and the two will begin writing together. (See opening entry for May.)

"[Brian and Van Dyke] met at my house," Melcher remembered. "I had lots of music-business gatherings. I had huge music speakers all over the house, all over the grounds, and these people would arrive from the studios in LA, New York, London and they would bring their acetates of unreleased material."

Parks will recall meeting Brian on Melcher's lawn: "'Brian needs a lyricist,' Terry [Melcher] announced ... as he introduced me to Brian. I knew him as a flatlander. That's what we called them: hoe dads. I lived on the beach and knew The Beach Boys couldn't surf. Brian said, 'Come on up and listen to some sounds.' I went up to his house on a mountain top in the Hollywood Hills. He had [recording] equipment that impressed me, along with a steaming swimming pool." Brian too is impressed by his new friend: "Listening to [Van Dyke Parks] talk, I said, 'That guy's articulate. I bet he'll make a good lyric writer.' And he was."

■ Wednesday 2nd
RECORDING *Pet Sounds* **session 6** Western Recorders studio (3) *Hollywood, CA* 2:00pm start; no fixed finish time. Further tracking work is done on '**Caroline No**' as Brian overdubs musicians playing keyboards, a second bass, drums and a saxophone on to the January 31st recording.
Musicians present Hal Blaine (drums), Al de Lory (harpsichord), Steve Douglas (tenor saxophone), Carol Kaye (bass guitar).

■ Thursday 3rd
RECORDING *Pet Sounds* **session 7** Western Recorders studio (3) *Hollywood, CA* 12:30pm start; no fixed finish time. Brian concludes tracking work on '**Caroline No**'.
• In Los Angeles, Carl marries 16-year-old Annie Hinsche (born December 27th 1949, in Manila, Philippines). She is the sister of Billy of popular American teenage singing group Dino Desi & Billy. Carl attempts to keep his marriage secret but the wedding is reported in several American entertainment and teen magazines. Once entwined, Carl and Annie move into Carl's recently purchased home in Beverly Hills.

■ Monday 7th
RECORDING *Pet Sounds* **session 8** Western Recorders studio (3) *Hollywood, CA* 1:00pm start; no fixed finish time. A music tracking session takes place for '**Hang On To Your Ego**', also known as '**Let Go Of Your Ego**' (take 12 marked as best). At the conclusion of the session Brian records a vocal for the song and completes two alternate mono mixes of the piece. 'Hang On To Your Ego' was written by Brian and Terry Sachen, the group's road manager, and pre-dates Brian's collaborations with Tony Asher.
Musicians present Hal Blaine (drums), Glen Campbell (guitar, banjo), Al de Lory (piano), Steve Douglas (saxophone), Jim Horn (saxophone), Barney Kessel (guitar), Larry Knechtel (organ), Jay Migliori (saxophone), Tommy Morgan (bass harmonica), Ray Pohlman (bass guitar), Lyle Ritz (upright bass), Julius Wechter (tambourine).
• *Summer Days (And Summer Nights)* album certified gold by RIAA in the US.

■ Wednesday 9th
RECORDING *Pet Sounds* **session 9** Western Recorders studio (3) *Hollywood, CA* 9:00am start; no fixed finish time. The Beach Boys have concluded their break after the Far East tour and excitedly head to Western to record vocals for '**Hang On To Your Ego**' (which for the album will become '**I Know There's An Answer**', supposedly changed on the insistence of Mike). Glen Campbell is present playing guitar and banjo; Chuck Britz again engineers the session. Slowly, The Beach Boys are initiated into Brian's new and unexpected musical direction. Coming so soon after the *Beach Boys' Party!* album and from singing about amusement parks, the beach, surfer girls and being "bugged at their ol' man", the changes are largely incomprehensible to the group.

Mike feels that the new album in production is too much of a departure and, according to Tony Asher, remarks to Brian: "Don't fuck with the formula." Brian will recall: "They liked [the new album] but they said it was too arty. I said, 'No, it is not! We need an album like this to prove that we can make good music.' I told them, 'Don't worry about it. It's only an album. We can always make more albums again after this one.' They agreed and said all right."

At the session Mike and Al begin taping solo vocal inserts for 'Hang On To Your Ego' and are surprised by what they are expected to sing. Al remarks, "Hey, Brian. This is a little tricky." When Mike begins his recordings, he mocks the lyrics and at one time sings the lines "They come on like they're peaceful / But inside they're so uptight" in the style of American comedian Jimmy Durante and character-actor James Cagney.

After several attempts, Al begins recording his line, the sequence ending, "Now what can you tell them / Now what can you say that won't make them defensive." No doubt still exhausted after the group's gruelling trip to Japan, Al soon says, "Hey, I need your help, Brian. I cannot hack this without your help. I mean it. I'm mentally destroyed." Mike does not help: his laughter and occasional belching is putting off Al. Immediately, Brian blasts through the studio intercom: "Hey, you guys. Don't fuck around. Please, we've got to do it, Mike. Come on."

Several attempts later, Brian is still not happy with Al's phrasing of some of the lyrics. While Al sings, Mike continues to snigger in the background, prompting Brian to ask: "Hey, what's the matter?" Mike interrupts, saying, "It's hilarious." Brian, now deeply frustrated, responds: "Come on! Let's make it." Al breaks into the conversation. "Look," he insists, "if I can cut it, man, that's what is important." Mike responds, "It looks like you're cutting it two ways." As laughter and nonsensical chat prevail, Brian blasts again: "Guys, let's cut this fucking thing!" His words go unheeded.

Al's next vocal attempt is again thwarted by laughter, prompted by Mike's comical antics. "I'm sorry Chuck," Al says to engineer Chuck Britz. "I'll get it this time." Brian, after several attempts to further coax the group, goes into the main studio from the control room and demonstrates how it should be done, singing the lyrics while accompanying himself on piano. After 17 further vocal attempts by Al, Brian admits he is happy with the recording. Al asks, "You're not just accepting it, uh?" Brian is happy, but only after Al has recorded his lines a further four times. Brian seems set on a course for perfection.

Vocal overdubs follow. Brian then joins the other Beach Boys in the studio to record an insert of the "I know there's an answer" vocal line. With the song's tracking master playing through their headphones, Brian counts down to the time when the group should tape their brief vocal part. "Here we go," he says. "Are you ready for it? Here it is. It's a bitch. It's a bitch." The ever-supportive Marilyn drops by the session at the end of the evening. Further backing-vocal insert overdubs are taped, first by Brian and then the whole group.

Al says later: "It was a whole new horizon for us. Brian introduced a whole new concept in pop music. We were a surfing group when we left the country at the start of 1966 and we came back to this new music. It took some getting used to. It was a different kind of singing. The vocals were arduous, tedious and long. We spent hours and hours working on the vocals."

Brian, covetous after listening to the great musical strides that The Beatles have made with their latest album, *Rubber Soul*, senses that musical changes are about to hit the staid record industry. His new songs for the album depart from the more traditional themes of The Beach Boys' current repertoire, and not surprisingly Mike – by now the 'leader' of the live-show Beach Boys – takes a less prominent role during the making of *Pet Sounds*. The fact that Brian has chosen a new lyricist, Tony Asher, probably adds to Mike's doubts. Subsequently, Brian will end up singing lead on most of the songs on the new album. Asher recalls later that he only attends a couple of sessions at this time, and admits that Mike, Al and Bruce were not happy with his presence. "They were cordial," Asher will tell BBC Radio-2, "but I could tell they weren't so sure about the music we'd written."

Musicians present Hal Blaine (drums), Glen Campbell (guitar, banjo), Al de Lory (piano), Steve Douglas (saxophone), Jim Horn (saxophone), Paul Horn (saxophone), Barney Kessel (guitar), Robert Klein (saxophone), Larry Knechtel (organ), Jay Migliori (woodwind), Tommy Morgan (harmonica), Ray Pohlman (bass guitar), Lyle Ritz (upright bass), Julius Wechter (percussion).

■ Friday 11th
RECORDING *Pet Sounds* **session 10** Western Recorders studio (3) *Hollywood, CA* 9:00am start; no fixed finish time. Four months since the song was first rehearsed in the studio (see October 13th 1965) Brian supervises instrumental tracking and vocal recordings for **'Don't Talk (Put Your Head On My Shoulder)'**. Inserts and a lead vocal track are also recorded today. As usual at Western, engineer is Chuck Britz. Brian says later that 'Don't Talk' is "one of the sweetest, most loving songs that I ever sang in my life. I thought that this song

would bring so much love to people". Dennis will recall that he's never heard anything like it before. "We'd be in the studio and [Brian] would play us a song, and we would start crying. We'd start crying because it was so great. It was like, 'How could this possibly be happening? How did he write this?' There is not one person in the group that could come close to Brian's talent."

Musicians present Hal Blaine (drums), Glen Campbell (guitar), Frankie Capp (kettle drum, percussion), Al de Lory (organ), Steve Douglas (percussion), Carol Kaye (bass guitar), Lyle Ritz (upright bass), Billy Strange (guitar).

■ Monday 14th
RECORDING *Pet Sounds* sessions 11/12 Western Recorders studio (3) *Hollywood, CA* 12 noon-approx 6:00pm; Gold Star studio (A) *Los Angeles, CA* 7:30-10:30pm plus one hour overtime. Brian supervises the recording of the instrumental parts for **'I Just Wasn't Made For These Times'**, but his creative juices are interrupted because the studio is booked for a Johnny Rivers session starting at 8:30pm. Determined not to be stopped in mid flow, he heads for nearby Gold Star where he completes instrumentation for the song (take 6 marked as master). The sessions at Gold Star with engineer Larry Levine are concluded with the recording of the song's lead vocal, backing vocal overdubs by the other Beach Boys, and various vocal inserts. (The union sheet notes the song's title as 'I Just Wasn't Made For These Things'. Also, Marilyn's sister Diane Rovell is logged as 'contractor', the person who arranges for the various musicians to play at the session; she will continue to do this job for a few years on many Beach Boys recording dates.)

It is the first time that Brian has employed the sound of a theremin, an early electronic instrument created in the 1920s by Russian Leon Theremin (also known as Lev Termen) and used for creepy sound effects on horror films, including Alfred Hitchcock's 1945 thriller *Spellbound*. For today's session Paul Tanner plays a simplified 'electro-theremin' – not really a theremin at all – developed specially for him by Bob Whitsell in 1958. A 'traditional' theremin is played by moving one's hand in space in relation to the instrument's antennae. Tanner's instrument duplicates the theremin's distinctive wobbly electronic sound, but here the desired pitch is achieved by moving a slider switch beside a stylised 'keyboard' strip that Tanner has marked on his instrument. He controls volume on the separate amplifier through which his instrument plays. Tanner is a noted jazz trombonist and session player, and a staff musician for the ABC Orchestra. Until today he has never heard of The Beach Boys. (Tanner's electro-theremin will appear on just two further Beach Boys recordings: 'Good Vibrations' and, in 1967, 'Wild Honey'.)

Musicians present (Gold Star) Charles Berghofer (upright bass), Hal Blaine (drums), Glen Campbell (guitar), Frankie Capp (percussion), Steve Douglas (saxophone), Plas Johnson (saxophone), Barney Kessell (guitar), Robert Klein (tenor saxophone), Michael Melvoin (harpsichord), Jay Migliori (saxophone), Tommy Morgan (harmonica), Ray Pohlman (bass guitar), Don Randi (piano), Paul Tanner (electro-theremin).

■ Tuesday 15th
RECORDING *Pet Sounds* session 13 Western Recorders studio (3) *Hollywood, CA* 2:00-5:00pm. First call this morning is at the San Diego zoo where the group participates in a photo-shoot with photographer George Jerman. The shoot takes place in the petting paddock at the zoo, an area designed to let children get close to some of the friendlier animals. Bruce accompanies Brian and the rest of the group to the shoot but again contractual restraints from

Phonograph Recording Contract Blank

^0374

AMERICAN FEDERATION OF MUSICIANS

105850

OF THE UNITED STATES AND CANADA

Local Union No. **47**

THIS CONTRACT for the personal services of musicians, made this **9th** day of **February**, 19 **66**, between the undersigned employer (hereinafter called the "employer") and **fifteen** musicians (hereinafter called "employees").

(including the leader)

WITNESSETH, That the employer hires the employees as musicians severally on the terms and conditions below, and as further specified on reverse side. The leader represents that the employees already designated have agreed to be bound by said terms and conditions. Each employee yet to be chosen shall be so bound by said terms and conditions upon agreeing to accept his employment. Each employee may enforce this agreement. The employees severally agree to render collectively to the employer services as musicians in the orchestra under the leadership of **Steven D. Kreisman – BEACH BOYS** as follows:

Name and Address of Place of Engagement **Western Recording, 6000 Sunset Blvd., Hollywood 28, California**

Date(s) and Hours of Employment **2-9-66   9:00 AM to 1:00 PM**

Type of Engagement: **Recording for phonograph records only**

WAGE AGREED UPON $ **Union Scale (including tracking and overtime)**

Plus pension contributions as specified on reverse side hereof.

(Terms and amount)

This wage includes expenses agreed to be reimbursed by the employer in accordance with the attached schedule, or a schedule to be furnished the employer on or before the date of engagement.

To be paid _____

(Specify when payments are to be made)

Upon request by the American Federation of Musicians of the United States and Canada (herein called the "Federation") or the local in whose jurisdiction the employees shall perform hereunder, the employer either shall make advance payment hereunder or shall post an appropriate bond.

Employer's name and **Capitol Records, Inc.**	Leader's name **Steven D. Kreisman**
authorized signature	Leader's signature
Street address **1750 No. Vine St.**	Local No. **47**
Hollywood 28, Calif. Ho. 2-6252	Street address **6950 Chisholm Ave.**
City State Phone	**Van Nuys, California**
	City State

(1) Label name **Capitol** _____ Session no. _____

Master no.	No. of minutes	TITLES OF TUNES	Master no.	No. of minutes	TITLES OF TUNES
		Let Go of Your Ego (track)			

(2) Employee's name (As on Social Security card) Last / First / Initial	(3) Home address (Give street, city and state)	(4) Local Union no.	(5) Social Security number	(6) Scale wages	(7) Pension contribution
(Leader)	6950 Chisholm Ave.				
Kreisman, Steven D.	Van Nuys, Calif.	47	556-46-1005	$244.04	$19.54
Britz, Charles D.	4501 Wawona St. Los Angeles 65, Calif.	47	567-26-4273	244.04	19.54
Campbell, Glen	8502 Allenwood Road Los Angeles 46, Calif.	47	452-54-0320	122.02	9.77
Blaine, Hal	2441 Castilian Drive Hollywood, Calif.	47	047-20-5900	101.68	8.14
Ritz, Lyle	1971 No. Curson Avenue Los Angeles 46, Calif.	47	549-38-1490	101.68	8.14
Pohlman, M. R.	6171 Rockcliff Dr. Los Angeles, Calif.	47	556-34-6698	101.68	8.14
deLory, Alfred V.	5524 Ruthwood Drive Calabasas, Calif.	47	559-36-9796	101.68	8.14
Morgan, Tommy	7111 Kilty Avenue Canoga Park, Calif.	47	556-40-5544	101.68	8.14
Wechter, Julius	12247 Hesby North Hollywood, Calif.	47	557-40-3644	101.68	8.14
Kessel, Barney	1727 Las Flores Drive Glendale 7, Calif.	47	447-12-3334	101.68	8.14
Horn, James R.	3225 Oakshire Drive Hollywood 28, Calif.	47	570-56-6753	101.68	8.14
Horn, Paul	2452 Horseshoe Cyn. Road Los Angeles 46, Calif.	47	579-34-1081	101.68	8.14
Klein, Robert H.	5854 Tujunga #2 North Hollywood, Calif.	47	467-36-8703	101.68	8.14
Migliori, Jay	1701 No. Lincoln Burbank, Calif.	47	208-24-6118	101.68	8.14
Knechtel, Lawrence W.	4847 Van Noord Ave. Sherman Oaks, Calif.	47	553-54-6386	101.68	8.14

NO ARR.

(8) Total Pension Contributions (Sum of Column (7)) $ _____

Make check payable in this amount to "AFM & EPW Fund"

LEFT Another *Pet Sounds* 'AFM sheet' logs musicians present on February 9th for 'Let Go Of Your Ego', soon to become 'I Know There's An Answer'. BELOW From the 9th Brian is joined in the studio by his bandmates, fresh from their Far East tour. Here Brian and Dennis work on a backing vocal.

Columbia Records prevent him from appearing in the selected photo from today's session that will grace the *Pet Sounds* album sleeve.

"The goats were horrible!" says Bruce. "They jump all over you and bite. One of them ate my radio. The zoo said we were torturing the animals but they should have seen what we had to go through. We were doing all the suffering."

This afternoon, the full Beach Boys line-up accompanies Brian to Western where they observe him taking charge of an instrumental tracking session for **'That's Not Me'** (take 15 marked as best). The song is unique because it's the only one that will appear on the album featuring any Beach Boy – including Brian – playing an instrument: Brian is on organ, Carl on guitar and Dennis on drums. Further recordings today focus on various instrumental insert pieces and a lead vocal overdub by Mike on the song.

Musicians present The AFM log suggests only Carl, Dennis, Al and Bruce are present, but evidence points also to Hal Blaine (drums), Terry Melcher (tambourine), Lyle Ritz (upright bass), and Brian Wilson (organ).

Wednesday 16th

MIXING Western Recorders studio (3) *Hollywood, CA* 12 noon start; no fixed finish time. The studio is booked but no recordings are made. Instead, Brian spends the first part of the day completing alternate mixes of **'You Still Believe In Me'** and **'Hang On To Your Ego'**. He also makes a rough mono mix of **'Wouldn't It Be Nice'** on this date, helped by engineer Chuck Britz, notable for Brian's lead vocal that transposes the lyrics of the verses. The tail end of the session is spent rehearsing vocals, but Brian and the other Beach

Boys are distracted from their work because Elvis Presley is recording at the nearby Radio Recorders studio. Brian notes: "I've worshiped that man for ten years and I just can't walk into his studio and say hello." So Bruce pays The King a visit, and when he returns Brian insists on hearing every single word muttered in his conversation with Elvis.

Thursday 17th

RECORDING *Pet Sounds* session 14, 'Good Vibrations' session 1 Western Recorders studio (3) *Hollywood, CA* 2:00pm onwards; Gold Star studio (A) *Los Angeles, CA* 11:30pm-3:00am. The day begins at Western with the first rehearsals of Brian's new song, **'Good Vibrations'**, which he will describe as his "little pocket symphony" (but today is noted on the union log simply as '#1 Untitled'). It will become his masterpiece. "I was an energetic 23-year-old," Brian will recall later. "That's when I cut 'Good Vibrations'. I said: This is going to be better than 'You've Lost That Loving Feeling'."

"My mother used to tell me about vibrations," he says on another occasion. "I didn't really understand too much of what it meant when I was just a boy. It scared me, the word 'vibrations'. She told me about dogs that would bark at people and then not bark at others, that a dog would pick up vibrations from these people that you can't see, but you can feel."

Later at Gold Star, working with engineer Cal Harris, Brian takes charge of the first recording of the song. Nine takes in, Brian, unsure of the workings of the electro-theremin, questions the volume of the instrument with musician Paul Tanner (see also February 14th). "Are you doing something to your volume out there?" Brian asks. "Do you make it louder or does it just get

BELOW Brian during the making of *Pet Sounds*. He is increasingly confident with the technicalities of recording and constantly seeks new techniques and sounds. RIGHT The first session for 'Good Vibrations', still noted as '#1 Untitled' on this union log for February 17th. It will become Brian's masterpiece.

louder?" Tanner explains that the volume varies. "OK, I'll be prepared for it," Brian replies. Take 10 begins immediately. By the final takes, Tanner's electro-theremin is mixed to feature more prominently in the recording. "When 'Good Vibrations' was forming itself in my mind," Brian will recall, "I could hear the theremin on the track. It sounds like a woman's voice or like a violin bow on a carpenter's saw. You make it waver, just like a human voice. It's groovy!" On the tape of the Gold Star session, Brian is also heard discussing organ effects with Phil Spector's keyboard player, Larry Knechtel. After 26 attempts, a satisfactory outline of the song is complete, and Brian makes a rough mono mix of the recording to complete the session.

Musicians present (Gold Star) Hal Blaine (drums), Frankie Capp (percussion), Al Casey (guitar), Steve Douglas (saxophone), Billy Green (woodwind), Plas Johnson (saxophone), Larry Knechtel (organ), Jay Migliori (saxophone), Ray Pohlman (bass guitar), Don Randi (piano), Lyle Ritz (upright bass), Billy Strange (guitar), Paul Tanner (electro-theremin).

■ Friday 18th

RECORDING *Pet Sounds* session 15, '**Good Vibrations**' session 2 Gold Star studio (A) *Los Angeles, CA*. Today sees the second tracking session for '**Good Vibrations**'. Not quite satisfied with the first set of recordings, Brian tapes a new instrumental base for the song with a fuller sound (28 takes required; take 28 marked as best). Later, he attempts to tape the song's first guide vocals (rough attempts that will be replaced later) but is unhappy with the results and begins questioning the lyrics provided by Tony Asher.

Musicians present Frankie Capp (percussion).

■ Tuesday 22nd

TV Brian's home *1448 Laurel Way, Los Angeles, CA*. BBC-1 *Top Of The Pops* filmed feature 'Barbara Ann' broadcast March 10th (7:30-8:00pm). Away from the studio, The Beach Boys take part in the shooting of a BBC television film. Wild, random scenes of the boys relaxing and having fun are shot exclusively for inclusion in the long-running UK music show *Top Of The Pops*.

■ Wednesday 23rd

RECORDING *Pet Sounds* session 16, '**Good Vibrations**' session 3 Western Recorders studio (3) *Hollywood, CA* 12 noon onwards. Enthused by the recordings done five days ago, Brian continues to build '**Good Vibrations**' by supervising insert recordings for the song. Instrumentation includes organ, drums, harpsichord, harmonica, electro-theremin (played again by Paul Tanner), piano (by Al de Lory), bass guitar (Carol Kaye) and drums (Hal Blaine). By take 11 Brian re-works the musical arrangements leading into the introduction to the song's chorus. As recordings progress, he also decides to have the organist play an octave higher. In total, 27 takes are required this afternoon. With that, Brian completes the first basic instrumental recordings for the verses of the song, which at this point still features Tony Asher's lyrics.

• A Capitol Records memo dated today lists a song titled 'Good Good Good Vibrations' as a preliminary track for the upcoming *Pet Sounds* album; see March 11th.

■ Thursday 24th – Friday 25th

RECORDING Western Recorders studio (3) *Hollywood, CA* 1:00pm onwards. This session focuses on Brian's musical arrangements for '**Good Vibrations**' with The Wrecking Crew, and the rehearsals are recorded. But Brian is still not happy with the way that the song is turning out. He realises its importance and the immense amount of work it will take to complete to his satisfaction and so decides to leave it off the album, putting it aside until March 24th. In the meantime he returns his immediate musical attentions to finishing the *Pet Sounds* album.

Phonograph Recording Contract Blank
AMERICAN FEDERATION OF MUSICIANS
OF THE UNITED STATES AND CANADA

№ 245226

Local Union No. **47**

THIS CONTRACT for the personal services of musicians, made this **17** day of **February**, 19**66**
between the undersigned employer (hereinafter called the "employer") and ____ **13** musicians
(hereinafter called "employees"). *(Including the leader)*

WITNESSETH, That the employer hires the employees severally on the terms and conditions below, and as further specified on reverse side. The leader represents that the employees already designated have agreed to be bound by said terms and conditions. Each employee yet to be chosen shall be so bound by said terms and conditions upon agreeing to accept his employment. Each employee may enforce this agreement. The employees severally agree to render collectively to the employer services as musicians in the orchestra under the leadership of

Steven Douglas Kreisman ____ as follows:

Name and Address of Place of Engagement **Gold Star Recorders, 6252 Santa Monica, Blvd.**
Los Angeles, Calif. 90038

Date(s) and Hours of Employment **Feb. 17, 1966 11:30 P.M. to 3:A.M. (½ hour overtime)**

Type of Engagement: **Recording for phonograph records only.**

WAGE AGREED UPON $ ____ **Union Scale**
(Terms and amount)

Plus pension contributions as specified on reverse side hereof.

This wage includes expenses agreed to be reimbursed by the employer in accordance with the attached schedule, or a schedule to be furnished the employer on or before the date of engagement.

To be paid **Within 14 Days**
(Specify when payments are to be made)

Upon request by the American Federation of Musicians of the United States and Canada (herein called the "Federation") or the local in whose jurisdiction the employees shall perform hereunder, the employer either shall make advance payment hereunder or shall post an appropriate bond.

Employer's name and **Capitol Records, Inc.**	Leader's name **Steven Douglas Kreisman** Local No. **47**
authorized signature	Leader's signature
Street address **1750 N. Vine St.**	Street address **6950 Chisholm Ave.**
Hollywood, Calif. 90028 **HO-26252**	**Van Nuys, Calif.**
City State Phone	City State

(1) Label Name **Capitol Records, Inc.**   Session No. ____

Master No.	No. of Minutes	TITLES OF TUNES	Master No.	No. of Minutes	TITLES OF TUNES
	2:29	#1-Untitled			

(2) Employee's Name (As on Social Security Card) Last First Initial	(3) Home Address (Give Street, City and State)	(4) Local Union No.	(5) Social Security Number	(6) Scale Wages	(7) Pension Contribution
(Leader) Kreisman, Steven D.	6950 Chisholm Ave. Van Nuys, Calif.	47	556-46-1005	254.24	20.33
Blaine, Hal	2441 Castilian Dr. L.A. 28, Calif.	47	047-20-5900	254.24	20.33
Capp, Frank	3017 Dona Nenita Pl. Studio City, Calif.	47	013-24-7193	127.12	10.16
Casey, Alvin W.	6355 Primrose L.A. Calif.	47	526-46-9373	127.12	10.16
Green William E.	4526 Don Miguel Dr. L.A. 8, Calif.	47	512-16-4687	127.12	10.16
Johnson, Plas	4120 W. 59th St. L.A. 43, Calif.	47	434-44-2284	127.12	10.16
Knechtel, Lawrence W.	4847 Van Noord Sherman Oaks, Calif.	47	553-54-6386	127.12	10.16
Migliori, Jay	1701 N. Lincoln Burbank, Calif.	47	208-24-6118	127.12	10.16
Pohlman, M.R.	6171 Rockcliff Dr. L.A. 28, Calif.	47	556-34-6698	127.12	10.16
Randi, Don	2906 Nichols Can. Rd. L.A. 46, Calif.	47	129-28-1617	127.12	10.16
Ritz, Lyle	1971 N. Curson Ave. L.A. 46, Calif.	47	549-38-1490	127.12	10.16
Strange, William E.	17312 Osborne St. Northridge, Calif.	47	547-36-8814	127.12	10.16
Tanner, Paul	12426 La Maida No. Hollywood, Calif.	47	015-16-3893	127.12	10.16

NO ARRANGER OR COPYIST THIS SESSION............................

(8) Total Pension Contributions (Sum of Column (7)) $ **152.42**
Make check payable in this amount to "AFM & EPW Fund."

FOR FUND USE ONLY: PAID MAR 7 ....

Date pay't rec'd ____ Amt. paid ____ Date posted ____ By ____

Form B-4 Rev. 4-59

March

'Barbara Ann' single peaks in UK *Record Retailer/Music Weekly* chart at number 3, and in Dutch chart at number 18.

• This month The Beach Boys move their management from Cummins & Currant to Julius Lefkowitz & Company. Nick Grillo takes charge of their account and is soon invited to become their personal manager. The band employs Derek Taylor as their publicist. Taylor has previously worked for The Beatles, and Brian sees the hip, humorous Liverpudlian as vital in establishing credibility for the group's image and for Brian's own new music. As Taylor recalls later, "Brian hired me to help *Pet Sounds* take them to what he called 'a new plateau'."

In matters of business, Taylor is regarded as a highly prestigious Los Angeles figure. In 1965, once installed in Los Angeles, Taylor's first job was to supervise publicity for the singing duo Bruce & Terry. Terry was Terry Melcher; Bruce was Bruce Johnston. Bruce introduced Taylor to Brian. The two hit it off immediately and Taylor is installed soon after as The Beach Boys' new publicist. Almost immediately, he begins to clash with the Wilsons' father, Murry.

Taylor, speaking on BBC Radio-1 in 1974, will remember one occasion when Murry Wilson rushed into his office. "The first thing he said to me was, 'Am I coming on too strong?' So I immediately said, 'Yes.' He wanted photographs, so I gave him some new shots of The Beach Boys with their hair protruding over their ears, touching the collar. He tossed them away, saying, 'Never mind that. I want them looking like Americans. It's for a six-foot … no, make that an eighteen-foot, stained-glass window.' He went on, 'Just imagine this. The boys looking like Americans, yeah, and Sea Of Tunes inscribed underneath.' He just kept throwing these photographs around and then suddenly he leapt up and ran out of the office. He never really intimidated me. Though I wouldn't have liked to have been one of his sons."

■ Tuesday 1st

RECORDING *Pet Sounds* **session 17** Western Recorders studio (3) *Hollywood, CA* 1:00pm onwards. Work begins on the instrumental tracks for **'I'm Waiting For The Day'**, a song apparently started two years earlier. After several run-throughs, Brian supervises the recording of the song's instrumental track (take 14 marked as best). *Musicians present* Gary Coleman (timpani, bongos), Al de Lory (piano), Jim Gordon (drums), Billy Green (flute), Len Hartman (English horn), Jim Horn (flute), Carol Kaye (bass guitar), Larry Knechtel (organ), Jay Migliori (flute), Ray Pohlman (guitar), Lyle Ritz (upright bass).

■ Thursday 3rd

MIXING Columbia studio *Los Angeles, CA*. Using the studio's impressive 8-track recorder at a time when 4-track machines are the standard, Brian completes an alternate early mono mix of **'Wouldn't It Be Nice'**. Meanwhile, Capitol Records issues an update to the memo issued 11 days ago, now omitting 'Good Good Good Vibrations' as one of the tracks intended for *Pet Sounds*. Its place is taken by the 1965-recorded instrumental 'Run James Run', renamed as **'Pet Sounds'**. (Also today, at Western Recorders, engineer Chuck Britz makes a mono mix tape featuring incomplete vocals for **'Wouldn't It Be Nice'** and **'I Know There's An Answer'**.)

TOUR STARTS US West/Midwest/East (Mar 6th-18th)

■ Sunday 6th

RECORDING *Pet Sounds* **session 18** Western Recorders studio (3)

Caroline No single by Brian Wilson

A 'Caroline No' (B. WILSON / T. ASHER)
B 'Summer Means New Love' (B. WILSON)

US release March 7th 1966 (Capitol 5610).
UK release April 1966 (Capitol CL 15438).
Chart high US number 32; UK none.

Hollywood, CA 2:00-5:00pm, 5:00-8:00pm. New strings and inserts of woodwind instrumental pieces are added to the March 1st recording of **'I'm Waiting For The Day'**. The session, engineered by H. Bowen David, concludes with the taping of a vocal overdub. Work is also done on an untitled song.
Musicians present (on 'Waiting'): Justin DiTullio (cello), Harry Hyams (viola), William Kurasch (violin), Leonard Malarsky (violin), Lyle Ritz (upright bass), Ralph Schaeffer (violin), Sidney Sharp (violin). (on untitled song:) Gary Coleman (tympani, bongos), Al de Lory (keyboards), Jim Gordon (drums), Billy Green (woodwind), Jim Horn (saxophone), Carol Kaye (bass guitar), Larry Knechtel (organ), Jay Migliori (woodwind), Ray Pohlman (guitar).

The McNeal Gymnasium *Southern Oregon State College Ashland, OR* 3:00pm; tickets $2.50
The live Beach Boys are back out on the road for this opening night of a brief five-date tour.

■ Monday 7th

'Caroline No' / **'Summer Means New Love'** single by Brian Wilson released in the US. This A-side marks the first public unveiling of some of Brian's new music; the B-side is an instrumental taken from 1965's *Summer Days (And Summer Nights!!)* album. It will be said later that before the master of 'Caroline No' is submitted to Capitol, Murry Wilson takes the recording and speeds it up in an effort to make his eldest son sound younger. In fact, the original master delivered to Capitol is at normal pitch – it is only speeded up during mastering, by wrapping splicing tape onto the playback machine's 'capstan', resulting in a song that plays eight percent faster than originally recorded.

The excitement surrounding Brian's 'new' style of music is so great that everyone close to him is certain the disc will be a monster hit. Anticipating that, Mike, Carl, Brian and Bruce tape several Thankyou radio spots, each aimed at a different station and complete with individual station ID. The pieces are approximately 23 seconds in length, typically going: "Hi, this is Brian Wilson of The Beach Boys. I'd like to thank WFVN for helping make my record 'Caroline No' a hit in Miami." Another spot goes: "Hi, this is Mike Love of The Beach Boys. I'd like to thank all the guys at KUNNZ for playing and making my cousin Brian's record 'Caroline No' a hit in Houston." In fact the single remains in the US *Billboard* Hot 100 chart for just seven weeks and peaks at a disappointing number 32.

■ Tuesday 8th

RECORDING *Pet Sounds* session 19 Western Recorders studio (3) *Hollywood, CA* 12 noon onwards. Brian begins work on the instrumental track for **'God Only Knows'** (take 20 marked as best) with engineer Chuck Britz as usual at Western. "We believe in God

as a kind of universal consciousness," Carl says to an interviewer this year. "God is love. God is you. God is me. God is everything right here in this room. It's a spiritual concept, which inspires a great deal of our music."
Musicians present Hal Blaine (drums), Jesse Ehrlich (cello), Carl Fortina (accordion), Jim Gordon (percussion), Billy Green (woodwind), Leonard Hartman (saxophone), Jim Horn (saxophone), Carol Kaye (bass guitar), Larry Knechtel (organ), Leonard Malarsky (violin), Frank Marocco (clarinet), Jay Migliori (saxophone), Ray Pohlman (bass guitar), Don Randi (piano), Lyle Ritz (upright bass), Alan Robinson (French horn), Sidney Sharp (violin), Darrel Terwilliger (violin, viola).

■ Wednesday 9th

RECORDING *Pet Sounds* session 20 Western Recorders studio (3) *Hollywood, CA* 12:30am-4:00am. In the early hours of the morning Brian takes charge of the second instrumental tracking session for **'God Only Knows'** as strings are overdubbed onto the previous day's recording (take 19 marked as best).
Musicians present Harry Hyams (viola), William Kurasch (violin), Lenny Malarsky (violin), Ralph Schaeffer (violin).

■ Thursday 10th

RECORDING *Pet Sounds* session 21 Columbia studio (A) *Los Angeles, CA* 12:30am-4:15am. Vocal overdubbing is done on **'I'm Waiting For The Day'**, **'Wouldn't It Be Nice'**, **'I Just Wasn't Made For These Times'** and **'God Only Knows'**. On the latter track Carl's lead vocal overdub is followed by work on a vocal harmony overdub from the other Beach Boys. The taping of vocal inserts rounds off the session. (Additional vocal overdubbing on 'I Just Wasn't Made for These Times' will take place on April 13th and on 'God Only Knows' on April 11th.) Brian is apprehensive about including the word 'God' in the title of a pop song because it has never been done before.

"When Brian has an idea, he'll phone us up and we'll do a recording session in the middle of the night," says Bruce. "We just about leave all the musical side of the business to Brian. He does the writing and arranging. We sit and put on record what he has worked out. When I walked in on 'God Only Knows' I realised that something wonderful was happening. Carl had kept telling me about how the new album was coming to life and how it was going to be. But I didn't realise just how great it was until I walked into the studio."

Carl agrees. "You'd hear all this sound coming out and it was indescribable what it did to the environment. You'd be in the room and you'd hear this noise coming over the speakers and you'd be resonating with it. 'God Only Knows' was written in five minutes. That was a special tune."

Even Brian is in awe. "I couldn't believe what I was hearing. There were moments when the group would all get tears in their eyes. That was probably when I learned emotional music, putting my heart in it. I think they thought this music was just for Brian Wilson only, a showcase for Brian Wilson, but it's still The Beach Boys. In other words, they gave in. They gave in to the fact that I had a little thing to say to myself, so they let me have my stint. I explained to them, 'It's OK. It is only a temporary rift where I have something to say.' I wanted to step out of the group a little bit and, sure enough, I was able to."

■ Friday 11th

RECORDING *Pet Sounds* session 22 Sunset Sound studio *Los Angeles, CA* 7:00-10:30pm. The first instrumental tracking session is

Carl, Bruce, Brian and Al in the studio working on an arrangement for a *Pet Sounds* vocal overdub.

done for a song bearing the working title of **'Good Good Good Vibrations'** (ten takes required) and Brian then takes charge of an insert musical sequence for the song (20 takes required). At this point he has no definite title or use for the piece and even considers incorporating its opening musical phrases into his ongoing 'Good Vibrations'. But at the end of today's session he decides to rework 'Good Good Good Vibrations' into a separate piece, ultimately to become **'Here Today'**. Work on the song continues the following day, while some of its phrases will reappear during the 'Good Vibrations' session on May 4th. The engineer at the session is Bruce Botnick.

Musicians present Frankie Capp (percussion), Al Casey (guitar), Mike Deasy (guitar), Steve Douglas (saxophone), Carol Kaye (bass guitar), Larry Knechtel (organ), Gail Martin (trombone), Nicholas Martinis (drums), Jay Migliori (saxophone), Jack Nimitz (saxophone), Ray Pohlman (bass), Don Randi (piano), Lyle Ritz (upright bass), Ernie Tack (trombone).

The Music Hall *Cleveland, OH* 8:30pm, with The Lovin' Spoonful, Noel Harrison

The live Beach Boys band performs a one-off sell-out concert in front of 3,000 fans tonight, and the show grosses more than $12,500.

■ Saturday 12th

RECORDING *Pet Sounds* session 23 Western Recorders studio (3) *Hollywood, CA* 2:00-9:00pm

The second tracking session for the now retitled **'Here Today'** takes place along with instrumental inserts for the song (20 takes required). Work on the piece will resume on March 25th. Later today Brian completes alternative early mixes of **'I'm Waiting For The Day'** (Mike on lead vocal) and **'God Only Knows'** (two versions: one featuring a saxophone solo, the other an a cappella song-end tag using vocals taped on March 10th).

• 'Barbara Ann' single and parent album *Beach Boys' Party!* both peak in the respective UK *Record Retailer* charts at number 2. The British success of the *Party!* album is a surprise: up to this point the group has had mostly minor hit singles, and the albums haven't fared much better. But *Party!* changes all that. Seemingly out of nowhere, the album reaches the lofty number 2 position in the UK charts, and Britain's love affair with the boys from California begins.

■ Sunday 13th

MIXING Western Recorders studio (3) *Hollywood, CA* 2:00-9:00pm. The studio is booked but no recordings are made. Brian spends part of the day mixing another rough cut of **'God Only Knows'** and engaged in conversation with American reporter Ken Grevatt. He begins by explaining why he doesn't join the other Beach Boys for concerts, for instance at tonight's show in Pittsburgh. "I don't go out on the tours at all," Brian says. "I just work on production. I'm at home while Bruce Johnston takes my place with the boys. I've spent five months working on this new album and I think that [it] and the batch of new singles I've been working on … well, it's like I'm right in the golden era of what it's all about. It's all just coming out, like breaking now. A lot of new things are already recorded, like our new single, 'Sloop John B'.

"I give a lot of credit to The Beatles," Brian continues. "They've had a tremendous universal influence. That *Rubber Soul* album was a great new contribution. It helped them reach a new plateau. I still give Phil Spector credit for being the single most influential producer. He's timeless. He makes a milestone whenever he goes into the studio and this has helped The Beach Boys evolve. We listen to what is happening and it affects what we do too.

"The trends have influenced my work but so has my own scene. I've got this terrific house high in the hills with a tremendous view.

Sloop John B single

A 'Sloop John B' (TRAD. ARR. B. WILSON)
B 'You're So Good To Me' (B. WILSON / M. LOVE)

US release March 21st 1966 (Capitol 5602).
UK release April 1966 (Capitol CL 15441).
Chart high US number 3; UK number 2.

It's stimulating and it's helped me to mature. I remember when I used to think marriage was a hang-up to the image. That's no more. The Beatles have brought so many things to the industry, like Lennon being married. His being married was so perfect, so beautiful because it enables so many other artists to be married and still be considered an artist. Three of our guys, Mike, Al and Carl, are already married."

Syria Mosque *Pittsburgh, PA*
The live band continues with the latest tour.

■ Tuesday 15th

RECORDING Western Recorders studio (3) *Hollywood, CA* 6:00pm onwards. Western is booked but again no recordings are carried out. Instead Brian spends the time working on arrangements with the Wrecking Crew musicians.

■ Thursday 17th
UP Fieldhouse, University of Dayton *Dayton, OH* 8:00pm

■ Friday 18th
Fordham College Bronx *New York, NY* 7:00 & 10:00pm
Last date of the tour; tonight's first show is a sell-out.

■ Monday 21st
'Sloop John B' / 'You're So Good to Me' single released in the US. Capitol Records puts out this new Beach Boys 45 in order to cover up the unimpressive performance of Brian's solo single 'Caroline No' on the chart. 'Sloop John B' will peak at number 3 on May 7th, selling 500,000 copies within the first two weeks of its release.

■ Tuesday 22nd
RECORDING United Recorders studio *Los Angeles, CA*; Western Recorders studio *Hollywood, CA*; Columbia studio (A) *Los Angeles, CA* 7:00pm-12midnight. At United, with engineer Chuck Britz, Brian tapes in mono the barking of his dogs Banana (a Beagle) and Louie (a Weimaraner), later used to close the new album. Meanwhile, a rough-mix session at next door's Western – also supervised by Britz – produces more alternative mixes of 'God Only Knows', 'I Know There's An Answer' and 'Wouldn't It Be Nice'. At Columbia, Brian continues to experiment with the mix of **'God Only Knows'** using Columbia's 8-track recorder, preparing a version that features his lead vocal. Still dissatisfied, he decides to tape new vocals for the song (see April 11th). It's possible that mixing work is also done today on **'Here Today'**.

■ Thursday 24th
RECORDING 'Good Vibrations' session 4 Columbia studio *Los Angeles, CA* 7:00pm-12 midnight. One month after the last recording

In the studio working on Pet Sounds *vocals. With their backs to camera are Bruce Johnston (left) and Carl Wilson (right); facing us are Al Jardine (left) and Brian Wilson.*

session for the piece, Brian continues with instrumental work on **'Good Vibrations'**. At the conclusion he joins up in the studio with the other Beach Boys and their recently installed publicist Derek Taylor to record several unscripted radio spots that will be played on selected US stations to promote the upcoming live shows, set to start on April 1st. The relatively short pieces feature humorous dialogue; some examples follow.

Dennis: "Hi, this is the greatest drummer on earth, Dennis Wilson of The Beach Boys."
Brian: "I wouldn't pay two cents to see you, anyway."
Dennis: "Well, I think I'm pretty darn good."
Brian: "Well, when's the show? One of these nights, right?"

Another segment alludes to Brian's continuing failure to appear on stage with The Beach Boys.

Brian: "Hey you. How come you look so much like me?"
Carl: "Because I'm your brother Carl."
Brian: "Is your dad Murry Wilson?"
Carl: "Yes he is."
Brian: "I'm gonna go with him to the show tonight."
Carl: "The Beach Boys show? Mike's going to be there. Al, Bruce, we're all gonna be there."
Mike: "Brian, I think you need a rest."

The group has decided to work without a script, so some of this amusing banter begins to wander aimlessly – and will remain on the cutting floor. The most interesting of these segments features a conversation between Mike and the well-spoken Derek Taylor, who plays a passer-by stopped by Mike.

Mike: "Hey you."
Derek: "Yes, pardon."
Mike: "You're kind of dressed funny, aren't you?"
Derek: "Maybe I am, yes."
Mike: "Well, you look like you've got some bread. How would you like to buy a ticket?"
Derek: "I don't know what you mean by bread."
Mike: "Money, dollars."
Derek: "Oh yes. I have some money. I have a pound note."
Mike: "What the heck's a pound note?"
Derek: "It's English money. I have it to spend. I want to do something with it. Something good."
Mike: "Well, the best thing I can tell you about is The Beach Boys."
Derek: "Oh, the Wilsons. Murry Wilson's sons." (At this point in the proceedings laughter is heard from the other Beach Boys present, filling the studio.)
Mike: "Well, I didn't know you knew them."
Derek: "I know Murry very well. Yes, I met him. I'd love to see those chaps. They're very good. Can I come?"
Mike: "Well, go to any A&W Hamburger stand."
Derek: "But they'd look at me and laugh, wouldn't they?"
Mike: "That's what I'm trying to get you to do. I like to see foreigners maligned."
Derek: "Well, I'd like to come but I'm not prepared to be insulted by you, sir. But I'd like to come to the show."
Mike: "I'm not insulting you. I'm just telling you you're kind of messed up and you look kind of funny for this country."
Derek: "I don't like your face at all."
Mike: "Well, maybe that's because I have a beard."
Derek: "That's because you're bald, isn't it?" (Laughter once more fills the room.)

■ Friday 25th

RECORDING *Pet Sounds* **session 24** Columbia studio *Los Angeles, CA*
At this session, engineered by Ralph Balantin, Mike adds a lead vocal to the **'Here Today'** instrumental tracks taped on March 11th and 12th and mixed on the 22nd. (The master released version of 'Here Today' comprises a mix of instrumental take 20 and vocals take 11. At 1:52 into the released version the group can just be heard in the background discussing the cameras they bought during their visit to Japan in January.)

"We worked long and hard on the vocals," Mike says later, "and if there was a hint of a sharp or a flat [there] we would have to do it again until it was right. Every voice had to be right. The timing had to be right." Carl too notices Brian's developing sense of perfection. "We'd be about eight or nine bars into the song and Brian would go, 'OK,' and stop us. Nobody else in the room would know what was wrong with it. But he'd know that a note was wrong, or somebody hadn't played, out of all the bits that were going on. It was amazing how he heard something at the time that it occurred."

■ Monday 28th

'Don't Run Away' single by Bruce & Terry released in the US, a song co-written by Mike Love.

April

'Caroline No' / **'Summer Means New Love'** single by Brian Wilson released in the UK. It fails to chart.

'Sloop John B' / **'You're So Good to Me'** single released in the UK. It will peak at number 2 in the *Record Retailer* chart.
The Beach Boys Today! album released in the UK.
• 'Barbara Ann' single peaks in German *Hit Bilanz* chart at number 2 and in French *Music Media Monthly* chart at number 7.

TOUR STARTS US South (Apr 1st-9th)

■ Friday 1st

Memorial Auditorium *Dallas, TX* 8:30pm, with The Lovin' Spoonful, Chad & Jeremy
Following a two-week break since the last live shows, the touring group starts a brief nine-date American outing.

■ Saturday 2nd

Will Rogers Coliseum *Fort Worth, TX* 8:30pm

■ Sunday 3rd

RECORDING *Pet Sounds* **session 25** Western Recorders studio (3) *Hollywood, CA* 10:00pm-1:00am. Using the instrumental tracks taped on February 11th (see entry), Brian oversees overdubbing of strings and two lead vocals onto **'Don't Talk (Put Your Head On My Shoulder)'**. Engineer is H. Bowen David. At the end of the session, Brian attempts three rough mono mixes, with and without strings.
Musicians present Arnold Belnick (violin), Norm Botnick (viola), Joe Saxon (cello), Ralph Scheaffer (violin), Sidney Sharp (violin), Tibor Zelig (violin).
Music Hall *Houston, TX* 6:30 & 9:30pm, with The Lovin' Spoonful, Chad & Jeremy

Sheet 1

Date: 11 APRIL 66

Program: BEACH BOYS

DEPT. OR CLIENT:

Reel No.:

Studio:

Start No.	Start Time	SELECTION TITLE SPOT DATA	Take No.	F.S.	Master No.	OK	REMARKS
1		VOCAL GROUP No. 1					
2		CARL – LEAD No. 1					
3		GROUP					
4		ORCH.					
5		CARL – LEAD No. 2					→ KILL BEFORE VG COMES IN
6		VOCAL GROUP No. 2					
7		BRYAN & BRUCE					
8		BRYAN & BRUCE					
9							
10							
11							
12							
13							
14							
15							

SPLICING DATA

GOD ONLY KNOWS

Producer:

Engineer:

CR-588

Sheet 2

Date: 13 APRIL 66

Program: BEACH BOYS

Tape Identification Data   Bryan

DEPT. OR CLIENT:

Reel No.:

Studio: A · HOLLY

Start No.	Start Time	SELECTION TITLE SPOT DATA	Take No.	F.S.	Master No.	OK	REMARKS
1		BRYAN – CHORUS					
2		BRYAN – LEAD No. 1					
3		VOCAL GROUP No. 1			MIGHT	HAVE	TO KEY OUT
4		ORCHESTRA					
5		BRYAN – LEAD No. 2					
6		BRYAN – CHORUS			BRYAN		w/ TAPE REVERB AT END
7		VOCAL GROUP No. 2			MIGHT	HAVE	TO KEY OUT
8		BRYAN – No 1 – ECHO			BRYAN		w/ TAPE REVERB AT EN.
9							
10							
11							
12							
13							
14							
15							

SPLICING DATA

JUST WASN'T MADE FOR THESE TIMES

Producer:

Engineer:

CR-588

Sheet 3

Sheet No. 5

Date: 3-23-66

Program:

DEPT. OR CLIENT:

JOB NO.:

Reel No. 8 TRK

Studio: CRA

Start No.	Start Time	SELECTION TITLE SPOT DATA	Take No.	F.S.	Master No.	OK	REMARKS
1		GROUP 2					
2		GROUP 1					
X 3		MIKE #3			CHORUS		GRP 3-25-66
4		BAND					FROM 4 TRK
O 5	Lead MIKE BRYAN MIKE #1			CHORUS MIKE		
X 6		MIKE #4			CHOR		GRP 3-25-66
7							
O 8	Lead	MIKE #2			CHORUS MIKE		
9							
10							
11							
12							
13							
14							
15							

SPLICING DATA

I DON'T HAVE A TITLE YET

HERE TODAY

Producer:

Engineer:

■ Monday 4th

Municipal Auditorium *San Antonio, TX* 7:30pm, with The Lovin' Spoonful, Chad & Jeremy
The latest US tour continues.

■ Tuesday 5th

Palmer Municipal Auditorium *Austin, TX* 7:30pm, with The Lovin' Spoonful, Chad & Jeremy

■ Wednesday 6th

Ellis Auditorium Amphitheater *Memphis, TN* 8:00pm; tickets $2.50-$4.00

An *Easter Spectacular* concert sponsored by WMPS radio station, in front of a sell-out audience of over 6,300. "The crowd that came out for The Beach Boys' second Memphis show surprised even the promoters," writes William Levy in the *Memphis Commercial Appeal*. "At 8:00pm, when the two-and-a-half-hour performance was scheduled to begin, the Amphitheatre was almost filled and an estimated 1,000 youngsters, enjoying the first day of the Easter School vacation, were still in front of the ticket window. To accommodate the huge overflow, the management opened the balcony of [tonight's venue] affording several hundred a birds-eye view of the back of the performers' heads. Unlike last year's performance when police and foremen had problems controlling the crowd, last night's audience was 'among the best-mannered and neatest-dressed I've ever seen for this type of performance', said Fire Captain G.B. Cleveland Jr. When asked how he planned to keep 6,300 autograph seekers away from the 15-member troupe when the show ended, the captain wiped his brow and remarked, 'Well, now, that's another subject.'"

Set-list 'Fun Fun Fun', 'Little Honda', 'Surfin' USA', 'Surfer Girl', 'Little Old Lady From Pasadena', 'Papa-Oom-Mow-Mow', 'You've Got To Hide Your Love Away', 'Sloop John B', 'Do You Wanna Dance', 'Hawaii', 'I Get Around', 'Help Me Rhonda', 'California Girls', 'Then I Kissed Her', 'Johnny B Goode', 'Barbara Ann'.

■ Thursday 7th

The Civic Auditorium *Jacksonville, FL* 7:00 & 9:00pm

■ Friday 8th

Bayfront Center Arena *St. Petersburg, FL* 8:30pm

■ Saturday 9th

RECORDING 'Good Vibrations' session 5 Gold Star studio (A) Los Angeles, CA 5:00-9:30pm plus one hour overtime for some musicians. Sixteen days after the last work on the piece, Brian takes charge of another tracking session for **'Good Vibrations'**, with Larry Levine engineering. The session is given a specific 'master' number in Capitol Records' tape filing system – in this case Master No. 55949 – meaning that it is considered a finished version potentially available for mixing and release. The filing system also notes that this version is of 2:28 duration. (Only Frankie Capp, Paul Tanner and Tommy Morgan stay on for the overtime.)

Musicians present Hal Blaine (drums), Frankie Capp (percussion), Al de Lory (keyboard), Steve Douglas (saxophone), Carl Fortina (accordion), Billy Green (woodwind), Carol Kaye (bass guitar), Larry Knechtel (organ), Michael Melvoin (harpsichord), Jay Migliori (woodwind), Tommy Morgan (harmonica), Ray Pohlman (guitar), Lyle Ritz (upright bass), Arthur C. Smith (possibly flute), Paul Tanner (electro-theremin).

Miami Beach Convention Hall *Miami Beach, FL* 8:30pm, with The Lovin' Spoonful, The Birdwatchers, The Dedd, The Morlocks

To end this brief tour the group plays another *Easter Spectacular* show, this one sponsored by local radio station WQAM. The nine-date tour has grossed $200,000.
• 'Sloop John B' single enters US *Billboard* Top 40 chart at number 35.

■ Monday 11th

RECORDING *Pet Sounds* session 26 Columbia studio (A) *Hollywood, CA*. With the band back from the recent tour, Brian and Carl record vocals for **'Wouldn't It Be Nice'** and **'God Only Knows'**. For 'God Only Knows' Carl overdubs a lead vocal and the two add harmony vocal overdubs and vocal inserts. (An 'insert' is a vocal or instrumental part, often of short duration, added usually to one tape track of the existing recorded performance.) Brian uses the 8-track recorder at Columbia for this work. Terry Melcher is on hand to provide additional backing vocals at the end of 'God Only Knows'.

Carl will recall: "Brian says he wrote ['God Only Knows'] especially for me. He says it fits my beautiful spirit. I know I shouldn't be embarrassed by a compliment but for so many years there was little communication between us three brothers, because we were … all near the same age and we were young and we were thrown into an adult world rather suddenly. Just recently we've been able to really talk to each other and appreciate the virtues rather than just complain about the faults."

Carl adds: "We really tried to make a good album. We wanted to take another step. 'Wouldn't It Be Nice' was the track that really brought that hope to all of us. We did at least ten sessions on that one, and still it wasn't right. I still think we sang it a little rushed." And Bruce: "We re-recorded our vocals for 'Wouldn't It Be Nice' so many times that the rhythm was never right. We'd slave … singing this thing and then Brian would say, 'No, it's not right! It's just not right!'"

■ Wednesday 13th

RECORDING *Pet Sounds* session 27 Columbia studio (A) *Los Angeles, CA*. Second vocal overdubbing session for **'I Just Wasn't Made For These Times'**. ('Overdubbing' is the recording of additional vocals or instruments onto an existing recorded performance on tape.) Seven of the eight tape tracks on Columbia's 8-track recorder are filled with vocals, and five of those are just Brian. With that work done – and after 27 recording sessions – the *Pet Sounds* album is complete. All that remains is to mix and master the record for release.

■ Saturday 16th

At a studio in the Capitol Records Tower HQ in Hollywood, Brian masters the *Pet Sounds* album. At the conclusion of the disc, he adds some closing sound-effects: a train roaring through a lonely railroad stop, courtesy of Capitol's tape library, and the barking of his dogs, Banana and Louie, which he taped on March 22nd.

Fred Vail, the Beach Boys concert promoter, remembers calling Brian and Marilyn at their home in Laurel Way, up in the Hollywood Hills, and that Brian invited him to Capitol where he was going to master the new record. "I was already down in Hollywood and he was in the hills so I got there first," says Vail. "Brian came into the studio: there was Brian, the mastering guy and me, just the three of us in the mastering facility. Back in the 1960s, these studios were clinical, technical, very sterile, had acoustic ceilings, neon lights, linoleum floors, nowhere to sit – it was very cramped. It was so stark that it took Brian back. In the recording studio itself you had rear lights which you could dim to create a mood, but in the mastering lab you couldn't do that. The lights were either on or off. So Brian had them turn off all the overhead lights. All there was in the room for

CAPITOL RECORDS, INC.
(Employer's name)

Phonograph Recording Contract Blank
AMERICAN FEDERATION OF MUSICIANS
OF THE UNITED STATES AND CANADA

~1394
Nº 247069

Local Union No. 47

THIS CONTRACT for the personal services of musicians, made this 9 day of April, 1966 16 musicians
between the undersigned employer (hereinafter called the "employer") and _____
(hereinafter called "employees").   (Including the leader)

WITNESSETH, That the employer hires the employees as musicians severally on the terms and conditions below, and as further specified on reverse side. The leader represents that the employees already designated have agreed to be bound by said terms and conditions. Each employee yet to be chosen shall be so bound by said terms and conditions upon agreeing to accept his employment. Each employee may enforce this agreement. The employees severally agree to render collectively to the employer services as musicians in the orchestra under the leadership of

Steven D. Kreisman   as follows:

Name and Address of Place of Engagement **Gold Star Recorders, 6252 Santa Monica Blvd.**
Hollywood, Calif. 90038

Date(s) and Hours of Employment **April 9, 1966 5:P.M. to 9:30 P.M. some man 1 Hour overtime only.**

Type of Engagement: Recording for phonograph records only.   Plus pension contributions as specified on reverse side hereof.

WAGE AGREED UPON $ **Union Scale**
(Terms and amount)

This wage includes expenses agreed to be reimbursed by the employer in accordance with the attached schedule, or a schedule to be furnished the employer on or before the date of engagement.

To be paid **Within 15 Days**
(Specify when payments are to be made)

Upon request by the American Federation of Musicians of the United States and Canada (herein called the "Federation") or the local in whose jurisdiction the employees shall perform hereunder, the employer either shall make advance payment hereunder or shall post an appropriate bond.

Employer's name and _____ CAPITOL RECORD _____   Leader's name Steven D. Kreisman   Local No. 47

authorized signature _____   Leader's signature _____

Street address _____ 1750 N. VINE ST. _____   Street address 6950 Chisholm Ave.

City _____ State _____ Phone   City Van Nuys, Calif. State

(1) Label Name _____ CAPITOL   Session No. 12265-A

Master No.	No. of Minutes	TITLES OF TUNES	Master No.	No. of Minutes	TITLES OF TUNES
57949	2:28	GOOD VIBRATIONS			

(2) Employee's Name (As on Social Security Card) Last First Initial	(3) Home Address (Give Street, City and State)	(4) Local Union No.	(5) Social Security Number	(6) Scale Wages	(7) Pension Contribution
1½ hr.O.T. (Leader) Kreisman, Steven D.	6950 Chisholm Ave. Van Nuys, Calif.	47	556-46-1005	284.72	22.78
Blaine, Hal (Contractor)	2441 Castilian Dr. L.A. 28, Calif.	48	047-20-5900	284.72	22.78
Capp, Frank 1-Hr.O.T.	3017 Dona Nenita Studio City, Calif.	47	013-24-7193	122.02	9.76
Delory, Alfred V.	5524 Ruthwood Dr. Calabasas, Calif.	47	559-36-9796	122.02	9.76
Fortina, Carl L.	838 No. Orange Dr. L.A. 38, Calif.	47	554-32-8082	122.02	9.76
Green William E.	4526 Don Miguel Dr. L.A. 8, Calif.	47	512-16-4687	122.02	9.76
Kaye, Carol	4905 Forman No. Hollywood, Calif.	47	555-46-5389	122.02	9.76
Knechtel, Lawrence W.	4847 Van Noord Sherman Oaks, Calif.	47	553-54-6386	122.02	9.76
Levine, Lawrence	19811 Itasca St. Chatsworth, Calif.	47	546-32-8261	122.02	9.76
Melvoin, Michael	5445 Corteen Pl No. Hollywood, Calif.	47	395-32-1757	122.02	9.76
Migliori, Jay	1701 N. Lincoln Burbank, Calif.	47	208-24-6118	122.02	9.76
Morgan, Tommy 1½ O.T.	7111 Kilty Ave. Canoga Park, Calif.	47	556-40-5544	142.36	11.39
Pohlman, M.R.	6171 Rockcliff Dr. L.A. 28, Calif.	47	556-34-6698	122.02	9.76
Ritz, Lyle	1971 N. Curson Ave. L.A. 46, Calif.	47	549-38-1490	122.02	9.76

SEE ATTACHED CONTINUATION SHEET FOR ADDITIONAL MUSICIANS **********************

(8) Total Pension Contributions (of Column (7)) $ **186.68**
Make check payable is amount to "AFM & EPW Fund."

FOR FUND USE ONLY:

illumination was the little red pilot lights that told you the machine was on or off, the VU meter lights, and a cutting light that they used on the lathe to make sure the needle was going down right. And that was it.

"We sat on the floor and Brian's left shoulder was against my right shoulder. The album started with 'Wouldn't It Be Nice'. Throughout the whole thing Brian gave instructions to the mastering guy. He'd say, 'Fade it here,' and, 'Turn up the highs a little bit.' Straight through to 'Caroline No' and the trains and his dogs at the end of the album. It faded out and I was just mesmerised by the sound. Brian said, 'Well, what do you think?' I said, 'It's great, Brian! I love it. It's fabulous! It's really different. It's unique. I love it.' Then he looked at me and said, 'What do you think the guys will think?' Meaning the other Beach Boys. I said, 'You know, Brian. I don't know. Whatever they think, it doesn't really matter, because it's your best effort yet. I think.' Brian said, 'Well, maybe I'll be that lucky with the guys. Maybe they'll like it too.'"

Marilyn Wilson later told *Rolling Stone*: "When they finished [*Pet Sounds*], dubbed it down and all that, Brian brought the album home. He prepared a moment and we went into the bedroom. He said, 'OK, are you ready?' He was serious. This was his soul in there. We just laid there all night, alone on the bed, listened and cried. It was really, really heavy. He was so proud of it."

■ Saturday 23rd

'Caroline No' single by Brian Wilson enters the US *Billboard* Top 40 chart at number 37.
• 'Sloop John B' single enters the UK *Disc & Music Echo* Top 50 chart at number 23.

■ Sunday 24th

TV Brian's home *1448 Laurel Way, Los Angeles, CA*. BBC-1 *Top Of The Pops* filmed feature 'Sloop John B' broadcast May 12th and June 16th (7:30-8:00pm), AVRO Dutch TV *Rooster* June 30th

The Beach Boys shoot the first promotional film for *Pet Sounds*, primarily to assist with the sales push in the UK where the group's popularity is rapidly increasing. The black-and-white 16mm clip, directed and scripted by their publicist Derek Taylor, is for 'Sloop John B' and intended for screening on the BBC TV show *Top Of The Pops*. It does not feature Dennis – who plays the role of cameraman.

In the film the group is welcomed at a door by Brian – who changes into Carl – and then they perform a short intricate dance step on the paving stones in Brian's back yard and, fully dressed, clown around in Brian's swimming pool with an inflatable rubber raft. Throughout the early part of the clip Mike wears a raincoat and swigs Coke from a bottle. Taylor makes cameo appearances in the film. (As well as the airings noted for the film, 'Sloop John B' has its first airing on *Top Of The Pops* during the April 28th broadcast when regular *TOTP* troupe The Go Jos dance to the record.)

■ Monday 25th

TV Mountainous areas above Lake Arrowhead *Hollywood, CA*. BBC-1 *Top Of The Pops* filmed feature 'God Only Knows' broadcast August 4th and September 1st (7:30-8:00pm). Derek Taylor scripts and directs a second, slightly longer film for *Pet Sounds*. In this slightly off-beat piece of celluloid pop the group – this time with Dennis but minus Bruce – appears from behind trees wearing horror masks. Mike is seen sitting drinking freshly brewed coffee from his boots

while the rest of the group (now without masks) sit nearby in the woods playing the card game Old Maid. Mike is stopped from joining them and takes solace in a nearby 'wood monster' (Al in a mask) who joins Mike in some brisk boot polishing. Slow-motion footage of Dennis jumping from a woodland tree is also included in the clip, and excerpts of the songs 'Wouldn't It Be Nice', 'Here Today' and 'God Only Knows' are used on the soundtrack. When this five-minute *Pet Sounds* film is submitted to the BBC for screening on *Top Of The Pops* the hierarchy at the Corporation fears that the group's fans may be unhappy to see The Beach Boys donning grotesque masks. Slight edits are made and the film is re-cut to accompany 'God Only Knows'.

TOUR STARTS US (Apr 28th-May 15th)

■ Thursday 28th
Circle Star Theater *San Carlos, CA*

Just three weeks after finishing their last junket, the live Beach Boys band starts another short tour.

• Around this time, with his Beach Boys colleagues away to begin another tour, Brian excitedly previews the group's new album *Pet Sounds* to Capitol executives at the Capitol Records Tower in Hollywood. They are unimpressed and tell him so. Plans to shelve the disc are discussed and several more meetings follow at the Tower. Brian is angry and hurt that his new heartfelt long-player has been received so negatively.

Tired of explaining why he has made an album like this, he attends the last Capitol meeting with a tape recorder on which are eight pre-recorded loops with Brian saying, 'No,' 'Yes,' and, 'Can you repeat that?' He refuses to speak to Capitol's hierarchy and instead responds to their questions by playing one of the loops as appropriate. Capitol see how proud Brian is of *Pet Sounds* and reluctantly agree to issue the LP, setting a release date of May 16th.

■ Friday 29th
Cornell University *Ithaca, NY*

■ Saturday 30th
Boston College *Boston, MA*

• 'Caroline No' single peaks in US *Billboard* chart at number 32. In the same issue, Capitol hastily insert a single-sheet advertisement for the forthcoming *Pet Sounds* album.

May

Beach Boys' Hits EP released in the UK: 'Help Me Rhonda', California Girls', 'The Little Girl I Once Knew', 'Barbara Ann'. The 'extended play' 45 will reach the number 1 position in the *Record Retailer* EP chart on June 4th, intermittently remaining there until the demise of the chart on December 2nd 1967 and spending a record-breaking 32 weeks in the top position.

• 'Barbara Ann' single peaks in Belgian chart at number 11, in Italian *Il Musichere* chart at number 5, in New Zealand *Listener Pop-O-Meter* chart at 3, in Norwegian chart at number 1, and in Rhodesian Broadcasting Corporation's chart at number 2.

• 'Sloop John B' single peaks in Canadian *RPM* chart at number 2, in Dutch chart at number 1, and in Swedish Radio 3 chart at 5.

• During this month at Brian's home on Laurel Way in Los Angeles he begins to write songs with Van Dyke Parks, three months after they first met. Parks is a sophisticated young wordsmith, sharp-tongued, bespectacled, and highly articulate. After five years of collaborating with Mike, Brian finds Parks a ray of fresh sunshine. The two are fascinated by one another. Once Tony Asher's work on *Pet Sounds* is concluded, Brian seeks out Parks for the next album project, initially titled *Dumb Angel*. His aim is to explore the innocence of youth and childhood, with an American theme, and to surpass *Pet Sounds*.

Usually they work together at Brian's Laurel Way home, and the songs come swiftly. Parks will recall later to KHJ Radio: "I went into a collaboration at his house, between the swimming pool operations and my jumping through his sandbox to get to his Steinway piano. Brian did all the music. All of it! He was the central source of what we call ideas." The duo put to paper a range of songs with titles such as 'Heroes And Villains' (the first track written by the pair; see also October 20th), 'Do You Like Worms' and 'Cabin Essence' (later retitled as one word, 'Cabinessence'). Some of the songs will be revised and, in some cases, rewritten as the pair devise songs for the new project between now and September (see September 8th).

■ Sunday 1st
Worcester Memorial Auditorium *Worcester, MA*

■ Wednesday 4th
RECORDING 'Good Vibrations' session 6 Western Recorders studio (3) *Hollywood, CA* 1:00-5:30pm. Brian works on the sixth tracking session for **'Good Vibrations'** (Master No. 55949), with Chuck Britz as usual engineering at Western. Capitol and the rest of The Beach Boys are beginning to lose patience at the seemingly endless work on this song, but Brian continues with his opus. Today he re-records and perfects the opening bass phrases of the song, the ones he had toyed with during sessions for 'Here Today' on March 11th.

Brian believes that time is not a concern because he is "creating art". He starts to lose his cool and threatens to take the track to another label, in particular Warner Brothers. All of Brian's production splendour from the last few years is being channelled into this one song. He feels that after working hard to make *Pet Sounds* the ultimate pop album he is now ready to make the ultimate pop single. Brian's quest for the perfect sound has taken him from Western to Gold Star studios and back now to Western. It seems as if every studio musician in Los Angeles has played on the song – and still there is no finished master.

Brian later tells BBC Radio-2: "We ran wild with [marijuana]. We were being very creative on drugs. To satisfy our fancy, we would try different studios with different parts of the song."

David Anderle, a friend of Van Dyke Parks, will recall: "When I first got in with Brian, it was right around the time of the fifth or sixth attempt of 'Good Vibrations'. It knocked me out and I said, 'Oh, there's something happening here that is unbelievable.' The next time I came into the studio, it was different again. The next time I came up, Brian told me that he decided to totally scrap 'Good Vibrations'. He was not going to put it out. The track was going to be sold to Warner Brothers and put out as an R&B record sung by a coloured group. I told [musician] Danny Hutton about this and he said, 'Well, let's see if I can't record the song myself and have Brian produce and finish the basic track.' So I called Brian back the next day and told him about this position. But Brian had decided to go ahead and finish his own version of the song."

The original so-called 'live' version of 'Good Vibrations' produced today at Western is an R&B number that many of the session musicians present will later recall as being as good as the released record. But Brian still isn't satisfied and has a complex vision that includes cellos – an idea from Van Dyke Parks – and the wobbly sound of the electro-theremin. This means he will continue to move the recording of the song from studio to studio in Los Angeles. "I wanted to experiment with combining studio sounds," explains Brian. "Every studio has its own marked sound."

Musicians present Hal Blaine (drums), Jimmy Bond Jr (upright bass), Frankie Capp (bongos, tambourine), Al Casey (guitar), Jerry Cole (guitar), Al de Lory (keyboard), Steve Douglas (saxophone), Sal Frohman (instrument unknown), Jim Gordon (percussion), Billy Green (woodwind), Jim Horn (woodwind), Jay Migliori (woodwind), Tommy Morgan (harmonica, jaws harp), Bill Pitman (guitar), Ray Pohlman (bass guitar), Paul Tanner (electro-theremin).

• A scheduled concert this evening at the Catholic Youth Center in Scranton, PA, is cancelled. Sid Benjamin writes in *Variety*: "Damages in excess of $10,000 are sought from The Beach Boys by a Scranton promoter in a lawsuit filed in Lackawanna County Court. It stems from failure of the troupe to take the stage as scheduled on Wednesday. With $7,300 in the till and the remaining half of a $6,000 guarantee awaiting them, the surfers remained holed up in their rooms at a motel several blocks away while an impatient crowd of some 2,500 teenagers awaited their appearance at the Catholic Youth Center.

"Their youthful manager, Richard Duryea, son of Dan, the film actor, said lack of proper police protection made it impossible for the performers to take the stage. A contract with Max Kearson, the promoter, specified that 20 policemen should be present to protect the Beachers from their followers.

"Duryea asserted that Kearson had only five [policemen] on hand, later added three more laymen and finally wound up ten short of the contractual requirement. 'We simply could not let the boys go on stage without proper policing,' he insisted. A reporter noted that Sammy Davis Jr and Harry Belafonte had taken the same stage with only three policemen on hand in each case. 'Nevertheless, we have to go by our own experience,' countered Duryea. 'We've had so many riots when there have been small crowds that we can't take a chance.' But the young crowd that waited in vain for the rock group appeared pretty tame. When Kearson announced that The Beach Boys would not appear, older observers feared a riot. Aside from a few scattered boos, the youngsters, assured that their money would be refunded, took it in their stride and filed out without any incidents. Kearson, who has been booking names here and in Syracuse for a number of years, said it was the first time that such an incident had occurred.

"Attorney Peter O'Malley, counsel for Kearson, may have thrown some light on the matter when he alleged that some of The Beach Boys troupe were disappointed because they weren't greeted by a full house of 4,000 and asked, 'What kind of hick town is this, anyway?' It was felt that the turnout was pretty good, since The Beach Boys had been some 15 miles away at the Kingston Armory just recently and Will Jordan was heading a variety show for a policeman's benefit the same night at the 1,800 seater Masonic Temple … . It was ironic that the snafu had to occur in Scranton, for millions of The Beach Boys' records have been pressed here. Capitol maintains its largest production plant in South Scranton."

■ Thursday 5th
RECORDING Capitol Records Tower *Hollywood, CA* 8:00-11:00pm. Recordings are made tonight for what will turn out to be an unreleased track, **'Excuse Me Baby'** (Master No. 55984; duration 2:40).

Musicians present Hal Blaine (drums), James Burton (guitar), Frankie Capp (percussion), Roy Caton (trumpet), Al de Lory (keyboard), Steve Douglas (saxophone), Melvin Pollan (upright bass).

■ Saturday 7th
Alumni Hall, Providence College *Providence, RI* 8:00pm
• 'Sloop John B' single peaks in the US *Billboard* chart at number 3, and in the UK *Record Retailer* chart at number 2.
• *Today!* album peaks in the UK *Record Retailer* chart at number 6.

■ Wednesday 8th
Civic Coliseum *Knoxville, TN* 8:00pm, with The Plesbians, The Krustations, The Echoes, King Kent

■ Friday 10th
Yankee Stadium Bronx *New York, NY* Sound Blast '66 show, with Ray Charles (headliner), The Byrds, Stevie Wonder, Jerry Butler, The McCoys, The Marvellettes, The Gentrys, Cowsills, Guess Who
A less-than-sell-out crowd for this big event totals 9,000.

■ Wednesday 11th
RECORDING 'Heroes And Villains' session 1 Gold Star studio (A) *Los Angeles, CA* 10:00am-1:30pm or 2:00pm. As the rest of the band continues a US tour, Brian works with his new songwriting collaborator Van Dyke Parks. Invigorated and excited by what they have produced so far, Brian anxiously books into Gold Star for an instrumental recording of one of their pieces. He sketches out his ideas to 14 session musicians led by Steve Douglas. Gold Star engineer Larry Levine is cast in the role as contractor, the person responsible for assembling the musicians. These players will help Brian and Parks achieve their lofty musical aspirations for **'Heroes And Villains'**, a song intended to evoke vivid images of an old Western town. The song is composed in segments and later strung together. Today's session (Master No. 55999, but later junked) is more an experiment than a full-blown recording, but Brian is happy with this try-out and decides to save the song for his next project. Proper recordings of 'Heroes And Villains' will not begin officially until October 20th.

Musicians present Hal Blaine (drums), Frankie Capp (bells, percussion), Al Casey (guitar), Jerry Cole (guitar), Al de Lory (percussion), Steve Douglas (saxophone), Billy Green (tenor saxophone, clarinet), Jim Horn (saxophone, flute), Carol Kaye (bass guitar), Larry Knechtel (keyboards), Jay Migliori (tenor saxophone, bass saxophone), Bill Pitman (guitar), Lyle Ritz (guitar).

■ Thursday 12th
Lansing Civic Center *Lansing, MI* with Sam The Sham & The Pharaohs
• In Britain, tonight's edition of *Top Of The Pops* broadcast on BBC-1 television between 7:30 and 8:00pm features the first screening of the BBC-commissioned 'Sloop John B' clip shot on April 24th (see entry for that date). A second airing of the film will come during the show broadcast on June 16th.

■ Sunday 15th
Bushnell Auditorium *Hartford, CT*
On the eve of the release of their latest album, The Beach Boys perform the last concert of their current tour.

■ Monday 16th
Pet Sounds album released in the US. The title for the new LP is apparently chosen by Mike because the music contained on the disc consists of Brian's 'pet' or favourite sounds. Mike will recall: "We were standing in one of the studios and we didn't have a title. So we were thinking of maybe a double entendre. We had taken pictures at the zoo with animals and there were animal sounds on the record. It's our

Capitol Records, Inc.
(Employer's name)

Phonograph Recording Contract Blank
AMERICAN FEDERATION OF MUSICIANS
OF THE UNITED STATES AND CANADA

1466

№ 247359

Local Union No. 47

THIS CONTRACT for the personal services of musicians, made this **11th** day of **May** 19 **66** between the undersigned employer (hereinafter called the "employer") and **fourteen (14)** musicians (hereinafter called "employees"). (including the leader)

WITNESSETH, That the employer hires the employees as musicians severally on the terms and conditions below, and as further specified on reverse side. The leader represents that the employees already designated have agreed to be bound by said terms and conditions. Each employee yet to be chosen shall be so bound by said terms and conditions upon agreeing to accept his employment. Each employee may enforce this agreement. The employees severally agree to render collectively to the employer services as musicians in the orchestra under the leadership of

Steven Douglas Kreisman (Beach Boys) as follows:

Name and Address of Place of Engagement **Gold Star Recorders, 6252 Santa Monica Blvd., Los Angeles 38, California**

Date(s) and Hours of Employment **May 11, 1966   10:00 AM to 1:30 PM**

Type of Engagement: **Recording for phonograph records only.**   Plus pension contributions as specified on reverse side hereof.

WAGE AGREED UPON $ **Union scale (including tracking)**
(Terms and amount)

This wage includes expenses agreed to be reimbursed by the employer in accordance with the attached schedule, or a schedule to be furnished the employer on or before the date of engagement.

To be paid **Within two weeks.**
(Specify when payments are to be made)

Upon request by the American Federation of Musicians of the United States and Canada (herein called the "Federation") or the local in whose jurisdiction the employees shall perform hereunder, the employer either shall make advance payment hereunder or shall post an appropriate bond.

Employer's name and authorized signature **Capitol Records, Inc.**

Street address **1750 North Vine St.**

City **Hollywood 28, Calif.** State Phone **HO. 2-6252**

Leader's name **Steven D. Kreisman**   Local No. **47**

Leader's signature

Street address **6950 Chisholm Avenue**

City **Van Nuys, California** State

(1) Label Name **Capitol**   Session No. **12072**

Master No.	No. of Minutes	TITLES OF TUNES	Master No.	No. of Minutes	TITLES OF TUNES
55999		Heroes and Villains (track)			

(2) Employee's Name (As on Social Security Card) Last First Initial	(3) Home Address (Give Street, City and State)	(4) Local Union No.	(5) Social Security Number	(6) Scale Wages	(7) Pension Contribution
(½ hr. O.T.) (Leader) Kreisman, Steven D.	6950 Chisholm Avenue Van Nuys, Calif.	47	556-46-1005	$203.32	$16.27
Levine, Lawrence Contr.	19811 Itasca St. Chatsworth, Calif.	47	546-32-8261	162.66	13.01
(½ hr. O.T.) de Lory, Alfred V.	5524 Ruthwood Drive Calabasas, California	47	559-36-9796	101.66	8.13
Tenor sax, bass sax Migliori, Jay (1 dbl.)	1701 No. Lincoln Burbank, California	47	208-24-6118	90.48	7.24
Tenor sax, clarinet Green, William E. (dbl)	4526 Don Miguel Drive Los Angeles 8, Calif.	47	512-16-4687	90.48	7.24
Sax, flute Horn, James R. (dbl)	3225 Oakshire Drive Hollywood 28, Calif.	47	570-56-6753	90.48	7.24
Bells, percussion Capp, Frank (dbl)	3017 Dona Nenita Studio City, Calif.	47	013-24-7193	90.48	7.24
Casey, Alvin M.	6355 Primrose Hollywood, Calif.	47	526-46-9373	81.33	6.51
Ritz, Lyle	1971 No. Curson Avenue Los Angeles 46, Calif.	47	549-38-1490	81.33	6.51
Pitman, William	9124 Nagle Avenue Pacoima, California	47	068-16-6762	81.33	6.51
Kaye, Carol	4905 Forman North Hollywood, Calif.	47	555-46-5389	81.33	6.51
Kolbrak, Jerry	11600 Kittridge North Hollywood, Calif.	47	394-36-7847	81.33	6.51
Knechtel, Lawrence W.	4847 Van Noord Avenue Sherman Oaks, Calif.	47	553-54-6386	81.33	6.51
Blaine, Hal	2441 Castillian Drive Los Angeles 28, Calif.	47	047-20-5900	81.33	6.51

ALR

PAID M' 2 6 1966

FOR FUND USE ONLY:

(8) Total Pension Contributions of Column (7) $ **111.94**
Make check payable amount to "AFM & EPW Fund."

paid_____ date posted_____ By_____

Pet Sounds album

A1 'Wouldn't It Be Nice' (B. WILSON / T. ASHER)
A2 'You Still Believe In Me' (B. WILSON / T. ASHER)
A3 'That's Not Me' (B. WILSON / T. ASHER)
A4 'Don't Talk (Put Your Head On My Shoulder)' (B. WILSON / T. ASHER)
A5 'I'm Waiting For The Day' (B. WILSON / M. LOVE)
A6 'Let's Go Away For Awhile' (B. WILSON)
A7 'Sloop John B' (TRAD. ARR. B. WILSON)
B1 'God Only Knows' (B. WILSON / T. ASHER)
B2 'I Know There's An Answer' (B. WILSON / T. SACHEN)
B3 'Here Today' (B. WILSON / T. ASHER)
B4 'I Just Wasn't Made For These Times' (B. WILSON / T. ASHER)
B5 'Pet Sounds' (B. WILSON)
B6 'Caroline No' (B. WILSON / T. ASHER)

US release May 16th 1966 (Capitol T2458).
UK release June 27th 1966 (Capitol T2458).
Chart high US number 10; UK number 2.

favourite music of that time, so we thought, 'Why not call it *Pet Sounds*?' I gave Brian the name." According to Brian in his 1990 autobiography, Mike asked Brian: "Who's going to hear this shit? The ears of a dog?" Hence the *Pet Sounds* title. Mike was also heard to call the album "Brian's ego music".

"The music of *Pet Sounds* was created solely for the purpose of making people feel good," Brian will recall, "and making them feel like, 'Hey, that's really cool.' I wanted to make people react to what I was doing. And it worked. I wanted to create music that people would feel would get to their feelings more. We basically centred the ideas around love. ... I find it possible to spill melodies, beautiful melodies, in moments of great despair. Good, emotional music is never embarrassing. If you take the *Pet Sounds* album as a collection of art pieces, each designed to stand alone, yet which belong together, you'll see what I was aiming at."

Carl says: "We're really saying something in this album. We spent a lot of time in the studio. It took a week full of sessions just to perfect the vocal tracks on 'Wouldn't It Be Nice'."

And Bruce: "[*Pet Sounds*] cost us so much money to make, you wouldn't believe it. But I'm happy to say we are knocked out with it. Brian recorded it in four different studios, which gives you some idea of the lengths he went to."

At Capitol's insistence 'Sloop John B', the latest single, is included on the album, much to Brian's annoyance. Although *Pet Sounds* is a huge breakthrough in production, arranging, performing and songwriting, it peaks at a disappointing number 10 in the US album charts (on July 2nd). Significantly, it becomes the group's first studio album in three years not to be certified as a gold record.

Nonetheless, the album shifts an impressive 200,000 copies shortly after its release, but Brian is still mortified. He desperately wants a number 1 hit album.

Marilyn Wilson will say later, in the film documentary *Brian Wilson: I Just Wasn't Made For These Times*: "When [*Pet Sounds*] wasn't received by the public in the way that [Brian] thought it would be received, it really hurt him. It made him hold back. He couldn't

understand it. He said, 'Why aren't people willing to expand and accept more and grow?'"

American music critics give the album several glowing reviews, hailing *Pet Sounds* as the ultimate rock masterpiece. *Billboard* uncharacteristically waits a few weeks to review the album, and in a very brief report calls it "an exciting, well-produced LP". Some musicians, notably John Lennon and Paul McCartney, are in awe (see May 17th).

But most record buyers in the States avoid the record. The country's teenagers are expecting another typical Beach Boys disc laden with fun, sun and driving rather than this effort that comes etched with unprecedented colour and production values, mixed with Brian's adult, soul-baring, heartfelt lyrics. The album certainly doesn't sound like anything that the group has produced before and is unlike any other record that currently resides in the American record charts.

Suddenly, The Beach Boys find themselves among a shift in taste of American fans. The group's once solid popularity among the teenybop audience begins to ebb, and in the place of those youngsters come a more hip, trendy and sophisticated crowd – many of who have so far regarded The Beach Boys as square and nothing more than surfing Doris Days.

Capitol Records too has wanted more of the bankable old-style Beach Boys. But that group is gone. The new LP clearly demonstrates how Brian, the architect of The Beach Boys' sound, has matured musically. Released at a time when popular music is not considered important enough to warrant analysis, *Pet Sounds* is a quiet revolution.

Brian is now about to take his experimentation a step further by channelling all his energy and creativity into a leftover *Pet Sounds* track, 'Good Vibrations'. Recordings for this song will begin again on May 24th.

• On this same day that *Pet Sounds* is released in the United States, Bruce and Derek Taylor arrive in London for a short five-day holiday, taking up residence at central London's Waldorf Hotel. Bruce brings with him a copy of the latest album, keen to promote the music within.

"We had five days off after our four-week tour of the States, so I thought I'd visit Britain and do a bit of hustling," Bruce tells the various UK music reporters on his first day in England. "I got a suite so I could have a drawing room and I could see people.

"I thought I'd better start promoting the album and the group for when we come over in November. I also wanted to find out what the scene was like in Britain. I've come here to work out the scene so I can go back and report what everyone is like and how we ought to approach Britain. I'm doing it in the same way that George Harrison came out to America before The Beatles arrived, to see what it was all about."

Hip LA musician and producer Kim Fowley, a friend of Bruce for the last ten years and currently resident in London, quickly spreads the word that a Beach Boy is in town. Fowley has been a publicist for Hollywood screen star Doris Day and her husband manager Marty Melcher, so Taylor has commissioned him to deliver to Bruce's hotel room some of the top names in the UK music industry. Fowley does not fail in his task.

Within hours, journalist Keith Altham of the *New Musical Express*, Rolling Stone frontman Mick Jagger and that group's manager, Andrew Loog Oldham, all visit Bruce's room at the Waldorf where they are played *Pet Sounds*. A procession of UK music journalists soon follows, each of whom is given an approximately 15-minute interview slot with Bruce and treated to advance selections from the new Brian Wilson masterwork.

Tuesday 17th

On the second day of their visit to London, Derek Taylor stages a press conference in Bruce's suite at the Waldorf Hotel to unveil The Beach Boys' latest long player. Kim Fowley is the unofficial master of ceremonies. Visitors include members of the UK music press such as Penny Valentine of *Disc & Music Echo* and pop people such as singer Marianne Faithfull, drummer Dave Clark of The Dave Clark Five, and pop group The Merseys. Guests of honour at this star-studded get together are John Lennon and Paul McCartney. Bruce recalls: "All day long, journalists were coming through and then, all of a sudden, I get this call saying, 'You're not going to believe this but John Lennon and Paul McCartney are in the room and they want to hear *Pet Sounds*.'"

Singer Tony Rivers of The Castaways, another visitor, will remember Lennon and McCartney coming to Bruce's room to hear the new album. "They came alone," says Rivers. "There were no bodyguards, no wives. Then, Bruce makes his grand entrance, wearing a white suit, white tie, white shirt and white shoes. He was brown and handsome, just as everyone thought [The Beach Boys] were. The all-American boys with a clean image – and this was it."

Fowley serves the two Beatles a drink of rum and coke. Sipping the beverage, McCartney announces that he has two requests. First, he asks for a piano to be wheeled into the room. Second, he requests that no one should speak when the album is being played. As *Pet Sounds* is put on this evening, the two Beatles sit attentively with their ears directed towards the small speakers, listening intently to the music that threatens to displace The Beatles as the dominant force in popular music. At the same time, John and Paul play a hand of canasta. When *Pet Sounds* finishes, the two rush over to the piano and play random chords while whispering to each other. McCartney will say later: "*Pet Sounds* blew me out of the water. I loved the album so much. The one thing that made me sit up were the basslines. It certainly is a totally classic album."

McCartney is keen to listen to the album once more. Bruce: "I played it for the second time and then they left." In fact McCartney heard the new Beach Boys LP last week on an advance test pressing during a visit to the London flat of Andrew Loog Oldham where he had arranged to meet Lou Adler, producer of the Mamas & The Papas. Oldham recalls, "McCartney was gobsmacked when he heard *Pet Sounds* for the first time." Oldham himself describes *Pet Sounds* as the "*Scheherazade* of pop."

In the early hours of Wednesday morning, after they have heard the album through twice, and after signing a playing card for Bruce, Lennon and McCartney get up, bid farewell to everyone, and head for Paul's shared accommodation in Wimpole Street. There, under the influence of Brian's groundbreaking music, the world's top songsmiths start to compose the song 'Here There And Everywhere'. (It will appear on The Beatles' next studio album, *Revolver*, released around the world in August.) After hearing *Pet Sounds* later this week, George Harrison will join his two Beatle colleagues in spreading the word about the marvellous new long-player by The Beach Boys. Beatles producer George Martin will say: "Without *Pet Sounds*, The Beatles' next album, *Sgt. Pepper*, wouldn't have happened. *Revolver* was the beginning of the whole thing. But *Pepper* was an attempt to equal *Pet Sounds*. Hearing *Pet Sounds* gave me the kind of feeling that raises the hairs on the back of your neck. You say, 'What is that? It's fantastic!'"

Tony Rivers: "John and Paul were so blown away by [*Pet Sounds*] it inspired them to come up with *Sgt Pepper*. I know that John and Paul were fans of The Beach Boys because I sat on the floor talking to John for about 20 minutes at the NEMS Enterprises Christmas party one year. And the main part of the conversation was The

Beach Boys, and how great they were. Praise indeed! Bruce also suggested I record one of the tracks off the album, 'God Only Knows'. We ended up releasing our version of the song a week before theirs. ... The same day I met Bruce Johnston at the Waldorf, I asked him if he'd like to meet one of The Who, Keith Moon. I told him that he was a big Beach Boys fan. Bruce said sure, so I called Moonie and told him to call Bruce."

Wednesday 18th

Tony Rivers and his band The Castways are playing a gig this evening at Romford Technical College in Romford, Essex. In the midst of the show Rivers spies Keith Moon and Bruce Johnston approaching through the crowd. "We got them on stage," says Rivers, "and proceeded to murder some classic Beach Boys songs. Ray Brown handed Bruce his bass, but he didn't really know what to play, or even how. He said, 'I'm really a piano player.' But we didn't use piano.

"We had just learnt 'The Little Girl I Once Knew', which had a quite involved bass line. Bruce looked terrified. Keith Moon was on drums and subtlety was not his strong point. At the end of every song I'd try to say, 'Let's hear it for Keith Moon and Bruce Johnston,' but Moonie would just say, 'What'cha doing next? Oh yeah, I know that one,' and on we played. Nice as it was to have such stars with us, it was great to get back to normal. That's probably the nearest that The Castaways ever got to playing jazz."

As the concert concludes, the promoter informs the teenage audience that there will be an extra charge for the unscheduled appearances by Messrs Johnston and Moon and could they pay for this on their way out. After the show Bruce joins Moon and Kim Fowley for a visit of nightclubs and meets members of The Animals. Moon tells Bruce: "I'm going to guide you through England and you're going to meet everybody." The idea of sampling the delights that the clubs have to offer is repeated the following evening, Thursday 19th, when Bruce and Moon visit the Phone Booth club, opposite the London Planetarium.

Friday 20th

Bruce's 'tour of England' continues when he accompanies Keith Moon to Rediffusion Television Studios in Wembley, Middlesex for a surprise, unplanned walk-on appearance on the weekly pop show *Ready Steady Go!*. During the 28-minute programme, transmitted live between 6:07 and 6:35pm in the London ITV region, the pair are interviewed by *RSG!* host Cathy McGowan. She asks Bruce about *Pet Sounds* and the possibility of a British tour by The Beach Boys.

Following the show and the regular tipple in the bar at the studio, Bruce accompanies Moon and Who bassist John Entwistle to Newbury's Ricky Tick Club where The Who are to perform. At 10:10pm, the trio arrives nonchalantly late from the *RSG!* party, with Paul & Barry Ryan and Samantha Juste, the disc girl on *Top Of The Pops*. They discover that Roger Daltrey and Pete Townshend are already on stage delivering a set. Incensed that his two bandmates have not bothered to wait, Moon starts a fight on-stage and (temporarily) quits the group. With The Who's wild antics filling his head, Bruce happily flies back to the States early the following morning.

• Back in the US, New York columnist Nat Hentoff writes, "The Beach Boys are now grossing at least $100,000 a year and have more American offers than they can handle."

Saturday 21st

'Sloop John B' single peaks in UK *Disc* Top 50 chart at number 2, kept from the top spot by Manfred Mann's 'Pretty Flamingo'.

• Also in *Disc & Music Echo* columnist Penny Valentine, fresh from hearing the new album on Tuesday, joins in the UK *Pet Sounds* hysteria. She writes: "Just out in America is a brand new, spanking hot Beach Boys LP, 13 tracks of Brian Wilson genius, packaged in a nice cover of The Beach Boys looking benignly at some pretty hungry pastel goats. Each track has that lovely distinctive smothered Wilson sound as though they're all singing through sugar cotton wool. ... The whole LP is far more romantic than the usual Beach Boys jollity. Sad little wistful songs about lost love and found love. I found the inclusion of 'Sloop John B' something of an irritation. But never mind, Brian has produced, arranged, written and sings on each beautiful track. One dismal note to the proceedings. So far, EMI Records in England have no plans to release this 'ahead-of-its-time' LP."

■ Tuesday 24th
RECORDING 'Good Vibrations' session 7 Sunset Sound studio *Los Angeles, CA* 10:00pm-1:30am. Almost three weeks after his last efforts on the song, Brian resumes work on **'Good Vibrations'**. After a long deliberation he decides to scrap the idea of taping the instrumental base in one take and instead records the music for the song in four separate sections (Master No. 55949).

Section one is the opening piece and requires 15 takes. Section two, focussing on organ, electro-theremin and saxophone – and later scrapped – requires seven takes. Section three features piano, bass, percussion and electro-theremin, and requires eight takes. Section four, the ending of the song, called the 'fade sequence' by Brian, features bass, tambourine, drums, saxophone, timpani, piano, flute, electro-theremin and guitar. It requires nine takes. Different arrangements for the latter section are also attempted.

Rehearsals for Carol Kaye's fuzz bass, accompanied by drums, tambourine, piano, timpani, harpsichord and percussion, round off the three-and-a-half-hour session.

Musicians present Gary Coleman (percussion), Al de Lory (keyboard), Steve Douglas (saxophone), Jim Gordon (drums), Billy Green (woodwind), Jim Horn (woodwind), Carol Kaye (bass guitar), Jay Migliori (saxophone, flute), Lyle Ritz (upright bass), Paul Tanner (electro-theremin).

• While at the studio, Brian hears via an API news report that either Bruce or Al has been involved in an accident on the East Coast.

■ Wednesday 25th
RECORDING 'Good Vibrations' sessions 8/9 Sunset Sound studio *Los Angeles, CA* 3:00-6:00pm, 10:00pm-1:00am plus thirty minutes overtime. Dissatisfied with the previous day's session, Brian takes charge of two new tracking sessions for **'Good Vibrations'** (2:40 duration) and works on section two of the song (seven 'takes', or attempts at a recording, are made). The lyrics "Gotta keep those lovin' good…" have already formed in Brian's mind.

Musicians present (3:00-6:00pm) Arthur 'Skeets' Herfurt (saxophone), Jim Horn (saxophone), Abe Most (clarinet); (10:00pm-1:00am) Gary Coleman (percussion), Al de Lory (keyboard), Steve Douglas (probably saxophone), Jim Gordon (drums), Billy Green (horns), Jim Horn (horns), Carol Kaye (bass guitar), Jay Migliori (saxophone), Lyle Ritz (upright bass), Paul Tanner (electro-theremin). (Glen Campbell plays on several sessions for 'Good Vibrations' but, mysteriously, his name is left off the union log sheets.)

■ Friday 27th
RECORDING 'Good Vibrations' session 10 Western Recorders studio (3) *Hollywood, CA* 9:00am-12:30pm. Another change of studio and a further tracking session for **'Good Vibrations'** (Master No.

55949), engineered by Western regular Chuck Britz. ('Tracking' is the term for the initial recording of backing instruments only.)

Musicians present Gary Coleman (tympani, percussion), Steve Douglas (probably saxophone), Jim Gordon (drums), Jim Horn (saxophone, flute), Plas Johnson (saxophone), Michael Melvoin (harpsichord), Jay Migliori (saxophone, flute), Bill Pitman (guitar), Emil Radocchia (percussion), Lyle Ritz (upright bass), Paul Tanner (electro-theremin), Artie Wright (probably saxophone).

June

Summer Days (And Summer Nights!!) album released in the UK. 'Barbara Ann' single peaks in Swedish Radio 3 chart at number 3.
• 'Sloop John B' single peaks in UK *Record Retailer/Music Weekly* chart at number 2, in New Zealand *Listener Pop-O-Meter* chart at number 1, in German *Hit Bilanz* chart at number 1, in Italian *Il Musichere* chart at number 11, and in Norwegian chart at number 1.
• Beach Boys friend and concert promoter Fred Vail leaves the group and takes up employment at Teenage Fair Incorporated, an organisation that stages Teen Fairs throughout the US.
• Much is made of Brian's mental and emotional state at this time. He took the hallucinogenic drug LSD for the first time in 1965, and some have argued that his interest in 'spiritual' music was a result of his experiences with the substance.

In a conversation this month with Los Angeles reporter Tom Nolan, Brian recalls: "I took LSD, a full dose of LSD, and later, another time, I took a smaller dose and I learned a lot of things, like patience and understanding. I can't teach you or tell you what I learned from taking it, but I consider it a very religious experience."

By now Brian has become interested in the occult, is reading about astrology and the I Ching, and begins an on-again-off-again obsession with his personal health.

Brian's bandmates will soon be out on the road promoting *Pet Sounds* so he is free to associate with a different, hipper LA crowd, including Van Dyke Parks. He finds this new way of life exciting, but to those who know him well – including his wife Marilyn – it seems out of character.

■ Thursday 2nd
RECORDING 'Good Vibrations' sessions 11/12 Western Recorders studio (3 and 2) *Hollywood, CA* 9:00am-5:00pm (some musicians employed only until 12:30pm). Further recording sessions take place for **'Good Vibrations'**, today focussing on a piece for the song that Brian will call **'Inspiration'** (Master No. 56065; duration 2:18).

The recordings in Studio 3 end prematurely, approximately just after 2:00pm with only drummer Hal Blaine still present, because there is a session for The Turtles booked to start at 3:30pm.

In order to continue, work on 'Inspiration' moves next door to Studio 2 where Brian is joined by Blaine, the drummer providing a timpani overdub (Master No. 56065; duration 2:18). Taping in Studio 2 concludes this afternoon at 5:00pm.

Musicians present 9:00am-2:00pm Hal Blaine (drums), Bill Pitman (guitar), Don Randi (harpsichord, piano), Lyle Ritz (upright bass), Carl Wilson (guitar).

■ Saturday 4th
Pet Sounds album hits US *Billboard* chart at number 49. Alongside the LP in the listings are such delights as the *Mary Poppins* movie soundtrack, *The Best Of Herman's Hermits*, the *Batman* TV show soundtrack album, and a comedy album titled *When You're In Love the*

During a year of remarkable achievements in the studio, the live band – with Bruce Johnston still taking Brian's place – performs regularly, here at the Cow Palace, San Francisco, on June 24th.

Whole World Is Jewish. Other LPs that will accompany *Pet Sounds* on its stay in the charts include *Andy Williams' Newest Hits*, the *Best Of Chad & Jeremy*, and *The Shadow Of Your Smile* by Johnny Mathis.

■ Sunday 12th
RECORDING 'Good Vibrations' session 13 Western Recorders studio (3) *Hollywood, CA* 1:00-5:00pm approx. Work continues on **'Inspiration'** (Master No. 56065; duration 2:18), which later becomes another piece in the **'Good Vibrations'** jigsaw. Today, Brian tapes further cello and electro-theremin parts for the song.
Musicians present Hal Blaine (drums), Jesse Ehrlich (cello), Paul Tanner (electro-theremin).

■ Monday 13th
RECORDING 'Good Vibrations' session 14 Western Recorders studio (3) *Hollywood, CA* 2:00-6:00pm. A further recording session for **'Good Vibrations'** concentrates on part three of the song (21 takes required). Musicians play piano, timpani, tambourine, flutes, drums, electro-theremin, percussion and guitar. Instrumental and percussion overdubs complete the session.

■ Thursday 16th
RECORDING 'Good Vibrations' sessions 15/16 Western Recorders studio (3) *Hollywood, CA* 1:00-8:00pm; Western Recorders studio (2) *Hollywood, CA* 5:00-9:00pm. Further instrumental tracking and overdub sessions for **'Good Vibrations'** (Studio 3 Master No. 12935; Studio 2 Master No. 55949) as Brian commandeers two separate, virtually simultaneous recording studios at Western.
Musicians present Studio 3: Hal Blaine (drums), Al de Lory (piano), Steve Douglas (saxophone), Michael Melvoin (harpsichord), Tommy Morgan (harmonica), Bill Pitman (guitar), Lyle Ritz (upright bass), Paul Tanner (electro-theremin). *Studio 2*: Jim Horn (horns), Jay Migliori (saxophone).

■ Saturday 18th
RECORDING 'Good Vibrations' session 17 Western Recorders studio (3) *Hollywood, CA* 9:00am-2:00pm (two musicians leave session at 1:30pm). Yet more **'Good Vibrations'** tracking (Master No. 55949; duration 2:35) for a 'sweetening' session with engineer Chuck Britz as saxophone, piano, bass, guitar, electro-theremin and harmonica inserts are added into the 'best' tracking take (28) from February 18th. Brian is happy with the recording – still featuring Tony Asher's lyrics – and feels at the end of the session that it is good enough to become the next Beach Boys single. But after several more listens he swiftly changes his mind about releasing it in its current state and decides to do further work. At the conclusion, dejected and frustrated at how the song is progressing, Brian shelves it for nine straight weeks, until August 24th – and, seemingly out of character, he will not return to the recording studio at all until August 3rd.
Musicians present Al de Lory (piano), Billy Green (saxophone), Plas Johnson (saxophone), Carol Kaye (bass guitar), Jay Migliori (saxophone), Tommy Morgan (harmonica), Bill Pitman (guitar), Paul Tanner (electro-theremin), Carl Wilson (guitar).

TOUR STARTS US West/Midwest/East (Jun 24th-Jul 8th)

■ Friday 24th
The Cow Palace *San Francisco, CA* 8:00pm, Beach Boys Summer Spectacular, with The Lovin' Spoonful, Chad & Jeremy, Percy Sledge, The Outsiders, The Leaves, Sir Douglas Quintet, Jefferson Airplane, The Byrds, Neil Diamond
  The touring band hits the stage again with a show attended by 16,100 and grossing $62,197. Ralph J Gleason writes in the *San Francisco Chronicle*: "The house was packed. It was close to a sell out. Despite the order of the billing, the stars of the show turned out to be The Lovin' Spoonful, who came on stage full of life, had the

benefit of excellent sound facilities, and produced a series of fine performances of their hits including 'Do You Believe In Magic?' and 'You Didn't Have To Be So Nice'. The Spoonful looks so great, their manner is utterly charming, and the spirit and feeling they evoke is a total blast. Jefferson Airplane, San Francisco's own, sounded and looked great. Jorma Kaukonen's guitar solos throughout the Airplane's set [were] really outstanding. The Byrds were something of a disappointment. They never really got started. Their set, which closed the first half, was delayed because of some mechanical problem with the microphones and it seemed to discourage the group. Percy Sledge sang well, especially his hit 'When A Man Loves A Woman' and his accompaniment was excellent. The Beach Boys are a very special thing. Their audience response was at least as great as the Spoonful's but they also inspire distaste and many left when they were on-stage. Personally, I can take them on record but in person I find them unbearable."

■ Saturday 25th
Hollywood Bowl *Los Angeles, CA* 8:00pm, Beach Boys Summer Spectacular, with Love, Captain Beefheart

The attendance totals 12,400 and the show grosses $51,000. Writing in the *Los Angeles Times*, Charles Champlin says: "At about 11:25 on Saturday night ... Beach Boy Mike Love said, 'The sound is terrible. I'm sorry. It's just dead wrong for rock music.' He was dead right. For whatever reason, the vocals were completely lost in a distorted blah of rhythm guitar and percussion. You could see mouths moving furiously at the microphones but you heard nothing."

■ Monday 27th
Pet Sounds album released in the UK. Six weeks after its American release, Capitol/ EMI finally bow to pressure from the public and the music press by issuing the new Beach Boys LP. The British label originally penciled in the disc for a release this coming November to coincide with the group's visit to the country. Within weeks of its release, *Pet Sounds* shoots to a heady number 2 position in the UK *Record Retailer* chart and will be one of the top five bestselling albums in Britain during 1966. The UK pop scene is turned around as critics and record buyers praise the LP.

Disc & Music Echo's reviewer writes: "Let the adjectives roll. A superb, important and really exciting collection from the group whose recording career so far has been a bit of a hotchpotch. At last they seem to have found their direction under the clever guidance of Brian Wilson, and this should gain them thousands of new fans. Instrumentally ambitious, if vocally over-pretty, *Pet Sounds* has brilliantly tapped the pulse of the musical times. 'God Only Knows' is a standard gem with its hymnal feel. 'Pet Sounds' is a fascinating instrumental track and 'Wouldn't It Be Nice' is fresh. Far and away our LP of the month. Don't miss it!"

Melody Maker says: "Now we know why Brian Wilson doesn't tour with The Beach Boys – he's far too busy at home, thinking up pet sounds. He's brought in the lot here, orchestral sounds, organs, bells, a train, and dogs barking for a start. This is the way pop LPs are going: months of preparation, unusual voicings, intricate writing, multi-tracking etc. It's good value for LP buyers though how they can ever do it in person is baffling. Like George Harrison says, 'They'll be going on with tape recorders.' The songs are not as strong as the production, but there are some good ones, particularly 'God Only Knows', 'Pet Sounds', 'Caroline No', 'Wouldn't It Be Nice' and 'Let's Go Away For Awhile'. Must be The Beach Boys' biggest seller to date."

In another feature in *Melody Maker* the paper asks, "Is This The Most Progressive Pop Album Ever? Or As Sickly As Peanut Butter?"

The article announces, "The record's impact on artists and the men behind the artists has been considerable." The piece gives contemporary pop celebrities the chance to have their say about the album. Eric Clapton, Cream: "It changed my life. All of us, Ginger, Jack and I, are completely knocked out with *Pet Sounds*. [We] listen to that album before and after rehearsals. I consider it to be one of the great pop LPs to ever be released. It encompasses everything that's ever knocked me out and rolled it all into one. We're all gassed by it. Brian is, without doubt, a pop genius."

Andrew Oldham, Rolling Stones' manager: "I think that *Pet Sounds* is the most progressive album of the year in as much as Rimsky-Korsakov's *Scheherezade* was. It is the pop equivalent of that, a complete exercise in pop technique. Personally, I consider it to be a fantastic album. The lyrics are tremendous. The way Wilson has suited them to the songs is outstanding. I see pop music as a form of escapism, and *Pet Sounds* is a great example of escapism."

Spencer Davis, The Spencer Davis Group: "It's fantastic! I've just bought it and finished playing it. 'God Only Knows' is the most fantastic track on the album. Brian Wilson is a great record producer. I haven't spent much time listening to The Beach Boys before, but I'm a fan now and I just want to listen to this LP again and again. Thirteen of the tracks are originals, which can't be bad."

But not everyone in *Melody Maker*'s feature is knocked out by the music on the new LP. Pete Townshend, The Who: "*Pet Sounds* is written for an audience sympathetic to Brian Wilson's personal problems. You've just got to listen to the words, like: 'I'm searching for places where new things can be found but people just put me down.' It seems that Brian has left The Beach Boys to be a record producer.

"The Beach Boys used to influence us a bit when we first started," Townshend continues. "Keith [Moon] likes all their surf music stuff and we once met two of them, Bruce Johnston and Mike Love. We do 'Barbara Ann' on stage because it gets the audience going. But The Beach Boys' new material is too remote and way out. It's written for a feminine audience."

Barry Fantoni, journalist and television presenter, is another dissenter: "I think *Pet Sounds* is probably one of the best produced albums out. But it suffers because of it. I managed to listen to one side of it, and I heard just about a bellyful. At times it was beautiful but the words were hazy, which may have been unintentional, or that may have been the idea. It was rather a lazy record. Sometimes boring. I've got *Beach Boys Today!*, which is rougher but exciting. ... I preferred them when they were young and more loose and rough. I agree that it's probably revolutionary but I'm not sure that everything that's revolutionary is necessarily good."

July

■ Friday 1st
Las Vegas Convention Center *Las Vegas, NV*
The current US tour continues.

■ Saturday 2nd
Earl Warren Showgrounds *Santa Barbara, CA*
• *Pet Sounds* album peaks in US *Billboard* chart at a disappointing number 10. In the same issue of the record-business magazine The Beach Boys place an ad thanking the industry for the sales of their latest album. It reads: "We're moved over the fact that our Pet Sounds brought on nothing but Good Vibrations." This is the first public hint of the title of the group's next single.

Camera fan Dennis takes photos during an afternoon soundcheck at the Hollywood Bowl on June 25th.

LEFT July 1966, and Brian works on at home, with a framed gold disc for the *Concert* album on the wall. BELOW During the same month the live band takes to the stage for another date, this one with a strong police presence.

Sunday 3rd
Convention Hall Ratcliffe Stadium *Fresno, CA*

Monday 4th
Community Concourse's Exhibit Hall *San Diego, CA*

Tuesday 5th

Best Of The Beach Boys album released in the US. The issue of this Capitol compilation LP is generally (and probably incorrectly) viewed as sabotage, given that the company has put so little promotional effort into selling *Pet Sounds*.

The *Best Of* album will outsell *Pet Sounds*, peaking at number 8, and soon goes gold, remaining in *Billboard*'s album chart for 78 weeks. (The UK version, showcasing a different line-up of tracks, peaks at an impressive number 2.) Stories soon circulate suggesting that when US record stores re-order *Pet Sounds* they in fact receive copies of *Best Of*.

Brian is upset by the release of the compilation, which features 'Surfin' USA', 'Catch A Wave', 'Surfer Girl', 'Little Deuce Coupe', 'The Warmth Of The Sun' among others. He sees it as evidence that Capitol have no faith in him and that his new musical direction is being undersold. But most of all he is angry that his older, sun-filled girls-on-the-beach music is outselling his newer, more mature offerings.

Bruce later tells BBC Radio-1: "Capitol didn't see the evolution. *Pet Sounds* was so radical compared to the nice 'Barbara Ann's we had been making, which Capitol had been successfully selling, and they just wanted more. So, instead of promoting *Pet Sounds* in America, even though 'God Only Knows' and 'Wouldn't It Be Nice' had been successful singles off that album, they turned around and put out the first *Best Of* album and promoted that. It went gold quickly and yet they didn't promote *Pet Sounds* because they said it

wasn't commercial enough and people wouldn't understand it. We were making our big gamble of growing up in music and Capitol just didn't think that this was the direction we should take. So they didn't promote it."

Al Coury, the vice president of promotions at Capitol Records, will recall later: "Some of the people at Capitol were carried away with [the *Pet Sounds* album] and felt it was important, while others probably couldn't relate to it, because I think the album was ahead of its time. I remember *Pet Sounds* did receive good exposure but yet it didn't sell. The retail activity of the album was not as much as the previously released Beach Boys albums."
Comiskey Park *Chicago, IL*
Meanwhile the tour continues.

Wednesday 6th
Peace Bridge Center *Buffalo, NY*

Thursday 7th
War Memorial Hall Syracuse, NY

Friday 8th
Convention Center *Asbury Park, NJ*
Last night of the tour.

Saturday 9th
Pet Sounds enters UK *Record Retailer* album chart at number 14.

Monday 11th
'Help Me Rhonda' / 'Do You Wanna Dance' single re-released in the US. Capitol Records in the United States further promotes the *Best Of* compilation by reissuing this record that combines A-sides dating back to last year.

TOUR STARTS US Midwest/East/South (Jul 16th-30th)

■ Saturday 16th – Monday 18th

Arie Crown Theater, McCormick Place *Chicago, IL* 8:30pm
(Sat), 7:30pm (Sun/Mon), with The Chieftones, Yesterday's Children
Just eight days after concluding their previous jaunt, the live Beach
Boys band heads off on the road again, beginning tonight with a
three-night residency in Chicago.

'Wouldn't It Be Nice' / **'God Only Knows'** single released in the US
(Monday 18th). Brian's decision to not yet release 'Good Vibrations'
as the group's new single means that Capitol must fill the gap, and
this, the third single taken from *Pet Sounds*, is the result. (*Pet Sounds*
itself stalled in the US album listings two weeks ago.) The single is a
big smash around the world: the A-side peaks in the US *Billboard*
chart at number 8 on September 17th, the B-side at 39 on the 24th.
(Some charts are still based on radio plays as well as sales, so B-sides
do occasionally chart separately from their As. 'God Only Knows' will
prove to be the last Beach Boys B-side to chart.)

"Originally Brian wanted to release ['God Only Knows'] as a
single under my own name," says Carl. "Then 'Good Vibrations',
which should have been our next single, didn't turn out the way
Brian wanted. We had to have another release and so ['God Only
Knows' came out as a Beach Boys single]. It's not the first time I've
sung lead. I start 'Sloop John B' and then Mike Love takes over on
the second verse."

■ Thursday 21st

Memorial Auditorium *Buffalo, NY* 8:00pm, Beach Boys Summer
Spectacular, with The Lovin' Spoonful, The Rogues, Stan & The Ravens

■ Friday 22nd

'God Only Knows' / **'Wouldn't It Be Nice'** single released in the
UK. It will peak at number 2.
• 'Sloop John B' single peaks in Belgian chart at number 5, and in
Rhodesian Broadcasting Corporation chart at number 4.
Onondaga County War Memorial *Syracuse, NY* 8:30pm

■ Saturday 23rd

Convention Hall, The Boardwalk *Asbury Park, NJ* 9:45pm

■ Sunday 24th

Iona College Institute for the Arts *New Rochelle, NY*
8:30pm, Iona Summer Music Festival

■ Tuesday 26th

During a break from the tour the group attends the opening-night

---

God Only Knows single

A/B 'Wouldn't It Be Nice' (B. WILSON / T. ASHER)
B/A 'God Only Knows' (B. WILSON / T. ASHER)

US release ('Wouldn't...' as A-side) July 18th 1966 (Capitol
5706).
UK release ('God...' as A-side) July 22nd 1966 (Capitol CL
15459).
Chart high US number 8; UK number 2.

---

performance by The Paul Butterfield Blues Band at New York City's
Cafe Au Go Go.

■ Friday 29th

Virginia Beach High School Stadium *Virginia Beach, VA*
with The Wild Kingdom, Bill Deal & The Rhondells
The concert is attended by 6,500 fans and sponsored by WGH
Radio, but is marred by problems with the $7,000 custom-built
sound system – rented by The Beach Boys at a cost of $1,000 per day.
The problem delays the start of the show by more than 30 minutes.
The sound system has recently been used, quite successfully, at the
Newport Jazz Festival.

■ Saturday 30th

Steel Pier *Atlantic City, NJ*
With the conclusion of The Beach Boys' East Coast tour of America
the group flies home to California the following day, Sunday 31st.
• 'God Only Knows' single enters UK *Disc & Music Echo* Top 50 chart
at number 30. It will peak at number 2 on Saturday August 27th,
kept from the top spot by The Beatles' single 'Yellow Submarine' /
'Eleanor Rigby'.

August

Throughout the wonderfully warm summer of 1966, Brian and Van
Dyke Parks continue to work on their new music intended for the
next Beach Boys album. Brian even asks Parks to rewrite the lyrics to
'Good Vibrations', but he refuses. Parks does not want to get involved
midway through the recording of the song, nor does he wish to
alienate Mike, Brian's traditional lyrics collaborator. Brian and
(mostly) Mike will eventually rework Tony Asher's original lyrics from
'Good Vibrations'.

The glowing praise for *Pet Sounds* from noted musicians and
critics around the world enables Brian to comfortably bask in his
growing status as a 'genius'. Publicist Derek Taylor says later, "I
started that off. It was my line, 'Brian Wilson is a genius.' It came
about because Brian told me that he thought he was better than most
other people believed him to be. So I went around town proposing
the contention to people like Danny Hutton (of the group Redwood)
and Van Dyke Parks and they all said, 'Oh yes, definitely. Brian
Wilson is a genius.' Then I thought, 'Well, if that is so, why doesn't
anyone outside think so?' Then I started putting it around, making
almost a campaign out of it. But I believed it. Brian Wilson *is* a
genius. It was something that I felt should be established."

The 'campaign' works. Brian Wilson's name is frequently uttered
in the same breath as pop music contemporaries such as John
Lennon, Paul McCartney and Bob Dylan, musicians who in turn
have become interested in Brian's way of life and his
groundbreaking, refreshing music. For the Beach Boy, just like the
California summer, it is a glorious time indeed.

■ Wednesday 3rd

RECORDING *Smile* session 1 Gold Star studio (A) *Los Angeles, CA*
10:00am-1:00pm (some musicians stay to 2:30pm; others leave by
1:30pm). After a gap of just over six weeks, Brian returns to the
recording studio where he supervises the first instrumental tracking
session for the beautiful **'Wind Chimes'** (take 9 marked as best:
Master No. 56448; duration 2:28). Working with Brian at the session
is engineer Larry Levine. Although not officially recognised as such
at the time, this session marks the start of work on the *Smile* album.

Brian in summer '66 with his most important musical instrument, the multi-track tape recorder.

The idea for the piece recorded today comes from the wind chimes hanging outside Brian and Marilyn's house in Laurel Way, Los Angeles.

Musicians present Hal Blaine (drums), Frankie Capp (percussion), Al de Lory (keyboard), Sam Glenn (tenor saxophone, flute), Billy Green (flute, clarinet, tenor flute, saxophone), Jim Horn (flute, tenor saxophone, clarinet), Carol Kaye (bass guitar), Larry Knechtel (organ), Jay Migliori (flute, tenor saxophone), Don Randi (keyboard), Lyle Ritz (upright bass), Carl Wilson (guitar).

■ Thursday 4th

In the UK, tonight's edition of *Top Of The Pops* broadcast on BBC-1 between 7:30 and 8:00pm features 'God Only Knows' set to a re-edited version of the group's *Pet Sounds* film (see April 25th). The short film will receive another screening on *TOTP* on September 1st.

■ Monday 8th

At the last minute Brian cancels a whirlwind three-day business trip to locations in London, Amsterdam, Stockholm and Paris planned to include meetings with Immediate Records to discuss Beach Boys publishing, recordings and distribution. Recordings for 'Good Vibrations' are uppermost in his mind.

Instead this evening he accepts an invitation from The Rolling Stones to join them at RCA Studios in Hollywood where they are recording and mixing their next album, *Between The Buttons*.

Brian will recall on 1980s cable-TV show *Art Fein's Poker Party*: "Just before I cut 'Good Vibrations' I heard the Rolling Stones track 'My Obsession'. I was invited to hear their dub-downs and the record producer Lou Adler gave me some marijuana. They got me all stoned, they laid all this stuff on me and I couldn't find the door. It wiped me out so much I didn't know where the door was to get out of the studio. I was just standing there saying, 'What is this? Hey, play that again.' And they'd say, 'No, we can't. It's playing now,' and I'd go, 'Oh, I see.' It really was quite an event to be there."

TOUR STARTS North America (Aug 9th-20th)

■ Tuesday 9th
Mile High Stadium *Denver, CO*

The Beach Boys begin a tour of one-nighters in the Pacific Northwest with this date in Denver.

■ Tuesday 9th – 11th

MIXING Western Recorders studio (3) *Hollywood, CA* 2:00pm start each day. Brian spends three days preparing an early mix of the instrumental tracks for **'Good Vibrations'**. By the end of the third day he feels confident enough to give the mix its first private airing (see 11th).

■ Wednesday 10th
Civic Auditorium *Omaha, NE*

■ Thursday 11th
Civic Memorial Auditorium *Fargo, ND* 8:30pm

The Beach Boys arrive at Hector Airport in Fargo to be greeted by a crowd totalling 1,500 and this evening perform a sell-out show at the Memorial Auditorium in front of an audience of 4,500. Afterwards at their hotel there is a significant telephone call. "The first time I ever heard the [completed] music to 'Good Vibrations', The Beach Boys were playing up in North Dakota," Carl recalls. "I came back up into my hotel room one night and the phone rang. It was Brian on the other end. He called me from the recording studio and played this

really bizarre sounding music over the phone. There were drums smashing, that kind of stuff, and then it refined itself and got into the cello. It was a real funky track."

■ Friday 12th

RECORDING *Smile* session 2 Western Recorders studio (3) *Hollywood, CA* 1:00-5:00pm. With Chuck Britz engineering, Brian oversees piano instrumental recording for **'I Ran'** (take 20 marked as best: Master No. 56473; duration 2:16). The piece is listed on the AFM (American Federation of Musicians) studio log sheet as **'Untitled Song #1'** and is also sometimes known as **'Look'**.

Musicians present Hal Blaine (drums), Jimmy Bond Jr (upright bass), Frankie Capp (vibes, bongos, tambourine), Al de Lory (keyboard), George Hyde (French horn), Richard Hyde (trombone), Barney Kessel (guitar), Larry Knechtel (organ), Jay Migliori (woodwind), Bill Pitman (guitar), Ray Pohlman (bass guitar).

Illinois State Fair *Springfield, IL* with Sam The Sham & The Pharaohs; admission $1.00

Just six policemen are on hand at this concert to help contain a crowd of 21,000 who are evidently keen to see the live band on its latest tour date.

■ Saturday 13th
Duluth Arena Auditorium *Duluth, MN* 8:00pm

At the grand opening night of this new venue 7,189 people are in attendance, setting an all-time record for indoor events in Duluth. Such is the demand from patrons to attend the show that local parking lots are full to bursting point. Some concertgoers have to park so far away from the venue that they need to take a bus to the concert.

■ Sunday 14th
Centennial Concert Hall *Winnipeg, MB, Canada*

■ Monday 15th
Municipal Auditorium *Minot, ND*

■ Tuesday 16th
Jubilee Auditorium *Calgary, AB, Canada*

Tonight's concert grosses $19,000, of which the group receives typically 60 percent.

■ Wednesday 17th
Empire Stadium *Vancouver, BC, Canada*

The show grosses $14,600.

■ Thursday 18th
Queen Elizabeth Theatre *Vancouver, BC, Canada* 6:30 & 9:30pm, with The Sunrays, Chad & Jeremy

■ Friday 19th
Coliseum *Spokane, WA*

Two shows, grossing $22,400.

■ Saturday 20th
Portland Coliseum *Portland, OR;* promoted by local radio station KISN

The one-nighters tour of the Pacific Northwest winds up this evening with a show that grosses $18,000 at the box office, while the entire tour has grossed a total of $93,000.

• 'Wouldn't It Be Nice' single enters US *Billboard* Top 40 chart at number 26.

■ Wednesday 24th

RECORDING 'Good Vibrations' session 18 Sunset Sound studio *Los Angeles, CA*. After a gap of just over two months and with the other Beach Boys now back from touring duties, Brian returns to his masterpiece, **'Good Vibrations'**. There is less pressure from Capitol, and Brian now has renewed interest in the song. Today he takes charge of yet another tracking session and begins overlaying a guide vocal using totally different lyrics to those that will appear on the released version. The first verse including the lines: "She's already working on my brain / I went and looked in her eyes / But I picked up something I just can't explain."

Later today, with that new rough vocal now cast aside, The Beach Boys collectively overdub the familiar as-released vocals on to the song. Al and Bruce appear on one tape track, Carl, Dennis and Brian on another, Mike on a third. Brian then doubles the lot and comes up with a chorus.

Mike Love will recall later that he wrote the released-version lyrics for 'Good Vibrations' on the Hollywood freeway, about ten minutes before the session. "I was dictating the words 'I'm picking up good vibrations' as we drove down the road. It was a kind of cliffhanger. Brian said, 'We need some words,' and I said, 'Well, OK. Let's see.'

"On one passage of 'Good Vibrations' we did it over and over, not only to get the note right, but we wanted the timbre and quality of each note and how the four parts would resonate together. Then, Brian would be hearing something that nobody else could hear, including a dog, y'know? He would say, 'Do it again,' and we'd say, 'Do it again? Are you crazy?' It was so exhausting! I can remember doing 25 to 30 vocal overdubs of the same part, and when I say part, I mean the same section of the record, maybe no more than two, three, four, five seconds long!"

When this passage of recording is played back, Brian is dissatisfied and attempts to re-record the group's vocals. He has himself and Carl singing on one track, Bruce, Carl and Al on a second, and Mike and Bruce on a third. But still he is not happy with the results – and will continue to re-work the track over the coming weeks.

■ Thursday 25th

RECORDING *Smile* session 3, 'Good Vibrations' session 19 Western Recorders studio (3) *Hollywood, CA* 2:00-7:00pm (some musicians only until 5:00pm). Instrumental tracking sessions are recorded for **'Good Vibrations'** and **'Wonderful'** (Master No. 56550; duration 1:55). Just after 5:00pm Brian attempts to record a harpsichord track for 'Wonderful' himself (18 takes required) but is hindered by the keys on the instrument. "Some of these notes are fucking up," he shouts at engineer Chuck Britz. "I swear to God. You push them and they don't go." Dennis joins his brother at the session – but not playing his customary instrument. "I played organ on 'Good Vibrations'," he will recall, "in the section where it slows down."

Musicians present Henry David (instrument unknown), Larry Knechtel (organ), Lyle Ritz (guitar), Alan Weight (trumpet), Brian Wilson (harpsichord), Dennis Wilson (organ).

■ Friday 26th

At the Los Angeles home of publicist Derek Taylor, Brian and Carl meet up with Beatles Paul McCartney and George Harrison.

■ Saturday 27th

'God Only Knows' single peaks in UK *Record Retailer* chart at number 2.

■ Monday 29th

Western Recorders studio (3) *Hollywood, CA* 1:00pm; session cancelled

■ Wednesday 31st

Western Recorders studio (3) *Hollywood, CA* 4:00pm; session cancelled

September

'Wouldn't It Be Nice' single peaks in Canadian *RPM* Chart at number 4, and in Australian chart at number 2.
• 'God Only Knows' single peaks in Canadian *RPM* chart at number 4, in UK *Record Retailer/Music Weekly* chart at number 2, and in France's *Music Media Monthly* chart at number 24.
• In Los Angeles, Brian rides around in a Rolls Royce purchased for $20,000 from Mamas & The Papas producer Lou Adler, who himself purchased the car from Beatle John Lennon. During nights free from recording Brian holds court at his modern $240,000 Laurel Way home and, after his guests have left, sits at his grand piano until dawn, writing new material.

■ Thursday 1st

RECORDING *Smile* session 4, 'Good Vibrations' session 20 Western Recorders studio (3) *Hollywood, CA* 4:00-7:30pm. What will be the penultimate musical recording session for **'Good Vibrations'** takes place today for a segment lasting one minute and 15 seconds. Carl and Dennis are also on hand to overdub additional backing vocals. Brian will complete the final mix of the song's basic track next Monday. Aside from a brief recording frenzy on September 12th, Brian will wait almost three weeks before completing the final mix of 'Good Vibrations' (see September 21st). Recordings conclude today with the first takes of **'He Gives Speeches'**, another new song that will be abandoned by Brian as the *Smile* sessions progress. It will eventually be recast in July 1967 as the first section of *Smiley Smile*'s 'She's Goin' Bald'.

Musicians present Hal Blaine (drums), Henry David ('instrumentation'), Tommy Morgan (harmonica, bass harmonica), Lyle Ritz (upright bass).

■ Saturday 3rd

MIXING Western Recorders studio (3) *Hollywood, CA*. Brian compiles a tape of recent recordings and tags it *Nu songs as of 9/3*. It contains **'Wonderful'** (see August 25th) and **'He Gives Speeches'** (see September 1st).

■ Monday 5th

MIXING Western Recorders studio (3) *Hollywood, CA*. Brian spends the day preparing a final tracking mix of **'Good Vibrations'**, restructuring the entire tail-end of the song as he strips off many painstakingly recorded parts. (A 'tracking mix' is a mix of instrumentation only, prior to recording any vocals.) At the end of the session Brian excitedly tells Derek Taylor, "OK, the track is ready to go."

■ Tuesday 6th

Western Recorders studio (3) *Hollywood, CA* 2:00pm start; overdub session cancelled.

■ Thursday 8th

RECORDING *Smile* session 5 Western Recorders studio (3) *Hollywood, CA* 2:00-7:00pm (some musicians leave at 6:00pm). With

Phonograph Recording Contract Blank

AMERICAN FEDERATION OF MUSICIANS

OF THE UNITED STATES AND CANADA

96413

Local Union No. ____

THIS CONTRACT for the personal services of musicians, made this **8th** day of **September**, 19__, between the undersigned employer (hereinafter called the "employer") and _____ **13** musicians (hereinafter called "employees").
(Including the leader)

WITNESSETH, That the employer hires the employees as musicians severally on the terms and conditions below, and as further specified on reverse side. The employer represents that the employees already designated have agreed to be bound by said terms and conditions. Each employee yet to be chosen shall be so bound by said terms and conditions upon agreeing to accept his employment. Each employee may enforce this agreement. The employees severally agree to render collectively to the employer services as musicians in the orchestra under the leadership of _____ **Charles D. Britz** _____ as follows:

Name and Address of Place of Engagement **Western Recorders, 6000 Sunset Blvd, Hollywood, Calif.**

Date(s) and Hours of Employment **September 8, 1966   2:00 P.M. to 7:00 P.M. (read will only**
until 6:00 P.M.)

Type of Engagement: **Recording for phonograph records only**   Plus pension contributions as specified on reverse side hereof.

WAGE AGREED UPON $ _____ **UNION SCALE** _____
(Terms and amount)

This wage includes expenses agreed to be reimbursed by the employer in accordance with the attached schedule, or a schedule to be furnished the employer on or before the date of engagement.

To be paid _____ **WITHIN 15 DAYS** _____
(Specify when payments are to be made)

Upon request by the American Federation of Musicians of the United States and Canada (herein called the "Federation") or the local in whose jurisdiction the employees shall perform hereunder, the employer either shall make advance payment hereunder or shall post an appropriate bond.

Employer's name and authorized signature	**Capitol Records, Inc.**	Leader's name **Charles D. Britz** Local No. __
		Leader's signature
Street address	**1750 N. Vine Street**	Street address **4501 Wavona St.**
City State Phone	**Hollywood 28, Calif. HO 26252**	City State **Los Angeles 65, Calif.**

(1) Label name **Capitol Records** _____ Session no. _____

Master no.	No. of minutes	TITLES OF TUNES	Master no.	No. of minutes	TITLES OF TUNES
	2:25	" Holidays "			

(2) Employee's name (As on Social Security card) Last First Initial	(3) Home address (Give street, city and state)	(4) Local Union no.	(5) Social Security number	(6) Scale wages	(7) Pension contribution
(Leader) Britz, Charles D.	4501 Wavona St. Los Angeles 65, Calif.	47	567-26-4273	325.40	26.05
Rovell, Diane J. (contract)	616 N. Sierra Bonita Los Angeles 36, Calif.	47	560-56-7005	325.40	26.03
Coleman, Gary L.	12237 La Maida North Hollywood, Calif.	47	571-42-3945	122.02	9.76
Estes, Gene P.	12212 Hartsook St. North Hollywood, Calif.	47	456-36-7156	122.02	9.76
Clarinet & Flute Glenn, Sam B. Jr. 1 Dbl.	P.O. Box 702 Tarzana, Calif.	47	227-48-7853	184.05	14.72
Clarinet & Flute Green, William E. 1 Dbl.	4526 Don Miguel Dr. Los Angeles 8, Calif.	47	512-16-4687	184.05	14.72
Clarinet & Flute Horn, James R. 1 Dbl.	3225 Oakshire Dr. Hollywood 28, Calif.	47	570-56-6753	184.05	14.72
Clarinet & Flute Migliori, Jay 1 Dbl.	1701 N. Lincoln Burbank, Calif.	47	208-24-6118	184.05	14.72
Parks, Van Dyke	72201 Melrose Ave. Hollywood, Calif.	47	151-28-1160	162.70	13.02
Ricord, Chester W.	6444 Elmer Ave. North Hollywood, Calif.	47	513-10-0116	122.02	9.76
Wilson, Brian D. POST OPEN	1448 Laurel Way Beverly Hills, Calif.	47	568-62-7150	162.70	13.02
Wilson, Carl D. POST OPEN	1902 Coldwater Cayn. Beverly Hills, Calif.	47	568-62-6168	122.02	9.76
Wilson, Dennis C. POST OPEN	2600 Benedict Cayn. Beverly Hills, Calif.	47	562-60-0767	122.02	9.76

NO ARRANGER OR COPYIST THIS SESSION

(8) Total Pension Contributions (Sum of Column (7)) $ 185.76
Make check payable in this amount to "AFM & EPW Fund"

FOR FUND USE ONLY:
Date pay't rec'd ____ SEP 28 1966 ____ mt. paid _____ Date posted _____ By _____
Form B-4 Rev. 4-59

recording work on 'Good Vibrations' wrapped up, today sees the first tracking session for a piece called **'Holidays'** (take 7 marked as master; duration 2:25) as Brian officially begins work on the new Beach Boys album, tentatively titled *Dumb Angel*. In fact, a few tracks scheduled to feature on the disc have already been taped – see entries for August 3rd, 12th, 25th and September 1st.

Around this time Brian gives the planned LP a new name, *Smile*. In an interview this year he explains: "*Dumb Angel* was just a passing title. *Smile* was more cheery, so we used the more cheery title. The whole album is going to be a far-out trip through the old west, real Americana, but with lots of interesting humour. I think it's going to be a big humour trip. There's even going to be talking and laughing between the cuts."

Capitol Records immediately schedules *Smile* for a Christmas release. Van Dyke Parks's artist pal Frank Holmes is commissioned to design a decidedly cheery album cover. The rear will feature a black-and-white snap of the Brian-less Beach Boys framed in astrological symbols. Capitol allots a catalogue number of DT 2580 to the album. Also assembled is a planned 12-page booklet containing pen-and-ink drawings also by Holmes alongside photos of The Beach Boys (these will be taken in Boston on November 17th by Guy Webster). Inspiration for Holmes's drawings comes from Parks who supplies him with an acetate of some of the album's early recordings and a selection of the lyrics.

Throughout the various early stages of *Smile*'s development, everyone surrounding Brian – friends, bandmates, press agents, Capitol personnel – has faith in the album. They all just know that it is going to be great and assume that it will be produced and released in the usual fashion.

From the album's onset Brian amasses a large batch of new songs, a result of his five-month songwriting collaboration with Van Dyke Parks. New songs by the pair include 'Barnyard', 'Wind Chimes' (later recycled into 'Can't Wait Too Long'), 'Friday Night', 'Wonderful', 'Child Is Father Of The Man', 'The Old Master Painter', 'You're Welcome', 'Prayer', 'Holidays', 'Surf's Up', and an ambitious four-part piece called 'The Elements' comprising 'Mrs O'Leary's Cow' (representing fire), 'Vegetables' (earth) and 'I Love To Say Da Da' (water). Brian's plan for the 'air' segment is unknown, though possibly it's a (later discarded) piano track. 'I Ran' (also known as 'Look') is recorded but abandoned as Brian's concept for the *Smile* album takes definite shape. Brothers Carl and Dennis join Brian at today's session, which warms up with a jam on Wilson Pickett's hit 'In The Midnight Hour'.

Thus work begins on *Smile*. Brian has a clear vision for the album, with all the individual songs written and lyrics completed. But the recording of the LP will turn into a nine-month journey filled with joy and despair, ending in chaos.

Musicians present Gary Coleman (percussion), Gene Estes (guitar), Sam Glenn Jr. (clarinet, flute), Billy Green (clarinet, flute), Jim Horn (clarinet, flute), Jay Migliori (clarinet, flute), Van Dyke Parks (instrument unknown), Chester Ricord (percussion), Carl Wilson (guitar), Dennis Wilson (drums).

■ Monday 12th

RECORDING 'Good Vibrations' session 21 Western Recorders studio (3) *Hollywood, CA.* A week after 'completing' his **'Good Vibrations'** masterwork Brian once more feels that he can improve the recording and hurriedly arranges another tracking session for the song. But again he is unhappy with the results – and threatens to discard all the recordings. In his anger he tells the session musicians present, "I'm gonna play all the instruments myself." But at the end of today's session Brian has to accept that the 'Good Vibrations' tracking tape he completed a week ago – on Monday the 5th – is the very best that he can do.

■ Saturday 17th

'Wouldn't It Be Nice' single peaks in US *Billboard* chart at 8.
• 'God Only Knows' single enters US *Billboard* Top 40 chart at 40.

■ Monday 19th

RECORDING *Smile* session 6 Columbia studio *Los Angeles, CA* 7:00pm start. Eleven days after the inaugural session for *Smile* Brian returns to Western to supervise the taping of **'Prayer'**, a beautiful, hymn-like piece featuring a superb vocal-only performance by The Beach Boys. Brian intends to use the recording as the new album's opening piece.

Recordings for the new record are halted when Brian is informed that vital tracking master tapes for 'Good Vibrations' have gone missing. He is paralysed with fear. In fact, they will mysteriously reappear in his Laurel Way home two days later. "All hell was breaking loose at this time," Derek Taylor later tells *Sounds*. "Tapes were being lost, ideas being junked, Brian thinking, 'I'm no good,' then 'I'm too good,' then 'I can't sing, I can't get those voices any more.' There was a time when there hardly seemed to be a Beach Boys at all."

■ Tuesday 20th

RECORDING *Smile* session 7 Columbia studio (A) *Los Angeles, CA* 7:00pm start. A 'sweetening' overdub session, featuring only Dennis.

■ Wednesday 21st

RECORDING/MIXING 'Good Vibrations' session 22 Columbia studio (A) *Los Angeles, CA* 7:00pm-12midnight (but recordings carry on until approx 3:00am Thursday morning). Just over two weeks after completing the instrumental track for **'Good Vibrations'** and two days after tapes of the song went missing, Brian takes charge of a final lead-vocal overdubbing session, and completes the final mixing, all in one seven-hour session. The only outside musician present is electro-theremin player Paul Tanner who again overdubs his instrument. Dennis has been waiting four months to sing the lead vocal on the song but tonight he can hardly speak and is found to be suffering from laryngitis. Carl replaces him.

In the early hours of the morning of Thursday September 22nd, after 22 sessions lasting around 94 hours in four different recording studios, Brian's masterpiece is finally completed. His four-year musical apprenticeship has paid off wonderfully. 'Good Vibrations', recorded intermittently since February 18th, is at last finished, complete with that final set of lyrics by Mike Love. Brian has recorded somewhere between 15 and 20 different versions of the song before he is satisfied.

Exactly how he makes the master instrumental track of 'Good Vibrations' is unclear, but by close listening we can attempt to unravel it. He seems to take the first verse and first chorus from take 28 of February 18th and overdubs them with cello. This new verse and chorus section, including the cello, is copied and edited together (there's an obvious edit at 0:25 between first verse and chorus, for example). The result provides the opening verse/chorus/verse/chorus sequence.

After this comes an edit at 1:42, half way through "excitation…", in order to change to the middle-eight section, possibly from May 4th, with 'tack' piano, jaws harp, flute and a little low-register electro-theremin ("I don't know where but she sends me there…"). The next edit is made at 2:14, switching to a new section with organ, harmonica and bass guitar ("Gotta keep those love good vibrations a-happening with her…"). A further edit at 2:56 ushers in another stripped-down and shortened chorus, again overdubbed with cello. There's no theremin, so it's not from the February sessions or the 'tack' piano recording, all of which have theremin throughout. The final edit comes at 3:13, into the half-tempo bass section with wordless vocals and then a short but elaborate orchestral fade, again on the chorus, complete with cellos and theremin.

'Good Vibrations' has cost around $50,000 to produce – and in 1966 this makes it the most expensive single ever made. No one has ever heard anything like it before. Bruce speculates that The Beach Boys will either have the biggest hit of their lives or that their careers will be ended by the song.

"I remember the time that we had ['Good Vibrations' just right]," Brian later tells *Rolling Stone*. "It was at Columbia [studio]. I remember I had it right in the sack. I could just feel it when I dubbed it down, made the final mix … down to mono. It was a feeling of power. It was a rush. A feeling of exaltation. I remember saying, 'Oh, my God! Sit back and listen to this.' It was a shock to hear that back. It was like, 'Wow! I created that?' I must have had help from upstairs. I felt that it was a plateau. … We started it at Gold Star, then we went to Western, then Sunset Sound and then finally we went to Columbia. Every studio had its own marked sound. Using four different studios had a lot to do with the way the final record sounded. There was no way of knowing how the track would turn out, because we were in so many places and it would be impossible to know."

Dennis remembers people saying that 'Good Vibrations' took a lot longer than it really did. "Actually it took four months," he says. "But we didn't record every day, and we didn't put in 90 hours. We went down one day and we recorded the soundtrack and we didn't like it. So we did it over again in sections. We wrote it as we were recording it. As we finished one part, we were inspired to do another. It just kept building and building."

Engulfed in the excitement of the recording, Brian immediately cuts the final mix of 'Good Vibrations' to two acetates – one for him, the other for the song's lead vocalist, Carl, who excitedly takes the disc home and proceeds to blast the recording through the speakers by the swimming pool in his garden. Considering that it is now way past 3:00am, those living close to him are not amused and immediately protest. Carl's wife Annie later remarks, "This was the first time that we had really met our neighbours."

The recording of 'Good Vibrations' sets a precedent for Brian's new style of studio working. His scheme now is to record a song from tiny fragments of inspirations, then re-record some sections, add a bridge or a new section, re-record the bridge, make trial mixes of the song, go back and re-record new sections, and finally piece it all together in a final mix.

While Brian manages successfully to link together all the pieces of 'Good Vibrations' and create one of the greatest pop singles of the 1960s, the method will prove problematic when it comes to crafting the next Beach Boys single, 'Heroes And Villains'. 'Good Vibrations' will be Brian's crowning achievement – but the completion of the song also marks the start of his undoing.
Musician present Paul Tanner (electro-theremin).

■ Thursday 22nd
RECORDING *Smile* session 8 Columbia studio (A) *Los Angeles, CA* 7:00pm-12midnight. Tonight sees an overdubbing session.

■ Friday 23rd
RECORDING *Smile* session 9 Columbia studio (A) *Los Angeles, CA* 7:00pm-12midnight. A further overdubbing session.

■ Saturday 24th
At Carl's home at 1902 Coldwater Canyon Avenue, Beverly Hills, CA, Carl and Annie Wilson film an appearance for the weekly ABC TV American music show, *Where The Action Is*. During the 4:05 slot the show's host Dick Clark asks Carl and his teenage wife how their marriage has affected their lives and they talk about how they met, their lifestyle, young marriage, and plans for the future. (Paul Revere & The Raiders, Stevie Wonder and Roy Head are among the other guests on tonight's show, which is transmitted on ABC TV on Friday, October 21, between 4:30 and 5:00pm.)
• *Best Of The Beach Boys* album peaks in US *Billboard* chart at number 8.
• 'God Only Knows' single peaks in US *Billboard* chart at number 39.

■ Friday 30th
Alabama State Coliseum *Montgomery, AL* 8:00pm, Big Bam Fall Spectacular, with Lou Christie, Ian Whitcomb, The Happenings, Peter & Gordon, The Hollies; promoted by WBAM Radio
A brief return to the concert stage for The Beach Boys.

October

'God Only Knows' single peaks in Dutch chart at number 11, in German *Hit Bilanz* chart at number 22, and in Norwegian chart at number 6.
• For the last few months, Beach Boys business manager Nick Grillo has been working on an idea to create an organisation for the group so that they can produce their own records and movies. It is designed to give them more control, certainly more than they could ever hope for under the wings of a large record company. For example, Brian will not have to get approval from Capitol for any of his future projects. The fact that Capitol has already dismissed his ideas for comedy and sound-effects albums hastens the action.

David Anderle, Brian's friend of five months and the manager of Van Dyke Parks, is put on The Beach Boys' payroll to run the new venture, which will eventually come to life as Brother Records. "I decided to become associated with Brian because his music was killing me," Anderle says later. "I loved it, Then, all of a sudden, there were new elements in his life. A lot of the contacts I had made here in the so-called underground I started bringing around to Brian. The press started paying attention – national press, underground press. He was getting phone calls from Paul McCartney and Andrew Loog Oldham. The mystique around Brian Wilson was growing." Brian agrees: "The mystique grew and I was getting fascinated with the fact that I was becoming famous and there was an interest in my style of life."

Elegant, cool and sharp, Anderle is an artist who has skipped back and forth between painting and the record business, with mixed results in both. As an executive for MGM Records he earns himself a reputation as a genius by purportedly thinking up the million-dollar movie-TV-record offer that will briefly lure Bob Dylan to MGM from Columbia in 1967 – until everybody has a change of heart and Dylan decides to go back home to Columbia.

His appeal to Brian is simple: everybody recognises Anderle as one of the hippest people in Los Angeles. In fact, some consider him as a sort of mayor of hipness, even a genius. Everything that Brian wants, he can now touch as, like a magic genie, Anderle produces miracles for him. The new Beach Boys record company, Brother Records, is set up with Anderle at its head and Nick Grillo as financial administrator. The organisation takes up residence at 9000

Sunset Boulevard, Los Angeles, CA. Anderle will also play a large role in the public's perception of *Smile* by rounding up journalists to preview the album. Interviews with Brian soon appear by Lawrence Dietz in *New York* magazine, Richard Goldstein in *The Village Voice*, and Paul Williams in *Crawdaddy*. Anderle and the reporters hang out with Brian, in and out of the studio, to bring to the world a prelude of Brian's Next Great Artwork.

• Meanwhile, at Brian's Laurel Way home in the Hollywood Hills, he tells dinner guests one October evening: "I'm writing a teenage symphony to God." In effect, the dinner party is his first hip social event. As far as Brian is concerned he is the star of the evening. The house is full of underground press writers. Several of Anderle's friends attend, including Michael Vosse and another (probably Jules Siegel, who is writing a story on Brian for *The Saturday Evening Post*).

A film crew from CBS-TV News is at the house shooting scenes for a new documentary to be called *Inside Pop: The Rock Revolution*. The buzz surrounding the *Smile* album has caught the attention of television producer David Oppenheim who is making *Inside Pop* about the powerful musical forces at work in 1966 (see November 29th, December 15th and 17th). Oppenheim, a middle-aged producer of decidedly high-brow documentaries, started work on the new show after producing a documentary on the Russian classical composer Igor Stravinsky. Leonard Bernstein, the highly-respected US-born composer and conductor, will present the *Inside Pop* documentary. These weighty credentials ensure that Brian sees it as pop music's first serious TV feature, and he is keen to participate. The chance to showcase *Smile* to a learned audience is an opportunity too good to miss.

Brian and Oppenheim will spend much time together. Some evenings, the pair will take some substances and just sit, staring at the night sky or talking until dawn as the steam from Brian's heated swimming pool surrounds them. In a 1971 interview for *Rolling Stone*, Oppenheim will recall: "So much was flowing from Brian. I was going into the studio and cutting sections, thoughts of music, and he was coming home and tying these thoughts together into songs. They would change daily. The beginning of 'Cabin Essence' becomes the middle of 'Vegetables', or the ending becoming the bridge. It was like changing colours or areas. The pieces were so musically interesting that they would fit. I would beg Brian not to change a piece of music because it was too fantastic. But when Brian did change it, I have to admit it was equally beautiful.

"When he got into something, he'd get into it right then. If he wanted to see the moon, he'd go out and buy a telescope that minute. I'd say to him, 'Brian, there's no place open at three in the morning to sell telescopes,' and he'd get angry. 'Well, let's buy a telescope place, man. We'll have it open 24 hours a day.' So I said, 'Brian, who's gonna want a telescope at three o'clock in the morning?' Brian replied, 'Well, somebody does and if someone does, then they should have it.' Or, 'Wouldn't it be great to play Ping-Pong? Let's get a Ping-Pong table.' 'Brian, it's four in the morning.' 'Get those *Yellow Pages*. Somebody must know. You must know somebody who knows how to get a Ping-Pong table.'"

At his Laurel Way home this late October evening, Brian plays the assembled crowd a collection of black acetate trial records that lay piled on the floor of his red imitation-velvet wallpapered bedroom. (If the guests visit the bathroom, they will see that above the washbasin there stands a plastic colour-picture of Jesus Christ with trick-effect eyes that appear to open and close when you move your head.) Brian shuffles through the acetates, most of which are unlabeled. He identifies each by the subtle differences in the patterns of the grooves. Most are instrumental tracks, recorded while The Beach Boys were preparing for their visit to Europe, and

for these Brian has supplied the vocal, managing to create complicated four and five-part harmonies with only his own voice. In the dining room a candlelit table with a dark blue cloth is set for ten guests. In the kitchen, his wife Marilyn is trying to prepare and serve the meal.

When everyone is seated and waiting for the food, Brian begins to tap his knife idly on a white china plate. "Listen to that," he says. "That's really great." Everybody listens as Brian plays the plate. "Come on, let's get something going here," he orders. A plate-and-spoon musicale begins to develop as each guest plays a distinctly different technique and rhythm under Brian's enthusiastic direction. "That's absolutely unbelievable," he says. "That's so unbelievable. I'm going to put it on the album. Michael, I want you to get a sound system up here tomorrow and I want everyone to be here tomorrow night. We're going to get this on tape." (Brian's plate-and-spoon musicale fails to reach the public – but only because he forgets about it.)

■ **Monday 3rd**
RECORDING *Smile* session 10 Gold Star studio (A) *Los Angeles, CA* 8:00pm-12:00midnight. After initial sessions, the most fertile period of *Smile* recording begins with an instrumental tracking session at Gold Star with engineer Larry Levine for '**Home On the Range**' (Master No. 56647; duration 3:20; later retitled 'Cabinessence' for the October 11th session). The first vocals for '**Wind Chimes**' are also recorded today. Brian and Van Dyke Parks oil their creativity with some substances. But soon their bliss turns to stress. As Brian will recall in his biography, *Wouldn't It Be Nice*, "The speed wrapped me tighter than a wind-up piano player."

Mike Love will soon admit to friends that the music on *Smile* means very little to him. Admissions that he cannot understand what is going on will become a regular occurrence. Van Dyke Parks will recall in the 1995 film *I Just Wasn't Made For These Times* that Mike Love says to him, "'Over and over the crow cries uncover the cornfield....' What does that mean?" Parks replies that he doesn't know. Carl will also remember Mike's difficulties: "A lot was said about Mike not liking the *Smile* music. His main problem was the lyrics were not relateable. They were so artistic and, to him, airy-fairy and too abstract. Personally, I loved it."

Musicians present James Burton (guitar), Jesse Ehrlich (cello), Carl Fortina (accordion), Jim Gordon (drums, tambourine), Armand Kaproff (cello), Carol Kaye (bass guitar), Jay Migliori (saxophone), Tommy Morgan (harmonica, bass harmonica), Van Dyke Parks (harmonium), Bill Pitman (guitar), Lyle Ritz (upright bass), Tommy Tedesco (guitar, bouzouki), Carl Wilson (guitar).

■ **Tuesday 4th**
RECORDING *Smile* session 11 Gold Star studio (A) *Los Angeles, CA*. Brian revisits the recording of '**Prayer**', a highlight of the *Smile* sessions and one of Brian's finest productions. He records The Beach Boys' vocals in segments and then later edits them into the minute-long version that will eventually appear on the 1969 album *20/20* as 'Our Prayer'. But from the outset Brian intends the piece to be an introduction for *Smile*. Its angelic, hymn-like refrains make a fine invocation. A mix of the recording completes the session.

Bruce will tell BBC Radio-1 in 1995: "We weren't at most of the *Smile* sessions; we were out on the road celebrating Brian's songwriting. While we were singing 'Fun Fun Fun' and 'I Get Around' he was back in LA musically expanding, growing and assembling incredible musicians around him. We only sang on the *Smile* recordings. The guy who put the blood, sweat and tears on the tracks is Brian. He would conceive the songs, hum the tune and would go into the studio and record the track. The last thing that would happen, really, would be to record the vocals."

■ Wednesday 5th

RECORDING *Smile* **session 12** Western Recorders studio (3) *Hollywood, CA* 3:00-6:30pm (some musicians leave at 6:00pm). Tracking session for **'Wind Chimes'** (9 takes required; Master No. 56648; duration 2:55). The Beach Boys are present to record a vocal track for the song's chorus. The session is wrapped with Brian re-recording the verse section and the multiple-pianos ending, recording his lead vocal over the group's chorus vocal harmonies, and mixing it together. Engineer as so often at Western is Chuck Britz.
Musicians present Charles Berghofer (upright bass), Van Dyke Parks (unknown instrument), Carl Wilson (guitar).

■ Thursday 6th

RECORDING *Smile* **session 13** Western Recorders studio (3) *Hollywood, CA*. Brian overdubs his lead vocal onto the **'Wonderful'** harpsichord instrumental taped on August 25th. Drums and additional instrumentation are also added to the recording during today's late-starting session, which is rounded off with a rough mix. Further work on the track is not done until December 15th. 'Wonderful' is one of the first tracks recorded for *Smile*, but Brian has difficulty in realising his visions for the song. In the space of 12 months he will record the song four times, but only one version is completed – an inferior one that will appear on the 1967 *Smiley Smile* album.

■ Friday 7th

RECORDING *Smile* **session 14** Western Recorders studio (3) *Hollywood, CA* 1:00-6:30pm. Today sees an instrumental tracking session for **'Child Is Father Of The Man'** (Master No. 56667; duration 2:40). Brian and engineer Chuck Britz tape the song in sections: section one of 22 seconds requires 8 takes while the song's verse requires 10 takes. At the end of this lengthy five-and-a-half-hour session Brian overdubs a piano track. Although lyrics are prepared, the song begins life as a foreboding ballad without words.
Musicians present Hal Blaine (drums), Jimmy Bond Jr. (upright bass), Frankie Capp (percussion), Carol Kaye (bass guitar), Bill Pitman (guitar), Carl Wilson (guitar).

■ Saturday 8th

At his home on Laurel Way in Los Angeles – away from the studio and aside from his increasing belief that his house is bugged – Brian confesses to his wife Marilyn about a strange incident. He has just been to see the recently released Paramount sci-fi thriller movie *Seconds* that stars Rock Hudson. Marilyn will recall later for BBC Radio-1 what Brian says. "I walked into that movie," he tells Marilyn, "and the first thing that happened was a voice from the screen saying, 'Good afternoon, Mr. Wilson,' and it completely blew my mind." Rock Hudson's character in the film is Antiochus 'Tony' Wilson. "That's not all," Brian continues. "The whole thing was there. I mean my whole life. Birth and death and rebirth. The whole thing. Even the beach was in it, a whole thing about the beach. It was my whole life right there on the screen." Marilyn tries to calm him, saying that it's just a coincidence. Brian is adamant that the film was made by Phil Spector.

Marilyn will tell Radio-1: "I think the drugs he was taking had started to confuse him. He had met a lot of strange people who had encouraged drugs and told him that they would expand his mind. I think he was caught up in experimenting and finding out who he was

as a person. He just got very confused."

As with the *Smile* album, everything in Brian's Laurel Way home is changing. There is always something new going on. Every week he re-arranges the house into 'fun zones' and, besides the house's sauna bath and the piano that is still sitting in a sandbox, Brian builds a tent in what was once the dining room. Meetings are carried out in the large, canvas-clad arena. Then, suddenly, in an attempt to get The Beach Boys in shape physically for recording sessions, Brian's living room is stripped down and turned into a gymnasium. Blue tumbling mats replace the house's exquisite furniture. Brian's den becomes stocked with overstuffed pillows and bubbling hookahs for smoking regular supplies of marijuana.

Brian does everything on the spur of the moment. When he gets into health food, various charts appear in the kitchen. He suggests to Marilyn she should turn their garden into an organic vegetable patch and sell veg from a new drive-through window at the rear of the house, but Marilyn immediately scotches the idea. Anyway, Brian will soon lose interest in the plan. To him, if it cannot be put together at that very moment then it cannot be put together at all.
• An interview with Brian appears in today's UK *Melody Maker* newspaper. He says, "Our next album will be better than *Pet Sounds*. It will be as much an improvement over *Sounds* as that was over *Summer Days*."

■ Monday 10th

RECORDING *Smile* **session 15** Western Recorders studio (3) *Hollywood, CA*. The Beach Boys overdub further vocals to the **'Wind Chimes'** instrumental track completed on October 5th.
'Good Vibrations' / 'Let's Go Away For Awhile' single released in the US. It sells over 293,000 copies in the first four days of its release and enters the *Cash Box* chart at number 61 on October 22nd. It will race quickly to the number 1 position in charts across the world. Almost immediately Brian is transformed into an even bigger superstar in the eyes of the media. The 24-year-old may well be the most popular American songwriter of his generation. For a short period, Capitol stops complaining about the 'new style' Beach Boys. Unlike *Pet Sounds*, this piece of work is instantly commercial. "After the poor sales of *Pet Sounds*," says Brian, "I felt that I had made my point. I have a feeling that this is a very spiritual song and I want it to give off good vibrations. I'm proud of 'Good Vibrations', it exemplifies a whole era."
• Four entirely different colour promotional films will be distributed by Immediate in Europe and Capitol in the US to promote 'Good Vibrations'. Film 1, made in Los Angeles on Sunday October 23rd, just prior to the start of their visit to Europe, opens with the group asleep in beds at a fire station. An alarm bell rings, the group wakes up and they slide down poles in the station. Scenes follow where they

---

Good Vibrations single

A **'Good Vibrations'** (B. WILSON / M. LOVE)
B-US **'Let's Go Away For Awhile'** (B. WILSON)
B-UK **'Wendy'** (B. WILSON / M. LOVE)

US release October 10th 1966 (Capitol 5676).
UK release October 28th 1966 (Capitol CL 15475).
Chart high US number 1; UK number 1.

are seen tearing along the street *Monkees*-TV-style, trying to jump on the back of a rolling fire engine. (Screening of this short includes a spot on UK BBC-1's *Top Of The Pops* on Thursday November 24th.)

Film 2 features the group at work rehearsing in the Western Recorders studio in Los Angeles. (Airings include a spot on French 1st Channel's *Cinq Colonnes à La Une*, a serious news magazine show, in February 1967.) Film 3 consists of footage shot during the making of Peter Whitehead's film *The Beach Boys In London*. It features the group arriving at London airport on November 6th alongside exclusive candid footage of the band rehearsing, relaxing and smoking in their dressing room at the first concert of the British tour later that evening. (Screenings include *Top Of The Pops* on BBC-1 on November 10th, and the *Beat Club* pop music show on Radio Bremen in Germany on December 31st.)

Film 4 is an alternative edit of Whitehead's footage, also prepared for an exclusive screening on BBC TV's *Top Of The Pops*, on November 17th. It too features film of The Beach Boys arriving in London but adds footage of them on their way to an EMI press conference (November 7th), Al and Dennis at London's Portobello Road, and clips from the group's evening concert at the Hammersmith Odeon (both November 14th).

Tuesday 11th

RECORDING *Smile* session 16 Western Recorders studio (3) *Hollywood, CA* 2:00-6:00pm. This is an instrumental and Beach Boys vocal overdubbing session for **'Cabinessence'** (Master No. 56716; duration: 2:50), now with a revised title as a single word. The segment taped today is known as the **'Who Ran The Iron Horse'** section. Carl joins Brian at the session to assist with guitar overdubbing onto the instrumental track taped on October 3rd. Brian completes a mix of the piece at the end of today's four-hour session.

Musicians present Jimmy Bond Jnr. (upright bass), Carol Kaye (bass guitar), Oliver Mitchell (trumpet), Bill Pitman (guitar), Carl Wilson (guitar).

Wednesday 12th

RECORDING *Smile* session 17 Columbia (A) *Hollywood, CA* 2:00pm. The Beach Boys overdub vocals onto the October 7th instrumental track of **'Child Is Father Of The Man'** and Brian compiles a mix. Later, following on from yesterday's rough mix, Brian produces the tracking tape for the **'Grand Coulee Dam'** section of **'Cabinessence'**. (A later session booked at Western for 10:00pm today is cancelled.)

Thursday 13th

RECORDING *Smile* session 18 Western Recorders studio (3) *Hollywood, CA*. Today sees a Beach Boys vocal overdubbing session for **'I Ran'** (Master No. 56473) onto take 20 of the August 12th piano track. ('I Ran' was formerly **'Untitled #1'** and **'Look'**. The session sheet was logged as 'Untitled Song #1', the tape box as 'Look', but the song is renamed 'I Ran [formerly Untitled Song #1]' for today's session.) The complete recording of this Beach Boys vocal session later goes missing from the group's tape library.

Monday 17th – Friday 21st

In readiness for their show in Michigan this Saturday and their tour of Europe and the UK set to begin on October 25th, The Beach Boys rehearse for five straight days in a rented hall at a secret location in Los Angeles. Sessions begin each day at 9:00am. After rehearsals on Monday and Friday they visit Brian at Western studio for vocal recordings.

Monday 17th

RECORDING *Smile* session 19, 'Heroes And Villains' session 2 Columbia studio (A) *Hollywood, CA*. Just three days before sessions on the song begin properly, the full Beach Boys line-up records a rough set of vocals intended for **'Heroes And Villains'** (Carl is again actively present at today's session). A small portion of the lyrics sung by the group during the session results in the song being logged on today's union sheet as 'I'm In Great Shape'. As the *Smile* sessions progress, Brian will toy with the idea of resurrecting the 'I'm In Great Shape' title for a completely different link track (see October 27th and November 29th).

Tuesday 18th

RECORDING *Smile* session 20 Western Recorders studio (3) *Hollywood, CA* 2:00-7:30pm (some musicians leave at 6:30pm). Today's session sees instrumental tracking for **'Do You Like Worms'** (Master No. 56729; duration 3:05), originally titled 'Do You Dig Worms'. To round off the session Brian tapes a rough guide vocal for the track and compiles a mix. (The other Beach Boys will overdub vocals on December 21st.) 'Do You Like Worms' consists of fragments recorded separately and then edited together as Brian employs his mosaic method that had worked so well for 'Good Vibrations'. He intends these identical fragments to unify the various tracks on the *Smile* album. "When you're stoned," he says, "30 seconds of music is like two hours."

After the session on December 21st, the melody of the recurring keyboard break in 'Do You Like Worms' will be lifted to become the chorus of 'Heroes And Villains', while 'Worms' itself becomes another casualty of the *Smile* sessions. 'Do You Like Worms' exemplifies the Americana theme of *Smile*, described by Van Dyke Parks as a deliberate attempt to counter the British mania ruling the musical world at the time. The song portrays the relentless European expansion across America, westward from Plymouth Rock to Hawaii.

Regarding *Smile*, David Anderle will remark: "Brian was obsessed with humour and the importance of humour. He was fascinated with the idea of getting humour into a disc." Brian first toyed with this idea back in November 1965. Several newspapers have reported that Brian is considering a separate 'humour' album, along with a health-food LP and a sound-effects record, but none of these will materialise – although some consider that the humour concept album will become *Smiley Smile* in 1967.

Brian continues to record several 'humorous' situations, the first of which is made at the end of today's session. A 24-minute tape features Van Dyke Parks, David Andrele, Michael Vosse, Diane Rovell, Brian, someone called Dawn, and Jules Siegel. Siegel tries to get the others to play the *Lifeboat* game, where players try to get shipwrecked sailors safely to a desert island in (leaking) lifeboats, necessarily discarding some of those on board as they go. But the idea soon gets tiresome, prompting one of the 'contestants' to enquire of Brian, "What are we doing in here?" Not surprisingly, nothing particularly amusing is committed to tape, but Brian will nevertheless return to the idea on November 4th.

Musicians present Jerry Cole (guitar), Gene Estes (percussion), Jim Gordon (drums, conga), Carol Kaye (bass guitar), Van Dyke Parks (instrument unknown), Lyle Ritz (upright bass).

Thursday 20th

RECORDING *Smile* session 21, 'Heroes And Villains' session 3 Western Recorders studio (3) *Hollywood, CA* 2:00-7:30pm (additional musician arrives at 5:00pm). After the fruitless session of May 11th, Brian holds the first proper instrumental tracking session for

Phonograph Recording Contract Blank
AMERICAN FEDERATION OF MUSICIANS
OF THE UNITED STATES AND CANADA

95362

Local Union No. 47

THIS CONTRACT for the personal services of musicians, made this 18th day of October, 19__, between the undersigned employer (hereinafter called the "employer") and ____ 6 musicians (including the leader) (hereinafter called "employees").

WITNESSETH, That the employer hires the employees as musicians severally on the terms and conditions below, and as further specified on reverse side. The leader represents that the employees already designated have agreed to be bound by said terms and conditions. Each employee yet to be chosen shall be so bound by said terms and conditions upon agreeing to accept his employment. Each employee may enforce this agreement. The employees severally agree to render collectively to the employer services as musicians in the orchestra under the leadership of Van Dyke Parks as follows:

Name and Address of Place of Engagement Western Recorders, 6000 Sunset Blvd.

Date(s) and Hours of Employment October 18, 1966 2:00 P.M. to 7:30 P.M. (some men only until 6:30 P.M.)

Type of Engagement: Recording for phonograph records only

Plus pension contributions as specified on reverse side hereof.

WAGE AGREED UPON $ UNION SCALE

(Terms and amount)

This wage includes expenses agreed to be reimbursed by the employer in accordance with the attached schedule, or a schedule to be furnished the employer on or before the date of engagement.

To be paid WITHIN 15 DAYS

(Specify when payments are to be made)

Upon request by the American Federation of Musicians of the United States and Canada (herein called the "Federation") or the local in whose jurisdiction the employees shall perform hereunder, the employer either shall make advance payment hereunder or shall post an appropriate bond.

Employer's name and authorized signature	Capitol Records
Leader's name	Van Dyke Parks
Local No.	47
Leader's signature	
Street address	1750 N. Vine Street
Leader's Street address	7220 Melrose Ave.
	Hollywood, Calif. HO 2-6252
	Hollywood, Calif.

(1) Label name Capitol Records   Session no. 1452

Master no.	No. of minutes	TITLES OF TUNES	Master no.	No. of minutes	TITLES OF TUNES
56729	3:05	"Do You Like Worms?"			

(2) Employee's name (As on Social Security card) Last First Initial	(3) Home address (Give street, city and state)	(4) Local Union no.	(5) Social Security number	(6) Scale wages	(7) Pension contribution
(Leader) Parks, Van Dyke	7220 Melrose Ave. Hollywood, Calif.	47	151-28-1160	366.06	29.29
Rovell, Diane (contract)	616 N. Sierra Bonita Los Angeles, Calif.	47	560-56-7005	366.06	29.29
Britz, Charles	4501 Wevona St. Los Angeles 65, Calif.	47	567-26-4273	183.04	14.64
Estes, Gene P. (Drums & Congo)	12212 Hartsook St. North Hollywood, Calif.	47	456-36-7156	142.36	11.39
Gordon, James Beck 1 DBL.	11616 Hartsook St. North Hollywood, Calif.	47	555-54-7854	160.66	12.85
Kaye, Carol	4905 Forman North Hollywood, Calif.	47	555-46-5389	142.36	11.39
Kolbrak, Jerry	5729 Irvine North Hollywood, Calif.	47	394-36-7847	183.04	14.64
Ritz, Lyle	1971 N. Curson Ave. Los Angeles 46, Calif.	47	549-38-1490	142.36	11.39

NO ARRANGER OR COPYIST THIS SESSION

(8) Total Pension Contributions (Sum of Column (7)) $ 135.18

Make check payable in this amount to "AFM & EPW Fund"

FOR FUND USE ONLY:

Date pay't rec'd PAID NOV 7 1966 Amt. paid ____ Date posted ____ By ____

Form B-4 Rev. 4

'Heroes And Villains' (Master No. 56727; duration 2:25), a piece he envisions as "a three minute musical comedy". Brian tells KHJ radio in 1977: "I said to my dad, 'I'm going to make a record that's better than "Good Vibrations", something that *you* could never do.' I don't know why in hell I said that. He goes, 'What are you talking about? What the hell do you mean I couldn't do it? Shut up!' And he started whacking me and we got into a fight. And then he started crying and goes, 'Oh, I'm sorry, son. I'm sorry. I didn't understand.' I was just in a playful mood. I get that way. Just before I go in and do something great, I get a little egotistical. I pump it up."

There will be further 'Heroes And Villains' sessions to come, each adding more pieces to a puzzle that will drive Brian to distraction over many months before the song's eventual release as a single in a totally different form on July 24th 1967. With a lyrical hint of 'El Paso', the Marty Robbins hit, 'Heroes And Villains' was the first song that Brian and Van Dyke Parks wrote together back in May. Brian played the long descending melody line on the piano to Parks who immediately came up with the line "I've been in this town so long …." Parks will later tell BBC Radio-1: "Brian always made a melody and the words were slapped on that melody. I had no input whatsoever in the music. I was a total lyricist and sometimes an instrumentalist."

More than any other songs intended for *Smile*, the dozens of musical themes and sections recorded for 'Heroes And Villains' demonstrate Brian's creativity at its peak as he tries to reach artistically for something totally new and epic in pop music. It is his attempt to surpass the monumental achievements of 'Good Vibrations'. 'Heroes And Villains' will undergo the most complex evolution of any song in Beach Boys history.

Another major piece of *Smile* is the **'Barnyard Suite'**, and work on its tracking tape begins today. The suite is a musical depiction of farm life, replete with animal sounds, hammers and saws, and lyrics about "eggs and grits". At this point it is intended to feature a compilation of short snatches from four different songs. "We never finished that one," Brian says later. "We got onto something else." There are several theories about what will happen to this song or fragment, some involving its possible assimilation as part of 'Heroes And Villains'.

Musicians present Gene Estes (timpani, percussion), Jim Gordon (drums, conga), George Hyde (French horn), Carol Kaye (bass guitar), Tommy Morgan (harmonica), Van Dyke Parks (unknown instrument), Bill Pitman (guitar), Lyle Ritz (upright bass).

■ Friday 21st

RECORDING *Smile* session 22 Western Recorders studio (3) *Hollywood, CA.* The Beach Boys overdub chorus vocals onto the October 18th tracking tape of **'Do You Like Worms'**. Lyrics written for the verses of the song but apparently not recorded include: "Once upon the sandwich isles, the social structure steamed upon Hawaii." Originally the chorus goes: "Ribbon of concrete, see what you done, done," but this is rewritten just before it recording at today's session. Later, working alone, Brian overdubs his vocal to the song's chorus, creating intricate four and five-part harmonies by multi-tracking his own voice. Brian sings, "Bicycle rider, just see what you've done, done to the church of the American Indian." With the session over, Brian prepares for a plane ride.

• The countdown to the arrival of The Beach Boys in Britain continues when a short audio-only preview of their new single 'Good Vibrations' is played during the rundown of this week's Top 20 singles on tonight's edition of *Ready Steady Go!*. (The show is transmitted between 6:15 and 7:00pm on certain regions of the ITV Network.) The official UK 45 release of 'Good Vibrations' is still seven days away.

■ Saturday 22nd

University of Michigan *Lansing, MI* two shows
This pair of performances marks the first time that the group plays Brian's musical masterpiece 'Good Vibrations' in concert. Fearing that his colleagues will be incapable of reproducing the song on stage, Brian accompanies the group to Michigan to oversee a lengthy and arduous day-long rehearsal for the song. Later he sits and watches faultless performances on-stage by The Beach Boys. At the very end of the second show Brian is coaxed into jumping up on stage to sing 'Johnny B Goode' as an encore. He receives a standing ovation from a packed University.

Set-list (both shows) 'Help Me Rhonda', 'I Get Around', medley 'Surfin' Safari' / 'Fun Fun Fun' / 'Shut Down' / 'Little Deuce Coupe' / 'Surfin' USA', 'Surfer Girl', 'Papa-Oom-Mow-Mow', 'You're So Good To Me', 'You've Got To Hide Your Love Away', 'California Girls', 'Sloop John B', 'Wouldn't It Be Nice', 'God Only Knows', 'Good Vibrations', 'Graduation Day', 'Barbara Ann'.

• In autumn 1966 everybody seems to want to be Brian's friend, but he is increasingly insecure. This evening, before his return from Michigan to Los Angeles, each of his friends and important acquaintances receives a call from wife Marilyn asking them to come to Los Angeles airport to greet Brian. They are told it is very important that they attend: Brian wants reassurance that he is loved. When he arrives and they all meet at the airport, Brian has a photographer take a series of group pictures. Around 30 people stare out from the photographs, including Danny Hutton, Mark Volman (The Turtles), Dean Torrence (Jan & Dean), Diane Rovell, Annie Hinsche Wilson (Carl's wife), Van Dyke Parks, David and Sheryl Anderle, Dick and Carol Maider, June Fairchild, Michael Vosse, and Terry Sachen. In the foreground is *The Saturday Evening Post*'s journalist, Jules Siegel, who looks out at the world with a sour expression.

For a long time afterwards a huge mounted blow-up of the best of these photographs hangs on Brian's living room wall at his home in Laurel Way. But within months it will be gone – and most of the people will no longer be his friends. One by one, each will step out or be forced out of the picture. The cycle has returned to its beginning. Brian started out in Hawthorne, California, with his two brothers and a cousin. Now, once more, he has surrounded himself with just his family and relatives. By April 1967 the Wilsons' house in Beverly Hills will be quiet and empty. Brian and Marilyn will be in their new Spanish Mission estate in Bel Air, living next door to John and Michelle Phillips of The Mamas & The Papas.

■ Monday 24th

'Surfin' Safari' / '409' single reissued in the US.
Surfin' USA and *Shut Down* albums reissued in the US.
• *Best Of The Beach Boys* album peaks in US *Billboard* chart at the number 8 position.
• A dub is made today at Capitol of the mono master for 'Good Vibrations' for use on a 16mm magnetic reel to accompany a promotional film the group made yesterday (see also October 10th).

TOUR STARTS Europe (Oct 25th-Nov 14th)

■ Tuesday 25th

RECORDING *Smile* session 23 Columbia studio (A) *Los Angeles, CA.* Today sees a dialogue session with Brian's friends for possible use in the *Smile* project.
Olympia Theatre *Paris, France* with The Coco Briavel Quartet, Michel Polnareff, Graham Bonney
The live Beach Boys outfit arrives in Paris on the 24th to begin the

This 'AFM sheet' for October 18th marks the 20th session for the doomed *Smile* album as Brian guides a small group of instrumentalists through a recording of 'Do You Like Worms'.

European leg of the tour. The entourage is greeted by freezing weather. The group immediately angers the French press by announcing that they will do no TV and radio appearances and no interviews for local newspapers. They kick off the tour tonight with a sell-out show at the Olympia, which will be aired on French radio station Europe 1's *Musicorama* show next month. Support artist Michel Polnareff is a fast-rising 21-year-old French pop idol.

There are some unforeseen problems with the group's equipment, mostly deriving from the electro-theremin played by Mike during the performance of 'Good Vibrations'. The instrument has been manufactured especially for The Beach Boys by a company in New York, possibly Moog. But the concert is well received by an ecstatic crowd. The critics, meanwhile, have mixed judgements. Mike Hennessey writes in *Melody Maker*: "Minus Brian Wilson and a few miles of electronic circuits, The Beach Boys have a tough time on stage to reproduce the increasingly complex sounds they are creating on disc. Beginning their European tour in Paris they did not quite live up to the high reputation they established on their first visit here in November 1964. Certainly they were handicapped by a rather muddy sound system, but this apart, they never seemed really to get into their stride and they admitted afterwards that they had not been happy about their performance.

"This said, The Beach Boys still remain a highly professional musical group with a wide range of harmonies, a surging rhythmic pulse and an excellent repertoire of originals," continued the *Melody Maker* reviewer. "On their well-established numbers like 'Fun Fun Fun', 'I Get Around', 'Barbara Ann' and 'Sloop John B' they produced that characteristic Beach Boys sound, a sort of big beat version of The Four Freshmen with added choirboys. But when it came to the more recent numbers like 'God Only Knows' and 'Good Vibrations' the interpretations sounded a little thin compared with the recorded versions. Even Mike Love's use of an oscillator, which the group have been employing on stage over the past five months, didn't completely fill the gaps."

Wendy Varnals, recent star of BBC TV teenage show *A Whole Scene Going*, reports on the concert for *Disc & Music Echo*: "For a preview of what Britain can expect from The Beach Boys when they come in this week, I flew to Paris to catch them at their sell-out performance … . They opened to a strangely mixed audience, teenage ravers from the US camp bases who started screaming directly the curtain rose and were screaming when Les Beach Boys had left the theatre, liberally mixed with an incongruous assortment of silent middle-aged devotees. I counted at least four bald heads in the audience. On balance, middle age won. I have no doubt that many bets were being made to see whether The Beach Boys can reproduce on stage their highly complicated but knockout new release, the product of many months in the recording studio in Los Angeles. I think they can – very successfully. It is their vocal strength that *is* The Beach Boys. On stage they have no act. Mike Love does a little clowning around when he introduces the numbers, but on the whole it's just a case of standing up and singing – beautifully."

The group spends Monday in Paris with Varnalls, taking in the sights, but at the top of the Eiffel Tower the driving rain is so bad they can't see a thing. A planned visit to Paris's sewers has to be cancelled because the system is not open on Mondays. Later on Tuesday evening, following their show, The Beach Boys attend a party in their honour at The Rolls Club in Montparnasse and, later still, with Varnalls still in tow, the entourage visits a French nightclub strangely adorned, top to bottom, with silver foil.
Set-list 'Fun Fun Fun', 'Barbara Ann', 'I Get Around', 'Sloop John B', 'You've Got To Hide Your Love Away' (Dennis lead vocal), 'God Only Knows', 'Good Vibrations', 'Little Honda'.

• Before the European tour schedule was completed, the group planned to open in London, England, with their first engagement an October 24th appearance on the BBC-1 television variety show, *Billy Cotton's Music Hall*. But this and a live November 11th appearance on the Associated-Rediffusion pop show *Ready Steady Go!* are cancelled. The group turns down the 15-minute three-track end-of-show *RSG!* appearance for financial reasons and for fears that they will be unable to replicate the sounds of their new single 'Good Vibrations'. The same reasons lead to them cancelling studio appearances on BBC TV's *Top Of The Pops* chart show on November 10th, 17th and 24th. Their visit to England is put back until November 6th.

■ **Wednesday 26th**

TV TF1 Studios Paris, France. TF1 *Tilt Magazine* lip-synch 'Good Vibrations' broadcast January 25th 1967. Following brief camera rehearsals, The Beach Boys mime to 'Good Vibrations' for this hour-long French television show, alongside other guests. Surprisingly, it will be their only European TV appearance for the duration of this tour.

■ **Thursday 27th**

RECORDING *Smile* session 24, 'Heroes And Villains' session 4 Western Recorders studio (3) *Hollywood, CA* 2:00-7:30pm (one musician arrives at 5:30pm). Back in California, Brian supervises a five-and-a-half-hour instrumental tracking session for **'Heroes And Villains'** (Master No. 56738; duration 1:25), again confusingly titled 'I'm In Great Shape' on the union log simply because of part of its lyric. It features piano, bass and saxophone, then harp, bass and saxophone. (By December, the piece recorded at today's session has evolved into the 'Barnyard Suite', intended to follow 'Heroes And Villains' on the *Smile* album.)
Deutchlandhalle *Berlin, West Germany* with Peter & Gordon, Graham Bonney, The Lords
Prior to the second date on the European tour, Al is the only one of the group who passes through the Berlin Wall and visits communist East Berlin. Mike says: "Germany was fantastic! They really believe in security precautions out there. When we arrived at the airport there were about 300 police to meet us. We just walked into the lobby, threw our hands up and surrendered. The people were real nice." Bruce befriends tour support singer Graham Bonney, and will later write and help arrange Bonney's German hit 'Thank You Baby' (see February 1967).

■ **Friday 28th**

Ernst Merck Halle *Hamburg, West Germany* 5:30pm, with Peter & Gordon, Graham Bonney, The Lords
Set-list 'Help Me Rhonda', 'Sloop John B', 'Barbara Ann', 'I Get Around', 'God Only Knows', 'California Girls', medley 'Fun Fun Fun' / 'Do You Wanna Dance' / 'Surfin' USA', 'You're So Good To Me', 'Good Vibrations'.

'Good Vibrations' / **'Wendy'** single released in the UK. (The B-side is taken from the 1964 album *All Summer Long*.) Music critics immediately celebrate the brilliance of 'Good Vibrations'.

New Musical Express: "A technically perfect and an impeccably performed disc by The Beach Boys (I should think so, with 40 attempts needed to make it) and one that's impossible to absorb completely until you've heard it a dozen times. The group's counter-harmonies are the most startling and complex even they have produced and, of course, there are the familiar falsettos in abundance. Tempo varies between a vigorous surf shake with tambourine, and a slow drag pace with organ and weird

Brian directs the first of four promo films for 'Good Vibrations' on the streets of Los Angeles on October 23rd.

oscillations. Colourful lyrics, highly electronic, a big one! Probably a number 1."

Melody Maker: "Instrumentally, the track is quite brilliant. No symphony was ever scored with more inspiration or patience. And because Wilson is as much a sound fiend as a maker of melodies, he has used four separate recording studios, each in a different neighbourhood, to build the four-tracked tape into a masterly record."

But once again Wilson's brilliance is lost on The Who's Pete Townshend. Just four months after his press attack on *Pet Sounds*, the guitarist and songwriter blasts Brian and 'Good Vibrations' in an interview for *Disc & Music Echo*. "Brian Wilson lives in a world of flowers, butterflies and strawberry flavoured chewing gum," Townshend rants. "His world has nothing to do with pop. Pop is going out on the road, getting drunk and meeting the kids. 'Good Vibrations' was probably a good record but who's to know? You had to play it about 90 bloody times to even hear what they were singing about. Pop is getting so complicated nobody knows what's happening, least of all the fans. Everything's so involved. Next year is going to be worse. We're going to have a batch of over-produced Beach Boys records and over-produced records in general. It needs The Beatles to come out of their hole and make a really simple pop record to sort things out."

■ Saturday 29th
Grugahalle *Essen, West Germany* with Peter & Gordon, Graham Bonney, The Lords
• 'Good Vibrations' single enters US *Billboard* Top 40 chart at number 38.

■ Sunday 30th
Halle Munsterland *Munster, West Germany* with Peter & Gordon, Graham Bonney, The Lords

■ Monday 31st
Messe Sportpalast *Hanover, West Germany* with Peter & Gordon, Graham Bonney, The Lords

November

God Only Knows EP released in the UK: 'God Only Knows', 'Here Today', 'Sloop John B', 'Wouldn't It Be Nice'.
Best Of The Beach Boys album released in the UK.
• 'Good Vibrations' single peaks in UK *Record Retailer/Music Weekly* chart at number 1, and in Canadian *RPM* Singles chart at number 2.
• 'Wouldn't It Be Nice' single peaks in New Zealand *Listener Pop-O-Meter* chart at number 12.
• The Beach Boys are voted 'Top Vocal Group' in Russia, Western Europe, Japan, and The Philippines.
• As 'Good Vibrations' takes off, The Beach Boys – without Brian, of course – head through Europe to the UK for their first tour there. By this time in the US it is common knowledge throughout the music industry that the title of the next Beach Boys album will be *Smile*. Reporters stream in to hear what Brian is doing and the legend begins to grow, with much of the media frenzy down to the group's press officer Derek Taylor.

■ Wednesday 2nd
Circus Krone *Munich, West Germany* with Peter & Gordon, Graham Bonney, The Lords

■ Thursday 3rd
Western Recorders studio (3) *Hollywood, CA* 2:00 start; session cancelled
Falkoner Centret *Torsdagm, Denmark* with Peter & Gordon, Graham Bonney
Mike acquires a pipe during a fleeting visit to a local market and will often be seen with it during the coming UK tour.

■ Friday 4th
RECORDING *Smile* session 25 Western Recorders studio (3) *Hollywood, CA* 2:00-6:00pm (some musicians employed only until 5:30pm). In California, Brian supervises the first tracking session for **'Surf's Up'** (listed on the American Federation of Musicians session sheet as **'1st Movement'**; Master No. 56842; duration 2:20), with engineer Chuck Britz. This beautiful track co-written by Brian and Van Dyke Parks is inspired by Dennis who has complained to Brian about having to wear the group's regular pin-striped shirts and that they still seem to be thought of as surfers. Parks guesses that the resulting song title is so square that it just has to be hip. Brian agrees. "'Surf's Up' was a masterpiece of a song," he says. "We wrote that in one night. We stayed up until six in the morning. It opened up on a minor seventh, unlike most songs, which open up on a major. From there it just started building and rambling. I thought it rambled beautifully and said a lot at the end. A children's song, a song of freedom. When we finished it, Van Dyke said, 'Let's call it "Surf's Up",' which is wild because surfing isn't related to the song at all. Special? That's right. Van Dyke and I really kind of thought we had done something special when we finished that one." But the lyrical tone of 'Surf's Up' soon takes on a dark side, and by the following year the song will be interpreted by many as Brian's swansong.

Just after 6:00pm, when the day's session is concluded, Brian demonstrates to Parks on the piano in the studio how he envisions the entire **'Heroes And Villains'** will sound. At this point, Brian's demo includes pieces of the *Smile* song 'Barnyard'. A tape from this session reveals Parks accompanying Brian with animal sounds and Brian explaining which pieces are finished and which are incomplete.

When the demonstration is complete, Brian begins taping another 'humorous' recording for his projected humour album. In front of an audience consisting of Van Dyke Parks, Danny Hutton, Michael Vosse and a fellow called Bob, this second party reel is slightly more amusing than the one recorded on October 18th. Brian performs an extended comedy routine about him "falling into the piano" and has the other participants trying to get him out by hitting certain keys. Then he falls into the microphone. The group does some chanting, a "rhythmic vegetable thing" with bongos, and another piece asking "Where's my beets and carrots" and "I've got a big bag of vegetables" (which will be used on the 'Vegetables' promo on the 2001 CD *Hawthorne CA*).

The party proceeds to an underwater "bottom of the ocean" chant and ends with a groaning section not unlike the 'Swedish frog' section recorded later for 'Heroes And Villains'. The underwater chant is likely the genesis of the 'Water chant' later performed by The Beach Boys for 'Heroes And Villains'. The sessions are interrupted by LA disc jockey 'Humble' Harv Miller who comes knocking on the door of the studio. After they exchange pleasantries, Brian sits at the piano in the studio and proceeds to play Miller the group's next single, 'Heroes And Villains'. Miller is knocked out by the tune and exclaims, "That is going to be the greatest record that anybody has ever heard!" (The surviving tape with Humble Harv will also become notable as containing the only known vocal versions of 'Barnyard' and 'I'm In Great Shape'. An

While the live band are in Europe, this union log notes the musicians present at Brian's session at Western Recorders on November 4th where part of 'Surf's Up' is committed to tape for the first time – and for now is given the subtitle '1st Movement'.

THE BEACHBOYS
TRACKING SCALE INCLUDED

CAPITOL RECORDS
(Employer's name)

Phonograph Recording Contract Blank
AMERICAN FEDERATION OF MUSICIANS
OF THE UNITED STATES AND CANADA

Local Union No. **47**

N⁰ **248099**

THIS CONTRACT for the personal services of musicians, made this **4 th** day of **November**, 19**66** **8** musicians
between the undersigned employer (hereinafter called the "employer") and _____ (including the leader)
(hereinafter called "employees"). The employer hires the employees as musicians severally on the terms and conditions below, and as further specified on reverse side. The leader represents that the employees already designated have agreed to be bound by said terms and conditions. Each employee yet to be chosen shall be so bound by said terms and conditions upon agreeing to accept his employment. Each employee may enforce this agreement. The employees severally agree to render collectively to the employer services as musicians in the orchestra under the leadership of
Charles D. Britz as follows:

Name and Address of Place of Engagement **Western Recorders, 6000 Sunset Blvd. Hollywood Calif.**

Date(s) and Hours of Employment **November 4, 1966   2:00 P.M. to 6:00 P.M. (Some men until 5:30 P.M.)**

Type of Engagement: **Recording for phonograph records only.**   Plus pension contributions as specified on reverse side hereof.

WAGE AGREED UPON $ **UNION SCALE**

This wage includes expenses agreed to be reimbursed by the employer in accordance with the attached schedule, or a schedule to be furnished the employer on or before the date of engagement.
(Terms and amount)

To be paid   **WITHIN 15 DAYS**
(Specify when payments are to be made)

Upon request by the American Federation of Musicians of the United States and Canada (herein called the "Federation") or the local in whose jurisdiction the employees shall perform hereunder, the employer either shall make advance payment hereunder or shall post an appropriate bond.

Employer's name and authorized signature	Capitol Records	Leader's name	Charles Britz	Local No. **47**
Street address	**1750 N. Vine Street**	Leader's signature	*[signature]*	
		Street address	**4501 Wavona St.**	
City State Phone	**Hollywood, Calif. HO 26252**	City State	**Los Angeles 65, Calif.**	

(1) Label Name **Capitol Records**   Session No. **19154**

Master No.	No. of Minutes	TITLES OF TUNES	Master No.	No. of Minutes	TITLES OF TUNES
56842	2:20	"SURF'S UP" (1st movement)			

(2) Employee's Name (As on Social Security Card) Last First Initial (Leader)	(3) Home Address (Give Street, City and State)	(4) Local Union No.	(5) Social Security Number	(6) Scale Wages	(7) Pension Contribution
Britz, Charles Dean	4501 Wavona St. Los Angeles 65, Calif.	47	567-26-4273	244.04	19.52
Rovell, Diane (contract)	616 N. Sierra Bonita Los Angeles 36, Calif.	47	560-56-7005	244.04	19.52
Bond, James E. Jr.	P.O. Box 8551 Los Angeles 8, Calif.	47	201-22-5657	101.68	8.13
Capp, Frank 1 Dbl. Drums & Latin	3017 Doss Benita Pl. Studio City, Calif.	47	103-24-7193	113.88	9.11
Casey, Alvin W.	6355 Primrose Ave. Hollywood, Calif.	47	526-46-9373	101.68	8.13
DeLory, Alfred V.	5524 Ruthwood Dr. Calabasas, Calif.	47	559-36-9796	122.02	9.76
Kaye, Carol	4905 Forman North Hollywood, Calif.	47	555-46-5389	101.68	8.13
Pellico, Nick	5700 Vantage Ave. North Hollywood, Calif.	47	035-12-2060	101.68	8.13

NO COPYIST OR ARRANGER THIS SESSION

FOR FUND USE ONLY:
Date payt rec'd   **PAID DEC 1 1966**

(8) Total Pension Contributions
Make check payable   n of Column (7)) $ **90.43**
this amount to "AFM & EPW Fund."

BELOW Live in Europe: LEFT Bruce, Carl, Al and Mike in Denmark on November 3rd; RIGHT Carl and Al three days later in London opening the British leg of the tour.

edited version of the tape will appear on the 1998 *Endless Harmony* soundtrack CD.)

Another tape with today's date will survive featuring sound-effect recordings, labelled 'Basketball', 'Chewing Terry's' (a dog's mouth sounds and barks), 'Chicago Cab Driver' (a cabbie giving directions around the city to Brian and friends), 'Kid At Fairfax', 'Tea Pot' (human whistling), and 'Water Hose' (the sound of a hose spraying water, with some traffic sounds in the background). In places heavy echo effects are added to these otherwise natural sounds.

Today, Brian's sister-in-law Diane Rovell is again studio contractor, the person who arranges for the various musicians to play at the session. Rovell continues to do this job for a few years on many Beach Boys recording dates.

Musicians present Jimmy Bond Jr (upright bass), Al de Lory (piano), Frankie Capp (drums, plus 'Latin'), Al Casey (guitar), Carol Kaye (bass guitar), Nick Pellico (percussion).

Konserthuset *Stockholm, Sweden* with Peter & Gordon, Graham Bonney

A planned visit to The Netherlands as part of the continuing European tour fails to materialise. Instead, The Beach Boys remain in Stockholm for one extra day before flying into London on Sunday morning.

■ Saturday 5th

'Good Vibrations' single enters the UK *Disc & Music Echo* Top 50 chart at number 14.

■ Sunday 6th

At 12:30pm, amid scenes replicating Beatlemania, The Beach Boys arrive at Terminal 2 of London's Heathrow Airport, en route from Stockholm on flight SK521. They are greeted by a horde of approximately 600 screaming fans. Marianne Faithfull intones during the *Beach Boys In London* film: "London on a grey, rainy morning became bright as a Californian surf when America's top group The Beach Boys flew into London Airport to be welcomed by thousands of their fans, many of whom had probably never ever seen their idols in person before."

Keith Altham writes in *New Musical Express*: "My first mistake was trying to escape from London Airport on Sunday morning through approximately 1,000 fans with drummer Dennis Wilson. We broke out of a side entrance from the Customs hall with PR Roger Easterby leading the charge, the man with the scream appeal, Dennis Wilson, a length behind, and myself bringing up the rear. A scream like several hundred Apache squaws in search of a scalp broke the air as a woman bearing a passing resemblance to Johnny Weissmuller embraced Dennis and attempted a step-over toe hold on his left leg while a smaller mortal clung barnacle-like to his right leg. This hampered his movements somewhat and with a supreme effort we made the inside of the Austin Princess limousine.

"Our successful arrival in the car was somewhat marred by the fact that Dennis discovered he still had the young lady in charge of his right leg," Altham continues. "We attempted to eject her through the car door, through which another 500 fans tried to squeeze. As the car moved forward, we discovered her reluctance to leave us had something to do with the door being jammed on her leg. After a further few yards it prised loose or broke off, I'm not sure which. 'Don't you love people,' Dennis said. 'I love people,' he smiled coolly, and waved from the windows to our self-appointed vanguard of scooters, motorbikes and cars with the placards bearing the words 'This Car Is Fitted With Good Vibrations'."

The Beach Boys' arrival and their time in London is captured for posterity by filmmaker Peter Whitehead's colour film (of 19:42 duration) produced by Immediate Records and suitably entitled *The Beach Boys In London*, with narration by singer Marianne Faithfull.

The Immediate connection comes from their handling of The Beach Boys' publishing in the UK. Excerpts from the feature will appear for the first time in two compilations screened on BBC TV's *Top Of The Pops* on November 10th and 17th to accompany 'Good Vibrations'.

The timing of the group's visit is perfect with the 'Good Vibrations' single riding high at number 15 in the UK *Record Retailer/Music Weekly* chart. Although they first visited the country back in November 1964, this is the first time that The Beach Boys have performed here. To coincide with their arrival, EMI in London arranges for 600 London double-decker buses to carry posters heralding the group's visit. The label had originally planned to have a fleet of fire engines to convey the group from the airport to the centre of London, but this proved impossible. The group takes residence at central London's Hilton Hotel, overlooking Hyde Park. It is here that Dennis plays a tape of the *Smile* track 'Child Is Father Of The Man' to *NME* reporter Keith Altham.

Finsbury Park Astoria *north London* 6:00 & 8:30pm, with Lulu, David & Jonathan, Sounds Incorporated, The Golden Brass, Jerry Stevens

The group play their first shows in the UK. Tickets for the performances sold out on the day they went on sale. Such was the demand that the venue's box office accidentally sold tickets set aside for photographers and reporters. Among the celebrities in attendance at the second concert this evening are Beatles manager Brian Epstein, John Walker of The Walker Brothers, Spencer Davis of The Spencer Davis Group, The Shadows, and Cathy McGowan, presenter of TV's *Ready Steady Go!*.

Backstage, Bruce wanders around aimlessly, worrying about his sore throat. He feels that his voice is about to give up thanks to the amount of singing he has done on this tour. Before the show, he remarks to a reporter: "They'll all be wanting to see Brian, not me." The group's PR man, Roger Easterby, notices that there is a strict build-up to this and every date on the tour. Each member of the group changes into his stage costumes at precisely the same time. The Beach Boys hold a team talk before each show and their production manager will insist that the group leaves the stage within 45 seconds of finishing their set. He will shout at the group if they take a second longer. Easterby later remarks, "The whole thing was a well oiled, extremely professional organisation."

Ray Coleman writes in *Disc & Music Echo*: "A Beach Boys fanatic said after their opening in London's Finsbury Park on Sunday, 'It was lovely, but I couldn't help feeling that there was something missing.' And without squashing one of the best groups since The Beatles, that just about summed it up. What was missing was a little bit of magic. The flame that ignites a stage show was not lit. And when that happens, the music must be dead right, to counter any moans that the show was a visual flop.

"The Beach Boys were on trial this week, their souls bared to the charge that they are products of studio sounds. Could they recreate in the flesh the brilliant inventiveness of Brian Wilson at the recording sessions? They just about made it. Carl Wilson's sweet voice braved 'God Only Knows' and it sounded pretty authentic. 'Good Vibrations' was less successful. But then nobody expected them to sound as good 'live' as on record. And this was where they fell down. Their stage act was nil. Bearded Mike Love clowned around a little before and during each number and that was just about that.

"It just isn't enough for five imageless Americans to stand and sing. They made no attempt to project personality unless it lay in

their fresh, California sun outfits of blue and white striped shirts and pure white trousers. ... 'Dennis! Dennis!' There were isolated calls for the handsome drummer, who is easily the most popular, despite the fact that the audience can hardly see him behind smiling Al Jardine. Perhaps that's part of the trouble. The one 'image' they've got is hidden. 'God Only Knows' drew the expected huge applause and 'Good Vibrations' went like a bomb. They went out with 'California Girls'. Very short rations: little more than 20 minutes."

Later this evening EMI Records holds a party to welcome The Beach Boys to England. During their time in London, Mike and Carl meet up with Motown singing group The Four Tops who are also in the UK on a promotional tour. On another day, Dennis, Carl and Mike walk into a London Rolls Royce showroom and purchase four $32,000 Phantom limousines, one for each of them and a fourth for Brian. Al and Bruce, the non-corporate members of Beach Boys Enterprises, settle for buying themselves some clothes instead. The salesman at the Rolls store tells the three Beach Boys that delivery to Los Angeles will take three months.

Set-list 'Help Me Rhonda', medley 'I Get Around' / 'Barbara Ann' / 'California Girls' / 'Sloop John B', 'Graduation Day', 'God Only Knows', 'Good Vibrations', 'California Girls'.

■ Monday 7th

RECORDING *Smile* **session 26** Western Recorders studio (3) *Hollywood, CA* 3:00-6:00pm. Brian is still busy in California, today overdubbing horns onto the November 4th instrumental track of **'Surf's Up'** (Master No. 56841; duration 2:20). A trial recording for horn effects featuring the assembled musicians talking through their instruments is also taped today and given the apt title **'George Fell Into His French Horn'**. The George in question is session musician George Hyde. Brian: "Five minutes after producer meets players, the men are creating laughing effects and having conversations with their horns."

Musicians present Arthur Briegleb (French horn, voice), Roy Caton (trumpet, voice), David Duke (French horn, voice, 'tubed horn'), George Hyde (French horn, voice), Claude Sherry (French horn, voice).

• This morning in London the touring Beach Boys face their first press conference of this trip, arriving in two lightweight Mini Moke open cars at EMI's central London Manchester Square headquarters where they are greeted by approximately 50 photographers. After posing for pictures the group faces the media in the conference room of EMI House.

Carl tells reporters, "I get annoyed at people who say we cannot reproduce our record sound on stage. It's idiotic to get hung up about not being able to reproduce the sound." Dennis jokingly remarks, "I like The Beatles but I am not pleased about being imprisoned in this room." The conference room, currently playing host to around 500 people, has been built to accommodate just 100. Once the get-together is over, Mike engages in conversation with Andrew Loog Oldham and Tony Calder of Immediate Records about the *Smile* album while a claustrophobic Carl heads to Carnaby Street where he purchases three trouser suits and a ring for his wife Annie. Dennis, meanwhile, pays a visit to Beatles tailor Dougie Millings.

■ Tuesday 8th

RECORDING *Smile* **session 27** Western Recorders studio (3) *Hollywood, CA* 2:00-6:00pm. Brian sweetens and completes the **'Surf's Up'** (1st movement) instrumental track taped on November 4th (Master No. 56850; duration 2:20) with brief percussion overdubs. The session concludes as Brian completes a mix of the song.

Musicians present Frankie Capp (drums), Nick Pelico (percussion).

Granada Theatre *Tooting, south London* 7:00 & 9:10pm, with Lulu, David & Jonathan, Sounds Incorporated, The Golden Brass, Jerry Stevens

In England, during the day before their two sell-out shows in Tooting, the touring group is at the BBC's central London Paris Studios for an appearance on the lunchtime BBC Light Programme show *Pop Inn*. Their interview is transmitted live on the station between 1:00 and 1:55pm.

■ Wednesday 9th

De Montfort Hall *Leicester* 6:35 & 8:50pm, with Lulu, David & Jonathan, Sounds Incorporated, The Golden Brass, Jerry Stevens

Derek Taylor tells the *New Musical Express*: "Leicester was the first provisional stop. A town I had never visited. I wasn't very amused when the car broke down on the edge of the motorway. ''Ad it,' said the driver. 'Completely mucked up,' and it was. So we sat there, lying back blandly in a swamp of swirling trucks manned by clever wrinkled-browed drivers who looked at us in a mixture of envy and contempt. A taxi came and took us to the theatre where Bruce thoughtlessly lost his voice and the song 'Graduation Day' was dropped because his is the very high harmony. For three days he vanished inside a cup of Friars Balsam."

■ Thursday 10th

Odeon Theatre *Leeds* 6:00 & 8:30pm, with Lulu, David & Jonathan, Sounds Incorporated, The Golden Brass, Jerry Stevens

Tickets for the Yorkshire show have sold out within three days of going on sale.

■ Friday 11th

RECORDING *Smile* **session 28** Western Recorders studio (3) *Hollywood, CA*. Meanwhile, Brian begins work on two versions of **'Vegetables'**. One features chanting; the other, with Brian on piano, has different and distinctly Van Dyke Parks-style lyrics: "Tripped on a cornucopia / Stripped the stalk green and I hope ya / Like me the most of all / My favourite vegetable." The track exemplifies Brian's vision of *Smile* as an album of 'humour with a message'. "I want to turn people on to vegetables, good natural food, organic food," he remarks at the time. "Health is an important element in spiritual enlightenment. But I do not want to be pompous about it, so we will engage in a satirical approach."

'Vegetables' will evolve from this fairly simple 'cornucopia' version into another complex *Smile* multi-part suite with numerous sections and fragments weaved together. Brian wants 'Vegetables' to be as innovative and groundbreaking a production as 'Good Vibrations'.

For now the 'cornucopia' version of 'Vegetables' is a part of 'The Elements' suite, representing earth. The planned *Smile* booklet includes an illustration by Frank Holmes with the title 'My Vega-Tables The Elements'. But by December Brian will separate 'Vegetables' as a self-contained song. Many of the 'Vegetables' recordings will later be lost or not catalogued, but at this stage the tapes most likely include remakes of the 'Fade To Vegetables' segue, several versions of the 'Do A Lot' sequence from the song, and a short 'With Me Tonight' section with identical bass and backing vocals to a section of 'Vegetables'. (A piece of today's recording will appear as the 'Vegetables' promo on the 2001 CD *Hawthorne CA*.) By December, Brian will have broken off 'Vegetables' into an individual song.

Odeon Theatre *Manchester* 6:15 & 8:45pm, with Lulu, David & Jonathan, Sounds Incorporated, The Golden Brass, Jerry Stevens

In England on the continuing tour, Derek Taylor tells the *New*

Musical Express: "Manchester was probably the wildest concerts. I can't be sure because the reception was excellent everywhere, but there is something about Manchester audiences, … more solid and vigorous than any other I have ever encountered. Also, let us recommend The Piccadilly Hotel there. It's new and cheerful and everything works. Also, the porters don't behave like leering automatons with right hands permanently hooked for a tip. We met two girls who had sent 100 letters to the cinema manager begging to meet the group. They had also written a message on 200 feet of toilet paper. This was the clincher and they met the group backstage and were photographed wreathed in the paper chain. In the city I met my mother, who fancied Mike and brought him a deerstalker hat."

Before the show, the group go for something to eat at a nearby hotel. After finishing their food, Carl, Dennis, Al and Bruce move on to the Odeon leaving Mike alone to finish his meal. This leaves the group's management with the problem of how to get him into the venue without alerting the hordes of screaming fans gathered outside the building. The group's publicist, Roger Easterby, comes up with an ingenious plan. He borrows a cloth cap and muffler belonging to an elderly newspaper-seller standing outside the theatre. Camouflaged by these strange items, Mike is able to walk unnoticed into the Odeon Theatre, straight through the growing crowd of excited Beach Boys fans.

Between the group's two performances and following another quick change in clothing, Bruce nips round to nearby Manchester University to introduce Freddie & The Dreamers to the stage for their November Ball concert. Later, immediately following the show, as the group rush towards their waiting car, they open the doors and find three teenage girls crouched in the back, lying on the floor. Beatlemania indeed!

■ Saturday 12th
Capitol *Cardiff, Wales* 6:15 & 8:50pm, with Lulu, David & Jonathan, Sounds Incorporated, The Golden Brass, Jerry Stevens
Bruce's voice has recovered so the song 'Graduation Day' is re-introduced into the group's repertoire. In between the two concerts Carl goes to hospital after he accidentally pushes his hand through a rusty window frame in a dressing room.
• *Melody Maker* in Britain publishes an article by Alan Walsh that asks, "Do The Beach Boys rely too much on genius Brian?"

■ Sunday 13th
Birmingham Theatre *Birmingham* 5:40 & 8:00pm, with Lulu, David & Jonathan, Sounds Incorporated, The Golden Brass, Jerry Stevens

■ Monday 14th
RECORDING *Smile* session 29 Gold Star studio (A) *Los Angeles, CA* 8:00-11:30pm. In California, tonight sees the first instrumental tracking session for **'You Are My Sunshine'**, also known as 'My Only Sunshine' (11 takes required; Master No. 56866; duration 2:20). During the recordings Brian explains to the musicians present, "The words are, 'The old master painter from the far away hills,' and the far away hills should sound far away." Brian's explanation produces brief but contagious laughter from bassist Carol Kaye.

Tapes of this Larry Levine-engineered session begin with a 16-second instrumental cover of the 1949 Gillespie/Smith tune 'The Old Master Painter' that runs neatly into the Davis/Mitchell composition 'My Only Sunshine'. Brian's new version of the classic 'Sunshine' begins with a cello, then a violin, followed by a stomping bass drum. A clarinet provides the bridge between the last verse and

the finale, where a plodding cello echoes the first chorus. The original version of this track fades with the "When skies are grey…" and "How much I love…" background vocals by Mike. (When Brian recasts 'Heroes And Villains' in January 1967 he will replace the 'Barnyard' ending with 'The Old Master Painter' tag, wiping the "When skies are grey…" vocals.)
Musicians present Arnold Belnick (violin), Norman Botnick (viola), Joseph DiTullio (cello), Jesse Ehrlich (cello), Jim Gordon (drums, 'conducting'), Carol Kaye (bass guitar), Ray Kelley (cello), Leonard Malarsky (violin), Jay Migliori (tenor saxophone, clarinet), Tommy Morgan (harmonica), Alexander Neiman (viola), Bill Pitman (guitar), Lyle Ritz (upright bass), Joseph Saxon (probably cello).
Hammersmith Odeon *west London* 6:45 & 9:00pm, with Lulu, David & Jonathan, Sounds Incorporated, The Golden Brass, Jerry Stevens
Meanwhile, the touring band is about to play an important London date. Before tonight's show, and taking advantage of their last full day in London, each of the group visits sights of interest. In a move instigated by Dennis, he and Al decide to pay a visit to west London's trendy Portobello Road area. Accompanied by filmmaker Peter Whitehead, the trio first visits an antique shop at number 123. Whitehead shoots the two Beach Boys fiddling with the shop's musical instruments and gadgets. Al's attempt to play a riff of 'Barbara Ann' on a secondhand trombone in the street outside the Princess Alexandra public house is also captured by Whitehead. Their excursion moves on to number 293, the site of the popular clothes shop *I Was Lord Kitchener's Valet*. Here Al and Dennis try on some of the shop's wares and fool around with the proprietor. During their time on the premises Dennis is excited to spot a fireman's hat, which he tries on and announces: "We've got to get Brian one. Brian absolutely loves fire hats." Al purchases an English policeman's cape. Later this evening, The Beach Boys' UK tour concludes with another performance in London, a concert added to their itinerary due to the big demand for tickets.

Mike will tell *Rave* just after the tour: "We originally intended to bring an orchestra with us on the [UK] visit in '66, but when we heard that the concerts were sold out in three days we figured that the screamers had moved in and that meant no one wanted to listen. We know now that we were wrong and next time we hope to bring the strings and brass. The introduction of some girl singers has been discussed and the possibility of doing comedy routines is not as remote as you might think."

Back at Hammersmith, a *New Musical Express* reporter writes: "On their last day, in The Beach Boys' dressing room, bearded Mike Love was lying prone across the middle of the floor. His right leg was propped up against the dressing room table and his eyes were tightly closed as he repeated softly to himself, 'I am co-operating. I am co-operating.' Peter Whitehead, making his second film for BBC TV's *Top Of The Pops*, collapsed into a chair and aimed his cine camera at Mike, saying soothingly, 'Now I don't want anything posed. Just try and imagine that I'm not here.' Mike opened one eye and said, 'That's going to be pretty difficult. Y'see, you're sitting all over my fucking stage clothes.'"

An end-of-tour party is thrown for the group at London's China Garden restaurant. They fly back to Los Angeles International Airport the following morning and find Brian waiting for them in his recently acquired Rolls Royce. Brian informs the jetlagged and weary Beach Boys that the group's new album *Smile* and single 'Heroes And Villains' must be completed by Christmas. A tiring recording schedule awaits them, with day and night sessions are planned. But first the group is forced to begin another American Thanksgiving Tour.

Set-list (first show) 'Help Me Rhonda', 'I Get Around', 'Papa-Oom-Mow Mow', 'Barbara Ann', 'Sloop John B' (filmed by Peter Whitehead), 'California Girls', 'You're So Good To Me', 'Good Vibrations' (filmed by Peter Whitehead), 'God Only Knows', 'Graduation Day', 'Wouldn't It Be Nice' (encore).

TOUR STARTS 4th Annual US Thanksgiving Tour (Nov 16th-24th)

■ Wednesday 16th

RECORDING Western Recorders studio (4) *Los Angeles, CA*. With the touring Beach Boys back from Europe and appearing tonight in Rhode Island to start another US tour, Brian and assorted friends are to be found at Gold Star attempting to record a third piece for his planned 'humour' album.

Today's recording, suitably titled 'Vegetables Arguments', features mock disagreements between Michael Vosse and Hal Blaine. It is the most entertaining of the party reels, almost entirely due to Blaine's contribution. Blaine, the regular Beach Boys session drummer, plays an irate man incensed at a younger individual, played by Vosse, who has trespassed into his garden just to look at the vegetables. But the conversations soon stray and turn into a discussion about the current movements of the planets.

Blaine explains, "At midnight, one planet is crossing another planet and there's gonna be explosions. The last time it happened was in 1860. They thought the world was coming to an end. It happens every 240 years." This prompts Vosse to ask, "Will we be able to see it?" Blaine replies, "Yes, it's supposed to be absolutely fantastic. You look east." Spooked by the story, Brian then relays a strange occurrence that had happened two hours earlier involving his two dogs, Banana and Louie. He tells how his animals had acted strangely, both facing the same direction, firmly to the east. "They were both lined up," Brian announces. "It must mean something." Blaine says, "I don't know a thing about it. But we'll be sure to see it. It'll be the most fireworks we'll see in our lifetime." Before going to watch the spectacle, Brian, Blaine and Vosse complete the recordings for 'Vegetable Argument' as follows.

Vosse: "Hi."
Blaine: "What do you mean 'hi'? What do you think you're doing on my property?"
Vosse: "Oh no, no. This is my garden. There are vegetables here."
Blaine: "This happens to be my property."
Vosse: "Those turnips. Oh, they're beautiful. They're the best turnips I've ever seen."
Blaine: "Hey man. I don't know who you are, or think you are. But this happens to be my property."
Vosse: "You're mistaken."
Blaine: "What do you think you're doing on my property?"
Vosse: "Can you believe these turnips?"
Blaine: "Don't talk to me about turnips. I have the most fantastic tomatoes on the other side of the hill."
Vosse: "Ah, that's a great tomato. You've got to eat this tomato."
Blaine: "Are they organically grown?"
Vosse: "What does that mean?"
Blaine: "Are you using fertilisers or chemicals?"
Vosse: "Oh yes, the best, the best."
Blaine: "Get that garden out. Get that garden out right now. You're gonna ruin my soil. I don't want any of your filthy tomatoes. I am the landlord of this property. Take this garden out immediately."
Vosse: "But this is my garden."
Blaine: "What do you mean? This is my garden ... I'm gonna call the cops."

Several more attempts to perfect an argument are made by Vosse and Blaine. The piece concludes with Brian taping an argument between himself and Blaine.

Brian informs Blaine, "You're not meant to be mean. You sound like a prick. You don't want to be." Blaine innocently reasons, "But you're taking my vegetables, Brian. You're either mad or you ain't." Another take follows. (At one point, it is believed that these recordings will somehow figure in the 'Vegetables' track itself. The arguments are similar to those that Brian will use later as the introduction to 'The T.M. Song' on the 1976 Beach Boys album *15 Big Ones*.)

Rhode Island Auditorium *Providence, RI* 7:30pm
Just a day after returning from their most successful tour of Europe, The Beach Boys resume their heavy duty of concert appearances in the US with an eight-day tour beginning tonight in Rhode Island.
• 'Good Vibrations' single peaks in UK *NME* Top 30 chart at the number 1 position.

■ Thursday 17th
Boston Garden *Boston, MA*
While in Boston the group poses for pictures taken by Guy Webster. These images – in a rowing boat, posing up an iron staircase without Bruce, and backstage at Boston Garden – are aimed for inclusion in the 12-page booklet planned for inclusion within the group's new album *Smile* due for release at Christmas.

■ Friday 18th
Indiana Fairgrounds Coliseum *Indianapolis, IN* two shows, with The Dawn Five, Boys Next Door, Chad & Jeremy; sponsored by radio station WIFE; tickets $4 ($3 advance)
Each of the sold-out evening shows at The Coliseum is attended by 12,000 fans (11,000 seated) and each grosses approximately $32,000. "The Beach Boys and their version of 'Good Vibrations' topped last week's list of disk faves among local high school students," writes Bea Acklemire in *Variety*, "so an overflow crowd of teenagers jammed into the 12,000 seat Coliseum when the combo came to town on Friday night. The Coliseum vibrated all right and so did the audience, right into a riot situation that scared the bejabbers out of assembled police, sponsors and talent.

"The show started quietly enough with short numbers by two local amateur groups, then on to Chad & Jeremy and a half-dozen or so songs heavy with suggestive lyrics, appropriate leers and repeated use of all the double entendres current in teenage patois. The young animals began to stir. Boys and girls started pushing into the aisles, upsetting seats and shouting. The seeds of a melee were planted but they didn't come to fruition until The Beach Boys appeared.

"The combo had hardly gotten a good start before all house lights had to be turned on. Part of the audience was busily dismantling some of the wooden chairs in the box seat sections. A flurry of slats soon began flying through the air, intended for the stage or anything or anyone that happened to be within firing range. Repeated threats to stop the show did no good. This only heightened the reaction of the kids. Before long, the stage was well crowded with members of the audience. Somebody was swinging a guitar, wildly. Police station personnel and Coliseum workers sought to protect the performers. Below and beyond, billy clubs drawn, other police grabbed hyped teenagers by the scruff of the neck and wrestled them to the doors. At long last, sponsors decided to terminate the show despite the number of Beach Boys ditties left unsung and chair slats left unslung. WIFE personnel and their guest talent left the premises as best they could. This is show biz?"

■ Saturday 19th

Fairleigh Dickinson College *Teaneck, NJ* (matinee show)
St. John's University, Alumni Hall *Jamaica, NY* (evening show)

The matinee concert grosses $9,700 while the early evening show takes in $32,000.

• 'Good Vibrations' peaks in UK *Disc & Music Echo* chart at number 1. The 45 stays at number 1 for two weeks until it is replaced by 'Green Green Grass Of Home' by Tom Jones.

• Back in California, at midnight Brian goes to see pop-rock group The Turtles in performance in Los Angeles, accompanied by record producer Lou Adler and Sonny Bono of Sonny & Cher.

■ Sunday 20th

Maple Leaf Gardens *Toronto, ON, Canada*

■ Monday 21st

Memorial Auditorium *Kitchener, ON, Canada* 8:00pm, with Chad & Jeremy, The Thanes.

■ Tuesday 22nd

The Forum *Montreal, PQ, Canada*

■ Wednesday 23rd – Thursday 24th

Civic Center *Baltimore, MD* 8:00pm, with Chad & Jeremy, Tony Van & The Echoes, The Minus Four

Two nights of shows in Maryland finish the Thanksgiving Tour. The opening show is attended by 10,003 fans and grosses $38,800.

■ Saturday 26th

Today's *New Musical Express* in Britain has the headline: "Beach Boys Challenge Beatles For World Group Title". The pop newspaper explains: "There could be a fantastic sensation in this year's *NME* International Poll. The Beach Boys are neck and neck with The Beatles for 'World's Outstanding Group' title. Any analysis of the first 1,000 coupons counted reveals that The Beatles are only two votes ahead of The Beach Boys. If the American group triumphs it would be the first time since The Beatles sprang to fame that they have been defeated in this section."

■ Monday 28th

RECORDING *Smile* session 30 Gold Star studio (A) *Los Angeles, CA* 2:00-5:30pm. This is a black day in the *Smile* sessions. Friends, family and colleagues of Brian generally regard it as the point where he loses track of the sessions – and of reality. The Beach Boys have returned home from touring and are ushered into the studio to record their meticulously arranged vocal parts. But when they hear the experimental, abstract recordings they begin to question Brian about the musical content – in particular Mike, who strongly opposes singing Van Dyke Parks's cryptic, pun-filled lyrics.

With engineer Larry Levine, recordings are made today at Gold Star of **'Mrs O'Leary's Cow'**, a track commonly called **'Fire'** (Master No. 56891; duration 2:50). Session tapes reveal that the track is referred to as **'The Elements – Part 1'** because it figures in the opening section of Brian's proposed four-part musical suite 'The Elements' which he has written to convey the primeval ancient elements of fire, earth, air and water. 'Love To Say Da Da' (see May 16th 1967) is intended for the water section; Brian will say that a piano instrumental will be the basis for air; and the track 'Vegetables' (or 'Vega-Tables') is the likely candidate for the earth section. With unrest filling the air, recordings focus on 'Mrs O'Leary's Cow', named for the cow that started the famous Chicago

fire of 1871. Against a backdrop of pounding drums and hypnotic, whirling sirens, Brian helps the session musicians get into the right mood for the music by having them wear fire helmets. The helmets were obtained by Marilyn Wilson, sent out by Brian on a mission to find as many as possible.

Eighteen takes are required to complete a satisfactory tracking master of the song. Brian halts some attempts because he is unhappy with the violins, then the fluctuating bass, and even the sounds emanating from the cymbals. Once completed, recordings are made of burning wood and this is then overdubbed onto the completed tracking master. A mono mix of today's three-and-a-half-hour session completes the day's recordings.

Jules Siegel of the *Saturday Evening Post* is present at the session and writes: "A gigantic fire howls out of the massive studio speakers in a pounding crush of pictorial music that summoned up visions of roaring wind storm flames, falling timbers, mournful sirens and sweaty firemen, building up to a peak and crackling off into fading embers as a single drum turned into a collapsing wall as the fire engine cellos dissolved and disappeared." Scenes of Brian sitting behind the studio's recording console today wearing a fireman's helmet are captured by Dennis on his colour home-movie camera. Brian's close musical friend Danny Hutton and the *Smile* album artist Frank Holmes are also present during the session.

A few days later, Brian is disturbed when a building across the street from Gold Star studio burns to the ground. He thinks that his recording has caused a spate of fires to break out in the area, apparently forcing him to check out the fire statistics in Los Angeles for the week. When he discovers that there has indeed been an abnormally high number of fires in the area he panics, believing that the fires are his fault. On most occasions when Brian talks of *Smile* in the coming years he claims that he now proceeds to burn every tape of the 'Fire' sessions of November 28th. Another story will circulate that when Brian tries to set fire to the tapes they refuse to ignite, further freaking out an already worried Beach Boy.

Brian will tell *Rolling Stone*: "We cut a song called 'Fire'. We used fire helmets on three musicians and we put a bucket with fire burning in it in the studio so we could smell smoke while we cut the track. About a day later, a building down the street burned down. We thought that maybe it was witchcraft or something. We didn't know what we were into. So we decided not to finish [the song]. I got into drugs and I began doing things that were over my head. It was too fancy for the public. I was getting too fancy and arty and doing things that were just not Beach Boys, at all. They were made for me."

A combination of Brian's increasing uncertainty and the group's uneasiness with the music he has produced will lead to a general unravelling of the *Smile* project.

Musicians present Arnold Belnick (violin), Norman Botnick (viola), Joseph DiTullio (cello), Jesse Ehrlich (cello), Gene Estes (bass), Jim Gordon (drums), Billy Green (horn), Jim Horn (horn), Plas Johnson (horn), Carol Kaye (bass guitar), Leonard Malarsky (violin), Jay Migliori (horn), Alexander Neiman (viola), Bill Pitman (guitar), Lyle Ritz (upright bass), Sidney Sharp (strings).

■ Tuesday 29th

RECORDING *Smile* session 31 Gold Star studio (A) *Los Angeles, CA* 2:00-6:00pm. The day after he records 'Fire' Brian is back in the same studio with the same musicians recording instrumental tracks for **'Jazz'** (one take only; duration 6:00), the Johnny Mercer song **'I Wanna Be Around'** (one take; duration 0:34) and **'Friday Night'** (take 11 marked as master; duration 1:38). 'Friday Night' is conceived by Brian as an 'after the fire' piece to convey the

(Employer's name) **CAPITOL RECORDS**

4018

Phonograph Recording Contract Blank

AMERICAN FEDERATION OF MUSICIANS

Nº 353630

OF THE UNITED STATES AND CANADA

Local Union No. **47**

THIS CONTRACT for the personal services of musicians, made this **28** day of **November**, 19 **66**
between the undersigned employer (hereinafter called the "employer") and _____ **17** ____ musicians
(hereinafter called "employees"). (Including the leader)
WITNESSETH, That the employer hires the employees as musicians severally on the terms and conditions below, and as further specified on
reverse side. The leader represents that the employees already designated have agreed to be bound by said terms and conditions. Each employee
yet to be chosen shall be so bound by said terms and conditions upon agreeing to accept his employment. Each employee may enforce this
agreement. The employees severally agree to render collectively to the employer services as musicians in the orchestra under the leadership of
Lyle Ritz
as follows:

Name and Address of Place of Engagement **Goldstar Recording Studio, 6252 Santa Monica Blvd. Hollywood, California**

Date(s) and Hours of Employment **November 28, 1966 2:00 P.M. to 5:30 P.M.**

Type of Engagement: **Recording for phonograph records only.**

Plus pension contributions as
specified on reverse side hereof.

WAGE AGREED UPON $ **UNION SCALE**
(Terms and amount)
This wage includes expenses agreed to be reimbursed by the employer in accordance with the attached schedule, or a schedule
to be furnished the employer on or before the date of engagement.

To be paid **WITHIN 15 DAYS**
(Specify when payments are to be made)
Upon request by the American Federation of Musicians of the United States and Canada (herein called the "Federation") or the local in
whose jurisdiction the employees shall perform hereunder, the employer either shall make advance payment hereunder or shall post an appropriate bond.

Employer's
name and **Capitol Records**
authorized
signature _____

Street
address **1750 N. Vine Street**

Hollywood, Calif. 90028 **HO 2-5432** 1966

Leader's
name **Lyle Ritz**

Leader's
signature

Street
address **1971 N. Curson Ave.**

Los Angeles 46, Calif.

Local
No. **47**

State

CONTRACT RECEIVED

(1) Label Name **Capitol Records**

Session No. **14199**

Master No.	No. of Minutes	TITLES OF TUNES	Master No.	No. of Minutes	TITLES OF TUNES
56891	2:50	"The Elements" (FINE)			

WARD ARCHER

(2) Employee's Name (As on Social Security Card) Last First Initial	(3) Home Address (Give Street, City and State)	(4) Local Union No.	(5) Social Security Number	(6) Scale Wages	(7) Pension Contri-bution
(Leader)					
Ritz, Lyle	1971 N. Curson Ave. L.A. 46, Calif.	47	549-38-1490	203.36	16.27
Rovell, Diane (contract)	616 N. Sierra Bonita L.A. 36, Calif.	47	560-56-7005	203.36	16.27
Belnick, Arnold	17107 Lisette St. Granada Hills, Calif.	47	074-12-1214	101.68	8.13
Botnick, Norman W.	543 N. Fuller Ave. Los Angeles, Calif.	47	560-18-3314	101.68	8.13
DiTullio, Joseph	1428 Ethel St. Glendale 7, Calif.	47	568-03-1024	101.68	8.13
Erlich, Jesse	6960 Whitaker Ave. Van Nuys, Calif.	47	025-18-9770	101.68	8.13
Estes, Gene P/	12212 Hartsook St. No. Hollywood, Calif.	47	456-36-7156	101.68	8.13
Gordon, James B.	11616 Hartsook St. No. Hollywood, Calif.	47	555-54-7854	101.68	8.13
Green, William E.	3733 Clayton Ave. L.A. 27, Calif.	47	512-16-4687	101.68	8.13
Horn, James R.	3225 Oakshire Dr. Hollywood 28, Calif.	47	570-56-6753	101.68	8.13
Johnson, Plas	3903 Burnside Ave. L.A. Calif. 90016	47	434-44-0284	101.68	8.13
Kaye, Carol	4905 Forman No. Hollywood, Calif.	47	555-16-5389	101.68	8.13
Levine, Lawrence	19811 Itasca St. Chatsworth, Calif.	47	546-32-8261	101.68	8.13
Malersky, Leonard	3891 Dos Palos Dr. L.A. 28, Calif.	47	555-04-0243	101.68	8.13
Migliori, Jay	1701 N. Lincoln Burbank, Calif.	47	208-04-6118	101.68	8.13

FOR FUND USE ONLY:
PAID DEC 14 1966

(8) Total Pension Contributions (S| Column (7)) $ _____
Make check ___ble in ___ amount to "AFM & EPW Fund."

reconstruction of the burned-down building. Half way through the recording of 'Friday Night' Brian halts the work and asks engineer Larry Levine to go out and buy a bunch of tools because he wants the sound of construction work on the piece. As requested, Levine purchases various saws, drills and hammers. Once he returns with the implements, Brian hands out the tools to the talented musicians – who are being paid around $80 an hour. The recording features sound effects of sawing, wood cutting, hammering and a drill, 'played' by Lyle Ritz. David Oppenheim, producer of the earlier *Inside Pop: The Rock Revolution* documentary, is present at the session and joins in the 'workshop' recordings.

At the end of the session, Brian edits together take 1 of 'I Wanna Be Around' and take 11 of 'Friday Night', overdubbing the sound effects and renaming it **'I'm In Great Shape'** (a line that originally appeared in a rough vocal for 'Heroes And Villains'; see October 17th). It will remain unreleased, but the hammering noises heard on 'Friday Night' (also known as 'Woodshop', 'Workshop' and 'The Woodshop Song') will later appear on the fade-out of the group's version of 'Do It Again' on their *20/20* album. (Dennis will later use the title 'Friday Night' for a song on his *Pacific Ocean Blue* solo album released on CBS Records in the US on September 16th 1977.)
Musicians present Gene Estes (vibes, percussion), Jim Gordon (drums, 'sound effects'), Carol Kaye (bass guitar, 'board drp'), Bill Pitman (guitar, vibes), Lyle Ritz (upright bass, drill).

■ Wednesday 30th
RECORDING *Smile* **session 32** Western Recorders studio (3) *Los Angeles, CA.* Dennis along with the other Beach Boys overdub vocals onto the November 14th tracking tape of **'You Are My Sunshine'**. Musicians have been booked but their session is cancelled.

December

'Good Vibrations' single peaks in Australian chart at number 2, in Dutch chart at number 4, and in French *Music Media Monthly* chart at number 1. It is voted 'Single Of The Year' in the UK's *Disc & Music Echo* and 'Best Single Of The Year' in UK pop weekly *Valentine*.
• The Beach Boys receive the heralded *Bronze Statuette* award from Germany's *Bravo* magazine and are voted 'Best New Group In The World' in Ireland's *New Spotlight*.
• The projected Christmas release date for *Smile* passes with the album far from completion. Guessing that an end-of-January 1967 release is now more probable, Capitol Records begins promotion for the album by syndicating to many American radio stations a 50-second radio commercial. Against a background of 'Good Vibrations' the narrator announces: "*Smile* is the name of the new Beach Boys album, which will be released in January 1967. And with a happy album cover, the really happy sounds inside and a happy in-store display piece, you can't miss. We're sure to sell a million units in January."

In readiness for the album's launch, promotional material for *Smile* has been sent to American record distributors and stores. Ads for the album are placed in music and teen magazines (*Billboard* and *Teen Set* respectively). At this point, Capitol is expecting the completed *Smile* album to be delivered to them by January 15th 1967. The only scheduled release date for any of Brian's new material is the 'Heroes And Villains' / 'Heroes And Villains' (Part II) single, which is set for release two days earlier, on January 13th. But by December 16th Capitol will have no alternative but to shift the release dates yet again.

• With paranoia overtaking him, Brian begins to have suspicions about the way Capitol deal with him and The Beach Boys, so he instructs the group's business manager, Nick Grillo, to check the label's financial papers. During one such search, Grillo discovers a $250,000 discrepancy in royalties paid to the group and uncovers the fact that the label is hitting The Beach Boys with a long-outdated clause known as 'breakages'. This dates back to the 78rpm-disc era when record companies would routinely deduct an amount from artist royalties to cover the inevitable breakages of a proportion of the fragile 78s when in transit.

Derek Taylor says: "[Brian] decided that Capitol were ripping him off and instigated a whole campaign against them. He employed people to audit Capitol, sue Capitol, and hate Capitol. The 'breakages' clause goes back to the old 78rpm discs and was simply a redundant clause that the label used to extort more money from a band. Brian employed a young lawyer guy, Nick Grillo, as the overseer of the campaign and was spurring him on. Nick was in the hottest seat in the world. In my life I have never seen a man under such pressure as Nick Grillo.

"Nick was a work freak. He worked 20 hours a day. He had no time for eating and no time for drinking. He had no time for anything. I used to wonder how he went through all this without moaning. Whatever he did for them, the reward was somewhere in heaven, because these people were rather heavenly people and it was OK, because it was the boys and boys will be boys. The Beach Boys were very aware of their money and very silly with it. They were all buying and selling cars, houses, whatever. But they all needed it. They were very interested in money. They were huge spenders and then the usual desire to wrangle with the record company [happened], which happens with every successful band's career. 'Where's our money?' and [then they] insist on audits and all that."

When news of Capitol's alleged underpayment reaches Brian it somehow adds to his belief that one of his recordings caused the several fires in Los Angeles and he becomes scared of the *Smile* project. His uncertainties are growing stronger.

Some indication of Brian's thinking now is revealed by his intense, perhaps paranoid reaction to a portrait that David Anderle paints of him. Anderle has expressed his desire to paint Brian, but knows he can't ask him to pose. That will never work: Brian is too active and would never stay still long enough. Instead, Anderle sits and talk with Brian for hours and then rushes home to paint what he remembers. This naturally proves to be a lengthy process. Also using a couple of photographs as a guide, Anderle takes a month to complete the painting. Now it is finished and he feels good about it, but hasn't told Brian what he is doing. One night, he requests that Brian comes to his apartment to "see something". Anderle is living with his wife, Sheryl, in a small apartment above a garage near the University of Southern California. Brian has never visited the place before. Once he arrives, the three sit and chat for a while with Anderle's painting standing in the corner, covered with a bedspread. Finally, Anderle pulls off the spread and unveils his masterpiece. Brian glares at the painting.

Anderle glances at Sheryl and Sheryl looks back at him. Brian does not utter a word. Instead, he walks up close to the painting and stares at his face in the portrait for the next hour. Those present do not utter one word. At last Brian turns around and remarks that the painting has captured his soul. He loves the painting and announces he wants it. Anderle tells him he can't have it right away because it is still wet and not yet finished. Anderle is caught off guard; he expected Brian to say that he didn't like it. Almost immediately, Brian begins counting the objects – circles, cars and so on – in the background of the painting. They match Brian's key

An 'AFM sheet' for the legendary 'Fire' session, part of *The Elements* suite, recorded at Gold Star, November 28th. From this point on, the *Smile* sessions begin to disintegrate.

numbers in numerology, a subject that has become important to Brian. Now the painting's numbers are mirroring the big things in Brian's history. This freaks out Anderle as much as it does Brian.

The following day, Anderle announces that he wants to sell the painting to Brian because is he financially restricted. But eventually he decides to give him the picture, and then Brian begins talking about having prints made so Anderle can keep the original. Strangely, from this night onwards, the closeness that once existed between Brian and Anderle seems to evaporate. The portrait appears to have come too close to capturing Brian as a person and this has scared him. Within four months, Anderle will be among those who will have left Brian's circle of close friends.

Friday 2nd
RECORDING *Smile* session 33 Columbia studio (A) *Los Angeles, CA* 6:00-9:00pm, 10:00pm–1:00am. Vocal sessions by The Beach Boys for **'Child Is Father Of The Man'**, overdubbing onto the instrumental track taped on October 7th. Van Dyke Parks will say that there are lyrics for this tune beyond those mentioned in the title, but these are never recorded. The chorus of 'Child Is Father Of The Man' will in time become familiar as the tag to the close of 'Surf's Up' as heard on the 1971 LP of the same name.

Monday 5th
RECORDING *Smile* session 34 Western Recorders studio (3) *Hollywood, CA*. Another recording session for **'The Elements – Part 1'** (also known as **'Fire'**) as The Beach Boys overdub further vocals. There is also evidence that some work may be done on **'Surf's Up'** at this session, possibly vocals.

Tuesday 6th
RECORDING *Smile* session 35 Columbia studio (A) *Los Angeles, CA* 6:00-9:00pm, 10:00pm–1:00am. Further sessions of vocal overdubbing onto the October 3rd recording of **'Cabinessence'**, notably Mike and Carl on **'The Grand Coulee Dam'** segment and the "Over and over the crow flies..." chorus. Also today Brian supervises another recording for **'Child Is Father Of The Man'** with more vocals overdubbed onto the October 7th instrumental track. The session concludes with Brian compiling his second mix of 'Cabinessence'.

Saturday 10th
Michigan State University *East Lansing, MI*
This is a one-off Beach Boys performance.
• In the annual year-end reader's poll in the British pop weekly paper *New Musical Express* (known as *NME*) The Beach Boys just beat The Beatles as Top World Vocal Group with votes of 5,373 to 5,272. It has been a spectacular year in music, so this is indeed an honour. Furthermore, Brian is voted to the number 4 position in the World Music Personality poll, behind Elvis Presley, Cliff Richard and John Lennon.

Tracy Thomas, a Hollywood music reporter, writes about the group's reaction. "'Who did we beat in the *NME* poll?' cried Mike Love when greeted with the news that The Beach Boys had indeed beaten The Beatles by one hundred votes. The faces of all The Beach Boys reflected awe rather than sheer joy, speechlessness rather than overflowing exuberance. 'I can't believe it,' said Al, sitting down, as if weighed down. The news that their album *Best Of The Beach Boys* had knocked the *Sound Of Music* soundtrack out of its perennial spot at the top of the LP charts was received similarly. 'I just can't believe that we're so popular,' Al remarked."
• 'Good Vibrations' single peaks in US *Billboard* Hot 100 chart at number 1, displacing 'Winchester Cathedral' by The New Vaudeville Band. Also on this date the single is at number 2 in the Eire, UK and Dutch charts.

Tuesday 13th
RECORDING *Smile* session 36, 'Heroes And Villains' session 5 Columbia studio (A) *Los Angeles, CA* 7:00-12midnight. Today sees a vocal session by the full Beach Boys line-up for **'Heroes And Villains'**. Mike: "Somebody bring me a dildo and a vibrator." Carl: "Somebody bring Mike a bag of money." Today's session also produces the track **'You're Welcome'**, a chant that will ultimately appear on the flip side of the 'Heroes And Villains' single.

"'Heroes And Villains' was already skeleton-formed in Brian's head when 'Good Vibrations' became number 1 all over the world," Beach Boys publicist Derek Taylor will recall. "With his new lyricist, Van Dyke Parks, Brian was working ... night after night in his Beverly Hills home when the other Beach Boys were touring Britain. As soon as The Beach Boys returned from their tour they went into the recording studio to hear the instrumental tracks and rehearsed the delicately intricate vocals which Brian had planned to weave with the music to make not a pop record but a rather cheerful oratorio."

Although the group is still confused and unsure about the other material recorded for *Smile*, they remain very excited about 'Heroes And Villains', which by now has turned into a full-blown Old West saga. But once vocals are added to the song Brian becomes dissatisfied and begins adding more sections, even cannibalising other *Smile* tracks for new pieces to add to it. For instance, the "Bicycle rider..." chorus from 'Do You Like Worms' is added – and then rejected.

The Beach Boys' optimism that this track could be another big hit like 'Good Vibrations' is outweighed by Brian's ever-increasing intake of drugs, a pastime shared by Dennis and Carl. What started out as a great musical adventure for Brian and the other Beach Boys has begun to turn sour.

Thursday 15th
RECORDING *Smile* session 37 Columbia studio (A) Los Angeles, CA 7:00-10:00pm (scheduled times). This evening sees a Beach Boys vocal session for **'Wonderful'** and a Brian vocal session for **'Surf's Up'**. On the first piece, The Beach Boys provide backing vocals to Brian's lead vocal recorded on October 6th. Before taping can begin, Brian guides his colleagues through the series of extensive vocals he has planned for the track. The first insert vocal features Mike singing, "C'mon pretty baby won't you rock with me Henry," but this is changed to the simple, repetitive, monotone line, "Mama, mama, mama, mama, mama, mama, mama." The second vocal insert features the other Beach Boys singing higher-pitched lines, hummed rather than with actual words. Brian notices that an out-of-breath Carl becomes exhausted when he tries to deliver the long line. For 'Surf's Up', Brian overdubs his vocals only – and a piano – onto the completed November 8th instrumental master of the song.

This afternoon television producer David Oppenheim arrives in LA to shoot Brian and The Beach Boys working on the group's new album, intended for use in his CBS TV News documentary *Inside Pop: The Rock Revolution*. This evening the crew covers The Beach Boys' vocal session for 'Wonderful', but this goes very badly. At midnight, the group has gone home and Brian sits in the back of his car smoking a joint. In the dark car, he breathes heavily. His hands are in his lap, his eyes are staring nowhere. "All right," he says to himself. "Let's just sit here and see if we can get into something positive, but without any words. Let's just get into something quiet and positive on a non-verbal level." There is another long silence.

"OK, let's go," he says. Then, quickly, he is in the Columbia studio rehearsing under a spotlight in the centre of the huge dark room. The cameramen hover about him unobtrusively and invisibly, outside the light.

"Let's do it," Brian announces, and the tape begins to roll. He sings **'Surf's Up'** for his audience in the control room, for the unreeling tape, and for the cameras that relentlessly follow as he struggles to make manifest what still only exists as a perfect, incommunicable sound in his head. For three minutes and 27 seconds he plays with delicate intensity, speaking moodily through the piano. In the control room no one dares or wants to move. Producer Oppenheim lies motionless on the floor, his hands clasped behind his head, his eyes firmly closed. Then Brian is finished. "That's it," he says as the tape continues to whirl.

The mood breaks. As if awakening from heavy sleep, the people stir and shake their heads. "I'd like to hear that," Brian says. As his music is replayed, he sings the lyrics in a high, almost falsetto voice. The cameras are on him for every second. "The diamond necklace played the pawn," Brian sings. However, although Brian's vocal performance is adequate – and will figure in the future studio recordings of the song, most notably the June/July 1971 re-recording – Brian and Oppenheim are unhappy with the visuals they have captured. A mutual decision is reached to re-shoot Brian's performance. A date is agreed, this time at Brian's house in Laurel Way (see 17th).

■ Friday 16th

RECORDING *Smile* session 38 Columbia studio (A) *Los Angeles, CA.* Brian does a vocals session for **'You're Welcome'**. After three months work, a great deal of the *Smile* material has been recorded, but the album is still not ready. With the label breathing anxiously down his neck, Brian informs Karl Engemann, Capitol's artist & repertoire director, that The Beach Boys' next album *Smile* and single 'Heroes And Villains' will definitely not be ready before January 1st 1967. But in all probability, in Brian's words, "I will deliver some time prior to January 15th." Upon hearing this, Capitol immediately moves back the release date for single and album to "sometime in March 1967".

In order to further ease the record company's fears and doubts over the album, Brian hands Engemann a handwritten note that contains the preliminary, out-of-sequence track listing for the *Smile* album. It reads: 'Do You Like Worms', 'Wind Chimes', 'Heroes And Villains', 'Surf's Up', 'Good Vibrations', 'Cabinessence', 'Wonderful', 'I'm In Great Shape', 'Child Is Father Of The Man', 'The Elements', 'Vega-Tables', 'The Old Master Painter'. Much future speculation about *Smile* will be based on this scrawled list.

With the proviso "see label for correct playing order", Capitol promptly inscribes Brian's running order onto the back of the album's printed cover slicks (proofs) which feature a dazzling, colourful *Smile* shop illustrated by artist Frank Holmes. At this point Holmes's original design does not feature the words 'Good Vibrations' repeated along the top, a feature that Capitol will add themselves early in 1967. In his haste Brian has accidentally omitted 'Prayer' from his list, already confirmed as the album's opening track. With the addition of that piece, the list indicates how Brian envisions *Smile* now, at the end of 1966, when everything in his camp is just about holding together. But all will soon begin to unravel.

■ Saturday 17th

At Columbia studio A in Los Angeles, Brian sets about compiling his first tapes of the *Smile* album, a day after telling Capitol that the

record is not ready and just hours after partaking in the shooting of footage of himself playing in his pool for the *Inside Pop* documentary. The first of two tape compilations features 'Cabinessence' (several sections), 'Do You Like Worms' (sections 1,2,4,5,6,7), 'Wonderful' (instrumental tracking with backing vocals only – the version that will be heard on the 1993 *Good Vibrations* boxed set), 'Child Is Father Of The Man' (several sections), 'Vega-Tables' ('cornucopia' version), 'Heroes And Villains' (two verses, one with vocals, one without: 'Heroes And Villains' introduction, chimes version; 'Heroes And Villains' barbershop Part 1), 'Barnyard Suite' (two versions, one with animal sounds, one without), 'Prayer'.

Following extensive work on *Smile*, Brian returns home this evening to be greeted once more by David Oppenheim and his TV crew. The re-filming of Brian's performance of 'Surf's Up' for Oppenheim's pop documentary is at the top of the agenda. With a delicately placed candelabrum sitting on top of his grand piano, Brian's one-take performance is perfectly captured by three simultaneously whirring film cameras. This time, Brian's live vocal and piano performance is deemed satisfactory by both artist and producer and will make its way into the completed CBS network news special *Inside Pop: The Rock Revolution* show, aired nationwide on April 25th 1967 between 10:00 and 11:00pm. (Footage of Brian playing in his pool at his Laurel Way home, shot this morning, and film from one of his dinner parties in October are cut from the finished programme.) During a 1968 interview for US Earth News Radio, Brian says that The Beach Boys almost broke up for good over the decision not to release 'Surf's Up' now.

• *Best Of The Beach Boys* album peaks in UK *Record Retailer* chart at number 2. It features a different track listing to its US counterpart.

■ Sunday 18th

At Columbia studio A in Los Angeles, Brian spends a second day compiling *Smile* recordings. The contents of this second tape are: 'Prayer' (mix from October 4th), 'Wonderful' (October 6th), 'Cabinessence' (October 11th), 'Cabinessence' (December 6th), 'Child Is Father Of The Man' (October 12th; two versions), 'Do You Like Worms' (October 18th).

■ Monday 19th

RECORDING *Smile* session 39, 'Heroes And Villains' session 6 Western Recorders studio (3) *Hollywood, CA* 1:00-6:00pm (some musicians employed only until 4:30pm). Brian moves back to studio recording work for *Smile* and takes charge of a new instrumental tracking session for **'Heroes And Villains'** (Master No. 57020) with engineer Chuck Britz. Possibly because Capitol is demanding the next Beach Boys single, Brian halts work on the majority of *Smile* tracks except this one. From December through to March 1967 Brian will hold over 20 sessions for the song but still does not complete it to his satisfaction.

"At any one time, Brian may have a change of ear," says Beach Boys publicist Derek Taylor. "One such change happened when he was called from a cinema to be told that two men had been caught robbing his Rolls Royce in the car park. At the police station later he watched with quiet dismay the heroes and villains scene played out with real heroes and villains, with real cops and robbers. As a result, he completely re-shaped one section of the song and had it re-recorded." Perhaps it is this incident that inspires the line, "Stop! You're under arrest!"

Musicians present Hal Blaine (drums), Arnold Belnick (violin), Harold Bemko (cello), Norman Botnick (viola), Joseph DiFiore (viola), Jesse Ehrlich (cello), Harry Hyams (viola), Armand Kaproff (cello), Raymond Kelley (cello), William Kurasch (violin), Leonard Malarsky (violin), Alexander Neiman (viola), Bill Pitman (guitar), Emmet Sergeant (violin or cello), Joseph Saxon (cello), Sidney Sharp (violin).

■ Wednesday 21st

RECORDING *Smile* session 40 Columbia studio (A) Los Angeles, CA 6:00-9:00pm. The Beach Boys overdub vocals onto the October 18th tracking tape of **'Do You Like Worms'** (24 takes required). Part of the vocals have The Beach Boys singing in the style of Hawaiian chants, including the line "Plymouth rock roll over". A Hawaiian-style slide guitar is also added during the session. Dennis has arrived at the session wearing his Royal Canadian Mounted Police hat, while Al turns up complete with his British policeman's cape, an item purchased from London's Portobello Road on November 14th.
• *Shut Down Vol. 2* album certified gold by the RIAA in the US.
• *Little Deuce Coupe* album certified gold by the RIAA in the US.
• 'Good Vibrations' single certified gold by the RIAA in the US.

■ Thursday 22nd

RECORDING *Smile* session 41, 'Heroes And Villains' session 7 Western Recorders studio (3) *Hollywood, CA*. Session for insert vocal and overdubbing on **'Heroes And Villains'** by members of The Beach Boys and by Brian. Today sees the infamous vocal taping session affectionately known as the "Swedish frog" sequence where the singers sound something like croaking frogs.

■ Tuesday 27th

RECORDING *Smile* session 42, 'Heroes And Villains' session 8 Western Recorders studio (3) *Hollywood, CA*. Brian records inserts and vocals for **'Wonderful'** and further vocals for the **'Who Ran The Iron Horse'** section of **'Cabinessence'**. Brian says that 'Who Ran The Iron Horse' is "about railroads, and I wondered what the perspective was of those Chinese labourers who worked on the railroads. They'd be hitting the thing but looking away too and noticing, say, a crow flying overhead. The oriental mind going off on a different track". Additional (unused) lyrics are written for this song, the first lines running: 'Reconnected telephone direct dialling / Different colour cords to your extension / Don't forget to mention this is a recording / Even though the echoes through my mind / Have filtered through the pines.' ('Cabinessence' will remain unreleased until its appearance over two years later on The Beach Boys' album *20/20*, released in the US on February 3rd 1969. This finished version, compiled by Brian on December 6th, will consist of 'Home On The Range' / 'Who Ran The Iron Horse' / 'Home On The Range' [second verse] / 'Who Ran The Iron Horse' / 'Grand Coulee Dam' and the "Over and over the crow flies" chorus.) Today's session concludes with Brian overdubbing another vocal onto **'Heroes And Villains'** (Master No. 57044).
The Coliseum *Seattle, WA* 8:00pm, with Don & The Goodtimers, The Emergency Exit, The Wailers, Sopwith Camel, The Royal Guardsmen, The Standells
Tonight sees the first of the live group's end-of-year holiday shows. This one does not begin until 8:40pm because a vast number of the 9,000 crowd are still waiting outside trying to get inside the venue at showtime. The Beach Boys' late-in-the-evening performance lasts for 42 minutes.

Wayne Johnson writes in the *Seattle Times*: "At 11 o'clock last night when The Beach Boys finally scrambled onto the revolving stage in the center of the Coliseum the predominately teenage audience cut loose with the expected response. The girls screamed, the boys shouted, everybody stomped. The noise reached the level at which sound creates pain. The enthusiasm was obvious, the excitement almost palpable. But up to this point in last night's

rock'n'roll show it was possible to believe that the teenagers were bored silly.

"There were isolated screams and cheers for the six groups that preceded The Beach Boys on the stage, but generally the audience was only perfunctory and occasionally it wasn't even that. The principal victim of this silent treatment was a San Francisco group called Sopwith Camel which twanged out something that sounded like an unhappy marriage between rock'n'roll and honky tonk piano. The teenagers not only did not applaud this group, they actually hooted at them to get off the stage. Later, however, it occurred to me that the teenagers were demonstrating that they, as much as their elders, are victims of the 'hit' psychology. They cheered the big, famous Beach Boys, but they sat on their hands when other less famous groups created their rock'n'roll sound.

"The Beach Boys, a freshly scrubbed group that exudes a good deal of healthy vigor, played enough of their hits to keep the audience satisfied. However, as with the other groups, while it was impossible not to hear the cranked-up volume of The Beach Boys' sound, it was also impossible really to hear the music they made."

■ Wednesday 28th

RECORDING *Smile* session 43, 'Heroes And Villains' session 9 Western Recorders studio (3) *Hollywood, CA*. Brian records a further brief vocal insert and overdubs another vocal track for **'Heroes And Villains'**. After that he breaks off from recording for the year. As 1967 dawns, Brian will become less productive and increasingly erratic. *Smile* is unfinished and so is 'Heroes And Villains', although he continues to work out new little pieces for the track ... and then scraps them.
Civic Auditorium *San Francisco, CA* 8:15pm, with Jefferson Airplane, The Seeds, Sopwith Camel, Music Machine, The Royal Guardsmen
The last Beach Boys concert of 1966 – and the end of a remarkable year for the group.

■ Saturday 31st

In Britain the year closes with further praise for *Pet Sounds* when *Melody Maker* names it joint Pop Album Of The Year alongside The Beatles' *Revolver*. "We argued, argued and argued," writes the paper's spokesman, "and still the *MM* Pop Panel couldn't agree which was the Pop Album Of The Year. The voting was evenly divided between The Beatles' *Revolver* and The Beach Boys' *Pet Sounds*. Cups of coffee were drunk and sheets of paper were torn up before we finally agreed to compromise and vote for both The Beatles and Beach Boys top.

"After a succession of brilliant previous albums, The Beatles came up with one of their finest in *Revolver*, which contains the new Beatles classic 'Eleanor Rigby'. Every track has something new to say, from the wry humour of 'Taxman' to the weirdness and reverse tapes of 'Tomorrow Never Knows'. From surfing USA sounds there came rumblings of new things from The Beach Boys during the summer [that] exploded with *Pet Sounds*. Because of the originality and exploratory character of the collection of Brian Wilson's compositions and productions, there was some reticence to release the album immediately in Britain. But the clamour of Wilson fans grew and finally we were transported by huge orchestral paintings that had never been heard before in pop music."
• Certainly 1966 has been a most amazing year both for Brian and his fellow Beach Boys. But their remarkable run of luck and success will be shortlived. Their hard-won accolades and acceptance from around the world will soon end in the most punishing circumstances. Tragically, they will do nothing to deserve it.

1967

Sessions for *Smile* and 'Heroes And Villains' continue ... Beach Boys file a lawsuit against Capitol for 'missing' royalties ... Brian plans a studio in his new Bel Air home ... Brian and songwriting partner Van Dyke Parks part company ... *Inside Pop* CBS TV documentary airs with Brian performing 'Surf's Up' ... European tour ... *Smile* album is abandoned ... work on *Smiley Smile* album starts, mostly at Brian's new home studio ... 'Heroes And Villains' is finally completed ... Beach Boys do not make their scheduled appearance at Monterey Pop festival ... Capitol dispute is settled and Brother Records is announced ... 'Heroes And Villains' single makes US number 12 and UK number 8 ... 'Gettin' Hungry' single, credited to Brian & Mike, fails to chart ... *Smiley Smile* album released, baffling fans and critics and charting at a disappointing US number 41 ... *Wild Honey* album is recorded, once more largely at Brian's home studio and with the group now playing their own instruments again ... *Wild Honey* album is released ... the group's critical hipness and record sales are in decline.

While the *Smile* album finally breaks apart with Brian in Los Angeles, the live band rehearses on stage in London in Ma

THE BEACH BOYS
TRACKING SCALE INCLUDED   (Employer's name) CAPITOL RECORDS

Phonograph Recording Contract Blank
AMERICAN FEDERATION OF MUSICIANS
00003
Nº 353637
OF THE UNITED STATES AND CANADA

Local Union No. 47

THIS CONTRACT for the personal services of musicians, made this __5th__ day of __January__ 19 67
between the undersigned employer (hereinafter called the "employer") and _____ 5 _____ musicians
(hereinafter called "employees").   (Including the leader)
WITNESSETH, That the employer hires the employees as musicians severally on the terms and conditions below, and as further specified on
reverse side. The leader represents that the employees already designated have agreed to be bound by said terms and conditions. Each employee
yet to be chosen shall be so bound by said terms and conditions upon agreeing to accept his employment. Each employee may enforce this
agreement. The employees severally agree to render collectively to the employer services as musicians in the orchestra under the leadership of
_____ Charles D. Britz _____
Name and Address of Place of Engagement ____ Western Recorders, 6000 Sunset Blvd. Hollywood, Calif. ____

Date(s) and Hours of Employment __January 5, 1967   6:00 P.M. to 10:00 P.M. (some men until 9:00)__

Type of Engagement: **Recording for phonograph records only.**   Plus pension contributions as
WAGE AGREED UPON $ ___UNION SCALE___   specified on reverse side hereof.
                                                    (Terms and amount)
   This wage includes expenses agreed to be reimbursed by the employer in accordance with the attached schedule, or a schedule
to be furnished the employer on or before the date of engagement.
To be paid __WITHIN 15 DAYS__
                  (Specify when payments are to be made)
   Upon request by the American Federation of Musicians of the United States and Canada (herein called the "Federation") or the local in
whose jurisdiction the employees shall perform hereunder, the employer either shall make advance payment hereunder or shall post an appropriate bond.

Employer's name and	**Capitol Records**	Leader's name	**Charles D. Britz**	Local No. 47

authorized
signature _____   Leader's
                                                 signature ___Charles D Britz___
Street   Street
address ___1750 N. Vine St.___   address ___4501 Wawona St.___

___Hollywood, Calif. 90028___ R026252   ___Los Angeles 65, Calif.___
   City   State   Phone   City   State

(1) Label Name___Capitol Records___   Session No. 14297

Master No.	No. of Minutes	TITLES OF TUNES	Master No.	No. of Minutes	TITLES OF TUNES
57045		Heroes & Villians- Part 2			

(2) Employee's Name (As on Social Security Card) Last First Initial	(3) Home Address (Give Street, City and State)	(4) Local Union No.	(5) Social Security Number	(6) Scale Wages	(7) Pension Contri- bution
(Leader)	4501 Wawona St.				
Britz, Charles D.	L.A. 65, Calif.	47	567-26-4273	260.02	20.80
	616 N. Sierra Bonita				
Rovell, Diane (contract)	L.A. 36, Calif.	47	560-56-7005	260.02	20.80
	7220 Melrose Ave.				
Parks, Van Dyke	Hollywood, Calif.	47	151-28-1160	130.01	10.40
	9124 Nagle Ave.				
Pitman, William	Pacoima, Calif.	47	068-16-6762	86.67	6.93
	1971 Curson				
Ritz, Lyle	L.A. 46, Calif.	47	549-38-1490	86.67	6.93
__NO COPYIST OR ARRANGER THIS SESSION__					

(8) Total Pension Contributions (Sum of Column (7)) $ __65.86__
Make check payable in this amount to "AFM & EPW Fund."

FOR FUND USE ONLY:

Date pay't rec'd _____ Amt. paid _____ Date posted _____ By _____
PAID JAN 19 1967

Form B-4 Rev. 4-66

January

■ Sunday 1st

Even though the *Smile* album and 'Heroes And Villains' single will not now be appearing this month, Capitol Records in California still takes delivery of its pre-ordered 466,000 copies of the album jacket, 419,200 copies of the accompanying LP-size 12-page booklet, and a vast number of picture covers for the single.

The back of the album cover still features a rundown of tracks based on Brian's handwritten track listing supplied to the label on December 16th last year. The inside of the booklet still features photos of the group in Boston as well as original artwork prepared by artist Frank Holmes relating to several of the tracks on the album – namely: "My Vega-tables" / The Elements ('Vega-Tables'); Do You Like Worms; "Two-step to lamps light"/ Surf's Up; "Diamond necklace play the pawn" ('Surf's Up'); "Lost and found you still remain there" ('Cabinessence'); "The rain of bullets eventually brought her down" / Heroes And Villains; "Uncover the cornfield" / Home On The Range ('Cabinessence').

Although a large majority of the *Smile* stock will eventually be pulped, the six-picture montage, as displayed on pages 8 and 9 of the booklet, will officially appear on the Canadian picture cover for the 'Heroes And Villains' single.

Meanwhile, Brian intends to deliver a master copy of the finished 'Heroes And Villains' single to Capitol within two weeks. But he knows that the chances of completing *Smile* in that time are slim. In truth, the album is already a month behind schedule. Brian is still recording and planning pieces for 'Heroes And Villains' and 'Surf's Up', while 'Vega-Tables' and 'I Love To Say Da Da' are not even started. In addition, the sessions are becoming crazier and weirder. Brian begins to insist that The Beach Boys record animal noises and tape their vocals while lying on their backs. Brian thinks this is hilarious. The group does not. When Mike Love again confronts Van Dyke Parks about Parks's cryptic lyrics, Brian will cower in the control booth at the studio. The once happy and joyous recording sessions have now turned into a chore.

■ Tuesday 3rd

RECORDING *Smile* session 44, 'Heroes & Villains' session 10 Columbia studio (A) *Los Angeles, CA* 6:00pm start. Capitol increases the pressure to have a single out before the album, so Brian halts work on all *Smile* tracks except **'Heroes And Villains'**. He recalls later: "'Heroes And Villains' sent me on a whole trip. I couldn't do it. I went on a bummer over it. I went on a two-month bummer over that record." Today, besides additional music recording, The Beach Boys perform an insert and vocal overdubbing session for the song.

A compilation tape of the work done includes pieces of the song given the following working titles: "Do a lot" (piano/drums version), "Tag to part one" (three takes), "Bridge to Indians" (vocal ascending), "Pickup to 3rd verse" (same as "Bridge" but without the Hmmm... vocal ending), "Bag of tricks" (instrumental, two takes), "Whistles", and "All day" (see May 16th). With this, work on 'Heroes And Villains' Part One is effectively concluded. Work on a proposed Part Two for the song will begin in two days.
• As recording for *Smile* drags into 1967, Brian for the first time in his career begins to work fewer hours and publicly admits that he doubts his own ability. Those close to him say that he appears unsure of The Beach Boys' future musical direction. There are major changes going on around him this month. His *Smile* collaborator, Van Dyke Parks, announces that he has been approached by Warner Brothers to become a solo artist in his own

right. Twenty-year-old Carl has received a US Army draft notice but refuses to be sworn in. He claims conscientious objections on the basis of a conflict of values. He tells *New Musical Express*: "My duty to God is far greater than any moral demand. I got a notice to report for a physical and I never got round to thinking about it and it never came up. Anyway, one day it did come up and I thought, 'OK, what's my position on this?' So I applied [to be a] Conscientious Objector on religious grounds. We ended up in court many times in a six-year period. I spent a lot of money on the thing." (See May 1st.)

■ Thursday 5th

RECORDING *Smile* session 45, 'Heroes & Villains' session 11 Western Recorders studio (3) *Hollywood, CA* 6:00-10:00pm (some musicians leave at 9:00pm). With Part One of 'Heroes And Villains' completed (or so it seems) Brian holds an instrumental tracking session today for **'Heroes And Villains'** Part Two (Master No. 57045), with engineer Chuck Britz. The piece is intended to feature as the B-side of the group's new single, a disc which, remarkably, has now been scheduled for release by Capitol in just eight days, on January 13th, with catalogue number 5826.

Today's four-hour session also has the full Beach Boys line-up taping "Bicycle rider", a vocal chorus once set for inclusion in the song 'Do You Like Worms' but now intended to feature in this second part of 'Heroes And Villains'. Lyle Ritz adds a fuzz bass to the piece. (At Western today Brian's sister-in-law Diane Rovell is the studio contractor, the person who arranges for the various musicians to play at the session. She will continue to do this job for a while on many Beach Boys recording dates.)
Musicians present Van Dyke Parks (instrument unknown), Bill Pitman (guitar), Lyle Ritz (fuzz bass).

■ Friday 6th

RECORDING *Smile* session 46, 'Heroes & Villains' session 12 Western Recorders studio (3) *Hollywood, CA*. Further tracking recordings for **'Heroes And Villains'** Part Two. Chuck Britz is as usual the engineer here at Western.
Musicians present Hal Blaine (drums), Van Dyke Parks (instrument unknown), Ray Pohlman (bass guitar), Lyle Ritz (cello).

■ Monday 9th

RECORDING *Smile* session 47 Western Recorders studio (3) *Hollywood, CA* 1:00pm start. A re-recording of **'Wonderful'** is completed with the taping of a musical sequence inserted into Brian's original piano track. Brian probably considers this as another potential candidate for the B-side of 'Heroes And Villains'.

■ Thursday 12th

RECORDING Western Recorders studio (3) *Hollywood, CA* 1:00-4:00pm. During the *Smile* sessions, Carl and Dennis each produces a track with studio musicians for the group's Brother label. Dennis is uncertain about the title for the piece recorded at his first solo session today and so it is given the thoroughly suitable working title of **'I Don't Know'** (Master No. 57063). (Dennis will record a different song called 'I Don't Know' for his solo album, *Pacific Ocean Blue*, in 1977.) Surprisingly, Brian is not in attendance at Western but fellow Beach Boys Carl (guitar) and Bruce (keyboards) are among the musicians, and Dennis plays drums throughout the three-hour session. These recordings may be part of a conscious effort to make the 1967 *Smile*-era sessions more of a group effort than effectively a solo Brian project, or may simply be for Carl and Dennis to test their own production mettle. (See also March 3rd.)

TRACKING SCALE INCLUDED

(Employer's name) **Capitol Records**

Phonograph Recording Contract Blank
AMERICAN FEDERATION OF MUSICIANS
OF THE UNITED STATES AND CANADA

№ 00170
№ 353622

Local Union No. **47**

THIS CONTRACT for the personal services of musicians, made this **23 rd** day of **January** 19**67**

between the undersigned employer (hereinafter called the "employer") and _____ **10** _____ musicians
(Including the leader)

(hereinafter called "employees").

WITNESSETH, That the employer hires the employees as musicians severally on the terms and conditions below, **and as further specified on reverse side.** The leader represents that the employees already designated have agreed to be bound by said terms and conditions. Each employee yet to be chosen shall be so bound by said terms and conditions upon agreeing to accept his employment. Each employee may enforce this agreement. The employees severally agree to render collectively to the employer services as musicians in the orchestra under the leadership of

Hal Blaine _____ as follows:

Name and Address of Place of Engagement **Western Recorders, 6000 Sunset Blvd. Hollywood, Calif.**

Date(s) and Hours of Employment **January 23, 1967   3:00 P.M. to 6:00 P.M.**

Type of Engagement: **Recording for phonograph records only.**   Plus pension contributions as specified on reverse side hereof.

WAGE AGREED UPON $ **UNION SCALE**

(Terms and amount)

This wage includes expenses agreed to be reimbursed by the employer in accordance with the attached schedule, or a schedule to be furnished the employer on or before the date of engagement.

To be paid **WITHIN 15 DAYS**

(Specify when payments are to be made)

Upon request by the American Federation of Musicians of the United States and Canada (herein called the "Federation") or the local in whose jurisdiction the employees shall perform hereunder, the employer either shall make advance payment hereunder or shall post an appropriate bond.

Employer's name and authorized signature	**Capitol Records** CONTRACT RECEIVED JAN 27 1967
Street address	**1750 N. Vine St.**
City **Hollywood, Calif. 90028** State Phone **HO26252**	

Leader's name **Hal Blaine**   Local No. **47**

Leader's signature _Hal Blaine_

Street address **2441 Castilian Dr.**

City **Los Angeles 28, California** State

(1) Label Name **Capitol Records**   Session No. **14262**

Master No.	No. of Minutes	TITLES OF TUNES	Master No.	No. of Minutes	TITLES OF TUNES
57087		" SURF'S UP "			

(2) Employee's Name (As on Social Security Card) Last First Initial	(3) Home Address (Give Street, City and State)	(4) Local Union No.	(5) Social Security Number	(6) Scale Wages	(7) Pension Contribution
(Leader)					
Blaine, Hal	2441 Castilian Dr. L.A. 28, Calif.	47	047-20-5900	173.34	13.87
Rovell, Diane (contract)	616 N. Sierra Bonita L.A. 36, Calif.	47	560-56-7005	173.34	13.87
Britz, Charles D.	4501 Wawona St. Los Angeles 65, Calif.	47	567-26-4273	86.67	6.93
Caton, Roy V.	3760 Willowcrest Ave. No. Hollywood, Calif.	47	192-20-7730	86.67	6.93
Green, William E.	3733 Clayton Ave. L.A. 27, Calif.	47	512-16-4687	86.67	6.93
Horn, James R.	3225 Oakshire Dr. Hollywood 28, Calif.	47	570-56-6753	86.67	6.93
Migliori, Jay	1701 N. Lincoln Burbank, Calif.	47	208-24-6118	86.67	6.93
Pitman, William	9124 Nagle Ave. Pacoima, Calif.	47	068-16-6762	86.67	6.93
Ritz, Lyle	1971 N. Curson Ave. L.A. 46, Calif.	47	549-38-1490	86.67	6.93
Wilson, Carl D. POST OPEN	1902 Coldwater Cnyn. Beverly Hills, Calif.	47	568-62-6168	86.67	6.93

NO COPYIST OR ARRANGER THIS SESSION

FOR FUND USE ONLY FEB 8 1967

Date pay't rec'd _____ Amt. paid _____ Date posted _____ By _____

(8) Total Pension Contributions (Sum of Column (7)) $ **83.18**
Make check payable in this amount to "AFM & EPW Fund."

Form B-4 Rev. 4-66

Musicians present Bruce Johnston (keyboards), Carol Kaye (bass guitar), Tommy Morgan (harmonica), Bill Pitman (guitar), Lyle Ritz (upright bass), Carl Wilson (guitar), Dennis Wilson (drums).

■ Friday 13th

Today's intended release date of the single 'Heroes And Villains' / 'Heroes And Villains' Part Two passes by in America with no single nor even a completed master tape in sight. Brian continues to work on the song but time is pressing. 'Good Vibrations' has begun to fall from the charts after selling more than two million copies.

• Brother Records is moving nearer to its launch. Even though Los Angeles offices for the company are open at Suite 808, 9000 Sunset Boulevard, Brian will continue to carry out company meetings in the swimming pool at his home. He says, "If you take a bunch of businessmen and put them in a swimming pool, with their heads bobbing out of the water, then they really get down to fundamentals because nobody can bullshit when they're in the water." And if they do deliver bullshit, then Brian will dunk their heads under the water.

■ Friday 20th

RECORDING *Smile* session 48, 'Heroes & Villains' session 13 Columbia studio *Los Angeles, CA* 7:00-8:00pm. Seven days after the anticipated release date for The Beach Boys new single went by with no record evident, and 17 days after 'completing' it, Brian now takes charge of a further instrumental recording for Part One of the ongoing puzzle called **'Heroes And Villains'** (Master No. 57079). The full Beach Boys line up is present to tape a new vocal track for the song. Today's piece is regarded as 'experimental' by Brian and at the end of the hour-long session he is unhappy with the way it has turned out and says that the recording will absolutely not be used.
Musicians present Nick Pellico (percussion), Alan Robinson (French horn), Claude Sherry (French horn).

■ Saturday 21st

Bruce Johnston leads a recording session today at Western Recorders studio 3 for one Jeanette Rado and Arwin Records. Nothing further is known of Johnston's participation in this project, though it's probable that he is the producer.

■ Monday 23rd

RECORDING *Smile* sessions 49/50 Western Recorders studio (3) *Hollywood, CA* 3:00-6:00pm; 6:30-10:00pm. Even though a satisfactory tracking-and-vocals master for the 1st movement of **'Surf's Up'** was completed last month, Brian takes charge this afternoon of a further instrumental tracking session for the song (Master No. 57087), overdubbing additional strings and horns onto the tape from December 15th 1966. Then later, in the company of a 16-piece string and horn section, Brian returns his attentions to the 1st movement of the song with additional recordings (Master No. 57086). Further work on **'Wonderful'** completes the day.
Musicians present (afternoon) Hal Blaine (drums), Roy Caton ('horn', probably trumpet), Billy Green (horn), Jim Horn ('horn', probably saxophone), Jay Migliori ('horn', probably saxophone), Bill Pitman (guitar), Lyle Ritz (upright bass), Carl Wilson (guitar).
• Session sheets for *Smile* maintain that eight of the 12 tracks intended for the album have been completed or are nearing completion.

■ Wednesday 25th

RECORDING Western Recorders studio (3) *Hollywood, CA* 3:00-6:00pm. Taking another break from *Smile* sessions, Brian participates in a further Brother Records project, this time for

Jasper Dailey, the official toupee-wearing photographer at the *Smile* recordings. The track is Brian's experimental, humorous and bizarre **'Teeter Totter Love'**, a 1:58 song about the ups and downs of a love affair. Work on the song will resume on February 9th. (Jasper will record two further tracks for the group's label, 'Crack The Whip' and 'When I Get Mad I Just Play My Drums', all of which will remain unreleased.)
Musicians present Hal Blaine (drums), Gene Estes (guitar), Jim Horn ('horn', probably saxophone), Richard Hyde ('horn', probably trombone), Bill Pitman (guitar), Frank Messina (horn), Jay Migliori ('horn', probably saxophone), Ray Pohlman (bass guitar), Chester Ricord (percussion), Lyle Ritz (upright bass).
• Although the 'Heroes And Villains' single and *Smiley Smile* album will be the first releases to bear the Brother Records logo, only one other record will appear on the label at the time, 'Gettin' Hungry', credited to "Brian & Mike". Capitol Records will continue to issue Beach Boys records until 1969. Brother will become active again in 1970 when the group signs with Warner/Reprise.

■ Friday 27th

RECORDING *Smile* session 51, 'Heroes & Villains' session 14 Western Recorders studio (3) *Hollywood, CA*. The Beach Boys – mainly Brian and Mike – record vocal parts for the "In the cantina" section of **'Heroes And Villains'**, replacing the "Eggs and grits" section of the song (see October 17th 1966). An instrumental tracking session for this section is also recorded, and Brian produces "Whistle in", a small musical piece also intended for 'Heroes And Villains' but not ultimately used. A rough mix made today of 'Heroes & Villains' has Mike and Brian trading off lead vocals on the first verse of the song.

■ Tuesday 31st

RECORDING *Smile* session 52, 'Heroes & Villains' session 15 Western Recorders studio (3) *Hollywood, CA*. A further **'Heroes And Villains'** vocal session by the full Beach Boys line-up.

February

While Brian and the other Beach Boys are busy working on the group's next album, Bruce hops on a plane to London, England, where he will assist with promotion of singer Graham Bonney's new record 'Thank You Baby', which Bruce has co-produced. While in London, Bruce also attempts to find a British market for more of his own compositions.

■ Friday 3rd

RECORDING *Smile* session 53, 'Heroes & Villains' session 16 Western Recorders studio (3) *Hollywood, CA*. A further Beach Boys vocal session for **'Heroes And Villains'**.

■ Tuesday 7th

RECORDING *Smile* session 54, 'Heroes & Villains' session 17 Columbia studio *Los Angeles, CA* 10:00pm start, but lasts just 45 minutes. A 'sweetening' session for guitar overdubs and additional Beach Boys vocals on **'Heroes And Villains'** (Master No. 57020).
Musicians present Tommy Tedesco (guitar).

■ Wednesday 8th

RECORDING *Smile* session 55 Columbia studio *Los Angeles, CA*. Further tracking recordings for **'Surf's Up'**. Dennis, Mike Vosse and

---

A session on the afternoon of January 23rd is logged on this 'AFM sheet' as Brian oversees further work on his developing song 'Surf's Up' – which will have to wait four years for release.

BELOW Working on *Smile* at Western Recorders in Hollywood in February: LEFT Brian at the recording console with trusted engineer Chuck Britz and RIGHT with his new songwriting partner Van Dyke Parks trying out a joint guitar part.

Van Dyke Parks are present at the session. Today's recording will feature in the June 1971 re-working of the song.

Thursday 9th
RECORDING *Smile* session 56, 'Heroes & Villains' session 18 Western Recorders studio (3) *Hollywood, CA* 2:00-6:00pm. Further session work on Jasper Dailey's track **'Teeter Totter Love'**. Chuck Britz engineers the 4-track recording with Brian producing. On the eve of The Beach Boys' first tour of the year, Mike joins Brian at the session for last-minute vocal additions to **'Heroes And Villains'**.

TOUR STARTS US South/Midwest (Feb 10th-19th)

Friday 10th
RECORDING *Smile* session 57, 'Heroes & Villains' session 19 Western Recorders studio (3) *Hollywood, CA*. Working as ever at Western with Chuck Britz, Brian tapes a solo vocal for **'Heroes And Villains'** and then later, still at Western, he completes a 2:56 mix of the "In the cantina" version of the song. (The original of this recording will later go missing from The Beach Boys' tape library. The version released on the *Smiley Smile / Wild Honey* 1990 CD and the *Good Vibrations* boxed set in '93 will be a safety copy of Brian's original mix-down tape, the only completed *Smile*-era Brian Wilson mix of the song available.) Shortly after completing the mix, Brian rejects this version and continues work on the song, recording numerous pieces for Part Two – many of which will be included in the *Good Vibrations* boxed set as 'Heroes And Villains (sections)'.

Miami Beach Convention Hall *Miami, FL* 8:30pm, with ? & The Mysterians, The Left Banke, The Electric Prunes, Keith
The Beach Boys start another short American tour, this one consisting of ten shows – and the first of five concert tours this year. As usual now, Bruce takes Brian's place in the live line-up. Irving Granz is the promoter and he pays the group a guaranteed $9,000 for each concert, from which they are responsible for paying the other acts on the bill.

Saturday 11th
Bayfront Civic Center Auditorium *St Petersburg, FL*
The concert grosses $29,150.

Sunday 12th
RECORDING Western Recorders studio (3) *Hollywood, CA*. Brian oversees another session for Jasper Dailey and **'Teeter Totter Love'** and the start of recordings with Dailey for two further Brian songs, **'When I Get Mad I Just Play My Drums'** and **'Crack The Whip'**.
Civic Auditorium *Jacksonville, FL* 6:00 & 8:30pm, with ? & The Mysterians, The Left Banke, The Electric Prunes, Keith.
The concert grosses $18,475.

Monday 13th
The Coliseum *Jacksonville, FL*
The live band continues the tour.

Tuesday 14th
RECORDING *Smile* session 58 Western Recorders studio (3) *Hollywood, CA* 7:00-10:00pm. Brian plays piano accompanied by just two session musicians during a low-key session this evening, taping an informal run-through of the Burt Bacharach/Hal David song **'My Little Red Book'**. Brian's rendition is more faithful to the Manfred Mann original than the version recently recorded by American group Love. He may be considering the song as a potential B-side for 'Heroes And Villains'. Hollywood reporter Tracy Thomas writes in her *NME* column *American Calling* on February 18th: "The Beach Boys' next single 'Heroes And Villains' will be released as soon as Brian Wilson decides on the B-side. Brian told me this week, 'I'm doing the final mix on the A-side tonight, but I can't decide what to do on the other side. The easiest thing would be to pull something off *Pet Sounds* but I feel that that would be cheating the record buyers. On the other hand, I want to keep as much of *Smile* a surprise as possible. I may end up just recording me and a piano. I tried it last night in the studio. It would be an interesting contrast, anyway.'"

Wednesday 15th

RECORDING *Smile* **session 59, 'Heroes & Villains' session 20** Western Recorders studio (3) *Hollywood, CA* 11:00pm-2:30am. Brian takes charge of a new, revised instrumental track for **'Heroes And Villains'** (Master No. 57020). The piece taped today becomes known as **"Prelude to fade"**, the Country & Western section of the song with strings, clip-clop percussion and a French horn ending.

Also tracked today is the tack-piano version of the song with the "Bicycle rider" theme from 'Do You Like Worms' in a different key (14 takes required). A tack piano is one with thumb tacks inserted into the felt hammers (or otherwise hardened hammers) to give a jangly, percussive sound.

Musicians present Hal Blaine (drums), Norman Botnick (viola), Joseph DiTullio (cello), Jesse Ehrlich (cello), Gene Estes (probably percussion), Carol Kaye (bass guitar), William Kurasch (violin), Tommy Morgan (harmonica), Alexander Neiman (viola), Van Dyke Parks (instrument unknown), Bill Pitman (guitar), Ray Pohlman (guitar), Jerry Reisler (violin), Lyle Ritz (upright bass), Ralph Schaeffer (violin), Sidney Sharp (violin), George Tyler (instrument unknown), John Vidusich (violin), Walter Wiemeyer (violin).

Friday 17th

RECORDING Western Recorders studio (3) *Hollywood, CA*. Further recordings by Jasper Dailey for **'Crack The Whip'**. Chuck Britz engineers the session.

Bradley University Fieldhouse *Peoria, IL* 8:30pm, with ? & The Mysterians, The Left Banke, The Electric Prunes, Keith.

Saturday 18th

RECORDING *Smile* **session 60, 'Heroes & Villains' session 21** Western Recorders studio (3) *Hollywood, CA*. Studio 'sweetening' for **'Heroes And Villains'** Part One. After five months of intermittent sessions, Brian announces that the track is (once more) finally ready for release.

Memorial Hall *Dayton, OH* 3:00pm & 7:00pm; The Memorial Auditorium Columbus, OH 5:00pm & 9:00pm, with ? & The Mysterians, The Left Banke, The Electric Prunes, Keith

An unusual arrangement for today's double-header of concerts means that as soon as the opening act finishes their set at the 2,500 capacity venue in Dayton they are driven the 60 miles to Columbus to repeat their performance in the next show of the day.

After that, they are returned to Dayton to perform again in the later show there, and then back again for the last show at the 4,500 seater venue in Columbus – and so on with all the acts.

Not surprisingly, it is one of the few times that such an elaborate stunt is attempted. The 3:00pm and 5:00pm sell-out shows gross a combined total of $27,775.

• In the UK, in response to 'Good Vibrations' being voted Single Of The Year last December, today's edition of *Disc & Music Echo* features a full-page message from The Beach Boys.

The group says that the award is "amply appreciated and benignly accepted. It was cautiously anticipated but not deliberately sought, yet, subconsciously, it was earnestly coveted and it is, in any case, frightfully nice of you to vote 'Good Vibrations' single of the year. ... We are The Beach Boys and we will see you in May and thank you".

Sunday 19th

Masonic Temple Auditorium *Detroit, MI*

The last night of the tour, and a concert that grosses $21,000. Eith that work out of the way, the live band now have just a relatively short four-week break from the road.

■ Tuesday 20th

RECORDING *Smile* **session 61, 'Heroes & Villains' session 22** probably Western Recorders studio *Hollywood, CA*.. There is evidence that work of some kind, probably vocals, is done today on **'Heroes And Villains'** Part Two.

■ Wednesday 21st

RECORDING *Smile* **session 62, 'Heroes & Villains' session 23** Western Recorders studio (3) *Hollywood, CA*. Three days after 'completing' the song, Brian becomes dissatisfied and takes charge of further Beach Boys vocal recordings for **'Heroes And Villains'** Part One.

■ Friday 24th

RECORDING *Smile* **session 63, 'Heroes & Villains' session 24** Western Recorders studio (3) *Hollywood, CA*. Working alone again, Brian cuts to tape a new vocal track for the still-developing **'Heroes And Villains'** Part One.

■ Sunday 26th

RECORDING *Smile* **session 64, 'Heroes & Villains' session 25** Western Recorders studio (3) *Hollywood, CA*. The Beach Boys are back in the studio with Brian to tape another (and final) new vocal track for **'Heroes And Villains'** Part One.

■ Monday 27th

RECORDING *Smile* **session 65, 'Heroes & Villains' session 26** Western Recorders studio (3) *Hollywood, CA* 12midday start. Almost immediately after completing the first part, Brian begins work today taping a new instrumental backing track for **'Heroes And Villains'** Part Two.

■ Tuesday 28th

RECORDING *Smile* **session 66, 'Heroes & Villains' session 27** Western Recorders studio (3) *Hollywood, CA* 1:00pm start. Another instrumental tracking session for **'Heroes And Villains'** Part Two as the "Fade to Heroes And Villains" segment is taped (25 takes required), with Carl providing live "doo doo" backing vocals.

Musicians present Van Dyke Parks (guitar), Lyle Ritz (cello).

• At this point, Brian's concept of *Smile* changes. Work is halted on the original 12 tracks of the handwritten list – 'Do You Like Worms', 'Wind Chimes', 'Heroes And Villains', 'Surf's Up', 'Good Vibrations', 'Cabinessence', 'Wonderful', 'I'm In Great Shape', 'Child Is Father Of The Man', 'The Elements', 'Vega-Tables', 'The Old Master Painter' – with the exception of the proposed singles 'Heroes And Villains', 'Vega-Tables' and 'Wonderful'.

• Also today, The Beach Boys file a lawsuit against Capitol Records asking for termination of their contract signed November 13th 1962 and $225,000 in outstanding royalties. They claim that they have not been given satisfactory audits of their royalties. The action serves as a less than perfect way to get Brother Records up and running.

March

■ Wednesday 1st

RECORDING *Smile* **session 67, 'Heroes & Villains' session 28** Western Recorders studio (3) *Hollywood, CA* 1:00-6:00pm. Instrumental tracking session for **'Heroes And Villains'** Part Two. Working with eight session musicians, Brian supervises the re-recording of the song's introduction.

■ Thursday 2nd

RECORDING *Smile* **session 68, 'Heroes & Villains' session 29** Western Recorders studio (3) *Hollywood, CA* 1:00-10:00pm (approx). An insert recording is made for the instrumental track of **'Heroes And Villains'** Part Two. With that, Brian at last completes work on the song.

He tells Derek Taylor: "The production of the record is like having a baby. I am emotionally involved in the pregnancy and all the pains and anguish and delight of birth is felt by me. It has taken a long time to arrive but you can't hasten these things. They come when they're ready, when they're formed and prepared."

At the end of today's session Brian and Van Dyke Parks split for the first time, following a disagreement – possibly about lyrics. In fact, Parks has not been a regular visitor to the studio since autumn 1966, but has recently returned, if only intermittently.

Furthermore, the presumed lack of enthusiasm by many of the other Beach Boys – notably, Al, Bruce and Mike – may have weakened Brian's confidence in *Smile*. Despite Brian's continuing work on 'Heroes And Villains', Parks's first exit from the scene will come to be seen as a symbolic end of the *Smile* era. This first rift between Brian and Parks will last precisely 29 days.

Musicians present Jay Migliori (saxophone), Van Dyke Parks (instrument unknown), Dorothy Victor (harp).

• With litigation against Capitol now underway, Brian holds the master tape of 'Heroes And Villains' hostage. And as a taunt to the label, he misleadingly announces that the long-awaited follow-up to 'Good Vibrations' will not be 'Heroes And Villains' at all, but rather 'Vega-Tables'. To help with mock promotion of the single, Brian partakes in a photo shoot at the Los Angeles Farmers Market where he poses in front of a large fruit and vegetable stand. The stand is located at Fairfax Avenue and 3rd Street – only feet away from where Brian will open his health-food store, The Radiant Radish, a few years later.

• Meanwhile at the annual Grammy awards ceremony in America 'Good Vibrations' loses out to 'Winchester Cathedral' by The New Vaudeville Band in the Best Rock'n'Roll Song category.

■ Friday 3rd

RECORDING *Smile* **session 69** Sound Recorders studio (A) *Los Angeles, CA* 9:30pm-12:30am. Having fallen out with Van Dyke Parks, Brian turns his attentions to taping the first tracking session for Carl's **'Tune X'**, possibly another 'solo' Beach Boys recording for *Smile*. (See also January 12th.) Armin Steiner is the engineer today at Sunset.

Musicians present Norm Botnick (viola), James Burton (guitar), Billy Hinsche (guitar), Jesse Ehrlich (cello), Norm Jeffries (drums), Jerome Kessler (cello), Irving Lipschultz (violin), Alexander Neiman (viola).

■ Monday 13th

RECORDING *Smile* **session 70** Western Recorders studio (3) *Hollywood, CA* 1:00-4:00pm. The Beach Boys overdub vocals onto the March 3rd tracking tape of **'Tune X'**.

■ Wednesday 15th

RECORDING *Smile* **session 71** Western Recorders studio (3) *Hollywood, CA* 1:00-4:00pm. Instrumental overdubbing is done today onto the tracking tape of **'Tune X'** that was recorded back on the 3rd (Master No. 57321). Chuck Britz is as usual the engineer at the Western Recorders studio.

Musicians present Carol Kaye (bass guitar), Bill Pitman (guitar), Lyle Ritz (upright bass).

TOUR STARTS US Midwest/South (Mar 17th-25th)

■ Friday 17th

UBB Western Hall *Macomb, IL* 8:00pm, with The Standard Deviationists, The Contents Are

A month after completing their last tour, The Beach Boys leave behind the debacle and disintegration of recording *Smile* and head out on the road again for a brief ten-date concert tour of the States, as usual now leaving Brian behind.

Lynn Jellema writes in *The Western Courier*: "If nothing else, The Beach Boys' concert on Friday night certainly proved that [the hall] is in need of a new sound system. Of course, the microphone going out during the first act didn't help matters any, but even with the mike on, the sound was different in every section.

"It's true that whether or not one could hear wasn't particularly important either. From the minute the sock-less wonders, also known as The Standard Deviationists, stepped on stage, it was the beginning of the end. At least their name was different, although the sound they made was nothing short of noise. As the second act tripped up on the stage, the only response from the audience was an audible groan. It might be more kind to say nothing at all about The Contents Are, except that the contents aren't much. The only spontaneous applause they got was when they announced their last song.

"By the time The Beach Boys arrived on the scene, the audience was ready to string someone up to the nearest tree. The name group was playing to an already dead audience. In spite of an obvious lack of practice, The Beach Boys put some life back into the show. Their one major failing was an attempt to get some response from the audience by chatter and clowning. But the crowd was in no mood for it. They started out their performance with 'Rhonda' and 'Get Around' with the added and, thus far, new attraction of looking like they enjoyed singing together. 'Wouldn't It Be Nice' would have been much nicer without the out of tune stretch in the middle and 'God Only Knows' lost a lot in the translation when Denny Wilson, the drummer, cracked up while it was being sung.

"Perhaps their most recent hit, 'Good Vibrations', was one of the better offerings of the evening, proving that the Beach Boy sound is more than just a beat. 'Barbara Ann' was still a great one. But when Mike Love announced 'New Orleans' with the comment that it was a 'rocker and roller and everybody should get up and mar the surface of the floor,' the only thing the audience wanted to do on the floor was a sit-in. Possibly the entire show would have been greeted with more enthusiasm if The Beach Boys had been the only performers, or if the preceding acts had been name groups. The last minute scramble for talent sold The Beach Boys down the river, which must be poetic justice since The Beach Boys dug them up in the first place."

■ Saturday 18th

Masonic Auditorium *Austin, TX* 7:00 & 9:30pm, with Keith, The Casinos, Harpers Bizarre.

■ Sunday 19th

Assembly Center Tulsa, OK

■ Monday 20th

Kiel Opera House *St Louis, MO* 8:00pm, with Keith, The Casinos, Harpers Bizarre; compère: KXOK DJ William A Hopkins
• There is some evidence to suggest that a piece titled 'Stop These Pangs' is recorded on or around this date, but nothing else is known of this item.

■ Tuesday 21st

Colonial Ballroom *Davenport, IA*

• In his regular weekly feature from Hollywood for Britain's *Disc & Music Echo*, Derek Taylor reports on the ongoing saga with The Beach Boys' next single. "Only a scoundrel would dispute the claim that 'Heroes And Villains' is the most famous single not yet recorded," Taylor suggests. "I don't know anyone in the industry who hasn't heard that 'Heroes And Villains' is the next Beach Boys release. But it is a fact that the single, at the time of writing, is not completed and many people here are troubled. But Brian Wilson is not one of them. Those who are troubled include disc jockeys who promised early copies to their station bosses and Capitol Records executives. The disc jockeys fear their rivals may get the first copies and Capitol fear that The Beach Boys may withhold the disc until a lawsuit between the group and the company is cleared up. Also troubled are The Beach Boys lawyers (who want product to keep their case intact) and the group's fans worldwide (they want simply to hear a new Beach Boys song).

"What then is the cause of the delay?" continues Taylor. "Brian Wilson does not believe there is a delay. And, in fact, there isn't. The Beach Boys were set no deadline, delivered no ultimatum nor offered any threats. The group's power is such that that they make their records in their own good time and release them when they're good and ready. Wilson's only concern is that when the music is ready, it is also good. And the very power which enables them to take time is based on a greatness of their past product. So there is logic on this situation. So much logic that one goes in a circle. But not a vicious circle. Rather a commercial/artistic infinite curve in which fine music makes great money in good time."

■ Wednesday 22nd

Mid-South Coliseum *Memphis, TN* 8:00pm, with The Buckinghams, The Casinos, Keith
The Commercial Appeal's reviewer writes: "The Beach Boys showed themselves masters of showmanship … by provoking approving squeals from 6,000 rock'n'roll fans with the old 'Sloop John B'. The proof of their performance with the song came with the last note…. The applause, whistling and yelling echoed against the domed ceiling when The Beach Boys ended the song.

"The group also pulled off another coup with an old, slow, sentimental, quiet tune, popular a few years back, 'Graduation Day'. But their antics during the singing got across the message that they thought it was strictly square. In introducing the number, the quintet called it 'a hot song, because we stole it from another group, The Four Freshmen.' This kind of ribbing of the audience and of themselves encouraged heckling. When they called for requests, one of The Beach Boys said, 'What? Leave town?' Before introducing the song 'God Only Knows', which several in the audience said they had never heard, the quintet warned, 'We're going to do a song that's kind of quiet, so you can all leave now … . If any one knows the words, just feel free to go ahead and shut up because *we're* going to do the song.' At the end of the song, which was a sentimental love ballad, sung with intelligible words, roars of approval came forth.

"The Beach Boys, apparently resisting the rush towards mod costumes, wore blue and white vertically striped shirts and white trousers. Their style, relaxed and filled with kidding, shows why they are fast becoming popular with the young set and popular as a live performance group."
Set-list 'Help Me Rhonda', 'I Get Around', 'Surfer Girl', 'Graduation Day', 'You're So Good To Me', 'Wouldn't It Be Nice', 'God Only Knows', 'California Girls', 'Barbara Ann', 'Papa-Oom-Mow-Mow', 'Good Vibrations', 'Sloop John B'.

■ Thursday 23rd

Municipal Auditorium *Austin, TX* 8:00pm, with The Buckinghams, The Casinos, Keith

■ Friday 24th

Memorial Auditorium *Dallas, TX* matinee show; Will Rogers Auditorium Fort Worth, TX 7:00pm

■ Saturday 25th

Music Hall *Houston, TX* 6:30 & 9:30pm, with The Buckinghams, The Casinos, Neil Ford & The Fanatics

Last night of the tour – but the group's respite from shows will last only until April 13th.

■ Tuesday 28th

Gold Star studio (A) *Los Angeles, CA.* Session cancelled without required notice period. A scheduled recording session for **'Tune X'** is cancelled. Brian also scraps the next three sessions due to 'bad vibes'. One evening, a studio full of violinists waits while Brian decides if the vibrations are friendly or hostile. They are hostile; the session is cancelled, at a cost of some $3,000.

Everything seems to be going wrong for Brian now. Even his long proposed lead story in *The Saturday Evening Post* falls through. Many of his friends are alarmed by his increasingly paranoid behaviour and bizarre demeanour. He thinks that Phil Spector is after him. Years of constant over-working and allowing his emotional distress to go untreated have finally caught up with him.

■ Wednesday 29th

Gold Star studio (A) *Los Angeles, CA.* Session cancelled without required notice period. Scheduled recording session for **'Tune X'** again cancelled.

■ Thursday 30th

Sunset Sound or Gold Star studio *Los Angeles, CA.* Session cancelled without required notice period. Scheduled recording session for **'Tune X'** yet again cancelled.

■ Friday 31st

RECORDING *Smile* session 72 Sunset Sound studio *Los Angeles, CA.* After three cancelled sessions, Brian returns to supervise another instrumental tracking session for Carl's **'Tune X'**. Today marks the return of Van Dyke Parks to the studio.
Musicians present Gene Estes (guitar), Van Dyke Parks (piano), Dennis Wilson (drums).

April

Surfer Girl album released in the UK. EMI issues this LP to meet consumer demand for new Beach Boys product and to complete the company's British catalogue of the group's output. It had been held back – US release was in September 1963 – due to Europe's initial reluctance to accept the group. This 1967 version comes complete with a sticker on its cover reading "Special Release – Early Beach Boys". *Surfer Girl* will peak in UK album chart at number 13.
• Brian is appointed to the board of the *Monterey International Pop Festival* along with other pop luminaries such as Paul McCartney, Donovan, Mick Jagger, Roger McGuinn, John Phillips and Paul Simon. The not-for-profit event is scheduled to run for three days from Friday June 16th to Sunday 18th. The show's performers are requested to appear for free and collectively have to provide $100,000 to finance the festival. Any takings above that figure will go towards providing musical scholarships and non-establishment youth projects. The Beach Boys are invited to headline Saturday night's 8:15pm show, along with Booker T & The MGs, The Byrds, Jefferson Airplane, Moby Grape, Hugh Masekela, Laura Nyro and Otis Redding.
• In an attempt to start afresh and free themselves from the hangers-on in their lives, Brian and Marilyn Wilson put up for sale their home on Laurel Way and move a mile or two east into their new property, a 14-room, two-storey Spanish-style mansion at 10452 Bellagio Road, Bel Air, northwest Los Angeles. Built in 1937, the spacious building once belonged to Edgar Rice Burroughs, creator of the fictional character Tarzan. The Wilsons instantly fall in love with the place and its open grounds and large rooms, and purchase the residence without even viewing the upstairs of the building.

Within days of moving in, Brian instructs workmen to paint the hacienda-style buildings a bright purple. It is an action that causes furore among their more conservative neighbours. Almost immediately a local residents' committee is set up and they force Brian to re-think his colour scheme. He relents and instructs workers to paint over the purple with a more subdued yellow. His plans to have a live giraffe installed in the back garden are thwarted when his application is turned down by the city. But his first priority is to create a studio in which he can record whatever and whenever he wants. This had been a major reason for Brian to form Brother Records. The music produced in the studio this spring will end up as the bulk of the *Smiley Smile* album and, later, *Wild Honey*.

■ Tuesday 4th

RECORDING *Smile* session 73 Western Recorders studio (3) *Hollywood, CA.* Brian takes charge of the first vocals-only recording session for **'Vega-tables'** following his assertion that this will replace 'Heroes And Villains' as the next Beach Boys single. Today is the first of four straight days working on the piece. (At this point, the song is still known as 'Vega-Tables' and is intended to represent the Earth segment in 'The Elements' suite of *Smile*. Perhaps the curious misspelling was inspired by The Vejtables, a group who supported The Beach Boys on January 1st 1966?)

■ Wednesday 5th

RECORDING *Smile* session 74 Western Recorders studio (3) *Hollywood, CA.* An instrumental tracking and Beach Boys vocals session for the piece now known as **'Vegetables'**.

■ Thursday 6th

RECORDING *Smile* session 75 Western Recorders studio (3) *Hollywood, CA.* Second instrumental tracking session for **'Vegetables'**.

■ Friday 7th

RECORDING *Smile* session 76 Columbia studio (A) *Los Angeles, CA.* Now over at Columbia, Brian takes charge of a further Beach Boys vocals-only and instrumental tracking session for **'Vegetables'**.

■ Monday 10th

RECORDING *Smile* session 77 Western Recorders studio (3) *Hollywood, CA* 8:00pm-2:00am. Beatle Paul McCartney, a week into his latest American visit, visits Brian who is producing another Beach Boys vocal session for **'Vegetables'**. McCartney helps out by crunching a stick of celery for a percussion effect on the track. During a lull in the proceedings, and prompted by Derek Taylor,

McCartney previews tracks from the forthcoming Beatles album, playing Brian an acetate of 'A Day In The Life' and performing 'She's Leaving Home' on the studio piano. When Brian's wife Marilyn hears the latter piece it makes her cry. Following a request from McCartney to hear a track from *Smile*, Brian replies by playing a snippet of 'Wonderful' on the piano. McCartney concludes by telling Brian to hurry up and finish the *Smile* album because the simultaneously recorded new Beatles album is due out in June and the two discs should not clash in the record stores.

Later, to round off the evening, McCartney grabs a guitar and joins the other Beach Boys for an impromptu version of 'On Top Of Old Smokey'. After that he accompanies Brian and Marilyn on a visit to their neighbours, John and Michelle Phillips of The Mamas & The Papas, and the five lightheartedly play instruments together. McCartney and Brian share demonstrations of how to play glasses filled with different amounts of water. In another jam session, McCartney picks up a cello and accompanies Michelle Philips who has taken to the drums.

The session lasts well into the early hours of Tuesday morning, at which point the entourage departs for the LA home of Derek Taylor, former Beatles but now Beach Boys publicist, where they have breakfast. After this, Brian and Marilyn return to their recently acquired Bellagio Road home while McCartney flies back to London (in a chartered plane) where he will conclude work on the new Beatles album, a disc to be called *Sgt Pepper's Lonely Hearts Club Band*. (After this event Brian is inspired to title one of his songs 'Paul & Jane' after McCartney and his girlfriend Jane Asher, but this is only a working title for one of his *Friends*-era compositions.)

■ Tuesday 11th
RECORDING *Smile* **session 78** Western Recorders studio (3) *Hollywood, CA* 2:00-5:00pm. Brian supervises the recording of another instruments track for Carl's 'Tune X' now retitled '**Tones – Part 3**' (Master No. 57321). A further vocal overdubbing session for '**Vegetables**' is also taped today. The union log for this session indicates it was cancelled after musicians arrived (and thus are paid). It is therefore possible that only the vocal session takes place, or that no successful recordings are made.
Musicians present Ron Benson (guitar), Frankie Capp (percussion), Jim Gordon (drums), Bill Pitman (guitar), Lyle Ritz (upright bass, mandolin).

■ Wednesday 12th
RECORDING *Smile* **session 79** Gold Star studio *Los Angeles, CA* 2:00-5:00pm. Instrumental tracking sessions for the "Fade to Vegetables" piece of '**Vegetables**'.

The day concludes with The Beach Boys laying down further, highly bizarre vocal tracks for the third part of the track. A strange deep-voiced "row, row, row, row, row" vocal track is added by Mike. After that, the full Beach Boys line-up overdubs a vocal track featuring the words "E-ola, e-ola, e-ola, e-ola, e-ola." A new group vocal recording of the phrases "Run-a-lot, do-a-lot" is then overdubbed onto the previous two vocal tracks, along with a new whistling track and additional laughing and quacking sounds. A mono mix of the recordings completes the session.
Musician present Ray Pohlman (upright bass).

TOUR STARTS US South/East/Midwest (Apr 13th-29th)

■ Thursday 13th
RECORDING *Smile* **session 80** Western Recorders studio (3) *Hollywood, CA*. With the rest of the group away ready to start another

American concert tour tonight, Brian works alone, adding finishing touches to '**Vegetables**', overdubbing additional percussion, bass, bongos and strings onto the track for a section lasting 1:42.
Animal Husbandry Service Building, State University *Starkville, MS*
The Beach Boys start a 17-day American tour that sees them moving gradually up the Eastern seaboard of the country. One thousand dollars' worth of tickets for the shows are sold six weeks in advance. After tonight's opening show the group discovers that two of their guitars, including a white Fender Jazz Bass, are missing and considered lost.

■ Friday 14th
RECORDING *Smile* **session 81** Western Recorders studio (3) *Hollywood, CA*. Brian completes the recordings for '**Vegetables**' as he overdubs a new lead vocal onto The Beach Boys' mixed vocal tracks taped on the 12th. A mono mix of the recordings completes the session. After that, Brian retires to his new home, mostly relaxing in the sauna and completely avoiding any recording studios for the next four weeks. (He will return on May 11th.)

Today's session is the last one with Van Dyke Parks. Following another argument, Parks, tired of defending his lyrics and tired of being constantly dominated by Brian, walks out of the *Smile* project. He leaves the madness that is surrounding the group's latest album to take up the offer of a recording deal with Warner Brothers. The following year he will release his debut solo album *Song Cycle*, destined to become a cult favourite. Parks tells US radio in 1974: "I was fired, that is I resigned, that is I dissolved my relationship with The Beach Boys. I was fired because it was already decided by Mike Love, as well as by the least known members, that I had written some words that were indecipherable and unnecessary. In short, they had a better lyricist on *Pet Sounds* than the one they had on *Smile*."

With Parks out of the equation and with Capitol and the other Beach Boys consistently at his throat, Brian effectively loses control of *Smile* and becomes unsure about what to do with it. He subconsciously realises that the album is dead. But Capitol is insistent that he delivers something. After all, the album is now four months late.

■ Sunday 16th
War Memorial Auditorium *Johnstown, PA* matinee performance; **The Penn Theater** *Pittsburgh, PA* 7:00 & 9:30pm Meanwhile out on the road, the two performances at the Penn Theater run approximately two hours late due to a late start in Johnstown. The three shows today gross a total of $33,000; typically the group would receive 60 percent of this.

■ Monday 17th
Municipal Auditorium *Kansas City, MO*

■ Wednesday 19th
Capital Theater *Davenport, IA*

■ Thursday 20th
Bradley Theater *Tulsa, OK*

■ Friday 21st
Morgan Gym, Western Illinois University *Macomb, IL*

■ Saturday 22nd
Western Illinois University Hall *Springfield, IL*

1967

■ Sunday 23rd
Cincinnati Gardens *Cincinnati, OH*

■ Monday 24th
Municipal Auditorium *Austin, TX*

■ Tuesday 25th
Westchester County Center *White Plains, NY*
• While Brian retreats from the world for the first time, the CBS TV News documentary *Inside Pop: The Rock Revolution* is aired throughout the US between 10:00 and 11:00pm (New York time). It will be critically acclaimed.

David Oppenheim gives a narrated introduction to Brian's clip: "Here's a new song, too complex to get all of, first time around ... Brian Wilson, leader of the famous Beach Boys and one of today's most important pop musicians, sings his own 'Surf's Up'." Brian's stunning solo performance of the song, filmed on December 17th 1966, arouses great expectations for the forthcoming, long-delayed Beach Boys album. *Inside Pop* also features contributions from music contemporaries such as Herman's Hermits, The Hollies, Byrds frontman Roger McGuinn, Frank Zappa, Janis Ian, Tim Buckley, and Graham Gouldman. The current Music Director of the New York Philharmonic orchestra, Leonard Bernstein, is the show's host.

■ Wednesday 26th
Long Island Arena *Commack, NY*
Before the concert, Carl is arrested because he has refused the draft to join the US Army. He is told to report to the Los Angeles Federal Court next Monday. Subsequently the group's coming tour of the UK and Europe is thrown into doubt.

■ Friday 28th
Back Bay Theatre *Boston, MA*
'Then I Kissed Her' / 'Mountain Of Love' single released in the UK. To coincide with the group's UK tour and appearance at Sunday 7th's *NME* Poll Winners Concert, Capitol/EMI rush-release this combination of tracks dating back to 1965. It will peak in the UK singles chart at number 4.

The release greatly angers Brian and the other Beach Boys and puts a serious dent in their position as 'world's number one group'. Brian says that the A-side "should be an interesting study in contrasts" between The Beach Boys in 1965 and 1967. Mike tells *New Musical Express*: "The record company did not even have the decency to put out one of Brian's compositions. The reason for the hold-up with a new single has simply been that we wanted to give our public the best, and the best isn't ready yet." Bruce tells the same paper's reporter Keith Altham: "It's really ridiculous. The record is in no way representative of the things we are doing now, or were doing even a year ago. This is not the music that won us the *NME*

Then I Kissed Her single

A 'Then I Kissed Her' (P. SPECTOR / E. GREENWICH / J. BARRY)
B 'Mountain Of Love' (H. DORMAN)

UK release April 28th 1967 (Capitol CL 15502).
Chart high UK number 4.

---

award as the World's Top Vocal Group. I've got some tapes at home of the new tracks to be on the *Smile* LP which would blow your mind. All the ideas are new and Brian is coming up with fantastic ideas all the time."

The British press are baffled too and slam the group for issuing a two-year-old track as the follow-up to the groundbreaking 'Good Vibrations'. *New Musical Express*: "This is a complete puzzlement ... . Well, if Mr Wilson can't get the new single ready, and they've got to release an old one, why *this* one, which reverts the group to a sound ages old. Why not something from *Pet Sounds*? Oh well, it will succeed, of course, because they have such power. But their version of this old Crystals number is so well known, it's a bore!"
• A Capitol-financed promotional clip to accompany 'Then I Kissed Her', featuring a montage of Beach Boys-related film clips, is sent to the BBC for screening on the British TV show *Top Of The Pops*. Screenings take place on the *TOTP*s broadcast on Thursday May 18th (between 7:30-8:00pm) and again during the *Best Of '67 Part One* show transmitted on Christmas Day (between 2:05 and 2:58pm).

■ Saturday 29th
Mosque Theatre *Newark, NJ* matinee show; Municipal Auditorium Schenectady, NY evening show
This double-header marks the close of this American tour.
• From his desk in Los Angeles, Derek Taylor announces in *Disc* that 'Vegetables' will be the next Beach Boys single. He writes: "All the 12 songs for the new Beach Boys album are now completed and with every indication that the group's dispute with Capitol Records is over, there are plans to release the album on a rush schedule at any moment. A rough draft of the cover depicts a nursery-like drawing of a smile shop, where people can go in and buy their smiles and grins to size." A press release from Taylor dated today and appearing in both *Record Mirror* and *New Musical Express* reveals that 'Heroes And Villains' has been held up "due to technical difficulties. There is a new single in the wind. ... The title of the new Beach Boys single, 'Vegetables', is a light and lyrical, day to day, green grocery song on which Al Jardine sings a most vigorous lead. The other side is 'Wonderful', which I only heard improvised at the piano with the boys humming the theme for Paul [McCartney]".

■ Sunday 30th
With their latest American dates completed, The Beach Boys depart for another tour of Europe, arriving at Dublin Airport in Ireland during the morning of Monday May 1st. Carl does not travel with the group because he has been forced to stay in the States where he is due to appear in court on the same day after his refusal of the Army draft. The Beach Boys' trip immediately runs into trouble and they are very nearly stranded in America when charter flight arrangements break down. Thankfully, Aer Lingus divert their New York-to-Shannon flight to Boston to pick up the group.

The temperature is decidedly chilly when they arrive in Dublin and the group's manager refuses to allow them to pose for waiting photographers gathered on the tarmac. The poor climate is also responsible for the poor turnout of fans to greet The Beach Boys.

Mike remarks to reporters in a hastily arranged press conference: "We don't know what the position is with Carl. The court will decide whether he will be able to join us here. For our part, we are hoping that the big, strong US will find it in their hearts to let him come. We admit that this will affect our act. Carl sings a lot of our leads and has done so on a couple of records, but by re-arranging our harmonies we will be able to carry on. We can assure Irish audiences we will be doing our very best and they will know it *is* The Beach Boys they are listening to."

RIGHT Performing 'Good Vibrations' in May, with Mike (right) playing the theremin part and Carl (left) on bass.
FOLLOWING PAGES In perfect harmony: the group sings 'Graduation Day' on-stage.

May

■ Monday 1st

Following his arrest last Wednesday for refusing to be drafted into the US Army, Carl is indicted by a Federal Grand Jury and enters a plea of not guilty at the Federal Court in Los Angeles. His attorney, J.B. Tietz, remarks during the hearing: "Carl's application is short circuited; that is, instead of handling it so that he could have the opportunity to talk to the board, and the opportunity to have an administrative appeal, the board handled it so that he was unable to have either." The denial of these rights forms the basis of Carl's defence. He is released on $40,000 bail, has his passport returned, and is free to join The Beach Boys on their European tour. Federal Judge Andrew Hauk gives him permission to fly to Dublin to join the rest of the group after Carl guarantees his court appearance on June 20th.

Following the ordeal, Carl returns home to prepare to join his colleagues in Europe. The following morning he flies the 6,000 miles to Dublin via Chicago in a specially chartered six-seater Lear Jet aircraft hired at a cost of $5,000.

Mike will tell Radio KCBS: "He went to the Federal Court in Los Angeles and explained everything. He doesn't mind serving the country but he will never touch a gun.

"He has had this point of view for years and he can prove it by showing newspaper articles of old interviews. Now they believe that he is true about what he says, I think that they will try and find him a reasonable job in the system. He will become a student at the UCLA."

Dennis says in an interview this year: "The only reason that Carl doesn't want to be drafted is because he feels, like me, that there is no reason for anyone to be connected with anything that could kill anyone. Why is there so much hate in the world? The belief of Carl's and mine is nothing to do with religion. It's ourselves. We won't kill. People must do things like Carl is doing to make the world realise that there never was and never will be any need for war at any time. I would not be drafted in if they called me. I'd serve my time in jail if necessary. But I'd never have anything to do with killing. I am anti anything that is not positive, and killing people is not positive. My brother ran into all this trouble because the draft authorities put him on the level of Cassius Clay [draft-refusing boxer Muhammad Ali]. Poor Carl, he is a beautiful person."

• A Western studio 3 session booked to start today at 1:00pm is cancelled.

• Some time during this month Brian records a spoken commentary regarding his thoughts on smog.

TOUR STARTS Europe (May 2nd–20th)

■ Tuesday 2nd

Adelphi Theatre *Dublin, Ireland* 6:30 & 9:00pm, with Derek Billy & The Freshmen, The Vampires, The Strangers, Joe Cahill

The Beach Boys are forced to perform the first show of this tour without Carl, and screams of "We want Carl" ring out from the audience. Bruce joins in by saying "We want Carl too" in between numbers.

Melody Maker writes of the first show: "It used to be, 'Where would The Beach Boys be without Brian Wilson?' But … the absence of brother Carl brought chaos and uncertainty for The Beach Boys and certain disappointment for the first-house audience. As Carl was jetting across the Atlantic, Al, Mike, Bruce and Denis took the stage. It was, to be as polite and charitable as possible, a disaster. The audience wanted Carl, but not as much as the four men who were struggling to make do without him. They seemed at a complete loss, like some amateur group struck with stagefright at the local talent contest. The numbers that came over best were 'Do You

Wanna Dance' and 'Then I Kissed Her'. The rest? Better forgotten by both Beach Boys and audience. Suffice to say that almost 70 members of the audience, who refused to leave their seats and demanded the return of their money, had to be ejected by the police. When Beach Boys time came round once again in the second house, the group refused to go on stage until word had been received that Carl had landed at Dublin Airport and was rushing to the theatre."

Carl is involved in a dramatic dash to the Adelphi, and about 11:00pm, following an escort by local police, an exhausted Beach Boy arrives at the theatre. For the band's second show, 30 minutes later than scheduled and after extra numbers from the rest of the bill to pad out the time, Al, Mike, Bruce and Dennis return to the stage and open with 'Help Me, Rhonda'.

Melody Maker takes up the story. "The sound was rough and the group, except for the hard working Al Jardine, looked dejected. Then, half way through 'I Get Around', Carl puffed on stage. 'We love you Carl,' erupted the audience. 'We love you Carl,' confirmed Mike Love. It was difficult to tell who meant it most. Still dressed in T-shirt and trousers, Carl tuned his guitar and The Beach Boys launched into the wistful 'Surfer Girl'.

"Then 'You're So Good to Me', with the Dublin version of teenyboppers singing along. From then on it was the same act, if rougher, that audiences heard on the last tour. We had 'God Only Knows', 'Sloop John B' (the number booed in the disastrous first house), 'Good Vibrations' and 'Graduation Day'. Thus The Beach Boys' opening night: an appalling first half and a better second half, with the wait, wait waiting for Carl to arrive."

Further problems befall the group when the British Musicians' Union prevents them from augmenting their act with the extra musicians they have brought from America. The four-piece band consists of leader Igor Horoshevsky (cello), Frank St. Peters (saxophone, flute, clarinet), Richard Thompson (flugelhorn, harpsichord, flute, organ, saxophone, clarinet) and Jim Carther (flute, saxophone). Igor & Co are able to perform on the non-UK dates on the tour. On a lighter, more luxurious note, The Beach Boys travel between dates in their own private jet.

Set-list (6:30 show) 'Help Me Rhonda', 'I Get Around', 'Do You Wanna Dance', 'Then I Kissed Her', 'Surfer Girl', 'California Girls', 'Sloop John B', 'Wouldn't It Be Nice', 'God Only Knows' (sung by Bruce), 'You've Got To Hide Your Love Away', 'Barbara Ann'.

Set-list (9:00 show) 'Help Me Rhonda', 'I Get Around', 'Surfer Girl', 'You're So Good To Me', 'God Only Knows', 'Sloop John B', 'Do You Wanna Dance', 'Then I Kissed Her', 'California Girls', 'Wouldn't It Be Nice', 'Good Vibrations', 'Graduation Day'.

■ Wednesday 3rd

ABC Theatre *Belfast, Northern Ireland* 6:45 & 9:00pm, with Derek Billy & The Freshmen, The Vampires, The Strangers, Joe Cahill

■ Thursday 4th

Odeon Hammersmith *west London* 6:45 & 9:00pm, with Helen Shapiro, Simon Dupree & The Big Sound, Peter Jay & The New Jaywalkers, The Marionettes, Nite People

The group's visit to the English capital does not begin well. At a press conference held at London's Hilton Hotel, Carl storms out. "The press attacked me with nasty questions about my draft resistance," he will recall on BBC radio. "They treated me like a criminal."

After the two evening concerts, Bruce pays a visit to London's Dolly's Club where he meets Beatle Ringo Starr and wife Maureen.

Nick Jones reviews the Odeon show for *Melody Maker*. "Maybe it is the polished perfection and the wealth of sound and orchestration that one is used to on their records that makes the live Beach Boys' group sound so comparably amateurish, floundering weakly as though their umbilical cord to Brian Wilson had been severed. One expects a group as experienced as The Beach Boys (and years of touring the States would be a good training ground) to have far more presence on stage. As the curtain slides up, the impact should strike you dumb. But one just hears the disjointed, empty, nervous instrumental sound.

"I have always imagined The Beach Boys as a hardened bunch of professionals but unfortunately they don't play like that. Carl Wilson's lead guitar playing lacks any drive or self confidence, amazing since he must have played most of the parts numerous times before, all over the world. Al Jardine seems to be the most conscientious worker on stage. But again his instrumental work lacks fire and power.

"In fact, it seems to be left to drummer Dennis Wilson to spur the group on to sadly uninspired heights. He is more conscious of sound and effect than his colleagues. The Beach Boys are mainly a vocal group, but is it their instrumental work that is finally going to kill them. They really should turn their amplifiers up and play with more conviction.

"But then, I suppose, this is really what Brian Wilson has done in the recording studio. He must have realised that the group couldn't possibly stay at the top of the charts unless they expanded instrumentally, hence the use of strings, woodwind and general orchestration to enhance the group's vocal talents. And vocally, The Beach Boys were good. Great when they were singing 'Help Me, Rhonda' or 'I Get Around' but less effective on numbers like 'Good Vibrations; or 'God Only Knows'. The time has come to get The Beach Boys in perspective. Their live performances aren't as outstanding as I, for one, was led to believe, although I enjoyed it and the music. They are good but not great and it's time they devoted their lives to recording studios and not live performances."

■ Friday 5th
Astoria Theatre *Finsbury Park, north London* 6:40 & 9:10pm, with Helen Shapiro, Simon Dupree & The Big Sound, Peter Jay & The New Jaywalkers, The Marionettes, Nite People

■ Saturday 6th
Odeon Theatre *Birmingham* 6:30 & 9:00pm, with Helen Shapiro, Simon Dupree & The Big Sound, Peter Jay & The New Jaywalkers, The Marionettes, Nite People
• A week after his optimistic statement, Beach Boys publicist Derek Taylor prematurely announces to the press the abandonment of *Smile*. Today's *Disc & Music Echo* reports Taylor saying: "In truth, every beautifully designed, finely wrought inspirationally-welded piece of music, made these last months by Brian and his Beach Boy craftsmen, has been SCRAPPED. Not destroyed, but scrapped. For what Wilson seals in a can and destroys is scrapped. As an average fan of The Beach Boys, I think it is utterly disappointing." The *Smile* project is apparently abandoned – but Brian has other ideas.

■ Sunday 7th
Empire Pool Wembley, *northwest London* NME Annual Poll Winners Concert with Dave Dee Dozy Beaky Mick & Tich, Cream, Dusty Springfield, Georgie Fame, Paul Jones, Lulu, The Move, Cliff Richard, Small Faces, The Spencer Davis Group, The Alan Price Set, Cat Stevens, The Tremeloes, The Troggs, Geno Washington & The Ram Jam Band, Steve Winwood; compèred by DJs Jimmy Savile and Simon Dee
The Beach Boys perform for the first and only time at the *New Musical Express*'s Poll Winners' Concert, in front of 10,000 screaming pop fans. Their brief set consists of 'Barbara Ann', 'God Only Knows' and 'Good Vibrations'. At the end of the show the group

receives their Best Group In The World award from actor Anthony Booth, co-star of BBC TV's comedy series *Till Death Us Do Part*. (For the first time since 1963 the show is not covered by ABC Television for screening on the ITV Television Network.) Bruce will recall: "Frankly, I was a little embarrassed to be receiving [a top] award from the *NME*. I mean, to all of us, there is only one number one and that's The Beatles. I told Ringo about this and he said that was nonsense and wishes us the best of luck in the poll again. I thought that was really nice."

Keith Altham reviews the show for *New Musical Express*. "Once Jimmy Savile introduced The Beach Boys, the reception was deafening. This was the biggest show the boys had played on their British tour and they were obviously knocked out by it all. The screams were ear-piercing, almost like standing behind a jet plane ... . Hearing those beautiful harmonies was quite a job with all the audience noise going on. ... In 'Good Vibrations' we had the fascinating experience of hearing the group's screaming theremin battling with the screams of fans. The theremin won, but only just. I had thought that The Beach Boys had lost some of their popularity because of the long gaps between their releases. But I was wrong. Nobody else on the bill could beat them."

Later this evening The Beach Boys join an all-star audience – including Beatle Ringo Starr, The Moody Blues, Spencer Davis, Rolling Stone Brian Jones and singer Georgie Fame – to watch a performance by The Jimi Hendrix Experience at London's Saville Theatre.

■ Monday 8th

Odeon Theatre *Manchester* 6:15 & 8:45pm, with Helen Shapiro, Simon Dupree & The Big Sound, Peter Jay & The New Jaywalkers, The Marionettes, Nite People

Following these two Manchester concerts the group flies on to Scotland to conclude the UK leg of their tour.

■ Tuesday 9th

Odeon Theatre *Glasgow, Scotland* 6:40 & 9:00pm, with Helen Shapiro, Simon Dupree & The Big Sound, Peter Jay & The New Jaywalkers, The Marionettes, Nite People

This morning at Eilean Donan Castle at Dornie, Kyle of Lochals in Scotland, where the group is staying, Al begins tinkering with the Leadbelly composition 'Cottonfields' on the castle's piano. Almost immediately, he suggests that The Beach Boys should record the song. Bruce uses the piano to continue work on his instrumental 'The Nearest Faraway Place'.

■ Wednesday 10th

ABC Theatre *Edinburgh, Scotland* 6:30 & 8:50pm, with Helen Shapiro, Simon Dupree & The Big Sound, Peter Jay & The New Jaywalkers, The Marionettes, Nite People

Tonight sees the last shows on the UK leg of the current tour. In contrast to their heavily promoted and highly successful excursion last November, this visit to the UK, while still a sell-out, receives a mixed bag of reviews. The poorly conceived idea of releasing 'Then I Kissed Her' as a single has damaged the group's once strong UK popularity. Some writers begin to suggest that the group's time at the top will be short.

DJ and television host Jonathan King writes in *New Musical Express*: "They came and went in their blond, sun-tanned, 1966

health image, surfing refugees from the glorious golden state. They came with a brilliant image on the crest of a wave of 'genius' records and a lately successful tour. But this time they were not conquering heroes. The indecision and temperament that led to the release of an inferior record after months of pregnant suspense had destroyed the magic. Three quarters of the country were unaware of their presence. The ballerina genius behind them, tripping a merry tarantella on a sandbox in Hollywood, has allowed a monumental gap to grow between the recording studios and the wooden stages of the world. Wax wizard Brian Wilson may still be, but it has to be said, in this country, The Beach Boys are finished. This tour and this record were the decline. Will The Beach Boys ever play to a capacity British audience again? I leave you to decide. Very sad."

Following the end of the UK tour The Beach Boys fly to the continent for a whirlwind visit. The group is told before their departure that because of permit problems a scheduled concert in France will not take place.

Thursday 11th
RECORDING *Smile* session 82, 'Heroes And Villains' session 30 Gold Star studio (A) *Los Angeles, CA*. Back in California, unaffected (and possibly invigorated) by Taylor's statement of the 6th, Brian returns to the studio and 'sweetens' his March 2nd mixdown of **'Heroes And Villains'**.

Saturday 13th
Finlandia Hall *Helsinki, Finland*
In order to sustain their strong European popularity the group begins a series of relatively low-key dates on the continental mainland, beginning tonight with an appearance in Finland.

Sunday 14th
This morning The Beach Boys arrive in Holland at Amsterdam's Schiphol airport in a private DC7 jet clipper plane adorned with the words "The Beach Boys & Igor are coming". Igor is the leader of the group's four-piece backing band, musicians reportedly capable of playing no fewer than 16 different instruments between them. (See May 2nd.)

In the afternoon The Beach Boys are at the Amsterdam Hilton for a press conference that starts two hours late and is attended by just a few Dutch pop-related newspapers, including *Hitweek*. The paper's subsequent report highlights the breakdown in communication between the group and Brian, revealing that they expected *Smile* to have been released before they arrived in Europe.

The group's only television appearance during this lightning visit occurs when they are interviewed for the VARA TV show *Fanclub*, aired on Nederland 1 on June 2nd between 7.00 and 7.56pm. During the show's short segment, reporter Judith Bosch asks The Beach Boys some weak questions, including: "Why do you own your own plane?", "How do you spend your money?", "Why have you come to Holland?" and "You have no wild stage show, why is that?" In response to the final question, the group replies, "Because the music is all that counts."

Answering Bosch's question about why the group is not performing in Holland, Carl says: "The Beach Boys were denied performing both in Holland and France because they had no working permit. Our trip of live concerts was reduced now to London, Helsinki, Munich and Cologne ." Carl's list of cities does not in fact tally with what will occur. He then turns his attention to Brother Records and the group's new single. "Capitol Records is worried about our new label," Carl announces. "'Heroes And Villains' will probably be cancelled in favour of 'Vega-tables', but

before this single is ready, they released 'Then I Kissed Her', not as sophisticated in production and quite an old song."

This evening, with no concert to perform, Mike, Bruce and the group's current support act, British singer Graham Bonney, visit the red light district in Amsterdam. Although this two-day visit to Holland turns out to be just a promotional visit, concert promoter Paul Acket had tentatively scheduled a concert appearance in Rotterdam around May 20th. But the group's Dutch concert debut will not take place for another 19 months (see December 14th 1968). Following further promotional appearances in the country, The Beach Boys leave Holland during the afternoon of the 15th and head for Germany.

Monday 15th
Gold Star studio (A) *Los Angeles, CA* session cancelled without required notice period. Back on the West Coast, Brian again cancels a recording session due to 'bad vibes'. The session was scheduled to initiate serious work on **'I Love To Say Da Da'**.

Tuesday 16th
RECORDING *Smile* session 83 Gold Star studio (A) *Los Angeles, CA* 2:00-5:30pm. Now almost two weeks after Derek Taylor's announcement about the abandonment of *Smile*, Brian continues work on the album, here with engineer Jim Hilton. One day later than planned, he begins work on **'I Love To Say Da Da'** (Master No. 57668), intended as the Water section of 'The Elements' suite. A solo piano try-out of the piece, titled as "All day", had appeared on a January 3rd 'Heroes And Villains' compilation reel, at which time it was most probably planned as a section of that song.
Musicians present Hal Blaine (drums), Gene Estes (percussion, bells, piano), Bill Pitman (guitar), Lyle Ritz (upright bass), Mike Rubini (keyboards).

Wednesday 17th
RECORDING *Smile* session 84 Western Recorders studio (3) *Hollywood, CA* 8:00pm-12:30am. Brian oversees a further tracking session for **'I Love To Say Da Da'** (Master No. 57668). This second day produces a different Part Two section of the song, with flutes making bird-like sounds, and there is a brief snippet of a third part with keyboards, though this immediately breaks down.
Musicians present Hal Blaine (drums), Gene Estes (guitar), Jim Horn ('horn'), Carol Kaye (guitar, bass guitar), Jay Migliori ('horn', probably saxophone), Bill Pitman (guitar), Ray Pohlman (bass), Lyle Ritz (upright bass), Mike Rubini (keyboards).
Sportshalle *Cologne, West Germany* with Small Faces, Graham Bonney
The European tour continues in Germany.

Thursday 18th
RECORDING *Smile* session 85 Gold Star studio (A) *Los Angeles, CA* 2:00pm start. Brian takes charge of a vocal and third tracking session for **'I Love To Say Da Da'** (Master No. 57668). While no one realises it, today's session will turn out to be the final one in the ill-fated *Smile* saga.
Musicians present Frank De Vito (probably percussion, possibly drums), Gene Estes (percussion), Billy Green (piccolo, whistle), Jay Migliori (piccolo, whistle), Bill Pitman (bass guitar, nylon-string guitar), Ray Pohlman (bass guitar), Melvin Pollan (upright bass), Mike Rubini (keyboards).

Friday 19th
Gold Star studio (A) *Los Angeles, CA* session cancelled without

The live group backstage on the European tour in May 1967. As the summer of love reveals itself, here they are still wearing the Beach Boy uniform of white pants and striped shirts.

required notice period. Brian does not show at a session intended for 'I Love To Say Da Da'. The musicians booked for today's session by contractor Diane Rovell – Hal Blaine, Gene Estes, Jim Gordon, Bill Pitman, Lyle Ritz and Mike Rubini – have to be paid at the union rate because Brian has cancelled the recordings without adequate notice. Capitol, tired of numerous delays with the album, is forced finally to abandon the recordings for *Smile*.

Those close to Brian feel that he has ceased work on the album in the interests of social harmony. Brian himself will reflect in *Rolling Stone* in 1976: "We didn't finish *Smile*, because we had a lot of problems, inner group problems. We had time commitments that we couldn't keep. So we stopped. Van Dyke Parks had written all of the lyrics and none were by The Beach Boys. The lyrics were so poetic and symbolic, they were abstract … . It didn't come out because I'd bought a lot of hashish. It was a really large purchase. I mean, perhaps two thousand dollars' worth. We didn't realise but the music was getting so influenced by it. The music had a really drugged feeling. I mean, we had to lie on the floor with the microphones next to our mouths to do the vocals. We didn't have any energy."

Carl will say in a later film documentary: "I think Brian was not able to finish the project due to the seriousness of his emotional problems, which were very much irritated and brought forward by his drug taking." And Brian again: "I wanted to do my kind of music and [the others] wanted to do theirs. It was like a tug of war. I felt that I was being pulled to pieces. I was being pulled all around and my life just fell to pieces."

Brian surely feels now that he has missed his and his group's most golden moment. He knows that if *Smile* had been completed to his satisfaction it would have shocked the world with its stunning originality. Those close to him feel that *Smile* would have been his magnum opus. But the album is not completed.

The loss of *Smile* is a disaster of immense proportions, not just for The Beach Boys but for the American music industry in general. Brian in particular is distraught and may even be feeling that his career in music is finished. His pursuit of the ultimate 'teenage symphony to God' has left him shattered. Although no one knows it now, the demise of *Smile* – perhaps the greatest unreleased pop album of all time – ends The Beach Boys' golden years of consistent fame and leads Brian to a gradual descent into dark depression. He returns home and begins to close the doors to his family, his friends and his music.

■ Friday 19th
Berliner Sportspalast *Berlin, West Germany* 4:30 & 8:00pm, with Small Faces, Graham Bonney
Meanwhile the European tour trundles on.

■ Saturday 20th
Konserthuset *Stockholm, Sweden*
Tonight sees the group's wives joining them at the conclusion of the slightly truncated European tour. A vacation on the continent follows.

■ Saturday 27th
'Then I Kissed Her' single peaks in UK chart at number 4.

June

■ Thursday 1st
Almost two weeks after *Smile* has been cancelled, The Beatles officially release in Britain their new, groundbreaking studio album, *Sgt Pepper's Lonely Heart Club Band*. The LP goes on sale in the US one day later.

■ Saturday 3rd
RECORDING *Smiley Smile* session 1 Hollywood Sound Recorders studio *Los Angeles, CA*. Just as the world is rejoicing to the breathtaking new sounds of *Sgt Pepper's*, The Beach Boys return to the studio to record more music. It is at this point that *Smile* segues into *Smiley Smile*.

It has been over a year since the landmark *Pet Sounds* album was released and six months since the remarkable 'Good Vibrations' single. At Brian's request most of the recordings made during the *Smile* sessions are now distinctly off limits, and The Beach Boys find themselves in a bind for new material. So over the next six weeks – until Friday July 14th – the group, with a partly lethargic Brian, begins to re-record many *Smile*-period songs in drastically simplified forms, including 'Wind Chimes' and 'Wonderful'.

During this period, Brian will never fully revisit the original *Smile* tapes, aside from the few recordings that will appear on *Smiley Smile* such as 'Heroes And Villains', which includes portions of the *Smile*-era recordings, and a small snippet of the original 'Vega-Tables' that appears at the end of *Smiley Smile*'s 'Vegetables'. There will also be elements of *Smiley Smile* tracks that echo parts of *Smile*, such as the melody of 'She's Goin' Bald', drawn from 'He Gives Speeches', and 'Mama Says' on *Wild Honey* will be based on a part of 'Vega-Tables'. Subsequent releases of *Smile*-era material – 'Cabinessence', 'Our Prayer' and 'Surf's Up' – will be overdubbed and completed by Carl and Dennis without Brian's co-operation in November 1968 and June/July 1971, although Brian does make an appearance during the recording of the "Child is father of the man" tag of 'Surf's Up' in June 1971.

Much later, during 2003, Brian and his keyboard player of the time, Darian Sahanaja, will prepare for a tour where they will perform a resurrected *Smile*. Vocals are roughly dubbed onto some unfinished pieces for this purpose, but these are all by Sahanaja, not Brian, and Van Dyke Parks will supply some vintage lyric sheets upon Brian's request. They re-organise the work into three segments for the 2004 live performances: *Americana* ('Our Prayer' / 'Heroes And Villains' / 'Do You Like Worms' / 'Barnyard' / 'Old Master Painter' / 'Cabinessence'); *Cycle Of Life* ('Wonderful' / 'Song For Children ['Look'] / 'Child Is Father Of The Man' / 'Surf's Up'); and *The Elements* ('I'm In Great Shape' / 'I Wanna Be Around' / 'Friday Night' / 'Vegetables' / 'Holidays' / 'Wind Chimes' / 'Heroes And Villains' [intro] / 'Mrs O'Leary's Cow' / 'Water' chant / 'I Love to Say Da Da' / 'Good Vibrations'). By March 2004 the intention will be for Brian and band to record a completely new studio version of *Smile*.

Back again to 1967, and some new songs are also concocted during the strained *Smiley Smile* sessions – so strained, in fact, that Bruce has little involvement. It is clear that Brian, after his recent turmoil, is not completely capable of producing or even leading The Beach Boys, even though he finds himself intermittently controlling the proceedings – mainly because the others know very little about the ways of record production. Carl says: "We'd just let the tape machines roll. We'd just make up stuff and just do it. There wasn't a real effort into that album. It was very simple. It was more like a 'jam' album." When released, *Smiley Smile* will bear the credit "Produced by The Beach Boys". Sessions today begin with a new vocal recording for **'Vegetables'** (Master No. 57450).

■ Monday 5th
RECORDING *Smiley Smile* session 2 Western Recorders studio *Hollywood, CA* 3:00pm start. The first tracking session for the new

'Vegetables' (Master No. 57450), with Chuck Britz engineering. Bass rehearsals and recordings are followed by the taping of a bass/piano track, and taping of instrumental inserts and special-effects tracks follow Beach Boys vocal overdubs. The effects include the munching and crunching of various vegetables by members of the group. Significantly, with no studio musicians in sight, it is the first time in three years that The Beach Boys have played all the instruments at a recording session.

Tuesday 6th
RECORDING *Smiley Smile* **session 3** Western Recorders studio (3) *Hollywood, CA* 2:00pm or 7:00pm start, or possibly double session. Today sees the second instrumental tracking session for **'Vegetables'** (Master No. 57450).

Wednesday 7th
RECORDING *Smiley Smile* **session 4** Western Recorders studio (3) *Hollywood, CA* 2:00pm start. This is the third tracking session for **'Vegetables'** (Master No. 57450). There is some evidence that three versions of 'Cool Cool Water' are taped today: the first a piano/vocal version, the second with just harpsichord, and the last with harpsichord and vocals.
Musician present Lyle Ritz (upright bass).

Friday 9th
A Beach Boys session is booked to start at 3:00pm today at Western studio 3; no further details are known.

Saturday 10th
At Brian's home studio in Bel Air, Los Angeles, The Beach Boys tape a phone conversation with the Radio London DJ, Keith Skues. The resulting interview is broadcast during Skues's show on the pirate station in Britain the following day.

Sunday 11th
RECORDING *Smiley Smile* **session 5** Brian's Home Studio *Bel Air, CA*. Vocals and instrumentation are recorded for what will remain an unreleased track, **'Good News'**. In an attempt to bring a dejected Brian back to the music, sessions for *Smiley Smile* leave Western Recorders and move into Brian's living room at his Bel Air home. A hastily constructed, makeshift, portable 8-track studio, paid for by The Beach Boys, is built in a non-soundproofed room to encourage further involvement from Brian. Throughout these sessions at Brian's home studio the group is joined by engineer Jim Lockert.

Lockert tells Byron Preiss: "When we started at the house we had remote equipment. It was rented and brought into the house. [There was] one large room which had been a music room for the former owner, and there was a hallway and an office, and the console and tape machines were set up in the office. The cables ran across the hall into the music room, and there was a closed-circuit television so you could see what was going on."

Carl will recall: "Most of *Smiley Smile* was done at Brian's house, with his own equipment and in his studio, which he had built in a couple of days. We did part of it in his gym, part in his backyard, and even in his swimming pool. ... All over the place."

As the sessions progress, Lockert says, they adapt and improve the set-up, moving the recording equipment out of the office. "We found a room adjacent to the large music room and built a control room in there, [installing] a remote console and speakers ... . We physically changed the music room into a recording studio with isolation and baffles and sound treatment so we could do some recording in there without problems."

Monday 12th
RECORDING *Smiley Smile* **session 6, 'Heroes And Villains'** session 31 Brian's Home Studio *Bel Air, CA*. The first of three straight sessions for the new version of **'Heroes And Villains'** (Master No. 57020). The recordings today include the taping of an entirely new vocal track and a re-recording of parts of the instrumental track. To create an echo-chamber effect the group records instrumental parts in Brian's drained swimming pool. A microphone is fed out through a window in the house, across the garden, and into the empty pool in Brian's back yard.

Tuesday 13th
RECORDING *Smiley Smile* **session 7, 'Heroes And Villains'** session 32 Brian's Home Studio *Bel Air, CA*. Further vocal sessions for **'Heroes And Villains'**. Engineer Jim Lockert recalls later: "We'd play the track and they'd work out their [vocal] parts until they got them … and if it was what they wanted they'd go in immediately and double it or overdub it with another part. Then the last thing they used to do is to go to the high parts. Brian would put his part on last most of the time. The high part."

Wednesday 14th
RECORDING *Smiley Smile* **session 8, 'Heroes And Villains'** session 33 Brian's Home Studio *Bel Air, CA* 3:00-6:00pm. The Beach Boys complete the vocal and instrumental recordings for **'Heroes And Villains'** (Master No. 57020). Following Brian's brief re-mixes and final edits, sessions for the song are concluded. This time, his decision is final. (See also July 11th.)
Musicians present Beach Boys: Al, Brian, Carl, Dennis.

Thursday 15th
RECORDING *Smiley Smile* **session 9** Brian's Home Studio *Bel Air, CA* 8:00-11:00pm. After an eight-day break, recordings are completed for **'Vegetables'** (Master No. 57450).
Musicians present Beach Boys: Al, Brian, Carl, Dennis.

Friday 16th – Sunday 18th
The last shift in Brian's attempt to win over the hip community is played out. The Beach Boys are scheduled to headline the *Monterey International Pop Music Festival*, a summit of rock music over these three days at the Monterey County Fairgrounds in California, with the emphasis on love, peace, flowers and youth. Although Brian is a member of the board of this non-profit event, The Beach Boys do not in fact appear – and thus squander their hopes of becoming the world's predominant pop group. The prime official reason for their non-appearance is that their negotiations with Capitol Records are at a crucial stage and that they have to get 'Heroes And Villains' out right away. A secondary official reason is that Carl was so upset by his recent arrest for refusing to report for induction into the Army that he won't be able to sing. An unofficial explanation is that Brian has had a disagreement with the festival's promoter.

Whatever the supposed reasons, the real one may be closer to something suggested by John Phillips of The Mamas & The Papas, another Monterey board member.

Phillips tells the *LA Times*: "Brian was afraid that the hippies from San Francisco would think The Beach Boys were square and would boo them." Apparently Brian didn't mind the prospect of playing alongside acts like The Mamas & The Papas, but was more concerned about how his group would measure up to performers such as impressive British bands such as The Who – especially as drummer Keith Moon would probably be screaming at The Beach Boys to play surf songs throughout their set.

(Employer's name) **CAPITOL RECORDS**

Phonograph Recording Contract Blank
AMERICAN FEDERATION OF MUSICIANS
OF THE UNITED STATES AND CANADA

02323

N⁰ 397209

Local Union No. **47**

THIS CONTRACT for the personal services of musicians, made this **15** day of **June** 19**67**
between the undersigned employer (hereinafter called the "employer") and _____ **5** musicians
(hereinafter called "employees"). *(Including the leader)*

WITNESSETH, That the employer hires the employees severally as musicians on the terms and conditions below, and as further specified on reverse side. The leader represents that the employees already designated have agreed to be bound by said terms and conditions. Each employee yet to be chosen shall be so bound by said terms and conditions upon agreeing to accept his employment. Each employee may enforce this agreement. The employees severally agree to render collectively to the employer services as musicians in the orchestra under the leadership of **Dianne Rovell** as follows:

Name and Address of Place of Engagement **BeachBoys Studio, 10452 Bellagio Rd. Bel-Air Calif.**

Date(s) and Hours of Employment **June 15, 1967 8:00 P.M. to 11:00 P.M.**

Type of Engagement: **Recording for phonograph records only.** Plus pension contributions as specified on reverse side hereof.

WAGE AGREED UPON $ **UNION SCALE**
(Terms and amount)

This wage includes expenses agreed to be reimbursed by the employer in accordance with the attached schedule, or a schedule to be furnished the employer on or before the date of engagement.

To be paid **WITHIN 15 DAYS**
(Specify when payments are to be made)

Upon request by the American Federation of Musicians of the United States and Canada (herein called the "Federation") or the local in whose jurisdiction the employees shall perform hereunder, the employer either shall make advance payment hereunder or shall post an appropriate bond.

Employer's name and authorized signature	**Capitol Records**
Street address	**1750 N. Vine St.**
City / State / Phone	**Hollywood, Calif. 4626252**

Leader's name	**Dianne Rovell** Local No. **47**
Leader's signature	*Dianne Rovell*
Street address	**616 N. Sierra Bonita**
City / State	**L.A. Calif.**

(1) Label Name **Capitol Records** Session No. **14377-N**

Master No.	No. of Minutes	TITLES OF TUNES	Master No.	No. of Minutes	TITLES OF TUNES
		VEGETABLES			

(2) Employee's Name (As on Social Security Card) Last First Initial	(3) Home Address (Give Street, City and State)	(4) Local Union No.	(5) Social Security Number	(6) Scale Wages	(7) Pension Contribution
(Leader)					
Rovell, Dianne	616 N. Sierra Bonita L.A. Calif.	47	560-56-7005	173.34	13.87
Jardine, Alan	1820 Westridge Brentwood, Calif.	47	566-54-3798	86.67	6.93
Wilson, Brian	10452 Bellagio Rd. Bel-Air Calif.	47	568-62-7150	86.67	6.93
Wilson, Carl	1902 Coldwater Cyn. Beverly Hills, Calif.	47	568-62-6168	86.67	6.93
Wilson, Dennis	10452 Bellagio Rd. Bel-Air Calif.	47	562-60-0767	86.67	6.93

NO COPYIST OR ARRANGER THIS SESSION

CONTRACT RECEIVED

(8) Total Pension Contributions (Sum of Column (7)) $ **41.59**
Make check payable in this amount to "AFM & EPW Fund."

FOR FUND USE ONLY:

Date pay't rec'd ___ Amt. paid ___ Date posted ___ By ___

Form B-4 Rev. 4-66

LEFT After the collapse of *Smile* the group has turned to a revised album, *Smiley Smile*, and this log notes Al, Brian, Carl and Dennis at a June 15th session to complete 'Vegetables' for the new record. BELOW The live group: Bruce Johnston, Mike Love, Al Jardine, Dennis Wilson and Carl Wilson.

As expected, the festival is a huge success and the public notes The Beach Boys' non-appearance as tacit agreement that they are no longer hip. Singer Otis Redding takes their place as Saturday evening's headlining act – and that night's show is the first to be totally sold out.

Guitarist Jimi Hendrix blows away the Monterey crowd with his stunning, visually exciting performance. For many years it will be thought that, to add insult to The Beach Boys' non-appearance at Monterey, Hendrix's lyric "You'll never hear surf music again" from 'Third Stone From The Sun' on his just-released debut album is actually directed at the group. While the guitar maestro does indeed sing this, it is not aimed at The Beach Boys at all. In fact, Jimi has in mind the seriously ill surf legend Dick Dale, to whom he dedicates the song.

The 50,000 crowd leave the Monterey concert thinking that The Beach Boys have run scared from the competition. Carl will tell BBC Radio-1 later: "Brian was on the board and [the festival] changed several times, the concept of it, and he decided, 'This is shit, let's not play it.' I think there were some people getting hostile about the group at the time, about the surfing thing and he figured, 'Fuck you,' or something like that."

Derek Taylor will tell BBC radio: "The Monterey thing did seem to get The Beach Boys in a very bad light. They dropped out and they shouldn't have dropped out. They were supposed to headline Saturday night. Nobody could believe it. Lou Adler [one of the show's organisers] shouted, 'What!' I told him, 'They won't do it.' He said, 'What do you mean, they won't do it? Everyone is doing it.' I don't know why they didn't do it. Possibly it was cold feet. [Brian had said] 'Yes' to me. He got so hellish at the end that I'm not sure when the 'No' came. It came by proxy. I think he shouldn't have said 'Yes'.

I don't think it was ever on. They were certainly very heavily criticised at the time for their cancellation. It seemed, in a way, rather like an admission of defeat. It was all down to Brian. Those sorts of decisions were always his, really. The festival was marvellous but … would have been better with them because they were representative of very good music. Everyone profited from the festival. It was a turning point, and it could have helped them for sure."

In truth, the group's new material is 'imprisoned' by their ongoing legal dispute with Capitol. With no new songs to play at the festival, Brian has no alternative but to withdraw The Beach Boys from the concert.

As The Beatles usher in the new, exciting psychedelic age with *Sgt Pepper*, The Beach Boys will be quickly left behind as unpopular, unfashionable and out of date, as throwbacks to 1950s doowop. Their rejection by the American press and the music-buying public will last for three long years.

■ Monday 19th

RECORDING *Smiley Smile* **session 10** Brian's Home Studio *Bel Air, CA* 2:00-5:00pm. With news of the success of the festival in Monterey filling many newspapers and television screens, The Beach Boys assemble in Brian's studio to record the inaugural tracking session for **'Hawaiian Song'** (Master No. 57863). A section of this will later be released on the *Smiley Smile* album as part of **'Little Pad'**.

Musicians present Beach Boys: Al, Brian, Carl, Dennis.

■ Tuesday 20th

RECORDING *Smiley Smile* **session 11** Brian's Home Studio *Bel*

THE BEACHBOYS
TRACKING SCALE INCLUDED   (Employer's name)   CAPITOL RECORDS

Phonograph Recording Contract Blank
AMERICAN FEDERATION OF MUSICIANS
OF THE UNITED STATES AND CANADA

02388

N? 397210

Local Union No. **47**

THIS CONTRACT for the personal services of musicians, made this **19** day of **June**, 19**67** between the undersigned employer (hereinafter called the "employer") and _____ **5** musicians (hereinafter called "employees"). (Including the leader)

WITNESSETH, That the employer hires the employees as musicians severally on the terms and conditions below, and as further specified on reverse side. The leader represents that the employees already designated have agreed to be bound by said terms and conditions. Each employee yet to be chosen shall be so bound by said terms and conditions upon agreeing to accept his employment. Each employee may enforce this agreement. The employees severally agree to render collectively to the employer services as musicians in the orchestra under the leadership of **Dianne Rovell** as follows:

Name and Address of Place of Engagement **BeachBoys Recording Studio, 10452 Bellagio Rd. Bel-Air California**

Date(s) and Hours of Employment **June 19, 1967 2:00 P.M. to 5:00 P.M.**

Type of Engagement: **Recording for phonograph records only.**

WAGE AGREED UPON $ **UNION SCALE**

Plus pension contributions as specified on reverse side hereof.

(Terms and amount)

This wage includes expenses agreed to be reimbursed by the employer in accordance with the attached schedule, or a schedule to be furnished the employer on or before the date of engagement.

To be paid **WITHIN 15 DAYS**

(Specify when payments are to be made)

Upon request by the American Federation of Musicians of the United States and Canada (herein called the "Federation") or the local in whose jurisdiction the employees shall perform hereunder, the employer either shall make advance payment hereunder or shall post an appropriate bond.

Employer's name and authorized signature	**Capitol Records**	Leader's name	**Dianne Rovell**	Local No. **47**
		Leader's signature		
Street address	**1750 N. Vine St.**	Street address	**616 N. Sierra Bonita**	
	Hollywood, Calif. HO26252		**L.A. Calif.**	
	City State Phone		City State	

(1) Label Name **Capitol Records**   Session No. **14477**

Master No.	No. of Minutes	TITLES OF TUNES	Master No.	No. of Minutes	TITLES OF TUNES
57863		" THE HAWAIIAN SONG			

(2) Employee's Name (As on Social Security Card) Last First Initial	(3) Home Address (Give Street, City and State)	(4) Local Union No.	(5) Social Security Number	(6) Scale Wages	(7) Pension Contribution
(Leader)					
✓ Rovell, Dianne	616 N. Sierra Bonita L.A. Calif.	47	560-56-7005	173.34	13.87
Jardine, Alan POST OPEN	1820 Westridge Brentwood, Calif.	47	566-54-3798	86.67	6.93
Wilson, Brian POST OPEN	10452 Bellagio Rd. Bel-Air, Calif.	47	568-62-7150	86.67	6.93
Wilson, Carl POST OPEN	1902 Coldwater Cyn. Beverly Hills, Calif.	47	568-62-6168	86.67	6.93
Wilson, Dennis POST OPEN	10452 Bellagio Rd. Bel-Air, Calif.	47	562-60-0767	86.67	6.93

NO COPYIST OR ARRANGER THIS SESSION

RECEIVED JUN 23 1967

(8) Total Pension Contributions (Sum of Column (7)) $ **41.39**
Make check payable in this amount to "AFM & EPW Fund."

FOR FUND USE ONLY:
Date pay't rec'd _____ Amt. paid _____ Date posted _____ By _____

Form B-4 Rev. 4-66

Air, CA. The second tracking session for **'Hawaiian Song'**.
Musicians present Beach Boys: Al, Brian, Carl (following his court appearance), Dennis.
• Carl's refusal to report for induction into military service means another appearance in court, at the Federal Court in Los Angeles. He is cleared and granted conscientious objector status but refuses to report for alternative civilian duty as a bed-pan changer at the Los Angeles veterans hospital, citing the fact that the alternative job will not make use of his talents. The case will drag on for the next two years. (See August 3rd 1969.)

■ Wednesday 21st
RECORDING *Smiley Smile* session 12 Brian's Home Studio *Bel Air, CA* 7:00-10:00pm. After three recording sessions, **'Hawaiian Song'** (Master No. 57863) is completed with the taping of an insert musical sequence. The complete piece will remain unreleased.
Musicians present Beach Boys: Al, Brian, Carl and Dennis. Session player: Charles Berghofer (probably upright bass).

■ Thursday 22nd
Instead of continuing his work on the next Beach Boys album, Brian travels to the Monterey County Fairgrounds, site of last weekend's *Monterey Pop Festival*, to collect programmes of the event.

During Brian's hiatus, UK music reporter Keith Altham pays a visit to Mike at his home in Los Angeles for a preview of a fabled and as yet unreleased Beach Boys recording.

"It was at Mike's house that I heard 'Heroes And Villains'," Altham writes in next week's *New Musical Express*. "His particular tape ran for about six minutes. The harmonies and melodies are as intricate and exciting as one would expect. The number sounds like a combination of 'Good Vibrations', 'God Only Knows' and 'I Just Wasn't Made For These Times'."

■ Sunday 25th
RECORDING *Smiley Smile* session 13 Brian's Home Studio *Bel Air, CA*. With Brian now back at the helm, The Beach Boys record **'Good Time Mama'**, inevitably unreleased.

■ Monday 26th
RECORDING *Smiley Smile* session 14 Brian's Home Studio *Bel Air, CA*. **'Good Time Mama'** is completed.

■ Wednesday 28th
RECORDING *Smiley Smile* session 15 Brian's Home Studio *Bel Air, CA* 2:00-5:00pm. **'Little Pad'** is recorded and combined with **'Hawaiian Song'** (Master No. 57933) during this afternoon's session. Most of the sessions recorded around this time are engineered by Jim Lockert.
Musicians present Beach Boys: Al, Brian, Carl, Dennis, Mike.

■ Thursday 29th
RECORDING *Smiley Smile* session 16 Brian's Home Studio *Bel Air, CA* 3:00-6:00pm. Work takes place for **'Fall Breaks And Back Into Winter (Woody Woodpecker Symphony)'** (Master No. 57934), with the instrumental track recorded and completed.
Musicians present Beach Boys: Al, Brian, Carl, Dennis, Mike.

■ Friday 30th
RECORDING *Smiley Smile* session 17 Brian's Home Studio *Bel Air, CA* 3:00-6:00pm. **'With Me Tonight'** (Master No. 57935) is recorded and completed.
Musicians present Beach Boys: Al, Brian, Carl, Dennis, Mike.

July

■ Wednesday 5th
RECORDING *Smiley Smile* session 18 Brian's Home Studio *Bel Air, CA* 2:00-5:00pm. The group tape backing tracks and overdub vocals onto three segments of a piece with the working title **'Untitled #1'** (Master No. 57941) and later renamed **'She's Goin' Bald'**. Jim Lockert continues as engineer at these home-studio sessions, and later recalls that on 'She's Goin' Bald' they decided to feature "the sound of a tape being rewound in an echo chamber at full speed".
Musicians present Beach Boys: Al, Mike, Brian, Carl, Dennis.

■ Thursday 6th
RECORDING *Smiley Smile* session 19 Brian's Home Studio *Bel Air, CA* 2:00-5:00pm. The Beach Boys record another instrumental. As you might expect, this one is entitled **'Untitled #2'** (Master No. 57942). It remains unreleased.
Musicians present Beach Boys: Al, Brian, Carl.

■ Monday 10th
RECORDING *Smiley Smile* session 20 Brian's Home Studio *Bel Air, CA* 2:00-5:00pm. Session for a new version of **'Wind Chimes'** (Master No. 58034). The Beach Boys tape new instrumentation – piano and harpsichord – and make vocal overdubs. Sessions conclude with rehearsals of the song's fade-out sequence (11 attempts). Despite the setbacks with *Smile*, tapes of today's session reveal that when the mood takes him, Brian is still actively in control.
Musicians present Beach Boys: Al, Brian, Carl, Dennis, Mike.

■ Tuesday 11th
RECORDING *Smiley Smile* session 21 Brian's Home Studio *Bel Air, CA* 2:00-5:00pm. This afternoon, after just two sessions, work is wrapped up on **'Wind Chimes'** (Master No. 58034) with the recording of an insert piece.
Musicians present Beach Boys: Brian, Carl.
• This evening, after being told by his astrologer Genevelyn that now is the time for the world to hear his new masterpiece, Brian delivers by hand an acetate containing a pre-release version of 'Heroes And Villains' to Tom Maule, a DJ at KHJ Radio (on Melrose Avenue in Los Angeles, next to the Desilu and Paramount studio lots). Brian has been holding on to the completed mix of the song for a month. Among those accompanying him on his journey is Terry Melcher.

Melcher recalls later in *Rolling Stone*: "This woman, I guess she was an astrologer of sorts, she came by Brian's house and said, 'Brian, the time is right.' He was waiting for the word from this woman to release the record, I guess. So he said all right and, shortly before midnight, he called the rest of the group and said, 'OK, look, here it is.' It was a small but weighty seven-inch disc. He said, 'Brace yourself for the big one!' All of the group had limos so a caravan of Rolls Royces took the record to KHJ.

"Brian was going to give the station an exclusive and just give it to them without telling Capitol. So we got to the gates at KHJ and the guard wouldn't let us in. A little talking, a little bullshit, and the guard was finally intimidated enough by four or five limousines to open the gates. We got into the building, got to the disc jockey who was presiding over the turntable, and Brian said, 'Hi, I'm Brian Wilson. Here's the new Beach Boys single and I'd like to give you and KHJ an exclusive on it.' It was like a gift from God, but this asshole turned around and said, 'I can't play anything that's not on

INCLUDED

(Employer's name) _____

Phonograph Recording Contract Blank
AMERICAN FEDERATION OF MUSICIANS
OF THE UNITED STATES AND CANADA

02600

№ 397221

Local Union No. 47

THIS CONTRACT for the personal services of musicians, made this __6__ day of __July__ 19__67__

between the undersigned employer (hereinafter called the "employer") and __4__ musicians (hereinafter called "employees"). (including the leader)

WITNESSETH, That the employer hires the employees as musicians severally on the terms and conditions below, and as further specified on reverse side. The leader represents that the employees already designated have agreed to be bound by said terms and conditions. Each employee yet to be chosen shall be so bound by said terms and conditions upon agreeing to accept his employment. Each employee may enforce this agreement. The employees severally agree to render collectively to the employer services as musicians in the orchestra under the leadership of

Dianne Rowell as follows:

Name and Address of Place of Engagement __Beachboys Studio, 10452 Bellagio Rd. Bel-Air, Calif.__

Date(s) and Hours of Employment __July 6, 1967   2:00 P.M. to 5:00 P.M.__

Type of Engagement: **Recording for phonograph records only.**   Plus pension contributions as specified on reverse side hereof.

WAGE AGREED UPON $ __UNION SCALE__

(Terms and amount)

This wage includes expenses agreed to be reimbursed by the employer in accordance with the attached schedule, or a schedule to be furnished the employer on or before the date of engagement.

To be paid __WITHIN 15 DAYS__

(Specify when payments are to be made)

Upon request by the American Federation of Musicians of the United States and Canada (herein called the "Federation") or the local in whose jurisdiction the employees shall perform hereunder, the employer either shall make advance payment hereunder or shall post an appropriate bond.

Employer's name and authorized signature	Capitol Records	Leader's name	Dianne Rowell	Local No. 47
		Leader's signature	Dianne Rowell	
Street address	1750 N. Vine St.	Street address	616 N. Sierra Bonita	
City	Hollywood, Calif.	State	Phone 4606052	L.A., Calif. City, State

(1) Label Name __Capitol Records__   Session No. __14507__

Master No.	No. of Minutes	TITLES OF TUNES	Master No.	No. of Minutes	TITLES OF TUNES
57942		UNTITLED #2			

(2) Employee's Name (As on Social Security Card) Last First Initial	(3) Home Address (Give Street, City and State)	(4) Local Union No.	(5) Social Security Number	(6) Scale Wages	(7) Pension Contribution
(Leader)					
Rowell, Dianne	616 N. Sierra Bonita L.A. Calif.	47	560-56-7005	173.34	13.87
Jardine, Alan POS. OPEN	1820 Westridge Brentwood, Calif.	47	566-54-3758	86.67	6.93
Wilson, Brian	10452 Bellagio Rd. Bel-Air, Calif.	47	560-62-7150	86.67	6.93
Wilson, Carl	1902 Coldwater Cyn. Bev. Hills, Calif.	47	560-62-6168	86.67	6.93

NO COPYIST OR ARRANGER THIS SESSION

(8) Total Pension Contributions (Sum of Column (7)) $ __34.66__
Make check payable in this amount to "AFM & EPW Fund."

FOR FUND USE ONLY:

Date pay't rec'd _____ Amt. paid _____ Date posted _____ By _____

Form B-4 Rev. 4-66

the playlist.' Brian almost fainted! It was all over. He'd been holding onto the record, waiting for the right time. He'd had astrologers figuring out the correct moment. It really killed him. Finally they played it, but only after a few calls to the program director or someone, who screamed, 'Put it on, you idiot!' But the damage to Brian had already been done."

As Brian and the entourage departs from the station, 'Heroes And Villains' is spun for the first time ever on radio. Just one year before, Brian was being branded a 'genius' and revered by almost everyone in the music business. Now, 12 months on, he is aware that people and critics alike are beginning to think that his stature as a genius was nothing more than a hollow ploy employed by the fickle media. But most importantly, he now feels hurt that "new music by Brian Wilson" no longer means anything. Immersed in a feeling of anonymity, he heads home.

■ Wednesday 12th
RECORDING *Smiley Smile* session 22 Brian's Home Studio *Bel Air, CA* 4:00-7:00pm. A new version of **'Wonderful'** (Master No. 58035) is started and completed. Five piano takes are attempted, and takes 3 and 5 notably feature the recurring 'Heroes And Villains' piano theme. Backing-vocal overdubs are followed by instrumental overdubs, and a recording of Carl's lead vocal completes the session. Jim Lockert again engineers many of the sessions around this time.
Musicians present Beach Boys: Al, Brian, Carl, Dennis, Mike.

■ Thursday 13th
RECORDING *Smiley Smile* session 23 Brian's Home Studio *Bel Air, CA* 2:00-5:30pm. Vocals by Carl and Mike and instrumentation for **'Whistle In'** (Master No.58036) are recorded and finished within one three-and-a-half-hour session.
Musicians present Beach Boys: Brian, Carl, Mike.

■ Friday 14th
RECORDING *Smiley Smile* session 24 Brian's Home Studio *Bel Air, CA* 2:00-6:00pm. The rocker **'Gettin' Hungry'** (Master No. 58037) is recorded and finished after 27 instrumental tracking takes followed by instrumentation and vocal overdubbing by Brian and Mike. With that, the *Smiley Smile* album is completed (and dubbed down in just one night). 'Gettin' Hungry' will be issued as a single on August 28th, credited to Brian & Mike, and becomes the second and last single to be released on the original Brother Records label.
Musicians present Beach Boys: Al, Brian, Carl, Dennis, Mike.

■ Tuesday 18th
Capitol Records in Hollywood announces that after nearly five months of litigation a settlement has finally been achieved with The Beach Boys. Brian announces the formation of Brother Records, with the label's product being distributed by Capitol.

■ Thursday 20th
At the Capitol Records Tower headquarters in Hollywood the company masters the *Smiley Smile* album (project No. 31-5526).

■ Tuesday 25th
A Capitol Records memo from the company's A&R director, Karl Engemann, bears the subject title "Beach Boys' Booklet" and reads in full: "The booklet which was originally prepared for the *Smile* album contains cartoon illustrations of 10 selections that will not be included in the *Smiley Smile* album. After discussing a number of alternatives with [Capitol staff] Schwartz, Polley and Brian Wilson, I agreed with Brian that the best course of action would be to not

include this booklet with the *Smiley Smile* package, but rather to hold it for the next album which will include the aforementioned 10 selections. The second album, which would be packaged with the booklet, would not include the selections 'Heroes And Villains' and 'Vegetables'. However, inasmuch as these two selections would have already been released, I believe the consumer would be quick to pick up the connection between the cartoons and these tracks. In fact, some word of explanation could be included in the liner notes of the second album. Unless anyone on this distribution has strong objections, we will then omit The Beach Boys' booklet from the *Smiley Smile* album and will include it in the next album." There are still 419,200 *Smile* booklets sitting in Capitol's warehouse. Despite Engemann's contention, there are in fact just seven cartoons in the *Smile* booklet, illustrating various portions of music that end up as parts of four songs: 'Surf's Up', 'Cabinessence', 'Heroes And Villains' and 'Vegetables' (see also January 1st this year).

• Brother Records ST9001 becomes *Smiley Smile* and Brother ST9003 will become the *Wild Honey* album. It seems likely that Capitol earmarked firstly *Smile* and then the ill-fated Hawaii concert album as Brother ST9002.

■ Thursday 27th
RECORDING Columbia studio *Hollywood, CA* 9:30am-1:00pm. Bruce Johnston records a song called **'Fanfare'** in a solo session paid for by Arwin Records.
Musicians present Charles Berghofer (upright bass), Louis Blackburn (trombone), Hal Blaine (drums), George Callender (tuba), Roy Caton (trumpet), Gary Coleman (percussion), Larry Knechtel (bass guitar or organ), Oliver Mitchell (trumpet), Don Randi (keyboards).

■ Monday 31st
'Heroes And Villains' / **'You're Welcome'** single released in the US. Just weeks after the group's last-minute cancellation at Monterey, the drastically reshaped and partly re-recorded centrepiece of *Smile*, 'Heroes And Villains', is issued as a single in America. The B-side is 'You're Welcome', a solo Brian Wilson chant from the *Smile* sessions. This first Brother Records release comes after eight months of silence from the Capitol-distributed label. The disc will fail to make the Top Ten, but is certainly a hit (peaking at number 12), though nowhere near the commercial success of 'Good Vibrations'.

Best Of The Beach Boys Volume 2 compilation album released in the US. This second Capitol compilation is also released this month and will peak in the US *Billboard* album chart at number 50. However marvellous are such tracks as 'When I Grow Up', 'Long Tall Texan', '409', 'Surfin' Safari', 'Little Saint Nick' and 'I Get Around', they are lost amid the current psychedelic pop revolution. The UK version of the album, as with the first volume, features a different track listing, and is another success. Following the group's controversial

Heroes And Villains single

A **'Heroes And Villains'** (B. WILSON / V.D. PARKS)
B **'You're Welcome'** (B. WILSON)

US release July 31st 1967 (Brother 1001).
UK release August 18th 1967 (Capitol CL 15510).
Chart high US number 12; UK number 8.

An intriguing 'AFM sheet' logs a *Smiley Smile* session on July 6th for an instrumental known only as 'Untitled #2'.

and well-reported failure to appear at the *Monterey Pop Festival*, this latest greatest hits album only helps to further the belief, brought on by the shelving of *Smile*, that The Beach Boys are yesterday's news.

Their biggest rivals, The Beatles, have released *Sgt Pepper's Lonely Hearts Club Band*. John Lennon is riding about London in a bright yellow Rolls Royce adorned with brightly coloured flowers. In the prestigious US magazine *Life*, Paul McCartney has come out about the notoriously trendy drug, LSD, and in the Haight-Ashbury district of San Francisco, George Harrison will soon be seen walking through the streets strumming a guitar, mingling and singing with the hippies. Ringo, meanwhile, is receiving accolades for his excellent drumming on *Sgt Pepper's*.

However good *Smile* might have turned out to be, it seems somehow that The Beatles have again outdistanced The Beach Boys. It is a dire time for the group from California.

August

■ Friday 4th – Monday 14th

During a break from Beach Boys duties, Bruce flies into London Airport on an 8:45am arrival from New York City. This is the start of a promotional trip arranged by the group's UK publicist, Roger Easterby. At a hastily arranged press conference Bruce tells reporters: "Brian Wilson is having a good time, only Brian doesn't relate to time. He keeps funny hours. The rest of the guys are keeping home with their family. You can't relax forever. I get bored resting. I really dig working and man, we're not working again until October. That's why I've come over to England because I can do some appearances on TV and radio."

Responding to a question about the latest events in Beach Boys land, Bruce says: "There isn't much to report. We haven't done anything that you don't already know about over here. 'Heroes And Villains' is out here in a few weeks and we have a new album prepared. Finished? Well, [*Smiley Smile*] sounds finished to me. I heard it a few times before I came over. It's a quiet record, like everybody's sliding around in socks. Definitely a 'listen to me' kind of record."

A reporter pipes up: "The Beach Boys have been criticised by some for the long gaps between releases. What do you think of this?" Bruce replies: "Well, I don't think there will be any more gaps now. 'Good Vibrations' and 'Heroes' came about because we were on the European tour; because we were involved in a lawsuit with our recording company in the States; and because Brian decided to record 'Heroes And Villains' again when we got back from the tour. He scrapped a finished version of the song and wrote it again. This version is completely different from the number he wrote first. We won't be doing so much work on the road in future and more in the studio, and now everything's a lot more peaceful." The reporter asks whatever happened to the *Smile* album, and Bruce concludes: "You can … expect *Smile* within the next two months."

During his visit to Britain, Bruce naturally takes the opportunity to promote the group's new highly anticipated 45, 'Heroes And Villains', set for release in the UK on August 18th. Bruce will tell US radio: "I was at the Speakeasy club in London when they debuted 'Heroes And Villains'. Everyone really cheered and got up to dance. But when the tempo on the track changed, I knew we'd blown it with that record."

■ Saturday 5th – Tuesday 8th

Bruce's ten-day promotional tour of the UK begins with an unscheduled appearance on Saturday at Studio B6 in the BBC's Broadcasting House in central London with DJ Chris Denning for the Light Programme radio show *Where It's At*, transmitted live between 4:00 and 5:30pm. Afterwards Bruce tapes some novelty jingles for the show, first aired the following Saturday. On Sunday 6th he's back at B6 for another live Light Programme radio show, *Easy Beat*, broadcast between 10:00 and 11:30pm, and on Monday at the Playhouse Theatre for a live appearance on the Light Programme's *Monday, Monday* show, transmitted between 1:00 and 2:00pm. And then on Tuesday 8th at 10:30am Bruce is at Studio S2 in Broadcasting House to tape an appearance for the Light Programme show *Saturday Club* transmitted on August 12th between 10:00 and 12:00 noon. Later, between 7:45 and 9:00pm, at the BBC's Paris Studios in central London, he tapes an interview for yet another BBC Light Programme radio show, this time *Disc Jockey Derby*, broadcast on August 15th between 1:00 and 1:59pm.

■ Saturday 12th

The flurry of BBC activity continues when Bruce travels to the Corporation's TV Centre in Shepherd's Bush, west London to appear as a panellist on the long running television music show *Juke Box Jury*, transmitted live on BBC-1 between 5:39 and 6:09pm. The programme, now in its eighth and final year, is famed for the panel's Hit or Miss evaluations of the week's new single releases. Tonight, Bruce sits in judgement on the following new discs: 'Omaha' by Moby Grape, 'Pleasant Valley Sunday' by The Monkees, 'The Day I Met Marie' by Cliff Richard, 'The World We Knew' by Frank Sinatra, and 'Thinkin' Ain't For Me' by ex-Manfred Mann singer Paul Jones. DJ David Jacobs hosts the show.

■ Monday 14th

Bruce's promotional visit to the UK concludes when he visits the Radio London ship, moored three and a half miles off Frinton-on-Sea in Essex. He partakes in a brief live conversation with the station's managing director, Philip Birch. Subsequently he becomes the last pop star to speak on the station. He says, "I wish the rest of The Beach Boys could be with me now. On behalf of the other members I'd also like to thank Radio London for promoting our records. Fellow American bands owe a lot to the work Radio London has done for us and it is sad to see it go."

Radio London ceases broadcasting at 3:00pm this afternoon, nine hours before the Marine, & c, Broadcasting (Offences) Act 1967 comes into operation. This legislation has been introduced by the Labour government to outlaw all the offshore 'pirate' radio stations. One by one, all the other pirates are closed down. Only the Radio Caroline North and South ships (one off the Isle of Man, the other off Frinton-on-Sea) continue in defiance of the law.

Following the farewell message from Bruce, the final record is played on Radio London: 'A Day In The Life' by The Beatles. Other (pre-taped) messages broadcast during the station's final hour of transmission come from Beatle Ringo Starr, Rolling Stone Mick Jagger and singers Dusty Springfield and Cliff Richard. After paying his respect to the axed pirate radio station, Bruce flies back to California, where preparations are being made for some unusual Beach Boys performances in Hawaii.

■ Friday 18th

'Heroes And Villains' / **'You're Welcome'** single released in the UK. Following already extensive radio airplay, and helped by Bruce's recent visit, EMI Records in London issues the new single, which will peak in the charts at number 8. Nick Jones writes in *Melody Maker*: "The hot, clear sound of The Beach Boys, especially in these

Mike Love and Brian Wilson consider the future.

summer months, is always to be reckoned with. This complex but exciting new mind child of Brian Wilson's is going to have a battle for that number one spot, though. Wilson mainly features the amazingly flexible voices of The Beach Boys as instruments, sighing and crying, glowing and growing in this intricate but propelling sound. Basically Wilson has succeeded because I think a lot of people expected him to eventually overload his material with unnecessary sounds that would turn your neck to stone after the first bar.

"However, 'Heroes And Villains' has an honest, jazzy, bell clear dimension and an enlightening, exhilarating feel to be explored when you have been conditioned to the interweaving vocals and numerous movements. Certainly another masterpiece of production from Wilson and another move in his flowery progression."

■ Friday 25th – Saturday 26th
HIC Arena *Honolulu, HI* 8:30pm, Beach Boys' Summer Spectacular, with Paul Revere & The Raiders, Bobbie Gentry, The Val Richards Five, Dino Desi & Billy (Saturday only), comedians The Pickle Brothers (Friday only)

While the group's new album is being prepared for the pressing plant, The Beach Boys travel to Hawaii on the 24th for this two-night engagement at Honolulu's International Center. Bearing a tentative but unconfirmed title of *Lei'd In Hawaii*, the two concerts are recorded for a proposed live album, and some parts are filmed. Local reports insist that this is the first time that a show in Hawaii has been committed to recording tape, for which purpose Capitol ships out to the island two state-of-the-art 8-track recording machines.

Surprisingly, Brian rejoins the group on stage, chiefly to oversee the recordings. Practically every fragment of The Beach Boys' performances over the two days is recorded on tape – even their rehearsal backstage prior to Friday's concert. Newspaper ads for the

shows announce that "the concert will be a live recording session" and request that concertgoers "wear flower leis and bring along a ukulele". Brian apparently envisions the sound of 10,000 ukuleles playing along with The Beach Boys performance.

Bruce does not appear at the concerts. At the time he tells *NME*: "This is definitely a one-off appearance by Brian. I was invited to take part in the Hawaii concerts but I shall not do so. However, I shall be playing with the group throughout its US Tour, beginning next month."

Wayne Harada writes in the *Honolulu Advertiser*: "The Beach Boys, who recorded their portion of the show for an upcoming album, probably will have to do a lot of studio editing. I particularly enjoyed the intricate harmony on 'Heroes And Villains', the quintet's latest chartbuster. It was an obligation to include a short chorus of 'Hawaii', but it came off quite nicely. 'California Girls', however, had more sparks, and yes, The Beach Boys are ageing. While they still put together a pretty good package of rock, I suspect The Beach Boys will soon follow The Beatles in concentrating on recordings and eliminating live concerts altogether. Leader Brian Wilson's participation here was the first anywhere in three years, and in his comeback he debuted his organ-playing talent."

Unfortunately, the taping is beset by technical difficulties and the group decides that most of the recordings are not usable. The chief problem is the grouping of vocal tracks, which are poorly mixed at the event. According to those closely associated with the group, the problem that prevents the official release of this concert isn't the recording quality but rather the somewhat mediocre performance, an ill-advised attempt to rearrange old hits in the minimalist style of *Smiley Smile*. The group – again featuring Brian – will make another attempt at recording a live Beach Boys performance on September 11th, but still using the live arrangements. (Footage of 'God Only Knows' from Friday's show will

Gettin' Hungry single by Brian & Mike

A 'Gettin' Hungry' (B. WILSON / M. LOVE)
B 'Devoted To You' (B. BRYANT)

US release August 28th 1967 (Brother 1002).
UK release September 1967 (Capitol CL 15513).
Chart high US none; UK none.

---

appear in the documentaries *The Beach Boys: An American Band* (1984), with sound from an entirely different and much later performance, and *Endless Harmony* (1998), with sound from the Hawaii show. Vacation footage taken by The Beach Boys during their stay in Hawaii will also appear in those two programmes.)
Set-list (Friday) 'The Letter' (sung by Brian; see October 13th), 'Hawaii', 'You're So Good To Me', 'Surfer Girl', 'Surfin'', 'Gettin' Hungry', 'Sloop John B', 'California Girls', 'Wouldn't It Be Nice', 'Heroes And Villains', 'God Only Knows', 'Good Vibrations', 'Barbara Ann' (see September 20th).
Set-list (Sat) 'Hawthorne Boulevard' (unreleased instrumental), 'Hawaii', 'You're So Good To Me', 'Help Me Rhonda', 'California Girls', 'Wouldn't It Be Nice', 'Gettin' Hungry', 'Surfer Girl', 'Surfin'', 'Sloop John B', 'The Letter', 'God Only Knows', 'Good Vibrations', 'Heroes And Villains', 'Barbara Ann'.
• 'Heroes And Villains' single peaks in US *Billboard* chart on Saturday at number 12.

Monday 28th

'Gettin' Hungry' / 'Devoted To You' single by Brian & Mike released in the US. Credited to "Brian & Mike", this is the second and final Brother single (until 1970), with a B-side lifted from the old *Beach Boys' Party!* album. It becomes the first Beach Boys-related release to fail to chart since their effort as Kenny & The Cadets with 'Barbie' in 1962, and the first ever on Capitol.

Thursday 31st

The BBC-1 TV channel in Britain is eager to showcase The Beach Boys' new disc on its show *Top Of The Pops* and screens on tonight's 7:30-8:00pm episode filmmaker Peter Clifton's hastily compiled 16mm clip for 'Heroes And Villains'. It features the song set against a backdrop of non-stop surfers riding the high waves in America and – par for the course for anything Beach Boys-related – a couple of attractive girls in bikinis also appear briefly.

This 'Heroes And Villains' montage will reappear two years later in Clifton's colour pop film, *Popcorn: An Audio-Visual Rock Thing*, a compilation of performances, interviews and promotional footage he has shot over the years and including Joe Cocker, Vanilla Fudge, Jimi Hendrix, Mick Jagger, Twiggy, Otis Redding and The Bee Gees. (See also September 2nd.)

September

Back in Los Angeles, Brian begins working with his friend Danny Hutton's new band, Redwood. Brian writes (and re-writes) two top

quality songs especially for the group, 'Time To Get Alone' and 'Darlin'', and will announce that he wants to produce them. But the other Beach Boys oppose this and Brian has to let Redwood go. They change their name the following year to Three Dog Night. (See October 13th, 14th, 15th, 26th, 27th.)

As the year slowly heads towards its final quarter, Brian's rate of activity grows more frantic – but nothing seems to be accomplished. He tears his Bellagio Road home apart and redecorates half of it. One section of the living room is filled with a full-sized Arabian tent and the dining room is draped with nursery curtains. His windows are stained grey and he puts a sauna bath in the bedroom. Brian continues to battle with his father, complains that his brothers aren't trying hard enough, and accuses cousin Mike of making too much money.
Gettin' Hungry / 'Devoted To You' single released in the UK.

Saturday 2nd

With no official Capitol film to accompany The Beach Boys' new disc, the BBC sends a film crew to Brian's Bellagio Road home in Los Angeles to shoot some miscellaneous scenes of the group for footage that can be married to the song 'Heroes And Villains'. In the UK, bosses at *Top Of The Pops* hope that the 16mm black-and-white clip can figure in the show broadcast on or around Thursday September 21st. But by that time the disc will have started to slip down the UK listings and the film remains unscreened (and is later junked).

Monday 11th

RECORDING Wally Heider studio *Hollywood, CA* 7:00-10:00pm. The Beach Boys are fast developing a worrying habit of not releasing their recorded material. The planned *Smile* album is classed as dead and buried by Capitol. So the label hastily begins planning the next album and presses ahead with plans to release the group's live recordings from Hawaii made on August 25th and 26th. There is some evidence that the original plan is to release the live tracks late in 1967, soon after the group's next studio album.

But when the live tapes are examined, The Beach Boys and Capitol decide that there isn't enough suitable material to comfortably fill an entire new album. The August 25th show is marred by technical difficulties while the 26th's is hindered by a below-par performance. Additional vocal and instrumental overdubs are urgently required to repair the band's inferior performance.

With that in mind The Beach Boys (including Bruce, and Brian) head to the Wally Heider studio in Hollywood today to try to fabricate a live performance for the album, tentatively titled *Lei'd In Hawaii* (though this is unconfirmed). Tracks recorded (and rehearsed) by the group today include **'You're So Good To Me'**, **'Help Me Rhonda'**, **'Surfer Girl'**, **'California Girls'**, 'Surfin'' (rehearsal), **'God Only Knows'** (seven takes or run-throughs required), **'Good Vibrations'**, **'Their Hearts Were Full Of Spring'**, **'The Letter'** and **'Heroes And Villains'**. The surviving audio tape of the group's performance in the studio includes Mike ridiculing the latter song. The group plans to re-record the one-off instrumental, 'Hawthorne Boulevard', performed on the 26th, but this fails to take place.

Although these songs will for the most part remain unissued, five recordings from The Beach Boys' live recordings on August 25th and 26th and today will see official release. 'Surfer Girl' (August 25th pre-concert rehearsal) is released on the 1993 Capitol five-CD boxed set *Good Vibrations*. 'Heroes And Villains' (August 25th performance) will appear on the 1990 Capitol CD *Beach Boys*

The original Boys on the Beach in Hawaii in August '67: Carl, Al, Brian, Mike and Dennis.

Concert / Live In London. 'Good Vibrations' (August 25th) will be released on Capitol's 2001 CD *Hawthorne, CA*. 'The Letter' (September 11th) is issued on the group's 1983 *Beach Boys Rarities* album, and 'God Only Knows' (September 11th) appears on Capitol's 1998 *Endless Harmony* CD.

For now, the group is still unsatisfied with the recordings – and so it is that the *Wild Honey* album is hastily born. (See September 26th.)

■ Monday 18th

Smiley Smile album released in the US. With unrest surrounding their latest as-yet unreleased recordings, The Beach Boys' new LP is issued in America. Dennis tells the US press: "It was not as ambitious an album as *Pet Sounds* was. But [*Smiley Smile* is] the most fun thing we ever did. I listened to it in a jungle in Africa and it sounded great."

Cut largely at Brian's new home studio, the album cobbles together inferior-quality versions of songs originally intended for *Smile* and hastily recorded new material. Only 'Good Vibrations' and 'Heroes And Villains' appear in their original versions. 'Good Vibrations' is here to help bolster sales, even though Brian is strongly against its inclusion. But he is outvoted by the other Beach Boys, the first time that the group has overruled him. Clearly, as he had feared, it is the end of an era.

Fans, critics and the music industry alike hang their heads in disbelief and sheer bewilderment when they first listen to *Smiley Smile*. There have been months of *Smile*-related hysteria, including the memorable appearance by Brian on the *Inside Pop* TV show just five months earlier, a performance that prepared everyone for the greatest album ever made. Now *Smiley Smile* appears – and becomes one of the most baffling and bizarre albums to appear from a major rock act. The underground rock aristocracy have already deemed The Beach Boys passé, and now they have the material with which to crucify them. The press wastes no time in effectively blacklisting the band, refusing to review their latest records, or reviewing them long after they have been released.

Carl will sum up the *Smiley Smile* LP as "a bunt instead of a grand slam" and says that it all but destroys the group's reputation for forward-thinking pop. The album is the first (and last) to be released by this incarnation of Brother Records, with a production credit to "The Beach Boys". It charts no higher than number 41 in the US. In the UK, where it is released in November, *Smiley Smile* will peak at number 9, but the album receives a severe mauling from the once appreciative UK music critics.

"Undoubtedly the worst album ever released by The Beach Boys," writes the *Melody Maker* reviewer. "It contains two single tracks, 'Good Vibrations' and 'Heroes And Villains', which are good, but the rest seem to be more a series of introductions to songs, which never start. There is a poor instrumental track called 'Fall Breaks And Back To Winter', and the rest are so childish and pointless they don't bear discussion, which is a tragedy in view of their past output. Prestige has been *seriously* damaged."

With the recordings for *Smiley Smile* over and the record out, it becomes clear that 25-year-old Brian Wilson has lost his control over The Beach Boys. It seems also that his drive and desire to create great artistic statements have deserted him. From now on Brian will be happy to let go and allow others to take over.

■ Wednesday 20th

RECORDING Capitol studio *Hollywood, CA* 8:00-11:00pm. On behalf of Brother Records, Carl produces a session for songwriter and future Beach Boy collaborator Steve Kalinich and his partner

---

Smiley Smile album

A1 **'Heroes And Villains'** (B. WILSON / V.D. PARKS)
A2 **'Vegetables'** (B. WILSON / V.D. PARKS)
A3 **'Fall Breaks And Back To Winter (W. Woodpecker Symphony)'** (B. WILSON)
A4 **'She's Goin' Bald'** (B. WILSON / M. LOVE / V.D. PARKS)
A5 **'Little Pad'** (B. WILSON)
B1 **'Good Vibrations'** (B. WILSON / M. LOVE)
B2 **'With Me Tonight'** (B. WILSON)
B3 **'Wind Chimes'** (B. WILSON)
B4 **'Gettin' Hungry'** (B. WILSON / M. LOVE)
B5 **'Wonderful'** (B. WILSON / V.D. PARKS)
B6 **'Whistle In'** (B. WILSON)

US release September 18th 1967 (Brother 9001).
UK release November 1967 (Capitol T9001).
Chart high US number 41; UK number 9.

Mark Buckingham, with engineer Jim Lockert on hand. Fifteen takes are made of **'Leaves Of Grass'** (take 15 marked as master, though this will remain a backing track with no vocal overdubs). They also attempt seven takes of **'Magic Hands'** and an unknown number of takes of **'If I Knew'**. All the recordings will remain unreleased.

■ Saturday 23rd

RECORDING Brian's Home Studio *Bel Air, CA*. A strange Beach Boys recording session where of all things they cover **'With A Little Help From My Friends'**, the Lennon & McCartney track from The Beatles' current album *Sgt Pepper's*. The recording will remain unreleased until the 1983 *Beach Boys Rarities* album.

• *Best Of The Beach Boys Volume 2* album peaks in US *Billboard* chart at number 50.

■ Tuesday 26th

RECORDING *Wild Honey* session 1 Brian's Home Studio *Bel Air, CA* 2:00-6:00pm. Today sees a session with engineer Jim Lockert for the R&B inspired track **'Wild Honey'**. Following the disappointment of their failure to headline at the *Monterey Pop Festival* and the fiasco surrounding *Smile* and *Smiley Smile*, The Beach Boys are totally exasperated. Now that they have also discovered the inadequacy of the recordings from their concerts in Hawaii the previous month, the group feels there is only one choice left: to start from scratch.

This means a return to their old ways, with the group members playing all their own instruments. For the first time the band as a whole will have a far greater say in the music they produce. This decision suits Brian because, following The Beach Boys' recent disappointments, he just isn't interested in producing the group any more on a full-time basis. From now on, his work with The Beach Boys becomes increasingly intermittent.

So today with Brian at his home studio Al, Bruce, Carl, Dennis and Mike regroup to begin work on the back-to-basics album *Wild Honey*. The group – and especially Carl – take over the main production reins that Brian has relinquished. Carl, now nearly 21, has almost instinctively begun to pick up where Brian has left off. Recorded in a matter of weeks, the sessions begin with the album's fine R&B-flavoured title track. Mike says on US radio: "Brian wanted

This September 27th 'AFM sheet' marks the second day of sessions for what becomes the Wild Honey album as Paul Tanner overdubs an electro-theremin onto the intro of the title track.

THE BEACHBOYS
OVERDUB FOR TRACK (SWEETENING)   (Employer's name) __CAPITOL RECORDS__

Phonograph Recording Contract Blank
AMERICAN FEDERATION OF MUSICIANS
OF THE UNITED STATES AND CANADA

03812
N⁰ 411714

Local Union No. __47__

THIS CONTRACT for the personal services of musicians, made this __28__ day of __September__ 19__67__

between the undersigned employer (hereinafter called the "employer") and _____ __1__ musicians
(hereinafter called "employees").   (Including the leader)

WITNESSETH, That the employer hires the employees as musicians severally on the terms and conditions below, and as further specified on reverse side. The leader represents that the employees already designated have agreed to be bound by said terms and conditions. Each employee yet to be chosen shall be so bound by said terms and conditions upon agreeing to accept his employment. Each employee may enforce this agreement. The employees severally agree to render collectively to the employer services as musicians in the orchestra under the leadership of
__Paul O.W. Tanner__ _____ as follows:

Name and Address of Place of Engagement __BeachBoys Studio, 10452 Bellagio Rd., Bel-Air, Calif.__

Date(s) and Hours of Employment __September 28, 1967   12:00 P.M. call (Session only lasted 1½ hrs.)__

Type of Engagement: **Recording for phonograph records only.**   Plus pension contributions as
                                                                                   specified on reverse side hereof.

WAGE AGREED UPON $ __UNION SCALE__
                                            (Terms and amount)

This wage includes expenses agreed to be reimbursed by the employer in accordance with the attached schedule, or a schedule to be furnished the employer on or before the date of engagement.

To be paid __WITHIN 15 DAYS__
                          (Specify when payments are to be made)

Upon request by the American Federation of Musicians of the United States and Canada (herein called the "Federation") or the local in whose jurisdiction the employees shall perform hereunder, the employer either shall make advance payment hereunder or shall post an appropriate bond.

Employer's name and authorized signature	__Capitol Records__	Leader's name	__Paul Tanner__	Local No. __47__
		Leader's signature		
Street address	__1750 N. Vine St.__	Street address	__12426 La Maida__	
	__Hollywood, Calif.__ 4626252		__No, Hollywood, Calif.__	
City	State Phone	City	State	

(1) Label Name __Capitol Records__   Session No. _____

No. of Minutes	TITLES OF TUNES	Master No.	No. of Minutes	TITLES OF TUNES
	Wild Honey			

(2) Employee's Name (As on Social Security Card) Last First Initial (Leader)	(3) Home Address (Give Street, City and State)	(4) Local Union No.	(5) Social Security Number	(6) Scale Wages	(7) Pension Contribution
Tanner, Paul O.W.	12426 LaMaida No,Hollywood, Calif.	47	015-16-3893	130.00	10.40
NO COPYIST OR ARRANGER THIS SESSION					

(8) Total Pension Contributions (Sum of Column (7)) $ __10.40__
Make check payable in this amount to "AFM & EPW Fund."

FOR FUND USE ONLY: OCT 13 1967
Date pay't rec'd _____ Amt. paid _____ Date posted _____ By _____

Form B-4 Rev. 4-66

to do an R&B influenced album. [He] was working on the track at his house and I went into the kitchen, opened the cupboard and there was a jar of honey and I thought, 'That's an interesting title.' When I wrote the words to 'Wild Honey' I was thinking of a Stevie Wonder kind of lyric."

'Wild Honey' features a brilliant piano riff and a raucous, impressive lead vocal from Carl. Today's first tracking attempt features organ, percussion, bass, tambourine and piano. Then, following Carl's lead vocal overdub, they record an instrumental insert featuring bongos, percussion and drums. To round off the session various overdubs are done, including vocals and organ.

■ Wednesday 27th

RECORDING *Wild Honey* session 2 Brian's Home Studio *Bel Air, CA* 12:00midday-1:30pm. Paul Tanner overdubs his distinctive electro-theremin part on to the opening of **'Wild Honey'**.

■ Friday 29th

RECORDING *Wild Honey* session 3 Western Recorders studio *Hollywood, CA* 10:00pm-1:00am. Harbouring plans for a single away from The Beach Boys, Bruce lays down a bass-and-drums-only demo recording for **'Bluebirds Over The Mountain'**. The song is a long-time favourite of Bruce's – and the group will come back to it on November 14th 1968.
Musicians present Jim Gordon (drums), Larry Knechtel (bass guitar).

Saturday 30th

Smiley Smile album hits the US charts.

October

The Many Moods Of Murry Wilson album by Murry Wilson released in the US. During this month Capitol Records issues an instrumental album by the Wilsons' father. It includes 'Italia', a composition by Al and an uncredited Brian Wilson production.
• Brian begins to grasp just how much he has lost inside a year. Once regarded as a successful musical prodigy, he is now no longer in charge of his own band, and his hip and trendy friends have long since departed from his company.

At home in Bellagio Road he begins to withdraw further and further into his own world. Marilyn Wilson will tell *Rolling Stone* in 1976: "One week, Brian [would] be active and go out. The next, he'd spend two weeks at home and not go anywhere. Then, he would spend a full day in bed or two days in bed and say, 'I don't feel good. I've got a sore throat.' Everybody loved Brian and they'd just say, 'He's OK. He'll just get over it.' Sometimes I'd think to myself, 'Is it me? Am I the one who's not seeing things right?'"
• In the midst of all this despair, Brian receives some good news from his wife. He is going to be a father.

■ Wednesday 4th

RECORDING *Wild Honey* session 4 Wally Heider studio *Hollywood, CA* 11:00pm-12:00midnight. Most of the *Wild Honey* album will be taped at Brian's home studio, but when it's necessary to overdub a number of session musicians the recording has to shift to a bigger, more suitable location. This is the case today when string and horn parts are recorded for the tracking tape of **'Aren't You Glad'**.

(At Wally Heider's today Brian's sister-in-law Diane Rovell is the studio contractor, the person who arranges for the various musicians to play at the session. Rovell will continue to do this job for a while

on many more Beach Boys recording dates.)
Musicians present Arnold Belnick (violin), Norm Botnick (viola), David Burk ('instrumentation'),.Bonnie Douglas (violin), Oliver Mitchell (viola, trumpet), Alexander Neiman (viola), Wilbert Nuttycombe (violin), Jerry Reisler (violin), Paul Shure (violin), Tony Terran (trumpet).

■ Saturday 7th

Cleveland Music Hall *Cleveland, OH* 7:00 & 9:00pm
The first of two weekend Beach Boys performances. Bruce is now present again in the line-up.

■ Sunday 8th

Civic Opera House Chicago, IL 5:00 & 8:00pm

■ Wednesday 11th

RECORDING *Wild Honey* session 5 Brian's Home Studio *Bel Air, CA*. Brian organises a session today, probably for overdubs. The song is unidentified.

■ Thursday 12th

RECORDING *Wild Honey* session 6 Brian's Home Studio *Bel Air, CA*. Another session for a song with unidentified title, probably the same one as yesterday. It is probably a bass overdub session: present are bassist Ron Brown, who often appears on live dates with The Beach Boys around this time, and session stalwart Ray Pohlman.

■ Friday 13th

Capitol Records in Hollywood announces that the next Beach Boys album will be *Wild Honey*, featuring production by Brian and released on Brother Records (catalogue number ST9003). Even though several of the tracks have yet to be recorded, the company lists the following songs: 'Wild Honey', 'Here Comes The Night', 'Let The Wind Blow', 'I Was Made To Love Her' (a cover of the Stevie Wonder track), 'The Letter' (live version from Hawaii), 'Darlin'', 'A Thing Or Two', 'Aren't You Glad', 'Cool Cool Water', 'Game Of Love', 'Lonely Days'. 'Honey Get Home' is listed but crossed out. ('Game Of Love' and 'Lonely Days' will remain unreleased. For more on 'Cool Cool Water' see October 29th.) The live version of 'The Letter' is intended to serve as a teaser for the forthcoming live concert album but is soon pulled because that LP is abandoned.

■ Saturday 14th

RECORDING Wally Heider studio *Hollywood, CA* 6:00-9:30pm. Today sees the original recording session by the group Redwood of the classic Brian composition **'Time To Get Alone'**. Redwood are a three-piece led by Brian's mate Danny Hutton alongside Chuck Negron and Cory Wells. Naturally, Brian produces the session, intended to form part of an album by Redwood for release on Brother Records. In fact only three songs will be taped for the proposed album. The Redwood/Brother deal will apparently be called off by Mike who feels that the group should be signed to the label for just one single. According to Beach Boys historians, Redwood's material is left unreleased because Mike feels that the group's vocals are not good enough.

Today's tracking tape for 'Time To Get Alone' will eventually be used by The Beach Boys for their recordings of the song which begin on October 2nd 1968. The lyrics of the 1967 and 1968 versions differ slightly. (Redwood's version of 'Time To Get Alone' will finally appear officially 26 years later, on the 1993 compilation *Celebrate: The Three Dog Night Story*.)
Musicians present Arnold Belnick (violin), Harry Bluestone (violin),

Norm Botnick (viola), Dwight Carver (probably French horn), Bonnie Douglas (violin), David Filerman (cello), Dick Forrest (trumpet, flugelhorn), William Kurasch (violin), Lenny Malarsky (violin), Jay Migliori (flute, clarinet), Joseph Saxon (cello), Leonard Selic (viola), Paul Shure (violin).

■ Sunday 15th

RECORDING Wally Heider studio *Hollywood, CA* 8:00-10:00pm. A 'sweetening' session is recorded for Redwood's **'Time To Get Alone'** with drummer Gene Pello on hand to overdub some licks.
Musician present Gene Pello (drums).

■ Monday 23rd

'Wild Honey' / **'Wind Chimes'** single released in the US. The group hopes 'Wild Honey' will help to re-establish them as a competent, self-contained rock band, especially after a couple of years living in the shadow of Brian's session players, the Wrecking Crew. The A-side sets the stage for the same-name LP, scheduled for December 18th, while the B-side is from *Smiley Smile*. But the 45 does precious little to reverse the band's ever declining fortunes, peaking at number 31 in the US charts and, following its release in November, at number 29 in the UK.

■ Wednesday 25th

RECORDING *Wild Honey* session 7 Brian's Home Studio *Bel Air, CA*. Session for a studio version of **'The Letter'**. Two tracking takes are required, followed by vocals recordings. A version of the Wayne Fontana & The Mindbenders hit **'Game Of Love'** is also attempted at this session. These recordings will remain unreleased. (Bill Halverson takes over for Jim Lockert as engineer at today's session at Brian's home studio.)

■ Thursday 26th

RECORDING *Wild Honey* session 8 Brian's Home Studio *Bel Air, CA* 1:00-4:00pm. Today's session sees work on two songs, **'Cool Cool Water'** and **'Here Comes The Night'**, with engineers Jim Lockert and Bill Halverson.

The basic instrumental track for 'Cool Cool Water' is recorded and then overdubbed with various musical inserts, followed by vocal work. A mixdown completes the song for now; work will resume on the 29th.

'Here Comes The Night' is also completed during this productive session; in 1979, re-recorded with a disco beat, it will become a chart hit for the group.

■ Friday 27th

RECORDING *Wild Honey* session 9 Wally Heider studio *Hollywood, CA* 2:00-5:00pm. The group returns to Wally Heider's with engineers Lockert and Halverson, once more freeing themselves from the space restrictions of Brian's home studio. Recordings begin with tracking for **'A Thing Or Two'** and **'Darlin''** and then the overdubbing of backing vocals onto 'Darlin''.

'Darlin'' was originally written back in 1963 as 'Thinkin' 'Bout You Baby', a record Brian produced for Sharon Marie (and it will reappear in that guise on the Spring album of July 1972). Now the song has been re-written and is intended for release by Brian's friend Danny Hutton and his group Redwood. But this fails to materialise, so today the full Beach Boys line-up set to work taping the song's instrumental track, which starts life featuring just piano, bass and drums. Carl then overdubs his lead vocal, and guitar, tambourine and percussion inserts are added. Strings, horns and a piano are then added to complete the song.

■ Saturday 28th

RECORDING *Wild Honey* session 10 Wally Heider studio *Hollywood, CA* 3:00-6:00pm. Recordings are made of **'Can't Wait Too Long'** (also known as 'Been Way Too Long'), **'I Was Made To Love Her'** (a cover of the Stevie Wonder classic), and **'Lonely Days'**. Drummer Hal Blaine is present at today's session. Even though *Smile* and *Smiley Smile* have seemingly sapped his creative juices, Brian's creative prowess returns when he begins work on his highly intricate piece 'Can't Wait Too Long'.

The tracking tape for the song's first verse features guitar and additional instrumentation, overdubbed onto Brian's simple piano demo. The second verse features drums, guitar, xylophone, bass, tambourine and backing vocals by Brian and the other Beach Boys. A rough mix of the two sections completes the recording; the group will return to it on November 1st.

Attention turns next to 'I Was Made To Love Her', which is completed in one swift, highly productive session. Backing vocal and lead vocal overdubs follow the taping of the song's tracking tape. 'Lonely Days' will remain unreleased until eventually issued on the 2001 *Hawthorne, CA* compilation.

■ Sunday October 29th – Fri November 3rd

RECORDING *Wild Honey* sessions 11/12 Brian's Home Studio *Bel Air, CA*. During this period, recordings are made of **'Cool Cool Water'**, with further extensive double-tracked vocals added to the work recorded and mixed on the 26th, and of **'Game Of Love'** and **'Let The Wind Blow'**.

After these sessions, 'Cool Cool Water' is put on the shelf and will not see the light of day again until July 1970. 'Game Of Love' will remain unreleased.

November

Smiley Smile album released in the UK.
'Wild Honey' / **'Wind Chimes'** single released in the UK.
• *Best Of The Beach Boys Volume 2* peaks in UK *Record Retailer* chart at number 3. The compilation features a different line up of tracks compared to the US version.
• Murry Wilson accompanied by wife Audree goes on a month-long tour of Europe and the UK to promote his album, *The Many Moods Of Murry Wilson*. During an interview with *Melody Maker* reporter Alan Walsh at London's Hilton Hotel, Murry announces: "Brian is a millionaire and well on his way to his second million now. Dennis and Carl aren't millionaires yet. I think it'll take another five years for them to reach that stage. They own, as a group, two corporations

---

Wild Honey single

A 'Wild Honey' (B. WILSON / M. LOVE)
B 'Wind Chimes' (B. WILSON)

US release October 23rd 1967 (Capitol 2028).
UK release November 1967 (Capitol CL 15521).
Chart high US number 31; UK number 29.

(Employer's name) __CAPITOL RECORDS__

Phonograph Recording Contract Blank

AMERICAN FEDERATION OF MUSICIANS
OF THE UNITED STATES AND CANADA

043396

№ 419037

Local Union No. __47__

THIS CONTRACT for the personal services of musicians, made this __26__ day of __October__ 19__67__
between the undersigned employer (hereinafter called the "employer") and _____ __9__ musicians
(hereinafter called "employees").   (Including the leader)

WITNESSETH, That the employer hires the employees as musicians severally on the terms and conditions below, and as further specified on reverse side. The leader represents that the employees already designated have agreed to be bound by said terms and conditions. Each employee yet to be chosen shall be so bound by said terms and conditions upon agreeing to accept his employment. Each employee may enforce this agreement. The employees severally agree to render collectively to the employer services as musicians in the orchestra under the leadership of
__Dianne Rovell__ as follows:

Name and Address of Place of Engagement __BeachBoys Recording Studio, 10452 Bellagio Rd. Bel-Air, Calif.__

Date(s) and Hours of Employment __October 26, 1967   1:00 P.M. to 4:00 P.M.__

Type of Engagement: **Recording for phonograph records only.**
WAGE AGREED UPON $ __UNION SCALE__   Plus pension contributions as specified on reverse side hereof.
                                                        (Terms and amount)

This wage includes expenses agreed to be reimbursed by the employer in accordance with the attached schedule, or a schedule to be furnished the employer on or before the date of engagement.
To be paid __WITHIN 15 DAYS__
                              (Specify when payments are to be made)

Upon request by the American Federation of Musicians of the United States and Canada (herein called the "Federation") or the local in whose jurisdiction the employees shall perform hereunder, the employer either shall make advance payment hereunder or shall post an appropriate bond.

Employer's name and authorized signature	Leader's name	Local No. __47__
__Capitol Records__	__Dianne Rovell__	

Leader's signature

Street address __1750 N. Vine St.__	Street address __616 N. Sierra Bonita__	
City __Hollywood, Calif.__ State Phone __4626252__	City __L.A. Calif. 90036__ State	

(1) Label Name __Capitol Records__   Session No. __14666__

Master No.	No. of Minutes	TITLES OF TUNES	Master No.	No. of Minutes	TITLES OF TUNES
58583		Cool, Cool Water			
58584		HERE COMES THE NIGHT			

(2) Employee's Name (As on Social Security Card) Last First Initial	(3) Home Address (Give Street, City and State)	(4) Local Union No.	(5) Social Security Number	(6) Scale Wages	(7) Pension Contribution
(Leader) Rovell, Dianne	616 N. Sierra Bonita L.A. Calif.	47	560-56-7005	173.34	13.87
Halverson, Bill	1921 Vista Del Mar Hollywood, Calif.	47	561-50-4891	86.67	6.93
Jardine, Alan POST OPEN	1820 Westridge Brentwood, Calif.	47	566-54-3798	86.67	6.93
Johnston, Bruce	4999 Coldwater Studio City, Calif.	47	573-54-9241	86.67	6.93
Lockert, James	1934 Dracena Dr. L.A. Calif.	47	409-14-2710	86.67	6.93
Love, Michael POST OPEN	9000 Sunset #808 L.A. Calif.	47	546-56-5698	86.67	6.93
Wilson, Brian POST OPEN	10452 Bellagio Rd. Bel-Air, Calif.	47	568-62-7150	86.67	6.93
Wilson, Carl	1902 Coldwater Bev. Hills, Calif.	47	568-62-6168	86.67	6.93
Wilson, Dennis	1902 Coldwater Bev. Hills, Calif.	47	562-60-0767	86.67	6.93

__NO COPYIST OR ARRANGER THIS SESSION__

CONTRACT RECEIVED

NOV 6 1967

WARD ARCHER
ASST. TO PRESIDENT

(8) Total Pension Contributions (Sum of Column (7)) $ __69.31__
Make check payable in this amount to "AFM & EPW Fund"

FOR FUND USE ONLY:
Date pay't rec'd _____ Amt. paid _____ Date posted _____ By _____

and their net worth is between four and five million dollars. They haven't let money or success go to their heads, although I have had to speak to them firmly, even sternly on occasions. They are human beings after all."

In another interview, this time with Mike Ledgerwood of *Disc & Music Echo*, Murry says: "I'm manager, nursemaid, banker, business agent, as well as The Beach Boys' father. I was like a mother bear watching over her cubs at the start. But now they've grown up and they virtually manage themselves, with just a little help from their dad.

"The Beach Boys will never, ever, in the foreseeable future be as big as The Beatles, even though this year alone they were the biggest money-earning group in the country. And they've been making records longer than The Beatles. When we started, we were going to conquer the world, of course.

"I had no idea, personally, that The Beach Boys would be such a success story as recording artists. But Brian sensed it. That boy has God-given talent. I hate the word genius. I see it as extraordinary God-given talent. Of course, you can't compare him with Mozart or Schumann, though he is [so] close to having musical genius it is pitiful. Do you know, he can think in five and six-part harmony at one time?

"The Beach Boys have always been big Beatles fans," Murry continues. "Carl even sported a giant picture of the group on the wall of his room. They had all their records. The Beatles could never have such ardent fans. I used to call Carl a traitor. But when The Beatles happened, my boys were quick to realise that here was the competition. Before then, they were set to conquer the world. Soon they realised they had no chance. ... I call them 'monsters', but they've never let me down. How could I be anything other than proud of them?"

• The Beach Boys send a message to France's Europe 1 radio station, previewing their arrival in the country next month for the Gala UNICEF Concert (see December 15th).

The short tape that the group provides for the station is aired throughout the month on the prestigious radio show *Dans Le Vent* (which translates into English as something like *'Trendsetters'*). The show is presented by famous French DJ Hubert, who also premieres the new Beach Boys single, 'Darlin''.

■ Wednesday 1st

RECORDING *Wild Honey* session 13 Brian's Home Studio *Bel Air, CA*. Meanwhile back in California, the group works on their instrumental tracks recorded on October 28th and overdub "Miss you baby" vocals onto **'Can't Wait Too Long'** (aka 'Been Way Too Long'). Also piano, xylophone, organ, bongos and tambourine are overdubbed onto the second section of the song. Further overdubbing of fuzz bass and a new xylophone part complete the session. Further work on the piece will not take place until July 24th 1968.

■ Saturday 4th

'Wild Honey' single hits the US charts.

■ Monday 13th

RECORDING *Wild Honey* session 14 Wally Heider studio *Hollywood, CA* 7:00-10:00pm. A run of three sessions at the Heider building in Hollywood begins now to record some additional material intended for the *Wild Honey* album. Today sees a session where **'I'd Love Just Once To See You'** is recorded. There is also some evidence that the group attempts some work today – possibly vocal overdubs – on **'Time To Get Alone'**.

■ Tuesday 14th

RECORDING *Wild Honey* session 15 Wally Heider studio *Hollywood, CA* 7:00-10:00pm. A further visit to the Wally Heider facility today sees the group starting and finishing the song **'Country Air'** in a three-hour session.

■ Wednesday 15th

RECORDING *Wild Honey* session 16 Wally Heider studio *Hollywood, CA* 7:00-10:00pm. During the third of this series of sessions, recordings are made of **'How She Boogalooed It'**, noted for now as 'Good Lord How She Boogalooed It'.
• At some time between the 8th and today at Brian's home studio, recordings are also made of **'Mama Says'** and, returning to the tape made on October 4th, work is concluded on **'Aren't You Glad'**. With that, the group's new album is completed.
• A Capitol Records memo refers to *Wild Honey* with catalogue number 2859 and as "Produced by The Beach Boys". The song list has now been altered to that which will appear on the released LP.

TOUR STARTS 5th Annual US Thanksgiving Tour (Nov 17th-26th)

■ Friday 17th

Masonic Auditorium *Detroit, MI* with Buffalo Springfield, Strawberry Alarm Clock, The Soul Survivors, The Pickle Brothers
The Beach Boys begin their annual Thanksgiving Tour, a nine-day excursion down the East Coast, with extra musicians Daryl Dragon (keyboards) and Ron Brown (bass) on-stage. Dragon will appear with the group again in the 1970s. The exhausting schedule sees the group performing up to three shows a day.

The Beach Boys make board (mixing-desk) recordings of several of the shows on this tour for their own archive, including tonight's performance. They play four songs from their new *Wild Honey* album, most of which will be dropped from later shows.
Set-list 'Barbara Ann', 'Darlin'', 'Country Air', 'I Get Around', 'How She Boogalooed It', 'Wouldn't It Be Nice', 'God Only Knows', 'California Girls', 'Wild Honey', 'Graduation Day', 'Good Vibrations', 'Johnny B Goode'.

■ Saturday 18th

Le Moyne College Athletic Center *Syracuse, NY* (matinee); **The Buffalo Memorial Auditorium** *Buffalo, NY* (evening)

■ Sunday 19th

The Richmond Arena *Richmond, VA* (matinee); **Daughters Of The American Revolution Constitution Hall** *Washington, DC* 7:00 & 9:30pm, with Buffalo Springfield, The Soul Survivors
The late show is recorded by the group on 2-track tape. (The Washington shows are rescheduled from postponed concerts originally on October 29th.)
Set-list (Washington 9:30pm) 'Barbara Ann', 'Darlin'', 'I Get Around', 'Surfer Girl', 'Wouldn't It Be Nice', 'God Only Knows', 'California Girls', 'Wild Honey', 'Good Vibrations', 'Graduation Day', 'Johnny B Goode'.

■ Monday 20th

The Bushnell Auditorium *Hartford, CT* (matinee); **Fairfield University Gym** *Fairfield, CT* (evening)

■ Tuesday 21st

Westchester Community Center *White Plains, NY*
Once again the group tapes their set, which includes 'Barbara Ann', 'California Girls', 'Darlin'', 'God Only Knows', 'Good Vibrations',

THE BEACHBOYS
TRACKING SCALE INCLUDED   (Employer's name) ___ CAPITOL RECORDS

034537

Phonograph Recording Contract Blank
AMERICAN FEDERATION OF MUSICIANS
OF THE UNITED STATES AND CANADA

Nº 419036

Local Union No. 47

THIS CONTRACT for the personal services of musicians. made this **15** day of **November** 19**67**

between the undersigned employer (hereinafter called the "employer") and _____ **4** musicians
(hereinafter called "employees").   (Including the leader)

WITNESSETH, That the employer hires the employees as musicians severally on the terms and conditions below, and as further specified on reverse side. The leader represents that the employees already designated have agreed to be bound by said terms and conditions. Each employee yet to be chosen shall be so bound by said terms and conditions upon agreeing to accept his employment. Each employee may enforce this agreement. The employees severally agree to render collectively to the employer services as musicians in the orchestra under the leadership of

Dianne Rovell

Name and Address of Place of Engagement **Wally Heiders, 6373 Selma, Hollywood, Calif.** ___ as follows:

Date(s) and Hours of Employment **November 15, 1967   7:00 P.M. to X 10:00 P.M.**

Type of Engagement: **Recording for phonograph records only.**   Plus pension contribution as specified on reverse side hereof.

WAGE AGREED UPON $ _____ **UNION SCALE** _____
          (Terms and amount)

This wage includes expenses agreed to be reimbursed by the employer in accordance with the attached schedule, or a schedule to be furnished the employer on or before the date of engagement.

To be paid _____ **WITHIN 15 DAYS** _____
          (Specify when payments are to be made)

Upon request by the American Federation of Musicians of the United States and Canada (herein called the "Federation") or the local in whose jurisdiction the employees shall perform hereunder, the employer either shall make advance payment hereunder or shall post an appropriate bond.

Employer's name and	**Capitol Records**
authorized signature	
Street address	**1750 N. Vine St.**
	Hollywood, Calif. 4626252
	City State Phone

Leader's name	**Dianne Rovell** Local No. **47**
Leader's signature	
Street address	**616 N. Sierra Bonita**
	L.A. Calif. 90036
	City State

(1) Label Name **Capitol Records**   Session No. **14702-A**

Master No.	No. of Minutes	TITLES OF TUNES	Master No.	No. of Minutes	TITLES OF TUNES
58688	"	Good Lord How She Boogaloo'ed It "			

(2) Employee's Name (As on Social Security Card) Last First Initial	(3) Home Address (Give Street, City and State)	(4) Local Union No.	(5) Social Security Number	(6) Scale Wages	(7) Pension Contribution
(Leader)					
Rovell, Dianne	616 N. Sierra Bonita L.A. Calif.	47	560-56-7005	173.34	13.87
Johnston, Bruce	4999 Coldwater Studio City, Calif.	47	573-54-9241	86.67	6.93
POST OPEN Wilson, Brian	10452 Bellagio Rd. Bel-Air, Calif.	47	568-62-7150	86.67	6.93
POST OPEN Wilson, Carl	1902 Coldwater Cyn. Bev. Hills, Calif.	47	568-62-6168	86.67	6.93
NO COPYIST OR ARRANGER THIS SESSION					

CONTRACT RECEIVED
NOV 17 1967
WARD ARCHER
ASST. TO PRESIDENT

(8) Total Pension Contributions (Sum of Column (7)) $ **34.66**
Make check payable in this amount to "AFM & EPW Fund."

FOR FUND USE ONLY:
Date pay't rec'd ___ NOV 17 1967 Amt. paid ___ Date posted ___ By ___

'Graduation Day', 'Help Me Rhonda', 'Surfer Girl', 'Wild Honey', 'Wouldn't It Be Nice'.

■ Wednesday 22nd
Penn Theatre *Pittsburgh, PA* two shows
The Beach Boys record their second set this evening.
Set-list 'Barbara Ann', 'California Girls', 'Darlin'', 'God Only Knows', 'Good Vibrations', 'Graduation Day', 'Help Me Rhonda', 'I Get Around', 'Johnny B Goode', 'Sloop John B', 'Surfer Girl', 'Wild Honey', 'Wouldn't It Be Nice'.

■ Thursday 23rd
Back Bay Theatre *Boston, MA* probably two shows
The group again tapes a set this evening.

■ Friday 24th
South Auditorium, West Point Military Academy *Highland Hills, NY* (matinee); **Rhode Island Auditorium** *Providence, RI* (evening)

■ Saturday 25th
US Military Academy Fieldhouse *West Point, NY* (matinee); **The St John's University Alumni Hall** *Jamaica, NY* (evening)

■ Sunday 26th
Walsh Auditorium, Seton Hall University *South Orange, NJ* (matinee); **Civic Center** *Baltimore, MD* (evening)
The audience at the Baltimore concert, the last on this tour, totals just over 5,000.

■ Tuesday 28th
RECORDING Western Recorders studio (3) *Hollywood, CA* 8:00pm-1:00am. Back at Western, with touring duties and recordings for The Beach Boys' latest album now completed, Dennis takes charge of a tracking session for the mysterious **'Tune #1'**, a further solo recording intended for release on Brother Records. It will remain unreleased. The multi-track tape of the session is labelled 'New Song' and 'No Name'; it has no vocals, so the tune probably never gets past this tracking stage.
Musicians present Michael Anthony (guitar), James Burton (guitar), David Cohen (guitar), Gene Pello (drums), Bill Pitman (guitar), Paul Tanner (electro-theremin).

December

During this month Dennis joins forces with Billy Hinsche (see February 3rd 1966), Dino Martin (son of Dean) and Desi Arnaz Jr. to write 'Away', a song that will remain unreleased.
• 'Heroes And Villains' is voted Record Of The Year by French radio listeners.
• The Beach Boys begin a weekly 15-minute broadcast of general chat to the USSR through the *Voice Of America* radio service.
• 'Sloop John B' single qualifies for a coveted silver disc in the UK. Since peaking at number 2 in May 1966 it has been selling consistently and has recently passed the qualifying 250,000 sales mark.

■ Saturday 2nd
'Wild Honey' single peaks in US *Billboard* chart at number 31 and in the UK *Record Retailer* chart at number 29.

■ Thursday 14th
The influential US *Rolling Stone* music paper prints an article by Jann Wenner who compares The Beach Boys unfavourably with The Beatles. This in effect seals the group's fate among discerning rock fans by excluding them from serious consideration.

The piece begins with praise for The Beatles and their album *Sgt Pepper's*, but then the matter appears to become personal. "Unfortunately for The Beach Boys," Wenner writes, "and leader Brian Wilson in particular, they won a British Poll two years ago [in fact it was in 1966] which ranked them one ahead of The Beatles. At the same time, just as *Revolver* was being released, their advertisements for *Pet Sounds* carried the line 'The most progressive pop album ever' and the English fans were saying that The Beach Boys were 'years ahead of The Beatles'. Of Brian Wilson they said 'Genius'.

"Such talk found its way back to Wilson and apparently he wigged behind it. His promotions men started to tell him and his audience that he was a 'Genius' and on a par with Lennon & McCartney.

"Brian Wilson is actually an excellent writer and composer and a superb composer, however his 'Genius' is essentially a promotional schuck. But Wilson believed it and felt obligated to make good of it. It left Wilson in a bind; a bind which meant a year elapsed between *Pet Sounds* and their latest release, *Smiley Smile*.

"Well before 'Good Vibrations' The Beach Boys were an excellent group; their surfing work continued for about ten albums with little apparent progress," Wenner continues. "'Sloop John B' was stupid, but transitional. John Lennon said he really dug 'God Only Knows' and the world perked up, and then came an honest-to-God monster, 'Good Vibrations'. The music is evocative of what they are saying in the lyrics; the vibrations are actually there. It's a song you can bathe in. And it works.

"'Heroes And Villains', one of their latest releases, is also on the new album. But for some reason, it just doesn't make it. The same is true for the rest of the songs, they just don't move you. Other than displaying Brian Wilson's virtuosity for productions, they are pointless.

"In person, The Beach Boys are a totally disappointing group. At the last minute, presumably afraid of a sophisticated audience, they pulled out of the Monterey Pop Festival.

"Brian also does not tour with the group, and in person they are nowhere near their records, especially with their surfing material. To please their fans, they do their old material but they make fun of it. Their old material is fine and they should do it with pride that they have every reason to take. But instead, they make fun of it on stage. The Beach Boys are just one prominent example of a group that has gotten hung up on trying to catch The Beatles. It's a pointless pursuit."
• There is some evidence to suggest that a piece roughly titled 'Come Back Home' is recorded on or around this date, but no further details are known.

■ Friday 15th
TV Au Palais de Chaillot *Paris, France*. France TF1 *Noel Des Enfants Du Monde (Christmas For The Children Of The World)*, UK BBC-1 *UNICEF Gala Variety From Paris*, live performance 'God Only Knows', 'Barbara Ann', 'Darlin'', 'Good Vibrations', 'Merry Christmas Baby' broadcast France December 24th ('God Only Knows', 'Merry Christmas Baby'), UK December 27th 10:15-11:38pm ('Barbara Ann', 'Darlin'', 'God Only Knows', 'Goods Vibrations'; with live English commentary by BBC DJ David Jacobs). Also appearing: Lena Horne, Victor Borge, Johnny Halliday, Ravi Shankar, Marlon

The group concludes their work for the *Wild Honey* album with 'How She Boogalooed It', logged on this 'AFM sheet' during a session at Wally Heider's Hollywood studio on November 15th.

Wild Honey album

A1 'Wild Honey' (B. WILSON / M. LOVE)
A2 'Aren't You Glad' (B. WILSON / M. LOVE)
A3 'I Was Made To Love Her' (H. COSBY / L. HARDAWAY / S. MOY / S. WONDER)
A4 'Country Air' (B. WILSON / M. LOVE)
A5 'A Thing Or Two' (B. WILSON / M. LOVE)
B1 'Darlin'' (B. WILSON / M. LOVE)
B2 'I'd Love Just Once To See You' (B. WILSON / M. LOVE)
B3 'Here Comes The Night' (B. WILSON / M. LOVE)
B4 'Let The Wind Blow' (B. WILSON / M. LOVE)
B5 'How She Boogalooed It' (M. LOVE / B. JOHNSTON / A. JARDINE / C. WILSON)
B6 'Mama Says' (B. WILSON / M. LOVE)

US release December 18th 1967 (Capitol T2859).
UK release March 1968 (Capitol T2859).
Chart high US number 24; UK number 7.

Brando, Elizabeth Taylor & Richard Burton. With repercussions from their withdrawal from the Monterey Pop Festival continuing to haunt them, The Beach Boys flew into Paris on the 13th ready to perform at today's televised Gala UNICEF Concert in Paris, suitably entitled *Gala Variety From Paris*.

It becomes the group's only studio appearance on television this year. Following an introduction by The Parisiennes, a famous French female vocal group, The Beach Boys perform live versions of five songs backed by a large multi-piece orchestra.

Also appearing on this one-hour-22-minute special is the Maharishi Mahesh Yogi, the new so-called guru to The Beatles. Their meeting with the Maharishi will bring mixed fortunes for The Beach Boys.

Mike Love will recall for Scott Keller in 1973: "We were the only rock group on the show. Beatles John and George were there because, at that time, they were intrigued by the Maharishi's practice of Transcendental Meditation. So we met the Maharishi in the hall at the rehearsals. We talked to him and asked what he thought about astrology. He replied, 'Oh, we recognise astrology but that's not what we teach. We're teaching this mental technique to give deep relaxation and create use of your mind.' It was great meeting him but we were very busy, running about, and after the show we – my wife and The Beach Boys' roadie – left and flew back to England. The other guys remained in Paris. I love England a lot and I've always preferred its atmosphere to France.

"No sooner had I reached my hotel in London than I received a call from Dennis saying, 'Hey, Mike. You've got to come back to Paris. The Maharishi is gonna teach us to meditate.' I said, 'Are you sure? Before I go flying back across the channel, make sure.'

"So, sure enough, a half-hour later he calls back and says, 'Yep, the Maharishi is gonna teach us to meditate at ten o'clock tomorrow morning. Be here. But you have to get to sleep early because you're supposed to get a lot of rest.' He told me the things I had to bring with me and I went to bed at eight o'clock in the evening and got up at four in the morning.

"We flew back across the channel, landed, got in a cab and the driver said, 'Have you been to Paris before?' And I said, 'Yes.' He

said, 'When?' I said, 'Yesterday!' We went to the hotel, met the other boys, and the Maharishi gave us an introductory lecture and then, in the afternoon, gave us another talk, and then he taught us the techniques of Transcendental Meditation.

"It was the most relaxed I had ever been in my whole life," says Mike. "I was very relaxed and it was very simple to do. I remember thinking, 'I wish everybody would do it,' because it is so simple and if everybody would do it, it would be a totally different world. So, from the very first time I meditated, I was intrigued by this. A couple of months later I found myself in India."

■ **Saturday 16th**

Smiley Smile album peaks in the US *Billboard* chart at number 41 and in the UK *Record Retailer* at number 9.

■ **Monday 18th**

Wild Honey album released in the US.
'Darlin'' / 'Here Today' single released in the US.
Just three months after the release of *Smiley Smile*, Capitol issues the R&B-flavoured 24-minute album *Wild Honey* along with the 'Darlin'' single (which comes coupled with a B-side from *Pet Sounds*).

Suitably enough given the location for most of the recordings, the cover of the *Wild Honey* album depicts a stained-glass window from Brian's home studio.

In the US, both records will reach a peak of number 24 in their respective *Billboard* charts. When the album is released in the UK early next year it will fare much better in the *Record Retailer* chart, peaking there at number 7.

In America the group's popularity hasn't completely ebbed away, but *Wild Honey* appears at a time when the new rock aristocracy – such as The Doors, The Jimi Hendrix Experience and Cream – have all released new LPs.

Subsequently The Beach Boys' simplistic style of musicianship does not stand a chance in the wake of the far-out psychedelic sounds currently filling the record charts. In addition, the group find themselves in direct competition with the *Magical Mystery Tour* compilation by The Beatles and the *Satanic Majesties Request* album by The Rolling Stones, both of which are issued this month.

The music on *Wild Honey* is respectable but Brian is disappointed and feels that the disc never equals his groundbreaking work on *Pet Sounds* or comes anywhere near the material he envisioned for *Smile*. In addition, and more alarmingly, he knows that The Beach Boys no longer stand shoulder to shoulder with The Beatles, and that his group is falling out of step with the rest of the rock world.

Further worries are heaped upon the group when the American record-buying public largely rejects The Beach Boys' new releases. Their year-long promise that great music was forthcoming again

Darlin' single

A 'Darlin'' (B. WILSON / M. LOVE)
B-US 'Here Today' (B. WILSON / P. ASHER)
B-UK 'Country Air' (B. WILSON / M. LOVE)

US release December 18th 1967 (Capitol 2068).
UK release January 1968 (Capitol CL 15527).
Chart high US number 24; UK 11.

On December 18th BBC radio DJ Alan Freeman presents the band with a gold disc for UK sales of the *Best Of The Beach Boys* compilation album.

goes to waste. As a result, fans, critics and radio programmers have become less well disposed towards new Beach Boys records.
• Meanwhile in Europe, after a day meditating in Paris with the Maharishi (see 15th), the group flies to London on the morning of Monday 18th to meet their British concert promoter, Arthur Howes, and discuss the next set of concerts in the country. America is now seemingly out of love with The Beach Boys, but the group knows they are still welcome in the UK. Tentative plans are set between the parties for a mid-spring 1968 excursion.

The Beach Boys also partake in a few radio interviews during their brief 48-hour London visit, including an appearance on a special Christmas Eve edition of *The Alan Freeman Show* taped at BBC Broadcasting House. During the visit Freeman presents the group with an award that recognises half-a-million sales of the first volume of the *Best Of The Beach Boys* album in the UK. (The interview is transmitted on BBC Radio-1 on the 24th between 5:00 and 7:00pm.)

■ Tuesday 19th
While Carl, Dennis and Al fly home to California for their Christmas holiday, Mike and Bruce remain in London for another promotional interview, this time a live appearance this afternoon at the BBC Paris Studios in central London on the Radio-1 music show *Pop Inn*, transmitted between 1:00 and 2:00pm.

■ Thursday 21st
On their last night in London, Mike and Bruce attend The Beatles' costume party at the Westbourne Suite of the Royal Lancaster Hotel in west London, held to celebrate the group's recently completed film *Magical Mystery Tour*, which is due for its television premiere on BBC-1 on the 26th.

Singers Cilla Black and Lulu and actor Robert Morley are among the other celebrities in attendance. At the end of the night the two Beach Boys jump on stage and perform an impromptu performance of 'Sloop John B' with members of The Beatles. Mike and Bruce return home to California the following morning to spend Christmas with their families.

■ Saturday 23rd
'Darlin'' single hits the US *Billboard* chart.

■ Saturday 30th
Wild Honey album hits the US *Billboard* chart.
• It has been a difficult year for the band, what with unreleased studio masterpieces and unsatisfactory live recordings, as well as a missed opportunity to enhance their hipness when they fail to appear at the Monterey Pop Festival. Their downward spiral will continue into the new year. A reversal of fortunes in their home country is still a long way off.

1968

The group, and especially Mike, become enthralled by the Maharishi and Transcendental Meditation ... recording sessions are held for the *Friends* album ... Mike flies to India to study alongside The Beatles with the Maharishi ... the group's Southern US tour is largely cancelled or re-scheduled following the murder of Martin Luther King ... Dennis meets Charles Manson ... a mostly ill-attended Beach Boys US tour with the Maharishi is halted after just seven dates ... sessions take place for *20/20* album ... *Friends* album released, but its chart peak at 126 marks the group's worst sales performance to date ... 'Do It Again' single makes US number 20 and a UK number 1 ... in a bizarre attempt to boost the group's flagging US sales, Capitol releases the *Stack-o-Tracks* backing-tracks-only album ... European tour takes place, with London performances recorded for a future live album.

The touring group in 1968: Dennis, Al, Mike, Bruce and Carl.

January

'Darlin'' / 'Country Air' single released in the US. It will peak at number 11.

• The group – and especially Mike – are keen for Brian to share in their new love for Transcendental Meditation. This month they cajole him into accompanying them to New York City where in a palatial suite at the Plaza Hotel they partake in a private meditation session with the Maharishi Mahesh Yogi.

Dennis is the first Beach Boy to speak to the Maharishi, whose opening words to Dennis are, "Live your life to the fullest."

Mike tells US radio: "One of the greatest things that interested me was that [the Maharishi] said, 'You don't have to give up your Rolls Royce and forsake all your pursuits of material pleasures to develop inner spiritual qualities.' That sounded real good to me."

Soon after this, Mike suggests to the group that Brother Records finances a documentary about the Maharishi, but the ambitious plan is soon vetoed by the rest of The Beach Boys. However, the Maharishi is excited by the idea and approaches US film company Four Star Television with the plan.

Meanwhile, undisturbed by his colleagues' rejection, Mike's liking for the guru becomes obsessive. He wastes no time in accepting an invitation to join in a forthcoming all-star gathering with the Maharishi (see February 28th).

■ Friday 5th

Back in England, miscellaneous film footage of The Beach Boys set to a soundtrack of 'Darlin'' is screened on BBC-1 (6:40-7:10pm) during tonight's edition of *All Systems Freeman*, a weekly pop music show hosted by BBC Radio-1 and *Top Of The Pops* DJ Alan Freeman. The clip will also be aired on BBC-1 in black-and-white during editions of *Top Of The Pops* broadcast on February 8th and 29th, 7:30-8:00pm.

February

RECORDING *Friends* **session 1** Brian's Home Studio *Bel Air, CA*. During this month Brian records an early version of **'When A Man Needs A Woman'** and a backing track for **'You're As Cool As Can Be'**, which will remain unreleased.

Another backing track recorded for Brother this month, **'I'm Confessin''**, may or may not be intended for The Beach Boys.

• 'Darlin'' single peaks at number 13 in Canadian RPM chart, at number 11 in UK *Record Retailer* chart, and at number 21 in Dutch chart.

■ Thursday 1st

Rainer Hall, College Gym, Everett Community College *Everett, WA* with Buffalo Springfield

With US bookings for the group apparently diminishing , their first concert duties of the new year consist of a scattering of concerts that they play with Buffalo Springfield, beginning tonight up in Washington state.

■ Friday 2nd

Seattle Sports Arena *Seattle, WA* with Buffalo Springfield

■ Saturday 3rd

The Agrodome *Vancouver, BC, Canada* with Buffalo Springfield

■ Sunday 4th

Portland Memorial Coliseum *Portland, OR* matinee show, with Buffalo Springfield; **St Martin's College, Capital Pavilion** *Lacey, WA* evening show, with Buffalo Springfield, The Surprise Package

■ Tuesday 6th

'Darlin'' single peaks in US *Billboard* chart at number 19, and in UK *Melody Maker* chart at number 10.

■ Sunday 11th

International Ice Palace *Las Vegas, NV* with Buffalo Springfield

■ Friday 16th

Capitol studio (B) *Hollywood, CA*. A session scheduled for today and paid for by Brother Records is cancelled. All 19 musicians – led by Nilsson arranger George Tipton – are paid because of insufficient notice of the cancellation. The ensemble would have featured strings, horns and keyboards.

■ Saturday 17th

Pawtuxet Ballroom *Cranston, RI* 8:00pm

After a five-day break, The Beach Boys return to the concert stage, appearing at approximately 9:05pm and performing for just 25 minutes. The large 3,000-plus crowd evidently expects a 50-minute performance. A reviewer writes in *The Providence Journal*: "Although the show did not start until 8:00pm, a line formed outside the door at 3 and more than 500 youngsters were screaming and pressing against the three closed glass doors by 6:00pm. There was some concern over whether the doors would hold and police thinned out the line until it was more than 50 yards long. At 6:30 shivering youngsters started filing into the ballroom.

"After their last number, The Beach Boys dropped their instruments, ran out of a backstage door and out of the front door of the building into a waiting cab. A fight broke out when an unidentified youth took a punch at one of The Beach Boys as the group was making a fast exit. But Captain Howard Gibbs, in charge of 12 Cranston policemen at the affair, stepped in. It was not known why the youth threw the punch. The group was pursued by several hundred youngsters as they left, but drove away with only 30 hanging on to the cab."

■ Wednesday 28th – Friday March 15th

Since meeting the Maharishi for the first time back in December, Mike's life has been greatly affected by the teachings of the Guru. Also enlightened by the Maharishi's teachings are Beatles John Lennon and George Harrison.

So when the four Beatles decide to fly out to India to sit at the feet of the Maharishi Mahesh Yogi and study Transcendental Meditation (TM) at the Maharishi's Academy of Transcendental Meditation in Rishikesh, Mike is happy to tag along and take time out from Beach Boys recording duties. But Ringo's longing for proper English food means the Beatle drummer will leave the camp shortly after Mike's arrival.

For two weeks Mike will live in the Maharishi's ashram, 150 feet above the Ganges and surrounded on three sides by jungle-covered mountains. Besides The Beatles and their respective wives and girlfriends – who began to arrive on February 15th – Mike will join American actress Mia Farrow and several others, including John Lennon's friend 'Magic' Alex Mardas and British pop star Donovan.

"The Maharishi was quite a relaxed guy," Donovan will recall in a 1998 documentary. "But once, there was quite an embarrassing

Mike arrives in India on February 28th for a two-week pilgrimage with the Maharishi Mahesh Yogi, alongside George Harrison and Ringo Starr.

silence in the room. It was just The Beatles, Mia Farrow, Mike Love and myself. Nobody was saying anything. We were all wondering what to say. John [Lennon] was so funny and so direct that, to break the silence, he went up to the Maharishi, who was sitting cross-legged on the floor, patted him on the head and said, 'There's a good little Guru.' We all laughed. It was so funny."

At first the entourage at the camp happily commit themselves to the enterprise. Over the next few weeks, Mike and the others take up residence in their own stone cottage.

The daily routine begins with some sleep-deprivation in the form of an early wake-up call to start meditation. Breakfast at the ashram is served from 7:00 to 11:00am and consists of porridge, puffed wheat or cornflakes, fruit juice, tea or coffee, toast, marmalade or jam.

Following breakfast, the entourage takes meditation practice. Lunch and dinner consists of soup followed by a vegetarian main dish, tomato or lettuce salad, turnips and carrots with rice and potatoes. The diet is strictly vegetarian, and students are required to participate in humbling chores such as latrine duty. But the atmosphere remains very happy and joyous. The participants affect a hip variant on local dress, and engage in contests to see who can meditate the longest.

Ninety-minute TM lectures are given by the Maharishi at 3:30 and 8:30pm. Soon Mike becomes an ardent convert to TM, convinced that its practice can not only change his life but also change the life of the world.

Mike tells US radio in 1972: "I was sitting in my room and the mantra I was given assumed a little melody. I was sort of singing it to myself and then, all of a sudden, from some other part of my mind, I was thinking, 'Well, I'm in India, so there's a little sitar-ish impulse to the melody.' And then I was thinking of the black kind of impulse, African, rhythmic drum impulses. Then the expression of the Latin kind of rhythm and sound and the Chinese sort of singsong approach and the Irish sort of hillbilly Appalachian music [occurred]: all elements all around the world, Eastern, Oriental, Indian, African and Russian. I mean, it was amazing, simultaneously this little original melody was being played in different instruments and voice expressions and rhythms until that sound built to a total cacophony, but it made sense.

"This whole world, in other words, in its expressions of the same sound, was in harmony, although there was a difference in each one. And then, once the whole world had attained that harmony, it became in harmony with the universe and the cosmos. And what I took it to be was a really far-out lesson that once everyone, starting with the individual, once all the nations and races became harmonious, even with their differences, only then will the world be in harmony with nature. It was neat to hear that melody building like that, like a symphony of nations."

Beatle Paul McCartney's interaction with Mike during this period results in 'Back In The USSR', a song later to appear on The Beatles' double '*White Album*' in November. Mike recalls: "I was there at the breakfast table in India when Paul came down to the table after he just wrote this song." Mike suggests to Paul that as a parody of past girls-inspired Beach Boys recordings, the Beatle should sing in the middle eight of the song about Ukraine girls.

Throughout the time that the entourage stays at the camp, members of the press wait outside, anxiously trying to catch a glimpse of one of the celebrities within.

■ **Thursday 29th**
RECORDING *Friends* **session 2** Brian's Home Studio *Bel Air, CA.*
Today's session is for **'Little Bird'** (take 7 marked as master) a song

co-written by Dennis and Stephen John Kalinich, a poet/songwriter and future Brother Records recording artist. The song will become Dennis's first released composition. Engineer is Jim Lockert on this and forthcoming sessions, which continue through April 13th.

March

Wild Honey album released in the UK. It will peak in the chart at number 7.
'Darlin'' single peaks at number 10 in New Zealand *Listener Pop-O-Meter* chart.

■ Wednesday 6th
RECORDING *Friends* session 3 Brian's Home Studio *Bel Air, CA*. With Mike away in India, the remaining Beach Boys record a preliminary instrumental track for **'Be Here In The Mornin''**, co-written by Brian, Carl, Mike, Dennis and Al. A new track will be recorded on the 29th.
Musicians present Jim Gordon (drums), Lyle Ritz (bass), Brian Wilson (probably keyboards), plus five more unknown.

■ Thursday 7th
MIXING Western Recorders studio (3) *Hollywood, CA*
Brian, Al, Dennis and Bruce travel to Western where they spend time experimenting with mixes of recent Beach Boys recordings. At least 15 mono mixes are made of Dennis's **'Little Bird'** with Brian at the helm. Only three of the mixes are wholly complete passes; the rest are false starts.

Meanwhile in an adjacent studio, Elvis Presley is taping songs for the soundtrack of his forthcoming film *Live A Little, Love A Little*. When told of the King's proximity, Brian shouts: "Don't bring him in here or I'll scream!" *NME* reports a visitor to the Beach Boys session is Monkee Peter Tork, who remarks, "I could really see the influence of the Maharishi on the guys. They used to be very confused but I talked to Dennis and he's a true spirit. He's got it. He's beautiful."

■ Saturday 9th
Wild Honey album peaks in the US *Billboard* chart at number 24.

■ Wednesday 13th
RECORDING *Friends* session 4 Brian's Home Studio *Bel Air, CA*. Today sees a session for **'Friends'**, co-written by Al, Brian, Dennis and Carl. The song's instrumental track is recorded in just six 'takes', or attempts at a recording (take 6 marked as master), followed by Carl overdubbing his lead vocal and then Brian, Al, Dennis and Bruce adding backing vocals. An alternate version of the song with a different arrangement is attempted but scrapped. Overdubbing of strings and guitar complete the session. ('Overdubbing' is the recording of additional vocals or instruments onto an existing recorded performance on tape.)

■ Thursday 14th
MIXING I.D. Sound studio *Hollywood, CA*. A mix session is held for **'Friends'** and at least three mono mixes are made.

■ Friday 15th
It is Mike's 27th birthday and his final day at the Academy of Transcendental Meditation in Rishikesh, India. Beach Boys recording commitments have forced him back to Los Angeles.

Professional rivalries between The Beach Boys and The Beatles are cast aside in the Himalayan humidity when the remaining Beatles, their wives, Donovan, Mia Farrow and miscellaneous friends give Mike a birthday send-off party, replete with musicians, magicians and fireworks.

The Beatles present Mike with a painting of the Maharishi's master, Guru Dev, and sing a medley of 'Thank You Guru Dev' (also known as 'Spiritual Regeneration') and 'Happy Birthday Michael Love', specially written by John, Paul and George and featuring the lines: "We'd like to thank you Guru Dev, but your children couldn't thank you enough, Guru Dev, Guru Dev, Guru Dev." Mike captures the performances on audio cassette (later broadcast on a 1976 US radio special and then widely bootlegged).

Afterwards, Mike leaves the Maharishi's ashram and takes a flight back to Los Angeles, and Paul and his girlfriend Jane Asher leave on March 26th.

For those remaining at the camp, bliss soon turns to disillusionment. A general consensus begins to emerge that a sophisticated businessman is conning The Beatles. According to Cynthia Lennon's *A Twist Of Lennon*, 'Magic' Alex Mardas remarks to Lennon that the Maharishi "is not what you think he is. He's just an ordinary hustler. The man's only in it for the money". Mardas is unimpressed by the Guru and confronts him, saying: "I know you! Didn't I meet you in Greece years ago?"

Almost immediately, unsubstantiated rumours about the Guru's behaviour with his students start to circulate, apparently instigated by Mardas. Lennon and Mardas conspire to catch the Maharishi in the act. On April 12th there is a sudden, bitter confrontation between Lennon, George Harrison and the Maharishi. The two Beatles storm out of the Academy and face a tense journey back to Britain, and subsequently their involvement with the Maharishi comes to a messy and unfortunate end. But The Beach Boys, chiefly through Mike, are about to take their entanglement with the Guru a step further.

• Also today, mono mixes of **'Friends'** and **'Little Bird'** are taken to Capitol's studio in Hollywood for mastering. However, it is likely that at least 'Friends' will be remixed later for the final mono single master.

■ Monday 18th
RECORDING *Friends* session 5 Brian's Home Studio *Bel Air, CA*. Back in California, sessions for the *Friends* album resume when The Beach Boys hold a further session for **'When A Man Needs A Woman'**. Brian's wife Marilyn's pregnancy with their first child, Carnie, has inspired him to write the song (although the lyrics "they make things like you my son" imply that Brian expected a boy).

Mike, freshly returned and invigorated by events in India, airs an idea for The Beach Boys to become professionally involved with the Maharishi. This time his colleagues are keen to hear Mike's proposal, and soon plans for a joint tour are formulated. A start date of May 3rd is arranged.
Musicians present David Cohen (guitar), Brian Wilson (probably keyboards), plus three unknown.

■ Wednesday 20th
RECORDING *Friends* session 6 Brian's Home Studio *Bel Air, CA*. A session takes place today for **'Our Happy Home'**, also known as 'Our New Home'. Take 5 of five takes is marked as master; following that, six takes of an insert are recorded, with the last again marked as best. No vocals are recorded, and the piece will remain unreleased.
Musicians present David Cohen (guitar), Jim Gordon (drums), plus four unknown.

■ Friday 22nd

RECORDING *Friends* session 7 Brian's Home Studio *Bel Air, CA.* Today sees a session for an instrumental, **'Passing By'**, recorded in 27 takes (take 27 marked as master). Brian has written lyrics for the track but they will remain unused. Brian, Bruce and possibly Carl play on this session.

Musicians present David Cohen (guitar), Alan Estes (percussion), Jim Gordon (drums).

■ Tuesday 26th

RECORDING *Friends* session 8 Brian's Home Studio *Bel Air, CA.* A tracking session proceeds for a song by Brian with working titles of 'Even Steven' or 'Even Time'. ('Tracking' is the term for the initial recording of backing instruments only.) Soon afterwards the piece is given its more permanent title of **'Busy Doin' Nothin'.** Today's recording of the song is faster than the released version, which is made on April 11th.

Musicians present Alan Estes (percussion), Gene Pello (drums).

■ Thursday 28th

RECORDING *Friends* session 9 Brian's Home Studio *Bel Air, CA.* A tracking session and a strings overdub session are held for **'Wake The World'**, Brian and Al's first co-composition.

Musicians present Dick Hyde (probably trombone), Tommy Morgan (harmonica), Lyle Ritz (bass), plus two unknown; and eight-piece string section.

• Also today a recording session paid for by The Beach Boys is held at I.D. Sound studio for potential Brother artists Benny & Sam. Twelve takes of their **'Everything That Is Good To You'** are taped.

■ Friday 29th

RECORDING *Friends* session 10 I.D. Sound studio *Hollywood, CA.* For a while from now, sessions move from Brian's home studio to the much larger I.D. facility where today the group undertakes a second instrumental tracking session for **'Be Here In The Mornin''** that produces the released version of the song (take 22 is the master).

Musicians present Alan Estes (percussion), Lyle Ritz (bass), plus four unknown.

■ Saturday 30th

RECORDING *Friends* session 11 I.D. Sound studio *Hollywood, CA.* Working with the backing track recorded on March 28th, the group overdubs vocals for **'Wake The World'**.

■ Sunday 31st

RECORDING *Friends* session 12 I.D. Sound studio *Hollywood, CA.* Using a tracking tape recorded on March 29th, the group overdubs vocals onto take 22 of **'Be Here In The Mornin''**.

April

TOUR STARTS US South/Midwest (Apr 1st-22nd)
The group sets out on another concert tour almost entirely in the South, originally set to run until April 22nd and taking in 33 shows in 18 days, but circumstances beyond their control will conspire against its completion. Accompanying them is a special PA system and eight musicians wearing black turtleneck sweaters and playing piano, organ, saxophone, cello, trumpet, flute, French horn, and congas. Brian tells *Melody Maker*: "The idea is to try to have the presentation as nice as possible." For each gig on this tour The

Beach Boys are paid $5,000 from which they are responsible for paying the guest musicians as well as the two regular support acts. The MC at the concerts is fast-talking South Carolina DJ Davy Jones – no relation to the singer with The Monkees.

■ Monday 1st

RECORDING *Friends* session 13 I.D. Sound studio *Hollywood, CA.* This morning the group is back at I.D. where they record the short song **'Meant For You'**. Originally titled 'You'll Find It Too', this simple song is recorded in just three takes.

Veterans Memorial Coliseum Columbus, OH with The Strawberry Alarm Clock, Buffalo Springfield; compère: Davy Jones
Recordings over, the touring band travels on to Ohio for the first date of this new concert tour – as ever now without Brian, who will not return to regular live appearances with the group until 1976.

■ Tuesday 2nd

RECORDING *Friends* session 14 I.D. Sound studio *Hollywood, CA.* An early-morning session finds the group back in Hollywood for **'Anna Lee The Healer'**, a musical tribute to a masseuse who "knew how to use her hands to make you feel a lot better". The song requires 37 takes to complete, with take 37 marked as master.

Cincinnati Gardens Cincinnati, OH with The Strawberry Alarm Clock, Buffalo Springfield; compère: Davy Jones
The group now travels again for the next live date in Ohio.

■ Wednesday 3rd

Indiana Theater Indianapolis, IN with The Strawberry Alarm Clock, Buffalo Springfield; compère: Davy Jones
After just three shows of the tour, the tour is about to face major disruption after the events of Thursday 4th.

■ Thursday 4th

RECORDING *Friends* session 15 I.D. Sound studio *Hollywood, CA.* Early today The Beach Boys are again back at I.D. in Hollywood to begin recording the instrumental track for **'Transcendental Meditation'**, a song resulting from the Maharishi's influence on Mike. The session concludes with Al overdubbing his lead vocal, which he shares with Brian.

Musicians present Jim Gordon (drums), Lyle Ritz (bass), plus ten unknown.

• Recordings over, the touring group prepares for a flight to Nashville. But events conspire against them as civil rights leader Rev Dr Martin Luther King Jr is assassinated in Memphis, Tennessee. Beach Boys business manager Nick Grillo tells *Amusement Business* magazine: "Exactly as we boarded the plane for Nashville, we got the news that Martin Luther King had been shot. When we landed in Nashville, the announcement was made that he was dead."

Further dates on the tour are cancelled now as riots erupt and curfews are imposed in many of the Southern cities where The Beach Boys are set to perform. Financial losses are devastating and the package tour turns into a disaster.

Cancelled or postponed concerts: Municipal Auditorium *Nashville, TN* (April 5th; promoter Lon Varnell says he hopes to reschedule a later date); East Carolina College, Minges Coliseum *Raleigh, NC* (6th 1:00pm); Dorton Arena *Raleigh, NC* (6th 8:30pm; rescheduled for April 23rd); Clemson University Field House *Columbia, SC* (7th 2:30pm); University of North Carolina *Greensboro, NC* (7th 8:00pm; rescheduled for April 25th); Charleston County Hall *Charleston, WV* (8th 7:00pm); Columbia Township Auditorium *Columbia, SC* (8th 8:45pm); George Jenkins Field House, Florida Southern College *Lakeland Township, FL* (9th 4:30pm); Orlando

Sports Stadium *Orlando, FL* (9th 7:00pm); Memorial Stadium *Daytona, FL* (9th 8:45pm); City Auditorium *Gainesville, FL* (10th); Civic Auditorium *Atlanta, GA* (11th matinee); Macon City Auditorium *Macon, GA* (11th 7:00pm); Curtis Hixon Hall *Tampa, FL* (13th); Robarts Sports Arena *Sarasota, FL* (13th 7:00pm); Florida Atlantic College *Ft Lauderdale, FL* (14th), Municipal Auditorium *Austin, TX* (15th); Robinson Auditorium *Norman, AR* (16th matinee); Civic Auditorium *Little Rock, AR* (16th evening); Mid-South Coliseum *Memphis, TN* (17th; rescheduled for April 24th); LA State University, John M. Parker Agricultural Center *Baton Rouge, LA* (18th).

■ Saturday 6th

With The Beach Boys' latest concert tour in complete disarray, and with no serious recording time scheduled until April 11th, Dennis takes it easy this afternoon. "I went up into the mountains with my houseboy to take an LSD trip," he tells British journalist David Griffiths. "We met two girls hitchhiking. One of them was pregnant. We gave them a lift and a purse was left in the car." The girls are Ella Jo Bailey and Patricia Krenwinkel. (See 11th.)

■ Monday 8th

'Friends' / 'Little Bird' single released in the US.

■ Wednesday 10th

University of Florida, Florida Field *Jacksonville, FL* 7:00pm, with The Strawberry Alarm Clock, Buffalo Springfield; compère: Davy Jones

This is the first concert of the group's current tour to go ahead since Martin Luther King Jr was assassinated on the 4th. Following the show, which attracts 5,200 people, The Beach Boys donate $1,000 from their own pockets towards the funding of a new basketball coliseum at the Field House.

■ Thursday 11th

With concerts today in Georgia cancelled and with time on his hands before the recording session scheduled for tonight, Dennis spends the afternoon cruising the streets of Malibu. He again sees the girls he'd given a lift to last Saturday. "I told them about our involvement with the Maharishi and they told me they too had a guru," says Dennis, "a guy named Charlie who'd recently come out of jail after 12 years. His mother was a hooker and his father was a gangster. Charlie had drifted into crime but when I met him I found out that he had great musical ideas. We began writing together. He taught me a dance, The Inhibition. You have to imagine you're a frozen man and the ice is thawing out. Start with your fingertips, then all the rest of you, then you extend it to a feeling that the whole universe is thawing out."

Friends single

A 'Friends' (B. WILSON / C. WILSON / D. WILSON / A. JARDINE)
B 'Little Bird' (D. WILSON / S. KALINICH)

US release April 8th 1968 (Capitol 2160).
UK release May 1968 (Capitol CL 15545).
Chart high US number 47; UK number 25.

He takes them back to his palatial home at 14400 Sunset Boulevard, a hunting lodge once owned by cowboy actor Will Rogers. Dennis impresses the girls by guiding them round his large, sprawling home and showing off his numerous gold records. After further conversations about their mysterious acquaintance Charlie, Dennis excuses himself, telling them that he has to leave for a recording session. He departs leaving Ella Jo and Patricia alone in his house.

RECORDING *Friends* session 16 I.D. Sound studio *Hollywood, CA.* Later this evening Brian oversees the recording with engineer Jim Lockert of a new tracking tape for **'Busy Doin' Nothing'** (formerly known as 'Even Steven' or 'Even Time'), first attempted on March 26th. Today 27 takes are recorded, with the last marked as master. Brian then overdubs a lead vocal and doubles his lead in sections onto the new tracking tape, completing the version that will be released. The autobiographical lyrics describe an average day in Brian's life around this time. If you follow the directions (provided you know where to start) you will arrive at Brian's Bellagio Road house in Bel Air. At the conclusion of the sessions, in the early hours of the morning, each member of the group returns home.
Musicians present James Ackley (probably keyboards), Lyle Ritz (bass), Al Vescovo (guitar), plus one unknown.

• At approximately 3:00am Dennis pulls into the driveway of his home on Sunset Boulevard. As he gets out of the car he notices a small, shadowy figure approaching him. Naturally startled, Dennis asks, "Are you going to hurt me?" The strange small man stands before him and replies, "Do I look like I'm going to hurt you, brother?" The stranger calms Dennis by sinking to his knees and kissing Dennis's training shoes. He says that he is "a philosopher, a god, and a musician". Dennis does not realise that the man has arrived at his home following an invitation from the two hitchhikers he picked up in Malibu earlier today.

The man is Charles Milles Manson – better known to some as 'The Wizard'. Manson cannot bear to be parted for too long from his girls. In Dennis's absence, Manson has already decided to take up residence in Dennis's home along with about a dozen more girls. Dennis is unaware of this until this morning when he finds his palatial house overrun and invaded by party animals. Dennis, not one to turn down an attractive young girl, does not mind allowing the strange man and his girls to stay the evening – or for as long as they like.

There is plenty of space at his home, and Dennis likes the idea of a dozen or more roommates. In his mind – and especially in light of his ongoing divorce from his first wife, Carol – there is no reason why they shouldn't all stay. In addition, Charlie offers free spiritual counsel. He and Dennis become friends and, over the next five months, Dennis's home becomes an open house to The Wizard and his 'Family'. Dennis's extravagance even stretches to giving Charlie a present of nine or ten of his gold discs received for Beach Boys record sales.

Immediately, Manson's Family begins to make full use of the luxurious amenities on offer, including Dennis's well-appointed alcohol cabinet and large swimming pool. In return for this, Dennis is given unlimited access to Charlie's stock of drugs and girls, who generally wander the house in a permanent state of undress. The girls, all mentally 'doctored' by Manson, have no inhibitions. They also have a craving for drugs, and work on orders from Manson to cook, clean and 'be nice' to all men. Charlie plays to Dennis the tunes he has composed, and Dennis begins to peddle Manson and his music to the other Beach Boys and anyone else who cares to listen. He tries to get everyone to listen to Charlie's work. But the act will not achieve success.

■ Friday 12th

RECORDING *Friends* session 17 I.D. Sound studio *Hollywood, CA.* 12midday-3:00pm. Back in the studio there's a tracking session with engineer Jim Lockert for the instrumental **'Diamond Head'**, co-written by guitarist Al Vescovo.

Musicians present James Ackley (probably keyboards), Lyle Ritz (ukulele), Al Vescovo (electric steel guitar), plus one unknown.

Jacksonville Coliseum *Jacksonville, FL* 8:00pm, with The Strawberry Alarm Clock, Buffalo Springfield; compère: Davy Jones

Before tonight's show – only the second of the planned tour to materialise in the last nine days – Mike presents Sister Shirley, supervisor of the local St. Vincent's Hospital operating room, with a $450 donation on behalf of The Beach Boys. The money contributes to the purchase of important equipment for open-heart surgery. The group has decided on the donation after viewing a film on the subject earlier today.

■ Saturday 13th

RECORDING *Friends* session 18 Brian's Home Studio *Bel Air, CA* 2:00-4:00pm. Dennis comes to Brian's studio where he records vocals and organ for his composition with Steve Kalinich, **'Be Still'**. With this, the sessions for the forthcoming *Friends* album are concluded. Further Beach Boys recording sessions will not take place until May 26th.

• The Wilsons' mother Audree recalls later in *Rolling Stone* that after the session Dennis asks if she will take him back to his home on Sunset Boulevard, where the Manson 'Family' is still in residence. "And I was very hesitant," says Audree, "because I thought, 'Oh god! Murry's not going to like this.' But I took him home and he said, 'Will you come in and meet them? Come on, they're nice.' And I said, 'Dennis, promise me that you won't tell dad.' So I went in and Charlie Manson was walking through this big yard with a long robe on. Dennis introduced me to him. I thought he looked older than he supposedly is – like an older man. We went into the house and I think three girls were in the house, just darling young girls, I thought, but leeches. I zipped through the house, got back in my car and left. And wouldn't you know Dennis told his dad [that I took him home]? He didn't like it."

■ Sunday 14th

Miami Beach Convention *Center Miami, FL* 8:00pm, with The Strawberry Alarm Clock, Buffalo Springfield, The Echoes; compère: Davy Jones

At last, some of the planned concerts on the tour begin to go ahead, with tonight's attended by a crowd of 8,000.

■ Monday 15th

San Antonio Municipal Auditorium *San Antonio, TX* 7:30pm, with The Strawberry Alarm Clock, Buffalo Springfield; compère: Davy Jones

■ Wednesday 17th

Arkansas State University *Jonesboro, AR* 8:00pm, with The Strawberry Alarm Clock, Buffalo Springfield; compère: Davy Jones

Tonight's concert is an addition to the original schedule.

■ Thursday 18th

Loyola Field House, Loyola University *New Orleans, LA* 8:45pm, with The Strawberry Alarm Clock, Buffalo Springfield; compère: Davy Jones

Eldridge Roark writes in *The Daily Reveille*: "The acoustics of the cow barn, while great for hog calling, did not do a thing for the super shattering amplified Beach Boys, Strawberry Alarm Clock and Buffalo Springfield. If it were not for the mass of teenyboppers in the place, the show would have been a complete flop!

"The Beach Boys, arriving in their super-cool white suits and sneakers, sang in the style that most of the upperclassmen on the campus twisted to at their High School prom. Songs like 'Help Me Rhonda' and 'Surfer Girl' were quite popular five years ago, but drew snide side comments and yawns from the older element of the crowd.

"Of course, the 12-year-olds completely blew their minds. The best contribution from The Beach Boys was 'Good Vibrations', which seemed to lend itself more to the styles of music enjoyed today. ... The Buffalo Springfield was easily the most enjoyable group heard this evening."

■ Friday 19th

Birmingham City Municipal Auditorium *Birmingham, AL* 8:30pm, with The Strawberry Alarm Clock, Buffalo Springfield, Randy's World; compère: Davy Jones

Gene Butts writes in the *Birmingham News*: "An evening well spent for pop music lovers all over Alabama. The near perfect program was exciting, both musically and visually, and the applause was frequent, spontaneous and energetic.

"The Buffalo Springfield, who took their name from the world's most powerful steamroller, lived up to their title. Dressed in Confederate uniforms, with a Confederate flag draping the amplifier, they established an immediate and close rapport with the audience. It was sustained throughout the program.

"Then came The Beach Boys. They declared that meditation gave them increased energy and they unleashed it all. Their ability to score in different musical styles was apparent from the first minute.

"They played a medley of their original surfing songs and other successes, including 'Sloop John B' and 'Good Vibrations'. Dennis, the barefoot drummer, leaped down from the bandstand to join the group in their newest release, 'Friends'. The evening came to an end on a note of exuberance as members of the entire cast danced and pranced about the stage in a happy finale."

■ Saturday 20th

Will Rogers Coliseum *Fort Worth, TX* 7:00pm; **Market Hall Dance** *Dallas, TX* 8:30pm; both with The Strawberry Alarm Clock, Buffalo Springfield; compère: Davy Jones

• 'Friends' single hits US charts. It will peak at number 47.

■ Sunday 21st

Moody Civic Center *Galveston, TX* 2:00pm; **McDonald Gym, Lamar Technical College** *Houston, TX* 4:30pm; **Sam Houston Coliseum** *Houston, TX* 7:30pm; all with The Strawberry Alarm Clock, Buffalo Springfield; compère: Davy Jones

■ Monday 22nd

Civic Auditorium *Little Rock, AR* matinee; **Municipal Coliseum** *Lubbock, TX* 8:00pm; both with The Strawberry Alarm Clock, Buffalo Springfield; compère: Davy Jones

■ Tuesday 23rd

Greensboro Coliseum *Greensboro, NC* matinee; **Dorton Arena, North Carolina State Fairgrounds** *Raleigh, NC* evening; both with The Strawberry Alarm Clock, Buffalo Springfield; compère: Davy Jones

The evening concert has been rescheduled from April 6th.

■ Wednesday 24th

Mid-South Coliseum *Memphis, TN* 8:00pm, with The Strawberry Alarm Clock, Buffalo Springfield; compère: Davy Jones

Rescheduled from April 17th. Radio station WMPS sponsors the concert, which is attended by 4,500.

Set-list 'Help Me Rhonda', 'I Get Around', 'Friends', 'Surfer Girl', 'Sloop John B', 'Wouldn't It Be Nice', 'Darlin'', 'God Only Knows', 'Good Vibrations', 'Surfin' Safari', 'Fun Fun Fun', 'Shut Down', 'Little Deuce Coupe', 'Surfin' USA', 'Papa-Oom-Mow-Mow', 'Graduation Day', 'Barbara Ann'.

■ Thursday 25th

University of North Carolina *Greensboro, NC* with The Strawberry Alarm Clock, Buffalo Springfield; compère: Davy Jones

Tonight's concert has been rescheduled from April 7th.

■ Saturday 27th

Fort Worth Tarrant County Convention Center *Dallas, TX* with The Strawberry Alarm Clock, Buffalo Springfield; compère: Davy Jones

After this, the final show of this ill-fated tour, The Beach Boys hold an autograph party for their fans back at their hotel and, at midnight, partake in an end-of-tour jam session with members of The Strawberry Alarm Clock and Buffalo Springfield. When the dust settles, it is estimated that the excursion has cost the group $350,000 in lost revenue. As if this isn't bad enough, their luck will continue to ebb away when on May 3rd the group's next foray into live performances again turns into a farce.

Their business manager Nick Grillo recalls in 1974 for BBC Radio-1: "After the disaster of our April tour, we re-grouped and started to prepare for the May tour with the Maharishi – and that tour was quite a fiasco. He was in Europe contemplating doing a film for Four Star Television, but he had already committed through his American representative to do the tour with The Beach Boys. We had major halls in major cities mapped out. The [plan was that the] boys would perform and, in the second half, the Maharishi would have a question-and-answer forum."

May

'Friends' / 'Little Bird' single released in the UK.

'How She Boogalooed It' single peaks in Swedish Radio 3 chart at number 10.

'Friends' single peaks in New Zealand *Listener Pop-O-Meter* chart at number 21.

■ Thursday 2nd

Just three weeks after his disagreement with John Lennon and George Harrison in India, the Maharishi Mahesh Yogi fails to show for a press conference at the Plaza Hotel in New York City arranged to promote his forthcoming concert tour with The Beach Boys. Waiting reporters are told, incorrectly, that the Guru is laid up with pneumonia in Kashmir, India. Beach Boys business manager Nick Grillo remembers on BBC Radio-1: "The Maharishi was delayed because he had signed an agreement to carry on with his filming with Four Star. It got to the point where we almost had to threaten litigation in order for him to acknowledge his responsibility to us, which he eventually did."

At this point the group's tour with the Maharishi Mahesh Yogi, promoted through Budd Filippo Attractions, is scheduled to run for 17 performances in various non-commercial venues. The plan is that the Maharishi will give a lecture on Transcendental Meditation following a performance by the group. It is Mike's idea, apparently one that only cultural outsiders and over-enthusiastic rock musicians are able to recognise as viable. The Guru insists that his share of the proceeds from the tour, after expenses, should go towards his Transcendental Spiritual Regeneration Centers throughout the world.

TOUR STARTS Beach Boys' US tour with Maharishi Mahesh Yogi (May 3rd-21st)

■ Friday 3rd

Washington Coliseum *Washington, DC* 7:30pm; Baltimore Civic Center Baltimore, MD 9:30pm

A 6:00pm press conference at Georgetown University's Gaston Hall in Washington kicks off the eventful schedule of the Maharishi/Beach Boys tour. Students are urged to sign up with the Student International Meditation Society, with a $35 donation invited from students, $75 non-students.

John Sherwood writes in Washington's *Evening Star*: "We were waiting for The Beach Boys' Guru at Georgetown University … but he was delayed en route from New York by a May storm. He was in a chartered jet and [I and the other reporters] wondered why he couldn't wave his hand and calm the skies. The students at the University were serving a mild wine punch spiked with strawberries. The press conference atmosphere was giggly in anticipation of the beacon of light of the Himalayas.

"The Maharishi arrived an hour late in a chartered black Cadillac Fleetwood limousine. He shuffled slowly in wooden sandals. His feet were nut brown and clean. His robes were of a cocoon silk, and his hair was shoulder length and streaked with grey. His beard was a rabbit tail, cotton white, and his moustache was black. And he smiled the contended smile of a new bridegroom coming down the aisle.

"His eyes were syrupy brown, dark and untroubled. His hands were the delicate hands of a potter. Childlike, innocent and bright-eyed naive, he was clearly not of this world at this time and this place. The Maharishi was coming to Mohammed on the sacred banks of the Potomac, but in search of what? He was coming with … he was coming with … The Beach Boys, a fading rock music group in white suits bent on a head-shrinking concert tour of 20 appearances in 19 days, from here to California.

"The holy man settled on an early American couch at Gaston Hall, sitting cross-legged in the traditional lotus position. He fingered a yellow flower, plucking petals from it while listening to a distant tinkle of bells. Photographers swarmed around him on stage as he relaxed on an antelope skin. His eyes remained closed in meditation for several minutes and then they opened and he smiled and looked around. He spoke softly about awareness and inner being and the underlying level of life. He talked of his Spiritual Regeneration Movement Foundation and full self-realisation.

"Someone asked him, 'How do you view Jesus Christ, his death and resurrection?' The Maharishi sniffed at a flower and said, 'With all admiration, I think.' When he left around 8:00pm for a scheduled 7:30pm concert at the Washington Coliseum with The Beach Boys, who began the performance after 8:00pm, there was not much of the Hindu con artist about him. Rather, there was the feeling of a Hindu Fakir being conned."

Maharishi tells the gathered reporters, "You don't want to miss the joys of the inner life, and you don't want to miss the joys of the outer world. Live 200 per cent of life as 100 per cent outer, material life and 100 per cent as inner spiritual life. All problems of all countries will be solved automatically when each country has fully-developed citizens. Meditation would end not only wars but also natural disasters, which are the results of eruptions and hostile influences in the atmosphere."

The opening concert of the Beach Boys/Maharishi tour also gets off to a rocky start, reaching farcical status when an audience of only 1,500 is present at the Washington Coliseum, nearly all of them students. The venue is capable of holding 8,000.

William Rice depicts the event for his readers in *The Washington Post*: "A foreigner once told me that Americans were the world's most polite people. Events at the Washington Coliseum almost convinced me he was right. A sparse gathering, not more than 1,000, applauded a dreadful concert by The Beach Boys. ... The group, in basic white suits, with shoes, shirts and ties to suit, performed before the intermission. A badly conceived sound system and the echoes that occur in the cavernous Coliseum contributed to make the group nearly inaudible.

"The songs they did, about 11 in all, sounded mediocre at the best when heard through the din of an under-rehearsed and over-modulated back-up orchestra. They are choral singers bred in the recording studio, and the tight harmony that gave them individuality as a group was lost in the arena. For their last effort ('Graduation Day') they dismissed the band, laid aside their electric instruments, stood as an old-fashioned campus singing group, and sang a cappella – badly! The whole performance had the air of a badly run wake for electrified pop music. One could only think of The Beatles' decision to stop touring and admire them anew."

Immediately after their short, 40-minute performance at the Coliseum, The Beach Boys call for an intermission and head off to Baltimore's Civic Center where they perform the second show of this tour, but the attendance there is also poor, with just 2,888 present in a venue comfortably catering for 11,500. The group's previous appearance at the venue on November 26th last year drew a 5,000-plus crowd.

"Even before The Beach Boys left for Baltimore," says Sherwood, "they were already 30 minutes late for their show – and the Maharishi hadn't even arrived at the Coliseum. When he finally arrived, the sparse crowd giggled when he sat Buddha-style front and center and closed his eyes in meditation. This was supposed to be the second half of the show, folks."

Rice continues: "The Maharishi held down the second half of the [Coliseum] event (somehow concert isn't the right word). He carried out a 30-minute sermon from a green couch. Only the occasional flower falling from his lap to the floor and an occasional hand gesture marred the calm." Sherwood takes up the story: "[The Maharishi] then spoke for some 25 minutes but the acoustics were bad and that's one thing the Maharishi can't afford, bad acoustics. He was trying to spread his philosophy of outer peace through inner peace, before returning to the seclusion of the Himalayas. He was trying to tell them that his meditation has nothing to do with booze, LSD, pot or speed."

■ Saturday 4th

Iona College New *Rochelle*, NY 5:00pm; **Philadelphia Spectrum, St. John's College *Philadelphia, PA*** 8:30pm
The bad vibes of the tour roll on when at 1:40pm, just 20 minutes before an afternoon show is due to begin at the Singer Bowl in Flushing, NY, it is called off because the audience within the 16,000-capacity venue totals just 800. There is better luck at nearby Iona College when a few hours later a show takes place before 1,800 spectators. But it is not well received. Brother Derby T. Ruane,

director of the school's Institute for the Arts, says: "The Beach Boys came on first but there was a considerable delay before the Guru came on. The crowd was edgy by the time the monologue was launched and he drew considerable heckling."

There is no great improvement later in Philadelphia. A spokesman for the 17,162-seater Spectrum says: "The Guru couldn't draw flies. Tickets went for just $5 and $3 and people walked out before and during the Guru's lecture. The attendance was about 5,800."

■ Sunday 5th

Bushnell Auditorium *Hartford*, CT 5:00pm; Providence Arena Providence, RI 8:30pm
Three days into the tour and at last there is good news as The Beach Boys/Maharishi tour plays to a audience of 3,000 in the 3,277-seater Bushnell Auditorium. But the luck doesn't last long: the next show, scheduled at the 6,887-capacity Providence Arena, runs into serious problems.

At 3:00pm the situation seems normal when Beach Boys road manager Dick Duryea contacts the Arena to check with the organisers that everything is OK for tonight's performance.

Edward Ellsworth, assistant treasurer of the Rhode Island facility, tells *Amusement Business*: "I talked with them at 3:00pm and they said they'd see me that evening. But at 6:00 I was informed that there would be no show and that the Guru had separated from The Beach Boys to fulfil a movie contract. I asked Duryea to bring the group to Providence without the Maharishi and [said] that I would make a public announcement offering refunds to anyone who wanted their money back. But it was no dice.

"I was told that the package was tied to the Guru and without him there was no package. Despite the lateness, we could have had between 3,500 and 4,000. The Beach Boys drew 6,400 here last November. Most of all, I feel bad for those 1,600 kids who bought tickets in advance. I feel bad that they didn't come for those kids."

Beach Boys business manager Nick Grillo says on US radio: "The problems on the tour came to a head when we played in Rhode Island. The Four Star Television people, who were at the concert, were trying to negotiate a way to have the Maharishi continue with our tour and, at the same time, fulfil his commitment to [make a film with] Four Star.

"We decided," says Grillo, "that rather than embark on the rest of the tour and lose money, and create a great deal of ill feeling with he Maharishi and the Four Star [people, we would] abandon the rest of the tour. A press conference was held and we told the press that the Maharishi was ill due to his trek through Europe prior to coming to the country. In fact, when he did arrive in America, he was ill and wasn't getting any better. We said he was convalescing somewhere in Santa Barbara but, in fact, he had left the country."

■ Monday 6th

With an absent Maharishi, The Beach Boys have no alternative but to cancel the rest of the tour after only seven performances. Al says later: "The tour completely fell on its ass. Talk about weird. That was the greatest mismatch of all time. There was no relevance to it. Our careers had distinct paths, neither of which belonged on the same stage together."

The cancelled performances are: Boston Gardens *Boston, MA* (May 6th); Brandeis University *Waltham, MA*, New Haven Arena *New Haven, CT*, Quinnipiac College *Hamden, CT* (7th); Vets Memorial Auditorium *Columbus, OH* (8th); Ohio State University *Buffalo, NY* (9th); Syracuse University *Syracuse, NY*, LeMoyne College, *Syracuse, NY* (10th); Richfield Coliseum *Cleveland, OH* (11th); Chicago

University *Chicago, IL* (12th); Capitol Theater *Madison, WI* (13th); St. Paul's Arena *St. Paul, MN* (14th); Veterans Memorial Auditorium *Des Moines, IA*, Municipal Auditorium *Kansas City, MO* (15th); Kiel Auditorium *St Louis, MO* (16th); Denver Auditorium *Denver, CO* (17th); Oakland Stadium *Oakland, CA* (18th); Hollywood Bowl *Los Angeles, CA*, University of Nevada *Las Vegas, NV* (19th); Frost Theater, Stanford University *Stanford, CA* (20th); Sacramento State College *Sacramento, CA*, San Diego International Sports Arena *San Diego, CA* (21st).

Mike tells *NME* shortly afterwards: "At first we were all enthused about [the Maharishi's] spiritual regeneration movement. It was not as flashy as the drug scene and at the time we believed in him – as I still do – and we wanted to bring him to American colleges campuses to spread the Transcendental Meditation word. The tour was not designed to enrich the coffers of the group. The show was not put together for commercial purposes.

"We did the tour with the Maharishi to help him establish meditation centres around the country because we believe in meditation and think it is good. We wanted to help him reach the young people on college campuses. The agreement was that we would perform and the Yogi would propagate his philosophy.

"The agents booked us into the wrong theatres, very commercial auditoriums, and charged too much money for entry so that we were getting the wrong crowd. We cancelled out and the Maharishi went home. The assassination of Dr Martin Luther King, not the allegation that the Yogi couldn't draw flies, was another reason for the demise of the tour."

Beach Boys road manager Dick Duryea rates the tour as "the biggest fiasco of my life. The Maharishi was a nice enough man, but no one wanted to listen to him. Everyone came to see The Beach Boys. When he came on stage and started talking, the audience just left. … Mike Love dearly loves the man and his philosophy. The Beach Boys must have lost a quarter of a million dollars on that tour."

Beach Boys business manager Nick Grillo says: "A lot of people felt that The Beach Boys were trying to capitalise on something that The Beatles had made popular, which wasn't the case at all. I felt that The Beach Boys were very serious about Transcendental Meditation, but at the time the Maharishi was receiving a lot of severe criticism from the American press. So the tour did not develop as well as anticipated."

It is estimated that the group's two disastrous tours this year have cost The Beach Boys a total of somewhere around half a million dollars. In reference to the rather ornate stage sets that have been used for the shows so far, Al tells *Newsweek*: "If anybody will benefit from this, it will be the florists."

Thursday 9th
TV Westinghouse Broadcasting Company, Group W Productions *Philadelphia, PA*. Syndicated *The Mike Douglas Show* lip-synch 'Friends', nationally broadcast from May 15th. This afternoon, free from their concert duties, The Beach Boys accept an invitation to tape their first appearance on this afternoon chat show. During their slot the group is interviewed; also on today's show are guests Michael Dunn and Lanie Kazan.

Saturday 11th
With their American popularity at an all-time low, The Beach Boys' once strong appeal in the UK also shows signs of weakening as one-time supporter Penny Valentine writes in today's *Disc & Music Echo*: "A carefully calculated warning to The Beach Boys – split up or get yourself together. There is something very stale in The Beach Boys camp. It is the smell of utter freedom run amok. It is the smell of staleness and inertia.

"It is not pleasant to reflect upon The Beach Boys and see what could have been and then face what is," Valentine continues. "This fact has been brought home to me by the group's latest release. 'Friends' is about the ultimate in sadness. Whither the progressive Beach Boys? Whither the same spine-tingling sensation one got with 'God Only Knows', The Beach Boys' answer to The Four Tops' 'Reach Out'? Gone, gone, gone. It has been suffocated in the same boring, muffled voices, the same trivial words, the same droning, friendly-dull atmosphere.

"If The Beach Boys are as bored as they sound, they should stop bothering and retreat to the Californian foothills. If they're not, they should stop boring their public and insulting them with below-par performances. Three years ago The Beach Boys gave us the throttled heady taste of Californian summer. The sun always shining, the surf always coming into land, brown young bodies on a beach, summery love in the long grass. They gave it to us through a record, frothy as the top of a Coca-Cola and burning as a 350cc Honda. They had a hardcore following here in gritty England, a mammoth one in America. Their final and complete connection with the pubic came with 'God Only Knows', 'Good Vibrations' and the beautiful *Pet Sounds*. It turned out to be their zenith.

"They had started something new and thrilling – a great kick in the stomach for pop music. Brian Wilson was lauded and acclaimed with all the power we could muster. But instead of leading us on and on to newer and more exciting things, they began a steady plunge downhill. Instead of thrusting us upwards, they led us round the maypole with nonsense like 'Then I Kissed Her'.

"Today, The Beach Boys are floundering pathetically in a mire of stodgy apathy. It is now time for them to stand still and take stock of themselves and the situation they are in today. They have been given too much freedom. Like greedy schoolboys in a sweetshop their sense has not prevailed – their control has snapped. They are no longer the brilliant Beach Boys. They are grey and they are making sad little grey records."

Wednesday 15th
With The Beach Boys' tour with the Maharishi now cancelled, Al and Bruce travel to Capitol Records' HQ in Hollywood to sign a contract that authorises the record company to use their name, signature, likeness, voice, sound effects and so on, as part of The Beach Boys.

Saturday 18th
'Friends' single peaks in US chart at 47 and in UK chart at 25.

Friday 24th
RECORDING *20/20* **session 1** Brian's Home Studio *Bel Air, CA*. There is some evidence that the group work on **'All I Want To Do'** on or around this date.

Sunday 26th
RECORDING *20/20* **session 2** Brian's Home Studio *Bel Air, CA*. After a six-week hiatus, Beach Boys recording sessions resume as they begin work on the album that will become *20/20*. Today the group records tracking tapes and vocals for a version of **'Walk On By'**, the Burt Bacharach and Hal David classic, and **'Old Folks At Home (Swanee River)'** / **'Ol' Man River'**. The first part of 'Old Folks' is a cover of Stephen Foster's traditional American classic, the second a cover of a song that originally appeared in the Broadway musical *Showboat*. Both recordings will remain unreleased until their appearance on the 1990 Capitol CD *Friends / 20/20*.

Sessions today also focus on **'Do It Again'** (originally entitled 'Rendezvous') with joint production by Brian and Carl. Mike has been inspired to write the song this month after surfing with an old friend, Bill Jackson. Mike's feeling of nostalgia is so vivid that he decides to turn it into a song, and Brian comes up with a catchy tune to go with the deja-vu lyrics. Brian will come to regard this song as the best of his collaborations with Mike.

Soon after a quick studio demonstration by Brian, the speedily recorded song begins life with Mike taping a vocal against the full Beach Boys line-up on guitar, organ, bass and drums. At first Mike's vocal has the lyric "Let's get back together and surf again" but he soon changes it to the released version's "…and do it again". Onto this, the group dubs additional backing vocals, a guitar/organ instrumental insert, and a new guitar solo. A saxophone track, additional percussion and handclaps are added to complete the 4-track recording. The heavy snare-drum beat on the very opening of the song becomes a strong hook when the recording is released as a single in the US on July 8th. It's not entirely clear how Brian achieves the distinctive sound of the drum, but it seems to be filtered with some kind of intense 'limiting'. The sound of hammering at the close of the *20/20* album version of 'Do It Again' is lifted from the unreleased *Smile* piece 'I'm In Great Shape' or 'Friday Night' (see November 29th 1966).

Carl admits in *Melody Maker*: "Yes, I suppose it has got the old Beach Boys surfing sound. It's back to that surfing idea with the voice harmony and the simple, direct melody and lyrics. We didn't plan the record as a return to the surf or anything. We just did it one day round a piano in the studio. Brian had the idea and played it over to us. We improved on that and recorded it very quickly, in about five minutes. It's certainly not an old track of ours; in fact it was recorded only a few weeks before it was released. We liked how it turned out and decided to release it."

• Brian is beginning to distance himself from the group – but sometimes, and only when the mood takes him, he will participate in the recording process. While the group is downstairs in the home studio, rehearsing and recording, Brian will lay on his bed, listening to the sounds rising up through the floorboards of his room. And if he hears something that he feels should be changed, he will come down the stairs, still in his pyjamas, and tell the group how the song should be recorded. This may last only a matter of minutes, and then he will return upstairs. The activities surrounding the studio naturally play havoc with Marilyn Wilson's home life.

■ Monday 27th
RECORDING *20/20* **session 3** Brian's Home Studio *Bel Air, CA*. Today sees the first tracking session for **'We're Together Again'**, a song by singer Ron Wilson, with whom Brian forms a company called Ron-Brian Music Productions (see also June 28th). Work on the recording continues two days later, and then will resume over three months later, on September 3rd.

■ Wednesday 29th
RECORDING *20/20* **session 4** Brian's Home Studio *Bel Air, CA*. A further session is held for **'We're Together Again'**.

June

■ Monday 3rd
RECORDING A backing track for a song titled **'Well You Know I Knew'** is recorded on or around this date, studio unknown. On the

same 8-track tape, Charles Manson runs through a number of songs on acoustic guitar, including 'Look At Your Game Girl'.

■ Tuesday 4th
In front of a large studio audience at ABC Television Studios in Los Angeles, The Beach Boys videotape an appearance on *The Les Crane Show*. During the 48-minute late-night chat show (transmitted in colour nationally by ABC on the 13th, 11:15pm-12:15am New York time, and hosted by former DJ Crane) the group talks passionately about their involvement with the Maharishi Mahesh Yogi. Surprisingly, the group does not perform during the show. Other guests include Harvey Von Bell, Ed Gray and Rudy Cole.

■ Wednesday 5th
RECORDING *20/20* **session 5** Brian's Home Studio *Bel Air, CA*. A tracking session takes place today for Brian and Carl's **'I Went To Sleep'** (six takes; take 6 marked as master). Also today the group records an organ and voice version of **'Old Man River'**, but no successful takes are made and it remains unreleased. Besides 'Sail Plane Song' (see June 8th), 'I Went To Sleep' will turn out to be Brian's only original song on the *20/20* album once it is passed over for *Friends*. Brian's other songs that will feature on *20/20* are not new: 'Time To Get Alone' was recorded by Redwood back on October 14th 1967, while 'Our Prayer' and 'Cabinessence' are leftovers from *Smile*.
Musician present Jimmy Bond Jr. (bass), plus one unknown.

■ Thursday 6th
RECORDING *20/20* **session 6** Brian's Home Studio *Bel Air, CA*. Vocal work is done on **'Do It Again'** this evening featuring Brian, Carl, Bruce, Al and Dennis.

■ Friday 7th
RECORDING *20/20* **session 7** Brian's Home Studio *Bel Air, CA*. An untitled track written by Dennis is recorded today. It remains unreleased.

■ Saturday 8th
RECORDING *20/20* **session 8** Brian's Home Studio *Bel Air, CA*. The group makes its first attempts at **'Sail Plane Song'**, a Brian and Carl co-composition that will evolve into 'Loop De Loop', and much later into 'Santa's Got An Airplane' when the band take on a Christmas project in the late 1970s (but it still remains unreleased until the 1998 *Ultimate Christmas* CD). Al provides guitar, Carl bass, Bruce organ, Dennis drums, and Brian organ. Tracking sessions for the song will begin afresh on March 5th 1969.

■ Monday 10th
RECORDING *20/20* **session 9** Brian's Home Studio *Bel Air, CA*. A second instrumental tracking session is done today for **'Old Man River'**.

■ Wednesday 12th
RECORDING *20/20* **session 10** Brian's Home Studio *Bel Air, CA* 2:00-5:30pm. Today sees overdubbing work on **'Do It Again'**, featuring John Guerin on various percussion to enhance Dennis's original track.
Musicians present John Guerin (drums, tambourine, wood blocks), Ernie Small (saxophone), John E. Lowe (reeds or woodwind).

■ Tuesday 18th
RECORDING *20/20* **session 11** Brian's Home Studio *Bel Air, CA*.

Friends album

A1 'Meant For You' (B. WILSON / M. LOVE)
A2 'Friends' (B. WILSON / C. WILSON / D. WILSON / A. JARDINE)
A3 'Wake The World' (B. WILSON / A. JARDINE)
A4 'Be Here In The Mornin'' (B. WILSON / C. WILSON / M. LOVE /
D. WILSON / A. JARDINE)
A5 'When A Man Needs A Woman' (B. WILSON / C. WILSON /
D. WILSON / A. JARDINE / S. KORTHOF / V.D. PARKS)
A6 'Passing By' (B. WILSON)
B1 'Anna Lee The Healer' (M. LOVE / B. WILSON)
B2 'Little Bird' (D. WILSON / S. KALINICH)
B3 'Be Still' (D. WILSON / S. KALINICH)
B4 'Busy Doin' Nothin'' (B. WILSON)
B5 'Diamond Head' (A. VESCOZO / L. RITZ / J. ACKLEY / B. WILSON)
B6 'Transcendental Meditation' (B. WILSON / M. LOVE / A. JARDINE)

US release June 24th 1968 (Capitol ST2895).
UK release September 1968 (Capitol ST2895).
Chart high US number 126; UK number 13.

Tracking session for an Al composition, **'Walkin''**. It will remain unreleased.

Wednesday 19th

RECORDING *20/20* session 12 Brian's Home Studio *Bel Air, CA*. Following yesterday's start, today sees a tracking overdub session for **'Walkin''** by two studio musicians.

Thursday 20th

RECORDING *20/20* session 13 Brian's Home Studio *Bel Air, CA*. Today the group records Bruce's 1967 instrumental **'The Nearest Faraway Place'**, which he composed, performs on, and produces. The title originates from a piece written by Shana Alexander for US magazine *Life*. Strings on the piece are arranged by Van McCoy, who will come to mainstream attention in 1975 with his hit dance classic 'The Hustle'.
Musicians present Jim Gordon (drums), Gene Estes (percussion), Bruce Johnston (piano), Don Peake (probably guitar).

Monday 24th

Friends album released in the US. For many pop music buyers, the low-key, harmonious pleasantries of *Friends* seem downright irrelevant in mid 1968. Many top groups – Cream and The Jimi Hendrix Experience, for example, who are at their apex – are playing full-out rock and venting their anger towards the ongoing war in Vietnam. The Beach Boys by contrast sound ambivalent. Nonetheless, some good reviews of the album do appear.

Arthur Schmidt will write with a flourish in *Rolling Stone* dated August 24th: "Everything on the first side is great. The cuts 'Wake The World', 'Be Here In The Mornin'' and 'When A Man Needs A Woman' all evoke the elation of *Wild Honey*. 'Passing By', reminiscent of [The Beatles'] 'Flying', is the best instrumental they've done, a smooth linear construction. On the second side, 'Anna Lee' is a trite melody and 'Diamond Head', except for a break in the middle, is uninteresting. But two cuts by Dennis Wilson and Steve Kalinich, 'Little Bird' and 'Be Still', are tight, emotional and beautifully done,

with fine lyrics that do not exploit the California-nature-youth idiom that is a vision and artistic as the music itself. 'Busy Doin' Nothing', words and music by Brian Wilson, is a real great lyric, a matter of fact, vernacular exposition that well evokes a quiet mood with its small beauties. A good melody tapers off into embarrassing sloppy jazz at its very end. Like an entity that creates its own idiom musically as well as culturally, The Beach Boys take getting into. Listen once and you might think this album is nowhere. But it's really just at a very special place, and after a half-dozen listens you can be there."

Such optimistic reviews come too late to influence sales. The disc is The Beach Boys' only new LP of the year and their first to be officially issued only in stereo (several, but not all, of their earliest albums were mixed and issued in true stereo, ending with the release of *All Summer Long* in July 1964). *Friends* will suffer the group's worst chart performance to date, peaking at a most disappointing 126 in the US *Billboard* listings. Brian, re-energised after recording the album, is devastated by the paltry US sales. From now, his influence on future Beach Boys recordings will falter at an alarming rate.

Wednesday 26th

RECORDING *20/20* session 14 Brian's Home Studio *Bel Air, CA*. A group session today results in another untitled and unreleased track.

Friday 28th

RECORDING I.D. Sound studio *Hollywood, CA*. Brian produces both sides for the single **'I'll Keep On Loving You'** / **'As Tears Go By'** for his partner in Ron-Brian Music, Ron Wilson. The 45 with its Jagger/Richards B-side will be released by Columbia Records on September 3rd.

July

RECORDING Brian's Home Studio *Bel Air, CA*. Charles Manson, who hopes that Brian can work wonders with his musical career, tapes a number of recordings intermittently during this period at Brian's Home Studio, allegedly co-produced by Brian and Carl. Dennis plays some part in the proceedings, as do members of the so-called Wrecking Crew, the elite team of LA studio musicians used by Brian, Phil Spector and others.

Nick Grillo will recall in *Rolling Stone*, "We recorded close to a hundred hours of Charlie's music at Brian's studio. The lyrics were so twisted and jaded." Mike tells *Rolling Stone* in 1971: "We've got several 8-track tapes of Charlie and the girls that Dennis cut … . Just chanting, fucking, sucking, barking. It was a million laughs, believe me. Maybe we'll put it out in the fall. Call it *Death Row*."

Charles Manson says in *Rolling Stone* that they "did a pretty fair session, putting down about ten songs".

Steve Desper, who engineers the sessions, remembers that some of the material is "pretty good … [Manson] had musical talent". Desper, who supervises three or four late-night recording sessions by Manson, thinks of Manson simply as a 'street musician' friend of Dennis's, and reckons that Manson is desperately in need of a good long bath.

Contrary to the writings of later rock revisionists, the songs taped by Manson are not demos but completed songs – or at least are as complete as Manson wants them to be. Reportedly, he rarely records more than one take of a vocal.

The precise titles recorded are not known, but it's safe to assume that they are the same songs that will appear later in different form on his *Lie* album, released not long after Manson's arrest following the Sharon Tate murders in summer 1969 but recorded sometime during 1968/69, shortly after he falls out with Dennis. The songs on that album are 'Look At Your Game Girl', 'Ego', 'I Am A Mechanical Man', 'People Say I'm No Good', 'Home Is Where You're Happy', 'Arkansas', 'Always Is Always Forever', 'Garbage Dump', 'Don't Do Anything Illegal', 'Sick City', 'Cease To Exist', 'Clang Bang Clang', 'I Once Knew A Man', and 'Eyes Of The Dreamer'.

The versions on the *Lie* album are not the Brian's Home Studio recordings. In 1971, when Manson murders investigating officer Vincent Bugliosi of the Los Angeles County District Attorney's office asks Dennis if he can listen to the musical tapes Manson made, Dennis claims he has destroyed them because "the vibrations connected with them didn't belong on this earth".

By this time, Charles Manson and his 'Family' have started to abuse Dennis's hospitality at the drummer's home on Sunset Boulevard. Around $100,000 of Dennis's money has been squandered by the gang.

Following The Beach Boys' decision not to promote Charlie and his music, the Family uses Dennis to try to get Charlie's music noticed by Dennis's friend, record producer Terry Melcher.

Van Dyke Parks recalls: "One day, Charles Manson brought out a bullet and showed it to Dennis, who asked, 'What's this?' Manson replied, 'It's a bullet. Every time you look at it, I want you to think how nice it is that your kids are still safe.' Dennis grabbed Manson by the head and threw him to the ground and began pummelling him until Charlie said, 'Ouch!' Dennis beat the living shit out of him. 'How dare you!' was Dennis's reaction. Charlie Manson was weeping openly in front of a lot of hip people. I heard about this, but I wasn't there. The point is, Dennis wasn't afraid of anybody."

Dennis's new housemates are clearly outstaying their welcome. There are almost twice as many of them since they first started living with Dennis three months ago.

His expensive Rodeo Drive wardrobe has been used and abused by the Family, and his $21,000 Mercedes Benz car has been severely damaged by a member of the entourage who drove the uninsured vehicle into a mountain outside Spahn Ranch, the Family's former lodgings in the northwest LA suburb of Chatsworth. Charlie and the girls continue to drain Dennis of his cash.

The Family lives splendidly and regularly takes free deliveries of food and drink from local suppliers, all paid for by Dennis. He has even recently paid for one of the girls, Sadie Mae Glutz, better known as Susan Atkins, to have her teeth fixed.

The situation reaches crisis point when the girls are brought to Dennis's Beverly Hills doctor for penicillin shots in order to treat their sexually transmitted diseases. Dennis says later he thinks that it was probably the biggest gonorrhoea bill in history. The bond between Dennis and Charlie is severely strained when the two get into a fight at Dennis's home and Charlie pulls out a knife. It is at this point that Dennis realises that he must get Charlie and the Family out of his home – and out of his life.

• Around this time Dennis, Terry Melcher and Gregg Jakobson form an exclusive, unofficial men's club called The Golden Penetrators. Membership is restricted to just the three, and activities include travelling the streets looking for attractive young females to take back to their homes for sex. When they find a suitable candidate, Dennis's introduction will usually consist of: "Hi, I'm Dennis Wilson, the drummer with The Beach Boys."

TOUR STARTS North America (Jul 2nd-Aug 24th)
With the noise of the disastrous time with the Maharishi still ringing in their ears, The Beach Boys dust themselves off and return to concert appearances with a long two-month schedule.

Do It Again single

A '**Do It Again**' (B. WILSON / M. LOVE)
B '**Wake The World**' (B. WILSON / A. JARDINE)

US release July 8th 1968 (Capitol 2239).
UK release July 19th 1968 (Capitol CL 15554).
Chart high US number 20; UK number 1.

■ **Tuesday 2nd**
RKO Orpheum *Davenport, IA* two shows

■ **Wednesday 3rd**
The Arena *Sioux Falls, SD*

■ **Thursday 4th**
Majestic Hills *Lake Geneva, WI*

■ **Friday 5th**
Chicago Auditorium Theater *Chicago, IL*

■ **Saturday 6th**
Fairgrounds Coliseum *Indianapolis, IN*
• *Friends* album hits the US *Billboard* chart.

■ **Sunday 7th**
The Arena *Duluth, MN*

■ **Monday 8th**
Civic Memorial Auditorium *Fargo, ND* two shows
'Do It Again' / 'Wake The World' single released in the US. This summer 45 proves to be the group's last US Top 20 hit for eight years. The A-side with its great melody and sound proves irresistible to the masses, peaking at number 20 in the US and reaching an impressive number 1 position in the UK charts after its release there on July 19th.

Penny Valentine reviews it for Britain's *Disc & Music Echo* paper. "This is a vast improvement on The Beach Boys' last single, and thank goodness for it," she writes. "It sounds like bees humming on a summer breeze and is so completely solid; there isn't room for a fly to creep in. It goes on very gently and easily and is very, very pleasant. In a way it reminds me of one of the tracks off *Pet Sounds*, which is nice to say the least, and a hit it will most certainly be. I can imagine a few people will be muttering, 'Well, she said they were finished,' but I didn't. I said they should get back to their competent, commercial sound and they have. So there."

To accompany the release of 'Do It Again' the group assists in the production of a promotional film. Directed by Peter Clifton and shot in Los Angeles, the colour 16mm clip features the group pulling up in a van and walking around a surfing shop, followed by scenes of the group arriving at a beach in their van and then surfing.

Screenings of the film occur in the UK on BBC-1's *Top Of The Pops* during editions broadcast on August 8th, 22nd and 29th (7:30-8:00pm) and in Germany during the ZDF TV music show *Hits A Go Go* in September.

The clip will reappear in Clifton's 1969 Australian "surf, drugs and rock'n'roll" film *Fluid Journey*, effectively a sequel to his *Popcorn* film released earlier that year with a montage of surfing scenes set to 'Heroes And Villains'.

(An original plan for Beatle Paul McCartney to make a cameo appearance in an alternative 'Do It Again' film as a clerk has been abandoned due to his prior commitments.)

■ Tuesday 9th
Municipal Auditorium *St Paul, MN* two shows

■ Wednesday 10th
Iowa State University *Ames, IA*

■ Thursday 11th
Ice Arena *Des Moines, IA*

■ Friday 12th
Bicentennial Center Arena *Salina, KS* two shows

■ Saturday 13th
Pershing Municipal Auditorium *Lincoln, NE*

■ Sunday 14th
KS Memorial Hall *Kansas City, MO*

■ Monday 15th
Civic Auditorium *Albuquerque, NM*
Best Of The Beach Boys Vol. 3 compilation album released in the US. The distinct lack of sales of the *Friends* album prompts Capitol to repeat their trick of the previous two years by issuing yet another Beach Boys greatest-hits package, this one released less than a month after *Friends*.

The compilation performs abysmally, charting at a new low of 153. Alarmingly, it fails even to outsell the previous Capitol best-of. This chart low will be swiftly beaten when *Stack-o-Tracks*, a bizarre compilation of classic Beach Boys recordings without vocals, is released by Capitol next month and becomes the first record bearing the Beach Boys' name not to chart.

■ Tuesday 16th
Hi-Corbett Field *Tucson, AZ*

■ Wednesday 17th
San Diego Convention Hall *San Diego, CA*

■ Friday 19th
University of Alaska *Fairbanks, AK*
'Do It Again' / **'Wake The World'** single released in the UK.
• At the Capitol Records studio in Hollywood a dub of the backing track for **'God Only Knows'** is made today. This is probably done in preparation for the label's forthcoming *Stack-o-Tracks* album, the without-vocals collection to be released in August. It is likely that dubs of some of the other backing tracks are made around this time for the same purpose.

■ Saturday 20th
West High Auditorium *Anchorage, AK*

■ Monday 22nd
Coliseum *Spokane, WA*

■ Tuesday 23rd
Memorial Arena *Victoria, BC, Canada*

■ Wednesday 24th – Friday 26th
The Steel Pier *Atlantic City, NJ*
A three-night residency for the group.

■ Wednesday 24th
RECORDING *20/20* session 15 Brian's Home Studio *Bel Air, CA*. Back in California, following the recordings made on October 28th and November 1st 1967, further tracking sessions take place today for Brian's experimental piece **'Can't Wait Too Long'** (also known as 'Been Way Too Long').
Musicians present Max Bennett (bass guitar), Frank Guerrero (percussion), Lyle Ritz (bass), plus four unknown.

■ Friday 26th
RECORDING *20/20* session 16 Brian's Home Studio *Bel Air, CA*. A further recording session takes place for **'Can't Wait Too Long'**, and possibly again on Tuesday 30th. The piece will remain unfinished and unreleased, but in 1990 a still clearly unfinished version made from several different recordings will appear on the Capitol CD *Smiley Smile / Wild Honey*, and another mix will appear on the 1993 *Good Vibrations* boxed set.

■ Saturday 27th
'Do It Again' single hits the US charts.

August

Early this month Dennis moves out of his home and begins living with his friend Gregg Jakobson in a basement apartment at Gregg's home in the Palisades near Santa Monica. Dennis has left his Sunset Boulevard home to get away from Charles Manson and his 'Family'. He is too afraid to ask them to leave, so three weeks before the lease is set to expire he takes off for the new place, conveniently leaving the Family to be evicted by the 'landlord', coincidentally Dennis's manager.

Beach Boys business manager Nick Grillo tells US radio that Manson and the Family "stayed at Dennis's house for six months. During this time Dennis was on the road with The Beach Boys, and Charlie or one of his girls would come up to The Beach Boys' office and pick up a cheque for food or an allowance, because they were supposedly looking after Dennis's home while he was away. They were driving Dennis's Ferrari, which really annoyed me".

Bruce tells *NME*: "Someone crashed [Dennis's] Ferrari, completely ruining it. Then someone came along with a tow truck and stole it!" Dennis's mother Audree Wilson says in *Rolling Stone*: "When they left Dennis's house, Manson or somebody stole Dennis's Ferrari and they stole everything in the house that could be moved. Everything was stripped! Dennis has them kicked out because they were into heavy drugs and he just wanted them out."

Grillo continues: "I wanted to know a little bit more about Manson and I found out that he was on probation in San Francisco. He was involved in some hold-up. He needed employment here and so, through the pressures put upon us by Dennis, we indicated to his probation officer that it would be fine for Manson to stay down here because we were thinking about signing him to Brother Records as a writer.

"He would come up to the office, serenade the office staff, and we'd have to shout him out of the office because it was interfering with us while we worked during the day. I believe Dennis was under a great deal of pressure from Charlie [who] was getting into a much heavier drug situation, which Dennis became concerned about. Charlie was taking a tremendous amount of acid and Dennis wouldn't tolerate it and asked him to leave. It was difficult for Dennis because he was afraid of Charlie."

• 'Do It Again' single peaks in UK *Record Retailer* chart at number 1.

■ Friday 2nd
New Civic Center, Lansdowne Park *Ottawa, ON, Canada*
8:30pm

■ Sunday 4th
Montreal Forum *Montreal, PQ, Canada*

■ Monday 5th
Metro Center *Halifax, NS, Canada*

■ Tuesday 6th
Civic Auditorium *Portland, ME*

■ Wednesday 7th
The Armory *Pittsfield, MA*

■ Thursday 8th
Pittsfield Boys Club *Pittsfield, MA* matinee; **New Haven Arena *New Haven, CT*** evening

■ Friday 9th – Sunday 11th
Steel Pier *Atlantic City, NJ*
A further three-night residency at the Steel Pier.
• On the 9th, with Dennis out of town, Gregg Jakobson arranges a recording session for their buddy Charles Manson at a studio in Van Nuys, California.

■ Monday 12th
TV ABC Television Studios *New York, NY*. ABC *The Dick Cavett Show* lip-synch 'Do It Again', broadcast colour August 13th, 10:30am-12:00 noon; ABC *Happening* lip-synch 'Wake The World', 'Do It Again', 'Friends', broadcast August 17th, 1:30-2:00pm. During a one-day break from their tour, The Beach Boys begin a frenzy of television appearances, beginning this morning with a slot for ABC's *Dick Cavett* morning chat show, including an interview with the host. Later, still at ABC studios, they tape an appearance to be slotted into the weekly Los Angeles-based pop show *Happening*.

■ Tuesday 13th
TV NBC Television Studios *New York, NY*. NBC *The Tonight Show* 'Graduation Day' broadcast 11:30pm-1:00am. This afternoon the group's current flurry of television appearances concludes when they tape an interview for NBC TV's highly influential nightly chat show hosted by the king of American talk shows, Johnny Carson. Besides the obligatory interview with the host, the group delivers an impromptu performance of 'Graduation Day' while still sitting on their chairs.
Wilkes University *Wilkes-Barre, PA*
Following the afternoon's TV recording, the group resume tour duties.

■ Wednesday 14th
State Farm Show Building *Harrisburg, PA*

■ Thursday 15th
Capital Music Hall *Wheeling, WV*

Stack-o-Tracks album

A1 'Darlin' (B. WILSON / M. LOVE)
A2 'Salt Lake City' (B. WILSON / M. LOVE)
A3 'Sloop John B' (TRAD ARR B. WILSON)
A4 'In My Room' (B. WILSON / G. USHER)
A5 'Catch A Wave' (B. WILSON / M. LOVE)
A6 'Wild Honey' (B. WILSON / M. LOVE)
A7 'Little Saint Nick' (B. WILSON)
B1 'Do It Again' (B. WILSON / M. LOVE)
B2 'Wouldn't It Be Nice' (B. WILSON / T. ASHER)
B3 'God Only Knows' (B. WILSON / T. ASHER)
B4 'Surfer Girl' (B. WILSON)
B5 'Little Honda' (B. WILSON / M. LOVE)
B6 'Here Today' (B. WILSON / T. ASHER)
B7 'You're So Good To Me' (B. WILSON / M. LOVE)
B8 'Let Him Run Wild' (B. WILSON / M. LOVE)

US release August 19th 1968 (Capitol DKAO2893).
UK release December 1976 (Capitol EAST24009).
Chart high US none; UK none.

■ Friday 16th
Civic Center *Charleston, WV*

■ Saturday 17th
Convention Center *Asbury Park, NJ*
• *Friends*, the poorest-selling Beach Boys album to date, peaks in the US chart at number 126.

■ Sunday 18th
Massey Hall *Toronto, ON, Canada*

■ Monday 19th
Winnipeg Arena *Winnipeg, MB, Canada*
Stack-o-Tracks album released in the US. Indicating just how low The Beach Boys' commercial stock has fallen at Capitol, the label issues what is easily one of the oddest albums ever by a major rock group in the 1960s. Issued for now in the United States only, the LP consists of instrumental backing tracks for 15 of The Beach Boys' most famous songs, stripped of their vocals to encourage karaoke-like singalongs. This is fast turning into the kind of year that The Beach Boys would rather forget.

■ Tuesday 20th
The Agridome At Exhibition Park *Regina, SK, Canada*

■ Wednesday 21st
Kinsmen Field House *Edmonton, AB, Canada*

■ Thursday 22nd
Jubilee Auditorium *Calgary, AB, Canada*

■ Friday 23rd – Saturday 24th
Pacific National Exhibition *Vancouver, BC, Canada*
Saturday night's Canadian performance marks the last date of this long and relatively unsuccessful tour.

FOLLOWING PAGES Relaxing with their jeep driver in the heat of the Mexican sun.

■ Monday 26th

TV Westinghouse Broadcasting Company, Group W Productions *Philadelphia, PA.* Syndicated *The Mike Douglas Show* live vocals over new pre-taped backing track 'Do It Again' broadcast nationally from August 29th. With their latest tour now completed, The Beach Boys videotape their second appearance on this show.

■ Saturday 31st

The Beach Boys' commercial appeal is at an all-time low in the US, but their latest single 'Do It Again' reaches number 1 in the UK.
• Around now the group is in Mexico for some promotional photo-shoots. They also make a colour film where they stroll down a road, play in a park and are chased by children. It is later used in the 1998 *Endless Harmony* DVD with 'Friends' as a soundtrack.

September

Friends album released in the UK.
'Do It Again' single peaks in Australian chart at number 1, in Dutch chart at number 5, in Swedish Radio 3 chart at number 5, and in Canadian RPM chart at number 10.

■ Tuesday 3rd

RECORDING *20/20* **session 17** Brian's Home Studio *Bel Air, CA* 2:00-6:00pm. A week after finishing their latest tour, The Beach Boys are ready to continue work on their next album. But following the poor sales of their latest LP they find Brian somewhat uninterested in creating new music, despite the fact that they are still working at his home studio. From this point, the group in general and Carl in particular will begin increasingly to take over the reins in the studio, even recording without Brian. Today work resumes on **'We're Together Again'**, a piece started three months ago; it seems likely that today's backing track is an all-new version.
'I'll Keep On Loving You' / **'As Tears Go By'** single by Ron Wilson released in the US. The 45 is co-produced by Brian.

■ Thursday 5th

RECORDING *20/20* **session 18** Brian's Home Studio *Bel Air, CA.* A further tracking session takes place today for **'We're Together Again'**.

■ Friday 6th

RECORDING *20/20* **session 19** Brian's Home Studio *Bel Air, CA.* Today sees the final tracking session for **'We're Together Again'**, after which the group adds backing vocals.

■ Monday 9th
RECORDING *20/20* session 20 Brian's Home Studio *Bel Air, CA*. Brian and Carl overdub vocals onto the last part of the completed September 6th tracking master of **'We're Together Again'**. After five long sessions, the recording will remain unreleased until its appearance on the 1990 Capitol CD of *Friends / 20/20*.

■ Wednesday 11th
RECORDING *20/20* session 21 Brian's Home Studio *Bel Air, CA*. The sessions this autumn produce an interesting array of new and exciting songs from almost every member of the band, but a song taped today comes from Dennis's erstwhile friend Charles Manson. Its original title was 'Cease To Exist', but with a slight re-wording of the lyrics its title has reverted to **'Never Learn Not To Love'**. The lyric includes the line: "Submission is a gift, give it to your lover / Love and understanding is for one another." It's possible that a further version of **'We're Together Again'** is also worked on during this session.

■ Saturday 14th
'Do It Again' single peaks in US *Billboard* chart at number 20.

■ Tuesday 17th
RECORDING *20/20* session 22 Brian's Home Studio *Bel Air, CA*. Work is completed today on **'Never Learn Not To Love'**.

October

'Do It Again' single peaks in German *Hit Bilanz* chart at number 4, in Norwegian chart at number 5, in New Zealand *Pop-O-Meter* chart at number 14, and in Rhodesian Broadcasting Corporation chart at number 5.

■ Tuesday 1st
RECORDING *20/20* session 23 Brian's Home Studio *Bel Air, CA*. Today's session sees The Beach Boys covering the Barry/Greenwich/Spector classic **'I Can Hear Music'**, a song once cut by The Ronettes. The first attempts today feature Carl singing a vocal accompanied by just his acoustic guitar and occasional drums from Dennis, while the second shot features a heavier drum sound, tambourine, sleigh bells, and Carl's acoustic guitar. Once a satisfactory 'guide vocal' has been completed – meaning a rough take intended to be replaced later – several attempts are made to add backing vocals by the group, and Carl's first serious lead vocal. Additional backing vocals are then taped but these are deemed not good enough, so a fresh backing vocal is recorded. Carl then records a new double-tracked and quite breathtaking lead vocal after several attempts. Carl and the full Beach Boys line-up then begin a series of insert vocal recordings for the song. (An 'insert' is a vocal or instrumental part, often of short duration, added usually to one tape track of the existing recorded performance.) Next, Carl takes charge of a series of guitar, drums, piano and keyboard inserts designed to pad out the sound. After watching and listening to Brian intently over the past six years, Carl emerges today having completed his first released session as sole producer. His developing expertise in the studio bodes well for the future, with Brian set to remove himself from recordings as well as the concert stage.

■ Wednesday 2nd
RECORDING *20/20* session 24 Brian's Home Studio *Bel Air, CA*.

Almost a year after the last session, The Beach Boys return their attentions to the wonderful **'Time To Get Alone'**, a song originally produced by Brian for Redwood, the American group led by his best friend Danny Hutton. (Redwood later becomes Three Dog Night.) Today's session begins with the re-recording of the song's harpsichord-led instrumental track. Work will resume on the song two days later.

■ Friday 4th
RECORDING *20/20* session 25 Brian's Home Studio *Bel Air, CA*. Recordings for **'Time To Get Alone'** are concluded when Carl's lead vocals and Brian and Al's backing vocals are overdubbed onto the October 2nd tracking tape. Overdubbing of vocal inserts follow. (The sessions today and on the 2nd are filmed and the results will be edited to form part of the 1969 promotional film for 'I Can Hear Music'. The footage is later seen in re-edited form in the documentary *An American Band* with 'Time To Get Alone' synched to it.)

■ Saturday 5th
Best Of The Beach Boys Vol. 3 album peaks in the US *Billboard* chart at a disappointing 153, in advance of the group's next American tour.
• Also today, the group mixes Brian's **'I Went To Sleep'**.

■ Tuesday 8th
MIXING I.D. Sound studio *Hollywood, CA*. The group makes a first attempt to mix down their version of **'Time To Get Alone'**. The result is slightly slower than the released version and will remain unreleased.

■ Friday 11th
Fillmore East *New York, NY* two shows, with Creedence Clearwater Revival
Today's performances mark the first appearance by the group at this venue and the first Beach Boys-related event to be promoted by well-known concert promoter Bill Graham. According to Steven Gaines in his book *Heroes And Villains*, Graham will later complain that the band insisted on a ticket-stub count at this show, questioning his honesty. Graham will not book the band again during the 1960s.

■ Sunday 13th
TV CBS TV (Studio 50) *New York, NY*. CBS *The Ed Sullivan Show* live vocals over new backing tracks 'Do It Again', 'Good Vibrations', broadcast live colour 8:00-9:00pm. The group's time in the Big Apple is almost over as they make their third and final appearance on CBS TV's top-rated Sunday night variety show. Live vocals are sung to newly recorded backing tracks, which have been taped this afternoon. The time was also spent taping special blue 'matte' video montages of the group playing their instruments and moving and appearing from behind mirrored studio partitions, the results of which are superimposed on-screen during the group's performance of 'Good Vibrations'.

■ Monday 14th
RECORDING/MIXING Capitol studio *New York, NY*. The Beach Boys happen upon a young boy who performs a rap titled **'Oh Yeah'**. They take this otherwise unknown performer into the studio and record the chant with him: "I got the spirit, I know you want it / But you can't have it, cos I've got it. / It's in my hand, I can't write / It's in my eyes, I can't see." Each line is answered by The Beach Boys, who sing, "Oh Yeah," in unison while clicking their fingers.

The stage band, white-suited and tanned, take time out in a photographic studio, September 1968.

The uplifting 43-second ditty, led by Carl, concludes with Bruce remarking: "Ain't that a groove?" Also at this session, the group make mono mixes for the single release of **'Never Learn Not To Love'**. The album and single mixes will differ considerably for this song. Bruce also attempts rough mono mixes of the backing track for **'Bluebirds Over The Mountain'** and **'The Nearest Faraway Place'**.

■ Tuesday 15th

The single mix of **'Never Learn Not To Love'** is mastered at Capitol's studio in New York City.

■ Saturday 19th

Friends album peaks in UK *Record Retailer* chart at number 13. *Best Of The Beach Boys Vol. 3* album peaks in the US at a disappointing number 153 and in the UK at an impressive number 13.

TOUR STARTS US South (Oct 20th-27th)

■ Sunday 20th

Memorial Coliseum *Greensboro, NC*

The group kicks off a week-long concert tour with a performance in North Carolina.

■ Tuesday 22nd

Fairgrounds Expo Center *Louisville, KY*

■ Thursday 24th

Civic Center, Bobyns Bennett High School *Kingsport, KY*

■ Friday 25th

Polytechnic Institute *Blacksburg, VA* afternoon; **Civic Center, Salem-Roanoke Valley** *Salem, VA* 8:30pm

■ Saturday 26th

Civic Center Auditorium *Charleston, WV* 8:30pm

■ Sunday 27th

Macon College *Macon, GA*

Last night of this short tour.

■ Tuesday 29th

The group works on preparing a single mix of Bruce's **'Bluebirds Over The Mountain'**.

November

Early this month, Dennis moves out of Gregg Jakobson's basement and into the woods in Death Valley, about 150 miles north-east of Los Angeles. He resides in a small room with just a tiny candle. He takes with him to the woods the 17 girls who usually accompany Charles Manson. Dennis calls his female entourage his 'Space Ladies' and toys with the idea of launching them as a group called The Family Gems.

■ Friday 1st

RECORDING Capitol studio (B) *Hollywood,CA*. Today's session produces a recording of the Dennis Wilson / Steve Kalinich composition **'A Time To Live In Dreams'**, which will remain unreleased until its appearance on the 2001 Capitol compilation *Hawthorne, CA – Birthplace Of A Musical Legacy*.

TV ABC Television Studios *Los Angeles, CA*. ABC *The Joey Bishop Show* lip-synch 'Do It Again', broadcast colour 11:30pm-1:00am. The group heads to ABC TV's studio this afternoon to record an appearance on a nightly entertainment programme hosted by a former member of the famous Rat Pack. During the 90-minute show the group is interviewed by Bishop as well as performing, joining guests Julie Andrews, James Garner and Zsa Zsa Gabor.

■ Saturday 2nd

RECORDING *20/20* session 26 Capitol studio (B) *Hollywood,CA*. Today sees a vocal and tracking session for Dennis's **'Be With Me'** (requiring 14 takes), one of two Dennis productions intended for the next Beach Boys album. Van McCoy again arranges the strings.

■ Wednesday 6th

MIXING Capitol studio *Hollywood, CA*. A stereo mixing session is held for Dennis's **'Never Learn Not To Love'**.

■ Monday 11th

RECORDING/MIXING Capitol studio *Hollywood. CA*. **'Be With Me'** and **'I Can Hear Music'** are mixed today. A spoken-word segment is also taped at today's session attended by Dennis, Brian and assorted friends. Carl is also present but declines an offer to join in on the recordings, which slowly turn into a farce. The piece is based on a tongue-twisting limerick that Dennis has: "I'm not the fig plucker, nor the fig plucker's son, and I'll pluck figs till the fig plucker comes." Inevitably, when repeated faster it sounds like they're saying 'pig fucker' – another Manson term.

■ Tuesday 12th

RECORDING *20/20* session 27 probably Capitol studio *Hollywood. CA*. The group work on **'All I Want To Do'**, in particular the song's tag. For this, Dennis enlists the help of a female friend who is recorded having sexual intercourse with the drummer in the studio. This 'sound effect' is layered onto the fade-out of the song's final mix, and is just about audible on the released version.

■ Thursday 14th

RECORDING *20/20* session 28 Bell Sound studio *New York, NY*. Working with Bruce's demo from September 29th 1967, The Beach Boys add vocals, instrumentation and a screaming lead guitar (by sessionman Ed Carter) to the September 29th tracking tape of **'Bluebirds Over The Mountain'**. The group through their Brother Music company purchase publishing rights in Ersel Hickey's song. The recordings, carried out in Manhattan's famed Bell Sound studio, mark Bruce's debut as a Beach Boys producer. Stereo mixes of 'Bluebirds Over The Mountain' are also made today at Capitol's New York studio. With the sessions completed, the group flies back to Los Angeles.

■ Friday 15th

RECORDING *20/20* session 29 I.D. Sound studio *Hollywood, CA*. The flurry of recordings continues as Dennis, working with the cream of LA session musicians, records a version of his grand Hawaiian instrumental **'Mona Kanau'** (Master No. 71522; running time 3:16). It will remain unreleased. Also today, the group works on mixing **'Time To Get Alone'** at Capitol.

■ Saturday 16th

RECORDING *20/20* session 30 Capitol studio *Hollywood, CA*. Instrumental work is done for a piece called **'The Gong'**. It seems likely that no vocals are ever recorded. Today is also probably when string overdubs are done for several of the *20/20* songs, including **'The Nearest Faraway Place'**, arranged once more by Van McCoy. Also at this Capitol session, 'The Nearest Faraway Place' is mixed into stereo in short sections, after which the final mix is edited together. There will be one further recording date for this song – see November 18th.

■ Sunday 17th

RECORDING *20/20* session 31 Capitol studio *Hollywood, CA*. With work on the forthcoming *20/20* album almost complete, Carl, Dennis and Bruce return to the Capitol Tower to record additional vocals onto Brian's October 4th 1966 recording of **'Our Prayer'**, another of the unreleased fragments originally intended for *Smile* (see also November 20th). Also at this session the group works on fine-tuning the stereo mix of **'I Can Hear Music'**.

■ Monday 18th

RECORDING *20/20* session 32 Brian's Home Studio *Bel Air, CA*. Eighteen months after initiating the idea, Al finally persuades the group to record a version of **'Cotton Fields (The Cotton Song)'**, a folk standard previously recorded by Huddie 'Leadbelly' Ledbetter. Brian produces the session, which continues tomorrow. Unhappy with this version, Al will push for a further recording – which does not take place until August 15th 1969 – but it will be this first version, produced by Brian, that will be issued on the group's *20/20* album.

■ Wednesday 20th

RECORDING *20/20* session 33 Capitol studio *Hollywood, CA*. For the second time in a week, and again to provide urgently needed material for *20/20*, The Beach Boys revisit the abandoned *Smile* tapes. Today they record additional vocals onto existing takes of **'Cabinessence'**. This version for *20/20* is compiled from three 1966 *Smile*-era pieces, 'Home On The Range', 'Who Ran The Iron Horse' and 'The Grand Coulee Dam'. Also at this session the group, possibly with Brian, works on mixing Brian's production of 'Cotton Fields' into mono. It is hoped that the version mixed today will be used for a single release, but that does not happen – at least not with this version. Special mixes are also made of the song for potential use in future television appearances.

■ Thursday 21st

RECORDING *20/20* session 34 Brian's Home Studio *Bel Air, CA*. The group returns to Brian's home studio to conclude work on Dennis's composition **'All I Want To Do'**, adding a lead vocal by Mike and backing vocals by session singers Julia Tillman, Carolyn Willis and Edna Wright. There is also some evidence that recording work is done to **'Time To Get Alone'** today. Stereo mixes of 'Our Prayer', 'Cotton Fields', portions of 'Cabinessence' and 'All I Want To Do' and a unique mono single mix of the latter are also made.

■ Friday 22nd

MIXING A further mix session for the elaborate *20/20* version of **'Cabinessence'** is held today, with work concentrating on the song's tag section and second chorus. With that, work on the next album, *20/20*, is complete.

TOUR STARTS 6th Annual US Thanksgiving Tour (Nov 23rd-27th)

■ Monday 23rd
Memorial Auditorium *Columbus, OH*
The group begins their annual Thanksgiving tour, this year a brief

five-day outing that also serves as a warm-up for their upcoming visit to Europe. The five-piece Beach Boys – Mike, Carl, Dennis, Bruce and Al – are joined on-stage by Daryl Dragon (keyboards), Mike Kowalski (percussion) and Ed Carter (guitar, bass). Dragon has been a regular extra musician on Beach Boys tours for some time now.

■ Tuesday 24th
Memorial Auditorium *Canton, OH*

■ Wednesday 25th
Bushnell Auditorium *Hartford, CT*

■ Thursday 26th
Stanley-Warner Theatre *Jersey City, NJ*
Set-list 'Darlin'', 'Sloop John B', 'California Girls', 'Wouldn't It Be Nice', 'I Get Around', 'Do It Again', 'Wake The World', 'Bluebirds Over The Mountain', 'God Only Knows', 'Their Hearts Were Full Of Spring', 'Good Vibrations', 'Barbara Ann' (encore), 'All I Want To Do' (encore).
• A filmed Capitol-financed promotional clip of The Beach Boys performing their forthcoming single 'Bluebirds Over The Mountain' is aired today on the Belgian TV show *Vibrato*.

■ Wednesday 27th
Music Hall *Boston, MA* two shows
The last night of the brief Thanksgiving tour, after which The Beach Boys spend a day relaxing at home in California before flying into London for the start of another lengthy European tour.

■ Friday 29th
Following a flight from Los Angeles hindered by fog, The Beach Boys arrive at London Airport at 9:10am on Flight BA562. British music reporters are aghast at the group's new longer hair and beards. Flying in with the group is £250,000 worth of brand new equipment designed to ensure faithful reproduction of their sound. Filmmaker Vic Kettle is on hand to record events for a proposed US/Europe TV documentary about the tour.

The group and entourage check in at the Hilton Hotel in central London where they will stay for the next four nights. First, they meet members of the UK press who are encamped in the hotel's conference room. Bob Dawburn writes in *Melody Maker*: "The Beach Boys were in remarkably good humour considering their urgent need for sleep when they met the press today."

'Bluebirds Over The Mountain' / **'Never Learn Not To Love'** single released in the UK. To coincide with the European tour Capitol/EMI issue this 45, which will peak in the charts at number 33. Penny Valentine writes in *Disc & Music Echo*: "It's probably the strangest record The Beach Boys have ever made. It really is so odd, disjointed and confusing. I can only see it being a hit because they're here in person."

Bruce, speaking to *Disc & Music Echo*, says: "'Bluebirds Over The Mountain' was kind of an accident. I was going to put it out as a solo record a year ago, then forgot about it. But Carl got interested and finished it with me. I did the arranging and we co-produced it. To be honest, our records are all very well, but I wanted us to be able to walk into London's Revolution Club and see people dancing to one of our records instead of just listening, and this is a danceable record! It doesn't signal any search for some new Beach Boys sound. It's just a single, pure and simple."

For the European release of 'Bluebirds Over The Mountain', Beatles publishing company Northern Songs acquires publishing

1968

Bluebirds Over The Mountain
single

A 'Bluebirds Over The Mountain' (E. HICKEY)
B 'Never Learn Not To Love' (D. WILSON)

UK release November 29th 1968 (Capitol CL 15572).
US release December 2nd 1968 (Capitol 2360).
Chart high UK number 33; US number 61.

rights for the song. When this information is picked up by the music industry, a rumour quickly spreads crediting Paul McCartney (under an alias of Ersel Hickey) as the song's composer. This is not true: Hickey is a real person who charted with his song back in 1958.

■ Saturday 30th

TV BBC TV (Studio G) *Lime Grove, west London.* BBC-1 *Top Of The Pops* lip-synch 'Do It Again', broadcast December 25th 1:28-2:11pm. After years of 'appearing' on the show through film clips, The Beach Boys finally get to make their studio debut on BBC television's prime pop programme, for inclusion in the Christmas Day edition. This appearance, as well as those recorded for the show on 3rd, 9th and 18th, are part of an 'exclusivity' deal between the group and the BBC that forbids the group from appearing on any other UK TV show between November 27th and December 26th 1968, in other words for the duration of their visit to the UK and Europe.

Once BBC duties are over today, Al, Bruce and Mike begin a round of socialising, including a visit to Bee Gee Barry Gibb's penthouse pad, near London's St Paul's cathedral, where the quartet sing songs and strum guitars until 4:00am.

December

TOUR STARTS UK and Europe (Dec 1st-16th)

■ Sunday 1st

London Palladium *central London* two shows, with Barry Ryan, Bruce Channel, Vanity Fare, Eclection, Sharon Tandy & Fleur De Lys, The Majority; compère: Roger Day
The Beach Boys' latest ten-day British junket kicks off this evening in London. Some reports have the group backed on-stage through this tour by British session musicians, but other sources specify the live line-up as the four-man Beach Boys – Carl, Dennis, Al and Bruce – plus American sessionmen Ed Carter on guitar and bass, Daryl Dragon on keyboards and bass, Mike Kowalski on percussion, and a four-piece horn section.

Bruce tells BBC TV: "It was unbelievable! A few months ago, The Beach Boys had drawn just 200 people to a gig in New York City and then we went to England and we sold out a whole tour. It was really crazy! The Beach Boys were really out of favour with the Americans and that's why England saw so much of us in '68 and '69. Every minute, it was: 'Here we are!'"

Bob Farmer reviews one of the Palladium shows in *Disc & Music Echo*: "You've heard expressions such as sorting out the men from the boys. Well, it applies to the current Beach Boys tour, which opened

at London's Palladium on Sunday to packed houses. The Beach Boys were a brilliant and faithful reproduction of all we've come to expect of them on record; the rest, with the sole exception of Eclection, can merely be discounted as there to fill in the first half. The Beach Boys' show is like eating Christmas cake. You leave the marzipan and icing until last. But first you have to plough through the puddingy part.

"A simple introduction [marked] the start of the second half," Farmer continues, "up swept the wine-red curtains, and there they stood, creating impact even before they began in their dazzling white suits. And then into 'Wouldn't It Be Nice', 'Darlin'', 'Sloop John B', bang, bang, bang. Timing to perfection and not a note out of place. 'Do It Again', deluges of applause, Dennis Wilson jacket discarded, demoniac on drums, hair flopping hectically, Keith Moon at 78rpm. For some reason, there follows the flipside of The Beach Boys' 'Do It Again', 'Wake The World', which gets a great reception, so what the hell? The Beach Boys have us eating out of their hands in any case. And if 'Bluebirds Over The Mountain' is a bit un-Beach Boyish to be their latest single, you wouldn't know it by the way the audience is wallowing in it. 'God Only Knows', chubby Carl Wilson coming to the front, and this brings the house down, which is not surprising. Of all that they do this night, perhaps this is the most perfect record reproduction – and then that seems to detract from the other songs they do.

"Pause for Mike Love to explain Brian Wilson's non-arrival, because he's pregnant. 'And it's embarrassing for him to go out.' Then 'Good Vibrations' and they are good vibrations and the curtains come down to encourage the audience to ask for more, as if they need any encouragement. 'Barbara Ann' and a rapping, rocking finish with a new album track titled 'All I Want To Do'. That's the lot, it's not enough, but it's been quite the most polished stage performance I and you have seen from the group in recent years. If there was any doubt about the on-stage ability of this recording ensemble, forget it. In fact, don't dare suggest it."

Later it will be claimed that tonight's shows are the source for the *Live In London* album (released later in the US as *Beach Boys '69*), but this is not the case. The American Federation of Musicians and the British Musicians' Union have blocked plans to record tonight's show. Harry Francis, assistant Musicians' Union secretary, speaking on November 26th, tells *Variety*: "It is no good. The Americans think they can come here and make records. But when the British act goes to America, there is no chance of them getting in the studios. If the reciprocal arrangement is to work, then it must be a two-way thing in all respects." Recordings on 1-inch 8-track tape are nonetheless made of tonight's show, but not used. An agreement is made with the unions, and the recordings that will appear on the *Live In London* album come from a show recorded next week, on December 8th at the Astoria in north London. ('All I Want To Do' from one of the sets recorded tonight is later issued on the 1983 *Beach Boys Rarities* album.)

Set-list (both shows) 'Wouldn't It Be Nice', 'Darlin'', 'Sloop John B', 'California Girls', 'Do It Again', 'Wake The World', 'Bluebirds Over The Mountain', 'God Only Knows', 'Good Vibrations', 'Barbara Ann', 'All I Want To Do'.

• Earlier today, bright and early, Bruce leaves his hotel for a sightseeing trip around central London, including Hyde Park. His conversation with Beach Boys fans who spot him is captured by filmmaker Vic Kettle for his European tour documentary. After tonight's shows at the Palladium, Al, Bruce and Carl visit the nearby Flanagan's public house where Bruce delights the regulars by bashing out tunes on the pub's piano. Carl and Al choose to eat instead of performing. After that, Bruce alone travels on to Blaises nightclub to see a show by The Bandwagon group.

Soundchecking on the European tour: Carl and Al adjust the group's electro-theremin that Mike plays for the distinctive wobbly electronic sounds on 'Good Vibrations'.

■ Monday 2nd

RECORDING Brian's Home Studio *Bel Air, CA*. While the other Beach Boys are away on tour in the UK, Brian is at the helm in his home studio back in California as a reunited line-up of The Honeys reconvene to begin a series of new recordings. They start today with a Murry Wilson composition **'Come To Me'** (take 6 marked best), but it will remain unreleased. (See also December 9th.)

Colston Hall *Bristol* two shows, with Barry Ryan, Bruce Channel, Vanity Fare, Eclection, Sharon Tandy & Fleur De Lys, The Majority; compère: Roger Day

After tonight's performances The Beach Boys return to London's Hilton Hotel in their Austin Princess car.

'Bluebirds Over The Mountain' / **'Never Learn Not To Love'** single released in the US. Aside from 1961's 'Surfin'', this becomes the lowest-charting Beach Boys US single of all time, peaking at number 61 in the American chart. Although not credited as such, the B-side is a Charles Manson song minimally altered and paid for by Dennis. When Manson hears the new version he is angered by Dennis's decision to change his lyrics and is threatening revenge.

■ Tuesday 3rd

Still on tour in Britain, the group this morning faces a press conference at London's Hilton Hotel. Dennis gives a most revealing interview to UK music reporter David Griffiths. "This could be our last tour," Dennis announces. "See, when you go on tour, you could be recording. I guess we've done more touring than just about any other group in the world. Now we're thinking of doing maybe just ten days a year and, for the rest of the time, getting right down to it in the studio. The public is evolving too. A couple of years ago, we got very paranoid about the possibility of losing our public. We were getting loaded, taking acid, and we made a whole album, which we scrapped! Instead, we went to Hawaii, rested up and then came out with the *Smiley Smile* album – all new material. Drugs played a great role in our evolution, but as a result we were frightened that people would no longer understand us, musically. We no longer feel that way. I know that I am now more in tune with my mind. I feel easier and more confident of myself and I am completely involved in communication with others. That's all there is, it's the most fascinating thing."

• Three days after their last visit, the group returns to the BBC Television studios at Lime Grove, west London this afternoon to record another appearance for *Top Of The Pops*, this time lip-synching to 'Bluebirds Over The Mountain'. But due to the song's less than impressive UK chart action the clip is not broadcast, and will remain unscreened.

• After the taping, each member of the group goes on a London sightseeing expedition. Carl and Mike visit a bookshop specialising in the occult, a trip instigated by Mike who has been harbouring plans to write a song about Atlantis, furthered by the title of Donovan's latest disc. Bruce meanwhile pays a visit to the home of Peter Noone of Herman's Hermits fame and later jams with Noel Redding of The Jimi Hendrix Experience at London's Revolution Club.

■ Wednesday 4th

Sheffield City Hall *Sheffield* 6:30 & 8:50pm, with Barry Ryan, Bruce Channel, Vanity Fare, Eclection, Sharon Tandy & Fleur De Lys, The Majority; compère: Roger Day

1968

Following tonight's concerts, a party is held backstage to celebrate Dennis's 24th birthday.

■ Thursday 5th

Odeon Theatre *Manchester* with Barry Ryan, Bruce Channel, Vanity Fare, Eclection, Sharon Tandy & Fleur De Lys, The Majority; compère: Roger Day

To publicise the concerts this evening The Beach Boys make a live personal appearance at Manchester's New Century Hall for the BBC's *Radio 1 Club* in front of hundreds of screaming fans. An interview with Al and Bruce recorded during the visit is transmitted between 12:00 and 2:00pm on Radio-1. (Anglo-American relations take a temporary dip at the Odeon this evening when, backstage, former *Mersey Beat* editor Bill Harry innocently asks the group, "Do you want a fag?")

■ Friday 6th

Odeon Theatre *Birmingham* two shows, with Barry Ryan, Bruce Channel, Vanity Fare, Eclection, Sharon Tandy & Fleur De Lys, The Majority; compère: Roger Day

■ Saturday 7th

Capitol Theatre *Cardiff, Wales* two shows, with Barry Ryan, Bruce Channel, Vanity Fare, Eclection, Sharon Tandy & Fleur De Lys, The Majority; compère: Roger Day

• *Disc & Music Echo* announces that The Beach Boys are to back a brand new group during 1969 ... made up of their own mothers. Bruce leaked the news to the music paper earlier in the week. "I know it sounds incredible and a gigantic gimmick but it's perfectly true," Bruce is quoted as saying. "The only thing is that they don't know yet. We haven't told any of them. We only had the idea this morning. We think we can persuade them to have a go. All of them can sing quite well and have a musical background.

"Al's mother plays violin, my mother a piano, Mrs Wilson the organ and Mrs Belcher, Mike's grandmother, sings. They definitely won't be along the lines of Mrs Miller. They're not meant to be laughed at. We'd like to launch them à la Ken Dodd. Perhaps even with a song like 'Tears' or with something Brian might write. I'm perfectly serious. I know it's probably the most extraordinary thing you've heard. But we've talked about it between us this morning and are going to approach our mothers as soon as we get home from this tour." Strangely, the idea fails to materialise.

■ Sunday 8th

Astoria Theatre *Finsbury Park, north London* two shows, with Barry Ryan, Bruce Channel, Vanity Fare, Eclection, Sharon Tandy & Fleur De Lys, The Majority; compère: Roger Day

Tonight's shows and rehearsals are recorded on 1-inch 8-track tape, while a separate recording of the audience only is made on quarter-inch tape. It is possible that some song orders are altered between the two sets performed this evening, with 'Aren't You Glad' and 'Their Hearts Were Full Of Spring' dropped entirely from one of the shows. Selected recordings are later released by Capitol as the *Live In London* album. It will be issued in the UK in May 1970, in Japan in 1971, in France, Germany and Holland in 1972 – and in America as *Beach Boys '69* in 1976. A heavily edited version of 'Good Vibrations' from today's rehearsal will be released on the 1998 CD *Endless Harmony*.

Set-list 'Darlin'', 'Wouldn't It Be Nice', 'California Girls', 'Sloop John B', 'Do It Again', 'Wake The World', 'Aren't You Glad', 'Bluebirds Over The Mountain', 'Their Hearts Were Full Of Spring', 'Good Vibrations', 'God Only Knows' (encore), 'Barbara Ann' (encore).

■ Monday 9th

RECORDING Brian's Home Studio *Bel Air, CA*. Back in California, Brian is again in the studio with The Honeys, continuing their comeback recordings today with **'Tonight You Belong To Me'** and **'Goodnight My Love (Pleasant Dreams)'** (see 13th).

• Meanwhile in London, during a break from their tour, the group spends a chilly morning in Chiswick on the River Thames embankment shooting another exclusive BBC film clip for *Top Of The Pops*. This segment is planned to accompany the song 'Friends' for a special December 26th show, *Top Of The Pops '68 – Part 2*.

At locations used by The Beatles more than three years earlier during the making of their second film *Help!*, The Beach Boys are seen drinking at the City Barge public house and ambling aimlessly by the river. They stumble upon an elderly man also strolling along the river and ask if he would like to participate in the film they are shooting. He agrees and poses as the captain of the boat that the group and BBC director Tom Taylor decide to use in the clip. Scenes follow of the group climbing into and floating off in a barge. At the end of the shoot, impressed by his acting in the piece, each member of the group chips in with some money to pay the 'captain' for his services. As the man walks away, pleased with his pocketful of money, another passer-by reliably informs the entourage that the quaint old character is, in fact, a 75-year-old millionaire.

The BBC decides against screening the clip and it is subsequently junked. Thankfully Vic Kettle is again on hand to capture the scenes for his tour film, and clips of these scenes will appear in the 1984 documentary *The Beach Boys – An American Band*.

In the afternoon the group takes a trip to The Beatles' Apple headquarters on Savile Row in central London. Their former pressman Derek Taylor escorts them around the elegant building and they come away with free copies of the Fabs' latest *White Album* double. After returning to their Hilton Hotel rooms, the group begins the long stretch up to Glasgow, Scotland to continue the tour.

■ Tuesday 10th

Odeon Theatre *Glasgow, Scotland* two shows, with Barry Ryan, Bruce Channel, Vanity Fare, Eclection, Sharon Tandy & Fleur De Lys, The Majority; compère: Roger Day

During the early hours the group arrives in Scotland and, as on their previous trip, takes up residence at Eilean Donan Castle at Dornie, Kyle of Lochalsh, considered to be Scotland's most romantic castle. The following morning, after tonight's concerts at the Odeon, the group and entourage board a plane to West Germany, where they take up residency in Bremen's Park Hotel.

■ Thursday 12th

TV Radio Bremen TV studio *Bremen, West Germany*. Radio Bremen TV *Beat Club* lip-synch 'Bluebirds Over The Mountain' broadcast December 31st, 'Do It Again' broadcast January 25th 1969, 'California Girls' broadcast March 29th 1969 (all black-and-white). This afternoon The Beach Boys videotape their first appearance on this top-rated German monthly TV pop show. The group's fee for appearing is a paltry equivalent of $140 or £60, the standard fee for every top group that appears on the programme. After the recording the group moves into the studio's control booth to watch playbacks of their performances with the show's production team and director Michael Leckebusch. Although the videotaping is in black-and-white, some behind-the-scenes colour footage of the band on the *Beat Club* set is captured by Vic Kettle's film crew – some of which is briefly seen in the 1984 *American Band* documentary.

Stadthalle *Berlin, West Germany*

This evening the group gives this first of two concerts in Germany.

■ Friday 13th

RECORDING Brian's Home Studio *Bel Air, CA*. Over in the US, recordings are completed for **'Tonight You Belong To Me'** and **'Goodnight My Love (Pleasant Dreams)'** by The Honeys, with Brian again producing. Take 2 of 'Tonight' and take 10 of 'Goodnight' will be coupled for a Honeys single released in the US on March 24th 1969.

TV Bavaria Television Studios *Munich, West Germany*. ZDF *4-3-2-1 Hot And Sweet* lip-synch 'Bluebirds Over The Mountain', 'Do It Again', broadcast colour February 15th 1969.

Kongresshalle *Dusseldorf, West Germany*

Their second day in West Germany sees The Beach Boys filming what will be their only appearance on this weekly ZDF colour TV pop show. 'Bluebirds Over The Mountain' features choreographed dance steps – but, strangely, without Dennis; 'Do It Again' has Dennis and instruments back in the line-up, accompanied by groovy female dancers. Afterwards, the group performs a further concert in Germany and then flies on to Holland, arriving in that country early on Saturday morning.

■ Saturday 14th

TV Theater De Brakke Grond *Amsterdam, Netherlands*. NCRV Nederland 1 *Twien* lip-synch 'Do It Again', 'Friends', 'California Girls', ' Darlin'', 'Wouldn't It Be Nice', 'Sloop John B', 'Good Vibrations', 'God Only Knows', 'Barbara Ann', broadcast black-and-white December 23rd, 3:50-4:10pm; Nederland 2 March 15th 1969, 7:30-7:55pm. During the afternoon the group records an appearance for a special 20-minute edition of this Dutch TV pop show. Although announced as filmed at Amsterdam's Club 67, the group in their regular all-white suits are videotaped at Amsterdam's Theater De Brakke Grond due to large public interest. Portions of this show will be used in the 1984 *American Band* documentary with a re-dubbed audio track.

Concertgebouw *Amsterdam, Netherlands* 12:00 midnight

The Beach Boys make their Dutch concert debut. Afterwards they attend a party at their hotel, and then during the afternoon of the 15th fly on to Paris, France where they will conclude their European tour.

• 'Bluebirds Over The Mountain' single hits the US *Billboard* chart.

■ Monday 16th

Olympia Theatre *Paris, France*

Tonight's Beach Boys performance completes the European leg of their latest excursion.

■ Wednesday 18th

With their European concert appearances now finished, The Beach Boys return to London to record their fourth (and final) exclusive film clip for BBC-1 TV's *Top Of The Pops*. Unfortunately, as with the films shot for 'Bluebirds Over The Mountain' (December 3rd) and 'Friends' (December 9th), today's studio performance of 'Darlin'' lip-synched at the BBC's Wood Lane, west London studios also ends up on the cutting-room floor, failing to make the final cut for the December 26th *Top Of The Pops '68– Part 2*. Commitments completed, the group flies back to California.

■ Saturday 28th

Reflecting a dismal year for The Beach Boys in America, the 'Bluebirds Over The Mountain' single peaks at a disappointing number 61 in the *Billboard* chart. The group's most traumatic and turbulent year is finally over – but 1969 will prove to be only marginally better.

The five-piece touring Beach Boys relax off-stage: (back row) Mike Love, Bruce Johnston, Dennis Wilson; (front) Al Jardine, Carl Wilson.

1969

Recording sessions begin for a new album, to become next year's *Sunflower* ... *20/20* album released ... 'I Can Hear Music' single makes US number 24 and UK number 10 ... The Beach Boys' record label Brother Records is again launched ... Brian announces that the group has severe financial problems, soon denied by Bruce ... European tour takes place, including dates in Czechoslovakia ... on tour in London, Carl spots South African group The Flames that includes future Beach Boys Blondie Chaplin and Ricky Fataar ... 'Break Away' single makes US number 63 and UK number 6 ... Capitol contract expires with one album still due ... deal with German label Deutsche Grammophon fails ... sessions for the album that becomes *Sunflower* continue ... The Beach Boys sign a new recording contract with Warner/Reprise ... Murry Wilson sells entire publishing rights to the group's original songs.

Mike works on his Czech stage announcements as the group waits backstage before one of their historic concerts in Prague in June. The Beach Boys are the first Western rock group to play there since the Soviet invasion last year.

1969

January

■ Thursday 9th
RECORDING *Sunflower* sessions Brian's Home Studio *Bel Air, CA*. Around this time, The Beach Boys, now sharing production duties, set to work recording a new album for Capitol. Probably today the basic recording is done for Dennis's **'San Miguel'**, written by Dennis and Gregg Jacobson (see 9th; unreleased until the 1981 *10 Years Of Harmony* compilation and then 1993's *Good Vibrations* boxed set), and possibly around now work starts on **'Forever'**. Recordings for the new album will continue intermittently over the next three months.

■ Saturday 11th
'Bluebirds Over The Mountain' single peaks in UK chart at number 33. Even though it receives extensive airtime on Radio Luxembourg, the 45's low position is reflected across most of the European charts.

■ Monday 13th
MIXING Sunset Sound studio *Hollywood, CA*. A 'reduction' mix is made on 8-track of the recording of Dennis's **'San Miguel'**. (A 'reduction' mix is one made to condense multi-track recordings into one or two tracks of another machine, here an 8-track, to provide free tracks for recording vocals.)

TOUR STARTS North America (Jan 15th-18th)

■ Wednesday 15th
The Queen Elizabeth Theatre *Vancouver, BC, Canada*
Leaving the comfort of the studio, the group heads off northwards for a brief four-date concert tour.

■ Thursday 16th
Memorial Arena *Victoria, BC, Canada*

■ Friday 17th
Seattle Center Coliseum *Seattle, WA*

■ Saturday 18th
PNE Agrodome *Vancouver, BC, Canada* with Tommy James & The Shondells
Last night of this short tour.

■ Sunday 19th
RECORDING Capitol studio (B) *Hollywood, CA*. Another tracking session for Dennis's **'San Miguel'**; no complete takes are made.

■ Wednesday 29th
MIXING Sunset Sound studio *Hollywood, CA*. Reduction mixes and edits are made to **'San Miguel'**.

■ Friday 31st
MIXING Sunset Sound studio *Hollywood, CA*. A stereo mix session is held for **'San Miguel'**.

February

■ Monday 10th
20/20 album released in the US. The album's title originates from its distinction as the 20th Beach Boys album released by Capitol – and

---

20/20 album

A1 'Do It Again' (B. WILSON / M. LOVE)
A2 'I Can Hear Music' (J. BARRY / E. GREENWICH/ P. SPECTOR)
A3 'Bluebirds Over The Mountain' (E. HICKEY)
A4 'Be With Me' (D. WILSON)
A5 'All I Want To Do' (D. WILSON)
A6 'The Nearest Faraway Place' (B. JOHNSTON)
B1 'Cotton Fields (The Cotton Song)' ALBUM VERSION (H. LEDBETTER)
B2 'I Went To Sleep' (B. WILSON / C. WILSON)
B3 'Time To Get Alone' (B. WILSON)
B4 'Never Learn Not To Love' (D. WILSON)
B5 'Our Prayer' (B. WILSON)
B6 'Cabinessence' (B. WILSON / V.D. PARKS)

US release February 10th 1969 (Capitol SKAO133).
UK release March 1969 (Capitol EST133).
Chart high US number 68; UK number 3.

---

for the eye chart that Brian hides behind in a photograph inside the gatefold cover. It will outsell *Friends* in the US, peaking at number 68 – a fair position considering recent chart performance – and in the UK will peak at a very impressive number 3, the group's best showing in that country since *Pet Sounds*.

The disc successfully combines impressive new material, recent singles, and re-workings of tracks from *Smile*. The new recordings mark the emergence of Carl and Dennis as producers and of Steve Desper as the group's engineer. Desper is now part of The Beach Boys' fold and remains as chief engineer of their work early into the next decade.

TOUR STARTS US Texas (Feb 11th-15th)

■ Tuesday 11th
The Municipal Auditorium *Austin, TX*
The group begins a short five-date tour of Texas.

■ Wednesday 12th
Heart O' Texas Coliseum *Waco, TX*

■ Thursday 13th
RECORDING *Sunflower* sessions Sunset Sound studio *Hollywood, CA*. Evidence suggests this is the tracking date for Dennis's **'Got To Know The Woman'**. Sixteen 'takes', or attempts at a recording of the song, are taped on 1-inch 8-track tape (take 16 is marked as master) with Bill Lazerus engineering, and take 16 is then overdubbed with fuzz guitar and organ.
Memorial Auditorium *Dallas, TX*

■ Friday 14th
Sam Houston Coliseum *Houston, TX*
'I Can Hear Music' / 'All I Want To Do' single released in the UK.

■ Saturday 15th
Tarrant County Convention Center *Ft Worth, TX*
Last night of the short Texan jaunt.

I Can Hear Music single

A '**I Can Hear Music**' (J. BARRY / E. GREENWICH / P. SPECTOR)
B '**All I Want To Do**' (D. WILSON)

UK release February 14th 1969 (Capitol CL 15584).
US release March 3rd 1969 (Capitol 2432).
Chart high UK number 10; US number 24.

■ Sunday 16th

TV NBC Television, Color City Studios *Burbank, CA*. NBC *Kraft Music Hall* lip-synch 'California Girls', 'I Can Hear Music', broadcast colour February 19th, 9:00-10:00pm. With current tour duties at a close, the group debuts this afternoon on the NBC weekly variety show, this one hosted by Don Adams of TV's *Get Smart* and comedian Don Rickles and so entitled *Don Adams And Don Rickles Are Alive And Well And Living In California*. For 'California Girls' the group performs on a large staging area surrounded by approximately 50 attractive bikini-attired women. They also mime to their new single, 'I Can Hear Music'. ('California Girls' from this show will be featured in the 1998 documentary *Endless Harmony*.)

■ Monday 24th

RECORDING *Sunflower* sessions Gold Star studio *Los Angeles, CA*. The group returns to the studio and continues work on the next album. Today they record 'tracking' (backing instruments) and vocals for '**Celebrate The News**', another composition by Dennis Wilson and Gregg Jakobson.

March

20/20 album released in the UK. It will peak in the chart at the number 3 position.

■ Monday 3rd

'**I Can Hear Music**' / '**All I Want To Do**' single released in the US. Lifted from the *20/20* album and a cover of the 1966 Ronettes 45, 'I Can Hear Music' is produced and arranged by 22-year-old Carl and is full of superb vocal and instrumental arrangements. It becomes a major turning point for the group. With this single they show they are able to work without Brian yet still recreate his classic sound and produce great, timeless records. It's a hit for the group, peaking at number 10 in the UK chart and at a strong number 24 in the US listings. As such it will mark their 25th and last Top 40 US hit of the decade.

A film to accompany 'I Can Hear Music' is compiled from footage shot at the recording sessions for 'Time To Get Alone' on October 2nd and 4th 1968. This colour 16mm clip is extensively aired, including appearances on *Happening* (ABC TV, US, April 22nd) and *Top Of The Pops* (BBC-1, UK, April 3rd).

■ Saturday 5th – Sunday 6th

RECORDING *Sunflower* sessions Sunset Sound studio *Hollywood, CA*. Sessions for the next studio album start again with the first proper tracking recordings of '**Loop De Loop**'. Recordings for this

song, a co-composition by Brian, Carl and Al, will resume later in the month when the first set of vocals are added at Brian's Home Studio. (In autumn 1977, this original 1969 backing track for 'Loop De Loop' will have lyrics about Santa Claus dubbed on to make 'Santa's Got An Airplane' during sessions for the group's planned but inevitably unreleased second Christmas album. It will remain unreleased until the 1998 *Ultimate Christmas* CD. In July 1998 Al will take the 1969 tracks as his basis and record new lead vocals, the result being released on 1998's *Endless Harmony* soundtrack CD.) An instrumental recognisable as '**When Girls Get Together**' is also recorded during this period.

■ Wednesday 9th

Murry Wilson records a session with a group called The Snow.

■ Saturday 12th

'I Can Hear Music' single peaks in UK chart at number 10.

■ Thursday 17th

RECORDING *Sunflower* sessions Gold Star studio (A) *Los Angeles, CA*. Dennis's song '**Forever**' is overdubbed on this date with strings and vocals. All additions are made to take 39, which is marked as master.

■ Saturday 19th

RECORDING *Sunflower* sessions Gold Star studio (A) *Los Angeles, CA*. Today, 39 takes are made of Brian and Mike's '**All I Wanna Do**', recorded on 1-inch 8-track tape.

■ Friday 21st

RECORDING *Sunflower* sessions Gold Star studio (A) *Los Angeles, CA*. Today sees the first tracking and vocal session for '**Deirdre**' (take 20 marked as master). Further work will be done on August 18th this year and January 9th 1970. The song is intended for the group's next Capitol album and ultimately released on the 1970 *Sunflower* LP. On that record Bruce and Brian share composition credits, although Bruce tells *NME*: "I tried to get Brian to do the lyrics. I gave him 50 per cent of the song and he wound up writing four lines. I said to myself, 'Most of this song is me, but what the hell. We'll just split it.'" The Deirdre in question is the sister of one of Bruce's former girlfriends.

■ Monday 24th

'**Tonight You Belong To Me**' / '**Goodnight My Love**' single by The Honeys released in the US. Capitol issues the group's final 45, with Brian producing both recordings.

Monday 31st

RECORDING Gold Star studio *Los Angeles, CA*. After the release of *20/20*, Murry Wilson calls his eldest son and tells him that the group needs his help. Murry desperately wants to write a great hit with Brian, who agrees. Thus is born the marvellous '**Break Away**', written in just an hour. By now the group probably know that this is likely to be The Beach Boys' last single for Capitol, as they are about to leave the label. Eager to leave on a high note, Brian rises to the challenge and becomes involved in the song's production, swiftly devising an impressive recording.

Sessions begin today with the group working on the song's basic instrumental track of guitars, drums and bass. With that completed, backing vocals are overdubbed by the whole group, followed by Carl and Al taping guide lead vocals – Carl on the verses, Al on the chorus. Next, new backing vocals are recorded and a fresh set of lead vocals are double-tracked. At the conclusion of the session Brian tapes a solo guide vocal for the track (see April 2nd). Work on the song resumes on April 23rd.

April

■ Tuesday 1st

TV Westinghouse Broadcasting Company, Group W Productions *Philadelphia, PA*. Syndicated *The Mike Douglas Show* live vocals over taped backing tracks 'I Can Hear Music', 'Never Learn Not To Love', broadcasts begin April 9th. The Beach Boys fly to Philadelphia and this evening record their third appearance on *Mike Douglas*. For 'Never Learn', Dennis sings up front as Carl takes over on drums. The 90-minute show also features Shirley Bassey and actor Glenn Ford.

■ Wednesday 2nd

MIXING I.D. Sound studio *Hollywood, CA*. Brian holds a mono mixing session for **'Break Away'**. A mix from this session, featuring just Brian on lead and backing vocals, will be issued on the 1998 CD *Endless Harmony*. Surprisingly, Brian will recall in a liner note he pens for Rhino Records that he was inspired by The Monkees to write 'Break Away'.

TOUR STARTS US South (Apr 3rd-13th)

■ Thursday 3rd

Dome *Virginia Beach, VA*

As usual now, the group is bolstered on-stage with extra musicians, often including at least Daryl Dragon (keyboards, bass), Mike Kowalski (percussion) and Ed Carter (guitar, bass).

■ Friday 4th

Curtis-Hixon Hall *Tampa, FL* with The Classics IV

■ Saturday 5th

Convention Hall *Miami Beach, FL*

■ Monday 7th

Peabody Auditorium *Daytona Beach, FL*

■ Tuesday 8th

Municipal Auditorium *Orlando, FL*

■ Wednesday 9th

Civic Auditorium *Jacksonville, FL*

Tonight's show is a sell-out charity event for the Heart Fund Benefit.

■ Thursday 10th

Municipal Auditorium *Atlanta, GA*

■ Friday 11th

Mid-South Coliseum *Memphis, TN*

■ Saturday 12th

Municipal Auditorium *Nashville, TN*

• Problems with Capitol Records come to a head today when The Beach Boys issue a lawsuit against the label for just over $2million. This consists of $622,618 in unpaid royalties and $1,418,827 in unpaid Capitol production fees for Brian, plus other losses incurred through alleged general mismanagement. According to the group's business manager Nick Grillo the lawsuit arises from his December 1966 audit of Capitol's books. The action effectively ends the group's seven-year association with Capitol and gives them the freedom to re-launch their own label, Brother Records.

The group announce at a press conference today that they "hope to create the furthest reaching music company ever established. Brother Records will have a different policy in dealing with artists than most record companies have. We hope to create a relationship with artists that will revolutionise the recording business by eliminating exploitation. All artists on Brother Records will participate in the company's profits, predicted on a formula still to be devised. Artists will be offered complete financial protection through Financial Concepts Inc, a management company that will perform complete accounting services and offer financial and investment advice to all personnel connected with Brother Records".

The released statement then concludes by marking out the group's intention to build a 16-track recording studio within their own studio complex.

Brother Records initiates a conglomerate of business enterprises including recording company, travel agency, business management operation, personal management company, and concert production firm. The directorship of the companies is divided between Nick Grillo and Dick Duryea, who also serves as a production co-ordinator. The Beach Boys are also running a real-estate syndicate and a cardio-vascular clinic in Jacksonville, Florida, under their already established Financial Concepts Inc.

"A lot of stuff detailed in the press release is still in the talk stages," Brian tells reporters. "This all hasn't happened yet. The fellows are never home long enough to make all their decisions." Shifting gear, he adds: "Our overheads in our office are so high. We have to go on the road every two weeks to stay even. Right now, Brother Records is just a logo. Before, when we started Brother the first time, it was formed because that was what we wanted to do artistically. But now it's an economic necessity."

When told of Brian's comments, Beach Boys manager Nick Grillo moves quickly to dismiss the remarks. "This is untrue," he blasts. "If Brian told you this, he's just putting you on. He hardly ever comes around the office. Brian's scared of corporate decisions, so he wouldn't know."

■ Sunday 13th

Oklahoma State Penitentiary *McAlester, OK*

The saga of Carl and his refusal to be drafted has been going on for two years, and as part of the deal The Beach Boys take time off from their tour of the South to play a morning concert at Oklahoma's State Penitentiary. Brian admits later in *NME*: "The prison concert and other charity bashes are not all motivated by the goodness of our heart. It's a kind of unofficial way for the group to pay off our debt to the American government for allowing Carl to become a conscientious objector. A few concerts here and there is the alternative to him emptying some bed pans in some hospital to substitute for military service." Their journey is made in a plane supplied by the Governor of Oklahoma. Reports at the time suggest that the group is accepting as many benefit shows as possible, especially for hospitals. A charity concert in Louisburg, North Carolina, is arranged soon after.

■ Wednesday 16th

Just four days after the group issued a lawsuit against their record company, it is perhaps surprising to note that The Beach Boys and Capitol evidently still share an interest in renewing their recording contract. Today the label's A&R director Karl Engemann drafts a letter explaining the position to Nick Grillo at Brother Records:

Dear Nick,
It was good speaking with you today and I am most happy to hear that in spite of the recent Billboard article [regarding the lawsuit], you and the group still have a desire to remain with Capitol if something satisfactory can be worked out. I, too, hope we have enough hits out of the product you plan to deliver to us between now and the end of the contract to give us cause to re-evaluate our most recent offer. Confirming our discussion, and as a reminder, you are going to talk with the boys about delivering the next single record by next Monday, April 21, and the album (The Fading Rock Group Revival or Reverberation) by May 1. Again I want to tell you how enthused I am about the single, 'Loop De Loop (Flip Flop)', and I'm most anxious to hear some of the things the boys have been working on for the next album.
Sincerely,
Karl Engemann

This deadline of April 21st for the single will pass with no delivery of suitable tapes. (See May 1st.)

Friday 18th
Beverly Hilton Hotel *Beverly Hills, CA*
The band's recent run of concert appearances concludes with this historic Senior Prom homecoming gig for Hawthorne High. The group performs for free and, contrary to later belief, the concert does not take place at the Hawthorne school itself.

Wednesday 23rd
RECORDING Brian's Home Studio *Bel Air, CA*. After a three-week break from the song, The Beach Boys supervise the taping of a horn insert and additional backing vocals onto the March 31st tracking tape of **'Break Away'**. Two alternative mono mixes of the song are made, completing the session.

Work on their next studio album is still not finished, however, even though Capitol has requested delivery of the new disc by May 1st, just over a week away.

Saturday 26th
'I Can Hear Music' single peaks in US chart at number 24.

Wednesday 30th
Mike arrives alone in Britain today for a business and social visit. His main aim is to finalise details for a special Beach Boys charity concert at the Odeon Theatre in Birmingham on June 6th. The show is in aid of The Spiritual Regeneration Movement, an organisation run by the Maharishi Mahesh Yogi, and will form part of the group's next UK tour, scheduled to begin on May 30th. During Mike's brief one-week excursion to the UK he also pays a visit to the Brighton Meditation School in Sussex.

May

The Beach Boys begin a weekly radio series for the *Voice Of America* transcription service in America, and plans are afoot for the group to appear in a series of lucrative commercials for Coca-Cola, but these fail to materialise.
• Early this month the group performs two shows at the Music Hall in Omaha, Nebraska, in front of crowds totalling 21,000, and possibly play other Midwest dates.

Thursday 1st
Today's deadline for delivery of The Beach Boys' latest (and last) Capitol album passes. Thus another projected LP by the group bites the dust. They fail to deliver because only seven of the album's ten recordings are complete, namely: 'Loop De Loop' (recorded March 5th and 6th); 'Break Away' (March 31st and April 23rd); 'San Miguel' (January 9th & 19th); 'Celebrate The News' (February 24th); 'Deirdre' (first version recorded March 21st); 'The Lord's Prayer' (the November 1963 recording in 'duophonic' or 'fake' stereo); and 'Forever' (January 9th).

Capitol documents name the proposed LP as *The Fading Rock Group Revival* or *Reverberation*. Despite Bruce later denying these titles, they are genuine working titles for now. The Beach Boys still owe the label one album to fulfil their contractual obligation. In the meantime, a new single is indeed delivered to Capitol (see June 16th and September introduction).

Tuesday 13th
MIXING. A stereo mixing session is held for **'Break Away'**, which now features full group vocals. The resulting single will be issued only in stereo in the US.

Monday 26th
At Brian's Home Studio the group set to work taping a 60-minute special for Radio Luxembourg, which broadcasts to Europe, including the UK. The show is their first for the station and is set for transmission to coincide with the group's upcoming European visit. Each member takes a turn at introducing a selected track from their impressive back catalogue. (The introductions by Mike to 'Surfin'', Dennis to 'Cotton Fields', and Al and Carl to 'Break Away' will appear on Capitol's 2001 Beach Boys compilation *Hawthorne, CA – Birthplace Of A Musical Legacy*.) Taping over, the group prepare for their next tour, an important and historic four-week excursion to the UK and Europe. As usual now, Brian will not be accompanying them – and anyway, he has plans of his own.

Tuesday 27th
Just three days before The Beach Boys' latest tour is due to start, Brian drops the biggest bombshell in the group's eight-year history. At a hastily arranged press conference at his house, he says: "The Beach Boys' empire is crumbling and in deep financial trouble."

He continues: "It's got so bad that The Beach Boys are considering financial bankruptcy. We're pretty low on money. We owe everyone money, and if we don't pick ourselves off our backsides and have a hit record soon we will be in worse trouble. Nick Grillo, our business manager, says if we don't start climbing out of the mess he will have to file bankruptcy in Los Angeles by the end of the year.

"Things started deteriorating about 18 months ago. Thousands of dollars were being frittered away and thrown away on stupid things. We spent a heck of a lot of corporation money on Brother Records, our own company, and in boosting other recording artists who just didn't make it and didn't have a single hit. When our records started to bomb out, we looked around desperately for something to save ourselves. We've had one recent hit, 'I Can Hear Music', but one hit isn't enough to pay for our tremendous overheads.

"Then recently Nick told us just how bad it really was. It was a big shock for all of us. A really tough blow. We all know that if we don't watch it and do something drastic inside a few months, we won't have a penny in the bank. I've always said be honest with the fans and I don't see why I should lie and say everything is rosy when it's not. Sure, when we were making millions, I said we were. But now the shoe is on the other foot.

"When we started earning good money, it was the same old story all over again. A lot of the guys started throwing their money around, buying cars, houses and other things, and pretty soon the cash started dwindling. When we didn't have hits there just wasn't enough bread coming in to pay for the overheads and we started to feel the ship sinking. Dennis now lives in a one-bedroom cellar in the basement of a friend's house in Beverly Hills. His car was smashed up in a traffic accident. He had loaned it to a friend and he has never replaced it. His room has a bed and a piano and nothing else, not even a bathroom.

"Nick wanted to check money individually with each member of the group, and he got different answers from each one. He was left hanging in the air because there was never a unanimous answer. We were all too busy with something else. Nick hasn't been with us for too long. He hasn't done badly but the job has given him two ulcers and he's working on a third. The other day, Mike Love had a battle of words with him and Nick said he wouldn't quit the group for anything. He is a member of our family as well as the other guys. We're even talking about doing a soft-drink commercial, something we have never done before, to beef up our bank balance." Brian concludes: "The Beach Boys' tour of Britain must be a success if the group is to survive."

There are further disruptions for the group when on June 4th, during the European tour, road and production manager Dick Duryea abruptly and unexpectedly leaves the group's organisation. Drafted in to replace him is the group's close friend and former concert promoter, Fred Vail, who left The Beach Boys back in summer 1966. "I was setting up a fair in Denver when The Beach Boys called," he recalls. "They asked if I'd come back as their co-manager. I replaced Dick Duryea. Nick Grillo was the group's business manager so I was hired to do the group's promotions, marketing and touring." Another change in personnel at this time sees Mike Love's brother Steve installed as the band's new road manager.

TOUR STARTS UK/ Europe (May 30th–Jun 30th) While Brian's startling comments are reverberating around the United States, his Beach Boy colleagues are in London preparing for another tour, a three-week excursion featuring an all-American line-up with support group Paul Revere & The Raiders and soul singer Joe Hicks.

Bruce tells *NME*: "We shouldn't have toured with The Raiders because they are a bubblegum kind of band. We were making our own decisions and some were very dumb. We wanted the group to happen in Europe, but we really should have taken Fairport Convention."

The Beach Boys arrive at Heathrow Airport on Thursday May 29th in a chartered Carvair plane. Clearance through customs is delayed for hours as officials insist on carefully examining every vitamin pill the entourage carries. Once through, the group is greeted by *New Musical Express* reporter Richard Green, and immediately the group and Green head across London, stopping for one night at the Royal Lancaster Hotel before heading off to Brighton, Sussex during this morning. Upon their arrival at the popular seaside resort the group takes up residence for the first time at the town's Transcendental Meditation School. Throughout their 31-day excursion Mike will regularly adopt a long white flowing robe, inspired by the Maharishi and reflecting his changing lifestyle.

Accompanying The Beach Boys on this visit is $200,000 worth of special musical equipment. Also along is cameraman Vic Kettle who has been assigned to capture further film footage of the group's activities for another proposed television special. Regular visits to the UK and Europe have become important to the group. In these territories, Beach Boys records continue to sell well and concert appearances by the band are commercially viable. But this current jaunt comes with an ulterior motive. The group is keen to impress successful Berlin-based record company Deutsche Grammophon, a label that has been showing strong inclinations to sign the group, who will soon be without a record company. Discussions have started between the group and DG and the first face-to-face meeting has been set for June 15th in Berlin.

■ Friday 30th
Brighton Dome *Brighton* 6:15 & 8:45pm, with Paul Revere & The Raiders, Joe Hicks; compère: Alan Field

The opening of this latest European jaunt takes place in front of two sell-out crowds. The backing band of musicians for the tour performs under the direction of John Deandreas and includes a brass section with baritone saxophonist John Warren.

Julie Webb writes in *Fabulous 208*: "The Dome was packed and the audience receptive. The Beach Boys were marvellous; Paul Revere & The Raiders were worried. ... The Beach Boys really do pack them in and put an end to those people who say pop tours are dead." A clip of the group performing a cover of Buffalo Springfield's 'Rock'n'Roll Woman' from this show will appear in the 1984 documentary *An American Band*.

After the evening concert Bruce and the *NME*'s Richard Green record an (inevitably unaired) appearance for the BBC's *Radio One Club*, joining Andy Fairweather-Low of Amen Corner and Richie Havens among other guests. The Beach Boys return to central London early the following morning and resume residence in their suites at the Royal Lancaster Hotel.

Set-list (8:45) 'I Can Hear Music', 'Wouldn't It Be Nice', 'California Girls', 'Darlin'', 'I Get Around', 'Rock'n'Roll Woman', 'Cotton Fields', 'Sloop John B', 'Do It Again', 'Break Away', 'Barbara Ann', 'The Nearest Faraway Place', 'God Only Knows', medley 'The Warmth Of The Sun' / 'Don't Worry Baby' / 'Please Let Me Wonder' / 'Surfer Girl' / 'In My Room', 'Their Hearts Were Full Of Spring', 'Good Vibrations'.

■ Saturday 31st
Hammersmith Odeon *west London* 6:45 & 9:15pm, with Paul Revere & The Raiders, Joe Hicks; compère: Alan Field

Following Brian's statement last week regarding The Beach Boys' apparently perilous financial situation, the group is almost prevented from continuing this tour. The charter aircraft company, the Royal Lancaster Hotel and some of the musicians accompanying the group are aware of Brian's words, and all demand payments for their services in advance. Subsequently the group is holed up in London while money is quickly raised and wired from a bank in Beverly Hills, California. Later, with adequate cash obtained, the first show in London takes place.

David Hughes writes in *Disc & Music Echo*: "If The Beach Boys are really in Britain just to make some quick money and get themselves in the black again ... they're certainly making sure they earned it! At the sedate Hammersmith Odeon on Saturday the world's most popular active group turned an uncommonly apathetic first-house audience into rousing cheers with 50 non-stop minutes taking in no less than 18 hits.

"The Beach Boys all looked happy, well fed and affluent. On stage they are a strange mixture of personalities and temperaments. Bruce, as always, is the crowd-conscious Beach Boy, always anxious to tell the audience how great it is to be in England again, slipping in little news snippets on the progress of Carl's baby, or the current health of Brian Wilson. Bruce is also the versatile one, switching from organ to bass guitar frequently and with great agility. Carl is still the leader and the voice, and either seriously or playfully (it's difficult to tell which) chooses to ignore all the 'asides' from the others and keeps the music going. His voice still misses the high notes on the loud numbers and he still becomes quite overwhelmed by the reaction to 'God Only Knows'. He should know by now that this will go down in history as the group's finest-ever recording.

"Mike Love has grown his beard, grown his hair (on those parts of his head where it still grows, that is) and has acquired an incredible white tunic/mini-habit. The overall effect is a cross between the Maharishi's younger brother and the original hermit from the hills. All very incongruous, especially when he bursts into 'Well, the East Coast girls are hip, I really dig those clothes they wear.' Mike has always looked the misfit in the group and gives the impression on stage that he doesn't really know what he's doing up there. His ad libs with the audience are becoming more and more outspoken.

"Al Jardine keeps himself to himself, and looks worried when his amplification equipment apparently doesn't work, though you can't hear his guitar anyway. [He sings solo on] 'Cotton Fields' from *20/20*. And Dennis Wilson, maybe because he never says anything, and always looks so wild and unpredictable, gets the bulk of the fan screams. Yet there were screams, plenty of them, and it will be a sad day when they stop. Dennis chews gum perpetually, occasionally mouths a few words of a song that takes his fancy, rebukes the band-leader for playing the wrong rhythm, and generally looks as if he can't wait to get off stage."

Set-list (6:45) 'I Can Hear Music', 'Wouldn't It Be Nice', 'California Girls', 'Darlin'', medley 'The Warmth Of The Sun' / 'Don't Worry Baby' / 'Please Let Me Wonder' / 'Surfer Girl' / 'In My Room', 'I Get Around', 'Rock'n'Roll Woman', 'Cotton Fields', 'Sloop John B', 'Do

It Again', 'Break Away', 'Barbara Ann', 'The Nearest Faraway Place', 'God Only Knows', 'Their Hearts Were Full Of Spring', 'Good Vibrations'. The 9:15 performance loses 'Rock'n'Roll Woman' but adds an impromptu Mrs Mills medley by Bruce on organ and a rousing version of 'Johnny B Goode' as part of the encore.

June

■ Sunday 1st
De Doelen Rotterdam, Netherlands 2:30pm; Concertgebouw, Amsterdam, Netherlands 8:15pm, with Paul Revere & The Raiders, Joe Hicks

■ Tuesday 3rd
TV Radio Bremen TV studio *Bremen, West Germany*. Radio Bremen TV *Beat Club* lip-synch 'Break Away' broadcast June 7th, 'Surfin' USA' broadcast August 2nd. This morning The Beach Boys fly into Germany and immediately head to Bremen to record their second appearance on this prestigious monthly pop show. Excerpts from the Peter Clifton-directed 'Do It Again' promotional film are played as a backdrop during 'Surfin' USA'.
• Back in California, the group's musical friend Terry Melcher visits Spahn's Ranch, a derelict site in the Santa Susana Mountains in the suburbs of Los Angeles once used for Westerns and other movies. There Melcher meets Charles Manson and his 'Family', who have been living at the ranch since they were thrown out of Dennis's home last August.

Accompanying Melcher is a trailer equipped with a mobile recording studio, along with Dennis's songwriting friend Gregg Jakobson, there to take photographs of Manson. Melcher is considering going beyond Manson's music and making a

documentary about his way of life, finally moving on a long-mooted idea to record and film Manson in his real environment. However, shortly after they arrive, and with Melcher and Jakobson watching, Manson gets into a fight with a drunken old stuntman who also lives on the ranch. It is the first time that Melcher has seen such anger and violence erupting from Manson, and the scenes shock him so much that he decides to end his involvement with Manson now.

When Melcher and Jakobson start to pack up and leave, Manson argues with them. Manson feels betrayed by Melcher and wants revenge. Family hanger-on 'Sunshine' will recount later that, after the argument, Manson approaches Sunshine and asks if he would help him to commit a murder. Later today, Manson puts out a contract on someone's life. Manson thinks he knows where Melcher lives because Manson was in the back seat when Dennis drove Melcher home one evening. But at present Melcher does not live at 10050 Cielo Drive. For the past four months the property has been rented out to screen actress Sharon Tate and her movie-director husband Roman Polanski.

■ Wednesday 4th

Olympia Theatre *Paris, France* with Paul Revere & The Raiders, Joe Hicks

Brian's controversial statements made last week continue to cause the group problems and this morning in Paris, Bruce is forced to reply on behalf of the rest of the group. Playing down Brian's allegation, he announces in a typed statement: "We're not broke at all, and it's been very upsetting to have spent the whole tour denying this instead of talking about the things we wanted, like music and meditation. While we all admire Brian immensely for what he does for the group, it's a fact that creative people are funny and don't know much about business. We have a business manager who handles all the financial side of the group's business, and personal wealth has nothing to do with our business wealth. But in view of the fact that we've just bought a new million-dollar office block to house all our companies and another studio to cope with all the recordings, you can't really say we're broke."

Beach Boys co-manager Fred Vail recalls in 2003: "It was more truth than fiction. Brian might have been exaggerating a little bit from his perspective. He's got a wife and kid and a house in Bel Air, and you start to panic easily. Brian might have overstated the situation, but The Beach Boys were in financial straits at this time. There is no question that they had financial problems. They had had two really bad tours in 1968, neither of which I was involved in. They were financial disasters for the band and they were really digging out from being under a mound of debt from creditors. They were not getting a lot of airplay and Capitol was not putting 110 percent into *20/20* because they knew it was going to be their last album. The Beach Boys were looking for another label and it was a kind of limbo period of their career.

"During that limbo period, and because of their two disastrous tours, a lot of my time was spent dealing with bill collectors, hotels, airlines, Diners Club cards, etc. I was working out terms for payments and looking at ways we could generate more revenue, like tours. But what was even worse was the fact that The Beach Boys had always been a touring band: the group had always relied heavily on doing 150 or so dates a year, and when you can't fill the calendar because promoters don't want you or are offering too little, it's devastating! It had a trickle-down effect. It affects everybody. It affects the front office, the staff, individual lifestyles, the families – and that's the real problem.

"I remember several tours where I had to advance the primary money for the tour out of my American Express and Diners Club credit cards," Vail continues. "And as we went along and played the gigs, I would take the money out to pay the bills. But there were some shortages, so I ended up being owed about $3,500. That wasn't paid, of course, and so the credit card companies came after me and not The Beach Boys. It was pretty tough. Things didn't start to pick up again for the group until about 1971/72 – it took a couple of years. By 1974, with *Endless Summer*, it was pretty much back on its feet."

Following the performance in France, the group spends the 5th relaxing in the country, before flying back to London Airport on the morning of June 6th.

■ Friday 6th

Odeon Theatre *Birmingham* 6:30 & 9:00pm, with Paul Revere & The Raiders, Joe Hicks; compère: Alan Field

The group returns to England for two special charity shows in aid of The Spiritual Regeneration Movement, an organisation run by the Maharishi Mahesh Yogi. The Move's Carl Wayne visits the group backstage. Valerie Mabbs writes in *Record Mirror*: "During the second half of the show The Beach Boys took to the stage with Mike Love dressed in a flowing white monk-style robe. The boys opened their set with 'In My Room' and, after making light-hearted quips about their financial status, they continued with 'I Get Around', 'Sloop John B' and 'Do It Again'. One of the highlights was their current release 'Break Away', which must renew every fan's faith in The Beach Boys' musical talent. Al Jardine was highlighted with 'Cotton Fields' and Carl Wilson excelled with 'God Only Knows'. The Beach Boys closed an enjoyable and memorable show with 'Good Vibrations' and left the capacity audience well satisfied."

■ Saturday 7th

Empire Theatre *Liverpool* 6:10 & 8:40pm, with Paul Revere & The Raiders, Joe Hicks; compère: Alan Field

Set-list (8:40) 'I Can Hear Music', 'Wouldn't It Be Nice', 'California Girls', 'Darlin'', medley 'The Warmth Of The Sun' / 'Don't Worry Baby' / 'Please Let Me Wonder' / 'Surfer Girl' / 'In My Room', 'I Get Around', 'Sloop John B', 'Do It Again', 'Break Away', 'Cotton Fields', medley 'Barbara Ann' / 'Papa-Oom-Mow-Mow', 'God Only Knows', 'Their Hearts Were Full Of Spring', 'Good Vibrations'.

■ Sunday 8th

King Edward Nurses Home, Leeds General Infirmary *Leeds* matinee; **Free Trade Hall** *Manchester* 6:00 & 8:30pm, with Paul Revere & The Raiders, Joe Hicks; compère: Alan Field

This afternoon in a special show arranged by the group's former road and production manager Dick Duryea and BBC DJ and *Top Of The Pops* presenter Jimmy Savile, The Beach Boys perform a concert for staff at Leeds Infirmary hospital. Savile tells BBC radio that Bruce Johnston phoned him from Los Angeles and offered to do the hospital show. "I put the phone down and thought, 'Well, this will never happen.' I went back to the hospital and I was faced with a problem. Should I say that The Beach Boys are coming over? Because I've got to make some provision if they are coming. How can I keep it quiet? Because if I say The Beach Boys are going to hit Leeds, where they weren't going to play anyway, there would be everyone and a dog crowding to see them. What a position! Plus, what if I made the arrangements and The Beach Boys didn't turn up? I would be crucified! Whichever way I looked at it, it looked bad, but at the same time, it was good. I crossed my fingers and toes and went ahead with the arrangements."

Savile only believes the concert will happen when he sees the group's coach pulling up to an ambulance parking area – and out step The Beach Boys. "They all came down to the boardroom and we had some lunch. I said, 'What have you brought with you?' They said, 'Nothing. We've just brought three acoustic guitars and a pair of drum sticks. What have you got here?' I said, 'Well, we've got about four operating theatres and about 940 people.' So they said, 'OK, never mind. We'll have a go.' We all teamed into the nursing home and, in front of about 150 incredibly delighted nurses, sisters and doctors, The Beach Boys marched up onto the stage and said, 'Here we are, The Beach Boys.' And with three acoustic guitars, and with Dennis sitting on a chair playing the top of a packing case and whacking a tambourine, and with one microphone between the three of them, they gave us a session, the like of which I could never ever remember. They sounded totally like The Beach Boys. They sounded so good! They knocked themselves out."

Savile watches them play for an hour and a quarter. "No one sat down. Aghast sisters, who happened to be Beach Boys fans, were standing on chairs; two sisters on one chair held on to each other so they wouldn't fall off. When The Beach Boys finished their set, the only thing they had left was ['Graduation Day'], without any instrumental accompaniment. At the end, I presented them with five operating gowns, which had just been cleaned from a recent heart operation … . The group was quite into this because they had just been to see a heart operation in California and it had turned them on. I stood on the yard as their coach rumbled out and I said to myself, 'I don't believe it.' It was too fantastic for words."

The hospital event is taped privately by a doctor, and captured professionally on film, partly screened for the first (and only) time on BBC-1's *Top Of The Pops* on June 19th, set to 'Break Away'. After the performance, Al ends up in casualty after he complains of feeling unwell; a doctor in the hospital says he is suffering from complications following a head cold. This evening, the group resume their UK tour proper with two shows in Manchester.

■ Monday 9th

Odeon Theatre *Glasgow, Scotland* 6:15 & 8:45pm, with Paul Revere & The Raiders, Joe Hicks; compère: Alan Field

■ Tuesday 10th

Astoria Theatre *Finsbury Park, north London* 6:00 & 8:30pm, with The Rainbow People, Marmalade

These two extra concerts are added through public demand, completing the UK leg of the European tour. Paul Revere & The Raiders and Joe Hicks do not appear tonight as they have flown back to America due to prior engagements.

Mike Ledgerwood writes in *Disc & Music Echo*: "Bruce Johnston sat down at a grand piano and, as the stage lights dimmed around him, gently picked out one of the prettiest pieces of musical poetry ever heard on a pop platform. It was his contribution to The Beach Boys' farewell British concert … and it went down a storm. The audience sat silent and attentive as he faultlessly played his own composition 'The Nearest Faraway Place' and then burst into wild applause. 'I'm glad everyone liked it,' he said afterwards. 'I wasn't sure about including it in the show at first.' I'm glad he did. It showed us the other side of Mr Johnston, the musically creative side few people imagined existed. And it made him much more than a singing, guitar-swinging pop star.

"Yes, The Beach Boys certainly left us with some good vibrations. A full-blooded power-packed bumper programme, which included most of their big hits and Carl Wilson's clever, if at times a tiny bit flat, rendering of 'God Only Knows'. On-stage together the group gagged and larked about with Mike Love, still sporting his flowing white robes and looking like a misguided monk, to the fore with his often unnecessary sarcasm. Musically, they might not exactly reproduce their famous studio sounds, but they have a damned good try and the result is not disappointing."

After the show and following a tip-off from Al, Carl visits Blaises nightclub where he watches a performance by South African group The Flames, with Blondie Chaplin (guitar/vocal) and the Fataar brothers Steve (guitar/vocal), Edries 'Brother' (bass/vocal) and Ricky (drums/vocal). Carl is greatly impressed and shortly afterwards invites the group to move to America and sign with Brother Records. The Flame, as they eventually become known, eventually settle in the States on July 21st 1970.

Early on the morning of June 11th, The Beach Boys catch a flight from London Airport to Budapest where they begin the European leg of their tour.

■ Wednesday 11th
Sporthall *Budapest, Hungary*

■ Friday 13th
Festhalle *Frankfurt, West Germany*

To coincide with two concerts in Germany, Vic Kettle's 1968 European tour documentary premieres this evening on German TV. David Morse directs the 53-minute colour presentation of footage shot between November 29th and December 16th 1968.

■ Saturday 14th
Deutschlandhalle *Berlin, West Germany*

■ Sunday 15th

A show due to take place in Munich today has been cancelled, so the group undertakes various promotional appearances and interviews.

Along with business manager Nick Grillo they also find themselves deep in discussion with Deutsche Grammophon at the German record company's headquarters in Berlin.

The label offers the group an advance of $100,000. Grillo will tell BBC Radio-1: "We negotiated a major 14-album deal with the label. We were in Berlin negotiating the deal but Mike Love did not feel satisfied with the offer and I criticised him about it. I could not understand why we had to return to America [on July 1st] before we accepted the deal, because we could have accepted the offer right there in Berlin."

With the meeting over, group and entourage head on to France late this evening.

■ Monday 16th
TV TF1 TV studio *Paris, France*. TF1 *Midi Première* lip-synch 'Break Away', broadcast 12:00 midday-1:00pm.
Olympia Théâtre *Paris, France*

The Olympia concert is recorded and filmed. The entire concert is aired on the Europe 1 French radio show *Olympia Musicorama* on July 14th, including 'California Girls', 'I Get Around', 'Barbara Ann' and 'Good Vibrations'. Their duties in France concluded, the group moves on to Prague in Czechoslovakia for a memorable visit.
'Break Away' / **'Celebrate The News'** single released in the US and (around this time) in the UK. The 45 is issued partly to fulfil a contractual obligation, with the ironically-titled A-side credited to Brian Wilson and 'Reggie Dunbar', the latter a pseudonym for Murry Wilson.

Packed with superb vocals and melodies and effective arrangements, 'Break Away' is a worthy hit in the UK where it peaks at number 6, but in the US manages only a poor 63, setting another low point for Beach Boys chart positions. It is a harsh and embarrassing outcome for such a marvellous single.

(A film to accompany 'Break Away' is screened in the UK on BBC1's *Top Of The Pops* on June 19th, 7:30-8:00pm.)

Break Away single

A '**Break Away**' (B. WILSON / R. DUNBAR)
B '**Celebrate The News**' (D. WILSON / G. JAKOBSON)

US release June 16th 1969 (Capitol 2530).
UK release June 1969 (Capitol CL 15598), reissued June 1975 (Capitol CL 15822).
Chart high US number 63; UK number 6.

■ Tuesday 17th
Lucerna Hall *Prague, Czechoslovakia*

Shortly after their arrival this afternoon the group prepares to play the first of three historic concerts in Czechoslovakia. They become the first Western rock group to play in this Communist Bloc country after the Russian invasion last year. During their performance this evening, they dedicate 'Break Away' to the recently replaced Prague Spring reformer Alexander Dubcek, who is sitting in the audience.

Mike later recalls in the *An American Band* documentary: "The invite to go to Czechoslovakia came through Poland. We were treated like visiting heroes because we represented the United States. The Czechoslovakian people were very nice to us. They seemed in favour of us, possibly because of our opposite poles, politically. Therefore they really appreciated us going there. It was the first time that an American group had gone to Czechoslovakia. The kids really dug us." Bruce says in the same documentary: "When we arrived in Prague it was only a few months after the Russian invasion. The city was still occupied so we didn't know what to expect. But to our amazement the kids were out in the streets, asking for our autographs. They wanted to know about America, the latest records, and rock'n'roll. They don't sell our records there. They have to get them in Finland and Yugoslavia."

In fact, to coincide with the group's appearance in the country, Czech label Supraphon issues a special Beach Boys album featuring tracks licensed from Capitol Records. Simply titled *The Beach Boys* (Capitol/Supraphon 1 13 0675) it is the group's first album released behind the Iron Curtain. Featuring liner notes in the local language, the disc features 'Barbara Ann', 'The Girls On The Beach', 'Fun Fun Fun', 'In My Room', 'California Girls', 'Do It Again', 'Help Me Rhonda', 'Sloop John B', 'God Only Knows', 'You Still Believe In Me', 'Wouldn't It Be Nice', 'Bluebirds Over The Mountain', 'Heroes And Villains', 'I'm Waiting For The Day' and 'Good Vibrations'.

■ Wednesday 18th
Hala Rondo *Brno, Czechoslovakia* matinee; **Bratislava Song Festival** *Bratislava, Czechoslovakia* evening

Following an afternoon show in Brno, the group's third concert in the country takes place on the opening night of the three-day *Gala Pop Festival* in Bratislava. The group proudly opens the first night's concert in front of an appreciative 2,000 crowd. But their impact as the event's top attraction is marred as the large audience has to watch some 20 helpers take three quarters of an hour on an uncurtained stage to set up the sound equipment. Slow handclaps, impatient jeers and whistles accompany the spectacle. The three nights of shows also feature various Czech musicians and singer John Rowles; The Beach Boys headline the opening night and The Tremeloes the third night.

Highly edited selections of the song festival will appear in a 25-minute programme produced by the InterVision television company, *The Bratislava Song Festival*, which is syndicated across Soviet Bloc countries from June 21st. Bruce says on the *Mike Douglas Show*: "There were loads of other groups from around the world there. The local Czechoslovakian groups were singing protest songs and the Russians blanked these parts out of the televised part of the festival."

Carl: "The audience was incredible. It was a real joy for them to be able to see someone from the West. It was a kind of symbol of freedom for them." Bruce: "They asked us about our homes and how much money we make. We had trouble spending our money over there." Al: "They wouldn't allow us to take all of our income home. So we had to spend half of the income while we were there. In the remaining two or three hours in the country, after we had done our work, we had to run around and try and get rid of this money." Bruce: "Everyone bought two suitcases. They're really beautiful. They cost $120 in the States but we only paid about $18. It was duty free. When we got back to the States I put my clothes in my new suitcase and just walked in."

■ Thursday 19th

While Al, Carl and Dennis fly on to Finland to continue the tour, Mike and Bruce fly to London to present a film of their visit to Leeds infirmary (see June 8th) on BBC-1 TV's *Top Of The Pops* tonight. When the live transmission from BBC Television Theatre in west London is completed, Mike and Bruce head up to the show's gallery and pose for pictures with the show's producer Johnnie Stewart and director Brian Whitehouse. Afterwards the two Beach Boys board their chartered plane and fly on to Finland to join their colleagues.

■ Friday 20th

Jaahalli *Helsinki, Finland* with Paul Revere & The Raiders, Joe Hicks

■ Saturday 21st

Antwerp Pop Festival *Antwerp, Belgium* with Paul Revere & The Raiders, Joe Hicks

After the Antwerp show the group heads back to London and their new operations base at the plush Londonderry Hotel in central London. The Beach Boys and their entourage will remain here until Tuesday morning. On the 23rd *New Musical Express* reporter Richard Green visits Dennis at the hotel to pursue Brian's comments made on May 27th regarding Dennis's current living arrangements. According to Brian, Dennis is living in a one-bedroom cellar in the basement of a friend's house in Beverly Hills, with just a bed and a piano and nothing else – not even a bathroom.

"Do you really live in a state of self-imposed near poverty?" Green asks Dennis. "I live there out of desire," he replies, backing up his brother's claim. "I'm living where I want. I look at the room as my mind. There's a piano in there, there's a bed, and that's all I need. What do you need in a home? People have so much rubbish in their homes … clocks and watches and they're scared of breaking them. I've lived in a beautiful home in Beverly Hills, in harems, in the mountains, with a family, but where I like best is where I am now. I want to achieve happiness. My goal is all the things we put out. It's a lot of personal satisfaction to have a hit record. You bump into friends and you say, 'Look what we've done.' It's great! I still give my money away. I give everything I have away. What I am wearing and what's in my case is all that I have. I don't even have a car. I have a 1934 Dodge somewhere."

This afternoon the group visits a film-editing studio in central London to view rushes of some of Vic Kettle's recently shot footage, in particular the film of their visit to Czechoslovakia on June 17th and 18th.

Tuesday 24th

Amerikaans Theater *Brussels, Belgium* with Paul Revere & The Raiders, Joe Hicks

The group check out of their London rooms early this morning and fly on to Belgium for tonight's televised show. Excerpts from their early-evening performance are transmitted live on the Belgium 1 TV music show *Vibrato* (7:30-8:25pm) including 'Good Vibrations', 'Cotton Fields', 'Do It Again', 'I Can Hear Music', 'Break Away' and a rare performance of 'Our Prayer'. Following the concert the group flies back to England and spend a few days relaxing in Brighton before flying on to The Netherlands on Monday.

■ Wednesday 25th – Sunday 29th

Largely due to Mike's insistence, The Beach Boys return to Brighton's Transcendental Meditation School and spend the next four days relaxing, meditating – and occasionally watching the Wimbledon Tennis Championships on BBC television. They sup immense amounts of tea, served by the retreat's spiritual man, known as George. During regular long and meaningful conversations, George tells Carl that he will make a good actor. A visitor to the hideaway is *NME* reporter Mike Ledgerwood who receives a 90-minute lecture from Mike. "I listened intrigued to Mike's views on meditation and his beliefs in the teaching of the Maharishi," writes Ledgerwood. "His conversation with the woman who studied life-after-death was captivating. Talk evolved about the planets, which Mike is currently writing a song about. But I must admit, a lot of it left me cold."

■ Monday 30th

TV Fietsotheek *Amsterdam, Netherlands*. NCRV Nederland 1 TV *De Raiders En De Beach Boys* lip-synch 'Good Vibrations', 'Break Away', 'I Can Hear Music', 'Cotton Fields', broadcast July 3rd, 7:07-7:35pm. This afternoon, shortly after their arrival from the UK, the group appears in another NCRV special. It is titled to reflect the inclusion of four songs by Paul Revere & The Raiders, and features footage of The Beach Boys backstage preparing to shoot their sequence and recalling their impressive string of hits. After the taping, Carl, Dennis, Al and Bruce fly back home to the US while Mike heads on to Ireland.

• Back in California, The Beach Boys' original seven-year recording contract with Capitol officially expires, two weeks after their last single was released. Carl tells *Disc & Music Echo*: "They were against *Pet Sounds* and all the albums that came after. They wanted us to stick with surfing and hot-rod records. But we said, 'We don't want to do that. We're doing other music now.' But they really weren't going for it. And so they had all these hundreds of people in their organisation pushing another thing, and people were bound to get the wrong impression about the group."

Although irritated by the somewhat fruitless results of Karl Engemann's optimistic conversation with Nick Grillo on April 16th about new product, Capitol still wants to work with the group. In readiness for the lucrative Christmas market, the label asks The Beach Boys to deliver their last contractually-obligated album by September. But the group is already gearing up for a fresh start with another top record label, Deutsche Grammophon. (As part of their eventual 1971 settlement with Capitol, The Beach Boys will retain ownership of all their post-*Party!* albums, although this is possibly a long term lease deal, as Capitol later appears to own outright the post-*Party!* and pre-*Sunflower* material. All unissued material from all eras – including the legendary *Smile* – is always owned outright by The Beach Boys.)

July

RECORDING *Sunflower* **sessions** Brian's Home Studio *Bel Air, CA.* The group is now partly free of the Capitol contractual obligations and has no touring commitments until July 19th, so at the start of this month they begin a new slew of recordings, including a resumption of work on Dennis's **'Got To Know The Woman'** and Brian and Mike's **'All I Wanna Do'**. (See November 11th.)

• Brian's attention is diverted away from music as he collaborates with his cousin Steve Korthof and Beach Boys road manager Arnie Geller to launch The Radiant Radish, a health-food store in West Hollywood. The store is opened when Brian feels like opening it. Because he goes there mostly at night and straight from his nearby home, Brian will be seen serving and taking cash while still attired in his pyjamas, bathrobe and slippers.

The group's UK public relations man and music reporter Keith Altham recently moved to the States and has become good friends with Dennis. One day Altham tells Dennis that he'd really like to see Brian again. No problem, says Dennis, and drives them to the Radiant Radish store. When they get there, Dennis parks outside, points to the front window and says, "There he is." Brian is inside, shuffling around the premises. When Altham suggests they go in and talk to him, Dennis replies in horror, "Nobody *talks* to Brian! I thought you just wanted to *see* him!" (See also September introduction.)

■ Tuesday 1st

As the group returns to the US after the recent European tour without a record contract, Beach Boys business manager Nick Grillo calls Deutsche Grammophon to inform them that The Beach Boys have accepted their offer of a major recording deal. But Grillo is told that because of the group's recent commercial failures and Brian's rapidly rising reputation in the record industry for unreliability, the German label has gone cold on the idea. Subsequently, this rebuff reverberates around the music industry and very few record companies will show an interest in signing the group.

Beach Boys co-manager Fed Vail recalls later: "When The Beach Boys left Capitol, after a seven-year stint, they and a lot of people, including Nick Grillo, thought they would be besieged with offers, because they were The Beach Boys. They were already a legendary band. But that wasn't the case, primarily because of this two-year-old thing called the Monterey Pop Festival. Because of that event, the whole landscape of the American music scene had changed drastically, and The Beach Boys were no longer a hot item. So when they left Capitol, they were shocked that they didn't get many offers. They really were! There just wasn't a clamouring for them." So it is that The Beach Boys find themselves cast aside in the American wilderness, still looking for a home for their new recordings.

■ Saturday 5th

'Break Away' single enters the US *Billboard* chart.

■ Tuesday 8th

RECORDING *Sunflower* **sessions** Gold Star studio (A) *Los Angeles, CA.* Evidence suggests this is the recording date for Dennis's song

'Slip On Through' and the inevitably unreleased **'I'm Going Your Way'**, a rocking song about picking up hitchhikers and the potential sex that might follow. 'Slip On Through' is tracked in 18 takes with a pick-up piece edited on to the song's ending. 'I'm Going Your Way' is a lengthier affair, taking 25 takes to complete. Also at this session, reduction mixes are made of 'Slip On Through' to make way for future overdubs. A rough vocal is also taped by Dennis, but this will be replaced for the master mix.

TV Westinghouse Broadcasting Company, Group W Productions *Philadelphia, PA.* Syndicated *The Mike Douglas Show* live vocals over taped backing tracks 'Break Away', 'Celebrate The News', broadcasts begin July 22nd. The group tapes their fourth appearance on this show, with Dennis taking the microphone and Carl moving to drums on 'Celebrate The News'.

■ Wednesday 9th

MIXING Gold Star studio (A) *Los Angeles, CA.* A further reduction mix is made of **'Slip On Through'**.

■ Saturday 12th

'Break Away' single peaks in UK chart at number 6.

■ Monday 14th

MIXING at Sunset Sound studio (3) *Hollywood, CA.* Further reduction mixes are made of 'Slip On Through' and 'I'm Going Your Way'.

TOUR STARTS US East/South (Jul 19th-Aug 2nd)

■ Saturday 19th

Long Island Arena *Commack, NY*

The group begins their latest tour, a relatively brief nine-date excursion.

■ Tuesday 22nd

Summer '69 Festival, Gaelic Park *Bronx, NY*

The Beach Boys appear as part of an eight-concert series of benefit shows for Manhattan College. The first show took place on July 17th, the last is due on August 19th, featuring artists such as The Association, Gary Puckett & The Union Gap, Pete Seeger, The Four Tops, The Rascals, and The Byrds.

■ Wednesday 23rd

Baltimore Civic Center *Baltimore, MD*

■ Thursday 24th – Saturday 26th

Steel Pier *Atlantic City, NJ*

Another three-day residence at this venue.

■ Sunday 27th

Oakdale Theater *Wallingford, CT*

■ Monday 28th

Merriweather Post Pavilion *Columbia, MD* 8:00pm, with The Box Tops

■ Wednesday 30th

TV Westinghouse Broadcasting Company, Group W Productions *Philadelphia, PA.* Syndicated *The David Frost Show* live vocal over pre-taped backing track 'Break Away', broadcasts begin August 8th 8:30-10:00pm. The group's first appearance on *David Frost*, with Carl's acoustic guitar the only live instrument.

FOLLOWING PAGES In Brian's home studio in July recording *Sunflower*: (left to right) Carl strums guitar, Al watches Dennis play an upturned bass drum, and Mike and Brian sit at the keyboard.

August

RECORDING Brian's Home Studio *Bel Air, CA*; Wally Heider studio *Hollywood, CA*. From this month through to November, Brian produces the album *A World Of Peace Must Come* by Stephen John Kalinich. The poet was introduced to The Beach Boys by Brian's friend Arnie Geller and cousin Steve Korthof, and was initially signed to Brother Records in 1968 as part of Kalinich's group, Zarathustra And Thelibus, for whom Carl produced the unreleased track 'Leaves Of Grass', based on a Walt Whitman poem.

Kalinich soon began collaborating with Dennis; two of their songs were included on *Friends* and one on *20/20*. (For unknown reasons, Kalinich is uncredited for the *20/20* song 'All I Want to Do'.) Now he collaborates with Brian on an album intended to marry his poetry with Brian's music.

The results are recorded during this three-month period and include 'Candy Face Lane' (poem set to musical backing), 'Birth Of God' (poem set to musical backing), 'Deer, Elk, Raven - The Magic Hand (Fury Palm)' (poem set to musical backing), 'Lonely Man' (instrumental), 'Be Still' (poem set to musical backing), 'Walk Alone With Love' (instrumental), 'A World Of Peace Must Come' (instrumental), 'If You Knew' (poem set to musical backing), 'America (I Know You)' (poem set to musical backing). One known recording date is for 'America (I Know You)', which Brian produces at Wally Heider studio on August 22nd.

• Possibly this month, Mike, Al, Dennis and Carl apparently arrive at the home of Carl's brother-in-law Billy Hinsche, one third of popular American combo Dino Desi & Billy, and offer him a permanent position in The Beach Boys as a replacement for Bruce. Hinsche reluctantly turns them down as he is due to go to college, but is promised a place in the group when he graduates. It seems that Bruce is not informed that the group is looking to replace him.

■ Friday 1st
Wollman Skating Rink Central Park, *New York, NY* 8:00 & 10:30pm, with Neil Young (co-headliner)
The group performs as part of the three-month annual *Schaefer Music Festival* in New York City.
Set-list (8:00) 'Do It Again', 'Darlin'', 'Wouldn't It Be Nice', 'Sloop John B', 'California Girls', medley 'The Warmth Of The Sun' / 'Don't Worry Baby' / 'Please Let Me Wonder' / 'Surfer Girl' / 'In My Room', 'I Can Hear Music', 'Break Away', 'Cotton Fields', 'Riot In Cell Block #9', 'God Only Knows', 'Their Hearts Were Full Of Spring', 'Good Vibrations', 'Rock'n'Roll Woman' (encore).

■ Saturday 2nd
Delaware State Fair Grounds *Harrington, DE* two shows
• 'Break Away' single peaks in US *Billboard* chart at number 63.

■ Sunday 3rd
Carl's troubles relating to his draft misdemeanours continue when he is indicted for failing to appear for community service work as a hospital orderly. A new service is immediately funded, meaning further free Beach Boys concerts at hospitals, prisons and the like.

To cheer him up, this evening the group (minus Brian) go to see Elvis Presley perform on the fourth night of his run at the Las Vegas Hilton. Elvis has returned to the stage after more than eight years away: his last concert was at a benefit at Pearl Harbor in March 1961. The Beach Boys sit happily among the crowd of 2,200 to watch the Las Vegas show, and then go backstage afterwards for an audience with the King.

■ Saturday 9th
Shortly after midnight tonight, film actress Sharon Tate, wife of film director Roman Polanski and star of the movie *The Valley Of The Dolls*, is brutally murdered at 10050 Cielo Drive, Beverly Hills, the former home of Terry Melcher. Also murdered during the siege is coffee heiress Abigail Folger, her boyfriend Voiytek Frykowski, internationally known hair stylist Jay Sebring, and Steven Parent, a friend of the caretaker managing the house. Some of the bodies are strewn across the estate; the bodies of Tate, who was more than eight months pregnant, and Sebring are hung by a rope over a rafter. Graffiti written in blood at the murder scene reads, "Death to Pigs." Charles Manson, who is not present at the slayings, expected Terry Melcher to be there, but Melcher sub-let the house to Polanski and Tate back in February. A so-called 'death list' of celebrities also targeted by Manson and his 'Family' includes Elizabeth Taylor, Richard Burton, Tom Jones, Steve McQueen, and Frank Sinatra.

■ Sunday 10th
A day after the Sharon Tate murders, a wealthy couple, Leo and Rosemarie LaBianca, are found stabbed to death in their home on the edge of Hollywood. The words "HELTER SKEALTER" (a misspelling of a song title from The Beatles' 1968 double '*White*' album) are painted on the refrigerator with the victims' blood. The grisly acts of these two days come to be known as the Tate-LaBianca murders.

■ Tuesday 12th
Charles Manson arrives at Dennis's new home in Los Angeles with a crazed look on his face. Dennis's friend Gregg Jakobson is quoted in a police report as saying, "The electricity was almost pouring out of him. His hair was on end." Dennis casually asks Manson where he has been. He replies, "To the moon," and then asks for $1,500,000 in order to be able to drive into the desert. Dennis refuses. Manson is incensed and snaps back, "Don't be surprised if you never see your kid again." A few days later, while Dennis is away in Canada, Gregg Jakobson is handed a .44 calibre bullet by Manson, who says to Jakobson, "Tell Dennis there are more where this came from." Jakobson keeps this statement to himself, knowing how upset Dennis was about Manson's first threatening comment.

■ Wednesday 13th
Centennial Concert Hall *Winnipeg, MB, Canada* with The Buchanan Brothers, The Box Tops
The first of two mid-week Beach Boys performances in Canada. The group arrives late because their driver takes them first to a hockey venue by mistake.
Set-list 'Do It Again', 'Darlin'', 'Wouldn't It Be Nice', 'Sloop John B', 'California Girls', 'I Can Hear Music', 'Help Me Rhonda', 'God Only Knows', 'I Get Around', 'Riot In Cell Block #9', 'Cotton Fields', 'Barbara Ann', medley 'The Warmth Of The Sun' intro only / 'Don't Worry Baby' / 'Please Let Me Wonder' / 'Surfer Girl' / 'In My Room', 'Good Vibrations', 'Johnny B Goode' (encore).

■ Thursday 14th
Wentworth Curling Club *Hamilton, ON, Canada* with The Buchanan Brothers, The Box Tops

■ Friday 15th
RECORDING Sunset Sound studio *Los Angeles, CA*. Unhappy with Brian's original production, The Beach Boys with Al again on lead vocal tape another version of '**Cotton Fields**' with sessionman Red Rhodes playing steel guitar.

■ Saturday 16th

TV Westinghouse Broadcasting Company, Group W Productions *Philadelphia, PA.* Syndicated *The Mike Douglas Show* live vocals over taped backing tracks 'Break Away', broadcasts begin August 22nd. The group's fifth and last collective appearance on the show.

■ Monday 18th

MIXING Capitol studio *Hollywood, CA.* Reduction mixes are made onto 8-track today at Capitol of Bruce's **'Deirdre'**. (A 'reduction mix' is one made to condense multi-track recordings into one or two tracks of another machine, here an 8-track, to provide free tracks, here for recording vocals.)

■ Tuesday 19th

TV ABC Television Studios *Los Angeles, CA.* ABC *Happening* lip-synch 'Cotton Fields', broadcast September 20th 1:30-2:00pm. The Beach Boys are special guests on this 77th and final show in the weekly live television series hosted by Mark Lindsay and Paul Revere.

Sidemen appearing with the group on this TV appearance include Red Rhodes (playing pedal steel guitar), Daryl Dragon (keyboards), Dennis Dragon (percussion), and Ed Carter (bass), as well as a number of horn players: Fred Koyen, Bill Byrne, Bill Peterson and David Edwards.

September

With what in hindsight will appear as unfortunate timing – just weeks after Charles Manson and his 'Family' carried out the gruesome Tate-LaBianca murders – *Rave* magazine in Britain publishes a 1968 interview with Dennis by UK music reporter and Beach Boys PR man Keith Altham.

In the two-page piece, Dennis acknowledges the talents of Manson and indicates that he will soon be appearing on the group's Brother Records label.

Altham: "You live in an apparently fearless manner, but is there anything that frightens you?" Dennis: "Fear is nothing but awareness. I was only frightened as a child because I did not understand fear, the dark, being lost, what was under the bed. It came from within. Sometimes The Wizard frightens me, Charlie Manson, who is another friend of mine, who says he is God and the devil. He sings, plays and writes poetry, and may be another artist for Brother Records."

• Although Capitol's desire to work with the group again has dissolved to a mere whim, the label still waits patiently for delivery of The Beach Boys' final album to fulfil their contractual obligation.

Internal Capitol documents suggest an album title of *The Fading Rock Group Revival* or *Reverberation* and note intended contents as 'Cotton Fields' (single version, mono, recorded August 15th), 'Loop De Loop' (recorded March 5th and 6th), 'All I Wanna Do' (March 19th and July), 'Got To Know The Woman' (mono, February 13th and July), 'When Girls Get Together' (instrumental track only, March 5th/6th), 'Break Away' (March 31st and April 23rd), 'San Miguel' (January 9th & 19th), 'Celebrate The News' (February 24th), 'Deirdre' (March 21st), 'The Lord's Prayer' (stereo remix of November '63 recording in 'duophonic' or 'fake' stereo), and 'Forever' (January 9th). (See also November 4th).

The group does get as far as preparing a master tape for the proposed LP, labelling it simply and straightforwardly as the "Last Capitol album". 'Loop De Loop', 'All I Wanna Do', 'San Miguel', 'Dierdre' and 'Forever' are later pulled from this tape and edited into the master reels for the *Sunflower* LP and the so-called 'Second Warner Brothers Album'.

But the group – possibly as a result of negotiations with Warner/Reprise – defaults on the Capitol agreement, deciding instead to remove from the tape a selection of recordings for their next album and whichever label they are signed to. In order to placate Capitol, they decide instead to deliver to the company the *Live In London* album.

■ Monday 22nd

Dennis is phoned at his home and the caller threatens to kill him; the call is later traced to Spahn's Ranch, where Charles Manson is living. The following day Dennis has his phone disconnected.

■ Tuesday 30th

MIXING Capitol studio *Hollywood, CA.* A mixing session is held for Al's production of **'Cotton Fields'**, though a final mix is not achieved.

October

■ Wednesday 1st

MIXING. A mix session is held for the single version of **'Cotton Fields'**. However, the results of today's work will remain unused, and further mixing is done on February 3rd 1970.

■ Friday 3rd

Murry Wilson is in the studio today working on various productions, including a song called 'Gonna Be Alright'.

■ Monday 6th

RECORDING *Sunflower* sessions Brian's Home Studio *Los Angeles, CA* 2:00-5:30pm. Today sees a horn overdub session for Dennis's **'Slip On Through'**. Brian's home studio is now identified by the musicians' union log as 'Brother Recording Studio'.
Musicians present John Audino (trumpet) Tony Terran (trumpet).

■ Monday 13th

RECORDING *Sunflower* sessions Brian's Home Studio *Los Angeles, CA.* 'Walkin'' is transferred from 1-inch 8-track to 2-inch 16-track tape to allow for further overdubs. Brian will record at least a partial lead vocal on this song, though he will announce prior to the take: "I don't want to sing it." The lyrics concern a little old lady with an electric car. Also today, The Flame work on their recording of **'See The Light'** for Brother Records.

TOUR STARTS Canada (Oct 14th-20th)
The group plays a seven-date Canadian tour at various locations, supported by Guess Who and Paul Revere & The Raiders, precise details unknown.

■ Monday 20th

RECORDING *Sunflower* sessions Brian's Home Studio *Los Angeles, CA.* Work takes place today on the song **'Games Two Can Play'**. It will remain unreleased until issued on the 1993 *Good Vibrations* boxed set.

■ Thursday 30th

MIXING Wally Heider studio (3) *Hollywood, CA.* A stereo mix session is held for Dennis's song **'Slip On Through'**.

November

RECORDING *Sunflower* sessions Brian's Home Studio *Bel Air, CA*. During this month recording on 2-inch 16-track tape is started for '**Our Sweet Love**'.

■ Monday 3rd

RECORDING *Sunflower* sessions Brian's Home Studio *Bel Air, CA* 8:00-11:00pm. Brian Wilson Productions pays for a session today; the piece recorded is untitled. (See also 10th.)

Musicians present Ron Benson (guitar), Allan Beutler (saxophone), Allen Breneman (drums), Marvin Brown (trumpet), David Cohen (guitar), John Conrad (bass), Billy Green (woodwind), Michael Melvoin (keyboards), Jay Migliori (woodwind), Tony Terran (trumpet), Al Vescovo (guitar).

■ Tuesday 4th

RECORDING *Sunflower* sessions Brian's Home Studio *Bel Air, CA* 1:00-7:00pm With US label Warner Brothers now showing strong indications that they wish to sign the group, The Beach Boys get back into the studio for the first time in a while and kickstart a busy period of recording. Today, tracking sessions take place for Brian and Mike's '**When Girls Get Together**'. Brian also tapes a solo piano demo of '**'Til I Die**', with no vocals or lyrics. It is a totally different recording to the one that will feature on the *Surf's Up* album in 1971.

'When Girls Get Together' will have a tortuous history. It is mooted for inclusion on several other Beach Boys albums, first as part of the scheduled early-1970 version of *Sunflower*. When that LP's name is temporarily changed to *Add Some Music* in May 1970, 'Girls' is still intended to appear on the record, but by the time the album is re-christened *Sunflower* for August 1970 release it has been dropped. As the group's next album is planned, the song is again considered for inclusion. The LP has a working title of *Landlocked*, which in turn becomes *Surf's Up*, released in the US in August 1971 – but between the changes 'Girls' is again dropped.

Five years later, in 1976, the song suffers the same fate when it is scheduled for inclusion on The Beach Boys' planned end-of-year *New Album*. Its first official release eventually takes place just over four years later, on March 17th 1980, on the Caribou album *Keepin' The Summer Alive*.

Musicians present Harold Bemko (cello), Douglas Davis (cello), Gene Estes (percussion), Jim Horn (horn), Armand Kaproff (cello), Jan Kelley (cello), Lew McCreary (trombone, bass trombone), Alexander Neiman (viola), Ray Pohlman (bass, mandolin), David Sherr (woodwind), Darrel Terwilliger (viola), Al Vescovo (guitar).

■ Thursday 6th

RECORDING *Sunflower* sessions Brian's Home Studio *Bel Air, CA*. Today sees the first vocal and tracking session for '**Soulful Old Man Sunshine**', a jazz-inspired song resulting from a summer '69 songwriting session between Brian and Rick Henn. Henn is the former leader of The Sunrays, a group once managed and championed by Murry Wilson as The Beach Boys' great rivals after his sons fired him as their manager in 1964. Henn arranges the instrumental backing for the song and Brian the vocal arrangements.

■ Sunday 9th

RECORDING *Sunflower* sessions Brian's Home Studio *Bel Air, CA*. The second vocal session takes place for '**Soulful Old Man Sunshine**'. Fans will have to wait until 1998 to hear the song when it appears for the first time on the *Endless Harmony* soundtrack CD (which also includes a segment from a 1969 writing session).

■ Monday 10th

RECORDING *Sunflower* sessions Brian's Home Studio *Bel Air, CA* 8:00-11:00pm. Brian Wilson Productions pays for another session today and the piece is again untitled – probably the same song as recorded on the 3rd.

Musicians present Bonnie Douglas (violin), Jay Rosen (violin), Paul Shure (violin), Brian Wilson (possibly keyboards).

■ Tuesday 11th

RECORDING *Sunflower* sessions Brian's Home Studio *Bel Air, CA* 10:00pm-1:00am. Today's session is for the Wilt Holt composition '**Raspberries Strawberries**', previously recorded by The Kingston Trio. Although unreleased in this version, the tracking tape – first attempted back in July – will be used for the Al/Brian composition '**At My Window**', which will appear on the group's 1970 *Sunflower* album.

■ Thursday 13th

RECORDING *Sunflower* sessions Brian's Home Studio *Bel Air, CA* 1:00-4:00pm. Today sees a tracking and vocal session for Brian's '**This Whole World**', for which Brian's heavily pregnant wife Marilyn and her sister Diane provide backing vocals.

The recording will not be released until March 1970 – when it is included on the US double album *The Big Ball* (PRO 358), a various-artists mail-order-only compilation – and then that August on *Sunflower*. An entirely different and later version, with a bridge not heard in the Beach Boys recording, will appear in medley form along with 'Starlight Star Bright' on Spring's eponymous United Artists album in July 1972; Spring consists of Marilyn and Diane Rovell. (The master take 5 of 'This Whole World' lasts several minutes longer than the released version, which fades on a vocal-only outro; the released ending is achieved by 'muting' all the non-vocal tracks on the 16-track tape.)

Musicians present David Cohen (guitar), Jerry Cole (guitar), John Conrad (bass), Dennis Dragon (drums), Gene Estes (chimes, bells), Ray Pohlman (bass guitar).

■ Monday 17th

Manson 'Family' member Danny DeCarlo implicates Charles Manson in a murder at Spahn's Ranch and suggests that persons at the ranch may also have been responsible for the Tate-LaBianca murders – but tells detectives he is afraid to testify. Five weeks earlier, on October 12th, Manson was arrested at Barker Ranch in Death Valley and charged with grand theft auto.

■ Tuesday 18th

RECORDING *Sunflower* sessions Brian's Home Studio *Los Angeles, CA* 10:00am-1:00pm. Tracking sessions take place for Bruce's '**Tears In The Morning**', another song earmarked for the group's ill-fated *Add Some Music* album but ultimately appearing on the 1970 LP *Sunflower*. The recording will also be issued in the US on October 12th 1970 as a single A-side, coupled with 'It's About Time'.

Musicians present Ron Benson (guitar, mandolin), Hal Blaine (drums), Daryl Dragon (keyboards), Carl Fortina (keyboards), Ray Pohlman (bass guitar), Carl Wilson (guitar).

• Following the decision of CBS, MGM, Polydor and Deutsche Grammophon not to sign The Beach Boys, and after several months of exploratory discussions, the group now signs an impressive

$250,000-per-album recording deal with the Reprise division of Warner Brothers Records. The company will be responsible for distributing Beach Boys records in the US. The deal enables the group to reactivate their Brother Records label, which has laid dormant since the releases of 'Heroes And Villains', 'Gettin' Hungry' and *Smiley Smile* back in 1967.

Signing with Warner/Reprise gives The Beach Boys the creative autonomy they sought but never achieved during their seven-year relationship with Capitol. As part of the agreement, Warners insist that Brian is involved in future Beach Boys recordings. The group agrees.

Beach Boys business manager Nick Grillo recalls : "In the long run, I think it was best that we didn't accept the deal with Deutsche Grammophon. So we came back to the States, and [Warner chief] Mo Ostin had tremendous belief in The Beach Boys and Brian Wilson. He wanted them on the label."

• Two years and seven months after leaving The Beach Boys' camp (see April 14th 1967) Van Dyke Parks, Brian's songwriting friend from the *Smile* era, re-enters the scene to assist with the group's signing. Parks tells Scott Keller in 1973: "I was working at Warner Brothers' Records at the time, both in A&R and in my newly developed office of Audio Visual Services. The Beach Boys were at a very low point in their career. They'd just left Capitol Records and they ended up at Warner Brothers because I personally begged Mo Ostin to sign them.

"My influence on Mr Ostin is best shown by a corporate 'org. chart' of that period, which shows that my only superior officer was Mr Ostin himself. I'd pressured Mo to sign the beleaguered Beach Boys to the label, in spite of industry-wide reservations about the group's ability to deliver. They were considered a problem at that time. They were an industry albatross, simply because there were so many egos involved. Everyone at the label just wanted Brian Wilson to come over and write some songs."

Nick Grillo says that Austin was naturally aware that the group hadn't been selling too many records recently. "But he had a gut feeling about signing the group. He was insistent that The Beach Boys would be a major force again in the music industry and he wanted them on his label. We negotiated a deal with the group. Their career came first and Brother Records came second. He wanted the group to get back into the mainstream and, once that had happened, he'd develop the other artists on their label."

For The Beach Boys, now free from Capitol, the new recording contract brings an immense sense of optimism, and their collective hopes for the future are high. During this month the group – including a temporarily rejuvenated Brian – develop work on their first album for Warner/Reprise. For this ambitious undertaking they bring in as many songwriting collaborators as possible, namely Gregg Jakobson, Daryl Dragon, Bob Burchman, and Joe Knott. The group is not taking any chances and regards the forthcoming album as a make-or-break disc. Failure never comes into the equation. A remarkable amount of new material appears.

• Just as everything seems to be running smoothly within The Beach Boys' camp and recordings are progressing well, disaster strikes in the form of Murry Wilson. Since 1965, Murry has had sole ownership of the Sea Of Tunes music publishing company, an organisation that retains the rights to all The Beach Boys' original songs. Brian allowed Murry to take total control to stop his father's continual hassling on the matter.

Now, witnessing the group's recently poor sales record, Murry thinks they have run their course and decides to cash in, selling the copyrights for all Brian and Mike's classic songs to Irving Almo Music, the publishing division of A&M Records, for the grand sum of $700,000. (Brian later tells a US radio interviewer that 'Surf's Up' is not included in the sale.) Murry allegedly tells Brian that the songs will never amount to anything. Estimates in 2004 put their value at around $25million.

Beach Boys co-manager Fred Vail says later: "I was not privy to all the details, but I do know that Brian was quite upset when he found out that Murry had done this all on his own. Irving-Almo got a real bargain.

"But at the time, Murry probably thought it was great money. No new Beach Boys records in the stores, *20/20* had not done much, and *Sunflower* had yet to be released. I remember thinking that's not a lot of money for an entire catalogue. Money was flowing pretty lavishly around the industry back then. Lots of the San Francisco bands were getting non-recoupable 'bonuses', limos were everywhere, and stars were stars. Huge billboards appeared on the Sunset Strip just to appease the artist's ego.

"Several labels that had initially looked good at signing the boys fell through," says Vail. "It was tough times, and Murry probably figured a bird in the hand is worth two in the bush. Little did he know. He never lived to see the revival and the commercials ... everything from cologne to orange juice to Sonic Drive-in spots ... all the merchandising. He probably would have known, deep down inside, and not admitted it that he'd made a huge mistake. But in 1969, he probably felt he had made a killing."

The whole group is furious with Murry. But their new recordings are enough to distract the band and keep their minds on finishing the next album.

Brian is inconsolable and spends several days in dark isolation at his Bellagio Road home in Bel Air, severely depressed and hardly uttering a word. Songs like 'Good Vibrations', 'I Get Around' and 'Help Me Rhonda' are his babies. They represent years of blood, sweat and tears. And suddenly they are gone.

■ Wednesday 19th

RECORDING Unknown studio. Today Carl works with Brother artists The Flame on songs such as **'Lady'** (no relation to Dennis's song also known as 'Fallin' In Love') and **'Get Your Mind Made Up'**.

TOUR STARTS 7th Annual US Thanksgiving Tour (Nov 25th-Dec 7th) A week after signing to Warner/Reprise the group sets off on the road again for a 13-day trek, their seventh (and final) annual Thanksgiving Tour. What was once an enjoyable and highly profitable jaunt has turned into a miserable, low-key operation with audience numbers struggling to reach even a couple of hundred at some shows. It is a dismal farewell to an otherwise memorable decade for the group. Beach Boys co-manager Fred Vail says that several dates had to be dropped, but at least those that went ahead provided some cashflow.

■ Tuesday 25th
The Arena *Sioux Falls, SD*

■ Wednesday 26th
Sioux City Auditorium *Sioux City, SD*

■ Thursday 27th
Mitchell Corn Palace *Mitchell, SD*

Fred Vail: "I don't think there were 200 in the audience! It was real depressing for everyone. I had the hotel fix box lunches of turkey for all the guys. Here we are, 'America's Band', thousands of miles from our families, eating Thanksgiving dinner from Styrofoam boxes. Life doesn't get much worse than that."

■ **Friday 28th**
Aragon Ballroom *Chicago, IL*

■ **Saturday 29th**
Minot State University Minot, ND

December

RECORDING *Sunflower* **sessions** Brian's Home Studio *Los Angeles, CA*. Recordings started on 2-inch 16-track tape during this month include **'Carnival'**, Dennis's **'Lady'** (also known as 'Fallin' In Love'), and **'Susie Cincinnati'** (see also November 22nd 1976) which will be released next year and in December 1974 as a single B-side.

■ **Tuesday 2nd**
The Jubilee Auditorium *Edmonton, AB, Canada*
Beach Boys co-manager Fred Vail receives a call telling him that that Dennis's son Scott is missing. Dennis wants to fly home immediately, but that proves impossible. Then news comes that Scott has been at a friend's house throughout the day. "The friend's Mom just 'assumed' that [Dennis's wife] Carole knew where Scottie was," says Vail. "It was all an innocent mistake, a simple breakdown of communication. Denny was so relieved. He was a great dad, despite all the negative stories that have been told about him. He loved his family, first and foremost. When we got back to LA the whole Manson thing broke. It dominated the news. I'm certain to this day that Denny felt Manson might have been involved in Scottie's disappearance. It ended up being merely a coincidence. Thank God for that."

■ **Friday 5th**
Centre Of The Arts *Regina, SK, Canada*

■ **Sunday 7th**
Centennial Concert Hall *Winnipeg, MB, Canada*
As this low-key tour ends, The Beach Boys and entourage return home. But more trouble awaits.

■ **Wednesday 10th**
A Los Angeles Associated Press report reads: "Bearded, long-haired and wearing fringe-trimmed buckskin clothing, Charles M Manson appeared bewildered as he arrived in Los Angeles to be jailed on murder-conspiracy charges in the deaths of actress Sharon Tate and six others. The 35-year-old leader of a communal clan he calls the 'family' was brought here Tuesday night in a five-hour, 300-mile automobile trip from remote Inyo County, where he had been held on charges of arson and receiving stolen property. Three women indicted with him Monday by the Los Angeles County Grand Jury were ordered to Superior Court today for arraignment. They are Susan Atkins, 21; Linda Kasabian, 20; and Leslie Sankstone, 19. Manson will be arraigned Thursday."

The Wilsons' mother Audree tells *Rolling Stone*: "When the horrible story came out about Manson's arrest for the Sharon Tate murders, Annie, Carl's wife, called me and said, 'Ma, do you realise?' I did not connect at all that that was the same person and the same family that had been with Dennis. When she told me, I just totally froze. The next day, Dennis was at Carl and Annie's home. I went there and we had dinner and we were all very quiet. Then, somebody said something, and Carl said, 'I don't think we should talk about it.' So we just watched television and had a very quiet evening. We were totally terrified. I remember Carl saying, 'Mom, let's all go back and stay at your house,' and I said, 'Carl, everybody knows where I live. What good would that do?' So I stayed at their house a couple of nights."

Following a sensational ten-month trial that grips public attention, Charles Manson and his followers Susan Atkins, Leslie Van Houten and Patricia Krenwinkel are convicted of murder and conspiracy in the killings of actress Sharon Tate and six others. Another Manson Family member, Charles 'Tex' Watson, is also found guilty in a separate trial.

Even though Manson was not physically present at the murders and his devotees attempted to assume full responsibility, he is seen as the malevolent power who directed their actions.

Vincent Bugliosi, the District Attorney instrumental in getting Manson and his followers convicted and locked away for life, calls Dennis to be interviewed in 1970. At first he refuses, but later admits he would feel better levelling with Bugliosi. It turns out that Dennis has just received another death threat. Bugliosi asks Dennis to testify against Manson but Dennis cannot agree. He fears for his life and that of his son. Dennis tells Bugliosi, "I'm the luckiest guy in the world, because I got off only losing my money."

■ **Thursday 18th**
MIXING Unknown studio. The Flame work on mixes of **'See The Light'** for Brother Records.

■ **Friday 19th**
MIXING Wally Heider studio *Hollywood, CA*. Twenty-three stereo mixes are made of **'Add Some Music'**, although at this point the song features a totally different set of lyrics to those eventually released. The backing track will be retained for the final released version, but the vocals featuring the original lyrics will be wiped from the 16-track tape to make way for the revised vocals.

■ **Sunday 28th**
RECORDING Unknown studio. Another recording session for Carl and Brother artists The Flame sees further work on **'Lady'** – no relation to Dennis's song also known as 'Fallin' In Love' – and **'Get Your Mind Made Up'**.

• Thankfully, the new year and fresh decade will bring better luck for The Beach Boys. The group's love affair with their homeland is about to be rekindled.

1970

Sessions conclude for *Sunflower* album, the first version of which is rejected by new label Warner/Reprise ... re-recordings and new work follow in the studio ... tour of New Zealand and Australia ... 'Cotton Fields' single fails to chart in the US but goes to number 2 in the UK and number 1 in Australia ... last Capitol album *Live In London* released in UK ... Warner/Reprise rejects a further version of the new album ... pressure builds as US-only single 'Slip On Through' fails to chart ... Warner/Reprise finally accepts the group's revised master tape and the *Sunflower* album is subsequently released to good reviews but poor sales ... Jack Rieley becomes The Beach Boys' new manager ... Dennis is filmed for his appearances in the *Two-Lane Blacktop* movie ... sessions start for next album, to become *Surf's Up* ... the group plays two acclaimed sets at the Big Sur festival in California that mark a return to critical hipness ... European tour, with support from Blondie and Ricky's group, subtly renamed as The Flame.

Master-of-ceremonies Mike performs on-stage.

January

RECORDING *Sunflower* sessions Brian's Home Studio *Bel Air, CA.* Recorded during this month are **'Back Home'** and **'Take A Load Off Your Feet (Pete)'**, a vocal session for **'Cool Cool Water'**, and a rehearsal of 1967's **'Let The Wind Blow'** which they are planning to include in live shows.
• **'Surfer Girl'** by The Beach Boys / 'New York's A Lonely Town' by The Tradewinds single released in the US.

■ Friday 2nd
RECORDING *Sunflower* sessions Brian's Home Studio *Bel Air, CA.* 10:00pm-1:00am. Another Brian Wilson Productions session (see also November 3rd & 10th 1969). The piece recorded today is noted as **'Untitled #3'**.
Musicians present Allan Beutler (saxophone), Norm Botnick (viola), Bonnie Douglas (violin), John Guerin (drums), Jay Migliori (woodwind), Don Peake (guitar), Ray Pohlman (probably bass), Mike Rubini (keyboards), Tom Scott (woodwind), Paul Shure (violin), Al Vescovo (guitar).

■ Monday 5th
RECORDING *Sunflower* sessions Brian's Home Studio *Bel Air, CA.* Now signed to a new label and with a fresh outlet for their music, an invigorated and optimistic Beach Boys return to the studio where they focus attention on recording vocals and instrumentation for their next studio album. Today they work on recording **'I Just Got My Pay'** and **'Carnival'** (also known as 'Over The Waves').

■ Wednesday 7th
RECORDING *Sunflower* sessions Brian's Home Studio *Bel Air, CA.* Today sees a tracking session, as usual now at Brian's home studio, for **'Susie Cincinatti'** and **'Good Time'**. Also today a keyboard-only version of The Beatles' recently released **'You Never Give Me Your Money'** is recorded.

■ Friday 9th
RECORDING *Sunflower* sessions Brian's Home Studio *Bel Air, CA.* Horns are overdubbed onto the August 18th 1969 tracking tape of **'Deirdre'**, with Bruce and Brian taking charge today. ('Overdubbing' is the recording of additional vocals or instruments onto an existing recorded performance on tape; 'tracking' is the term for the initial recording of backing instruments only.)
Musicians present Gary Barone (trumpet), Mike Barone (trombone), Marion Childers (trumpet), David Duke (French horn), Bob Edmondson (trombone), Chuck Findley (trombone), Steve Huffsteter (trumpet), Randall A Locroft (trombone), Arthur Maebe (French horn).

■ Monday 26th
RECORDING *Sunflower* sessions Brian's Home Studio *Bel Air, CA.* Work draws to a close on the new album. During today's three-and-a-half-hour session, strings are overdubbed onto **'Tears In The Morning'**, **'Our Sweet Love'** and **'Take A Load Off Your Feet (Pete)'**. Work is done too on Dennis's **'Lady'** (also known as 'Fallin' In Love').
Musicians present Michel Colombier (arranger/conductor), Alvin Dinkin (viola), Sam Freed (violin), David Frisina (violin), Allan Harshman (viola), Igor Horoshevsky (cello), Alexander Kaminsky (violin leader), Nathan Kaproff (violin), George Kast (violin), Marvin Limonick (violin), Abe Luboff (upright bass), Edgar Lustgarten (cello), Virginia Majewski (viola), Robert Ostrowsky (viola), Dorothy Wade (violin).

■ Tuesday 27th & Wednesday 28th
Over these two days it is very likely that the live recordings made in the UK in December 1968 are mixed down from 8-track to 2-track stereo tape for potential release. It is not clear if any Beach Boys are involved in these mixes.

■ Wednesday 28th
RECORDING *Sunflower* sessions Valentine studio *Studio City, CA.* Bruce records the solo piano tag for **'Tears In The Morning'**. Also, probably at a different studio, **'Slip On Through'** is remixed in stereo.

February

■ Tuesday 3rd
MIXING Unknown studio. The final mix session is held for the single version of **'Cotton Fields'**.

■ Friday 6th
MIXING Unknown studio. The group works on mixing Al's **'Susie Cincinatti'**, which will be released later in the month as a single.

■ Wednesday 18th – Friday 20th
Twelve days after completing the latest batch of recordings, the group sets to work mastering the new album, the first for their new label.

They title the disc *Sunflower*. Featuring production by The Beach Boys collectively and by Brian, Bruce, Dennis and Al individually, it features 'Slip On Through', 'Take A Load Off Your Feet (Pete)', 'Forever', 'Games Two Can Play', 'Add Some Music To Your Day', 'When Girls Get Together', 'Our Sweet Love', 'Tears In The Morning' (original version with some different lyrics), 'Back Home', 'Fallin' In Love' (which becomes better known as 'Lady'), 'I Just Got My Pay', 'Carnival', 'Susie Cincinatti' and 'Good Time'.

The recordings have been made intermittently over the past 15 months. A photograph for the jacket is taken by the group's friend, Ricci Martin, son of Dean, of the six Beach Boys sitting and standing on the grass in the blazing sun, surrounded by their children.

(A long-lived rumour will build up over the years that at one stage a 16-song version of *Sunflower* is planned. This stems from a tape in the Beach Boys library labelled "Sunflower 16 track". This is simply the first reel of *Sunflower* 16-track tape masters: the reference is to 16-track tape, not 16 tracks or songs. A second reel is also labelled "Sunflower 16 track" and contains only three songs. Certainly *Sunflower* is originally intended as a 14-song album.)

Within days, the master tape is submitted to Warner/Reprise Records. However, the company cannot hear an abundance of potential hits and rejects it, considering the album too weak as a debut for the label.

Instead, as a way of testing the group's new material on the weary Beach Boys consumer, the label decides to release two of the new recordings as a single (see 23rd). The label requests that another batch of songs be written and recorded; The Beach Boys, dejected but undeterred, duly oblige (see May 15th).

■ Friday 20th
MIXING Unknown studio. The Flame mixes **'See The Light'** for their first Brother Records single.

On the opposite page and those following is a series of Brother Records promotional shots released in 1970, this first one featuring Mike.

Mike Love

BUSINESS MANAGEMENT:
GRILLO AND GRILLO, INC.

PERSONAL APPEARANCES AND PROMOTION:
FREDERICK S. VAIL
1654 NORTH IVAR
HOLLYWOOD, CALIFORNIA 90028
(213) 461-3661

1970

Add Some Music To Your Day
single

A 'Add Some Music To Your Day' (B. WILSON / J. KNOTT / M. LOVE)
B 'Susie Cincinnati' (A. JARDINE)

US release February 23rd 1970 (Brother/Reprise 0894).
Chart high US number 64.

■ Monday 23rd

'Add Some Music To Your Day' / 'Susie Cincinnati' single released in the US. Despite the rejection of the album, optimism again fills the air as the first Beach Boys record is issued on the Brother/Reprise label.

■ End of month

RECORDING *Sunflower* sessions Brian's Home Studio *Bel Air, CA*. Following the rejection by Warner/Reprise of their completed album, The Beach Boys set to work from now periodically through June overdubbing and re-recording some of their latest material for a new LP.

■ Saturday 28th

Seattle Coliseum *Seattle, WA* with Paul Revere & The Raiders
First of a weekend's worth of Beach Boys live performances (see also March 1st).

March

■ Sunday 1st

Paramount Theater *Portland, OR* with Paul Revere & The Raiders

■ Monday 9th

TV ABC Television Studios *New York, NY*. ABC *Get It Together* lip-synch 'Add Some Music To Your Day', broadcast March 14th 12:00-12:30pm. In an attempt to boost the lacklustre sales of the new single, The Beach Boys make their debut on this shortlived weekly pop music show produced by Dick Clark, partaking in an interview with hosts Mama Cass (formerly of The Mamas & The Papas) and Sam Riddle.

■ Friday 20th

Queen Elizabeth Theatre *Vancouver, BC, Canada* two shows, with Paul Revere & The Raiders
In readiness for the group's four-week tour of New Zealand and Australia next month they commence a short series of concerts, performing six shows in the space of three days. Surprisingly, Brian returns to The Beach Boys' touring line-up to take Mike's place; Mike has been hospitalised for three days suffering from malnutrition after following the Maharishi's teachings and undertaking a three-week fast. During the self-imposed fast – he could take only water, fruit juice (out of his ever-present and occasionally dangerous jug), and a little yoghurt – everything had apparently become blown out of proportion and he became quite sensitive to the positive and negative forces around him. Mike began

to look at things metaphorically. For instance, the birds in the sky seemed to have a purpose in flying southwesterly. Furthermore, Mike felt that if he could try a little harder he could perhaps talk to the birds.

Brian recalls on US radio: "When Mike Love was sick, I went with the group up to Seattle and Vancouver and the Northwest for some appearances. I was scared for a few minutes in the first show because it had been a while since I was in front of so many people." In fact, Brian has not appeared regularly on-stage with his group since December 1964. "But after it started to cook, I really got with it. It was the three best days of my life, I guess. If Mike were ever to get sick again, I suppose I'd appear, depending on how far away the tour was."

These first two shows, postponed from February 27th, feature Carl singing Mike's vocal parts and Brian on backing vocals and keyboards. They are attended by a total of 5,500 fans.

■ Saturday 21st

Civic Auditorium *Portland, OR* two shows
The two concerts are seen by a total audience of 2,000.

■ Sunday 22nd

Seattle Center *Seattle, WA* two shows
Attendance at the shows is 6,700 in total. Afterwards the group returns to Los Angeles where they take a brief break before rehearsals for the Antipodean tour.

■ Friday 27th

Back in Los Angeles, work is done to mix The Flame's recording of 'Don't Worry Bill', a song that will later turn up in The Beach Boys' live set.

April

■ Saturday 4th

'Add Some Music To Your Day' single peaks in US *Billboard* chart at a disappointing number 64, spending just five weeks in the listings. Meanwhile, the tireless Fred Vail is busy out in the field selling all things Brother. "In 1970 I was out on the road for seven months promoting 'Add Some Music To Your Day', *Sunflower*, The Flame's album and their 'See The Light' single," he says. "In those days, if a top radio station in all the big cities had a record on their playlist, all the other stations in that area, maybe within 300 miles, would add that record to their playlist because the 'big dog' stations had been playing it."

Vail visits the influential station WFIL in Philadelphia and its powerful program director Jay Cook. Cook proceeds to tell Vail how much he loves Brian Wilson's work. "He tells me what the music means to him. He tells me about how, when he started in some in small station, one of the first records he remembers adding to the playlist was the 'Surfin' USA' / 'Shut Down' single. He tells me that Brian is a genius and blah, blah, blah, all these great things about The Beach Boys and how they created this mythical, powerful Californian sound." Vail decides this is a good moment to ask Cook to add the new single, 'Add Some Music To Your Day', to the WFIL playlist. "He looked at me and said, 'Fred, I can't add your Beach Boys record.' Surprised, I said, 'Well, you've just been telling me how great The Beach Boys are and how great Brian is.' He replies, 'Yeah, they are.' I said, 'Well, why can't you play "Add Some Music To Your Day"?' He looked at me straight and said, 'Fred, The Beach Boys

Carl Wilson

BUSINESS MANAGEMENT:
GRILLO AND GRILLO, INC.

PERSONAL APPEARANCES AND PROMOTION:
FREDERICK S. VAIL
1654 NORTH IVAR
HOLLYWOOD, CALIFORNIA 90028
(213) 461-3661

aren't hip any more.' Those were his exact words. That was the reality. That was what we were up against, and it just crushed me. At the same time, The Beach Boys themselves realised that they weren't hip any more. Unfortunately, they were no longer America's favourite band."

■ Saturday 4th – Friday 17th

RECORDING Wally Heider studio *Hollywood, CA.* Over the course of five sessions that span the next two weeks, Brian produces a country & western album for Fred Vail. Vail, whose association with The Beach Boys began in May 1963 and continued as he became promoter, co-manager and Brother Records employee, also listens to country radio stations a lot. "A lot of times when I'd pick The Beach Boys up I'd have the country stations on, and I'd sing along sometimes and they'd be teasing me. And then they'd put on the pop music stations and I'd put it back on the country stations. We were just fooling around. So they knew I sang and liked country music."

Fifteen songs are recorded for the LP, which has a provisional title of *Cows In The Pasture*: '**Bethany Ann**' (with Fred's vocals), '**There's Always Something There To Remind Me**' (with Fred's vocals), '**Kittens Kids & Kites**' (tracking only), '**Lucky Billy**' (tracking), '**Black Man In Georgia**' (tracking), '**One Woman Won't Hold Me**' (tracking), '**Why Don't You Give Her To Me**' (tracking), '**If You're Not Loving You're Not Living**' (tracking), '**All For The Love Of A Girl**' (with Fred's vocals), '**Only The Lonely**' (with Fred's vocals), '**Carolina On My Mind**' (tracking), '**My Way Of Life**' (tracking), '**A Fool Such As I**' (with Fred's vocals), '**You Pass Me By**' (tracking), and '**I Can't Help It If I'm Still In Love With You**' (tracking).

Brian loses interest half way through the project, and the disc remains unreleased. "I think once he got into it, he realised that he wasn't as comfortable doing that kind of music," says Vail. "Brian was kind of out of that loop, really. He was in the control room – but he just wasn't into it. It wasn't like a Beach Boys session. It was never finished. I think Brian did it to get out of the house."

Musicians present James Burton (guitar), Buddy Emmons (steel guitar), Glen D. Hardin (piano), Red Rhodes (steel guitar).

■ Friday 10th

The world is in shock with the news that The Beatles have split up. Naturally, members of The Beach Boys are asked for their opinions on the demise of one of their greatest pop rivals. "We didn't get as rich as they did," Al Jardine remarks to *Disc & Music Echo*, "and it didn't happen so quickly for us either. I don't think the things that members of The Beach Boys are into now can be considered dangerous for the group's future. We don't have the same sort of scene that The Beatles had with John and his association with Yoko. I mean, it's difficult to see how that sort of individuality could be contained within a team. And if one [member] goes from an entity, it can only serve to weaken that entity. It's a very difficult thing to be in a team and grow up together as well."

■ Monday 13th & Tuesday 14th

Just prior to going on tour, Carl works with The Flame on final mixing and mastering of their debut Brother single '**See The Light**' and '**Get Your Mind Made Up**'.

■ Tuesday 14th

Around this time, Warner A&R man Lenny Waronker decides to visit Brian at his Bellagio Road home in Bel Air. During the visit Brian plays Waronker a piano-and-vocal performance of 'Cool Cool Water',

a song by Brian and Mike. (This is another piece from the infamous 1966/67 sessions for *Smile*, one that started life called 'I Love To Say Da Da'; see May 16th 1967; after that the song was partially recorded for *Wild Honey* and recently revisited in January 1970 with a new vocal session.) Waronker is moved by the song's beautiful simplicity and insists that Brian include it on the group's first album for the label. Brian agrees. (See also July 1st.) When executives at Warner/Reprise are told about 'Cool Cool Water' and the chance that it will feature prominently on the next version of the album, a new single is pencilled in for June 29th release as a 'taster'.

■ Wednesday 15th

Just days before embarking on their first major tour of the year, Dennis breaks away from a game of chess with his girlfriend Barbara to give an interview to American reporter Wayne Schuster. "I am planning, right now, to leave [Los Angeles] or even the country," the Beach Boy announces in *Pop Weekly*. "I don't now where I'm going but I'm going to live somewhere else. I don't like America. The land is OK, it's the government. I don't like seeing wealth used so that every ten months they make the Beverly Hills roads wider for the drunks to drive their fast cars, while people are starving in the ghettos. I don't have the power to control this, but I don't have to stay amongst it. The smog in Los Angeles makes me sick. Maybe I'll go and live in Scotland. This isn't a cop out. I'm a citizen of the world."

TOUR STARTS New Zealand (Apr 18th-22nd)
With a revitalised Mike back in the fold, the group flies into Auckland, New Zealand on the 17th for the start of a four-day tour, their first major excursion of the year. Supporting them on this visit is the "exciting new comedian-singer", Englishman Dave Allenby, and in Auckland local pop-folk quartet The Rumour.

Accompanying Carl, Dennis, Mike, Al and Bruce as part of the live Beach Boys band are Ed Carter (guitar) and Daryl Dragon (keyboards). Dragon is the son of composer Carmen Dragon and will become better known in the mid 1970s as the 'Captain' of Captain & Tennille fame. Also joining the entourage on this tour are three reporters from Sydney-based radio station 2SM, who record and compile interviews for a Beach Boys documentary to be transmitted on the station on April 28th.

One newspaper ad on the tour features a photo of the group from 1964 with the misleading line attached: "The Fabulous Beach Boys – including Brian Wilson", even though Brian is as usual nowhere to be seen on this visit. Most ads for the concerts run the slogan: "A part of your life is remembered in a Beach Boys hit."

■ Saturday 18th

Auckland Town Hall *Auckland, North Island, New Zealand*
6:00 & 8.15pm, with Dave Allenby, The Rumour
The opening night of the group's short tour of New Zealand.

■ Monday 20th

Wellington Town Hall *Wellington, North Island, New Zealand* 6:00 & 8.15pm, with Dave Allenby, The Kal-Q-Lated Risk
'**Cotton Fields (The Cotton Song)**' / '**The Nearest Faraway Place**' single released in the US. Completely unexpectedly, at a time when The Beach Boys are out of the country performing concerts in New Zealand, Capitol back in America issues this 45 coupling the re-recorded 1969 version of 'Cotton Fields' with 'The Nearest Faraway Place' from *20/20*. The group expects a release of the disc in Britain and some other places, but certainly not in America – where it becomes the first ever Beach Boys single to fail to chart. But it does

Al Jardine

BUSINESS MANAGEMENT:
GRILLO AND GRILLO, INC.

PERSONAL APPEARANCES AND PROMOTION:
FREDERICK S. VAIL
1654 NORTH IVAR
HOLLYWOOD, CALIFORNIA 90028
(213) 461-3661

Cotton Fields single

A 'Cotton Fields (The Cotton Song)' (H. LEDBETTER)
B 'The Nearest Faraway Place' (B. JOHNSTON)

US release April 20th 1970 (Capitol 2765).
UK release May 1970 (Capitol CL 15640).
Chart high US none; UK number 2.

become a huge hit in other countries, reaching number 1 in the Netherlands and South Africa and the top 5 in the UK, Australia, Japan and Spain. (In the UK it will peak at number 5 in the BRMB charts, and in June will make number 2 in the *Melody Maker* chart and number 3 in the *NME*.)

■ Tuesday 21st

Majestic Theatre *Christchurch, South Island, New Zealand*
6:00 & 8:15pm, with Dave Allenby, Tap Haperi, The Chapta
Rob White writes in the *Christchurch Star*: "'Good Vibrations', 'Sloop John B', 'Barbara Ann', all these sounds were blasted to Christchurch last night by the American Beach Boys … . Strangely enough, the falsetto voices and the surfing songs did not seem dated, and although at times The Beach Boys seemed sick of playing the same melodies for the thousandth time, some of the excitement of the mid 1960s rubbed off on the audience. Probably the only disappointment of the five men (plus two musicians) … was the lack of new material. The group tried what they called a 'slow medley' of their softer and not so popular numbers but it got bogged down a bit. They quickly recovered the audience's attention with the faster paced numbers. Then the expected climax came, their incredible 'Good Vibrations'. The record took a long time to produce in the studio and The Beach Boys were not expected to be able to reproduce the same full sound. But they did!"

■ Wednesday 22nd

Dunedin Town Hall *Dunedin, South Island, New Zealand*
8.15pm, with Dave Allenby
After finishing tonight's show the group flies on to Australia.

TOUR STARTS Australia (Apr 23rd–May 13th)

■ Thursday 23rd

Festival Hall *Melbourne, Victoria, Australia* 8.30pm, with Dave Allenby
The Beach Boys arrived at Essendon Airport yesterday at midnight, an hour later than expected, and at 9:30 sharp this morning at their hotel face their first press conference of the tour. Later at the Festival Hall the group play their debut concert of this Australian tour. Their late arrival on stage for the Channel 7/3DB-sponsored show is a result of problems with their sound equipment. (An excellent quality recording survives in private hands, taped by a member of the audience on a portable tape recorder smuggled into the venue.)
Set-list 'Do It Again', 'Darlin'', 'I Get Around', 'Wouldn't It Be Nice', 'Sloop John B', medley 'The Warmth Of The Sun' / 'Don't Worry Baby' / 'Please Let Me Wonder' / 'Surfer Girl' / 'In My Room', 'California Girls', 'Help Me Rhonda', 'God Only Knows', 'Cotton Fields', 'Their Hearts Were Full Of Spring', 'Good Vibrations', 'Riot

In Cell Block #9', 'Barbara Ann', 'Johnny B Goode', 'Papa-Oom-Mow-Mow' (encore), 'Surfin' USA' (encore).
• Back in California, Murry Wilson prepares a tape with two of his recent productions – 'So Much In Love' and 'Love To Be Your Lover' – at Sunset Sound's studio 2. The tape features a spoken interlude from Murry, pitching his latest material to The Beach Boys and imploring them to cover these songs because he "doesn't have long to live".

■ Friday 24th

Perry Lakes Stadium *Perth, Western Australia, Australia*
8:00pm, with Dave Allenby
The group flies from Melbourne to Perth, making a brief 20-minute stopover at Adelaide airport where they pose for waiting photographers gathered on the tarmac, and hold a low-key press conference. Soon after their arrival in Perth the group faces a further obligatory press conference. Dennis again talks of leaving his hometown. "I'd like to quit the pollution of Los Angeles and buy a small place here, just a few acres to grow a little food. Smog? I've just got to get away from it. It's terrible in Los Angeles, truthfully terrible." Later, 3,500 fans brave the cold to attend tonight's show.

■ Saturday 25th

Apollo Stadium *Adelaide, South Australia, Australia*
8:00pm, with Dave Allenby
• Today's issue of *Go-Set*, Australia's national music newspaper, mentions that The Beach Boys' new album, said to be titled *Cool Water*, is due for release in the US. It is also announced that the band will make a colour TV film about their Australian tour, filmed by Emerald Films, produced by the BBC's Steve Turner, and made for worldwide release. It will "send up many of the age-old myths about Australia". (See May 2nd.)

■ Sunday 26th

Canberra Theatre *Canberra, Australian Capital Territory, Australia* 5:00 & 8:00pm, with Dave Allenby

■ Monday 27th

Sydney Stadium *Sydney, New South Wales, Australia*
8:00pm, with Dave Allenby
The concert, advertised as "one and a half hours of their hits", is reported by the *Sunday Telegraph* as "marred by the temporary loss of their equipment on the day and the far from perfect acoustics".

■ Tuesday 28th

Capitol Hall *Wollongong, New South Wales, Australia* 7.30 & 10.30pm, with Dave Allenby, Tamam Shud, Fantasy, The Turkish Green Electric Band
The Beach Boys are touted in the local press as the most famous group ever to play a concert in this inland city. The owners of the venue have paid the large sum of nearly AU$7,000 to bring the band to Australia, while other reports suggest the tour is costing The Beach Boys AU$200,000 to stage. The Beach Boys perform to sell-out crowds of over 2,000 at each show, netting the group AU$3,600. Murry Wilson has tagged along for the tour, and despite his pleas for the group to wear matching white shirts for the shows, they take the stage wearing casual clothes, Mike adding a blue-and-white Cossack hat and Al a black beret for the 7:30 concert.

■ Wednesday 29th

The Century Theatre *Newcastle, New South Wales, Australia* 7.30 & 9.30pm, with Dave Allenby

Brian in a Brother promo photograph.

Brian Wilson

BUSINESS MANAGEMENT:
GRILLO AND GRILLO, INC.

PERSONAL APPEARANCES AND PROMOTION:
FREDERICK S. VAIL
1654 NORTH IVAR
HOLLYWOOD, CALIFORNIA 90028
(213) 461-3661

1970

■ Thursday 30th
Festival Hall *Brisbane, Queensland, Australia* 8:00pm, with Dave Allenby

May

'Cotton Fields (The Cotton Song)' / 'The Nearest Faraway Place' single released in the UK. It will peak at number 5 in the BRMB charts, and in June will make number 2 in *Melody Maker*'s chart and number 3 in the *NME*.
Live In London album released in the UK. EMI/Capitol issues this LP consisting of Beach Boys performances at the Astoria Theatre on December 8th 1968. It will not be released in the US until 1976.

■ Saturday 2nd
The Beachcomber Tiki Village Motel, *Surfers Paradise Queensland, Australia* 8:00pm, with Dave Allenby
High-quality sound equipment, considered to be some of the most sophisticated ever heard in Australia, is transported to the tropical surroundings of the venue's poolside garden in preparation for the group's concert. The event is filmed with four separate cameras; the footage will be used as the centrepiece for an unusual Beach Boys colour documentary of the tour, planned for worldwide television screenings. It is partly financed by the BBC in London, and scriptwriters for the Corporation have written comedy send-ups and jokes for inclusion. However, the finished version of this TV special is never screened, although one clip – a live 'I Get Around' featuring the group dressed as pirates and sailors chasing support artist Dave Allenby around the pool – is evidently screened on an episode of *Sounds* on Channel 7 in Australia during the 1970s.

■ Monday 4th – Wednesday 13th
Silver Spade, Chevron Hotel *Sydney, New South Wales, Australia* with Lorrae Desmond

---

Live In London / Beach Boys '69 album

A1 'Darlin'' (B. WILSON / M. LOVE)
A2 'Wouldn't It Be Nice' (B. WILSON / T. ASHER)
A3 'Sloop John B' (TRAD ARR B. WILSON)
A4 'California Girls' (B. WILSON / M. LOVE)
A5 'Do It Again' (B. WILSON / M. LOVE)
A6 'Wake The World' (B. WILSON / A. JARDINE)
B1 'Aren't You Glad' (B. WILSON / M. LOVE)
B2 'Bluebirds Over The Mountain' (E. HICKEY)
B3 'Their Hearts Were Full Of Spring' (B. TROUP)
B4 'Good Vibrations' (B. WILSON / M. LOVE)
B5 'God Only Knows' (B. WILSON / T. ASHER)
B6 'Barbara Ann' (F. FASSERT)

UK release as *Live In London*, May 1970 (Capitol ST21715).
US release as *Beach Boys '69*, November 15th 1976 (Capitol ST11584).
Chart high UK none; US number 75.

The group begins a week of concerts as the headline act at the Chevron's Silver Spade room in Sydney, a cabaret-style nightclub more suited to a mature audience than the young, excitable teenage crowd. At first the shows are scheduled to run until Saturday 9th but are extended to Wednesday due to popular demand, and extra seating is arranged on the dancefloor to accommodate the bigger than expected audience. Support act Lorrae Desmond is a well known Australian performer and TV entertainer.

The Silver Spade concerts provoke a string of positive newspaper reviews. "The Beach Boys live up to their reputation," suggests Sinclair Robieson in *The Australian* newspaper, continuing: "Many pop groups, smash hits on record, turn out dismal flops in person. Not so The Beach Boys. If anything they're even better live than on disc. And although this is their first ever stint in a nightclub, they handle the situation as if they've been doing it all their lives. The patter sounds just unrehearsed enough to be natural and the show itself has enough informality to produce a spontaneous reaction from the audience. The sound, naturally, is the thing and this The Beach Boys have in plenty, despite some bugs in the amplifying system on opening night. ... The show itself nicely mixes up-tempo numbers with ballads and includes many of their past hits, although it doesn't include 'Heroes And Villains' which is a pity because it's probably the best thing they've done so far. In fact, the whole show proves, if it needed proving, that The Beach Boys are still right up there with the very best." A further good review appears in the *Daily Telegraph*, which mentions the group's "better than average musicianship and solid beat", and "as this is their first ever appearance in cabaret, it is enormously entertaining and impressive".

■ Thursday 14th
TV ATN-7 Studios, Television Centre *Sydney, New South Wales, Australia*. National Seven Network *The Tommy Leonetti Show* live performance 'Barbara Ann', 'I Get Around', 'Graduation Day' broadcast May 20th 7:30-8:30pm. The group's tour of Australia concludes with a last-minute appearance on Network Seven's top-rated variety show, hosted by actor, singer and composer Leonetti. Australian performer Samantha Sang is another guest on the show.

■ Friday 15th
With their first major tour of the year completed, The Beach Boys fly out of Australia and head back to Los Angeles. Uppermost in their thoughts now is the need to hand over an acceptable studio album to Warner/Reprise, following the rejection in February, and work on this will occupy most of the following ten days.

By the end of the month, they deliver a reworked new album to the record company's headquarters in Burbank, California. Entitled *Add Some Music (An Album Offering From The Beach Boys)* and allocated catalogue number Brother-Reprise 6382, the LP is intended to feature the following recordings: on side one 'Susie Cincinnati', 'Good Time', 'Our Sweet Love', 'Tears In The Morning' (with different lyrics in one verse), 'When Girls Get Together', and 'Slip On Through'; on side two 'Add Some Music To Your Day', 'Take A Load Off Your Feet (Pete)', 'This Whole World', 'I Just Got My Pay', 'At My Window', and 'Fallin' In Love' (perhaps better known as 'Lady'). The recordings have been made over the previous 16 months and feature production by The Beach Boys collectively and by Brian and Carl, Bruce, Al and Dennis individually.

Warner/Reprise again rejects the recordings. They are somewhat disappointed by the music on the album, but also wish to distance themselves from anything that bears the name *Add Some Music*, an abridged title of the group's first and unsuccessful single with the

Bruce Johnston

BUSINESS MANAGEMENT:
GRILLO AND GRILLO, INC.

PERSONAL APPEARANCES AND PROMOTION:
FREDERICK S. VAIL
1654 NORTH IVAR
HOLLYWOOD, CALIFORNIA 90028
(213) 461-3661

1970

label. The relationship between the two parties is at a low, and The Beach Boys are told once again to come up with a new batch of stronger recordings.

■ Thursday 28th

TV various locations *New Orleans, LA*. Syndicated *Something Else* lip-synch 'Good Vibrations', 'Cotton Fields', broadcast July 4th & 5th. The group flies to New Orleans to film a two-song appearance for the weekly 25-minute pop show, this one hosted by John Bryner and sponsored by the Milk Marketing Board. They mime and act out sequences to accompany 'Good Vibrations' in the afternoon, then mime a performance to 'Cotton Fields' in the evening as darkness sets in.

June

■ Friday 12th

MIXING Brian's Home Studio *Bel Air, CA*. The group works on final mixing and mastering for their next single **'Slip On Through'** and **'This Whole World'**.

■ Friday 19th

A master is assembled for what the group considers contractually to be their final Capitol album release. The line-up is as follows: 'All I Wanna Do' (a different mix to the one eventually included on *Sunflower*), 'Breakaway', 'Celebrate The News', 'Cotton Fields' (duophonic fake-stereo mix of the single version), 'Deirdre', 'Forever', 'Got To Know The Woman' (a different mix to the one eventually included on *Sunflower*), 'Loop De Loop', 'San Miguel', 'The Lord's Prayer', and an instrumental-only mix of 'When Girls Get Together'. This assembly will never be released.

■ Saturday 20th

'Cotton Fields' single peaks in UK *BRMB* chart at number 5.

■ Friday 26th

Varsity Stadium, University of Toronto *Toronto, ON, Canada* with Alice Cooper, Bread, Steppenwolf, Lighthouse, Chilliwack, Bloodrock
The group returns to the concert stage for the *Beggar's Banquet Festival*.

■ Monday 29th

'Slip On Through' / **'This Whole World'** single released in the US. Still eager to promote their group, Warner/Reprise issues the label's second Beach Boys 45, intended to serve as a taster for the forthcoming album. But like the first it is another massive flop,

---

Slip On Through single

A **'Slip On Through'** (D. WILSON)
B **'This Whole World'** (B. WILSON)

US release June 29th 1970 (Brother/Reprise 0929).
Chart high US none.

---

failing to break into the US chart at all. Clearly the group is still regarded as unhip by America's record-buying public.

■ End of month

As problems for The Beach Boys continue to mount now and into July, each member spends time away from the group to develop other projects. Carl produces The Flame group, featuring the Fataar brothers; Bruce produces a folk singer called Amy; Brian composes music for a chorus of frogs to go with Steve Kalinich's poetry. Brian also produces black country artist Larry Strong and tells *Melody Maker* he is contemplating writing music for an Andy Warhol film about a "gay surfer".

July

RECORDING *Sunflower* **sessions** Brian's Home Studio *Bel Air, CA*. Probably around the first days of this month **'It's About Time'** is recorded. The song is recorded on 2-inch 16-track tape; take 21 marked as master.
• In the UK, Isle Of Wight Festival promoter Ron Foulk tells the music press: "We are still considering The Beach Boys [for the Festival] but, though they are musically brilliant, we are not sure that their act would be quite right for a festival audience." The group does indeed not play at the event.
• 'Cotton Fields' single peaks at number 1 in Australian chart, at number 5 in UK *Record Retailer* chart, and at number 13 in New Zealand *Listener Pop-O-Meter* chart.

■ Wednesday 1st – Saturday 9th

RECORDING/MIXING *Sunflower* **sessions** Brian's Home Studio *Bel Air, CA*. Following the visit in May by Warners A&R man Lenny Waronker and his approval of the song, the collective Beach Boys line-up begins a lengthy six-day recording session for **'Cool Cool Water'**, working with engineer Steve Desper. Final mixing is done on the 8th and 9th. The group is now optimistic that the song will provide the finishing touch for their first Warner/Reprise album.

■ Friday 8th

MIXING Brian's Home Studio *Bel Air, CA*. The group works on mixing **'Cool Cool Water'**, **'It's About Time'** and **'Tears In The Morning'**.

■ Tuesday 21st

RECORDING *Sunflower* **sessions** Brian's Home Studio *Bel Air, CA*. Bernie Krause is employed to overdub Moog synthesiser parts onto recent Beach Boys recordings – and possibly only **'Cool Cool Water'**. Bob Moog's pioneering voltage-controlled keyboard synthesisers use electrical currents to simulate the vibrations that create musical sounds. The Beatles' *Abbey Road* LP, released towards the end of last year, had strong use of the Moog synthesiser and has influenced many musicians to try the new instrument. The Beach Boys will buy a 'modular' Moog system, intrigued by its potential to emulate existing sounds and create new ones (see for example sections on recording 'Surf's Up', June/July 1971, and 'Leaving This Town', June-August 1972). Carl in particular is attracted to the synthesiser and will record a number of experimental, unreleased pieces: see April 1971, March 1973, and April and September 1974.
• After this session the final master for *Sunflower* is delivered to Warner Bros. This is the third time in five months that the group has tendered a proposed new LP – and the label finally announces itself

satisfied. The record is scheduled for a US release on August 31st. Almost all the recordings made during this period and not included on *Sunflower* will see subsequent release, although none in their original forms. For instance, 'Back Home' is recorded with several sets of lyrics, and the version originally intended for the Warner/Reprise album is completely different to that which will appear on the 1976 album *15 Big Ones* (and different to the 1963 Wilson/Norberg demo). Dennis's 'Fallin' In Love' is released as 'Lady' on a single in December 1970, while 'Take A Load Off Your Feet', 'Susie Cincinnati', 'Good Time', 'When Girls Get Together', 'I Just Got My Pay' and 'Games Two Can Play' will be released respectively on *Surf's Up*, *15 Big Ones*, *The Beach Boys Love You*, *Keepin' The Summer Alive* and the 1993 *Good Vibrations* boxed set. 'Carnival', a wordless vocal rendition of the standard 'When You Are In Love (It's The Loveliest Night Of The Year)', will remain unreleased, as will 'Walkin''. Another unreleased piece from this period is 'Where Is She', a haunting song by Brian.

Tuesday 28th – Thursday 30th
With the group's *Sunflower* album at last complete, attention returns to mixing The Flame's debut LP. Over these three days mixes are made of 'Highs And Lows', 'Dove', 'Lady', 'See The Light' (reprise), 'Help Me I'm Falling Down', and 'Hey Lord'.

Wednesday 29th
Following poor management and diminishing interest from Brian, The Radiant Radish health food store in West Hollywood closes for business.
• This evening Brian accompanied by Mike and Bruce gives his first ever full-length radio interview, to KPFK Pacifica Radio DJ John Frank, also known as Jack Rieley III. Rieley first met Brian at the Radiant Radish. Mike arrives at the station in his shiny 1939 Rolls Royce touring car. During the broadcast on the Los Angeles station the unreleased songs 'San Miguel', 'I Just Got My Pay' and 'Good Time' are aired.

Beach Boys co-manager Fred Vail arranges the radio interview. "We go out to this station," says Vail, "and Jack Rieley is all excited and becomes very enthusiastic about The Beach Boys. He tells them, 'This is what you need.' He's talking to Bruce, he's talking to Mike, and he's telling them all these things that he would do to make the group popular again." As it turns out, that is precisely what Rieley will do. Rieley recalls in *Rolling Stone*: "I had read some articles about Brian. They first got me interested in meeting him. I thought, 'Nobody could be that far out.' I found out they could be."

Brian says during the broadcast interview: "In the first half of our career, the surf thing was projected so much. It was so clean, the sound was clean, and we looked clean. Around 1966 I think people started rejecting the image. We got a little funkier about that time, but they didn't know it. As we went along, our sound picked up a little R&B. But the name 'Beach Boys' was still like a clean name. I wanted to change it. But we just didn't." Mike adds: "We came up with a bunch of names, [to] shorten the name to just 'Beach' or something like that. But nothing came of it."

Brian: "I'm proud of the group and the name. But I think the clean American thing has hurt us. And we're really not getting any kind of airplay today. Haven't had as much as we should for two years. But it's our fault too. I don't think we're putting enough spunk into our production and I don't know who to blame. We're working on them and we're all really producing. Another thing is that we haven't done enough to change the image, though."

Bruce cuts in. "Brian, I think there's too much equality in our group," he says. "I've always felt you should run the group more than

you do." Brian says: "Yeah, we sort of operate a democracy thing in our productions. Maybe that's the problem. I don't know. But look at The Beatles, and it seems you have to sort of look to their example in some things. They don't appear to have one person as leader – unless there's one none of us has ever known about."

Brian also talks about past Beach Boys recordings. "Probably the best record we've done was 'Don't Worry Baby'. It has about the best proportion of our voices and ranges. But my favourite has to be 'Good Vibrations'. Just that cello on that song alone. I never heard a guy play cello like that before, playing triplets. Also, I really go for 'The Little Girl I Once Knew' and the intro for 'California Girls' – although I can't listen to the vocal on that one, the dub-down on that one just didn't make it for me. If I could, I'd re-record that one and maybe 'The Girl From New York City'. We rushed the beat on that one."

When asked about his still unreleased *Smile*-era recording of 'Surf's Up', Brian explains: "It's just that it's too long. Instead of putting it out on a record, I would just rather leave it as a song. It rambles. It's too long to make it for me as a record, unless it were an album cut, which I guess it would have to be anyway. It's so far from a singles sound. It could never be a single."

During the broadcast, Dennis puts a phone call through to the radio station and announces: "They shut off my phone because I forgot to pay the bill," before adding, "I'll be down as soon as I can get a ride." He fails to show.

Friday 31st
RECORDING Brian's Home Studio *Bel Air, CA* 2:00-6:30pm. The Beach Boys minus Dennis return to the studio to tape a version of **'Seasons In The Sun'**, a tune written in 1961 as 'Le Moribond' ('the dying man') by Belgian poet/composer Jacques Brel and translated into English by singer-songwriter Rod McKuen in 1964, the same year that Bob Shane of The Kingston Trio recorded the song. The idea for a Beach Boys attempt comes from the producer of today's session, Canadian-born Terry Jacks. Earlier this year Jacks had a huge US chart hit with his group The Poppy Family's 'Which Way You Goin' Billy?' – and he will have a big worldwide hit with 'Seasons In The Sun' in 1974.

By all accounts it is not an easy session. Besides Dennis's non-appearance, Brian leaves dissatisfied after three hours. Jacks tells US radio in 1974: "When The Beach Boys asked me to produce them, it was a real honour because I was the first producer outside of Brian who had been asked to [do that]. I thought 'Seasons In The Sun' was a great song for The Beach Boys. It would fit just perfect. I had this idea for the song [and] I went down there and worked real hard on it. But I think it was too much for Brian to have someone from the outside come in and produce. Unfortunately, the song never got going. We put some tracks down but we never finished it." (See August 4th).
Musicians present Sonny Curtis (guitar), Mike Deasy (guitars), Earl Palmer (drums), Lyle Ritz (upright bass).

August

'Cotton Fields' single peaks in Swedish Radio 3 chart at number 1, and in German *Hit Bilanz* chart at number 29.

Tuesday 4th
RECORDING Brian's Home Studio *Bel Air, CA* 3:00-6:00pm. Determined to achieve a satisfactory recording, the group

reconvenes for additional overdubs onto the July 31st recording of **'Seasons In The Sun'**, again produced by its composer, Terry Jacks. Besides overlaying various guitar parts, the song is 'sweetened' with a trumpet overdub from session musician Virgil Evans. But the recording, with a lead vocal by Carl, will remain unreleased. The group feels the song is not right for them and that it will do little to reverse their diminishing fortunes. (Bizarrely, the group will later consider the song for release on their failed 1977 Christmas album.)

Mike says on US radio in 1974: "We did record a version [of 'Seasons'] but it was so wimpy we had to throw it out. It was the wrong kind of song for The Beach Boys. Carl sang it and I don't think he sang it great. We might have spent years living it down. It was just the wrong song for us. I was glad that Terry had a hit with it [later]." Dennis is again absent from the session, instead choosing to marry his girlfriend, Barbara Charren.

• Following the sessions, engineer Steve Desper compiles a tape of recordings potentially suitable for a second Warner/Reprise album, aptly labelling it "Second Brother Album" (and omitting 'Seasons In the Sun'). The tape is cut to an acetate disc. (The Beach Boys will take a tape dubbed from this acetate to an interview they give to New York's WPLJ Radio on February 19th 1971 during which they say that the tape contains cuts that "might be on an album, but it's *not* a new album".)

■ Thursday 13th

On the streets of Los Angeles, Dennis begins shooting *Two-Lane Blacktop*, a Universal Pictures road movie inspired by *Easy Rider* and also featuring US singer-songwriter James Taylor and noted character actor Warren Oates. Oates is the only professional actor in the pack; neither Taylor nor Dennis has ever acted in a film before. Nor has Laurie Bird, a 17-year-old high school graduate who plays the girl they pick up in Arizona. She was found during casting calls in New York. Taylor secured his role after director Monte Hellman had spotted a poster of him on a billboard on Sunset Boulevard advertising his first album.

The shoot will last until late October for a period lasting just over eight weeks, and in various locations including: the Lakeland International Raceway, near Memphis, Tennessee, for the racetrack sequences; Boswell, Oklahoma, for gas station exteriors; and locations in Needles, California, Flagstaff, Arizona, Santa Fe and Tucumcari, New Mexico, Boswell, Oklahoma, Little Rock, Arkansas, and others. All scenes in the film are shot in the sequence that they will appear on the screen.

The role of The Mechanic has proved hardest to cast. Four days before shooting was due to begin, the part was still not settled. The producers felt that it had to be someone who really knew and 'felt' cars. Hellman became desperate, even testing people he chanced upon in garages. Finally, Fred Roos, a friend of the film's producer, suggested Dennis – who immediately and quite happily accepted the role, temporarily leaving The Beach Boys and his drums in Los Angeles. Hellman tells *US Cinema*: "Finally, Dennis came in. He had actually lived the part and had spent half his life taking apart automobiles and putting them back together. It was love at first sight. It was instant love between us. He was just so right for the part."

Accompanying Dennis throughout his time on the film is Barbara, his wife of nine days. It will become an extended and frequently unglamorous cross-country honeymoon. For the first week, only night shooting is done. The cast and crew sleep all day and work from six at night until sunrise. Singer Joan Baez becomes a regular visitor to the film sets.

Dennis tells *Disc & Music Echo*: "It was the hardest work I've ever done. It was quite an experience working on that. It had nothing to do with music. It's another art form – a very beautiful art form. It was good to work for someone, to know that you had to be where he said, when he said. It was a humbling experience. We can all use that. By 'we', I mean everyone on earth. ... With the exception of Warren [Oates] they wouldn't let us see our lines until just before we actually shot the scenes. They made us read them day by day. We read them through once and that was it. James [Taylor] was pissed off about this. He was a control freak and, half way through the film, he told the director he couldn't go on unless he saw the scripts. So the director was forced to give him a copy of the film's script. But James did not bother to read it."

Hellman: "Dennis was the only actor ... who completely forgot that he was on camera. A couple of times in the movie he laughed in front of the camera because he was caught up in the scene and was laughing at what was going on. He was totally natural. He was amazing. Sometimes he would have trouble with his lines and we'd have to do ten or fifteen takes and he'd get really, really furious at himself for having to do it over and over again."

Dennis tells *Disc* around this time: "It's hard to say what the film is about. It shows what people go through under pressure. At one time, I thought that our car represented youth and the other car the establishment. You can take it a thousand different ways. ... The film is good and James [Taylor] is good. A true friendship developed there. We'd never met before and all of a sudden we were there in front of a camera. What are we doing here? It was that sort of thing. We got on well and argued a lot. That was my first acting role and probably my last. Not because I didn't think I was any good, I think I was great. It was eight weeks' hard work but I didn't mind that. It's just that I have a choice, and music, for me, is more rewarding. I'd like to be involved in films, musically."

The opening scenes of the film were shot with the help of the LA Street Racers Association, a real-life group who race illegally on the streets of Los Angeles. The film's producers spend a long time with the group trying to convince them that it will be OK to be portrayed in the film and that they will not be arrested following their appearance on celluloid. The other characters – most notably the bar workers, policemen, and even the kids seen playing baseball – are all real-life people drafted in by Hellman for the relevant scenes. The movie costs Universal $850,000 to produce and is one of four currently in production by the company.

■ Friday 14th

RECORDING *Surf's Up* **sessions** Brian's Home Studio *Bel Air, CA.* Recording takes place for **'Lookin' At Tomorrow'** (take 6 is master).

■ Saturday 15th

RECORDING *Surf's Up* **sessions** Brian's Home Studio *Bel Air, CA.* Recorded today are version one of **'Big Sur'**, in a different time signature to the familiar released version, and the *Surf's Up* version of **'Til I Die'**, which requires five 'takes', or attempts at a recording. This version of 'Big Sur' will remain unreleased.

■ Monday 17th

RECORDING Brian's Home Studio *Bel Air, CA.* Today the group record **'H.E.L.P.'** This song will later be used as the basis of 'Santa's On His Way' for the aborted 1977 Christmas album, while the original version will remain unreleased until the 1993 *Good Vibrations* boxed set.

■ Thursday 20th

At Brian's Home Studio some old recordings are revisited: **'Can't**

1970

Sunflower album

A1 'Cotton Fields (The Cotton Song)' SINGLE VERSION (H. LEDBETTER) UK ALBUM ONLY
A1/A2 'Slip On Through' (D. WILSON) US/UK
A2/A3 'This Whole World' (B. WILSON) US/UK
A3/A4 'Add Some Music To Your Day' (B. WILSON / J. KNOTT / M. LOVE) US/UK
A4/A5 'Got To Know The Woman' (D. WILSON) US/UK
A5/A6 'Deirdre' (B. JOHNSTON) US/UK
A6/A7 'It's About Time' (D. WILSON / B. BURCHMAN / A. JARDINE) US/UK
B1 'Tears In The Morning' (B. JOHNSTON)
B2 'All I Wanna Do' (B. WILSON / M. LOVE)
B3 'Forever' (D. WILSON / G. JAKOBSON)
B4 'Our Sweet Love' (B. WILSON / C. WILSON / A. JARDINE)
B5 'At My Window' (A. JARDINE / B. WILSON)
B6 'Cool Cool Water' (B. WILSON / M. LOVE)

US release August 31st 1970 (Brother/Reprise 6382).
UK release November 1970 (Stateside SSLA8251).
Chart high US number 151; UK number 29.

Wait Too Long' is dubbed from 1-inch 8-track to 2-inch 16-track tape for possible overdubbing, and the 3-track tape of **'Sherry She Needs Me'** is also transferred, although no vocals will be added until 1976.

■ Wednesday 26th

MIXING Brian's Home Studio *Bel Air, CA*. A mix session is held for **'Big Sur'** (version one), **'Til I Die'**, **'H.E.L.P.'** and **'Lookin' At Tomorrow'**.

■ Monday 31st

Sunflower album released in the US. After considerable revision, including a title change, the new LP – with its charming jacket shot of the group and some of their children relaxing on the grass – is finally released in America on Brother/Reprise Records. *Sunflower* is in effect a reworked version of *Add Some Music*: it consists of 'Slip On Through', 'Add Some Music To Your Day', 'This Whole World', 'Tears In The Morning', 'At My Window' and 'Our Sweet Love' from that album, rejected by Reprise in late May, the strongest tracks from the aborted so-called 'last Capitol album', and the recently completed 'Cool Cool Water'.

Although filled with impressive music, the album swiftly becomes the group's least successful studio album in terms of its sales performance, peaking at a lowly 151 and only selling to the group's faithful fans – who are dwindling in numbers. When the album is released in November in the UK, where The Beach Boys are still very popular, the record peaks impressively at 29 after several glowing reviews, the best since *Pet Sounds*. Two tracks, 'Cool, Cool Water' and 'Got To Know The Woman', are presented in 'quadraphonic', a shortlived system designed to provide surround-sound.

Carl tells *Sounds*: "*Sunflower* is the truest group effort we'd ever had. Each of us was deeply involved in the creation of almost all the cuts. Someone would come down to the studio early and put down a basic track, and then someone else would arrive and think of a good line or overdub." But Bruce has reservations about his two songs on the album when he speaks to BBC Radio-1 in 1974. "I thought 'Tears In The Morning' was too pop," recalls Bruce. "It just didn't fit the group and it was my mistake. I think it's a lovely song with a lovely arrangement, but it just isn't right for the group. As for 'Deirdre', I wish I hadn't recorded this with the group. It didn't help them at all." Later still, Bruce will nonetheless name *Sunflower* as his favourite Beach Boys album.

Brian tells *Rolling Stone*: "I think we threw away at least one good song on [*Sunflower*]. Overall the record is good but it doesn't please me as much as I wish. In 'Cool Cool Water' there's a chant I wish we hadn't used. It fits all right, but there's just something I don't quite think is right in it. But, all in all, with some good airplay, the record should do very well."

Shortly after *Sunflower's* release, *Rolling Stone* gives the album a generally positive review.

"After a long period of recovery, mediocrity and general disaster," Jim Miller writes, "The Beach Boys have finally produced an album that can stand with *Pet Sounds*. The odd vocal and instrumentation complexity has returned and the result largely justifies the absurd faith some of us had that The Beach Boys were actually still capable of producing a superb rock album or, more precisely, a superb rock 'Muzak album'. ... Hip supermarkets might program this album for contented perusing among the frozen vegetables and canned fruits. ... 'Slip On Through' hints of the soft hard rock that marked 'I Get Around', 'Help Me Rhonda' etc, transferred to the domain of contemporary Motown. All of these tracks are executed with a certain aplomb that often was lacking in post-'Good Vibrations' Beach Boys music, and the self consciousness of such homogenising enterprise of making a new Beach Boys record has been overcome.

"As a result, the naiveté of the group is more astounding than ever. I mean, it's 1970 and here we have a new, excellent Beach Boys epic, and isn't that irrelevant? In any case, Brian's new stuff is great, especially 'This Whole World' and 'All I Wanna Do', which brings up the engineering and production work on this album. It's flawless, especially in view of the number of overdubs. There is a warmth, a floating quality to the stereo that far surpasses the mixing on, say, *Abbey Road*. *Sunflower* is, without doubt, the best Beach Boys album in recent memory. A stylistically coherent tour de force. It makes one wonder, though, whether anyone still listens to their music or could give a shit about it."

Almost immediately, several other American publications follow suit and dish out good reviews. But it is too late. The damage done by their non-appearance at Monterey in 1967 seems irreversible among rock's opinion-formers. The Beach Boys are poorly considered by the general record buying public. The album's low ratings in the US *Billboard* chart knock any optimistic juices out of a despondent, demoralised group. It's a sad moment for them and for Warners, which has sunk a good deal of money into the group and is left wondering if it has made a big mistake. The bosses at the record company need a change in fortune to recoup their investment.

Beach Boys co-manager Fred Vail: "I remember a Beach Boys meeting. All the guys were sitting around this table and we were talking about the 'Add Some Music' single not happening and *Sunflower* not charting, and they were wondering why. I said to them, 'Listen, this is a phase right now. If you stay the course, your real audience won't forget you. They won't desert you.' But The Beach Boys really didn't believe in themselves."

Just as the album is about to be released, the group meets again with the American Pacifica Radio DJ Jack Rieley, a journalist with an

apparently impressive resumé, who again insists that he knows how to help them regain their popularity. He says he can update their image for the 1970s and make them more relevant, and in the process make them more palatable to a wider audience, thus appeasing the record label and pleasing the group. Taking up the challenge, the group (primarily Mike and Bruce) install Rieley as their new manager and director of public relations at Brother Records – at the expense of their longtime friend Fred Vail. "One day I came back off the road and I walked into my office," recalls Vail, "and there was Jack sitting behind my desk. I said, 'Jack, what are you doing?' He said, 'Oh, I'm just using the phone. I'll get out. Don't worry.'" But Vail sees the writing on the wall, and decides to leave. Later, he describes Rieley as "a great manipulator".

Rieley takes up the post as The Beach Boys' new manager and insists on a few conditions. First, there will be no more candy-striped shirts or matching outfits. Second, Carl will become the official musical leader of the band. Third, he announces his intention to turn the group into a socially conscious band of songwriters, ditching typical love songs and pop-oriented lyrics in favour of a more topical stance. And finally, the group should appear in a series of commercials saying, "It's now safe to listen to The Beach Boys." The phrase soon becomes the headline in a number of newspaper ads for the group.

Rieley tells Radio-1: "I had a letter from a man in Houston, Texas. He said he went into his record shop and bought a Beach Boys album and sandwiched it between albums by Jethro Tull and Led Zeppelin. He didn't want it to be known to his buddies that he still listened to The Beach Boys. I used that story in one of our ads. It sounds silly, but people in America at this time were afraid to listen to The Beach Boys. *20/20* and *Sunflower* were real disasters sales-wise. But *Sunflower* is one of the finest recordings I have ever heard by anybody. So, I changed the group. I dropped their white suits and we started doing concerts unlike the concerts that The Beach Boys had been doing previously."

September

Beach Boys Greatest Hits album released in the UK and Europe. This new compilation LP will peak at number 5 in the UK chart.
• 'Cotton Fields' single peaks in Norwegian chart at number 1, and in Dutch chart at number 12.

■ Tuesday 1st
Just weeks after mastering their latest album, the group takes charge of assembling another LP from existing recordings. The new record is given what turns out to be a shortlived working title of *Landlocked*. The group's new manager Jack Rieley tells *Rolling Stone*: "*Landlocked* came to me as an album title because it represented departure. It was meant as a demarcation line, separating striped-shirted bullshit that had become irrelevant, an object of public scorn, from artistry, new creativity and great new songs. We even had a cover designed, which featured stark bright white san-serif letters on a stark black field."

Thirteen songs are selected from the material recorded: 'Loop De Loop', 'Susie Cincinnati', 'San Miguel', 'H.E.L.P. Is On The Way', 'Take A Load Off Your Feet', 'Carnival' (also known as 'Over The Waves'), 'I Just Got My Pay', 'Good Time', 'Big Sur' (version one), 'Fallin' In Love' (also known as 'Lady'), 'When Girls Get Together', 'Lookin' At Tomorrow', and "Til I Die'

This version of 'Big Sur', taped in August, is a completely

different recording to that which will appear on the *Holland* album. 'Lookin' At Tomorrow' and a shorter version of "Til I Die' will both appear on *Surf's Up*. 'San Miguel' will finally appear in 1981 on the *Ten Years Of Harmony* compilation and, along with 'H.E.L.P. Is On The Way', on the 1993 *Good Vibrations* boxed set. (See also entry for January-April 1971.)

Rieley: "I heard the songs, among which were titles like 'Loop De Loop' and others which were even more forgettable. I was totally perplexed. No strategy was worth anything without the goods, and the goods were just not there. Embarrassed, I met with Mo Ostin, a true Brian Wilson fan, at Warner Brothers, who listened to the songs, and he declared: 'No way.'"

In truth, there never was going to be a *Landlocked* album. At best, it can be considered as a working title for what became *Surf's Up*.

■ September / October
The Beach Boys spend the majority of these two months rehearsing in Brian's Bel Air mansion for their forthcoming concert appearances. Dennis misses the rehearsals due to continuing filming for *Two Lane Blacktop*.

October

During the first two weeks of October, and still at Brian's home studio, the group also begins work on their second one-hour Radio Luxembourg spectacular. As with the presentation taped on May 26th 1969, this Bruce Johnston-produced show is intended as a curtain-raiser for their forthcoming UK and European tour, set to begin on November 16th. Radio Luxembourg's Don Wardell says in *Fab 208* magazine: "The show won't be just a series of individual tunes like last year's programme, but a radio spectacular of special Beach Boys sounds." The station sets a tentative air date of November 18th.

'See The Light' / 'Get Your Mind Made Up' single by The Flame released in the US. The group includes the Fataar brothers, future Beach Boys members; this first single is produced by Carl.
• Reports circulate this month that Brian and Van Dyke Parks are working together again, penning the music for an upcoming Beach Boys TV special to be called *H-2-0*.

■ Saturday 3rd
Big Sur Folk Festival, Pattee Arena, Monterey County Fairgrounds *Monterey, CA* two shows matinee/evening, with Joan Baez, John Hartford, Linda Ronstadt, John Phillips, Kris Kristofferson, Mimi Farina, Country Joe McDonald, Merry Clayton, Love Ltd
Following an invitation last month by Brian's friend Van Dyke Parks, the group plays two acclaimed sets at the eighth annual *Big Sur Folk Festival* in California.

These shows will come to be seen as landmark events in the chequered history of The Beach Boys. The performances in front of a crowd of 6,000 help to establish the group's image in the eyes of the rock hierarchy, and they are subsequently 'rediscovered' as an important live act.

They close the afternoon section of the show and appear first during the evening. Only Mike, Bruce, Al, and Carl are present: Dennis is still away filming *Two-Lane Blacktop*, and Mike Kowalski takes his place behind the kit. California-born session drummer Kowalski has played with Sonny & Cher, Nick Drake and John

Martyn, among others. Also joining the live band is Beach Boys stage regular Daryl Dragon on keyboards and bass.

Carl tells *Sounds*: "It went fine. I only wish we had had a little more time. There were a lot of acts on the bill, so even with two sets we didn't get a chance to play as much as we'd like to. After the show, you'd see one person turn to another and say, 'Did you dig it?' And the other person would say, 'Well, I don't know. Did *you* dig it?' They were a little paranoid about committing themselves."

"We did it without Brian but the group was successful," manager Jack Rieley says later in *Rolling Stone*. "It was just what we wanted to get things moving. They hadn't done festivals before – and I'm not sure why. Some people in the group seemed apprehensive about doing them.

"We changed the order of the songs in the performance around drastically. We dropped some numbers entirely, introduced some album cuts, which they hadn't done on stage much, and I thought it was a great show. That's what started things. Shortly after, we got an offer to play Carnegie Hall." (See February 24th 1971.)

Jann Wenner reviews the afternoon show for *Rolling Stone*: "They did 'God Only Knows', 'Sloop John B', 'Vegetables', some superb stuff from their new album, 'Cotton Fields', 'Wouldn't It Be Nice', 'Darlin'. ... The Beach Boys quite obviously were excellent. They could have gone on for another two hours and no one would have known. They were the best act of the day."

A recording of the group's performance of 'Wouldn't It Be Nice' will be included on a *Live At The Big Sur Folk Festival* single and album (see April 23rd 1971).

Today's Festival appearance also enables the group to gauge the public's reaction to an old song they are considering as the next single. Mike tells *Melody Maker* shortly after the *Big Sur* appearance: "'Riot In Cell Block #9' is a Leiber & Stoller song from way back, which I've rewritten with more contemporary lyrics. It deals with student demonstrations and troubles at places like Jacksonville State and Kent Universities. The message is, 'Stay away, there's a riot going on. Don't get involved.' It's a really strong blues-cum-R&B piece and it may be our next single in the States." The 'new' song, 'Student Demonstration Time', will not in fact appear as a single, but will be on the 1971 *Surf's Up* album.

Set-list (evening) 'Wouldn't It Be Nice', 'Sloop John B', 'Country Air', 'California Girls', 'Darlin'', 'Aren't You Glad', 'Tears In The Morning', 'Wake The World', 'Vegetables', 'God Only Knows', 'Cotton Fields', 'Their Hearts Were Full Of Spring', 'Riot In Cell Block #9', 'Good Vibrations'.

■ Monday 12th

'Tears In The Morning' / 'It's About Time' released in the US. This latest 45 continues the dismal run of Beach Boys releases as it fails to break into the American charts.

Tears In The Morning single

A 'Tears In The Morning' (B. JOHNSTON)
B 'It's About Time' (D. WILSON / B. BURCHMAN / A. JARDINE)

US release October 12th 1970 (Brother/Reprise 0957).
UK release November 1970 (Stateside SS 2181).
Chart high US none; UK none.

■ Saturday 17th

Sunflower album peaks at a lowly 153 in the US Billboard chart.

■ Tuesday 27th

Nick Grillo announces that the group's Brother Records label has made a deal with EMI for "foreign distribution" including the UK. It is an ironic twist, considering that Brother has severed ties with Capitol and has a damages suit pending against them – and that Capitol is an EMI-owned US company. Grillo announces that the first record to go out through EMI's Stateside label will be *Sunflower*, The Beach Boys' current album, presently without UK release.

■ Saturday 31st

RECORDING Brian's Home Studio *Bel Air, CA*. On this Halloween night, The Beach Boys with Billy Hinsche record **'My Solution'**, which will remain unreleased – although Brian will revisit the melody later for the opening of the song 'Happy Days' on his 1998 album *Imagination*.

November

Sunflower album released in the UK. 'Cotton Fields', a British number 2 single, is added to the existing US running order for this issue. The LP fares better in the UK charts, peaking at number 29. **'Tears In The Morning'** / **'It's About Time'** released in the UK. It fails to chart.

■ Wednesday 4th – Saturday 7th

Whisky A Go Go *Los Angeles, CA* with The Flame
The Beach Boys return to the concert stage, making their first Los Angeles appearance since June 25th 1966. Dennis, fresh from his solo film debut, returns to the group's drumming stool. These Whisky dates, which also serve as a warm-up for the forthcoming concerts in Britain, mark Brian's first live performances with The Beach Boys since August 26th 1967. Also on-stage with the group are regular extra musicians Ed Carter (guitar, bass) and Daryl Dragon (keyboards) and a number of others, including possibly as many as nine horn players and at least one percussionist (probably Mike Kowalski).

American reporter Judy Sims writes in the British *Melody Maker*: "I was down at the Whisky, which is something akin to torture, no matter who's there. This time it was crowded; people sitting in the tiny spaces between tables that the waiters facetiously call aisles. Somebody said Paul McCartney was there, but I never saw him. The occasion for all this madness? The first Los Angeles appearance by The Beach Boys in four years. The Beach Boys at the Whisky must be likened to The Rolling Stones at London's Speakeasy. A bit crowded... . I arrived early, so I could sit at a table and not in the aisle, which meant I had to sit through The Flame. They must have played for two hours, a long set of unmitigated dullness! They were introduced as the next great international sensation. Spare us!

"The Beach Boys didn't play so long but they covered a wide range of old and new songs. There were 15 people on that stage: five horns, two percussion, an extra bass, and an extra keyboard, plus the much-heralded appearance of Brian Wilson, who hasn't performed in years! Brian looked slimmer and more handsome than the last time I saw him. He sat down at the electric piano near the Moog and didn't really seem to do a heck of a lot. Carl still carries the group, with Mike and Al close by. Carl's voice and guitar are the mainstays, and he handles that role with enthusiasm, something which seemed to be lacking in the others. Dennis, traditionally the heartthrob, came out from behind the drums to sing one song, looking uncomfortable. He slouches; I never noticed that before.

"Listening to The Beach Boys is an exercise in balancing intellect and emotions. When I hear their new stuff, I feel like I'm listening to jazz: I know it's good, but it doesn't move me. But when they play the oldies, I perk right up and feel like singing along. They encored with 'I Get Around' and for me it was the high spot. I almost wish that wasn't true because, while The Beach Boys have evolved and progressed, most of their audiences want the earlier teenage stuff, which the group must have tired of playing about five years ago."

Rolling Stone's reviewer writes: "Just like the surfers they sang so much about in their first records, The Beach Boys are travelling a precarious course these days, full of ups and downs. [They] set house records at the Whisky, with long lines around the Sunset Strip block for four straight nights. The Whisky is a small club and The Beach Boys had their full entourage, including a nine-horn section with them. There was talk that Paul McCartney would fly in from New York, having heard that Brian would be making his first appearance with the group in five years."

Brian tells *Melody Maker*: "It was good to get up there again. When I first got up on stage, I felt a little self-conscious. A lot of eyes were on me. So I thought, 'OK, I'm gonna have some fun.'" But his comeback is shortlived. As *Rolling Stone* concludes: "Paul never made it and Brian only lasted a night and a half." Brian: "On the second night, I started to feel dizzy from the amps and from the sounds. After about half an hour I realised that I couldn't go on. I started feeling dizzy and I told the guys I had to stop. It felt like I was killing myself. I thought for a minute I was going to have a blackout. I couldn't see the audience. There were faces out there swimming at me and I had to stop singing. My eardrums ached and it got worse whenever there was loud drumming from Dennis. I had trouble focusing on anything and my right ear was killing me. I knew then that I wasn't going to make it and so I asked Marilyn to help me out."

On that second night, Thursday 5th, Brian is helped off stage by his wife and some doctors, and taken by car to rest at his home in Los Angeles.

Just days later, still at home, he gives a revealing interview to *Melody Maker*. "I certainly wouldn't call myself a leader," Brian announces. "I'm not as creative as I once was and I'm not participating as much as I should have done. I guess I'm a kind of drop-out. I go to bed in the early hours of the morning and sleep until the early afternoon. I potter around doing nothing much, and lately I haven't even been writing music. I'm a bit overweight now [he's 14 and a half stones] but I hope to start swimming again and lose a few pounds. I'm not unhappy with life; in fact I'm quite happy living at home. After the Whisky thing, I came home and started thinking about a new song. I haven't done the words yet, but I'm going to call it 'The Wise Man Stayed Home'. I'm that wise man."
Set-list (6th) 'Darlin'', 'Aren't You Glad', 'Wouldn't It Be Nice', 'Wake The World', 'Cotton Fields', 'Country Air', 'Sloop John B', 'Riot In Cell Block #9', 'God Only Knows', 'Good Vibrations', 'It's About Time', 'I Get Around', 'Johnny B Goode'.

■ Friday 13th

RECORDING Capitol studio *Hollywood, CA*. Dennis is working on his first solo album and today tapes a version of his composition **'Settle Down'**. The session also includes overdubbing and additional recording onto his January recording of **'Lady'** (formerly known as 'Fallin' In Love') in readiness for its release in the UK as the B-side

of his single 'Sound Of Free' on December 4th. Dennis produces the recordings, which feature a selection of session musicians from the LA scene. No other Beach Boys are present.

TOUR STARTS UK/Europe (Nov 19th-December 20th)
The Beach Boys, again minus Brian, fly into London Airport on the 16th to start only their second major tour of the year. Their first assignment is an obligatory press conference, held the same morning aboard the floating discotheque Sloop John D, a boat moored on the River Thames. During the get-together the group announces details of their new British album *Sunflower* and Dennis once more complains about being too hot and claustrophobic. True to form, the photographers and reporters present at the conference far exceed the room's capacity and crowd into every available space on the overheated boat. Afterwards the group takes up residence at the Inn On The Park Hotel in central London, and later they party into the early hours of the morning.

■ Tuesday 17th

Over breakfast at about 11:00am, Dennis gives a revealing interview to British music paper *Disc & Music Echo*. Photographer at the session is Michael Putland, who recalls: "Dennis had been up all night. He hadn't a clue where he had been and who he had been with. He was exhausted."

In the feature, Dennis once again sums up his apparently unmotivated but contented lifestyle, reiterating many points he made during the group's last major visit to the country 17 months ago. "My style of living changes every year," he reveals. "I always had to have mansions, limousines and 20 women. Then I threw it all away. I wanted to live alone. I haven't had a car now for three years. I don't have a home either. I move around every couple of weeks. For the last couple of months I've lived in hotels. Before that, I rented a place for a while, and before that I had a shack. I suppose the idea of a small cottage in the hills appeals to me.

"Music is the biggest thing in my life, and apart from my music I like the idea of being a father. Here's my life: music, making love, being happy, making a family, fishing and gardening. That's about it. I don't want any money. I've had a lot and spent a lot. I've been wealthy and poor as a Beach Boy. I've been looking for myself for the last four or five years. I used to think that there was nothing but music, [that] music is God and that everything would evolve to one thing, a song. That has been my thought, the one big thought behind everything I did. But I realise now that it's not really true. I'm just a guy who plays drums and plays piano. I figure that I'll find myself by the time I die, maybe. I have that to look forward to."

■ Wednesday 18th

TV BBC TV Centre *west London*. BBC-1 *Top Of The Pops* live vocal over new backing track 'Tears In The Morning', broadcast colour November 19th 7:05-7:44pm. The group record their fourth studio appearance for *TOTP*, for which they are paid £200.

■ Thursday 19th

New Theatre *Oxford* two shows, with The Flame
Opening night of the group's UK tour, and for the first time on a British stage The Beach Boys do not wear their matching stage uniforms. Accompanying the group on-stage for this tour is guitarist Ed Carter and keyboard player Daryl Dragon.

The Flame, the first signing to the Brother label, will stay on in Britain for a further ten days after their support slot on the tour, playing live dates and promoting their new single 'See The Light'.

BELOW Carl and Mike on-stage at the Hammersmith Odeon in London on November 20th.
BELOW RIGHT Experiencing northern Britain in late November as the European tour continues.

■ Friday 20th

Hammersmith Odeon *west London* two shows, with The Flame
Ray Coleman writes in *Melody Maker*: "The Beach Boys always seemed the embodiment of Young America: sun, surf, sand and some irresistible songs that projected happiness. Without that natural high school effervescence they are nowhere, and [Friday's show] damaged their reputation. First, their sound was atrocious, and they repeatedly ignored pleas from the audience to improve it. The result was that the very core of their act was lost and they were forced to rely on other assets. Secondly, the chat by Mike Love and Bruce Johnston was slow, boring and lacklustre, so they were leaning even more heavily on a true Beach Boys sound to create a good performance. Thirdly, The Beach Boys' panache was missing.

"If you like their music, you are perhaps clutching at memories of open-topped cars and summers and 'Wouldn't It Be Nice', 'Good Vibrations', 'God Only Knows' and 'I Get Around' wafting from the radio. Well, they sang these and other specialities but they all came across like clockwork. There wasn't any spark. Bruce Johnston bubbled as he always does; Al Jardine played guitar with the furrowed-brow concentration of a chess player; Mike Love looked like a principal boy in a panto and clowned about embarrassingly. If their future shows are not going to reach the standards of previous years, we will all be better off staying at home and playing *Pet Sounds*. There is nothing sadder than diminishing magic."

Beach Boys manager Jack Rieley tells BBC Radio-1: "The group did 45 minutes and they were terribly dissatisfied with it. Some of the critics didn't like it and it just wasn't the group. The shows had that strange guy introducing the group. I remember some of his jokes and they were very sad. We had The Flame with us but it was just so bad. From an artistic stance, it was a disastrous tour."

Set-list 'Cotton Fields', 'Darlin'', 'Wouldn't It Be Nice', 'Country Air', 'I Can Hear Music', 'Sloop John B', 'Vegetables', 'Riot In Cell Block #9', 'Tears In The Morning', 'God Only Knows', 'Forever', 'Good Vibrations', 'I Get Around' (encore), 'It's About Time' (encore).

■ Saturday 21st

The Palace *Manchester* 6:00 & 8:30pm, with The Flame

■ Sunday 22nd

Coventry Theatre *Coventry* two shows, with The Flame

■ Monday 23rd

Gaumont Theatre *Southampton* two shows, with The Flame

■ Tuesday 24th

Capitol Theatre *Cardiff, Wales* two shows, with The Flame

■ Wednesday 25th

Odeon Theatre *Birmingham* two shows, with The Flame

■ Thursday 26th

Green's Playhouse *Glasgow, Scotland* two shows, with The Flame

■ Friday 27th – Sunday 29th

Fiesta Night Club *Stockton-on-Tees, Co Durham* with The Flame

■ Monday 30th – Sunday December 6th

Fiesta Night Club *Sheffield* with The Flame

December

■ Friday 4th

'**Sound Of Free**' / '**Lady**' single by Dennis Wilson & Rumbo released in the UK. Following a discussion between Dennis and EMI's Sir Joseph Lockwood, the Stateside/EMI label in the UK rush-release this 45.

'Rumbo' is Daryl Dragon, keyboard player in The Beach Boys' touring band. The A-side is written by Dennis with additional lyrics by Mike, guitar playing by Carl, and backing vocals by Brian. The B-side is one of the tracks intended for the *Sunflower* album but rejected by Warner/Reprise (see February 18th).

Dennis's single is released to coincide with the group's current visit and in anticipation of his solo album, planned for release some time in 1971 but ultimately unreleased.

Two further recordings intended for the solo record – 'Cuddle Up' and 'Make It Good' – will appear in 1972 as part of the *Carl And The Passions – "So Tough"* album. Furthermore, 'Lady' will covered by American Spring and issued by them as a single in the US on April 6th 1973.

■ Saturday 5th

With the group's UK/European tour well underway, British music paper *Melody Maker* picks up on the story first announced by Dennis on April 19th.

"The Beach Boys may be going to live in Britain and may build a recording studio in the Surrey area," suggests *MM*. "The group have been thinking seriously about leaving their Los Angeles base for several months because of he smog problem there."

Carl also comments to *Melody Maker*: "I can't see us living [in Los Angeles] any longer because to be there is really not to live at all. I

want to get a place in the country and I want to get the hell out of Los Angeles immediately."

Mike adds: "I have only rented my Los Angeles home and I no longer have any ties there. I see no reason why we should live in Smog City."

And manager Jack Rieley concludes: "No decisions about this have been made yet because we have recording commitments in the US to get through. But the group is definitely leaving Los Angeles because of the smog. There is a chance that Carl may buy a farm in Northern California at a place called Carmel, which is 400 miles north of Los Angeles, and Dennis's wife is expecting a baby in March and he doesn't want the child to grow up in Los Angeles. He wants to live in the country."

■ Monday 7th

Following the last date of their residency at the Fiesta Night Club in Sheffield, England on Sunday (see November 30th) the group flies on to Paris to start a round of three shows in Europe.

Sound Of Free single by Dennis Wilson & Rumbo

A '**Sound Of Free**' (D. WILSON / M. LOVE)
B '**Lady**' (D. WILSON)

UK release December 4th 1970 (Stateside SS 2184).
Chart high UK none.

BELOW Relaxing at a club with The Flame, the support band on this European tour. Ricky Fataar and Blondie Chaplin (top right) will later become members of The Beach Boys. BELOW RIGHT Dennis takes to the microphone with his four bandmates during a concert on the continuing European tour.

■ Tuesday 8th

Gaumont Palace *Paris, France* with The Flame

This show, added to the original itinerary, is a special charity concert in aid of the families of 142 dancers tragically killed in a recent French beat-club fire.

Only around 500 people turn up for the concert, and Bruce and Mike encourage them to gather around the stage for the cameras present to record the event for French television.

Extracts from tonight's performance – 'Wouldn't It Be Nice', 'Their Hearts Were Full Of Spring', 'Cotton Fields' and 'Vegetables' – will be shown on the 45-minute French TF2 TV show *POP2* on April 17th 1971.

Earlier in the day the group films an interview for the show with noted French rock reporter P.F. Blancard.

■ Wednesday 9th

Palais D'Hiver *Lyon, France* with The Flame

The second of the group's two French shows on this tour.

■ Thursday 10th

Ahoy Halle *Rotterdam, Netherlands* with The Flame

Following tonight's show in Rotterdam the group flies back to London the next morning.

■ Friday 11th

Astoria Theatre Finsbury Park, *north London* two shows, with The Flame

Mike Ledgerwood writes in *Disc & Music Echo*: "I watched … from the wings, and it was obvious throughout that Mike Love, Dennis Wilson and Bruce Johnston were competing against each other for the solo spotlight. [Mike], of course, is officially The Beach Boys' lead singer, and makes a damn good job of it. But lately it's become blatantly obvious that Bruce and Dennis are struggling for personal stardom. Dennis, for instance, did solo numbers in the second show, yet appeared sadly devoid of either enthusiasm or presence out front. But he struggled defiantly through three songs, when one would have been enough.

"Later, seemingly not to be outdone, bouncy Bruce interrupted the group during 'Tears In The Morning' to take his solo entirely alone except for his own piano accompaniment. I must admit it went down a storm, as the song benefited from the simple piano-voice presentation. But if you'd seen the expressions and heard the mutterings of the others in the group as they were ordered off stage, it looked decidedly as though Bruce could find himself in the doghouse!"

Who drummer Keith Moon, a long-time admirer of The Beach Boys, is present tonight and happily accepts an invitation to

accompany the group on the train ride to their shows in Bournemouth the following day.

Saturday 12th
Winter Gardens *Bournemouth* two shows, with The Flame
As part of the show's finale, Keith Moon jams with the group on stage.

Sunday 13th
The Empire *Liverpool* two shows, with The Flame
Last night of The Beach Boys' UK Tour. The following morning, while the rest of his colleagues stay on in England, Bruce heads off to France to meet his girlfriend in Paris. The pair then travel on to the Netherlands.

Tuesday 15th
This afternoon in the Netherlands, working alone and still travelling separately from the other Beach Boys, Bruce accepts an invitation to film an appearance for the AVRO TV show *Toppop*, lip-synching a performance of 'Tears In The Morning' in Bellevue, Leidseplein, Amsterdam. The black-and-white clip is aired later this evening on the Nederland 1 television station (7:04-7:30pm). Aside from the filming, Bruce also visits the studios of Veronica Radio in Hilversum to record a jingle for the station. Two days later he flies back to London.

Thursday 17th
Royal Albert Hall *London* with Magna Carta, The Flirtations; compère: DJ Mike Quinn
The Beach Boys perform their first Royal show, topping the bill at the *Save Rave* charity show in the presence of Princess Margaret. Bruce has invited Princess Anne to the concert but she is unable to attend. The *Save Rave* show is organised by The Invalid Children's Aid Association. Following the show The Beach Boys attend a party held at the nearby Revolution discothèque.

Friday 18th
Concertgebouw *Amsterdam, Netherlands* scheduled 12:30am; actual start 4:00am, with The Flame
It is a bad winter in England, and when The Beach Boys arrive at London Airport this afternoon for their flight to Amsterdam to conclude their tour they find themselves fogged in. They scramble for a jet at neighbouring Gatwick Airport but still cannot get a flight to Amsterdam.

They are forced to fly to Brussels, Belgium where they are met by seven Mercedes taxis and driven hastily to Amsterdam. A minute-by-minute account of their progress is broadcast to the waiting audience at the Concertgebouw, where the group were set to perform at 12:30am.

As dawn approaches, The Beach Boys sincerely doubt there will be an audience if and when they make their destination. But as they stride on stage at four on Saturday morning, the house is still full and clamouring for the group.

When the show starts, the enthusiastic audience shouts for new songs from the group instead of the old favourites. In an interview for Dutch magazine *OOR*, Carl later announces: "I love this audience. Our last albums sold poorly in the US, our financial situation is disastrous – and here we have success. I like this country." Carl and the group will later follow up on this affection for Holland.

Saturday 19th
De Doelen *Rotterdam, Netherlands* 12:15am, with The Flame
Another late-night/early-morning show. Just before the concert, Bruce is interviewed by Radio Caroline DJ/presenter Robbie Dale. Bruce too is impressed by the Dutch, telling Dale: "The audience is very respected by me and the band. ... They listen to the lyrics. I might consider living here." At the end of the interview the station announces they will air tonight's concert in 1971 in two parts, but this does not materialise.

Sunday 20th
Concertgebouw *Amsterdam, Netherlands* 8:30pm, with The Flame
A return appearance to the Concertgebouw rounds off their trip to Holland and their year. The Beach Boys fly home to California the following afternoon. Their great comeback is well underway.

1971

Recordings continue for *Surf's Up* album ... Dennis injures his hand badly in an accident and will not play drums again until 1974 ... Ricky Fataar takes Dennis's place on the drum stool for live dates ... *Surf's Up* album released ... the hip-again Beach Boys make the cover of *Rolling Stone* ... sessions begin for the next album, to become *Carl And The Passions – "So Tough"*.

Performing at the Fillmore East in New York City in June.

January

'Another Day Like Heaven' / 'I'm So Happy' single by The Flame released in the US. This is the group's second 45, produced by Carl.
• 'Tears In The Morning' single peaks in Dutch chart at number 6.
• Along with several other celebrities, The Beach Boys feature in one of a series of television commercials for Eastern Airlines. Bruce speaks for the group, while the song 'This Whole World' features on the soundtrack of each 30-second slot.

■ Tuesday 19th
Whisky A Go Go *Los Angeles, CA*
The group's first live appearance of 1971 is at this legendary venue.

■ Saturday 23rd – Sunday 24th
Civic Auditorium *Santa Monica, CA*

■ January through early April
RECORDING *Surf's Up* sessions Brian's Home Studio *Bel Air, CA*. Intermittently during these three months the group works on their next studio album.

Beach Boys manager Jack Rieley tells Scott Keller in 1974: "Carl and I began to write. 'Long Promised Road' was created. Then came 'Feel Flows' and 'A Day In The Life Of A Tree'. Mike Love, Al Jardine and Bruce Johnston began to get irritable about it all. There was a long meeting during which they tried to force me to march into [Warners boss] Mo Ostin's office and sell him on their 1969 track 'Loop De Loop'. I refused and Brian, Dennis and Carl backed me up. Love, sensing that I might be on to something by rejecting their 'string-of-hits' crap as out of date, suddenly came up with 'Student Demonstration Time', which had Carl and I blushing with embarrassment and which thoroughly disgusted Dennis. Then Jardine demanded that his track 'Take A Load Off Your Feet' should go on the album."

Recordings made up to and during this time include **'Don't Go Near The Water'** (written by Al and Mike, with lead vocal from Mike and Al; see April 3rd), **'Long Promised Road'** (written by Carl and Rieley; lead vocal Carl; see April 3rd), **'Take A Load Off Your Feet'** (by Al and his schoolfriend Gary Winfrey; lead vocal Al, with Brian on first verse), **'Student Demonstration Time'** (based on Leiber & Stoller's 'Riot In Cell Block #9' with new lyrics and lead vocal by Mike), **'Feel Flows'** (by Carl and Rieley; lead vocal Carl, probably Charles Lloyd on flute), **'Lookin' At Tomorrow (A Welfare Song)'** (by Al and Winfrey; lead vocal Al), **'4th Of July'** (written by and lead vocal by Dennis; see April), **'Wouldn't It Be Nice To Live Again'** (written by and lead vocal by Dennis), **'A Day In The Life Of A Tree'** (by Brian and Rieley; lead vocal Rieley; see April), **''Til I Die'** (by Brian; group vocal with Brian on chorus), and **'Disney Girls (1957)'** (by Bruce; lead vocal Bruce; see June 3rd).

Brian will say in later press material that ''Til I Die' had its origins in a late-night visit to the beach. "One night, I drove to the beach, parked the car, and walked out onto the deserted sand. If Marilyn had known where I was going she would've hidden the car keys, perhaps robbing me of the inspiration that led to one of my best and least-known songs. Of course, she would've had good reason. Lately, I'd been depressed and preoccupied with death. I'd ordered the gardener to dig a grave in the backyard and threatened to drive my Rolls off the Santa Monica pier. Looking out toward the ocean, my mind, as it did almost every hour of every day, worked to explain the inconsistencies that dominated my life; the pain, torment, and confusion and the beautiful music I was able to make.

Was there an answer? Did I have no control? Had I ever? Feeling shipwrecked on an existential island, I lost myself in the balance of darkness that stretched beyond the breaking waves to the other side of the earth. The ocean was so incredibly vast, the universe so large, and suddenly I saw myself in proportion to that, a little pebble of sand, a jellyfish floating on top of the water; travelling with the current I felt dwarfed, temporary.

"The next day I began writing ''Til I Die', perhaps the most personal song I ever wrote for The Beach Boys," Brian contonues. "In doing so, I wanted to re-create the swell of emotions that I'd felt at the beach the previous night. For several weeks, I struggled at the piano, experimenting with rhythms and chord changes, trying to emulate in sound the ocean's shifting tides and moods as well as its sheer enormity. I wanted the music to reflect the loneliness of floating a raft in the middle of the Pacific. I wanted each note to sound as if it was disappearing into the hugeness of the universe. ''Til I Die' was my postcard to the outside world. The song summed up everything I had to say at the time." Aside from Dennis's '4th Of July' and 'Wouldn't It Be Nice To Live Again', all songs recorded in this period will appear on *Surf's Up* in August.

February

■ Tuesday 2nd – Monday 8th
Newport Hotel *Miami Beach, FL*
Away from the studio, the group plays a six-night residency in Florida, joined on stage by keyboardist/bassist Daryl Dragon.

■ Saturday 13th
Princeton University *Princeton, NJ*

■ Friday 19th
The Beach Boys are guests of New York FM radio station WPLJ and bring with them a tape dubbed from Steve Desper's acetate compiled from recent recordings (see August 4th 1970). As they air 'Good Time', 'I Just Got My Pay', 'San Miguel' and ''Til I Die', the DJ asks Carl, "Is that a new album?" Carl replies, "You could say that some of the cuts might be on an album, but it's *not* a new album."

■ Saturday 20th
Santa Monica Civic Auditorium *Santa Monica, CA* 8:00pm, with The Flame

■ Tuesday 23rd
Symphony Hall *Boston, MA*
During 'Surfer Girl' ex-Beach Boy David Marks joins in on-stage.

■ Wednesday 24th
Carnegie Hall *New York, NY* 8:00pm
The group is booked for the first time into the famous New York venue by Mike Klenfer, Chip Rachlin and George Brown, three longtime Beach Boy fans who own Krab Productions. Their first-choice venue was the Fillmore, but the group's concert there in October 1968 was not successful enough to warrant a return. Instead Krab, after four months' work, choose the legendary Carnegie Hall.

A two-hour set covering the group's entire career is enthusiastically received by the sell-out crowd. (Eighty percent of the tickets were sold five days prior to the event. Shortly after announcing a second show the promoters call it off. The Beach Boys will go on to play eight shows at Carnegie Hall during the following

21 months.) Manager Jack Rieley says on US radio in 1974: "There was no support. There was no opening act. Instead of The Beach Boys coming on and being a jukebox of 45 minutes of their hits, they did two hours and they did good artistic material. I started to sell the group on just being themselves. Certainly, a lot of people had come to the concerts just to hear Brian Wilson's music. But I also knew that there is other music they do as well."

Set-list 'Heroes And Villains', 'Help Me Rhonda' (Carl lead vocal), 'Aren't You Glad', 'Cotton Fields', 'Okie From Muskogee', 'Country Air', 'Wouldn't It Be Nice' (rarely-performed full-length version), 'Vegetables', 'Cool Cool Water', 'Lady', 'Forever', 'Darlin'', 'Caroline No', 'Riot In Cell Block #9', 'Tears In The Morning', 'Your Song' (Bruce sings lead), 'You Still Believe In Me', 'Their Hearts Were Full Of Spring', 'Sloop John B', 'In My Room', 'God Only Knows', 'Good Vibrations', 'California Girls', 'Surfer Girl', 'It's About Time', 'I Get Around', 'Johnny B Goode' (last five as encores).

■ Thursday 25th

TV Westinghouse Broadcasting Company, Group W Productions *Philadelphia, PA*. Syndicated *The David Frost Show* live performance 'Forever', 'Vegetables', 'Lady', broadcast March 24th, 4:30-6:00pm. The group tapes their second appearance on the *Frost* show, performing acoustic live versions. By this point Dennis's role in the group has developed to the extent that he has almost become the frontman, highlighted tonight as he sings lead on two of the show's three songs. Furthermore, during the interview Frost's questioning focuses on Dennis's soon-to-be-released movie *Two-Lane Blacktop*.

March

The Flame album by The Flame released in the US. Produced by Carl, this will be the only non-Beach Boys album issued on Brother Records. A second album, produced by engineer Steve Desper, is recorded but the band breaks up and it remains unreleased.

'Cool Cool Water' / **'Forever'** single released in the US. It becomes the latest Beach Boys single to miss the charts.

■ Monday 15th

Dennis works on a vocal-and-piano recording; no more is known.

April

RECORDING *Surf's Up* sessions Brian's Home Studio *Bel Air, CA*. At some point this month The Beach Boys work on 2-inch 16-track recordings of Dennis's **'4th Of July'**, **'Old Movie'**, as well as **'A Day**

Cool Cool Water single

A 'Cool Cool Water' (B. WILSON / M. LOVE)
B 'Forever' (D. WILSON / G. JAKOBSON)

US release March 1971 (Brother/Reprise 0998).
Chart high US none.

Wouldn't It Be Nice live single

A 'Wouldn't It Be Nice' LIVE (B. WILSON / T. ASHER)
B (ANOTHER ARTIST)

US release April 23rd 1971 (Ode 66016).
Chart high US none.

In The Life Of A Tree', and Carl records a Moog synthesiser sound collage titled **'Telephone Backgrounds (On A Clear Day)'**. Rieley recalls in *Rolling Stone* that he is in the studio for hours as the group tries to achieve a vocal for 'A Day In The Life Of A Tree'. "I think everybody took a crack at it but it just wasn't right. I was disgusted and heading for the door to go home when Brian said, 'Wait a minute, Jack. Come back. I want you to try the vocal.' Well, the last thing I ever expected I'd have to do was sing a song. But I went out and did it. Brian went on and on about how much he loved it. It was perfect and just what he'd wanted all along. Other people in the booth testified he had tears in his eyes when he heard it. But you know, I still don't know whether he was putting me on."

The sessions for The Beach Boys' latest album are concluded some time in April but will resume unexpectedly at the start of June. Dennis records a demo of his track **'Barbara'**, another heavenly piano ballad, written about his second wife. It is another piece intended for his inevitably unfinished first solo album. The song is composed and recorded on two pianos, played by Dennis and Daryl Dragon. Dragon says later that his piano melody is a guide for a string part intended to be overdubbed at a future session. 'Barbara' will remain unreleased until its inclusion on the 1998 Beach Boys compilation *Endless Harmony*.

■ Saturday 3rd

RECORDING *Surf's Up* sessions Brian's Home Studio *Bel Air, CA*. Today's session produces **'Don't Go Near The Water'** as well as rough versions of **'Long Promised Road'** (piano tracks only) and Dennis's **'Old Movie'**.

■ Saturday 10th
Shrine Mosque *Springfield, MA*

■ Tuesday 13th – Wednesday 14th
The Whisky A Go Go *Los Angeles, CA*
Return performances by The Beach Boys just three months after their previous shows at the venue.

TOUR STARTS US East/Midwest (Apr 22nd-May 9th)

■ Thursday 22nd
John F Kennedy Coliseum Stadium *Manchester, NH*
Opening night of an 18-day tour. In addition to Mike, Carl, Dennis, Bruce and Al, the live band at this time includes regular stage Beach Boy Daryl Dragon (keyboards, bass) and his brother Dennis Dragon (percussion).

■ Friday 23rd
'Wouldn't It Be Nice' by The Beach Boys / 'The Times They Are A-Changin'' by Merry Clayton single released in the US. These are live

recordings from the *Big Sur Festival* (see October 3rd 1970) and issued here on the Ode label. An album containing the Beach Boys track (and Clayton's) is also issued around this time.

Saturday 24th

A turn in the group's fortunes is noted in a US trade magazine: "The Beach Boys have now signed with the Millard Agency, who have offices at the Fillmore East in New York and in San Francisco, Bill Graham affiliated. In addition, the group have lined up 16 dates in 18 days between April 22nd and May 9th. The Beach Boys are guaranteed a fee of $125,000 upwards for these shows."

Monday 26th

University of Notre Dame Convocation Center *Notre Dame, IN*

Tuesday 27th

Fillmore East *New York, NY* with The Grateful Dead (headliners) Three nights into the Dead's five-night residency The Beach Boys are surprise guests during tonight's second show, which is broadcast on FM radio. As the headliners play their sixth song, our boys arrive in time to join in on 'Searchin'' and 'Riot In Cell Block #9'. The Dead then depart from the stage, leaving them to sing 'Good Vibrations' – introduced by Bruce who says, "How about a song that reflects these really fucked up times?" – and 'I Get Around' before being rejoined by the Dead. The two groups then jam versions of 'Help Me Rhonda' (a slower arrangement, with Carl on lead vocal), 'Okie From Muskogee' and, to conclude, 'Johnny B Goode'. Amid audience applause, The Beach Boys depart from the stage and the Dead close tonight's concert with three more songs. The Beach Boys were on stage for approximately 38 minutes. A reporter notes Bob Dylan watching from the sound booth and hears him remark aloud, "You know, they're fucking good, man."

Despite later reports, the Grateful Dead crowd do not welcome The Beach Boys warmly; there are loud cries of "Bring back the Dead" between the performances of 'Good Vibrations' and 'I Get Around'. During 'Good Vibrations', Mike tells the crowd of an occasion in 1968: "We did this one night on the bus with the Buffalo Springfield, all stoned and drunk, and it really sounded great."

Wednesday 28th

Merrimack College *North Andover, MA* matinee; **Lowell Auditorium** *Lowell, MA* evening

Thursday 29th

Loew's State Theater *Providence, RI*

Friday 30th

Painters Mill Music Fair *Owings Mills, MD*

Just as it seems that the group is on an upward spiral, they find themselves performing to an audience of only 200 or so tonight.

May

Saturday 1st

The Washington Monument *Washington, DC* afternoon; **Springfield College** *Springfield, MA* evening

Days after performing to one of their smallest ever crowds, The Beach Boys' status as a notable live act returns when, shortly after noon and in front of 500,000 people, they kick off the May Day anti-

war rally concert, *The Peace Treaty Celebration Rock Show*. The event is organised by the Mayday Collective, a body that has grown out of The Ann Arbor Student and Youth Conference, and is in protest over the war in Vietnam. It is the first of five non-violent nationally-organised protests that will run daily in Washington DC until May 5th. The goal is to halt business in the nation's capital through non-violent civil disobedience, with the main aim to stop and stall the flow of traffic on 22 key Washington roads.

The Washington Post reports: "By dawn, more than 1,000 young people, sipping wine, flipping Frisbees, but mostly napping in sleeping bags, had already claimed the pieces of lawn closest to the rock concert stage on a polo field in West Potomac Park. Two hundred yards north, 5,000 more slept in Peace City, the West Potomac Park tent encampment in which young people opposing the war have lived since Monday. Leaders of this demonstration have estimated that between 35,000 and 50,000 will participate in traffic-blocking on Monday and Tuesday. At West Potomac Park the atmosphere much resembled that of a rock festival. Attire ranged from nudity in a few instances to combat fatigues and helmets at the other extremes. ... Several thousand federal troops were readied for possible trouble." This event is filmed; portions of the group's performance of 'Student Demonstration Time' will be seen in the later documentary *An American Band*.

Following their 60-minute set, The Beach Boys perform an evening concert at Springfield College in Massachusetts.

Sunday 2nd

Trinity College *Hartford, CT* afternoon, with Sea Train; **Paris Cinema** *Worcester, MA* 7:00pm, with The Psychedelic Magician

Tuesday 4th

CW Post College *Greenvale, NY*

Thursday 6th

New Paltz State University College *New Paltz, NY*

Friday 7th

The Spectrum *Philadelphia, PA*

TV Westinghouse Broadcasting Company, Group W Productions *Philadelphia, PA.* Syndicated *The David Frost Show* live performance 'Wouldn't It Be Nice', 'Cool Cool Water', broadcast May 28th, 4:30-6:00pm. During the afternoon the group tapes their third (and final) studio appearance on the *Frost* show, with Al messing up the lyrics to 'Wouldn't It Be Nice'. 'Cool Cool Water' from this show will later be seen partially in the *Endless Harmony* documentary. Afterwards they head over to The Spectrum for this evening's performance.

Saturday 8th

University of Bridgeport *Bridgeport, CT*

Sunday 9th

New York State University *Plattsburg, NY*

Last night of the current tour.

Tuesday 11th

Manley Field House, Syracuse University *Syracuse, NY*

Two days after finishing their latest excursion, the group performs at a fund-raising benefit concert for the Berrigan brothers' defence fund. Roman Catholic priests Daniel and Philip Berrigan are leaders of the anti-war movement in the US, having achieved notoriety as members of the Catonsville Nine, who in May 1968 removed and burned records from the local draft board located in Catonsville,

June

Long Promised Road single

A **'Long Promised Road'** (C. WILSON / J. RIELEY)
B1 **'Deirdre'** (B. JOHNSTON)
B2 **''Til I Die'** (B. WILSON)

US release (A/B1) **May 24th 1971** (Brother/Reprise 1015).
US release (A/B2) **October 11th 1971** (Brother/Reprise 1047).
UK release (A/B1) **June 1971** (Stateside SS 2190).
Chart high US May none, October 89; UK none.

Maryland. The Berrigans and others involved were arrested, tried, and convicted on charges of conspiracy and destruction of government property. Daniel was sentenced to three years in a federal prison; Philip to three-and-a-half years, to run concurrently with a six-year sentence imposed previously for a conviction on similar charges. (Dennis is absent from tonight's show.)

■ Sunday 23rd
RECORDING Brian's Home Studio *Bel Air, CA*. Dennis records his inevitably unreleased **'Wouldn't It Be Nice To Live Again'** with the help of Carl, taped on two-inch 16-track.

■ Monday 24th
'Long Promised Road' / **'Deirdre'** single released in the US. This is the sixth consecutive miss for the group in the US singles charts.
• *Warm Waters* album by Charles Lloyd released in the US. The record features Mike, Brian, Carl and Al on backing vocals and Carl on Moog synthesiser.

'Long Promised Road' / **'Deirdre'** single released in the UK. The Stateside-label 45 fails to chart.

■ Early June
For years, Brian has been living in terror of public failure. It was because 'Heroes And Villains' had failed to impress Capitol and the critics that he has withdrawn from the world, adopting the persona of "Brian Wilson, eccentric recluse". But his desire for public recognition is returning. At the last minute, and with The Beach Boys' new album already in the can, he gives the go-ahead to Carl and Jack Rieley to finish his unreleased *Smile*-era recording, 'Surf's Up'.

Rieley will tell BBC Radio-1's series *The Beach Boys Story* in 1974: "We always encouraged Brian to go back into the studio more frequently. This culminated one day when I was going to Warner Brothers and I thought I would stop at Brian's house. I was going to meet [Warner boss] Mo Ostin and I said, 'Brian, why don't you come with me?' Surprisingly, he said, 'OK. I will. The President of Warner Brothers, I don't know what I'm going to say to him.' We then drove to Burbank from Bel Air.

"Suddenly Brian said, 'Well, OK, if you're going to force me, I'll do it.' I asked, 'Force you to do what, Brian?' And he said, 'Force me to put "Surf's Up" on the album.' I had asked him about putting 'Surf's Up' on the next album, which at that point was tentatively titled *Landlocked*, … the first Beach Boys album with which I was involved. I said to Brian, 'Are you really going to do it?' And Brian said, 'Well, if you're going to force me.' We got into Warner Brothers and, with no coaxing at all, Brian said to Mo, 'I'm going to put "Surf's Up" on the next album.' I think this was a great thing because it did provide a commitment on Brian's part and he became very active in the studio."

Sessions for *Surf's Up*: LEFT Mike and Bruce at the piano; BELOW Carl and Mike await a cue during a vocal session; FOLLOWING PAGES Brian reaches for the headphones in preparation for a vocal recording.

Thursday 3rd

RECORDING *Surf's Up* sessions Brian's Home Studio *Bel Air, CA*. Bruce's **'Disney Girls'** is recorded during today's session. Bruce will tell BBC Radio-1 that his haunting song emerged from a positive wave of nostalgia. "I came up with that song because I saw so many kids in our audiences being wiped out on drugs. I tried to think of a time when I was really young and what it was like being real naive. I thought of 1957 and remembered what was going on in 1957 in my life, and I thought of a funny record called 'Old Cape Cod' by Patti Page. It was a big hit. … I wrote a song about going back in time. I was 13 and I was afraid to go on to high school because I [might] get beaten up. Now, 14 years later, I realise how tame those times were and I was thinking, 'Gee, how great it would be to go back there for a minute.' Because it's so hard these days, with everybody overdosing … and that is what that song is about. People being a little naive but a little healthier."

Friday 4th

Today David Sandler, Brian's co-producer on the Spring project, records a piano demo of 'Sing Out A Song' at the Home Studio.

Mid June through early July

RECORDING *Surf's Up* sessions Brian's Home Studio *Bel Air, CA*. The new arrangement of **'Surf's Up'** comes as the result of many talks between Carl, Rieley and Brian and a careful examination of some of the original *Smile*-era recordings, which are removed from the Beach Boy vaults following Brian's approval. A selection of the multi-track tapes are then taken to Carl's home in Coldwater Canyon, where night after night Carl and Rieley listen to the songs, snippets and outtakes. With no engineer present, the two also set about mending and splicing the tapes.

The primary reason for the trawl through the tapes is to locate the master recordings of 'Surf's Up'. Once they find them, they discover that the song survives in several disjointed sections. After many nights of listening at Carl's home, with Brian joining the pair on at least two occasions, Carl and Rieley set about reconstructing the masterpiece.

However, shortly before the new recordings are set to begin, Brian changes his mind about revisiting the song. Rieley stands firm and reminds him of his promise, and Brian relents. But generally Brian stays away from the song, presumably because of the negative memories associated with the *Smile* era. Recordings go on for several weeks, with Carl in charge of the effort. Everyone present seems to know this is going to be a masterpiece.

The new version of **'Surf's Up'** is assembled in three parts at Brian's Home Studio in his living room at Bellagio Road in Bel Air. The result will see section one lasting from 0:00 to 1:36, based on the 'Surf's Up' backing track of February 8th 1967; section two 1:37 to 3:09, based on the vocal-and-piano 'Surf's Up' recording for *Inside Pop* of December 15th 1966; and section three from 3:09 to the fade around 4:11, based on the 'Child Is Father Of The Man' recording of December 2nd 1966. The 4-track backing track for section one of this new version is taken from recordings made on February 8th 1967 and is transferred to the 16-track machine at Brian's studio. At first, the group attempts to record an entirely new instrumental track for this section. "But we scrapped it," Rieley tells *Rolling Stone*, "because it didn't quite come up to the original." The group decides instead to use the existing February 1967 track for section one. Two organ overdubs are made, along with Brian's car keys providing percussion. Several studio musicians are also brought in to re-record and add brief parts to the original track. A new lead vocal is required. During an exceedingly brief visit by Brian to the

studio, Rieley asks if he wants to record a new vocal, but Brian insists that Carl does it. Rieley: "Carl didn't want to sing the lead in the first portion of the record. He just didn't want to. We originally wanted Brian. ... [He] was the only person who could sing that part, but when he decided not to, it put Carl in a difficult position because, just like the rest of us, he felt that Brian had to sing it. Carl was in the studio at Brian's house and he hit that high note, in the first portion of the song, and he really did it well. He read that lyric beautifully. Carl did an immense amount of work on the track."

Section two of the newly constructed song again comes from the tape vaults. The recording dates from December 15th 1966, featuring just Brian and a piano. Carl believes this to be a demo that Brian recorded for his own purposes, but in fact it is the recording of 'Surf's Up' made at Columbia studio for the CBS TV programme *Inside Pop: The Rock Revolution* but unused (the TV show used the version filmed two days later). The group now uses this recording virtually untouched, only overdubbing a Moog synthesiser bass that continues into section three. Carl adds vocals, doing an excellent and almost imperceptible job as he sings the same parts, blending his voice with Brian's, and creates backing vocals.

Section three of the new 'Surf's Up' is based on the vocal refrain from a *Smile*-session song, 'Child Is Father Of The Man', as taped on December 2nd 1966. After the original 4-track recording from that session is again transferred to the 16-track machine at the Home Studio, vocal 'ooohs' are added, which will be placed in deep reverberation in the final mix. Carl feels that something should be done to move the rhythm along, but wants to avoid overdoing the car keys. After much experimentation he decides to emphasise the 'ch' sound of the word 'child' at certain points as it is sung by the group, accomplished through manual control of stereo position, equalisation and volume at mix-down. Rieley says in *Rolling Stone*: "The final ... tag, 'Child Is The Father Of The Man', is something which we all got involved in. I know Al has an important part in that, Carl sings a couple of parts, so do Mike and Bruce. Even I'm on it. So is a guy who worked for us part-time. He just sings, 'Hey, hey.' But it is vital to the tag on the record. It was a lot of fun doing [that]."

After long hours of preparation, the song becomes ready to mix. About 30 minutes into the process, which will complete the production, Brian pays another surprise visit to the working area. He has been listening to the recording of the song as the sounds come through the floor into his bedroom directly above the studio.

Dishevelled, with his stomach hanging out over striped pyjama bottoms, Brian comes bursting into the studio, excitedly proclaiming that they should stop the mix and add just one more part to the ending. A microphone is hastily set up in the studio along with headphones and Brian arranges the 'Child Is Father Of The Man' coda. It is almost as if it was always in Brian's mind from the song's conception, forgotten until now.

Engineer Steve Desper recalls: "Brian didn't want to work on 'Surf's Up'. But after three days of coaxing, and of him walking in and out of the studio, he was finally convinced to do a part. He came down in his pyjamas, sang this new 'Child Is Father Of The Man' tag part, and then ran out."

As a postscript, a further line is added, doubled-tracked at the last minute: "A children's song, and we listen as they play, their song is love, and the children know the way". With 'Surf's Up' now ready for inclusion on the new record, the album is retitled accordingly. *Surf's Up* will be issued in the US on August 30th.

■ Friday 11th

Dennis accidentally puts his hand through a glass window, badly severing nerves and tendons. He will not play drums again until late

in 1974. For several weeks after the incident, music publications around the world incorrectly state that Who drummer Keith Moon will stand in for Dennis on forthcoming Beach Boys concert appearances. In fact Ricky Fataar from The Flame (and briefly Michael Kowalski) takes his place in the live Beach Boys line-up, although Dennis does continue to appear live with the group occasionally, usually singing or playing keyboards.

Stories circulate in the press insinuating that the injury was the result of a bar-room brawl. Dennis: "You know what really happened? I got drunk on my ass, walked into the house, threw off my wife's clothes and ripped off mine. It was cold and I went to slam the door, only we had just moved and I'd forgotten that the door was made of glass and I put my hand right through it! You know how it is when you're drunk. Barbara saved my life by putting a tourniquet on it. I was scared shit! I knew I'd play drums again. The doctor told me that if I followed his instructions I'd be using my hand again in two or three years. I was playing piano again in six months. I really worked at it. It felt weird making love, touching someone and not feeling anything. But it all came back, just like the doctor said it would, except for the two little fingers."

■ Saturday 19th

On the eve of his 29th birthday, Brian stands in the kitchen of his home in Bel Air and flips through an atlas made by *The Times* in London that Jack Rieley has given to him as a present. "Look," Brian says to Rieley, "it's got all these different countries ... Afghanistan ... Yugoslavia ... Bolivia ... Portugal." Brian begins perusing further parts of the atlas, reading them out loud. "World climatic regions ... Face of the moon ... Geodetic Satellites? What does geodetic mean?" When the novelty of the atlas wears off, Brian joins Rieley in the pool and talks excitedly about The Beach Boys' next album.

Later, back in the house, Tom Nolan of *Rolling Stone* has a discussion with Carl about Brian. "He's not too accessible, you know," Carl announces. "There's probably about three people that know him and four people that really know him. He must not want to talk to journalists. I guess that Jules Siegel stuff and a lot of that other stuff really turned him off. Most of the stuff about Brian is grossly inaccurate. Most of the stuff is in the past anyway. He's a pretty vulnerable guy and I think that anybody that really knows him would probably regard it as a private friendship and wouldn't really be into thing of 'What's Brian like?' or something like that.

"It's quite natural really that the weird stories circulate. Oh, he is something of an eccentric, that's true. There are lots of stories about him being flipped out and him 'spending a lot of time in his room'. I mean, that really cracks me up, that he 'spends a lot of time in his room'. He's all over the place! But he's not co-operative with the press at all. And Brian, I'm sorry, he is a put on. Yeah, he's out there. He's a very highly evolved person and he's very sensitive at the same time, which can be confusing. Brian's Brian, you know?"

■ Sunday 20th

On the occasion of Brian's 29th birthday a small party at his home studio is taped in quadraphonic sound by Steve Desper. Everyone sings 'Happy Birthday' to Brian, with Bruce providing piano accompaniment. Mention is made that Brian has received 29 records for his birthday. Jack Rieley then steps up and asks Brian how he feels. Brian replies, "Hungry."

■ Thursday 24th

Celebration Island *Pointe Coupee, LA* with Pink Floyd, Miles Davis, B.B. King

The Beach Boys – without Dennis – perform on the opening night of a special series of *Festival Of Life* concerts in Louisiana, scheduled to run until the 28th. But the festival is shut down after only three days due to insufficient supplies of food, poor sanitation facilities and few medical staff.

■ Sunday 27th

Fillmore East *New York, NY* with Mountain, The Allman Brothers, The J. Geils Band, Albert King, Edgar Winter's White Trash, Country Joe McDonald

The Beach Boys perform on the closing night of Bill Graham's legendary rock venue following three years of business. The show goes on until 4:00am. The lucky invitation-only ticket holders find a rose on each seat as they enter the hall, one of the many little touches for which Graham has become famous over the years. Tonight's concert is broadcast live on WNEW-FM Radio.

Set-list 'Heroes And Villains', 'Do It Again', 'Cotton Fields', 'Help Me Rhonda' (Carl on lead vocal), 'Wouldn't It Be Nice' (full-length version), 'Your Song' (Bruce on lead vocal), 'Student Demonstration Time', 'Good Vibrations', 'California Girls' (encore), 'I Get Around' (encore), 'It's About Time' (encore).

■ Tuesday 29th

Kingsbridge Armory *New York, NY*

The group performs on the opening night of the eight-day *International Youth Expo* event. The series of shows, which run until July 6th, also include performances by Ike & Tina Turner, Wilson Pickett, Alice Cooper, Chuck Berry, John Lee Hooker, Moby Grape, Illusion and many others. During this evening's performance Dennis returns to the group, playing keyboards and singing 'Lady'.

■ Late June

At the end of the month former Beatle George Harrison visits a Beach Boy session, but does not play on any of the recordings.

July

Reports in the US music press suggest that The Beach Boys' income is now five times greater than it has been for many a year. Further features reveal that the group is now rated as "the hottest grossing act in America" – next to Grand Funk Railroad.

■ Friday 2nd

Wollman Rink Central Park *New York, NY* 8:00pm

The Beach Boys give an open-air performance on the opening night of the annual two-week *Schaefer Music Festival*, which also features the likes of Ike & Tina Turner, Ravi Shankar, Carole King, Carly Simon, Boz Scaggs, and The Byrds. Highlights will appear in the NBC TV special *Good Vibrations From Central Park*, aired on August 19th, 9:30-10:30pm. During the broadcast The Beach Boys are seen performing 'Good Vibrations' at the start of the show and, at the tail-end of the programme, 'Heroes And Villains', 'Okie From Muskogee', 'Forever', 'It's About Time' and 'I Get Around' (as part of the encore). Following Dennis's hand injury, Michael Kowalski takes his place on drums. Former Beatle George Harrison is seen chatting with the group backstage, further to his visit to a Beach Boy recording session the previous month.

■ Wednesday 7th

Dennis's film *Two-Lane Blacktop* makes its worldwide theatrical debut at the Beekman Theater in New York City, backed by heavy

advertising in *The New York Times*. The opening is greeted with critical acclaim but public indifference.

Archer Winston, *New York Post*: "The picture has soul! The cars are the language. ... It can't be put into words, but it is there to be felt. The gist is very clever and the realism and the drama are shocking." Jay Cocks, *Time* magazine: "One of the most ambitious and interesting American films of the year! It is immaculately crafted, funny and beautiful. Not a single frame in the film is wasted. *Two-Lane Blacktop* is an American pop epic!"

Despite such reviews, cinemagoers remain largely unaware of the film's existence. It is a box-office disaster, and Universal Pictures fails to recoup its outlay on the film. Legal hassles over the film's soundtrack, most notably The Doors' 'Moonlight Drive', will prevail for 25 years, preventing the film's home-video release until 1996.

August

■ Tuesday 24th

A recording is made – probably without the Beach Boys – of a new Brian and Murry Wilson song called 'Won't You Tell Me'. Reportedly, Brian will record a rough lead vocal for this song at some point. Murry is the session's producer.

■ Monday 30th

Surf's Up album released in the US. It's issued just one day short of a year since The Beach Boys released their last album. Manager Jack Rieley says: "The cover was something that caught my eye at an antique shop near Silver Lake. It was a painting and I bought it. It reminded me a bit of the Brother Records logo, but it was different."

The album had once had the shortlived working title of *Landlocked*, but has been renamed in honour of the great title song. The shift was instigated by Rieley who wants to show Brian he is serious about making Brian's great work shine again. *Surf's Up* does much to restore the group's critical and financial standing, peaking at number 29 in the US charts.

Time magazine's reviewer writes: "The Beach Boys ... have

Surf's Up album

A1 'Don't Go Near The Water' (A. JARDINE / M. LOVE)
A2 'Long Promised Road' (C. WILSON / J. RIELEY)
A3 'Take A Load Off Your Feet' (A. JARDINE / G. WINFREY)
A4 'Disney Girls (1957)' (B. JOHNSTON)
A5 'Student Demonstration Time' (BASED ON 'RIOT IN CELL BLOCK #9' J. LEIBER / M. STOLLER, NEW LYRICS M. LOVE)
B1 'Feel Flows' (C. WILSON / J. RIELEY)
B2 'Lookin' At Tomorrow (A Welfare Song)' (A. JARDINE / G. WINFREY)
B3 'A Day In The Life Of A Tree' (B. WILSON / J. RIELEY)
B4 ''Til I Die' (B. WILSON)
B5 'Surf's Up' (B. WILSON / V.D. PARKS)

US release August 30th 1971 (Brother/Reprise 6453).
UK release October 1971 (Stateside SSL 10313).
Chart high US number 29; UK number 15.

matured considerably. Brian is now 29, brothers Dennis and Carl 27 and 25 respectively, Al Jardine 27, Bruce Johnston 27, and Mike Love 30. As men they have more to say. All those beaches are dirty, for one thing, and they do not mind at all if adults listen. The group's latest LP *Surf's Up* … is a case in point. Always noted for their pop polish, they have this time turned out one of the most imaginatively produced LPs since last fall's *All Things Must Pass* by George Harrison and Phil Spector.

"Al and Mike's 'Don't Go Near The Water' is probably the best song yet to emerge from rock's current ecology kick. 'Student Demonstration Time' is a hard-rock parody that ponders the wisdom of violence. The title song, 'Surf's Up', finds Brian as close as he probably will ever come to something he has long searched for: a floating, ethereal tone painting that he modestly describes as 'the sound of heaven'.

"The essential message of *Surf's Up*, a celebration of the return to childhood, may exasperate mature listeners but seems to have worked wonders for gloomy Brian. His music has a high, soaring, quasi-religious vocal and instrumental character that even The Beatles of *Abbey Road* could envy. At long last he may be on the verge of coming out of his house. Brother Carl reports that Brian has pledged to appear at a Beach Boys concert in Manhattan's Carnegie Hall this month. That may take some doing."

Surf's Up will peak at number 15 in the UK, where rave reviews follow its October release. Richard Williams writes in *Melody Maker*: "Here's one that won't disappoint anybody at all. Suddenly, The Beach Boys are back in fashionable favour and they've produced an album that fully backs up all that's recently been written and said about them. The title track, 'Surf's Up', [was] originally written for the never-released *Smile* album [and] the best thing I can say is that, had it been released back at *Pepper*-time, it might have kept many people from straying into the pastures of indulgence and may have forced them to focus back onto truer values. I've rarely heard a more perfect, more complete piece of music. From first to last it flows and evolves from the almost lush decadence of the first verses to the childlike wonders and open-hearted joy of the final chorale.

"But that ain't all: you'll love Carl's two songs, with words by Jack Rieley, 'Feel Flows' and 'Long Promised Road', which are quite simply the best 'inner quest' songs I've ever heard, and they lack nothing in terms of jewelled arrangements. Brian and Jack contribute the sad, delicate 'A Day In The Life Of A Tree' but all of them are nearly upstaged by Bruce Johnston, whose 'Disney Girls (1957)' says a lot of what many of us are beginning to feel about our fading youth. The only bummers are those in which Al Jardine and Mike Love are involved and, of course, EMI had to choose one of those, 'Don't Go Near The Water', as the new [UK November] single, when 'Surf's Up' cries to be heard. Forget all that, though, this album is a blast of truth at the time we need it most. Let's just hope that Brian feels like sticking around a while longer."

When asked about this version of 'Surf's Up', Brian will describe it on BBC Radio-1 in 1995 as "atrocious", adding: "I'm embarrassed. Totally embarrassed. That was a piece of shit in my eyes. I was the wrong singer for it in the first place. It's not my favourite vocal I ever did. And in the second place, I don't know why I would ever let a record go out like that."

Another Beach Boy not happy with the track or indeed the album is Bruce, who rants: "To me, *Surf's Up* is, and always has been, one hyped up lie! It was a false reflection of The Beach Boys and one which Jack [Rieley] engineered right from the outset. … It made it look like Brian Wilson was more than just a visitor at those sessions. Jack made it appear as though Brian was really there all the time." Rieley's only complaint about the *Surf's Up* album is the way it's

handled in the UK. "It came out eight weeks after it was released in the States," he blasts, "and they sold more import copies than they sold of British pressings."

Notably, this is the last Beach Boys album to feature Bruce Johnston until *LA (Light Album)* in 1979 and the first to feature lyrical contributions from Rieley, who will play a substantial role in songwriting for the next two Beach Boys albums.

Dennis's songs '4th Of July' and 'Wouldn't It Be Nice To Live Again' as well as the previously recorded 'Lady' are all left off the album. According to Rieley, speaking on US radio, there are two reasons. First, there is political infighting within the group and Dennis's songs are sacrificed to maintain harmony and prevent the disc from being an almost completely Wilson-brothers album. Second, Dennis is working seriously on his solo album and intends to save his songs for that record. Breaking free from The Beach Boys and going alone is an important part of Dennis's thinking now. During the relatively short period from August to early September his wish will be granted.

September

■ Saturday 4th

Disc & Music Echo reports in Britain: "The Beach Boys' UK dates this autumn are off. They've been postponed until next spring when the group will probably only do one major concert here. UK representative Russ Mackie revealed: 'Tour plans for November have been postponed. Instead the trek will run from April 15th [1972] for one month, taking in the continent also. Offers for the London date haven't come from the right venues. Either the places were too big for an enjoyable concert or the acoustics were terrible.'"

■ Monday 6th

"One afternoon last week," says *Time* magazine, "[our] correspondent Timothy Tyler was invited out to the Wilson house for what was promised to be Brian's first interview in four years. Brian never came downstairs. 'The meeting was a test for him,' reports Tyler. 'He thought he could do it, but he failed.' Brian did manage to phone down to Tyler as he sat in the back yard with Carl. 'I'm sorry I couldn't make it down, but I just got to sleep,' Brian explained. 'Let me talk a while on the phone before I drift off again … What'm I doing? Getting back into arranging, doing that more than writing now … I'm really excited about "Surf's Up" as a single. It has a very virile sound … Well … um … I'm drifting off again.' Click. Whatever Brian does, *Surf's Up* is doing well enough. Barely out, it is fast approaching $250,000 in sales."

■ Saturday 11th

"Beach Boy Dennis Wilson is out of The Beach Boys for good: that's the unconfirmed report from America this week," says British music paper *Disc & Music Echo*. "The news follows his enforced departure from the band following an accident at his home when he severed nerves in his right hand and was ordered not to play drums for at least three months. Ricky Fataar from Flame currently replaces Dennis. *Disc* understands from a close friend of the group, 'Dennis contends that he has left the group once and for all and is setting up a production and publication company with his father, Murry Wilson. Dennis is quite into writing and producing commercials for various products. He was in New York last week to finish negotiations with a major company.'" The 'major company' is the Bristol-Myers ad agency. Dennis attempts to persuade them to use his song 'It's A

New Day' in commercials for Dry Command anti-perspirant. He says the song – sung by Blondie Chaplin and written by Dennis and Daryl Dragon – will cost Bristol-Myers a cool $1million. Incensed at the extortionate sum, executives apparently give Dennis ten seconds to leave their offices before they attempt to throw him out of the sixth floor window. Dennis leaves within five seconds.

■ Monday 13th
Indiana University of Pennsylvania *Indiana, PA*
The Beach Boys (without Dennis) perform a one-off concert tonight, serving as a warm-up for the tour set to begin next week.
Set-list 'Good Vibrations', 'Don't Go Near The Water', 'Darlin'', 'Wouldn't It Be Nice', 'Long Promised Road', 'Student Demonstration Time', 'Disney Girls (1957)', 'Sloop John B', 'Surfin' USA', 'It's About Time', (intermission), 'Caroline No', 'Cool Cool Water', 'Okie from Muskogee', 'God Only Knows', 'Surf's Up', 'Cotton Fields', 'Heroes And Villains', 'California Girls', 'I Get Around', 'Help Me Rhonda', 'Fun Fun Fun' (last four as encores).
• Carl's four-year legal battle with the US Army ends when the Los Angeles Federal Court reverses its previous decision and now gives Carl his right to perform at prisons, hospitals and orphanages in order to satisfy his obligations under the US Military Selective Service Act.

Federal Court judge Harry Pregerson delivers his ruling that Carl's wish to help and provide some sort of entertainment for hospital patients, orphans and prison inmates is certainly in the national interest.

Carl says on US radio: "The judge was very fair and he gave me the chance to do the alternative service. It went down to the very last appeal, on the very last day, and the judge cooled out. But I was still convicted by the jury for failing to report for alternative service at the LA County General Hospital."

TOUR STARTS US East (Sep 22nd-Oct 2nd)

■ Wednesday 22nd
Roger Williams College *Bristol, RI*
For this tour, Ricky Fataar, drummer with The Flame, continues to take Dennis's place in The Beach Boys' line-up. Despite recent reports of his departure from the group, Dennis returns to the fold and is seen on-stage tonight alternating between keyboards and microphone. The extended live band around this time also includes Ed Carter (guitar, bass), Daryl Dragon (keyboards, bass), Glenn Ferris (trombone), Billy Hinsche (guitar, bass, keyboards), Mike Kowalski (percussion), Sal Marquez (trumpet), Roger Newman (saxophone), Joel Peskin (saxophone), Mike Price (trumpet) and Bobby Torres (percussion).

■ Thursday 23rd
Music Hall *Boston, MA*

■ Friday 24th
Carnegie Hall *New York, NY* 7:30 & 11:00pm
The shows have sold out two weeks in advance, but mixed reviews follow. Don Heckman writes in *The New York Times*: "The audience for the first show was extremely restive, interrupting song announcements to shout out demands for their favourites, usually tunes from The Beach Boys' surf-music days, and demonstrating a particularly excessive degree of rudeness when Mike Love recited a few moments of poetry.

"The audience finally got what it wanted to hear in the encores when the group ran through hit after hit. No one seemed particularly concerned that the playing was sloppy and the singing uncertain. The genuine highlight came earlier in two particularly brilliant songs from the new album, Bruce Johnston's stunning trip through nostalgia 'Disney Girls (1957)' and Brian Wilson and Van Dyke Parks's 'Surf's Up'. The latter tune," writes Heckman of the *Times*, "bears easy comparison with the best of The Beatles' *Sgt. Pepper* songs."

Circus magazine reports: "Lines extend around the corner of 57th Street with people awaiting entry to a concert, a concert that has been sold out long in advance. It's Carnegie Hall and the tickets are expensive, the room restrictive (no smoking or anything, no horsing around, no going near the stage, no going backstage).

"The security guards are hostile but none of that matters because this is now about the only place you can go in Manhattan to see a rock concert, or more importantly, *this* rock concert – The Beach Boys.

"The size of the crowd seems to imply that their latest album, *Surf's Up*, is indeed re-uniting The Beach Boys with the public. Or maybe the crowd is just there to listen to 'Surfin' Safari'?

"To a full house, they open with 'Good Vibrations'. Is it going to be an oldies show after all? Not at all! Just a little warm-up to do exactly what the song says, send out some good vibrations. Right after that, they go into 'Student Demonstration Time', complete with sirens, and have the crowd standing and clapping from the second song.

"Carl does his 'Feel Flows', Al his 'Lookin' At Tomorrow', Bruce his 'Disney Girls' and Mike his 'Don't Go Near The Water'. Dennis presents the audience with one of his new songs, dedicated to his best friend, his wife.

"They end the set after numerous requests for Brian's 'Surf's Up', with just that. The whole orchestra, four tiers of balconies, and all those standing or sitting in the aisles were all on their feet, creaming, clapping and begging for more.

"The Beach Boys have made it, not for what they were but for what they are. Now that they've been accepted for what they are singing today, they feel free to sing yesterday's songs.

"For their encores, all three of them, they dig into 'California Girls', 'Surfin' Safari', 'Heroes And Villains', 'Help Me Rhonda' and 'I Get Around', one right after the other so that the audience can't take any more.

"After all the screaming requests have been played," concludes the *Circus* reviewer, "all the eyes tearing from excitement, all the voices hoarse from yelling, all the faces smiling with delight, there is no doubt in anyone's minds that they were great then, boy they were great. But now they are even better!"

■ Saturday 25th
Villanova University *Villanova, PA*

■ Sunday 26th
State University Of New York *Stony Brook, NY*

■ Tuesday 28th
University Of Rhode Island *Kingston, RI*
A concert planned today for Concord College, Athens, WV, is cancelled.

■ Wednesday 29th
Taft Auditorium *Cincinnati, OH*

■ Thursday 30th
Penn State University *Erie, PA*

October

Surf's Up album released in the UK. It will peak at number 15.

■ Friday 1st

Clowes Hall, Butler University *Indianapolis, IN*
Dennis plays keyboards throughout this evening's show.
Set-list 'Good Vibrations', 'Take A Load Off Your Feet', 'Don't Go Near The Water', 'Wouldn't It Be Nice', 'Darlin'', 'Student Demonstration Time', 'Cool Cool Water', 'Long Promised Road', 'Pom Pom Play Girl', 'God Only Knows', 'Sloop John B', 'It's About Time', 'Looking At Tomorrow', 'Caroline No', 'Disney Girls (1957)', 'Okie From Muskogee', 'Surf's Up', 'Heroes And Villains', 'Do It Again', 'Little Deuce Coupe', 'I Get Around', 'Help Me Rhonda' 'Surfer Girl', 'Johnny B Goode'.

■ Saturday 2nd

Notre Dame University *South Bend, IN*
Last night of the tour.

■ First week

RECORDING Brian's Home Studio *Bel Air, CA*. Brian and musician friend David Sandler record demos for **'Silly Walls'** and **'Awake'**, tracks intended for the planned album by Spring, the group featuring Brian's wife Marilyn Wilson and Diane Rovell, former members of The Honeys. (See October 20th.) 'Silly Walls' features backing vocals from Spring and The Beach Boys. Brian records at least three different demo takes of 'Awake': the first features slide guitar and his vocal; the second is simply an a cappella rendition from Brian; and the third is a piano-and-vocal version.

■ Monday 11th

'Long Promised Road' single re-released (from May) in the US with a new B-side, **''Til I Die'**. It ends a 19-month period during which no Beach Boys single charted, but with a peak of just 89 it's still the lowest charting Beach Boys single ever released – a record it will hold for some 18 years.

■ Wednesday 20th

'Now That Everything's Been Said' / **'Awake'** single by Spring released in the US. Spring consists of Marilyn Wilson and Diane Rovell, former members of The Honeys. The songs on this debut single, on United Artists, are produced by Brian and David Sandler and were recorded at Brian's Home Studio earlier in the month.

■ Wednesday 27th

Today sees a mixing session for The Flame's inevitably unreleased recordings **'Seven Sisters'**, **'Thank Someone'** and **'I'm A Man'**.

Surf's Up single

A 'Surf's Up' (B. WILSON / V.D. PARKS)
B 'Don't Go Near The Water' (A. JARDINE / M. LOVE)

US release November 1971 (Brother/Reprise 1058).
Chart high US none.

Don't Go Near The Water single

A 'Don't Go Near The Water' (A. JARDINE / M. LOVE)
B 'Student Demonstration Time' (BASED ON 'RIOT IN CELL BLOCK #9' J. LEIBER / M. STOLLER, NEW LYRICS M. LOVE)

UK release November 1971 (Stateside SS 2194).
Chart high UK none.

■ Tuesday 28th

The Beach Boys appear on the cover of the latest issue of *Rolling Stone*; inside is the first of an important, lengthy two-part interview with the group by Tom Nolan and David Felton. Part two will appear in the issue dated November 11th.

■ Thursday 30th

Surf's Up album peaks in the US *Billboard* chart at number 29.

■ Friday 31st

A Dennis Wilson-led rehearsal is recorded today, most likely at Brian's home.

November

'Surf's Up' / **'Don't Go Near The Water'** single released in the US. It fails to chart.
'Don't Go Near The Water' / **'Student Demonstration Time'** single released in the UK. It too fails to chart.

■ Monday 1st

A Dennis Wilson-led rehearsal is recorded, probably at Brian's home.

■ Sunday 7th

Georgetown University *Washington, DC*

■ Thursday 11th

Princeton University *Princeton, NJ*
Following further heated rows between group members, Dennis again leaves The Beach Boys, announcing that he may not return.

■ Saturday 20th

Cleveland Music Hall *Cleveland, OH*
• 'Long Promised Road' single peaks in US chart at a disappointing 89.

■ Sunday 21st

Hiram Bithorn Stadium *San Juan, Puerto Rico*
The Beach Boys perform without Dennis on this the second night of the eight-day *Fiesta Del Sol Festival*, an event that also features performances by The Allman Brothers, The Chamber Brothers, Ike & Tina Turner, John Mayall, Jose Feliciano, Mountain, Stevie Wonder, and Ten Years After.

■ Monday 22nd

The Performing Arts Center *Milwaukee, WI* two shows, with Yes, Jackson Browne

December

Beach Boys business manager Nick Grillo is sacked by the group, nine months before his contract is due to expire, and Jack Rieley immediately assumes sole managerial duties. Grillo tells *Rolling Stone* in 1973: "My departure from the boys came quite suddenly. We were having some problems, in particular regarding their career directions and their finances. Some of the boys wanted to be more involved with the financial side of things and this really bothered me. I wish some of them showed this kind of enthusiasm when it came to cutting some new material. The Beach Boys have the choice to dismiss anyone, I appreciate that, but what concerned me was the way in which it was done. A colleague notified me on the road that I was not to return to their office after a certain point.

"I did receive a call from Carl and it occurred to me that some of these differences between myself and the boys could be resolved. Carl said he would call me back, but he never did. I believe there was an attempt, by certain people in The Beach Boys' organisation, to shield the boys from me. I never had the opportunity to defend myself against certain allegations that had developed, and this was very painful. I felt an injustice had been perpetrated. A year later, further dismissals in The Beach Boys' organisations took place and I think that this exonerated me from a lot of the ill will that had taken place."

When told about Nick's sacking, Derek Taylor, former Beach Boys press officer, will remark to BBC Radio-1's *Beach Boys Story* in 1974: "Nick Grillo was in the hottest seat in the world. I never saw a man under such pressure. Nick was a work freak, working 20 hours a day. No time for eating and no time for drinking, poor fellow. I used to think, 'How can this man go through all this without moaning?' Nick never complained about anything because he thought that whatever he did for [The Beach Boys] or whatever hell he went through for them, the reward was somewhere in heaven, because these people were rather heavenly people. But it all turned to ashes in the end."

A series of law suits follow Grillo's dismissal. Grillo sues The Beach Boys and their manager Jack Rieley for money he alleges they still owe him. In turn, the group and Rieley counter-sue, claiming mismanagement of some of their financial affairs. (See May 1972.)

• 'Don't Go Near the Water' single peaks in New Zealand *Listener Pop-O-Meter* chart at number 21.

• 'Student Demonstration Time' single peaks in Dutch chart at number 21.

Friday 3rd
Long Beach Arena *Long Beach, CA* 8:00pm, with Elvin Bishop, Seatrain; tickets $3.50-$5.50

Manager Rieley has cajoled Brian into making an appearance with the group on-stage tonight, his first since November 5th 1970. But it lasts a matter of minutes, just long enough for 'Surfer Girl'. The show is also marked by Dennis's return from his three-week sabbatical from the group to sing and play keyboards.

Saturday 4th – Friday 10th
RECORDING *Carl And The Passions* sessions Brother studio *Santa Monica, CA*
San Diego Sports Arena *San Diego, CA*

Today's session for vocals and instrumental tracking is the first carried out at the group's new recording studio at 1454 5th Street in Santa Monica, an impressive complex converted from an old cinema. It boasts state-of-the-art equipment, stained-glass windows, and a room where kids can play.

Working with engineer Steve Moffitt, Mike and Al work alone recording **'All This Is That'**, a song co-written by Al, Carl and Mike and based on a poem by Robert Frost, *The Road Not Taken*. Following this brief start to their latest recordings, the group performs another show in California later this evening (the 4th).

Further tracking sessions at the new Santa Monica studio continue intermittently until the 10th of this month as the group starts recording work on **'Beatrice From Baltimore'** (later to become 'You Need A Mess Of Help'), **'Here She Comes'** and **'He Come Down'**.

Brian and Bruce are occasional visitors to the studio, but the bulk of recording during this seven-day period focuses on completing 'One Arm Over My Shoulder', an "ode to a masseuse" that soon becomes better known as **'Marcella'**.

Carl sings lead vocal, with Mike on the tag and Brian on backing vocal. The completed recording of 3:51 duration – featuring joint production by Brian, Carl, Dennis, Mike and Al along with ex-Flame members Ricky Fataar and Blondie Chaplin – will eventually appear on the group's album *Carl And The Passions – "So Tough"* released next year, along with the four other pieces on which they start during this period.

After working on various vocal arrangements for 'One Arm Over My Shoulder', the group and Rieley earmark the completed recording as a potential new single. Recordings for the *Carl And The Passions* album will resume on April 3rd 1972. Carl takes charge of most of the record's production chores.

■ Friday 10th – Saturday 11th
Winterland *San Francisco, CA* with Stoneground, Mason Proffit
TOUR STARTS North America (Dec 15th-19th)

■ Wednesday 15th
Queen Elizabeth Hall *Vancouver, BC, Canada*

■ Thursday 16th
Salem Armory *Salem, OR*

■ Friday 17th
Paramount Theater *Seattle, WA*

■ Saturday 18th
Paramount Theater *Portland, OR*

■ Sunday 19th
Kennedy Pavilion *Spokane, WA*

• Bruce tells *New Musical Express*: "I noticed that the group had now gotten kind of 'clubby' again. You had two guys, Mike and Al, that were deeply involved in meditation. You had Carl and Ricky that were kind of tight, and Dennis wasn't sure of his role because of the accident with his hand. He couldn't play drums for a while [and] was trying to get used to the role of singing. The group felt kind of uncomfortable with each other."

• After ten years with more or less the same group line-up, Carl now suggests that fresh blood is needed to invigorate The Beach Boys, both musically and personally. In truth, the group is barely holding together. They travel to and from every concert separately: Carl and Dennis in one car with some of the musicians; Mike and Al in their vehicle. At some shows, members are seen arriving on stage from different entrances, just to avoid being with each other. It seems that only their music and business interests are keeping them together.

1972

The group decides to shift their recording base from Los Angeles to The Netherlands ... drummer Ricky Fataar and guitarist Blondie Chaplin officially join The Beach Boys ... sessions continue in California for the new album *Carl And The Passions – "So Tough"* ... Bruce Johnston leaves the group ... *Carl And The Passions* album released ... sessions start in The Netherlands for a new album, which becomes *Holland* ... Warner/Reprise rejects the first version of *Holland* and so the group replaces 'We Got Love' with the more commercial 'Sail On Sailor'.

Two new Beach Boys: ex-Flame musicians Blondie Chaplin (left) and Ricky Fataar.

January

Dennis records his jingle for the Dry Command product. The recording is commissioned by Brian and Murry's Bri-Mur Publishing company.

■ Sunday 9th
Murry Wilson works on a song titled 'Take Back The Time'.

■ Friday 21st
RECORDING Brian's Home Studio *Bel Air, CA*. Brian records **'Funky Pretty'** under the working title of 'Spark In The Dark' on 2-inch 16-track tape. The backing track for the song, with Brian on organ, is completed today; vocals will be recorded later in the year as sessions begin for the *Holland* album, starting June 3rd.

■ Monday 24th
Cass Elliot album by Mama Cass Eliot released in the US. The RCA LP by the ex-Mamas & The Papas singer features Carl on backing vocals for a cover of Bruce's 'Disney Girls (1957)'.

February

Even with moderately successful sales of *Surf's Up*, communication between The Beach Boys and their record company Warner/Reprise has now reached a perilous position. The distinct possibility of signing with a new label looms. With that in mind, the group withholds their finished December 1971 recording of 'Marcella' as bait for any potential new record deal. The Beatles' record company Apple is among those showing an interest in signing the group.

■ Thursday 24th
TV Studio 6, NOS Studios *Hilversum, Netherlands*. AVRO Nederland 1 *Toppop* lip-synch 'Marcella' broadcast May 2nd 7.05-7.30pm. This morning the group – Carl, Mike, Al, Bruce and Dennis, with guitarist Blondie Chaplin and drummer Ricky Fataar – fly into Holland at Amsterdam's Schipol Airport and immediately head to the NOS studios, eager to preview their only recently completed 'Marcella' (formerly 'One Arm Over My Shoulder'). The clip does not feature Blondie. Immediately following the afternoon taping, the group heads to the Congrescentrum for photo sessions and camera rehearsals in readiness for their appearance tomorrow on the annual *Grand Gala Du Disque* show.

■ Friday 25th
TV RAI Congrescentrum *Amsterdam, Netherlands*. AVRO Nederland 1 *Grand Gala Du Disque Populaire 1972* live performance 'Heroes And Villains', 'Sloop John B', 'Surf's Up', 'Student Demonstration Time', broadcast 8:30pm-12:00midnight. Following further camera rehearsals this afternoon, the group (once again without Blondie) perform at this televised concert. Their invitation to appear comes just over five years since they declined an offer to perform at the *Grand Gala* of October 1st 1966. Johnny Cash, Gene Pitney, Helen Reddy, Charles Aznavour, Labi Siffre, Middle Of The Road, The New Seekers, The Bee Gees, and Gilbert O'Sullivan are among the other recording artists on the this evening's show, transmitted live in colour. The Beach Boys take to the stage around 10:00pm.
• Returning to Holland following their amiable visit at the end of 1970, the group intends to stay for just a week. But this will turn into

several months as they happily succumb to the country's all-encompassing calm. They decide that The Netherlands – where the surf is never up – will be the base from which they will administer their forthcoming UK/European tour, and that the excursion will wind up in Holland where they will stay to record their next album. After many years of recording in Los Angeles the group feels that they need a change of location.
Beach Boys manager Jack Rieley tells *Rolling Stone*: "I wanted to [shift our base] and so did Carl. It seemed like an interesting place. But most importantly, I felt that The Beach Boys had to do a record outside of California, to get away from that whole scene, find a new scene, and create in that new scene." At first they want to make an album in the south of France, where The Rolling Stones have just finished recording. But this idea is shelved in favour of the peace and tranquillity that Holland can bring.

The group mistakenly assume that they will be able to just book and use the facilities on offer. Soon however they learn that the country's few studios are already over-booked and that it is impossible to reserve enough time to record an LP. But they have come too far to turn back. Sick of the poison atmosphere and strain that California has brought them, they rashly decide to commission the creation of a studio based on the technology of the future in sleepy, rural Holland. The group eagerly discusses these plans during February 25th and 26th.

(Geographical note: 'The Netherlands' and 'Holland' are words used interchangeably to describe the same country, and you'll see both used here. Things relating to The Netherlands, including its people, are described as Dutch. The resulting Beach Boys album is only ever called *Holland*.)

■ Sunday 27th
The Beach Boys temporarily separate. Bruce returns home to the US while Mike and Al fly on to the Spanish island of Majorca for a meditation holiday with the Maharishi Mahesh Yogi. On the morning of the 28th Carl, Dennis, Blondie, Ricky and Rieley fly to London.

The group's line-up has now officially increased by two. Drummer/singer Ricky Fataar will tell Sylvie Simmons in 2002: "I was with Jack Rieley one evening in his home in Topanga [California] and he brought up the suggestion that Blondie [Chaplin] and I should join the band full-time. I looked at him as though he was out of his mind. Sure we were playing with the band and all of that, but joining … on a permanent basis just seemed a bit ludicrous. He suggested it to the rest of the band and I guess they agreed. But I think the idea had come from Carl originally."

Guitarist/singer Blondie Chaplin, like Fataar a South African, says: "Carl wanted a couple of other voices in the line-up and he thought maybe we could do something to help. Carl was the closest to us and asked us if we wanted to join up. I think he liked the idea of going out on the road and playing with us [and] wanted to get some new blood and stir it up a little bit. I like to think that it was just because of how we played that Carl made the effort. He didn't care about the group's squeaky-clean look. He liked the way we played and I think he just wanted to spend more time with us on the road and in the studio."

Another effect of the addition to the group is less welcome, as the news strikes the white liberal nerve of the US press. A headline in the *San Francisco Chronicle* reads: "Beach Boys Now Include Non-Whites." Speaking at the time, manager Rieley remarks: "The main reason we hired them was because their voices add so much to the blend. The only reason the racial thing has any relevance is the repercussive effects the announcement is having in South Africa.

Posing backstage during an appearance on Dutch TV to promote 'Marcella' on February 24th.

The Beach Boys are now forbidden to play in the country. But it gets silly. I mean, Blondie is no darker than I am."

Monday 28th

En route from Amsterdam to their homes in California, Carl, Dennis, Blondie, Ricky and Rieley arrive in London and hold a press conference this evening in central London's Royal Garden Hotel. During the brief get-together in the presence of a handful of reporters the group ratifies Blondie and Ricky as full-time members of The Beach Boys. They are the first new members to join the group since Bruce Johnston in April 1965. Blondie Chaplin (guitar/vocals) was born July 7th 1951 and Ricky Fataar (drums/vocals) on September 5th 1952, both in Durban, South Africa.

Carl tells the gathering: "This will add two more personalities and two more emotions to our music. Blondie and Ricky both sing and they both compose and they'll be allowed to express themselves within the group."

Rieley says: "We called Brian up last night and he says he feels inspired by the whole thing. It's fresh blood." Dennis pipes up: "We've been playing with the same people for ten years and that's not necessarily a bad thing, but I don't remember ever having this much fun just listening to the band. It's like having stereo sound with your colour TV." Blondie Chaplin recalls later on US radio: "I thought it was so ridiculous. It just didn't seem possible to join The Beach Boys because it was such a tight knit family. When we first joined the group, it was really weird adjusting. The most annoying question we kept getting asked was, 'How does it feel being a Beach Boy?' We're not Beach Boys, you know!"

During the conference, Carl surprises everyone by announcing the imminent arrival of the famous unreleased 1967 album *Smile*. Naturally, Carl's statement produces a barrage of questions. Have you been working on the *Smile* tapes, asks one reporter? Carl: "I was working on the tape of 'The Old Master Painter' [in June 1971] and somebody put the tape out with the garbage by mistake. It got shredded into a thousand pieces. I had to go out, find it, and put it back together again. It's OK now, but we've made safety copies of everything, just in case, like the 'Fire' suite. These old things were done on 4-track tape and they're very fragile."

They're asked for the latest news in the legal dispute between The Beach Boys and Capitol Records. The group sued the label alleging underpayment of just over $2million in royalties. Manager Rieley says: "The problem has been resolved. We settled out of court for a large sum of cash, the exact size of which we're not prepared to disclose, and the total rights to the last five albums for Capitol, which they didn't exploit sufficiently in America, although they did well in Europe. That's *Pet Sounds* onwards." Another reporter asks, "How is Brian?" Carl is diplomatic. "He will, as always, play a vital

and basic role in the future development of The Beach Boys' music."

Rieley closes the conference by announcing a British visit. "We'll be back touring this country in May but we're sure not going to be doing the usual round of Odeons with three supporting acts and a compère. We'll be playing for two hours or more with material off the recent albums and new songs. It's definitely not going to be the old 45-minutes-of-hits thing."

The following morning, Carl, Dennis, Blondie, Ricky and Rieley continue their journey back to Los Angeles.

March

'Student Demonstration Time' single peaks in Belgian chart at number 27, and in Australian chart at number 62.

■ March through early April

Back home in California, the group continues to make plans for recording in Holland. The idea poses a mass of logistical problems. The first person the group call on to assist is Bill de Simone, their erstwhile Hollywood PR man. His job is to find houses and transportation for the entire entourage. With no prior knowledge of Holland's critical and chronic housing shortage, de Simone begins by trying to retain the necessary 11 houses in Haarlem, a handsome residential area to the southwest of Amsterdam that is convenient for EMI's studios. Two weeks later, he has done well to find four. The Beach Boys go back to Holland early in March before returning once again to California where rehearsals with their new band members will continue at their Santa Monica studio.

■ Mid March through April and May

Steve Moffitt is engineer at the group's Santa Monica studio during the continuing sessions for the album that becomes *Carl And the Passions – "So Tough"*. Moffitt gets a call from The Beach Boys while they're in Amsterdam asking him to design and construct a new mixing desk (console), disassemble it, ship it to Holland, and reassemble it there. While Moffitt has been involved in the discussions about the possibility of one day recording overseas, the idea of a 'portable' console has never been proposed before. He is given a deadline of June 1st.

Moffitt's first move is to contact all the best makers of mixing consoles in New York and Los Angeles, requesting prices and specifications for standard models. The deadline is a problem: none of the manufacturers can promise delivery in less than 90 days. With no alternative, Moffitt decides to create a dream console from scratch. He will need help. His friend and physics genius Gordon Rudd is the only man with whom Moffitt feels the project has a chance, but at first Rudd is understandably reluctant. In the *Holland* booklet, Moffitt admits: "It was a ridiculous task to start with, with only two men working on it. But the manufacturers were proposing [mixers] twice the size with half the functions. Most of the people who design consoles have never actually had to use them."

When Moffitt and Rudd complete their design, construction takes place in a 2,000-square-foot warehouse cum laboratory located in the back of a beachside porn movie theatre in Santa Monica. The place also serves as an inventory of all the Brother Records gear, including the earthly remains of Brian's Home Studio. Once the job starts, assemblers work 24 hours a day in shifts to complete it.

With his work finished in co-ordinating the console in the US, Moffitt flies to Amsterdam to supervise assembly. For four-and-a-half weeks Beach Boys equipment travels on every single flight from Los Angeles to Amsterdam (of which there are four daily) and, to correct breakdowns, on every Amsterdam to Los Angeles flight (three daily). The gross weight of all the gear is an alarming 7,300 pounds. The specially made crates alone cost over $5,000. The heaviest single item is a crate containing the racks of ancillary gear, including limiters, gates, noise reduction and a prodigious patch bay. This crate cracks the tarmac as it is rolled out to the plane for loading.

■ Saturday 4th

The *New Musical Express* reports in Britain: "The Beach Boys have become a septet with the addition of two new members. They have been joined by musicians Blondie Chaplin (guitar) and Ricky Fataar (drums), both of whom were previously with the South African group, Flame. Russ Mackie, communication director for The Beach Boys, told the *NME* the group is expected to sign a new recording deal within the next week. Negotiations are taking place with several companies, with Apple favourite to secure The Beach Boys. As soon as a new deal is finished, a new single, ['Marcella'] will be issued."

TOUR STARTS US East/South (Mar 16th-Apr 2nd)

■ Thursday 16th
New York State University, State University Plaza *Albany, NY*

The group hosts its first concert of the year and the first public performance with Blondie Chaplin and Ricky Fataar as official new members. This run of concerts is the first in a series of warm-up shows for the upcoming dates in Europe. Tonight they perform 'Wonderful' in a medley alongside 'Don't Worry Bill', a track on the eponymous album by Ricky and Blondie's old group, The Flame. The Beach Boys nickname this medley 'Wonderbill'.
Set-list 'Wouldn't It Be Nice', 'Long Promised Road', 'Sloop John B', 'Take A Load Off Your Feet', 'Cool Cool Water', 'Disney Girls (1957)', 'Do It Again', 'Heroes And Villains', 'Wild Honey', 'Surfin' USA', (Intermission), 'Surf's Up', 'Let The Wind Blow', 'Darlin'', medley 'Wonderful' / 'Don't Worry Bill', 'God Only Knows', 'Help Me Rhonda', 'Student Demonstration Time', 'Good Vibrations', 'California Girls', 'Surfer Girl', 'I Get Around', 'Fun Fun Fun' (last four as encores).

■ Friday 17th
The Spectrum *Philadelphia, PA*

■ Saturday 18th
Montclair State College *Montclair, NJ*

■ Monday 20th – Wednesday 22nd
Carnegie Hall *New York, NY* **8:00pm**
Each of these three concerts is a sell-out.

■ Thursday 23rd
Kleinhans Music Hall *Buffalo, NY*

■ Friday 24th
Roberts Center, Boston College *Boston, MA*

■ Sunday 26th
Muhlenberg College *Allentown, PA*

■ Tuesday 28th
University of Maryland, Cole Field House Arena *College Park, MD*

Gathered at the Brother studio in early April, just before Bruce Johnston announces his sudden departure the group.

■ Thursday 30th
Alexander Memorial Coliseum, Georgia Tech *Atlanta, GA*

April

This month The Beach Boys abandon plans of signing a deal with another label, deciding instead to commit themselves to a new long-term recording contract with Warner/Reprise. Plans are immediately put in place to issue the group's new long player *Carl And The Passions – "So Tough"* and a US release date of May 15th is set.

■ Saturday 1st
Miami Beach Convention Center *Miami, FL*

■ Sunday 2nd
Ft Hesterly Hall *Tampa, FL*

Last night of the tour; following the show the group flies back to California.

■ Tuesday 3rd – Thursday 13th
RECORDING *Carl And The Passions* **sessions** Brian's Home Studio *Bel Air, CA*; Village Recorders studio (B) *West Los Angeles, CA*; Sunset Sound studio *Los Angeles, CA*. Taking advantage of a ten-day gap in their schedule, and once more working with their busy engineer Steve Moffitt, the new Beach Boys line-up wraps the recordings for their first studio album together, ultimately to be called *Carl And The Passions – "So Tough"*. Songs completed during this period include those first tracked in December 1971: **'Here She Comes'** (written by

Ricky and Blondie), **'He Come Down'** and **'All This Is That'** (both by Al, Carl and Mike), and **'You Need A Mess Of Help To Stand Alone'** (by Brian and Rieley).

Bruce tells *NME* that 'Mess Of Help' was originally titled 'Beatrice From Baltimore'. "I didn't play on it but I watched Brian make the track. I'm disappointed at the vocal. I didn't think there was much energy or unique arrangements put into the background vocals and I don't like Carl's lead. It sounds a little forced and it's a double lead, which didn't sound right to me."

Started and completed during this period are **'Hold On Dear Brother'** (by Ricky and Blondie), and **'Cuddle Up'**, originally called 'Old Movie', and **'Make It Good'** (both by Dennis and Daryl Dragon). These last two songs were planned for the duo's album recorded during 1971 but unreleased; another unissued song recorded for the duo album was 'Baby Baby', which is performed at least once live by The Beach Boys. Bruce Johnston was due to contribute one song to *Carl And The Passions*, '10 Years Harmony', but only piano tracks were taped for this song prior to Johnston's departure from the group (see 10th). The title will later be used for a compilation of Brother-era material, *Ten Years Of Harmony*, and the song becomes the basis of Bruce's 'Endless Harmony' song.

Mike says later in *Melody Maker* that he's pleased with most of the recordings done at this time. "[They were] recorded mostly at Brian's house. He was there with 'Marcella' and 'Mess Of Help' to help with the vocal harmonies. The recordings were very spontaneous. Some … were done in late 1971. [We] branched out and did types of songs that we hadn't done in the past: gospel, some with the sound of a choir, and a couple from Ricky and Blondie that have a rock feel. When Carl writes now, he has that Brianesque feel, but before Carl began writing, the overwhelming force was always

Brian. Three or four years ago the production was entirely handled by Brian, then Carl started doing the production in terms of engineering and Brian moved on and lost interest in the mechanical aspect of things. He just moves from one thing to another continually."

In order to finish the disc quickly, separate sections of the group simultaneously take up residence in three different LA studios. Blondie will tell Sylvie Simmons: "We recorded some tracks in the studio at Brian's home. But most of the time he was up in his bedroom while we were working downstairs. He would come down occasionally and work with us, but most of the time we were down there and he was up there. I didn't make any judgement. I just thought that maybe he needs to recharge his battery or take it easy for whatever reason. I wasn't about to go to his bedroom and say hello. When he came down his contribution was amazing."

Ricky: "It was just all done very piecemeal. Somebody would be cutting a track over at Village Recorders and somebody else would be recording at Sunset … . It was an 'in between touring' kind of an album. We'd sleep and go back, sleep and go back. There was always a deadline that had to be met: record as quickly as you can and go back out on the road. We kept changing studios all the time. Perhaps that's why it sounds so bad. If Carl had mixed it, it would have been really good. But it ended up really terrible."

■ Monday 10th

With recordings for *Carl & The Passions* nearly at an end, Bruce Johnston unexpectedly leaves The Beach Boys. Bruce has been a Beach Boy for exactly seven years and one day. First reports suggest that he has become dissatisfied with Jack Rieley's style of management and with the division of the group into factions. He cites "differences in musical policy" as his main reason for departure. Other reports suggest that Rieley has fired Bruce. Rieley tells *Rolling Stone*: "Something just wasn't gelling. The guys felt that Bruce's talent musically was more of a solo artist. No personal animosity was involved. It's one of those things you can't quite put your finger on." The official statement released by the group and their management reads: "Bruce has left The Beach Boys by mutual consent."

Bruce tells the *New Musical Express*: "I guess I left because there was an uncomfortable feeling around in the band. We all felt uncomfortable with one another. I'm surprised that we all didn't quit. I have other ambitions in producing and arranging and I felt very restricted. I felt that in order to achieve these ambitions and save friendships I should leave – and I left. Also I was getting lazy. I was making too much and only writing about two or three songs a year. I also realised that Brian probably wouldn't be playing an active role in The Beach Boys again and that the group was like a beautiful harmonic orchestra without a composer or arranger. It actually took me three years to figure out that he was not coming back to the group. Unfortunately, he set standards for the group, and even though some of the records The Beach Boys did after he quit were very good, they didn't reach Brian's standards."

Mike: "We had a meeting and we discussed the personal problems within the group and the relationship between the various members within the group – and some of us had no relationship at all! Bruce said, 'If that's the way you feel about it, maybe I should just leave. I don't want to leave but maybe it's for the best.' All I know is that he left because he wasn't too happy about things. It was decided that, because of a couple of feelings harboured by different members of the group, and the way that things went with Bruce developing a solo career, it made it more or less an uncompromising situation. It was very amicable. The Beach Boys never threw him out. He was just on a tangent that was outside The Beach Boys for so many years. ...

He's just doing his own thing now and it remains to be seen what happens. It's not a closed thing. Bruce is free to write with us or record with us. We'll just see if he comes up with any good songs for the group."

Bruce: "I suppose I should make an official statement regarding my departure from The Beach Boys but I'm kind of superstitious about discussing the future. I had a lot of hopes and dreams for The Beach Boys but now I think it's time to transfer all those things to me. There are things that I've wanted to accomplish on my own and you just have to strike off on your own and do it.

"I went home and began writing songs. I wrote 'I Write The Songs' and couldn't get anyone to record it. I sent it to the *Yamaha Song Festival* in Japan and they sent it back saying it wasn't acceptable!" Bruce's 'I Write The Songs' is later recorded by Beach Boys associates Captain & Tennille, and by Barry Manilow, who has a hit with it.

"I also phoned Terry [Melcher] and he was asleep," Bruce continues. "I phoned him again and he was out. So I phoned him again and he was in hospital for six months with two broken legs. This gave me a year to plan my future, and travel, and read, and think and speak with Terry, and see what we both planned to do." Bruce and Melcher's first project together, the Equinox record label, will take shape in July 1973 but does not become operational until a full year later. In the interim, Bruce will make occasional appearances on stage with The Beach Boys, which he calls 'visitation rights'. In January 1975, Equinox records an album by legendary US songwriters Barry Mann and Cynthia Weil.

■ Saturday 15th

RECORDING Larrabee Sound *West Hollywood, CA*. Today sees a Beach Boys tracking session for '**Rooftop Harry**', which will remain unfinished and unreleased. ('Tracking' is the term for the initial recording of backing instruments only.)

• With recordings for their new album finished, a depleted Beach Boys line-up and their ever-increasing entourage return to Holland where they will take up residence, preparing for their forthcoming tour and recording the new album. The group's personnel is scattered within a 30-mile radius of central Amsterdam. Dennis settles with wife and child; Carl with wife, two children, mother, brother-in-law, housekeeper and two dogs; Mike and Al each lives with wife, two kids and a maid; Ricky with wife and in-laws; Blondie with his girlfriend. Then there are Beach Boys chief engineer Steve Moffitt with his secretary and son, and additional engineers Gordon Rudd (plus wife) and Jon Parker (plus girlfriend). There is Russ Mackie, the group's travelling attaché, and manager and Brother Records senior officer Jack Rieley, with secretary Carole Hayes and her husband, plus Rieley's dog. Last but not least is Bill de Simone, the group's erstwhile Hollywood PR officer and the man who has successfully found homes for everyone.

Rieley, Hayes and Mackie are based right in Amsterdam, and the others are at various locations not far from the city. Carl and Blondie are in Hilversum (15 miles south-east of Amsterdam), Ricky in Vreeland (12 miles southeast of east of Amsterdam, near Hilversum on the River Vecht), Parker and Gellert in Haarlem (just to the southwest of Amsterdam) and Rudd in nearby Heemstede, Moffitt in Assendelft (eight miles northwest of Amsterdam), and Mike and Al in Bloemendaal (just to the north of Haarlem). Before the houses are ready, however, everyone is put up in hotels. When they eventually move into their homes they find that each has been fitted with a rented stereo and piano. They hire nine Mercedes and an Audi, and purchase three Volkswagens and a van. Before the group obtains an Amsterdam office, the children's room at Rieley's rented duplex

Al and Mike on-stage in May during the European tour.

apartment becomes the European headquarters of Brother Records, resplendent with bears, dolls and tiny tables. A Telex is installed with an obliging Dutch answering service that apparently handles on average 45 minutes' worth of messages every day, the printed sheets unfurling like an endless paper towel. So many transatlantic calls are placed that the international operators in Pittsburgh, through whom all such calls are relayed, soon get wise to the number and note it to save time.

May

At the Los Angeles Superior Court, the group's ex-business manager Nick Grillo successfully sues The Beach Boys to recover the $17,500 he loaned the group, amongst other charges. He also wins damages totalling $1million against the group and manager Jack Rieley. All parties regard the eventual (undisclosed) settlement figure as unjust. Grillo remarks to *Variety* at the end of the case: "The only people who have made money in this deal were the attorneys. They ripped everybody off."

■ Monday 1st
'Good Time' / 'Sweet Mountain' single by Spring released in the US. It is produced by Brian, who also co-wrote the A-side. This is the second 45 by the female duo that features two-thirds of The Honeys – Brian's wife Marilyn and her sister Diane – and has been at the centre of Brian's recent musical interests. The A-side uses the same backing track as the Beach Boys *Sunflower*-era recording, and the lyrics are changed to suit the gender of the group. The Beach Boys'

own released recording of 'Good Time', again using this backing track, will surface on the 1977 *Love You* album. 'Sweet Mountain' is a musical tribute to one of Brian's favourite oldies, 'Mountain Of Love', as recorded by the group on the *Party!* album. It is also significant as the one Brian original from this period that will not be recycled for a later Beach Boys project.

TOUR STARTS Europe/UK (May 5th-June 3rd)

■ Friday 5th
Koncerthuset *Stockholm, Sweden*
Using their homes and offices in Holland as their base, the group opens their European tour in Sweden. With Bruce no longer a part of the group, The Beach Boys' 14-strong line-up now consists of Mike, Carl, Al, Dennis, Blondie (on bass guitar), Ricky (drums) and an eight-piece backing band including Ed Carter (guitar), Carl's brother-in-law Billy Hinsche (guitar), Daryl Dragon (keyboards) and Toni Tennille (keyboards and backing vocals), plus a horn section, another keyboard player, and two extra percussionists (possibly Dennis Dragon and Mike Kowalski). Throughout this excursion there is no support act.

■ Saturday 6th
Scandinavium *Gothenburg, Sweden*

■ Sunday 7th
Grugahalle *Essen, West Germany*

■ Monday 8th
Festhalle *Frankfurt, West Germany*

At the windswept "muddy marsh" of the Lincoln festival in England: BELOW keeping warm backstage (left to right) are Carl, Blondie, Mike, Dennis, Al and Ricky. BELOW RIGHT the frontline on-stage.

■ Tuesday 9th

Circus/Krone/Bau Munich, West Germany
Set-list 'Sloop John B', 'Long Promised Road', 'Wouldn't It Be Nice', 'God Only Knows', 'Here She Comes', medley 'Wonderful' / 'Don't Worry Bill', 'Do It Again', 'Heroes And Villains', 'Wild Honey' (sung by Blondie), 'Surfin' USA', 'Cool Cool Water', 'Let The Wind Blow', 'I've Got A Friend' (sung by Dennis), 'Surf's Up', 'Darlin'', 'You Need A Mess Of Help To Stand Alone', 'Student Demonstration Time', 'Good Vibrations', 'Help Me Rhonda' (sung by Carl), 'I Get Around', 'Fun Fun Fun', 'Johnny B Goode', 'Barbara Ann' (the last six of these played as encores).

■ Wednesday 10th

RADIO Concert Hall Of The Villa Louvigny, Luxembourg.
The Beach Boys perform specially for Radio Luxembourg in the station's own concert hall, the first time that a major American act has done so.

During the two-hour broadcast – beamed to homes in Britain, France and Holland – the group delivers 'Heroes And Villains', 'Long Promised Road', 'Wouldn't It Be Nice', 'Here She Comes', 'Help Me Rhonda' (Carl on lead), medley 'Wonderful' / 'Don't Worry Bill', 'Cotton Fields', 'Do It Again', 'Wild Honey' (sung by Blondie), 'Surfin' USA', 'Blues Jam' (one-off instrumental).

After a brief intermission there follows 'Let The Wind Blow', 'I've Got A Friend', 'Caroline No', 'Darlin'', 'Student Demonstration Time', 'Good Vibrations', 'I Get Around' and 'Fun Fun Fun'.

The show is performed in front of a specially invited audience and is compèred by the Luxembourg DJ Paul Burnett. The station transmits the performance live between 10:00pm and 12 midnight. The normal news bulletins and advertising breaks are dropped throughout the broadcast.

Carl And The Passions – "So Tough" album

A1 'You Need A Mess Of Help To Stand Alone' (B. WILSON / J. RIELEY)
A2 'Here She Comes' (R. FATAAR / B. CHAPLIN)
A3 'He Come Down' (A. JARDINE / C. WILSON / M. LOVE)
A4 'Marcella' (B. WILSON / J. RIELEY)
B1 'Hold On Dear Brother' (R. FATAAR / B. CHAPLIN)
B2 'Make It Good' (D. WILSON / D. DRAGON)
B3 'All This Is That' (A. JARDINE / C. WILSON / M. LOVE)
B4 'Cuddle Up' (D. WILSON / D. DRAGON)

US release May 15th 1972 (Brother/Reprise 2MS 2083) twinned with 1966 Pet Sounds album.
UK release May 15th 1972 (Reprise K44184).
Chart high US number 50; UK number 25.

■ Thursday 11th
Martinihall Groningen, Netherlands 8:15pm

■ Saturday 13th
Sportpaleis Ahoy Rotterdam, Netherlands 8:15pm

■ Sunday 14th
Stadthalle Vienna, Austria 8:15pm

You Need A Mess Of Help To Stand Alone single

A *'You Need A Mess Of Help To Stand Alone'* (B. WILSON / J. RIELEY)

B *'Cuddle Up'* (D. WILSON / D. DRAGON)

US release May 15th 1972 (Brother/Reprise 1091).
UK release May 1972 (Reprise K14173).
Chart high US none; UK none.

■ Monday 15th

Queen Elizabeth Hall *Antwerp, Belgium* 8:15pm

'You Need A Mess of Help to Stand Alone' / 'Cuddle Up' single released in the US and (around this time) UK. It fails to crack the US or UK charts.

Carl And The Passions – "So Tough" album released in the US and UK. The Beach Boys' new album is issued in America in a gatefold package with *Pet Sounds*, a move that provokes unfavourable comparison with the landmark 1966 LP and contributes to the album stalling at a disappointing number 50 in the US charts.

In Britain, where the new single-LP will peak at number 25, *New Musical Express*'s reviewer is erstwhile Beach Boy, Bruce Johnston. "To sum up the album," Bruce writes, "I don't think it's as good as *Surf's Up* and I don't think it matches anything that *Sunflower* did. I like *Sunflower* better than any album we've made in four years, but I know it didn't do well in the US or England. I would like to see more Brian Wilson involvement with The Beach Boys. I spoke to Brian a

couple of weeks ago and he told me that he really didn't have too much to do with this album. ... I don't hear his voice very much on this album."

• Meanwhile back in California, Van Dyke Parks goes to Brian's Bel Air home.

"Once upon a time, I visited him there one day, with a trusty Sony tape recorder in hand," Parks tells US radio. "I went to Bellagio Drive to work on a song with Brian. The entire group [had been] working on a record for delivery to the Warner Brothers label. Mo Ostin held great expectations for that record and suggested that my working with Brian again might goad him to similar creative heights we had reached in *Smile*.

"Mo was astonished that Brian wasn't participating in the album, and feeling somewhat deceived, thought I should step forward, as I was in large part the reason for their commitment to the group. Having only gotten a partial song out of that one meeting with Brian, I put the tape away, and lay low. I wanted to avoid getting involved with the internecine group dilemmas once again." The song in question is 'Sail On Sailor' (and for more on this, see October 10th and November 28th).

■ Tuesday 16th

TV BBC TV Centre (Studio B) *White City, west London*. BBC-2 *The Old Grey Whistle Test* live vocals over taped backing track 'You Need A Mess Of Help To Stand Alone' broadcast colour 10:55-11:45pm.

City Hall *Newcastle Upon Tyne*

At approximately 9:30am, shortly after flying into London from Belgium, the group heads to the BBC to tape their first (and only) collective studio appearance for the station's late-night adult-orientated *Whistle Test* rock show. Following brief camera rehearsals, three takes are required to achieve a suitable performance for transmission of the new single. Immediately following the recordings the group travels north for tonight's concert.

■ Thursday 18th
Kinetic Circus *Birmingham*

Mark Plummer writes in *Melody Maker*: "They had a strange audience. Half of the people there were obviously along to see a 'Beach Boys' that no longer exists and the other section were hippy and hairy. 'They were better at the Odeon two years ago,' one fellow told his mate as they took leave in the gent's toilets. That was their opinion. But for me, it was one of the best gigs I have ever been along to see for a long time. They still play a lot of the old numbers – 'Darlin'', 'Surfin' USA', 'Good Vibrations', 'Sloop John B' and 'Wild Honey' – but their set has changed. It's no longer 45 minutes. They blow for anything up to three hours now."

Record Mirror's reviewer adds some detail: "The Kinetic Circus [is] part of a cold, reinforced concrete block near to where the old Bull Ring used to be. Starting the show with 'Heroes And Villains' warmed the place up a bit, but for the first hour at least there was no great crash of Californian surf on these Birmingham shores. Though there is no actual leader of the group, Carl Wilson is certainly the hub around which the show revolves. And revolve they do. After each number there's a unique Beach Boys shuffle, a sort of musical chairs, and whoever has the bass guitar in their hands when the music starts, plays it.

"Carl took most of the vocals in the first half of the show, while the rest of the group weaved a soft gentle pattern of harmony around him. It's a fascinating pattern to see in the making, everyone on stage playing a part in it, and it's hard to tell what combination of voices is creating the harmonies at any one time.

"Al Jardine holds centre stage with guitar and looks out at the audience from under a buckled pirate's hat. Dennis Wilson, ex-drummer, now busy versatile frontman, looks fit, handsome and lively as he moves across stage from organ to electric piano with his shirt tails hanging out. Blondie Chaplin works hard. Ricky Fataar is heard on drums to great effect but not seen through the stage clutter. Mike Love, red beard under a motoring cap, is cool, casual and competent.

"At the break, it is hard to tell whether The Beach Boys were being cool, too casual or just slow. In the second set, it came strong. 'Do You Wanna Dance', 'Sloop John B' and 'Do It Again' were familiar as nursery rhymes to a young audience. The last numbers, 'I Get Around' and 'Good Vibrations', once again made the point that these Beach Boys standards are second only to The Beatles' songs in their universal appeal, and left the audience hot and happy."

Backstage during the group's brief ten-minute break, Martin Lewis of *New Musical Express* catches a few words with Dennis:

NME: What's the atmosphere like in the re-modelled Beach Boys?
Dennis: "I don't know how it looks outside, but it's more fun inside. There's less tension since Bruce left."
NME: Was there one turning point in the association with him?
Dennis: "No, not anything dramatic. Musically, we didn't click [and] appreciate each other, so one day we both said, 'OK, that's it.' He's a good guy but he was writing stuff for a solo album. ... We're a band."
NME: Do you ever look back on your records?
Dennis: "Sometimes I have company over and we put on *Pet Sounds* or something, and to me it's camp. It brings back memories, good and bad. That *Pet Sounds* really hit it."
NME: Will we be seeing Brian on stage?
Dennis: "Well, he's coming over in a couple of days, and sometimes, if he's in the audience, he'll come up and mess around. So it's possible. He does what he wants." (There is no evidence that Brian does come on now.)

■ Friday 19th
Kings Hall Belle Vue, *Manchester* 7:45pm

■ Saturday 20th
Empire *Liverpool* 6:15 & 8:35pm

■ Sunday 21st
De Montfort Hall *Leicester* 8:00pm; tickets 50p

■ Monday 22nd
Reading Suite, Top Rank Ballroom *Reading, Berks* 7:00 & 10:00pm
Tickets on door £1.25.

■ Tuesday 23rd
Bristol Suite, Top Rank Ballroom *Bristol*

■ Wednesday 24th
The Dome *Brighton*
Set-list 'Heroes And Villains', 'Long Promised Road', 'God Only Knows', 'Here She Comes', medley 'Wonderful' / 'Don't Worry Bill', 'Do It Again', 'Sloop John B', 'Wild Honey', 'California Girls', 'Cool Cool Water', 'Let The Wind Blow', 'Caroline No', 'Transcendental Meditation' (a poem by Mike), 'Surf's Up', 'Darlin'', 'Cotton Fields', 'You Need A Mess Of Help To Stand Alone', 'Student Demonstration Time', 'Good Vibrations', 'Help Me Rhonda', 'I Get Around', 'Fun Fun Fun' (last three as encores).

■ Thursday 25th
During a day off from concerts the group shoots two films for the *Music Unlimited* pop series intended for screening in UK cinemas. The first colour clip filmed is for 'You Need A Mess Of Help To Stand Alone', to which the group mimes on top of the Brighton Dome, and then later 'Don't Go Near The Water', shot inside one of the small promenade buildings adjacent to the seafront. When the series starts running at cinemas later in the year, the group's performances are credited to 'The Beachboys'. Apparently the desire to change their image has even led to thoughts of a change of name, and at one time they toy with the idea of calling themselves simply 'Beach'.

■ Saturday 27th
Royal Festival Hall *central London* 6:15 & 9:00pm
The group performs on the first day of a three-day *Festival Of Progressive Music*. Keith Altham writes in *New Musical Express*: "I am, it should be emphasised, a Beach Boys freak from way back and so I went to the Royal Festival Hall prepared not to like the new-look band with their auxiliary members Blondie Chaplin and Ricky Fataar. I was completely converted. They were superb! What they have done successfully is to add a new dimension to the band in terms of 'heavy' rock without dissipating the charm and quality of their three-part harmonies and earlier works like 'Wild Honey', 'Sloop John B' and 'God Only Knows'. Particularly impressive was their second-half set, which began with 'Cool Cool Water' and 'Let The Wind Blow', with Carl in better voice than I have ever heard him and an on-stage version of the brilliant studio production, 'Surf's Up', which certainly does credit to the recording. ... I missed some of the high harmony touches which Bruce Johnston used to add, but overall the new Beach Boys thoroughly deserved the standing ovation they received."
Set-list (6.15) 'Long Promised Road', 'God Only Knows', 'Here She Comes', 'Wonderful', 'Do It Again', 'Sloop John B', 'Wild Honey',

'California Girls', 'Cool Cool Water', 'Let The Wind Blow', 'Caroline No', 'Surf's Up', 'Darlin'', 'Cotton Fields', 'You Need A Mess Of Help To Stand Alone', 'Student Demonstration Time', 'Good Vibrations', 'Help Me Rhonda', 'I Get Around', 'Fun Fun Fun'.

■ Sunday 28th

Tupholme Hall *Bardney, Lincs* 10:30pm, with Brewers Droop, Spencer Davis, Lindisfarne, The Average White Band, Slade, Monty Python's Flying Circus; compère BBC DJ John Peel
This is day three of the four-day *Great Western Express Festival*, staged at this site east of Lincoln. Because of the non-appearance of Sly & The Family Stone, The Beach Boys are top of the bill this evening. But the impressive array of acts cannot stop the organisers from incurring a reported £50,000 loss.

The *Lincolnshire Echo* reports: "Hundreds of pop fans made the long 12-mile walk from Lincoln ... as winds blowing up to 45-50 miles an hour howled around them. And to make matters worse, rain showers hindered their progress. A number of disappointed fans told how they had made journeys from Scotland, Devon, London and Wales only to find they had a long, long walk to get to the site where a four-day pop festival is being held.

"But unfortunately, the pop festival site, Tupholme, is a muddy marsh. There has been rain, cold and high winds but nothing can stop the fans pouring in. At the latest count 50,000 youngsters were either inside the site or near the entrance and local police reported no major problems or incidents with the fans. By the time the day's music began, several hundred youngsters had been treated for exposure. This, dealt with by medical staff laid on by the festival organisers, was mainly due to the overnight storm, which had caused havoc for fans trying to erect tents and makeshift sleeping accommodation. The high winds and torrential rain overnight caused widespread damage and discomfort for thousands trying to camp at the site. Some visitors to Tupholme have travelled as far as 12,000 miles albeit indirectly to be a part of the event. Flags of many nationalities were clearly visible, billowing in the wind, including an Australian flag perched on the top of the Abbey. Many of the fans arrived days early to pitch their tents in the space immediately adjacent to the entrance."

■ Wednesday 31st

TV BBC TV Centre *White City, west London*. BBC-1 *Top Of The Pops* live vocals over taped backing track 'You Need A Mess Of Help To Stand Alone' broadcast June 8th 7:25-7:59pm. The Beach Boys return to London to tape a studio appearance for *TOTP* with Daryl Dragon on piano.

■ Late this month

Meanwhile in Holland, Beach Boys engineer Steve Moffitt finds an existing studio in a barn in Baambrugge, about ten miles south of Amsterdam, that sits among a collection of unprepossessing farm buildings, adjacent to a defunct greenhouse. The acoustics of the building are dreadful. But Moffitt thinks it can be successfully converted into the group's new studio.

He starts work by having a new floor laid six inches above the old one so that cables can be run underneath. Sand is poured between the uprights to avoid sound resonating. Even the speakers are made containing specially imported Malibu sand, again to prevent resonance. Sound-friendly angles are built into the ceilings, which are covered with spun glass. The fluorescent lighting already in the barn is quickly replaced with a multitude of Study-Buddy lamps stuck to the walls, covered with different coloured gels and controlled by dimmer switches.

June

■ Saturday 3rd

Crystal Palace Sports Stadium *south London* 12:00midday-9:00pm, with Joe Cocker, Richie Havens, Melanie, Sha Na Na; tickets £1.75 (advance), £2.00 (today)
The Beach Boys perform at the *Crystal Palace Concert Bowl Third Garden Party* in front of an audience estimated at 15,000. NBC TV from the US videotapes the proceedings and broadcasts highlights in a show titled *Good Vibrations From London*, aired on the national Public Broadcasting Service on June 28th, 9:00-10:00pm. In The Beach Boys' segment the group is seen performing 'Do It Again', 'Wild Honey' (sung by Blondie) and 'Help Me Rhonda' (sung by Carl and with guest Elton John on keyboards).

The last-minute unannounced compère of the event is Who drummer Keith Moon who jumps on stage as The Beach Boys leave during one of their two encores. Problems with the inadequate sound system and NBC TV's intricate technical equipment forces long delays between each act. Although scheduled to appear around 3:45pm, The Beach Boys do not take the stage until about an hour and a half later. Poor sound mars portions of The Beach Boys' rain-drenched performance and to compensate, the group offers to perform a free open-air concert in London's Hyde Park on or before August 13th, but this will fail to materialise.

Tony Stewart writes in *NME*: "Announcing a track from *Surf's Up*, they said it was a most apt album title, implying they had deserted the surfing days. But then they went on to give us all those good oldies. We had 'Good Vibrations', a rocking version of 'Sloop John B' (still with its initial beauty), 'Help Me Rhonda' and 'I Get Around'. An excellent act, which even had the odd one or two swimming in the lake. They were wet enough, so it made no difference."

After the show, The Beach Boys return to Holland where they will spend the next three weeks working on their new studio album.

■ Saturday June 3rd – Wed August 2nd

RECORDING *Holland* sessions Beach Boys Dutch Studio *Baambrugge, Netherlands*. The Beach Boys start recording sessions at the Baambrugge studio at Rijksstraatweg 45 for the album that becomes *Holland* – the last group LP where Carl rules supreme. The work continues in The Netherlands to Thursday June 22nd and then intermittently until August 2nd.

The description in the booklet that will accompany the resulting album is a romantic one. "Baambrugge is about a 20-minute drive from Amsterdam along a four-lane highway flanked on both sides by flat fields, cows and canals. Sea birds fly overhead. The windmills are there, just like in the pictures, all turning with spatulate grace. It is said that in Holland, the highway patrol drive Porsches and that the gypsies drive Mercedes."

Although the individual components of the group's new hi-tech recording studio have been tested back in the US, there has been no time to try out the system as a whole. It's possible that parts may have been affected by the extreme cold in the plane's freight bay. Even back in California it could take a full month to get all the parts of a new system working compatibly together. Engineer Moffitt will recall in the *Holland* booklet, "We finally got it all hooked up in Holland ... and nothing worked right! You learn in electronics to expect anything." Moffitt and Gordon Rudd attend to the studio and begin working 18-hour troubleshooting shifts.

The group is ignorant of European voltage standards. Local electronic experts, summoned by The Beach Boys, begin adapting

The new line-up poses for a Fender Guitars promo shot at the studio in Baambrugge, Holland, with drummer Ricky Fataar switching convincingly to pedal steel guitar.

the studio to Holland's 230-volt/50-cycle electrical current. The aggregate delay of four-and-a-half weeks halts the group's plans for extra touring intended to defray the staggering expenses they are incurring.

As if all that isn't bad enough, there is the problem with brother Brian. Except for his fleeting visit to Hawaii in August 1967, he has not ventured out of Los Angeles since he gave up touring with The Beach Boys in December 1964. For some time, Brian has had suicidal thoughts and, allegedly, has even asked his gardener to dig a grave for him in his backyard. The group is naturally pained by Brian's withdrawal and are at a loss to explain what is happening to him, besides his drug abuse, so they simply refuse to talk about it. They figure that a change of scenery might change Brian's perplexing character.

Trying to get Brian to Amsterdam proves complex. Manager Jack Rieley helps to get Brian to leave his palatial Bel Air home by describing the journey to Holland as nothing more than a little vacation. Brian's wife Marilyn along with their two kids and housekeeper come over first. Twice, Brian gets as far as the airport but changes his mind about the flight and returns home. Frantic transatlantic phone calls follow between various Beach Boys and Brian as they attempt to coax him into making the journey. Another flight is booked for Brian for the following day and this time he appears to get on the plane. A phone call to Los Angeles Airport confirms it. But three hours after the plane lands in Holland there is still no sign of him. A search of the aircraft finds his ticket and passport abandoned on his seat. Oblivious to the panic, Brian has shuffled off the plane and fallen asleep on a couch in the duty-free lounge at Amsterdam's Schiphol Airport, where he is eventually found. Brian at last sets up home in Laren, near Hilversum, with his wife, two children, sister-in-law, and housekeeper.

Carl later tells Dutch TV: "Brian lived in a Dutch house called

Flowers. It had a very artistic, moody, fairytale sort of feel. It can seem like that to you when you're there for a while. It is a very beautiful place, calm and natural. When he was there, he started making up a story, wanting to express that feeling. It was fun, and it appeared as [the] seven-inch *Fairy Tale* record that accompanied the *Holland* album [see January 8th 1973]. The crickets you hear [on *Fairy Tale*] were all from one cricket. We overdubbed many times just to make it sound like it was a backyard full of them.

"I lived [in Holland] for seven months, first in Hilversum and then in Laren," Carl continues. "It was a very creative time for me. Brian had me working on the album very hard so he could have some time for himself. He wasn't really up for doing much, as far as going into the studio every day. I remember leaving the house in the early afternoon and going home in the morning, when the sun was coming up. The days were very long in the summer. I rode my bike to the studio one day, … about ten miles away. It was a very good experience for me. It was also a very spiritual time for me."

Throughout this period as *Holland* is recorded, engineer Steve Moffit tends regularly to the temperamental 4-track equipment, running it for four hours before recording begins each day and for another two after taping has concluded. The hi-tech studio has a streamlined, multi-coloured mixing desk (console) supported on two pedestals with no cables visible. It glows futuristically in the dark. Once operational, the studio is the best ever seen in The Netherlands. The building has in fact been a studio before, primarily for Dutch TV and radio commercials and the odd Christmas album. Out front it still bears the imposing name BBC2 – no relation to the BBC-2 TV channel of the British Broadcasting Corporation in Britain. That 4-track studio was originally run by Piet Visser (who under the name Pi Veriss wrote a famous Dutch song, 'Geef Mij Maar Amsterdam', or 'Just Give Me Amsterdam'). Now, just inside the door stand 15 empty cases of Coke, conclusive

LEFT AND BELOW Carl at the studio in Baambrugge in The Netherlands where work is starting on the album that becomes *Holland*. The group has had the new recording console shipped out piece by piece from California.

evidence of American occupation. The carpet tiles are littered with ash, empty cigarette packs, glutinous coffee cups, and foul ashtrays.

Soundproofing of the barn has been attempted with fibreglass, specially flown in from Los Angeles, but it does not work. Blondie will tell Sylvie Simmons in 2002: "There were microphones and wires everywhere. You had to tiptoe through the studio like a war-zone. There was a train [line] a couple of hundred yards away, and every time you heard the train you had to stop [recording] for a minute because you could pick up the rumble on the microphones. It was funny. In between the trains and us, there were tons of cows grazing." Ricky: "There were times when we were recording when we had to shoo away the cows because they were mooing too loud. I don't think a moo made it onto any of the tracks. Half of the time when we were recording there would be some engineer lying under the console with his legs sticking out, fixing something or moving a channel around because we'd run out of channels to record."

Ricky recalls no fixed daily schedule. "Carl and Blondie and myself would get together a lot and play, and then Dennis would come in and play, and then Al. Carl and Blondie and myself seemed to be the core of the group who consistently wanted to play and mess around in the studio. We seemed to be the most enthusiastic people. We just wanted to get out of the house, go to the studio and play. There was no 'We've got to get this thing done'. It was an album made at leisure. The studio was there and if you had some music and you wanted to work it out, you'd just go down. Al would call and say, 'Ricky, would you come down and play on this?' It was all totally casual and leisurely."

Blondie says: "Sometimes I'd play guitar, sometimes I'd play bass, Ricky would play drums and Carl would play piano or guitar. Work was really very focused, not chaotic at all. You'd have the song and you'd start playing it and we'd start to fall in, and you'd focus on a good groove and just keep it going. Carl had his hands on the reins, put it that way. When Brian wasn't around, it was up to baby brother Carl to keep everything together. For me it was Carl who was holding things together, completely in charge, the organisation and everything, and [he] played a big part in helping us all keep going."

To Ricky it hardly seems as if an album is being made. "It was just moving along at this leisurely, idyllic pace. I remember having wonderful, delicious summery days lying out in the backyard, and getting in a boat and going fishing, things like that. It was very idyllic and charming and sweet. But there were obstacles in the way, like 'We can't use the studio today because they have to tear this down'. It was kind of a pioneering thing to do, to take a studio to another country."

During breaks in the recordings, the group and engineers eat in a bar across the street from their studio. Some of the locals there are surprised that Blondie and Ricky can speak a bit of Dutch, until they realise they are South African. The group knows when fans are approaching for autographs because of the sound of their wooden shoes on the concrete outside the studio. Breaks for Transcendental Meditation are a regular occurrence during the *Holland* sessions.

Dennis is frustrated at how his music is being frozen out of the sessions and becomes increasingly restless, moving out to the Spanish Canary Islands, off the west African coast, and then flying back for certain sessions. During one memorable night, Dennis's restlessness even led him to fly to Los Angeles just to get a chilli from the noted Chasen's restaurant there.

Brian apparently visits the studio mostly late at night, preferring to work on his own. The early sessions are hindered by the building's delighted owner rushing around making home movies and gathering autographs. Little more than basic tracks are recorded in Holland and much additional work will be required on the group's return to California. In contrast to *Surf's Up*, *Holland* will reflect the potentially idyllic surroundings in which it is made and reveal a new side to The Beach Boys.

Carl tells Dutch radio: "We've all been wanting to leave Los

PACKARD ORGAN

Angeles for a couple of years now. Holland is friendly in every sense. The environment eliminates distractions. The only kind of tension is the good kind of working tension – not the kind you get crossing LA in rush hour. There is a subliminal feeling of safety here. We worked long hours, usually waking in the afternoon and then working until five in the morning. It was so perfectly still at night. Sometimes we'd walk out and see Venus like a headlamp, amazingly bright."

A number of recordings for *Holland* are made in the June, July and August 1st and 2nd period, chiefly supervised by Carl. **'Steamboat'** is written by Dennis and Jack Rieley; Carl sings lead and co-produces with Dennis; musician Tony Martin adds steel guitar. **'California Saga: Big Sur'** was first worked on in August 1970 and marks the first time that Mike has composed music as well as the words for a song. It's the first part of the group's collaborative 'California Saga' trilogy for the album that examines what's left of the ghettos in California. Mike sings lead and Al and Carl co-produce. The trilogy's second part, **'California Saga: The Beaks Of Eagles'**, is composed by Al, who bases it partly on a poem by Robinson Jeffers.

The last section is **'California Saga: California'**, which author Al also refers to as 'On my way to sunny Cal-i-forn-eye-ay', the line emanating from the now seldom-heard vocal cords of Brian. The song, co-produced by Al and Carl, uses a flashback montage to create a highly descriptive lyric. The 'California Saga' sequence is subsequently played and recorded by the whole group in one take, and a homesick Al remembers it as "the last thing we did on the *Holland* album", by which time homesickness was setting in. Al tells Scott Keller: "We came down to the studio to do a mix-down so [Brian] could get home. Then suddenly, [he] came in and said, 'Give me a microphone.' He walked straight in. I hadn't see him for a month. He walked up to the microphone and started singing, 'I'm on my way to sunny Californi-i-a.' He then left the microphone and walked out. That's my favourite part of the whole record. Brian was apparently homesick too."

'The Trader' is a two-part Carl composition, his first since 'Feel Flows' and 'Long Promised Road' on *Surf's Up*, with lyrics by Rieley. Carl sings lead and produces. **'Leavin' This Town'** is a beautifully simple song created by Ricky with help from Carl, Blondie and Mike. Blondie sings lead; Ricky produces and performs the Moog solo. "Everybody would come in with a piece of a song or a completed song and kind of play around with it and then figure out how we wanted to record it," says Ricky. "It was very casual. I wrote 'Leavin' This Town' in Holland at the piano in the house I lived in. I had parts of it and Carl came in the studio and suggested other things, so we were just making it up as we went along. The tracks were always cut with two or three people playing at the same time, and the vocals were always done later. I used to love to watch when they all sang together. That was a great thrill. People would come up with parts right there on the spot. They'd sung together for so long they could do that, and it was a great thing to see."

'Only With You' is by Dennis, with words by Mike and Carl singing lead. **'Funky Pretty'**, first tracked on January 21st, is completed in The Netherlands and incorporates every member of the group equally; even the lead vocal is shared by several group members, singing the counter-melodies that run concurrently through the verse. The lyrics by Mike and Rieley are humorous, mystical and perverse. The song's tag incorporates perhaps a dozen moving parts. Brothers Brian and Carl produce, and Brian plays some instruments. Ricky tells Sylvie Simmons: "I think [Brian] might even be playing drums on the song. I missed playing on that because I was sick. I had a cold or something that week. I didn't see Brian all that much. I can't even remember seeing him in the studio in

Holland. Everyone had their own family situation and we'd just go to work and occasionally see each other. It wasn't like a one-big-family thing."

"On 'Funky Pretty'," says Blondie, "Brian came down while we were trying to work out the vocals and he was doing a mix that I thought was even better than what eventually came out on the record." Brian will recall in the 1998 *Endless Harmony* film: "It was during a period of my life when I didn't know for sure what I wanted to do. So I just laid there in the booth while the other Beach Boys would be working."

'We Got Love' is an anti-apartheid song written, sung and played by Blondie, Ricky and Mike, and **'Carry Me Home'** is written by Dennis. Both songs will be dropped from the album before release (see January 8th 1973), although the early French release of *Holland* (Brother/Reprise 54008) mentions 'We Got Love' on its jacket. A live version will appear on the 1973 double album *The Beach Boys In Concert*.

Carl tells *Melody Maker*: "We know now want we want to do individually. We can tell what the arrangements should be without Brian having to tell us everything. But he gets a lot done without looking like it. You could swear he isn't doing anything and he could have a whole thing together."

There is an incident that temporarily threatens the apparent tranquillity during this period. The Dutch musicians' union ANOUK is suspicious of the group's presence in the country. They think that The Beach Boys might be taking away work from Dutch musicians and want the group investigated and, if necessary, deported. In the group's defence Brother Records prepares a dossier to explain how they're working, and that in fact they use Dutch sidemen on occasions, for example for the strings on 'Only With You'. The group says that they hope their activities will give a boost to Holland's music scene. ANOUK is agreeable. Their only regret is that Dutch musicians can't hope to do the same thing in the US because of America's notoriously strict immigration service.

■ Wednesday 7th
TV NOS Studios *Hilversum, Netherlands*. NCRV Nederland 2 *Eddie Ready Go!* lip-synch 'You Need A Mess Of Help To Stand Alone' broadcast colour 7:05-7.55pm.

■ Saturday 24th
O'Keefe Center *Toronto, ON, Canada*

■ Monday 26th
Borough of York Stadium *Toronto, ON, Canada* with Steppenwolf, Bread, Bloodrock, Alice Cooper, Lighthouse, Chilliwack
As a rehearsal for their next concert tour in August, the group's second Canadian show takes place at tonight's *Beggar's Banquet Dance*. To fulfil their promise of appearing in Canada, the group has

---

Marcella single

A 'Marcella' (B. WILSON / J. RIELEY)
B 'Hold On Dear Brother' (R. FATAAR / B. CHAPLIN)

US release June 26th 1972 (Brother/Reprise 1101).
Chart high US none.

cancelled a scheduled appearance in Benidorm, Spain at Club 3000, a new nightclub that opened just five days ago. Next, the group flies back to Holland where they will reside until August 5th. **'Marcella' / 'Hold On Dear Brother'** single released in the US. The 45 continues the group's run of American chart misses.

July

Spring album by Spring is released in the US (and later in the UK as *American Spring* to prevent confusion with another group called Spring). The LP, produced by Brian, Steve Desper and David Sandler in various combinations, is critically acclaimed but will see zero chart action. It features more involvement from Brian as a producer than any released album since *Friends* in 1968 and until *15 Big Ones* in 1976. Brian will also record a solo promotional interview during this period in an effort to promote the release, a recording later distributed on reel-to-reel tape.
• *Carl And The Passions – "So Tough"* album peaks in US chart at 50.

August

■ Thursday 3rd

To celebrate the end of their recording work, The Beach Boys attend a party organised by Dutch record company Bovema-Negram at the Belle Amie Club in Scheveningen, near The Hague, in a venue owned by a Dutch band, Tee Set. Also present is the Wilsons' mother Audree who has flown in specially from Los Angeles. During the party the group's manager Jack Rieley announces to local journalists that the group's latest recordings will feature on a double album to be called *Holland*. Each member of The Beach Boys and their entourage receives a photo-book of Amsterdam. The Beach Boys' dream trip to Holland is over.

■ Saturday 5th

The group leaves Holland, flying back today to the US.

■ Tuesday 8th

Nassau Coliseum *Uniondale, NY*
Three days after leaving Holland the group are in New York State for this one-off, another show designed to prepare them for the US tour starting next week. Afterwards they fly back to California.

■ Friday 11th

MIXING Brian's Home Studio *Bel Air, CA*. Mixing **'Funky Pretty'**.

TOUR STARTS US East/Midwest/South (Aug 16th-Sep 9th)

■ Wednesday 16th

Mississippi River Festival, Southern Illinois University *Edwardsville, IL*
Tonight's show is attended by 22,573 people. In addition to the core Beach Boys live group – Mike, Carl, Dennis, Ricky, Blondie and Al – extra musicians joining them on-stage at this time include Daryl Dragon (keyboards, bass), Billy Hinsche (guitar, bass), Charles Lloyd (saxophone, flute) and Toni Tennille (keyboards).

■ Thursday 17th

Arie Crown Theater, McCormick Place *Chicago, IL*

■ Friday 18th

Dillon Stadium *Hartford, CT* with The Kinks, Phlorescent Leech & Eddie, The Doors
The Kinks and The Beach Boys share the same booking agency in the US, hence the pairing on this and the next few dates. The post-Jim Morrison Doors are promoting their *Full Circle* LP.

■ Saturday 19th

Roosevelt Stadium, New Jersey Fairgrounds *Jersey City, NJ* 7:30pm, with The Kinks, Looking Glass

■ Sunday 20th

Allentown Fairgrounds race track *Allentown, PA* 7:00pm, with The Kinks, Orleans; tickets $3.50
The concert is sponsored by the Allentown Council of Youth, promoted by William Honney, and MC'd by local radio personality Danny Somach.

Karen Burgio writes in the *Allentown Morning Call:* "With 10,000-plus in attendance, the show didn't pass without incident as local officials were upset by The Kinks bringing a case of beer on stage and passing cans out to people at the front of the stage, and the band had been troublesome before going on. However, performances by The Beach Boys and The Kinks were both very highly rated and the evening is deemed a large success for all parties involved."

■ Monday 21st

Nassau Veterans Memorial Coliseum *Uniondale, NY* 8:00pm, with The Kinks
The crowd totals 18,000.

■ Wednesday 23rd – Thursday 24th

Boston Common *Boston, MA*
One of a series of *Concerts On The Common*, part of a city-sponsored *Summer Thing* programme. After the intermission The Beach Boys perform songs with members of the Boston Symphony Orchestra, but this does not go over well with the party-atmosphere crowd.
Set-list (23rd) 'Marcella', 'Wouldn't It Be Nice', 'Long Promised Road', 'Here She Comes', 'Heroes And Villains', 'Only With You', 'Wild Honey' (Blondie on lead vocal), 'Surfin' USA', 'Student Demonstration Time', (Intermission), 'God Only Knows', 'Let The Wind Blow', 'Cuddle Up', medley 'Wonderful' / 'Don't Worry Bill', 'Surf's Up', 'Do It Again', 'Sloop John B', 'Good Vibrations', 'I Get Around', ' Fun Fun Fun', 'Jumpin' Jack Flash' (last three as encores).

■ Friday 25th

Hampton Rhodes Coliseum *Hampton Rhodes, VA*

■ Sunday 27th

Alexandria Roller Rink *Waynesboro, VA*

■ Wednesday 30th

Merriweather Post Pavilion *Columbia, MD*

September

■ Friday 1st

Wildwood Convention Hall *Wildwood, NJ*
Part of a summer-long series of concerts down on the New Jersey shore near Atlantic City

■ **Sunday 3rd**
Ocean City *Baltimore, MD*

■ **Monday 4th**
Pine Knob Musical Theater *Independence, MI*

■ **Saturday 9th**
University of Notre Dame *Notre Dame, IN*
The last night of the current tour.

■ **Monday 11th**
Just as everyone thinks that The Beach Boys may have settled down in Holland for good, the group travels to relaxed Baambrugge to pack up their $500,000 studio and return it to frantic Los Angeles. The equipment is shipped back piece by piece and re-built in the group's studio in Santa Monica alongside their existing and impressive 24-track facility. With all this recording gear comes, naturally enough, The Beach Boys along with their entourage. (Years later the shed that once housed the Dutch studio will be unceremoniously demolished.)

Brian's wife Marilyn tells *Rolling Stone*: "[Holland] was a vacation for Brian and me. He loved it and didn't like coming back to Los Angeles. Everything's slower in Holland, you can relax and you can enjoy the air. Brian used to go on a bicycle every day."

Brian returns to his home in Bel Air to find that his home studio has been dismantled by Marilyn. Meanwhile, Brother Records have become so enamoured with Holland that they set up a permanent office in Amsterdam in an exquisite 17th century house overlooking a mossy green canal. Even though the group's time in Holland is over, manager Jack Rieley decides to remain in the country and manage the band long-distance.

Everyone in the group's camp is agreed that the trip to Holland has been worthwhile – everyone, that is, except Dennis, who is becoming increasingly frustrated at being a Beach Boy. He feels that he is now typecast simply as the group's drummer – despite not having drummed for a while now – and that he is not being recognised for the songs he is composing.

■ **Late September through early October**
RECORDING/MIXING *Holland* sessions. Village Recorders studio (B) *West Los Angeles, CA*. The Beach Boys complete overdubbing and start mixing of the *Holland* album. ('Overdubbing' is the recording of additional vocals or instruments onto an existing recorded performance on tape.)

October

■ **Monday 2nd**
MIXING Village Recorders studio *West Los Angeles, CA*. Blondie and Ricky work on mixing their song **'Leaving This Town'**.

■ **Wednesday 4th**
RECORDING *Holland* sessions. Village Recorders studio *West Los Angeles, CA*. Blondie records **'Hard Times'** and although fully completed it will remain unreleased. (This song should not be confused with the later Brian composition, 'Hard Time'.)

■ **Friday 6th**
RECORDING Unknown studio. Murry Wilson records an unsolicited jingle for the Kentucky Fried Chicken chain of restaurants.

■ **Saturday 7th**
MIXING Village Recorders studio *West Los Angeles, CA*. Blondie and Ricky conduct a further mixing session.

■ **Monday 9th**
The master for the *Holland* album is assembled, at this point including the song 'We Got Love'.

■ **Tuesday 10th**
The group submits the completed master of *Holland* to executives at Warner/Reprise in Burbank, California, who are expecting something good after their disappointment with *Carl And The Passions – "So Tough"*. The group feels confident that they have a strong album, and a November 5th release date is tentatively set. But they are aghast when the company rejects the disc. Warner/Reprise wants a hit single but says they cannot hear one, saying they need a strong single in order to promote the album. The group is forced to drop the weakest track, 'We Got Love', from the album's line-up and replace it with a song that has hit potential.

Van Dyke Parks once again enters the scene and reminds Brian of the song they composed (allegedly with Ray Kennedy and Tandyn Almer) around May 15th.

Brian and Parks now re-structure the song, adding a middle-eight that allegedly receives a last-minute lyrical overhaul from Jack Rieley. 'Sail On Sailor' is thus reborn and made ready for recording (see November 28th). Parks tells Scott Keller: "*Holland* arrived at the Burbank offices and it was the consensus of everyone in A&R, promotion, and distribution, that the album was 'un-releasable'. Knowing the company's enormous investment, and the high stakes involved, I got out the tape cassette from [the May] session with Brian … , gave it a listen, and delivered it to the company with my assurance that it would solve all their problems.

"I came up with that lyric when I was working with Brian, as well as the musical pitches those words reside on. I did nothing with that tape until I saw The Beach Boys' crisis at the company where I was working, earning $350 a week. Well, they recorded the song, and it was a hit. And I'm glad that everyone then came out of their little rooms to claim co-writing credit on that song. But I never questioned it, just as I never questioned the various claims on the residuals.

"On the tape, it's clear from the contents that I authored the words and the musical intervals to 'Sail On Sailor'. It's also clear that I composed the chords to the bridge, played them, and taught them to Brian. You could say I did the Beach Boys a nice turn there. It was just a nice thing to do." In 2004 the song's publishers will list the composers as Tandyn Almer, Ray Kennedy, Van Dyke Parks, Jack Rieley, and Brian Wilson.

■ **Monday 16th**
Murry Wilson returns to work on his 'Take Back The Time' song, among other titles.

November

TOUR STARTS North America (Nov 1st-23rd)

■ **Wednesday 1st**
University of Georgia *Atlanta, GA*

■ **Thursday 2nd**
Paramount Northwest Theater *Seattle, WA*

1972

■ **Saturday 4th**
Agrodome *Vancouver, BC, Canada*

■ **Monday 6th**
University of Georgia *Athens, GA*

■ **Thursday 9th**
Dane County Memorial Coliseum *Madison, WI* with Poco

■ **Saturday 11th**
Oklahoma Civic Center Music Hall *Oklahoma City, OK*

■ **Tuesday 14th**
Palace Theater *Albany, NY*

■ **Thursday 16th**
War Memorial Auditorium *Syracuse, NY*

■ **Sunday 19th**
Capitol Theater *Passaic, NJ* two shows
Both tonight's shows are professionally recorded by the group for a future live album project. Among the songs performed are 'Wouldn't It Be Nice', 'You Need A Mess Of Help', 'Only With You', 'Don't Worry Baby', 'Help Me Rhonda', 'Wonderful', 'God Only Knows', 'Good Vibrations', 'Surfin' USA', 'Fun Fun Fun', and 'Jumpin' Jack Flash'.

■ **Tuesday 21st**
New Haven Coliseum *New Haven, CT*

■ **Wednesday 22nd**
DAR Constitution Hall *Washington, DC*

■ **Thursday 23rd**
Carnegie Hall *New York, NY* 8:00 & 11:30pm
These performances gross $34,000 at the box office. Both shows are again recorded in full. Among the songs performed are 'Darlin'', 'Only With You', 'Heroes And Villains', 'Long Promised Road', 'Don't Worry Baby', 'Student Demonstration Time', 'I Get Around', 'Marcella', 'California Saga: California', 'Help Me Rhonda', medley 'Wonderful' / 'Don't Worry Bill', 'God Only Knows', 'Do It Again', 'Wouldn't It Be Nice', 'Wild Honey', 'Good Vibrations', 'Surfin' USA', 'Fun Fun Fun', 'Jumpin' Jack Flash', 'You Need A Mess Of Help', 'Leaving This Town', and 'Sloop John B'. Tonight's recording of 'Wonderful' / 'Don't Worry Bill' will appear on the 1998 CD *Endless Harmony*.

■ **Tuesday 28th – Wednesday 29th**
RECORDING *Holland* sessions Village Recorders studio *Los Angeles, CA*. Carl, Blondie and Ricky begin recording the backing track for **'Sail On Sailor'** in a desperate bid to persuade Warners to issue the group's latest album, *Holland*. Carl produces the sessions. Near the end on Wednesday, Gerry Beckley from the group America and musician friends Tony Martin and Billy Hinsche ably assist the trio as they record backing vocals.

According to Ricky, Brian does not appear at the session. "I remember Carl called Brian to say 'Is this the right chord?' and 'What kind of a groove is it?'," Ricky tells Sylvie Simmons. "Brian was at home on the telephone telling us what to do with the song. He came up with this idea that Carl should play a part that was sort of like an SOS, Morse code signal … 'Dd-dd-dd dd-dd-dd', and Carl went out and played that and it was just right."

■ **Thursday 30th**
RECORDING/MIXING *Holland* sessions Brother studio *Santa Monica, CA*. Following attempts by Dennis and Carl, Blondie adds the final lead vocal to **'Sail On Sailor'**.

"Dennis tried it once," says Blondie. "but he wanted to go surfing. He gave it one shot and then literally went off with his board and went surfing. Then Carl tried it, and then he looked at me and said, 'I think it sounds pretty good with my voice but why don't you give it a bash?'

"So I sang it and everybody thought that was the right timbre for the song. I think I did two takes on it and I was just getting warmed up, because there's a whole mouthful of words in that song. I was reading and singing them at the same time and I said, 'I'll give it another shot,' but after the second, Carl said, 'No, that's fine.'" The song is immediately mixed.

Warner/Reprise is satisfied with the up-tempo song and feels that the track has given the album the necessary potential hit.

Van Dyke Parks says on US radio: "When the song was delivered back to Warner Brothers it was designated as the single for the album. My name appeared as co-author on that first-issue copy, with Brian's. After Ray Kennedy's lawsuit [claiming authorship of the lyrics] my name and participation diminished, and in some ensuing cases I've been given no royalties or credit at all. I understand that there was a general feeding frenzy around the tune's lyrics, as The Beach Boys regrouped back in LA. I have no idea how many people may have been at those final vocal sessions, now claiming additional credit. That's none of my business."

The record company sets a release date for the *Holland* album of December 29th, but that is soon changed.

December

■ **Thursday 2nd**
MIXING Unknown studio. Today sees a mixing session for **'California Saga'**.

■ **Saturday 4th**
The first side of the group's forthcoming *Holland* album is today re-mastered at Warner/Reprise to include the new recording 'Sail On Sailor' as the opening track. A new US release date of January 8th 1973 is set.

TOUR STARTS US West/East (Dec 10th-13th)

■ **Friday 10th – Saturday 11th**
Winterland Ballroom *San Francisco, CA*

■ **Sunday 12th**
Georgetown University *Washington, DC*

■ **Monday 13th**
Capitol Theater *Passaic, NJ*
Last night of the current tour.
• As the year draws to a close, The Beach Boys and their families reflect on what has been an eventful and exciting 12 months, exhilarated by the imminent release of their latest batch of recordings. What they do not know is that the new album will mark the start of a barren time for studio recordings from the once so prolific group.

1973

Holland album released, including Brian's *Mount Vernon And Fairway* EP ... 'Sail On Sailor' single released ... Murry Wilson dies of a heart attack at 56 ... Brian withdraws further from the world while the live band continues to tour ... *In Concert* double-album released, becoming the group's first gold record for Warner/Reprise ... Blondie Chaplin leaves The Beach Boys.

The group takes time out in a relatively quiet year.

1973

January

■ Monday 8th

Holland album released in the US and (around this time) UK. Jim Miller writes in *Rolling Stone*: "Like the finest Beach Boys' work, *Holland* makes me consistently smile, as much at its occasionally unnerving simplicity of viewpoint as its frequently ornate perfection. Although the Beach Boys may be an acquired taste, once the listener has granted them their stylistic predilections, their best records become irresistible. Their music long ago transcended facile categorization, and they now play what might as well be described simply as Beach Boy music. Unlike last year's disappointing *So Tough*, *Holland* offers that music at its most satisfying. It is a special album." Following such general critical approval, *Holland* peaks at number 36 in the US chart where it will remain for seven months, and at number 20 in the UK. Some reports have it outselling *Surf's Up*, even though that album charted higher. This is sweet music to the group because reports estimate that *Holland* has cost a mighty $250,000 to produce.

Early copies of the album include Brian's 7-inch EP, *Mount Vernon And Fairway (A Fairy Tale): A Fairy Tale In Several Parts*. This is a self-consciously ironic spoken children's story inspired by Brian's fond recollection of teenage nights spent listening to the radio at Mike Love's family home, which was situated at the junction of Mount Vernon Drive and Fairway Boulevard in Baldwin Hills, Los Angeles. Brian wrote the words, music and text in Holland last year as he listened to Randy Newman's *Sail Away* album. Carl compiled the recordings, which feature narration by Jack Rieley, a few snippets of Brian playing the piano, and Brian providing the voice of the Pied

Holland album

A1 'Sail On Sailor' (B. WILSON / T. ALMER / V.D. PARKS / J. RIELEY / R. KENNEDY)
A2 'Steamboat' (D. WILSON / J. RIELEY)
A3 'California Saga: Big Sur' (M. LOVE)
A4 'California Saga: The Beaks Of Eagles' (R. JEFFERS / A. JARDINE)
A5 'California Saga: California' (A. JARDINE)
B1 'The Trader' (C. WILSON / J. RIELEY)
B2 'Leavin' This Town' (R. FATAAR / C. WILSON / B. CHAPLIN / M. LOVE)
B3 'Only With You' (D. WILSON / M. LOVE)
B4 'Funky Pretty' (B. WILSON / M. LOVE / J. RIELEY)

Mount Vernon And Fairway (A Fairy Tale): A Fairy Tale In Several Parts (bonus 7-inch disc with early copies)
A1 'Mt. Vernon And Fairway: Theme' (B. WILSON)
A2 'I'm The Pied Piper: Instrumental' (B. WILSON / C. WILSON)
A3 'Better Get Back In Bed' (B. WILSON)
B1 'Magic Transistor Radio' (B. WILSON)
B2 'I'm The Pied Piper' (B. WILSON / C. WILSON)
B3 'Radio King Dom' (B. WILSON / J. RIELEY)

US release January 8th 1973 (Brother/Reprise MS 2118).
UK release January 1973 (Reprise K54008).
Chart high US number 36; UK number 20.

Sail On Sailor single

A 'Sail On Sailor' (B. WILSON / T. ALMER / V.D. PARKS / J. RIELEY / R. KENNEDY)
B 'Only With You' (D. WILSON / M. LOVE)

US release February 1973 (Brother/Reprise 1138), reissued March 10th 1975 (Brother/Reprise 1325).
UK release June 1975 (Reprise K14394).
Chart high US number 79 (1973), number 49 (1975); UK none.

Piper. The EP, with a picture sleeve drawn by Brian, is his major contribution to *Holland*. He is disappointed and hurt when it does not feature on the LP itself. Warners are upset too: the extra disc means that the already expensive project costs even more.

Several overseas Warners affiliates are sent early *Holland* master tapes made prior to the inclusion of 'Sail On Sailor' and still featuring 'We Got Love'. Corrected master tapes quickly follow, but in Germany there is a mix-up and the album is sent to the pressing plant. It is said that 600 copies with the 'wrong' contents are shipped to record stores before the mistake is caught.

While *Holland* is a respectable commercial success, the disc marks the start of a depressingly unproductive period for the group. From this point, The Beach Boys go into a creative dead end. Over the next three years they record very little. Exceptions include notable guest appearances on Chicago's 'Wishing You Were Here' and Elton John's 'Don't Let The Sun Go Down On Me', both of which will be Top 40 hits in 1974.

Al takes advantage of the inactivity by moving to the Big Sur area of California, while Dennis reconciles his feelings for his father and begins to socialise with Murry. The two regularly go fishing together or share a beer while watching boxing on TV. Audree Wilson tells *Rolling Stone*: "They were buddies. It's the most amazing thing. … Dennis called his father on Mother's Day and Murry told him, 'I'm just going to live about a month.' Dennis didn't tell me this, thank God! I didn't need to know that, but he could tell Dennis that."

■ Tuesday 30th

Just as *Holland* hits the racks, the group tries to assemble a new live album culled from their winter 1972 tour. This single album will ultimately be rejected by Warner Bros and replaced by a double album in November. The version of 'Heroes And Villains' intended for the single-LP version of the live album will eventually be released on the 1998 CD *Endless Harmony*. (See also February 28th.)

February

'Sail On Sailor' / 'Only With You' single released in the US. It will peak in the US chart at number 79.
'California Saga: California' / 'Sail On Sailor' single released in the UK. It will peak in the UK chart at number 37.

■ Thursday 8th

A Bri-Mur Publishing (Brian and Murry) tape dated today features a song called 'Go Tell Her'. No further details are known.

California Saga: California single

A 'California Saga: California' (A. JARDINE)
B 'Sail On Sailor' (B. WILSON / T. ALMER / V.D. PARKS / J. RIELEY / R. KENNEDY)

UK release February 1973 (Reprise K14232).
Chart high UK number 37.

■ Sunday 18th
The Haze *Riverside, CA*
The first of two Beach Boys dates serving as warm-ups for the tour scheduled to start on March 7th.

■ Monday 19th
Cow Palace *San Francisco, CA*

■ Wednesday 28th
Beach Boys' engineer Stephen Moffitt assembles some of the live recordings made on the winter 1972 tour for the proposed single-disc version of a live album. These include 'Don't Worry Baby', 'Heroes And Villains', 'Let The Wind Blow', 'Marcella', and 'Wouldn't It Be Nice'.

March

■ Thursday 1st
New York City Center Joffrey Ballet makes its debut performance of *Deuce Coupe Ballet* set to Beach Boys music by choreographer Twyla Tharp and designed by New York graffiti artists.

■ Tuesday 6th
MIXING probably Brother studio *Santa Monica, CA*. The group works on remixing **'California Saga'** for single release. Additional vocals are recorded around this time, and the single version will indeed feature more of Brian's vocals than the original album mix. (See also March 8th.)

TOUR STARTS US (Mar 7th-May 17th)

■ Wednesday 7th
Colby College *Waterville, ME*
Supported by an impressive new backing band, the group begins another lengthy American tour, a ten-week excursion that will run until May 17th. The core live group – Dennis, Carl, Mike, Al, Blondie and Ricky – are joined by Billy Hinsche (guitar), Carlos Munoz (keyboards), Joe Pollard (drums), Ed Carter (bass guitar), and Richard 'Didymus' Washington (percussion), providing a very full band sound. However, the tour draws some criticism for unusually long pauses between each song and the group's sometimes negative reaction to any audience requests for oldies.

■ Thursday 8th
Just one day into their latest tour Steve Love, Mike's brother and Beach Boys assistant manager, types a memo to the group, namely Brian, Dennis, Carl, Mike, Al, Blondie, Ricky and manager Jack Rieley. "The purpose of this memo is to inform you that, pursuant to the terms of the contract between Warner Brothers and Brother Records Inc., The Beach Boys' *Smile* album is supposed to be delivered to Warner Brothers no later than May 1st or $50,000 is to be deducted from any advance to the group after May 1st."
MIXING probably Brother studio *Santa Monica, CA*. The group do further work today remixing **'California Saga'** for single release.

■ Friday 9th
Following Steve Love's memo, Carl takes it upon himself to fly out to Holland to discuss the matter with manager Jack Rieley, who is still living in the country six months after the rest of the group flew back to Los Angeles. By a strange coincidence, Carl's visit coincides with the annual Edison Awards, the Dutch equivalent of the American Grammys. *Surf's Up* has just been voted Best Pop Album of 1971 by the Edison committee so Carl happily accepts an invitation to receive the award live on the AVRO TV show *Edisons Voor De Vuist Weg* (transmitted on Nederland 1 9:10-10:35pm). Immediately after, Carl flies on to Canada to rejoin the tour.

■ Saturday 10th
Memorial Arena *Victoria, BC, Canada* with Chilliwack

■ Sunday 11th
Pacific Coliseum *Vancouver, BC, Canada* with Chilliwack
After this date, the group flies back to California.

■ Monday 12th
RECORDING Brother studio *Santa Monica, CA*. A session for **'Dr. Tom',** another of Al's folk adaptations. In this case the song is based on 'Tom Dooley'. Although Al records a partial lead vocal, the recording remains unfinished and inevitably unreleased.

■ Friday 16th
Hollywood Palladium *Hollywood, CA* 8:00pm
Rescheduled from March 9th.

■ Friday 23rd
Pirate's World Arena *Dania, FL*

■ Saturday 24th
Californian Polytechnic, State University *Pomona, CA*

■ Thursday 29th
RECORDING probably Brother studio *Santa Monica, CA*. Carl is recorded experimenting with Moog synthesiser and piano; his keyboard improvisation does not feature vocals.

■ Friday 30th
Arie Crown Theater *Chicago, IL*

April

'Shyin' Away' / 'Fallin' In Love' single by American Spring released in the US. The two songs are from recordings made in Iowa by the group formerly known as The Honeys and Spring. 'Fallin' In Love' uses the same basic track as The Beach Boys' version from the *Sunflower* era, albeit with keyboard overdubs. Nevertheless, the basic string and drum machine tracks are intact. Alternative mixes of both sides of this single will appear as bonus tracks on Rhino's 1998 reissue of *Spring*, alongside another outtake, 'Had To Phone Ya'.

■ Wednesday 4th
Warner Bros prepares the masters for the next Beach Boys single, 'California Saga' and 'Funky Pretty'.

■ Friday 6th
The Spectrum *Philadelphia, PA*

■ Saturday 7th
Scope Arena *Norfolk, VA* with Bruce Springsteen
Support tonight is from a 23-year-old guitarist promoting his debut album *Greetings From Asbury Park NJ*.

■ Tuesday 10th
University Of North Carolina *Chapel Hill, NC*

■ Wednesday 11th
Omni Coliseum *Atlanta, GA* with Bruce Springsteen

■ Thursday 12th
University of Florida *Gainesville, FL*

■ Friday 13th
University of Alabama *Tuscaloosa, AL*

■ Saturday 14th
Pirate's World *Dania, FL* 8:00pm

■ Tuesday 17th
Civic Arena *Los Angeles, CA* 8:00pm with Steely Dan

■ Thursday 19th
Winterland Arena *San Francisco, CA* with Jesse Colin Young, Barbara Mauritz
Portions of this concert are shot on 16mm film for Dennis's archive.

■ Friday 20th
The Palladium *Hollywood, CA*
The concert is highlighted by the return appearances of Brian Wilson and Bruce Johnston. Brian appears exceedingly briefly during the encore, his first stage moment with the group since December 3rd 1971. He has been talked into appearing by his friend, Three Dog Night singer Danny Hutton. Carl recalls in *The Los Angeles Times*: "They were just messing around. I think what [Brian] was really doing was checking the audience out. He wanted to come out and see what all the fuss was all about. I think that it probably was nerve-wracking to him. He's not exposed to that because he doesn't tour." The show is professionally recorded by the group for possible use on their revised live album.

Judith Sims writes in *Rolling Stone*: "The Beach Boys recently decided to come back and live in Los Angeles after last year's escapade in Holland, but this was the first concert in their home town in almost two years. As they loped on-stage, it wasn't the old recognisable group. For one thing, Bruce Johnston was missing and there were six new musicians (see March 7th).

"They started with 'Help Me Rhonda', ragged and uneasy with Dennis singing lead instead of Al Jardine. But when they hit 'Darlin'' it was a smooth, joyous example of their professional innocence. Two and a half years ago, at the Monterey Big Sur Festival, The Beach Boys introduced their new act. They would perform no tunes

recorded before *Pet Sounds* except in the encore and then only 'I Get Around'. They've since modified that, probably because of audience demand, and now they put a few oldies in the middle: 'Don't Worry Baby', 'Surfin' USA' and 'Sloop John B'.

"Carl sang Brian's solo on 'Caroline No' and they jumped back to the present day with Chaplin singing lead on 'Sail On Sailor' from *Holland*. He sounded just like... a Beach Boy. 'Heroes And Villains' sagged in the middle with feedback screeches and spotty harmonies, but they eventually pulled it together.

"Voices cracked and equipment failed, but the occasional lapses were lost on the ecstatic audience. Most of the crowd looked too young to remember the Boys' vintage striped-shirt stuff, but when 'Good Vibrations' began, the whole, huge Palladium erupted in the singalong.

"Brian Wilson was there. He occasionally walked across the edge of the audience, looming larger than ever in a long dark coat, and though the audience kept calling out for him, he didn't emerge. They did four encores, 'Surfer Girl', 'I Get Around', 'Fun Fun Fun' and, surprise, 'Jumpin' Jack Flash'. Former Beach Boy Bruce Johnston joined in, and by that time Mike Love was bare-chested and dancing a modified Jagger across the stage. He screamed 'Los Angeles!' and the group went off.

"The crowd kept up a steady, pounding encore call for eight minutes and the group finally came back with 'California Girls'. Gerry Beckley of America sang with them. They went into 'Barbara Ann' and, in the last minute, Brian himself came out, shy and uneasy, and sang a few lines until they all left for the last time."

■ Saturday 21st
Houston Civic Center *Houston, TX*

■ Sunday 22nd
Bronco Bowl *Dallas, TX* with The Doobie Brothers

■ Wednesday 25th
Celebrity Theater *Phoenix, AZ*

■ Thursday 26th
Red Rocks Community College *Denver, CO*

■ Friday 27th
Kiel Opera House *St. Louis, MO*
Set-list 'Heroes And Villains', 'Funky Pretty', 'Darlin'', 'Do It Again', 'Leavin' This Town', 'Help Me Rhonda', 'Caroline No', 'Don't Worry Baby', 'Surfin' USA', 'Marcella', 'California Saga: California', 'Let The Wind Blow', 'Sail On Sailor', 'Sloop John B', 'Wouldn't It Be Nice', 'Wild Honey', 'Good Vibrations', 'California Girls', 'I Get Around', 'Jumpin' Jack Flash' (last three as encores).

■ Saturday 28th
Hoch Auditorium *Lawrence, KS*

■ Sunday 29th
Omaha Civic Auditorium *Omaha, NE*

May

'California: On My Way to Sunny Californ-i-a' / 'Funky Pretty' single released in the US. This remixed A-side charts at an unexceptional number 84.

California single

A 'California: On My Way to Sunny Californ-i-a' (A. JARDINE)
B 'Funky Pretty' (B. WILSON / M. LOVE / J. RIELEY)

US release May 1973 (Brother/Reprise 1156).
Chart high US number 84.

■ Tuesday 1st

The Warners deadline for delivery of the *Smile* album passes with no sign of the tapes. As threatened, the label holds back $50,000 from the next payment due to the group.

■ Sunday 6th

Fairleigh Dickinson University *Teaneck, NJ* with John David Southern
The Beach Boys perform on the final day of the three-day *Miracle Weekend* that takes place under a 4,400-capacity tent.

■ Wednesday 9th

Grove City College *Grove City, PA* 8:30pm

■ Friday 11th

Albany Theater *Albany, NY*

■ Saturday 12th

Fairleigh Dickinson University *Paramus, NJ*

■ Sunday 13th

Colby College *Waterville, ME*

■ Thursday 17th

Kiel Auditorium *St. Louis, MO*
Closing night of the tour.

■ Monday 28th

University of Notre Dame *Notre Dame, IN*
A one-off performance for the group.

■ Tuesday 29th

Al copyrights 'Canyon Summer', his failed attempt at a jingle for the Coppertone sun-tan lotion company.

June

■ Monday 4th

Murry Wilson dies suddenly of a heart attack, a month short of his 56th birthday. When told of their father's death, Brian flees to New York City with Marilyn and her sister Diane Rovell. During the trip Brian and Diane are interviewed by WNEW's Pete Fornatale, to whom Brian mentions he has been planning to record one of Murry's tunes, 'Lazaloo'. Meanwhile, Dennis escapes to Europe. Neither Brian nor Dennis can bring themselves to attend the funeral but Dennis will visit his father's body in the morgue. Carl tells *Rolling Stone*: "I really loved my dad a lot. It just about killed Brian when our dad died. He went to New York. He just could not handle it. He left so he wouldn't have to be there and go to the funeral." Murry's wife Audree tells *Rolling Stone*: "Carl was very angry that Brian didn't go to the funeral. I said, 'Carl, I understand perfectly.' It didn't bother me. Brian couldn't face it, no way."

• Following Murry's death, The Beach Boys release the following statement prepared by management: "Murry Wilson was a hard oyster shell of a man, aggressively masking a pushover softness which revealed itself at the sound of a beautiful chord or the thought of his wife and three sons. An unending source of high-powered energy, he could wear down the strongest souls just by explaining his thoughts in a telephone call. A jealous guardian of the incredible career he helped built for his sons, he was the enthusiastic champion of any who sought to help them, and the scourge of those who used the Wilson name for personal gain.

"He was a proud man, who wanted more than anything for his sons to be 'good boys'. In his eyes they remained 'boys' until the end, though Brian is now 30, Dennis 28, and Carl 26. They were not the 'tough' men he used to say he wanted then to be but, over his last years, Murry Wilson whittled down the generation gap through increased confidence in all three, despite their 'soft' ways. Although there were periods of storm for Murry and his wife Audree, the last 18 months found them together nearly all the time. And, as if out of a gallant other-age, he almost always referred to her as 'Mrs. Wilson' when others were about.

"When it came to his machinery business, which fed the Wilsons until The Beach Boys were born, Murry worked harder than any man. The shop had to be absolutely clean and the demanding father shouted to his sons, 'Get in the cracks,' as they scoured the place on Saturday mornings. On the business side Murry said he wasn't a financial wizard, that he spent money too lavishly. But it was he who would first raise the alarm when his sons were about to embark on questionable business deals. Of one man who laid out a complex real estate scheme, Murry screamed, 'Sophisticated businessman? Hell no, he's just a son of bitch and a crook. Get rid of him.'

"His continuing pleasure for years was music. He relished writing songs, anguished over lyrics and drove studio musicians like a construction foreman in his role as producer. His unbelievable energy could be applied equally to a studio session for the Beach Boys or a demonstration of a musical commercial he created. In a recent transatlantic telephone call, Murry devoted nearly a quarter of an hour to playing tapes of a tune he had written and was hoping The Beach Boys would record. As the tapes squeaked through the overseas connection, Murry enthused: 'Here's where Mike will come in … this part is a natural for Carl' … and on and on.

"Murry Wilson remained his sons' most enthusiastic adviser even in 1973, years after his formal managerial ties with The Beach Boys had ended. His compassion for their good fortune was enthusiastic, but critical when he saw them performing live about two months ago. After the concert Murry told someone: 'Tell the boys to sing out more, especially Carl. He's not projecting enough. And tell Dennis to keep his hand out of his pockets. But don't let him know the old man said it.'"

• In the middle of June, following his visit to New York, a heartbroken Brian withdraws further into himself. He returns to his home in Bellagio Road in Bel Air, goes to his bedroom situated above the garage, and retires to his large four-poster bed. He will stay there intermittently for the next two and a quarter years. During this period he supposedly writes a song in tribute to his dad, 'Just An Imitation'. Permanently dressed in his bathrobe, he will pass time in a state of self-destruction, drinking heavily and smoking five packs of cigarettes a day. His daily rituals include watching television shows such as *Mr. Rogers* and Johnny Carson's *Tonight Show*. His eating habits will include eggs and toast for breakfast, four hamburgers for lunch, and an array of steaks, cookies and candy bars last thing at night. Beside his bed is a record turntable on which Brian will play The Ronettes' 1963 single 'Be My Baby' up to a hundred times a day. His daughter Carnie will recall being awoken early every morning by the sound of the record.

Alongside his exceedingly brief excursions to the studio and his visits to his friend Danny Hutton, Brian's only ventures outside his bedroom will be to replenish his plate with large quantities of food and drink and to rush out to the school bus that brings his two daughters home from school – to ask the driver for a cigarette. This strict lack of activity means his weight increases rapidly and, alarmingly for Marilyn, he becomes increasingly dependent on cocaine.

Brian later tells Scott Keller: "The chief reason I dropped out was because I had taken too many drugs and they had messed my brain up. I was hiding in my bedroom from the world. Basically, I had been just out of commission. I mean I was out of it. I was totally overweight. I was unhealthy. I was totally a vegetable. In other words, my life just got all screwed up. My brain got screwed up and my thinking process went somewhere else. I started taking a lot of cocaine and a lot of drugs and it threw me inwards. It made an explosion and I withdrew from society."

Carl tells Keller: "Brian worked really hard for the first seven years and he needed a break. I think he was pretty confused at the time by his environment. He just took a look at it and saw how fucked up the world was and said, 'The world is so fucked up. I can't stand it. I can't stand it.' I think it broke his heart."

Audree Wilson tells *Rolling Stone*: "I would go over [to Brian and Marilyn's house] and he'd stay in his room all the time. ... There'd be a house full of people and he just wouldn't come down. He just wanted to be alone. Sometimes he'd say, 'I'm really so tired,' or 'I'll be down in a little while,' and I'd think to myself, 'You might or you might not. And if not, that's OK with me.' I knew he had a problem. I'd go upstairs to say hi to him and gave him a kiss and he would always be sweet to me and say, 'Hi mom, how are you?' or 'I have a cold,' or 'My stomach is upset,' or something."

Brian says on US television: "I believed the devil was chasing me around and I think the devil came in the form of other people that were competing with me and had ideas of killing me. Everywhere I looked, even in the shower heads, I went, 'Aaarrrgh, the devil's after me.' I was taking some drugs and I experimented myself right out of action. That was what my life was all about for me: staying in bed. I was hiding away from everyone and everything. It was just one big hideaway. I used my room as my little castle. Added to that, I was very depressed with The Beach Boys. I couldn't talk to them and nobody in the band would relate to me. This went on for about two and a half years. But, on and off, I'd sometimes go and record. But basically I just stayed in my bedroom. I was under the sheets and I watched television."

• Meanwhile this summer, as Brian is self-destructing, The Beach Boys' Brother studio in Santa Monica, which the group has been using since December 1971, is officially opened.

August

During this month the legendary US disc jockey and record collector Dr Demento tapes an interview with the group for a proposed Reprise promo release, but the interview disc never materialises.

TOUR STARTS North America (Aug 9th-Sep 9th)

■ Thursday 9th
Grove City College *Grove City, OH*
The live band for this tour includes Carl (guitar, electric piano), Blondie (guitar), Ricky (drums), Dennis (electric piano) and Al (guitar), plus Ed Carter (bass), Billy Hinsche (guitar, keyboards), Robert Kenyatta (saxophone, flute), Mike Kowalski (percussion), and Carlos Munoz (keyboards).

■ Sunday 12th
Football Field, University of Cincinnati *Cincinnati, OH*
The show is properly recorded for possible use on the revised live LP.

■ Tuesday 14th – Thursday 16th
Auditorium Theatre *Chicago, IL*
Shows on the 15th/16th are taped for the revised edition of the live release. During this stint they perform Dennis's 'River Song', which will eventually appear on his 1977 solo album *Pacific Ocean Blue*.
Set-list (15th) 'Wouldn't It Be Nice', 'Leavin' This Town', 'The Trader', 'California Girls', 'You Still Believe In Me', 'Marcella', 'Funky Pretty', 'Surfin' USA', 'Caroline No', 'Surfer Girl', 'California Saga', 'We Got Love', 'Surf's Up', 'Sloop John B', 'Help Me Rhonda', 'Sail On Sailor', 'Good Vibrations', 'I Get Around', 'It's About Time', 'Fun Fun Fun'.

■ Friday 17th
Tiger Stadium *Massillon, OH*

■ Saturday 18th
The Mosque *Richmond, VA* 8:00pm
The group performs the entire show without any support acts. Linda Ronstadt was scheduled to appear but can't make it, and attempts to bring singer Jonathan Edwards down from Washington fail. The show is professionally recorded for possible use on the revised live LP.

Dave Noechel writes in the *Richmond Times*: "It has always been difficult to review Beach Boys shows because, although they are one of the supergroups, they have always been more of a studio band than a live band. Last night at the Mosque they displayed these same tendencies. The concert suffered from lack of momentum. There was so much tuning up and changing of instruments that the group never really got any pacing. The sets, however, mixed old and new material, which made for a nice variety and showed just how far The Beach Boys have come. Their songs are much more solid now.

"The addition of Blondie Chaplin and Ricky Fataar has helped the group. Chaplin easily has the best solo voice of the group. His best numbers and the group's best were 'Sail On Sailor' and 'Leavin' This Town', both off their latest album that's easily the best they've done. Al Jardine has sort of slipped into the background. But he still sounds good on the old numbers. His best lead parts were on 'You Still Believe In Me' and 'Heroes And Villains'.

"With all these good things going for them, it may be difficult to understand how the concert failed. Basically, the problem is that The Beach Boys are not an exciting group. Their songs have always been … nifty but not all that good. Their new phase has produced better songs, but they do not require an exciting group."

■ Sunday 19th
Nassau Coliseum *Uniondale, NY*
Tonight's performance is professionally recorded by the group for possible inclusion on their revised live album. The set includes 'Sloop John B', 'California Girls' and 'I Get Around'.

■ Monday 20th
Schaeffer Stadium *Foxboro, MA*
This show too is professionally recorded by the group for potential use on the forthcoming live album.

■ Thursday 23rd
Danbury Prison *Danbury, CT*

■ Friday 24th
Dillon Stadium *Hartford, CT*
Tonight's show is professionally recorded by the band for possible use on their revised live album, and sees one of the few Beach Boys concerts to feature the three songs 'Long Promised Road', 'California Saga' and 'River Song'. Audree Wilson is present tonight.

■ Saturday 25th
Roosevelt Stadium *Jersey City, NJ* 7:30pm, with Poco, The Stanky Brown Group
This performance is another professionally recorded for possible inclusion on the group's upcoming live album, and the set includes 'We Got Love'. The show grosses $129,800 from a potential $137,500.

■ Sunday 26th
Hampton Rhodes Coliseum *Hampton Rhodes, VA*

■ Monday 27th
Saratoga Arts Festival *Saratoga Springs, NY*

■ Thursday 30th
Merriweather Post Pavillion *Columbia, MD*
The show is professionally recorded by the group for possible use on their revised live album.

■ Friday 31st
Syria Mosque *Pittsburgh, PA*
This show too is recorded by the group for potential use on the coming live album.

September

■ Saturday 1st
Century Theater *Buffalo, NY*
Tonight's performance is yet another of those on this tour that is professionally recorded by the group for possible use on their revised live album. Among the songs taped are 'Darlin'', 'Barbara Ann', 'Fun Fun Fun' and 'Jumpin' Jack Flash'.

■ Sunday 2nd
Massey Hall *Toronto, ON, Canada* two shows
Both shows tonight are sell-outs, and a portion is recorded by the group for potential inclusion on their forthcoming live album.

■ Monday 3rd
Pine Knob Musical Theater Independence Township *Detroit, MI*
The last night of the gruelling tour, much of which has been recorded. The group takes a five-week break before starting another round of concert appearances, but first they need to take care of some other important matters.

October

In a rare act of unity, the group fires Jack Rieley as their manager. Rieley has performed the role for three years. He receives news of the termination of his employment from Carl who again visits Rieley at his home in The Netherlands.

Rieley tells BBC Radio-1 shortly after the event: "I pulled away from The Beach Boys' organisation because of terribly complex, complicated and horribly distasteful situations involving aspects of their business and financial management. It was horrible and it put a terrible amount of pressure on me in an area that I never thought I would be involved in. What I think they need now is trust. They need to get someone in there now who has enough faith in The Beach Boys and has enough creativity in him to go and do something about it. They are in another one of those mini strange points in their career where they are gonna need another big boost." Steve Love, Mike's brother and the band's assistant manager, takes over more of the management duties.

November

'Little Saint Nick' / 'The Lords Prayer' single released in the UK. In effect it is a re-release in Britain of a 1963 US-only single.

■ Monday 12th
Warner Bros today prepares a series of radio spots for the forthcoming Beach Boys live album.

TOUR STARTS US West, Midwest, South, East (Nov 14th-Dec 29th)

■ Wednesday 14th
Convention Center Complex *Denver, CO*
Portions of this concert are shot on 16mm film for Dennis's archive.

■ Thursday 15th
Celebrity Theatre *Phoenix, AZ*

■ Friday 16th
Anaheim Convention Center *Anaheim, CA* 7:30pm, with Three Man Army
Portions of this concert are shot on 16mm film for Dennis's archive.

■ Saturday 17th – Sunday 18th
Winterland Arena *San Francisco, CA* with Commander Cody & His Lost Planet Airmen, Three Man Army

■ Monday 19th
The Beach Boys In Concert double-album released in the US and (around this time) in the UK. Originally rejected by Warners as a single LP, the album will peak in the US charts at number 25, easily the best performance of a Warner Beach Boys release so far, and becomes the group's first gold album for the label. Surprisingly, it fails to dent the UK listings. It is their third authorised live album (and will be their last). The content is heavily weighted towards older songs, but the package serves as a document of The Beach Boys' impressive live powers at this time, perfectly capturing excellent performances from the US in November 1972 and in April, August and September this year. Dennis's friend Ed Roach shoots a TV ad for the album with footage of the band in concert.

1973

The Beach Boys In Concert album

A1 'Sail On Sailor' (B. WILSON / T. ALMER / V.D. PARKS / J. RIELEY / R. KENNEDY)
A2 'Sloop John B' (TRAD ARR B. WILSON)
A3 'The Trader' (C. WILSON / J. RIELEY)
A4 'You Still Believe In Me' (B. WILSON / T. ASHER)
A5 'California Girls' (B. WILSON / M. LOVE)
A6 'Darlin'' (B. WILSON / M. LOVE)
B1 'Marcella' (C. WILSON / T. ALMER / J. RIELEY)
B2 'Caroline No' (B. WILSON / T. ASHER)
B3 'Leavin' This Town' (R. FATAAR / C. WILSON / B. CHAPLIN / M. LOVE)
B4 'Heroes And Villains' (B. WILSON / V.D. PARKS)
C1 'Funky Pretty' (B. WILSON / M. LOVE / J. RIELEY)
C2 'Let The Wind Blow' (B. WILSON / M. LOVE)
C3 'Help Me Rhonda' (B. WILSON / M. LOVE)
C4 'Surfer Girl' (B. WILSON)
C5 'Wouldn't It Be Nice' (B. WILSON / T. ASHER)
D1 'We Got Love' (R. FATAAR / B. CHAPLIN / M. LOVE)
D2 'Don't Worry Baby' (B. WILSON / R. CHRISTIAN)
D3 'Surfin' USA' (C. BERRY)
D4 'Good Vibrations' (B. WILSON / M. LOVE)
D5 'Fun Fun Fun' (B. WILSON / M. LOVE)

US release November 19th 1973 (Brother/Reprise 2MS 6484).
UK release November 1973 (Reprise K84001).
Chart high US number 25; UK none.

■ **Tuesday 20th**
North Gym, Chicago State College *Chicago, IL* with Three Man Army

■ **Wednesday 21st**
Memorial Auditorium *Sacramento, CA* 7:30pm

■ **Friday 30th**
Louisiana State University *Baton Rouge, LA*

December

■ **Saturday 1st**
Ellis Auditorium *Memphis, TN*

■ **Sunday 2nd**
Civic Auditorium *Knoxville, TN*

■ **Monday 3rd**
Kiel Auditorium *St. Louis, MO*

■ **Wednesday 5th**
Dane County Memorial Coliseum *Madison, WI* with New Riders Of The Purple Sage

■ **Thursday 6th**
Eastern Illinois University *Charleston, IL*

■ **Friday 7th**
Music Hall *Cleveland, OH*

■ **Saturday 8th**
Music Hall *Boston, MA*

■ **Sunday 9th**
University Of Rhode Island *Kingston, RI*

■ **Monday 10th**
University Of New Hampshire *Durham, NH*

■ **Wednesday 12th**
DAR Constitution Hall *Washington, DC*

■ **Thursday 13th**
Newark State College Theater For The Performing Arts *Union, NJ* two shows, with Henry Gross

■ **Friday 14th**
The Spectrum *Philadelphia, PA*

■ **Sunday 16th**
Seton Hall University *South Orange, NJ*

■ **Tuesday 18th**
Brooklyn College *Brooklyn, NY*

■ **Wednesday 19th**
Madison Square Garden *New York, NY*
Last night of the tour. Bruce Johnston joins the group on-stage for their encore.
Set-list 'Happy Birthday Salute', 'Wouldn't It Be Nice', 'Sail On Sailor', 'The Trader', 'Leavin' This Town', 'Long Promised Road', 'California Girls', 'Funky Pretty', 'Marcella', 'Surfer Girl', 'Darlin'', 'Caroline No', 'We Got Love', 'Sloop John B', 'Help Me Rhonda', 'Surfin' USA', 'Good Vibrations', 'Little Saint Nick', 'Barbara Ann', 'I Get Around', 'Don't Worry Baby', 'Fun Fun Fun'.
• Following the Madison Square Garden concert, The Beach Boys lose another member. Blondie Chaplin quits after a backstage fight with the group's new manager, Steve Love. Although Love has been in post for less than two months, bad feeling has grown between Steve and Blondie almost from the time they met. Blondie says later: "I didn't show up for the next couple of gigs. I didn't want to be treated that way so I just said 'screw it'." When told about the fight, Carl is busy taking care of his sick four-year-old son, Jonah, who is with him at the gig. Blondie, who seems to have the classic 'musical differences' with the rest of the group, does not return to The Beach Boys.

■ **Saturday 29th**
Swing Auditorium *San Bernardino, CA*
The group performs in California, now permanently without Chaplin.

■ **Monday 31st**
Long Beach Arena *Long Beach, CA*
The Beach Boys give their final concert performance of 1973, a New Year's Eve show in their home state.
• After several years in the American musical wilderness the group is set to return to major prominence in their homeland – but this will come at a price. Their days of forward-thinking music are about to come to an end.

1974

Chicago's producer/manager James Guercio joins the group as occasional stage bassist and part-time manager ... *Endless Summer* compilation double-album released by Capitol, becoming a great success and introducing many new fans to the group's rich seam of past successes ... a tour is done with the group supporting Crosby Stills Nash & Young ... attempts to record a new studio album are abandoned ... Ricky Fataar leaves the group and Dennis returns to the live band's drum stool ... 'Child Of Winter' single released, the first new Beach Boys material on record for nearly two years.

Brian hoists a gold disc for this year's *Endless Summer* compilation just clear of the water.

1974

January

With Blondie Chaplin now departed from the group, James William Guercio joins The Beach Boys as occasional bass player on-stage and part-time manager.

Guercio is producer and manager of Chicago and Blood Sweat & Tears, which takes up a good deal of his time, and owner of the Caribou Ranch studio in Nederland, Colorado.

■ Tuesday 29th
RECORDING probably Brother studio *Santa Monica, CA*. Ricky holds a recording session today for a couple of songs, including **'Share Your Love'**, which will remain unreleased.

February

TOUR STARTS US West (Feb 18th-Mar 16th)

■ Monday 18th
The Gymnasium, Airforce Academy Colorado Springs, CO
with Jim Stafford
The group today begins a low-key 13-date trek, starting with this evening's concert in Colorado and then moving through some undocumented concerts that take place at a number of venues until March 16th.

■ Tuesday 19th
Colorado State University *Ft. Collins, CO*
A further date takes place this evening in Colorado, this one at a university venue.

March

■ Saturday 2nd
RECORDING probably Brother studio *Santa Monica, CA*. Brian records run-throughs of **'Shortenin' Bread'**, **'Clangin''** – which will develop into 'Ding Dang' – and the *Carl & The Passions* track **'Marcella'**.

■ Tuesday 5th
RECORDING probably Brother studio *Santa Monica, CA*. Carl experiments today with a song he is working on that for now consists simply of guitar, drum-machine and a hummed melody, logged as **'Guitar Demo'**.

■ Saturday 16th
Pacific Lutheran University *Tacoma, WA* with Jim Stafford
The Beach Boys' latest concert tour ends – though it's probable that the group played other dates in the Pacific Northwest during this period. Evidence of this comes in the form of film in Dennis's archive dated later this month that includes footage shot in Vancouver and Seattle.
Set-list 'Wouldn't It Be Nice', 'The Trader', 'Long Promised Road', 'California Girls', 'Funky Pretty', 'California Saga: California', 'Marcella', 'Surfer Girl', 'Darlin'', 'Little Deuce Coupe', 'Caroline No', 'God Only Knows', 'We Got Love', 'Sloop John B', 'Help Me Rhonda', 'Surfin' USA', 'Good Vibrations'.

April

■ Monday 1st
RECORDING probably Brother studio *Santa Monica, CA*. Carl holds a tracking session for a piece provisionally titled **'Carl's Moog Riff'**. This is the second version of this piece that he has recorded, though nothing further is known about the composition. Ricky is also involved in today's session.

■ Thursday 4th
Michigan State University *Lansing, MI*
Just three weeks after concluding their last tour, the group performs a concert in Michigan in preparation for their next, which will kick off on the 9th.
• In Los Angeles, former Beatle Paul McCartney and his wife Linda pay a visit to Brian at his Bel Air home. The McCartneys bang on his door for over an hour but Wilson refuses to let them in. Paul and Linda know he is there because they can hear him inside, crying quietly to himself. With no alternative, the McCartneys leave the residence and head on their way.

TOUR STARTS US South, East, Midwest, West (Apr 9th-25th)

■ Tuesday 9th
University Of Mississippi *Oxford, MS*
The group begins a 16-day excursion, and announce that they anticipate playing 80 concerts this year, sometimes two shows a day. For this purpose they have just purchased a second sound system and lights.

■ Wednesday 10th
Municipal Auditorium *New Orleans, LA*

■ Thursday 11th
Municipal Auditorium *Atlanta, GA* matinee
Auburn College Fieldhouse *Auburn, AL* evening
The afternoon show of this pair of appearances grosses $27,083 from a potential $31,000.

■ Friday 12th
Curtis Hixon Convention Hall *Tampa, FL*

■ Saturday 13th
Hollywood Sportatorium *Hollywood, FL* 8:30pm

■ Sunday 14th
Orlando Sports Stadium *Orlando, FL*
Set-list 'Wouldn't It Be Nice', 'Darlin'', 'Little Deuce Coupe', 'The Trader', 'Long Promised Road', 'Surfer Girl', 'Funky Pretty', 'California Saga: California', 'Marcella', 'God Only Knows', 'We Got Love', 'Don't Talk (Put Your Head On My Shoulder)', 'Heroes And Villains', 'Surf's Up', 'Don't Worry Baby', 'Sloop John B', 'Help Me Rhonda', 'Surfin' USA', 'Good Vibrations', 'California Girls', 'Barbara Ann', 'I Get Around', 'Fun Fun Fun' (last four as encores).

■ Monday 15th
Edinboro State University *Edinboro, PA*

■ Tuesday 16th
University of Scranton *Scranton, PA*

The live band in Joliet, Illinois, on May 19th: (left to right) Al, Mike, Carl, Ricky and Dennis.

■ **Wednesday 17th**
Pittsburgh Civic Arena *Pittsburgh, PA*

■ **Thursday 18th**
University of West Virginia Coliseum *Morgantown, WV*

■ **Friday 19th**
St John's Arena, Ohio State University *Columbus, OH*
8:30pm, with Steely Dan; tickets $4 & $5

■ **Saturday 20th**
Calvin College *Grand Rapids, MI* matinee
University of Notre Dame, Convocation Center *Notre Dame, IN* evening

■ **Sunday 21st**
Bedley Auditorium, Youngstown State College *Youngstown, OH* matinee
Slippery Rock State College *Slippery Rock, PA* evening

■ **Tuesday 23rd**
University of Michigan *Ann Arbor, MI*

■ **Thursday 25th**
Memorial Auditorium *Sacramento, CA*
The last night of the current tour.

■ **Monday 29th**
RECORDING probably Brother studio *Santa Monica, CA*. The group is recorded rehearsing an early version of Brian's **'Good Timin''** as well as a jam with Ricky.

May

'All Summer Long' / 'Surfin' Safari' single released in the UK. EMI Records issues this single coupling two of the group's old recordings in an attempt to capitalise on the fact that several Beach Boys songs are featured in the hit movie *American Graffiti*. However, the 45 fails to make the chart.

■ **Wednesday 1st**
Still in the UK, the BBC2 *The Old Grey Whistle Test* broadcasts (between 11:38 and 00:11am) an interview with Carl, conducted by Bob Harris in California in February.

■ **Thursday 2nd**
Cedar Point *Sandusky, OH*
Just a week after concluding their latest jaunt, The Beach Boys perform a one-off show in Ohio as a prelude to their next US tour, scheduled to begin on the 11th.

TOUR STARTS US Midwest (May 11th-19th)

■ **Saturday 11th**
Millett Hall, Miami University *Oxford, OH*
Set-list 'Wouldn't It Be Nice', 'Darlin'', 'Little Deuce Coupe', 'The Trader', 'Long Promised Road', 'Surfer Girl', 'Funky Pretty', 'California Saga', 'Marcella', 'Sail On Sailor', 'Caroline No', 'Heroes And Villains', 'Surf's Up', 'We Got Love', 'Sloop John B', 'Help Me Rhonda', 'I Get Around', 'Good Vibrations', 'California Girls',

'Barbara Ann', 'Surfin' USA', 'Fun Fun Fun'.
• In Britain, BBC Radio-1 begins broadcasting a six-part series entitled *The Beach Boys Story* written and produced by Jeff Griffin and narrated by DJ and *Old Grey Whistle Test* presenter Bob Harris. The series features exclusive interviews with members of the group and their associates carried out by Harris mostly in California between February 10th and 18th this year. Locations for the recordings included Carl's home in Coldwater Canyon and the group's recording studio in Santa Monica. Dennis was interviewed while taking a shower at a Beach Boys gig in Colorado on the 18th, while a meeting with Brian and Marilyn at their Bel Air home proved fruitless for interview material.

■ **Monday 13th**
The 1966 *Pet Sounds* album is reissued in the US, on the Brother-Reprise label.

■ **Tuesday 14th**
Western Illinois University *Macomb, IL*

■ **Wednesday 15th**
Municipal Auditorium *Kansas City, MO* 8:00pm

■ **Saturday 18th**
Michigan State University *Lansing, MI*

■ **Sunday 19th**
Joliet Memorial Stadium *Joliet, IL* with Bachman Turner Overdrive
Trouble erupts following the group's performance as fighting breaks out among the 3,000-plus crowd.

June

■ **Saturday 8th**
Alameda County Coliseum *Oakland, CA* with The Grateful Dead, Three Man Army
The group begins a run of four one-offs at this Bill Graham-promoted *Day On The Green*.

■ **Sunday 9th**
RECORDING probably Brother studio *Santa Monica, CA*. Brian records a version of his **'Ding Dang'**. Also taped at this session is a song called **'Is It Really Love'**, though it is unclear if there is any Beach Boy involvement.
Cape Cod Coliseum *South Yarmouth, MA*
A further live date this evening in the series of one-offs.

■ **Thursday 13th**
Cow Palace *San Francisco, CA*

■ **Friday 14th**
Nassau Coliseum *Uniondale, NY*
The last of four one-offs, this concert includes some songs played infrequently live: 'California Saga: California', 'All This Is That' and 'Feel Flows'. A local newspaper reporter writes: "An awesome show. The band was in fine shape and the crowd was totally into it. In my opinion this was the best Beach Boys concert ever!" Singer-songwriter Elton John joins the group on stage, singing and performing on two songs during the encore

and joined on one by Paul Simon. The show is broadcast live on FM radio.

Set-list 'Wouldn't It Be Nice', 'Sail On Sailor', 'Funky Pretty', 'Marcella', 'California Saga: California', 'We Got Love', 'Little Deuce Coupe', 'The Trader', 'All This Is That', 'Feel Flows', 'Surfer Girl', 'God Only Knows', 'Heroes And Villains', 'Don't Worry Baby', 'Sloop John B', 'Help Me Rhonda' (vocal by Dennis), 'I Get Around', 'Good Vibrations', 'California Girls' (encore), 'Barbara Ann' (encore, with Elton John and Paul Simon), 'Surfin' USA' (encore, with Elton John), 'Fun Fun Fun' (encore).

■ Sunday 23rd
Cleveland Municipal Stadium *Cleveland, OH* with REO Speedwagon, Lynyrd Skynyrd, Joe Walsh (co-headliners)

■ Monday 24th
Endless Summer compilation double-album released in the US. Five years after the group left the label, Capitol Records issues this compilation with a title conceived by Mike and a selection of songs covering the years from 1962 to 1965. It will be an enormously successful record, soon selling more than a million copies and becoming a catalyst that changes the career of the group. In a matter of weeks, The Beach Boys are back once again as the biggest act in America. Their legacy and timeless back-catalogue launches them as superheroes to a new generation.

Heavily advertised on TV and radio, *Endless Summer* becomes the US record phenomenon of the year and, backed by the group's acclaimed live show, it reaches the top spot in the US charts, remaining on the listings for a remarkable three years. It is only their second American chart-topping album; the other was the 1964 *Concert* LP. Carl recalls later: "There was a whole new generation of fans out there and some of them weren't even as old as the songs themselves. Our concerts were selling out and we were singing and playing better than ever."

■ Thursday 27th
In a report on the release of *Endless Summer*, NBC News in the US airs a film of Mike Love performing 'California Girls' alongside Charles Lloyd (on flute) and John McLaughlin (acoustic guitar).

July

Wild Honey & *20/20* double-album released in the US. Doubtless riding on the success of *Endless Summer*, Warner's set of two reissued LPs will peak in the American charts at a respectable number 50.

'Surfin' USA' / **'The Warmth Of The Sun'** single released in the US. Not to be outdone, Capitol reissues 'Surfin' USA', which reaches number 36, easily outclassing any of the Warners singles released since the group signed to the label in late 1969.

• Revelling in The Beach Boys' sudden resurgence in popularity, Dennis buys a 50-foot sailing boat, *The Harmony*. Besides using it to cruise the Californian waters, he puts it into service as a temporary home when it is harboured at Marina Del Ray in Los Angeles. Dennis is proud of his Japanese vessel and lavishes thousands of dollars on refurbishment, customising it to accommodate a drum kit, an electric organ and an impressive recording facility. The boat also serves as an escape for Dennis when he wishes to retreat from the discord within The Beach Boys' organisation, and he will regularly sail up the Baja peninsula in Mexico. *The Harmony* will serve as a base for Dennis until 1981.

■ Saturday 6th
The group was due to appear third on the bill tonight at the Los Angeles Coliseum. The scrapped show promoted by Bill Graham was also due to feature The Allman Brothers Band and The Marshall Tucker Band. The Beach Boys' new tour will now kick off on the 9th.

■ Tuesday 9th
Seattle Coliseum *Seattle, WA* with Crosby Stills Nash & Young (headliner), Jesse Colin Young

Three days later than anticipated, tonight's performance marks the first night of a nine-show CSNY reunion tour with The Beach Boys as the main support act.

CSNY's great get-together is exhaustively touted around the States as "the rock comeback of the year", but for The Beach Boys the concerts come at a strange time.

Just as America is rediscovering the group through the immense success of *Endless Summer*, the group, now quite capable of headlining and selling a big tour of their own, find themselves fulfilling this commitment to play second fiddle to CSNY. The Beach Boys' appearance on the tour receives virtually no press recognition.

■ Thursday 11th
RECORDING probably Brother studio *Santa Monica, CA*. The group and several other friends record a birthday greeting for their fellow musician Roger McGuinn.

■ Friday 19th
Harry S. Truman Sports Complex (Royals Stadium) *Kansas City, MO* with Crosby Stills Nash & Young (headliner), Jesse Colin Young

■ Sunday 21st
County Stadium (Milwaukee Baseball Stadium) *Milwaukee, WI* with Crosby Stills Nash & Young (headliner), Jesse Colin Young
The audience tonight is a massive 52,000.

■ Monday 22nd
Civic Center Arena *St Paul, MN* with Crosby Stills Nash & Young (headliner), Jesse Colin Young

■ Tuesday 23rd
Civic Center Coliseum *Minneapolis, MN* with Crosby Stills Nash & Young (headliner), Jesse Colin Young

■ Thursday 25th
Red Rocks Amphitheater *Denver, CO* with Crosby Stills Nash & Young (headliner), Jesse Colin Young

■ Saturday 27th
'Don't Let The Sun Go Down On Me' single by Elton John, featuring backing vocals by Carl and former Beach Boy Bruce Johnston, peaks at number 2 in the US chart.

■ Sunday 28th
Jeppesen Stadium *Houston, TX* with Crosby Stills Nash & Young (headliner), Jesse Colin Young

■ Wednesday 31st
Texas Stadium *Dallas, TX* with Crosby Stills Nash & Young (headliner), Jesse Colin Young

August

'California Saga: California' / 'Sail On Sailor' / 'Marcella' / 'I'm The Pied Piper' EP released in the UK. Early copies of this Reprise release come in a special picture bag.

• Who drummer Keith Moon begins work this month on his first solo album at the Record Plant studio in Los Angeles. The disc is to be called *Two Sides Of The Moon* with production by former Beatles roadie Mal Evans. Erstwhile Beach Boy Bruce Johnston is among the all-star array of musical celebrities present at the intermittent sessions that continue over a four-month period. Brian is also in attendance, albeit very briefly, as he makes a rare excursion from the seclusion of his bedroom to play the Record Plant's recently acquired pipe organ. Neither Bruce nor Brian's musical contributions will feature on the completed disc. Among the songs recorded for the album is 'Don't Worry Baby', Moon's all-time favourite Beach Boys track.

■ Saturday 3rd

A *Summer Jam West* show due to take place today at the Ontario Motor Speedway Stadium in Los Angeles – with Crosby Stills Nash & Young, The Beach Boys, Joe Walsh & Barnstorm, Jesse Colin Young, and The Band – is cancelled. Excessive heat, rumours of lagging ticket sales, and CSNY's apparent reluctance to play before crowds larger than about 80,000 are variously offered in explanation. The Beach Boys will not perform on the same bill with Crosby Stills Nash & Young again until September 8th.

■ Sunday 11th

RECORDING probably Brother studio *Santa Monica, CA*. Ricky holds a tracking (backing instruments) session for **'Foolin''**, later overdubbing a lead vocal. Ricky makes a further recording at the session, simply logged as **'Drum Song'**.

TOUR STARTS North America (Aug 17th-Sep 3rd)

■ Saturday 17th

Chicago Stadium *Chicago, IL*
The group returns to headlining concert performances.

■ Wednesday 21st

Warner Bros prepares masters for another Beach Boys reissue single, coupling 'I Can Hear Music' with 'Let The Wind Blow'.

■ Friday 23rd

Roosevelt Stadium *Jersey City, NJ* 8:00pm, with The Eagles

■ Saturday 24th

Capital Center *Largo, MD* 8:00pm

■ Wednesday 28th

Concert Bowl, Maple Leaf Gardens *Toronto, ON, Canada*

■ Thursday 29th

Ohio State Fair *Columbus, OH* 6:30 & 9:00pm
Set-list (6:30) 'Wouldn't It Be Nice', 'California: California Saga', 'Marcella', 'We Got Love', 'Do It Again', 'I Can Hear Music', 'Little Deuce Coupe', 'Long Promised Road', 'Sail On Sailor', 'Feel Flows', 'All This Is That', 'Sloop John B', 'Surfer Girl', 'Help Me Rhonda', 'I Get Around', 'Fun Fun Fun', 'Good Vibrations', 'California Girls', 'Barbara Ann', 'Surfin' USA'.

Set-list (9:00) 'Wouldn't It Be Nice', 'California Saga: California', 'Marcella', 'We Got Love', 'Do It Again', 'I Can Hear Music', 'Little Deuce Coupe', 'Long Promised Road', 'Sail On Sailor', 'The Trader', 'Feel Flows', 'All This Is That', 'Sloop John B', 'Surfer Girl', 'Heroes And Villains', 'Help Me Rhonda', 'I Get Around', 'Fun Fun Fun', 'Good Vibrations', 'California Girls', 'Barbara Ann', 'Surfin' USA'.

■ Saturday 31st

Pocono International Raceway *Long Pond, PA* with The Allman Brothers, Edgar Winter

September

■ Sunday 1st

Assembly Hall, Indiana University *Bloomington, IN* with The Eagles, Kansas

■ Tuesday 3rd

Pine Knob Musical Theater Independence Township, Detroit, MI
Last night of the current tour.

■ Sunday 8th

Roosevelt Raceway *Westbury, NY* with Crosby Stills Nash & Young (headliner), Joni Mitchell, Jesse Colin Young
Another Bill Graham concert and the final night of the CSNY reunion tour, a ten-hour four-act open-air extravaganza attended by 80,000 music fans and the largest rock concert of the summer in New York.

The *New York Times* reports: "Mike Love of The Beach Boys said that his group enjoyed outdoor concerts more than the indoor variety. 'We're an outdoor kind of a group,' Mr Love said. 'Outdoors brings good vibrations.' All four acts are associated with California rock and it's post-1960s image of inner peace and outer pleasures – the perfect musical complement for a balmy late summer day like today. Certainly Mr Love's 'good vibrations' seemed plentifully in evidence among the crowd. People had begun to fill up the Raceway early in the morning, and by late this morning were packed tightly into the muddy mid-field area. Bill Graham, the San Francisco promoter who is one of the producers of the event, said that 'the rain fouled up the logistics of our preparations, but it's beautiful today, and that's what counts'. Chief Edward F Curran of the Nassau County Police reported no serious incidents as of late afternoon today. 'It's been a very well-behaved, orderly crowd,' he said."

Following a two-month lay off, The Beach Boys will return to live performances on November 2nd.

■ Thursday 19th

RECORDING probably Brother studio *Santa Monica, CA*. Carl records a demo session, the rough tape featuring him humming a melody over tracks of piano and Moog and ARP synthesisers.

October

Friends & Smiley Smile double-album released in the US. The set of two reissued LPs will peak in the American charts at number 125.
• Al, Carl and Dennis contribute backing vocals to Chicago's Top 20 hit single 'Wishing You Were Here'.

Dennis back on drums at last, pictured here on-stage in December behind Al, Mike and Carl.

■ Early part of October

RECORDING Caribou Ranch studio *Nederland, CO*; Brother studio *Santa Monica, CA*. Since the release of *Holland* 21 months ago, new studio recordings by the group have been virtually non-existent. Now, after continuous cajoling from James Guercio, The Beach Boys agree that the time is right to record again. Initially working at Guercio's Caribou Ranch in Colorado the group, including Brian, attempts to record a new studio album. But only two songs are recorded, one of which is **'The Battle Hymn Of The Republic'**, an American patriotic anthem dating from the Civil War. Work on this piece will resume on November 5th.

Recordings in Colorado are halted when Brian insists on returning to his home in Bel Air. Later, a fire that destroys the Colorado studio also destroys the tapes of these sessions, with the exception of those taken to the group's Brother studio in Santa Monica for further work (see November 5th). Another song taped at the Caribou sessions that survives is a Brian song, **'Hard Times'** with a melody based on his 'Ding Dang'. Also, it is believed that more than two songs are taped at these sessions. Mike tells *Melody Maker* that these include 'Our Life Our Love Our Land' and 'Don't Let Me Go'.

■ Saturday 5th

Endless Summer, the Capitol compilation double-album, tops the US album charts. It will reside in the listings for a total of 155 weeks.

November

Drummer Ricky Fataar gives notice of his decision to leave The Beach Boys and join Joe Walsh's group, Barnstorm. Ricky will continue to appear on-stage with the group until the middle of December. He tells *NME*: "Joe Walsh offered me a gig to go play with him and it just seemed an appropriate time to do it. I called up Carl … and said, 'I want to leave the band and go play with Joe Walsh,' and that's what I did."

Endless Summer compilation double-album released in the UK.

■ Friday 1st

TV ABC Television Studios *New York, NY*. ABC *Chicago's New Year's Rockin' Eve* live performance 'Surfer Girl', 'Darlin'', 'Wishing You Were Here' broadcast December 31st 11:30pm-1:00am. The Beach Boys are special guests on this World Wide Special Presentation hosted by US rock group Chicago. 'Darlin'' is performed backed by Chicago's horn section, and 'Wishing You Were Here' with backing vocals from Chicago (Al, Carl and Dennis recently contributed backing vocals to this Top 20 hit single). The performance today by the two groups together triggers an idea for a joint tour (see May 2nd 1975).

■ Saturday 2nd
Paramount Northwest Theater *Seattle, WA*

■ Tuesday 5th

RECORDING Brother studio *Santa Monica, CA*. Hoping to salvage the work carried out in Colorado last month, the group, with Brian, reconvene in their own studio for another attempt at **'The Battle Hymn Of The Republic'**. They go on to make tracking recordings for **'Child Of Winter (Christmas Song)'**, **'Here Comes Santa Claus'**, and **'Good Timing'**. The group also tracks an early version of **'It's OK'** (to which they will not return until March 1976). Neither the group nor Warners are happy with the meagre results and the album project is abandoned.

TOUR STARTS US North America (Nov 14th-Dec 31st)

■ Thursday 14th – Friday 15th
The Spectrum *Philadelphia, PA*

Ricky Fataar and a returning Dennis will alternate on the drummer's stool through the first month of this six-week tour. Throughout the tour the musicians backing The Beach Boys – Mike, Carl, Dennis, Ricky and Al – include Bobby Figueroa (drums), Carlos Munoz (keyboards), Ron Altbach (keyboards) and Jim Guercio (bass), and five years after declining the first offer, Billy Hinsche becomes a full-time member of The Beach Boys, playing guitar.

Set-list (14th) 'Marcella', 'I Can Hear Music', 'Little Deuce Coupe',

'Do It Again', 'The Warmth Of The Sun', 'California Saga: California', 'Sail On Sailor' (Billy Hinsche on lead vocal), 'All This Is That', 'Feel Flows', 'Darlin'', 'Heroes And Villains', 'Surfer Girl', 'Catch A Wave', 'I'm Waiting For The Day' (Billy Hinsche on lead), 'God Only Knows', 'Don't Worry Baby', 'Sloop John B', 'Wouldn't It Be Nice', 'I Get Around', 'Good Vibrations', 'Help Me Rhonda', 'California Girls', 'Barbara Ann', 'Fun Fun Fun' (last three as encores).

■ Monday 18th
RECORDING Brother studio *Santa Monica, CA*. During a break from their current tour, and with Brian back in the producer's chair, The Beach Boys overdub vocals onto **'Child Of Winter (Christmas Song)'** tracked on November 5th.

They consider it as a salvageable song from the scrapped album. It features lead vocals by Brian and Mike. The session becomes a Wilson family affair as Carl adds guitar, Dennis drums and Brian all the other instruments, along with Brian's daughters Carnie and Wendy on sleigh bells. The song will be issued as a single in the US on December 23rd.

■ Wednesday 20th
Vermont Memorial Hall *Burlington, VT*
• Reprise prepares masters for the next Beach Boys single, coupling 'Child Of Winter' with 'Susie Cincinnati'. However, the A-side will still be late for the Christmas and new-year holiday season.

■ Thursday 21st
Madison Square Garden *New York, NY*
Former Byrds frontman Roger McGuinn joins the group on-stage playing guitar.

■ Friday 22nd
Baltimore Civic Center *Baltimore, MD*
Another date with Dennis and Ricky alternating as Beach Boy drummer.
Set-list 'I Can Hear Music', 'Marcella', 'Little Deuce Coupe', 'Do It Again', 'The Warmth Of The Sun', 'California Saga: California', 'Sail On Sailor' (Billy Hinsche on lead), 'All This Is That', 'Feel Flows', 'Surfer Girl', 'Heroes And Villains', 'Darlin'', 'Catch A Wave', 'I'm Waiting For The Day' (Billy Hinsche on lead), 'God Only Knows', 'Don't Worry Baby', 'Sloop John B', 'Wouldn't It Be Nice', 'I Get Around', 'Good Vibrations', 'In My Room', 'Help Me Rhonda', 'California Girls', 'Barbara Ann', 'Surfin' USA', ' Fun Fun Fun' (last four as encores).

■ Saturday 23rd
Music Hall *Boston, MA*
• In the UK, *Melody Maker* publishes an interview with former Beach Boy Bruce Johnston, currently in London to promote his new band California Music and his new record label, Equinox, that he runs with long-time friend Terry Melcher.

The interview by Chris Charlesworth took place last week at London's Inn On The Park hotel.

"No, I'm not with The Beach Boys any more," Bruce tells Charlesworth. "I didn't want to go on singing oldies for the rest of my life. ... Once in a while I may go out and do a show with The Beach Boys. I really miss performing live. But I know I couldn't do that all the time because I am getting more and more business orientated, more than the rest of that group. I get too frustrated being [considered as] a fifth of something – which was what I was with The Beach Boys."

■ Wednesday 27th
Warner Bros prepares yet another Beach Boys reissue single, this time by coupling the old recording 'Good Vibrations' with 'Susie Cincinnati'. But for reaons unknown the proposed record never gets past the lacquer stage of mastering and its release is officially cancelled in March 1975.

December

■ Thursday 5th
Convention Center Complex *Denver, CO*

■ Friday 6th
Terrace Ballroom *Salt Lake City, UT*

■ Saturday 7th
Boise County Fairgrounds *Boise, ID*

■ Monday 9th
Spokane Coliseum *Spokane, WA*

■ Tuesday 10th
Seattle Center Arena *Seattle, WA*

■ Friday 13th
Memorial Coliseum *Portland, OR*

■ Saturday 14th
Pacific Coliseum *Vancouver, BC, Canada*

■ Wednesday 18th
Warner Theater *Fresno, CA*
Tonight's performance marks Ricky Fataar's last concert appearance with The Beach Boys.

■ Thursday 19th
Bakersfield Civic Center *Bakersfield, CA*
With Ricky no longer a part of the group, tonight's is the first show in three years where Dennis is regarded as the group's official drummer.

American show-business reporter Elliott Cahn writes in *Melody Maker*: "Riding the crest of their enormous comeback wave, The Beach Boys delighted a Bakersfield Civic Center audience with a powerful 90-minute presentation of a decade of their hits. ... Carl Wilson has assumed all the lead guitar-playing duties, which he performs admirably. The normally dignified Carl was down on his knees for the solo to 'Help Me Rhonda', much to the delight of all.

"Dennis Wilson returned to the drums tonight. Carl admitted to having been so nervous for his brother on his first night back at the drums that his legs were shaking for most of the set.

"At Bakersfield, their harmonies were full and, for most of the time, perfectly in tune," Cahn continues, "though there was a scattering of ragged moments. I've heard them better, especially Al Jardine, who sounded strained and hoarse at times. A better sound engineer would certainly have helped, as the balance was badly off on several songs.

"Their set ended with 'Good Vibrations' and, after a three-minute stomping and screaming ovation, The Beach Boys returned with an encore of 'In My Room', 'Help Me Rhonda', 'California Girls', 'Surfin' USA', 'Barbara Ann' and 'Fun Fun Fun'. When the

---

Child Of Winter single

A 'Child Of Winter (Christmas Song)' (B. WILSON / S. KALINICH)
B 'Susie Cincinatti' (A. JARDINE)

US release December 23rd 1974 (Brother/Reprise 1321).
Chart high US none.

---

house lights went up, only a few die-hards shouted for more. What could you possibly do to follow that? Like most Beach Boys audiences, this one went home smiling."
• Following tonight's successful show, Mike and Al put a phone call through to erstwhile Beach Boy Bruce Johnston, who is about to embark on another promotional visit to London, England. Bruce recalls on British TV: "I spoke to Mike before I flew over and they said, 'Bruce, you won't believe it. We've just made $60,000 playing one concert.' It was the most money that the group had ever made in a night playing in America."

■ Friday 20th
San Francisco Civic Center, Civic Auditorium *San Francisco, CA*

■ Saturday 21st
National Exhibition Hall *Sacramento, CA* two shows
The attendance tonight breaks The Beatles' record set at the venue in 1964. Each concert attracts a sell-out 17,500 crowd, and 5,000 fans have to be turned away.

■ Sunday 22nd
Earl Warren Community Convention Center *Santa Barbara, CA*

■ Monday 23rd
'**Child Of Winter**' / '**Susie Cincinnati**' single released in the US. It features the first new Beach Boys material issued on record for nearly two years, and an A-side that bears Brian's first Beach Boys production credit for some seven years. But the 45 fails to chart – presumably no great surprise to the record company as it is released just two days before Christmas and, it is rumoured, only 5,000 copies are pressed and distribution is poor. This single is notable as the only Beach Boys release between the 1973 *Holland* album and the *15 Big Ones* album and 'Rock'n'Roll Music' single in summer '76. (Although once intended for the group's 1977 Christmas LP, 'Child Of Winter' remains unreleased on album until the 1998 *Ultimate Christmas* CD.)
• In an end-of-year poll *Rolling Stone* magazine makes The Beach Boys 'Band Of The Year', entirely on the strength of their immensely popular live show.

■ Friday 27th
The LA Forum *Los Angeles, CA* 8:00pm, with Honk
TV BBC TV Centre, Studio B *west London*. BBC-2 *The Old Grey Whistle Test* live performance (Bruce) 'Disney Girls (1957)' broadcast January 24th 1975 8:10-9:00pm. Bruce's second UK promotional tour of the year wraps up with an interview with *Whistle Test* host bob Harris, after which Bruce plays 'Disney Girls (1957)' on the piano in

the studio because, as he admits to Harris, "I never got to play the song in England because I left the group too soon."

■ Saturday 28th
Swing Auditorium *San Bernadino, CA*

■ Sunday 29th – Tuesday 31st
Long Beach Arena *Long Beach, CA* with Honk
Three sell-out concerts to a total of over 40,000 paying customers. (Portions of this concert are shot on 16mm film for Dennis's archive.) Harvey Kubernik, American show-business reporter, writes in *Melody Maker*: "Tonight's gig coincides with the group's 13th birthday. A Beach Boys Bar Mitzvah? The Beach Boys' melodic re-acceptance has been highly documented in 1974. Platinum awards for tunes that are ten years old and sell-outs in the US's most respected venues. ... 1974 has also been the year that Brian Wilson's brew of musical drink is tasting good again. It's cool to dig The Beach Boys again.

"Some groups are afraid to take chances on stage. They offer the same programme year after year. With the exception of Dylan, the song repertoire never deviates and even the encore is fairly predictable. The 1974 Beach Boys differed from the norm. Rather than structure the show for the adoring masses, The Beach Boys lately have changed the concert experience into an invigorating time for themselves as well as the fans.

"This time around they are not doing songs like 'Caroline No', 'Trader' or even 'Funky Pretty'. The show now includes tunes like 'In My Room', 'Warmth Of The Sun' and 'I Can Hear Music', the show's opener, which has been absent from recent Beach Boys concerts over the year.

"Yet, as the evening rolls on in Bakersfield, San Francisco, or LA, it seems no matter what songs the group does, the audience loves it. Sure, old freaks get off on the offerings from *Surf's Up* and *Holland*, but at 23, I'm one of the oldest in the crowd. There's a whole new breed of Beach Boys fans that have been getting into their 1960s efforts through Capitol Records reissues and repackages, and Warner Brothers have made their late-1960s records available again.

"It's been four years since The Beach Boys started to regain prominence as a live band. I've often wondered how embarrassing it must have been to play the [tiny] Whisky A Go Go in 1970 after selling 60 million records. Then The Beach Boys would answer audience shouts for oldies with, 'We'll get to them'.

"All areas of the group's existence were touched upon in their two-hour set. 'Surfin' USA', 'Don't Worry Baby', 'Surfer Girl', 'I Get Around', 'Little Deuce Coupe' ... and they pay homage to their 1966 epic *Pet Sounds* with 'God Only Knows', 'Sloop John B' and 'Wouldn't It Be Nice'. The concert ended with 'Good Vibrations', possibly one of rock's finest songs. The crowd wouldn't leave. Then came the opening notes of their first encore, 'California Girls', with 'In My Room', and a song of desperation, 'Help Me Rhonda'. Then 'Barbara Ann' and, to close, 'Fun Fun Fun'."
• On New Year's Eve the group performs at Long Beach at the same time as their appearance on Dick Clark's *Rockin' New Year's Eve* show is being transmitted on ABC TV.

■ Monday 30th
Three new Brian/Steve Kalinich songs are copyrighted today: 'California Feeling', 'You're Riding High On Music' and 'Lucy Jones'.
• It has been a most amazing year for The Beach Boys' live touring show and for the group's archive record sales. Remarkably, it is about to get even better.

1975

'Sail On Sailor' single re-released in the US, making number 49 ... Capitol releases another successful compilation album, *Spirit Of America* ... 'Beachago' US tour sees The Beach Boys and Chicago joining forces ... brief visit to the UK for a show at Wembley Stadium with Elton John ... Warner/Reprise also releases a compilation album, *Good Vibrations* ... psychiatrist Dr Eugene Landy is hired to treat Brian's continuing insecurity.

Dennis backstage at a show in Wembley, England in June.

January

■ Thursday 2nd

Madison Square Garden *New York, NY*

The group's first concert of the year takes place at the legendary New York venue.

■ Monday 20th

Plug Me Into Something album by Henry Gross released in the US. The A&M LP features backing vocals by Carl on 'One More Tomorrow', which is released as a single on March 31st.

■ Friday 31st

HIC Arena *Honolulu, HI*

The first of three warm-up shows in readiness for the two-week American tour set to begin on March 22nd. Tonight's concert is attended by 8,423 people and grosses $47,607.

February

■ Monday 3rd

Municipal Auditorium *Atlanta, GA*

■ Wednesday 5th

Ralph Swing Auditorium, National Orange Showgrounds *San Bernardino, CA* with Honk

The concert is a 7,200 sell-out grossing $48,672.

■ Wednesday 12th

RECORDING Brother studio *Santa Monica, CA*. A session today for Dennis's **'Pacific Ocean Blues'** and **'Old Man Booze'**. The latter piece will remain unreleased.

• Warner Bros prepares the master for a reissue of the two-year-old single 'Sail On Sailor' and 'Only With You'.

March

Dennis is frustrated at artistic restrictions within The Beach Boys' camp and so teams up with writing partner Steven Kalinich. The two harbour plans for a project to be called *Life Symphony* that will focus on a series of poems reflecting life from childhood to death.

'Take It To Mexico' / **'Rebecca'** single by Bruce & Terry released in the US. Bruce Johnston and Terry Melcher issue a 45 on their Equinox label.

■ Monday 10th

'Sail On Sailor' / **'Only With You'** single re-issued in the US. The 45, first released in February 1973, this time peaks in the American chart at number 49, easily the group's best performance so far with a Warners single.

■ Tuesday 11th

RECORDING probably Brother studio *Santa Monica, CA*. An early version of Dennis's song **'Rainbows'** is recorded today.

■ Wednesday 12th

RECORDING RCA studio *Los Angeles, CA*. Brian enters the RCA studio to work on some new music just weeks before he is due to sign a recording contract with Equinox Records, a subsidiary of RCA set up by Bruce Johnson and Terry Melcher.

During a break in the recordings, Brian decides to pay a visit to Elvis Presley who is three days into a combination of rehearsals and recording in an adjacent studio in the same building. Presley's appearance in a studio is quite rare these days: he did not do so during the whole of 1974. But in the opening days of this month Elvis is back, recording through the night, usually in three-hour sessions, and evidently in a newly productive mood. During sessions on March 10th and 11th, for example, he completed eight songs, mostly cover versions.

During Presley's second session today, from 12.30 to 3.30am on Thursday morning – the last of these recordings – he begins work on 'Pieces Of My Life', which he'd heard on Charlie Rich's album *Silver Fox*. But any additional work on the track is prevented when the studio door suddenly bursts open and Brian Wilson forces his way in. He is fresh from recording material next door and insists on meeting Elvis. This will make it third time lucky for Brian.

Surrounded by their respective entourages, the two biggest recluses of pop music create a commotion as they meet, preventing further recording. According to Jerry Schilling, a long-time member of Presley's group of close buddies affectionately known as the Memphis Mafia: "Brian walked straight in and said, 'Hey man, its great to see ya!' I don't think he introduced himself and I don't think Elvis recognised him because he'd put on a lot of weight and had this big beard. Brian said, 'I've been recording some songs for a new album. Do ya wanna come and hear them?' And Elvis said yeah." The entourages follow as they move into another studio room where Brian starts playing his new songs to Elvis. After a few tracks, Brian says, "Well? Do you think they're any good?" Elvis looks up and replies, "Nah," before leaving. Schilling recalls, "I don't think he had any idea that the guy was Brian Wilson."

TOUR STARTS US West, South (Mar 22nd-Apr 7th)

■ Saturday 22nd

Tempe Arizona Hall *Tempe, AZ* 1:30pm

At the start of another Beach Boys tour Dennis immediately falls into trouble with the rest of the group by breaking their new rule: do not take drugs on the road. His fine is $2,000 for taking two Quaalude sedative drugs and drinking a bottle of wine before the show. Dennis tells *Melody Maker*: "I walked out on stage and fell over my drum set. I knocked them over. The rest of the band got them together and propped me up on the drums. I laughed at Carl and said, 'How'm I doing? Ha, ha.' I embarrassed the band. I took Quaaludes because I wanted to. Just because there's a drug rule, that doesn't mean I have to follow it. I mean, once in a while I'll take drugs."

■ Sunday 23rd

University of California, Campus Stadium *Santa Barbara, CA* 1:00pm, with Jesse Colin Young, Honk

This *Outdoors On The Grass* concert attracts an audience of 2,300.

■ Friday 28th

Peabody Auditorium *Daytona Beach, FL*

The show includes rare performances of 'The Warmth Of The Sun' and a cover of the Stones song 'Jumpin' Jack Flash', which both go into the regular set around now.

■ Saturday 29th

Mann Theater *Fort Myers, FL*

■ Sunday 30th
Hollywood Speedway Sportatorium *Hollywood, FL*

April

Ex-professional basketball player Stanley Love, brother of Mike and Steve, is hired to be Brian's minder. His first task is to try to arrest Brian's physical decline. Stanley's employment is temporary and, at the end of the summer, he returns to basketball.
• Also this month Brian signs a production deal with Bruce Johnston and Terry Melcher's RCA-distributed Equinox label, but the agreement soon lapses.

■ Tuesday 1st
Freedom Hall *Louisville, KY*
US radio reporter Larry Froebe interviews Carl and Al backstage at this date in Kentucky and asks them about the origins of the logo for the group's Brother Records label. Carl tells Froebe he calls the logo "the last horizon".

■ Wednesday 2nd
Stokely Athletic Center *Knoxville, TN*

■ Thursday 3rd
Omni Coliseum *Atlanta, GA* with Billy Joel
Set-list 'Sloop John B', 'You're So Good to Me', 'California Saga: California', 'The Warmth Of The Sun', 'Marcella', 'Help Me Rhonda', 'Little Deuce Coupe', 'Do It Again', 'Sail On Sailor', 'Feel Flows', 'All This Is That', 'Surfer Girl', 'Heroes And Villains', 'Catch A Wave', 'I'm Waiting For The Day', 'Don't Worry Baby', 'Darlin'', 'Wouldn't It Be Nice', 'I Get Around', 'Good Vibrations', 'California Girls', 'Surfin' USA', 'Jumpin' Jack Flash', 'Barbara Ann', 'Fun Fun Fun' (last five as encores).

■ Friday 4th
Coliseum *Charlotte, NC*

■ Saturday 5th
Coliseum *Greensboro, NC*

■ Sunday 6th
Coliseum *Charlotte, NC*

■ Monday 7th
William & Mary Hall, College of William & Mary *Williamsburg, VA*
Last night of the tour.

■ Monday 14th
Spirit Of America compilation album released in the US. Capitol's collection is essentially *Endless Summer* volume two, and includes the 1969 non-album single 'Break Away'.

The group has had no opportunity to air their opinions about the selection of tracks on the compilation, which will peak in the US chart at number 8.

■ End of month
The Beach Boys spend a good deal of the latter half of April at their Brother studio in Santa Monica, California, rehearsing for the upcoming tour.

May

TOUR STARTS *Beachago* Beach Boys/Chicago Summer Of '75 US South, East, Midwest, West (May 2nd intermittently to Jul 6th) The idea for this tour was spawned back on November 1st 1974 during a TV appearance when The Beach Boys and Chicago teamed up together. Also last year, Carl, Dennis and Al supplied harmonies in the studio for the recording of Chicago's Top 20 hit 'Wishing You Were Here'. Now the two groups join forces for the musical event of the summer, a heavily promoted 12-city 21-date concert tour across the US. Jim Guercio devises the joint tour, no doubt with cash tills ringing in his ears. Guercio, producer of Chicago, is bass player for The Beach Boys on this tour and shares managerial duties for the group with Steve Love. He tells *Time* magazine: "The American experience is found in Southern California and the streets of Chicago. These bands sing about youth, love and marriage in an American context. America – it's the common denominator."

Each band performs a set and then combines forces for a joint finale. Accompanying the two groups for some shows are various high-wire trapeze artists who perform their skills high above the concert stage. The Beach Boys' stage musicians include Billy Hinsche (guitar, bass), Carlos Munoz (keyboards), Ron Altbach (keyboards), Bob Figueroa (drums) and Guercio on bass.

The tour is a huge success, grossing $7.5million, and will nearly eclipse The Rolling Stones' excursion taking place concurrently across America. In the space of just four or so years The Beach Boys have gone from performing in front of a crowd of just 200 Americans to an audience totalling 50,000. The group is now as profitable as in their heyday in the 1960s.

■ Friday 2nd
Jefferson Stadium *Houston, TX* with Chicago
Tonight's opening performance is in front of a sell-out crowd of 15,000.

■ Saturday 3rd
Cotton Bowl Stadium *Dallas, TX* with Chicago
The concert is attended by 30,000 fans

■ Saturday 10th
Madison Square Garden *New York City, NY*
The first of two concerts away from the joint Chicago tour.

■ Sunday 11th
Myriad Arena *Oklahoma City, OK*
This second show away from the Beach Boys/Chicago tie-up attracts 10,000 fans and generates $58,000 gross.

■ Saturday 17th
Arrowhead Stadium, Harry S. Truman Sports Complex *Kansas City, MO* with Chicago
Rolling Stone's reviewer writes: "Outside the gates of Arrowhead Stadium, just a mile from the birthplace of our 33rd president, a shiny new sign proclaims the arena part of the Harry Truman Sports Complex. But though Chicago headlined with Harry Truman, The Beach Boys, playing more than 1,000 miles from an ocean, stole the show. The riotous greeting accorded the group was ironic, since most of the audience was still toddling when The Beach Boys began to sing about surfing.

"They opened with pure greatest hits. 'Help Me Rhonda', 'Heroes And Villains', 'Wouldn't It Be Nice', 'I Get Around', 'Little

Deuce Coupe' and 'Good Vibrations' were exactly what the crowd wanted. The songs are still perfect for a hot, sunny day. Jardine and Love cranked out the incredible harmonies as if it were the summer of '65 instead of '75. So much so that when Chicago were introduced for the first of two joint sets and Bob Lamm was given the lead on 'Surf's Up', the drop off in vocal quality was obvious. The Beach Boys, with a potent backing band [that includes] Jim Guercio, producer and creator of Chicago, living out a teenaged fantasy on guitar, sounded better than ever. When they broke into 'Little Deuce Coupe', without help from the headliners, the crowd went nuts.

"After a half-time of aerial acts, Chicago came on-stage to a deafening roar. As the show continued, however, it became clear that something was ever so slightly off: a little sluggishness, a few ragged edges, some mis-cues.

"The crowd, high-spirited and dying for a good time, had sung along with The Beach Boys, but spontaneous clap-alongs for the less catchy Chicago songs soon trailed off into limbo. And so did Chicago's compressed, brassy energy. The energy peak of the Chicago set came only when The Beach Boys returned to help out with 'Wishing You Were Here' and 'Saturday In The Park'. On their own again, Chicago's 'Make Me Smile'/ 'Colour My World'/ 'Beginnings' segue mustered a response that was appreciated but controlled.

"But when The Beach Boys returned for the everybody-on-stage finale, the applause turned ecstatic. With the surfer boys behind it on harmony, 'Harry Truman', a song taken seriously by some in Kansas City, turned into a special event. 'California Girls' provoked lines of snake dancers and 'Jumpin' Jack Flash' was, as always, a great set closer, perhaps the best ever written. As the show ended, the 30,000 fans who hadn't left after the Chicago set began straggling home, tired, happy and a little sunburned. On the third date of the *Summer Of '75* tour, The Beach Boys had caught a perfect wave."

■ Sunday 18th
The Arena *St Louis, MO* with Chicago
Tonight sees a crowd of 20,000.

■ Monday 19th
The Arena *St Louis, MO* with Chicago
Beach Boys set-list 'Sloop John B', 'Do It Again', 'Help Me Rhonda' (Al back on lead vocal), 'In My Room', 'Sail On Sailor' (Billy Hinsche lead vocal), 'California Saga: California', 'In The Back Of My Mind', 'God Only Knows' (with Chicago horn section), 'Surf's Up' (Bobby Lamm of Chicago lead vocal), 'Darlin'' (Peter Cetera of Chicago lead vocal, with Chicago horn section), 'Their Hearts Were Full Of Spring', 'Surfer Girl', 'Heroes And Villains', 'Little Deuce Coupe', 'Catch A Wave', 'Wouldn't It Be Nice', 'I Get Around', 'Good Vibrations', 'Barbara Ann' (encore), 'Surfin'' USA' (encore). *Beachago set-list* 'Wishing You Were Here' (Chicago/Beach Boys), 'Saturday In The Park' (Chicago/Beach Boys), 'California Girls', 'Fun Fun Fun', 'Feelin' Stronger Ever Day' (Peter Cetera and Mike Love lead vocals), 'Jumpin' Jack Flash'.

■ Friday 23rd
Anaheim Stadium *Anaheim, CA* with Chicago
The concert makes $483,710 gross from 48,371 fans. Stadium director T.F. Lieger tells *Rolling Stone*: "The second tier in the stadium moved up and down two to 18 inches during The Beach Boys' set, prompting a message board request for the clapping and stomping upstairs crowd to sit down." Concertgoers remark that the yo-yoing tier was most noticeable during The Beach Boys' performance of 'Fun Fun Fun'.

■ Saturday 24th
Oakland Alameda County Coliseum *Oakland, CA* with Chicago, Bob Seeger
Promoted by Bill Graham, the concert generates $408,737 gross from a sell-out crowd of 55,000.

■ Monday 26th
'**Little Honda**' / '**Hawaii**' single released in the US. Capitalising on The Beach Boys immense popularity, Capitol reissues these two old recordings.

■ Thursday 29th
RECORDING RCA studio *Los Angeles, CA*. Brian's first session for Bruce's Equinox Records, as he begins work on '**Why Do Fools Fall In Love?**' with California Music, a group signed to Equinox. Brian produces the recording, contributes vocals, and conducts the orchestra. Equinox's Jimmi Seiter tells *Rolling Stone*: "This is Brian's first attempt in getting back into it. There'll be a lot more better things ahead." It's possible Brian also records tracks for '**Money Honey**' and yet another take of '**Ding Dang**' at this session.

■ Saturday 31st
Municipal Auditorium *Cleveland, OH* with Chicago
Tonight sees a $210,000 gross from 26,000 fans.
• 'Sail On Sailor' reissued single peaks in US *Billboard* chart at number 49.

June

'**Break Away**' / '**Celebrate The News**' single released in the UK. Capitol reissues this 45, first released in June 1969. It fails to chart. '**Sail On Sailor**' / '**Only With You**' single released in the UK. Reprise in Britain issues this competing single, first released in the US in February 1973 and doing well there now after a re-release earlier this year. But in Britain it fails to chart.

■ Sunday 1st – Thursday 5th & Saturday 7th
Chicago Stadium *Chicago, IL* with Chicago
These six performances mark the highest grossing concerts of the Beach Boys/Chicago tour with a total attendance figure of 120,000 and a box-office gross of $1,080,000.

■ Monday 2nd
'**Get It Up For Love**' single by David Cassidy released in the US. The Bell 45 is co-produced by Bruce Johnston and features Carl on backing vocals.

■ Thursday 12th – Sunday 15th
Madison Square Garden *New York, NY* with Chicago
Four sell-out shows grossing $750,000. Audience figures during the concerts set a new indoor concert box-office record for the venue. Henry Edwards writes in the *New York Times*: "Rather than earnestness, The Beach Boys have always projected an air of ebullience. Purveyors of 'good vibrations', this vocal quartet accompanied by four back-up musicians is also relatively clean-cut in appearance, with the exception of lead singer Mike Love who on past occasions has shown a preference for salmon-coloured meditation outfits and crocheted beanies. His costuming lends colour to the kind of musical joy created by The Beach Boys as they

Performing at Wembley Stadium, north-west London, on June 21st: (left to right) Mike, James Guercio (bass, with back to audience), Al, Dennis, Bob Figueroa (drums), Carl, and Carlos Munoz (keyboards).

conjure up their vision of a mid-1960s Southern California adolescence touched by sun, surfing, convertibles, cruising and girl watching.

"As effective as it ever was, The Beach Boys' sound – complex, imaginative, rich, swirling vocal harmonies backed by a series of pulsating rhythm lines – can still cause audiences to dance in the aisles. Many have hailed The Beach Boys as 'the quintessential American white middle-class rock'n'roll band'. It is an apt description. Reports from the road have indicated that the performance, which in some locations has lasted as long as six hours, begins with a long and bouncy set by The Beach Boys featuring many of their most beloved songs. Chicago then joins The Beach Boys for a greatest-hits swap, but The Beach Boys are allowed to finish the first half by themselves. A lengthy medley of Chicago's greatest hits opens part two, and the evening is concluded as both bands join in a wild jam highlighted by The Beach Boys' lush harmonies, Chicago's piercing horns, and as many other musical hi-jinx as the 16 musicians can muster up."

■ Saturday 14th

An interview with Dennis, carried out by Elliot Cahn in Hollywood two weeks ago, is published in this week's edition of the UK music paper *New Musical Express*. Dennis takes the opportunity to reply to Carl's recent statement that The Beach Boys have about two years left as a group. "I think that's utter bullshit," Dennis storms. "We'll keep making it as long as we want, because we're not trying. The Beach Boys haven't made a big statement. ... We're just five horny guys on the road doing our thing. It's so simple. If the group broke up tomorrow and it turned out that I didn't have a penny, it wouldn't freak me out at all. I'd be a gardener or a fisherman."

■ Friday 20th

'Help Me Rhonda' single by Johnny Rivers released in the US. The song features backing vocals by Brian. Speaking on US radio a few years later, Rivers recalls, "I was backstage at a Beach Boys concert. The last song they did was 'Help Me Rhonda' and it kept going round my head for days. So, a week later, I was recording in the studio and I told my band, 'Listen, we've got an hour left and I want to record a track just for fun' So we recorded the track [for] 'Help Me Rhonda'. I put a rough vocal on it and then some friends of mine came in to do some backing vocals. But we still needed that high harmony part. So I called Brian Wilson. I played the version I'd just recorded over the telephone to him and he said, 'Wow! That sounds like a big hit.' I told him we were finishing it tomorrow night and asked if he would like to come down to the studio. He said,

'Yeah, yeah. I'll be there.' I didn't really think he would show up. He had become a recluse and hadn't recorded in a long time. But he did come down. He came with his wife, Marilyn. She held his hand while he stood there and sang his part on 'Help Me Rhonda'. He did it in one take. It was perfect. We went, 'Wow! Thanks Brian.' He was so excited to hear his voice on a record again. Shortly after that, he began recording with The Beach Boys again."

■ Saturday 21st

Wembley Stadium Wembley, *north-west London* Elton John (headliner), The Eagles, Rufus with Chaka Khan, Joe Walsh, Stackridge; compère BBC Radio-1 DJ Johnnie Walker

The Beach Boys break from their concert tour with Chicago to return briefly to the UK for this *Midsummer Music Show*, an 11-hour all-day event attended by a crowd of 75,000. Among the celebrities present to watch the show are former Beatles Paul McCartney and Ringo Starr, who sit apart in the Royal Box area of the stadium, alongside American singers Harry Nilsson and David Cassidy. Joe Walsh's band features former Beach Boy Ricky Fataar.

Chris Welch writes in *Melody Maker*: "Unfortunately for Elton, [who played] endless songs from his new album *Captain Fantastic*, The Beach Boys had already stolen the show hours beforehand as they played their marvellous surfing songs under the blazing sunshine of the longest day. ... Elton was topping the bill, but it was The Beach Boys who stole the show, and for a very good reason, they simply played their greatest hits. The band, augmented by James William Guercio on bass guitar plus two new keyboard players and a percussionist, provoked an immediate response, right from the opening number, 'Wouldn't It Be Nice'.

"But how could the band fail? They went through the motherlode of their repertoire, from 'Help Me Rhonda' and 'Little Deuce Coupe' to 'Sail On Sailor' and 'Surf's Up'. The audience was on their feet for the entire set. The force of the music and familiarity of the songs were enough for the band to take the audience with them. 'Do It Again', 'Sloop John B', 'I Get Around' and of course 'Good Vibrations' ... they just came one after another. For the encore, The Beach Boys returned to sing 'Surfin' USA', 'Barbara Ann' and 'Fun Fun Fun'. It was an object lesson in upstaging, and Captain Fantastic, who followed, couldn't hope to better The Beach Boys. Elton made a mistake by starting his set with the doom-laden track 'Funeral For A Friend'."

Max Bell agrees in *New Musical Express*: "Elton John might be the world's biggest-selling rock star at this point, but it was The Beach Boys who presented the estimated audience of 72,000 with a slice of rock history that stole the show at Wembley. The balding

superstar played it all wrong. Do all those people want to listen to over an hour's worth of new material after already sitting through seven hours of music? For sure they didn't, and a lot of them said so with their feet, so that halfway through Elton's set there was a long stream of concertgoers leaving the stadium with the memory of those four guys from Southern California ringing around in their heads. ... Dennis sang 'You Are So Beautiful' and dedicated it to England. There was 'Barbara Ann', the inevitable 'Fun Fun Fun' and Love doing his Jagger bit. ... It's apparent that The Beach Boys can make you feel like laughing and crying. ... They are, quite simply, the best." *Set-list* 'Wouldn't It Be Nice', 'I Can Hear Music', 'Do It Again', 'Help Me Rhonda', 'In My Room', 'Sail On Sailor', 'The Trader', 'Surf's Up', 'California Saga: California', 'Surfer Girl', 'Heroes And Villains', 'Little Deuce Coupe', 'Catch A Wave', 'Don't Worry Baby', 'Darlin'', 'Sloop John B', 'California Girls', 'I Get Around', 'Good Vibrations', 'You Are So Beautiful', 'Surfin' USA', 'Barbara Ann', 'Fun Fun Fun' (last three as encores).

■ Monday 23rd

Good Vibrations – Best Of The Beach Boys compilation album released in the US. Warners rush-release this single LP covering the group's career from 1966 to 1973. *Good Vibrations* will equal 1973's *In Concert* as the best performing Warners LP in the US chart, where it peaks at number 25.

■ Tuesday 24th – Saturday 28th

Capital Center Landover, MD 8:00pm, with Chicago
Back in America after the UK visit, The Beach Boys continue their highly successful joint tour with Chicago. The *Washington Post* reviewer writes: "There was no doubt that The Beach Boys were back, stronger than ever. Cotton-candy vendor Tam Cole, who said she expected her sales to top 700 sticks, was so excited by The Beach Boys' music that she found it hard to keep her mind on her work. 'I'm going crazy,' she said. 'I can't go in there.' But she did manage to peer around the curtain as The Beach Boys broke into 'I Get Around' and jumped up and down and clapped her hands just like everybody else in the house. Even promoter Jack Boyle seemed to be excited by The Beach Boys. 'You know me,' he said. 'I don't usually like rock'n'roll but this is the greatest show I've ever seen. Just wait until The Beach Boys and Chicago play together.'

"At first there were only a few thousand on their feet. Then there was 10,000 and then almost everyone. By the time they sang 'Wouldn't It Be Nice' there was no need for Beach Boy Mike Love, garbed in turban and sequinned jacket, to urge the crowd to stand up and join in. As Love sang the words of what may well be the most idealistically adolescent rock love song of all time, there was an outpouring of emotion from the audience that surprised even the most regular attendees of Capitol Center concerts. There was a feeling in the air, pure, innocent and without the false hipness that is standard at most rock shows, and even The Beach Boys themselves were amazed.

"And finally, there was Chicago. ... When Chicago finished, maybe a few hundred in the crowd made their way to the exits but the majority stayed and stomped and cried for more. Shortly, back came The Beach Boys to join Chicago, and if they did not combine to raise the Capital Center roof it was only because it's fastened tight. Everybody standing, arms raised, hands clapping, bodies swaying, cameras flashing, the sounds were of 'Wishing You Were Here', 'Saturday In The Park' and a half dozen other tunes, including 'Fun Fun Fun' and 'California Girls'. The difference between the two groups was perhaps best illustrated in 'Wishing You Were Here', a Chicago song, for which The Beach Boys sing background vocals.

Chicago was simply no match for the tight, lilting vocal harmonies of Beach Boys Mike Love, Carl Wilson and Alan Jardine. They closed the show with a rousing version of The Stones' 'Jumpin' Jack Flash', complete with a vamping Mick Jagger imitation by Mike Love."

■ Sunday 29th – Monday 30th

Schaefer Stadium Foxboro, MA with Chicago
Sixty thousand advance tickets have been sold for the shows, including a further date on July 3rd.

■ Monday 30th

'Barbara Ann' / 'Little Honda' single released in the US. Capitol reissues these old recordings to help promote the *Spirit Of America* compilation. It does not chart.

July

■ Tuesday 1st

The Spectrum Philadelphia, PA with Ambrosia
A Beach Boys gig away from the *Beachago* tour.

■ Thursday 3rd

Schaefer Stadium Foxboro, MA with Chicago

■ Sunday 6th

Colorado State Stadium Fort Collins, CO with Chicago
The final night of the Beach Boys/Chicago *Beachago* Summer Of '75 tour. Larry Fitzgerald, Chicago's manager, says in *Amusement Business* magazine: "This was the most significant concert tour for 1975 and perhaps 1976 if we do it again next year. The concerts delivered four hours of music with two of America's premiere supergroups. There is an incredible identification for both groups with the audiences. Both acts are at the roots of contemporary American music."
• Several shows on the tour are taped for a possible live *Beachago* album. A tentative release date is set for the end of the year, but the album is never released. Reports suggest that the tapes are lost in the Caribou studio fire. Apparently they reappear in late 2002 in the possession of Jim Guercio.

■ Saturday 12th

Marcus Amphitheater Milwaukee, WI
Just a week after the conclusion of the *Beachago* tour, The Beach Boys headline the annual *Milwaukee Summerfest Festival*.

■ Monday 14th

A concert due to take place today at North Western University in Evanston, Illinois, is cancelled when Mike is stranded after a visit to Indianapolis.
The Higher They Climb – The Harder They Fall album by David Cassidy released in the US. The LP is co-produced by Bruce Johnston and features backing vocals by Carl.

■ Wednesday 16th

Masters for the next Beach Boys Reprise single – a reissue of the *Pet Sounds* classics 'Wouldn't It Be Nice' and 'Caroline No' – are prepared for release.

■ Monday 28th

'Wouldn't It Be Nice' / 'Caroline No' single released in the US. A further re-issue of old recordings.

August

RECORDING possibly Western Recorders *Los Angeles, CA*. Working with Terry Melcher, Brian continues his slow comeback as he co-produces the A-side of the **'Why Do Fools Fall In Love'** / **'Don't Worry Baby'** single by California Music. The backing track for 'Fools' was recorded in May. The single is released on the 22nd by RCA-Equinox. (Bruce Johnston produces the B-side.)

■ Friday 1st

King Harvest album by King Harvest released in the US. Carl and Mike are featured on backing vocals on 'Vaea (Vy-ya)', which is issued as a single on September 15th.

■ Thursday 7th

Nassau County Coliseum *Uniondale, NY* with Gary Wright
In preparation for the next tour, due to begin on the 21st, the group performs a couple of warm-up shows, one tonight and another on Saturday.
Set-list 'Sloop John B', 'Do It Again', 'Help Me Rhonda', 'In My Room', 'The Trader', 'Sail On Sailor' (Billy Hinsche lead vocal), 'California Saga: California', 'Surfer Girl', 'Heroes And Villains', 'Little Deuce Coupe', 'Catch A Wave', 'Darlin'', 'California Girls', 'Wouldn't It Be Nice', 'I Get Around', 'Good Vibrations', 'You Are So Beautiful' (sung by Dennis), 'Barbara Ann', 'Surfin' USA', 'Fun Fun Fun' (last four as encores).

■ Saturday 9th

Balboa Stadium *San Diego, CA* with Jesse Colin Young, Pure Prairie League

■ Friday 15th

New Arrangement album by Jackie DeShannon released in the US. The LP features a backing vocal by Brian on 'Boat To Sail', which is released as a single on September 22nd.
New Lovers And Old Friends album by Johnny Rivers released in the US. It includes backing vocals by Brian on 'Help Me Rhonda'. The recordings Brian has made recently with Bruce, Terry Melcher, Jackie DeShannon and Johnny Rivers are his only serious musical activities during this very lean period.

TOUR STARTS North America (Aug 21st-Sep 20th)

■ Thursday 21st

Iowa State Fair *Des Moines, IA*
This opening night of the new tour takes place at the annual Iowa State Fair in front of a crowd totalling 25,400.

■ Friday 22nd

Pine Knob Theatre *Clarkston, MI*

■ Saturday 23rd

War Memorial Auditorium *Rochester, NY*

■ Sunday 24th

Allentown Fairgrounds *Allentown, PA* 3:00pm, with Captain & Tennille
Support duo Captain & Tennille are Daryl Dragon and Toni Tennille, both former touring members of The Beach Boys. WFIL Radio and the Seafood Shanty Company sponsor this afternoon's concert in Pennsylvania.

■ Monday 25th

New Haven Coliseum *New Haven, CT* with Captain & Tennille
At the end of tonight's concert Gerry Beckley and Dewey Bunnell of the group America get up and jam with The Beach Boys.

■ Thursday 28th

Nassau Coliseum *Uniondale, NY*

■ Saturday 30th

National Exhibition Grandstand *Vancouver, BC, Canada*

■ Sunday 31st

The Montreal Forum *Montreal, PQ, Canada*
Set-list 'Sloop John B', 'Do It Again', 'In My Room', 'Help Me Rhonda', 'The Trader', 'Sail On Sailor' (Billy Hinsche lead vocal), 'California Saga: California', 'Heroes And Villains', 'Little Deuce Coupe', 'Catch A Wave', 'Surfer Girl', 'Darlin'', 'California Girls', 'Wouldn't It Be Nice', 'I Get Around', 'Good Vibrations', 'You Are So Beautiful', 'Barbara Ann', 'Surfin' USA', 'Fun Fun Fun' (last four as encores).

September

Worried by Brian's almost hermit-like existence, Marilyn approaches the highly respected doctor Eugene E. Landy (born November 26th 1934 in Pittsburgh, Pennsylvania) to treat her husband.

Landy's clients have included actors Rod Steiger, Gig Young and Richard Harris and singer Alice Cooper. Marilyn admits that she can't deal with Brian's situation any longer. After two years of severe inactivity his weight has now ballooned to 240 pounds (about 17 stones).

Marilyn tells *Rolling Stone*: "I just couldn't stand to see Brian, whom I love and adore, unhappy with himself and not really creating, because music is his whole life. So one of my friends told me about Landy and I went and talked to him for an hour." When Marilyn describes Brian to Landy, he says he thinks her husband is an "undiagnosed and untreated schizophrenic".

Marilyn: "[Landy] then came to my house to see me and Brian kept peeking his head in and said, 'What are you doing with my wife?' Then one day, as I was talking again to Landy, Brian just walked in the room and said, 'Something's wrong with me. I need your help,' and that started it all."

Landy agrees to help her husband, quotes a $90 per 50 minutes fee, and insists to Marilyn that "he does his own thing" with Brian. Marilyn agrees. Acting on Landy's instructions, she throws out of the house any drugs, cigarettes, alcohol and fattening foods she finds. A lock is placed on the refrigerator. Soon, Brian's phone calls are monitored.

Landy's form of treatment is centred on total control of his patient's daily life, even barring some of Brian's friends from the house. Landy wants to keep his patient away from negative influences. He also begins bossing Brian around like an army major. Soon, Brian will partake in his doctor's 24-hours-a-day therapy sessions. At 9:00am each morning Brian will take a jog. Two hours later, he will sit and talk with Landy. At 1:00pm Brian will eat a healthy fat-free lunch. Further exercising, washing, dressing and participation in family discussions follow. The first results are encouraging.

• *Spirit Of America* compilation album released in the UK.

1975

■ Monday 1st
Nassau Coliseum *Uniondale, NY*
Meanwhile, The Beach Boys' tour presses on.

■ Tuesday 2nd
New York State Fairgrounds *Syracuse, NY* with The Doobie Brothers (co-headliners), America, Jefferson Starship, New Riders Of The Purple Sage, The Stanley Brown Group
The *Great American Music Fair* is disrupted when a mob of 500 armed with rocks and bottles tries to gatecrash the event, but their attempts are thwarted by a strong police presence and strict security.

■ Friday 5th
Wings Stadium *Kalamazoo, MI* with Ambrosia

■ Saturday 6th
Civic Arena *Pittsburgh, PA* with Ambrosia
Attendance at today's show totals 12,000.

■ Friday 12th
Civic Center *Hartford, CT* with Ambrosia

■ Saturday 13th
Veterans Memorial Coliseum *New Haven, CT* with Ambrosia

■ Friday 19th
Seattle Center Coliseum *Seattle, WA*

■ Saturday 20th
Memorial Coliseum *Portland, OR*
Final night of the current tour. The group takes a five-week break before resuming concert duties on October 27th.

■ Tuesday 23rd
Union Pacific Railroad Shop *Omaha, NE*
Just days after completing the latest tour, Mike gives his first solo performance away from the other Beach Boys at a benefit concert for the US Revolution Bicentennial Freedom Train.

■ Friday 26th
RECORDING probably Brother studio *Santa Monica, CA*. An early version of '**Come Go With Me**' is recorded today.

■ Saturday 30th
Good Vibrations: The Best Of The Beach Boys compilation album peaks in US *Billboard* chart at number 25.

October

RECORDING Unknown studio. Brian and Van Dyke Parks reportedly make a new recording of Parks's '**Come To The Sunshine**' during this month. Brian hopes to use the song, which was a US hit for Harper's Bizarre, for the Beach Boys' next album, but following a dispute the tape cannot be used.

■ Monday 6th
RECORDING probably Brother studio *Santa Monica, CA*. A recording is made today of Dennis's composition '**Rainbows**'.

■ Monday 20th
'**Stop Look Around**' / '**I Had A Dream**' single by Ricci Martin released in the US. Carl produces the disc with assistance from brother-in-law Billy Hinsche, and Dennis plays drums.

TOUR STARTS US Midwest (Oct 27th-Nov 2nd)

■ Monday 27th
Market Square Arena *Indianapolis, IN* 7:30pm
The first concert of this week-long tour is attended by 8,500 people and grosses $52,185.

■ Tuesday 28th
University of Illinois *Champaign, IL*

■ Tuesday 29th
Bowens Fieldhouse, Eastern Michigan University *Ypsilanti, MI*
Eight thousand people attend the show, which grosses $55,000.

■ Thursday 30th
University of Missouri *St. Louis, MO*

■ Friday 31st
St Paul Civic Center *St. Paul, MN*
This show is attended by 15,817 fans and grosses $92,877.

November

■ Saturday 1st
The University, Allen Field House *Lawrence, KS*
Attendance tonight is 13,232, grossing $72,873.

■ Sunday 2nd
Civic Auditorium *Omaha, NE*
Last night of this tour; performances resume on the 16th.

■ Friday 7th
Chicago IX: Chicago's Greatest Hits album released in the US. Carl, Dennis and Al sing background vocals on 'Wishing You Were Here'.

TOUR STARTS US Midwest, East, South (Nov 16th-30th)

■ Sunday 16th
Olympia Stadium *Detroit, MI*

■ Tuesday 18th
Providence Civic Center *Providence, RI*
A sell-out show grossing $91,000 and attended by 13,000.

■ Wednesday 19th
Boston Garden *Boston, MA* two shows
The performances gross $204,000 with a combined attendance of 27,000.

■ Thursday 20th
University of Vermont *Burlington, VT*
Another sold-out show.

■ Friday 21st
Niagara Falls Convention Center *Niagara Falls, NY* 8:00pm

■ Saturday 22nd
Convocation Center *Athens, OH*

■ Sunday 23rd
Riverfront Coliseum *Cincinnati, OH* with Dave Mason, Eric Carmen
The concert tonight in Cincinatti is attended by 15,666 and grosses $94,000 at the box office.

■ Tuesday 25th
University of Vermont *Burlington, VT*

■ Wednesday 26th
Mid-South Coliseum *Memphis, TN*

■ Thursday 27th
Boutwell Municipal Auditorium *Birmingham, AL*

■ Friday 28th
University of South Carolina *Columbia, SC*

■ Saturday 29th
Jacksonville Memorial Coliseum *Jacksonville, FL*

■ Sunday 30th
Orlando Sports Stadium *Orlando, FL*
Last night of the tour.

December

The proposed UK release by Reprise of the single 'Child Of Winter' / 'Susie Cincinnati' as K14411 is cancelled. The 45 was issued in the US back in December 1974. Another British release of the disc will be attempted, with A and B sides reversed, in April 1976.
• Around this time, Mike spreads the word on Transcendental Meditation, appearing at a seminar held at Mount Vernon College. He also pays a visit to the first daughter at The White House, supplying her with TM literature.

TOUR STARTS US North America (Dec 12th-17th)

■ Friday 12th
Municipal Auditorium *Birmingham, AL*
The opening concert of this short tour takes place in Alabama and is attended by a crowd totalling 5,000 and grosses $35,000 at the box office.

■ Sunday 14th
Pacific Coliseum *Vancouver, BC, Canada*

■ Monday 15th
Portland Coliseum *Portland, OR* 8:00pm
Attended by a crowd of 11,000, grossing $71,500.

■ Tuesday 16th – Wednesday 17th
Seattle Center Coliseum *Seattle, WA*
These shows are attended by a total of 30,000 fans and gross $210,000.
• It has been another successful year for The Beach Boys. Remarkably, 1976 will be even better. But for the individual members of the group the new year will be tinged with a hint of musical sadness.

1976

Recording sessions begin for a new album, to become *15 Big Ones* ... 'Rock And Roll Music' is the first Beach Boys single for 16 months and makes number 5 in the US ... *15 Big Ones* released, marking Brian's 'comeback', and is the group's first studio album since 1973 ... *20 Golden Greats* compilation album released in the UK, leaping to number 1 ... in the US an NBC TV special and a *People* magazine cover-story mark the group's 15th anniversary ... Dennis works on solo-album recordings, to become *Pacific Ocean Blue* ... Brian begins essentially solo sessions for a new album, which becomes 1977's *The Beach Boys Love You* ... a show at The LA Forum coincides with the 15th anniversary of the first concert by The Beach Boys.

Brian is back: The Beach Boys celebrate the return of their erstwhile producer.

January

■ Friday 2nd

Dennis is arrested in Los Angeles for carrying a .38 revolver that he has taken from his girlfriend, Karen Lamm. He is released after charges are dropped.

■ Monday 19th

Civic Arena *Pittsburgh, PA* 7:30pm

■ Friday 30th & Saturday 31st

RECORDING *15 Big Ones* **sessions** Brother studio *Santa Monica, CA*. Brian is making progress under Dr Eugene Landy's treatment regime. He is eating healthily, isn't smoking or drinking, and his drug taking has been curtailed. So with Warner Bros screaming for new music, the group asks Brian to produce their next (well overdue) album. They feel that Brian back in the producer's chair will generate great publicity. Ill-at-ease and still far from rehabilitated, Brian nonetheless agrees and immediately calls upon members of the so-called Wrecking Crew band to help out. Along with the other Beach Boys and Dr Landy, who hovers constantly around his patient, the *15 Big Ones* album is recorded. Brian's suggestion to call the disc *Group Therapy* is soon vetoed by the others.

Brian tells *Sounds*: "It was a little scary because [The Beach Boys and I] weren't as close. We had drifted apart, personality-wise. A lot of the guys had developed new personalities through meditation. It was a bit scary and shaky. But we went into the studio with the attitude that we had to get it done. After a week or two in the studio, we started to get the niche again."

Already recorded and now considered afresh for this project is **'Come Go With Me'** (see September 26th 1975). Over these two days they record the oldies **'Palisades Park'** and **'Blueberry Hill'**, and Brian's **'Honkin' Down The Highway'**, with a lead vocal by Billy Hinsche. Other material is recorded in March, April, May and June (see entries). Stephen Moffitt and Earle Mankey are engineers.

Brian is in charge of the album's production but according to Al, because the group are not all sure of his competence to do the job, some members will sneak into the studio at night to add extra background vocals to songs, which Brian had wanted done 'dry'. Carl says: "Once we had finished a certain batch of songs Brian said, 'That's it. Put it out.' That's why the album sounds unfinished. Brian just wanted to do one cut and capture the moment rather than working on something."

February

Sessions for the LP grind to a halt. The theme of the album centres on a return to the good old days, with brother Brian – who now weighs 240 pounds (about 17 stones) – back at the studio helm. But the group is divided and arguments now arise. Brian is intent on making an 'oldies' album, with a disc of originals to follow. Dennis and Carl are adamant that they should forget about oldies and concentrate on well-developed new Brian Wilson songs. They think – correctly, as it turns out – that an oldies programme will damage their credibility.

But Warner Bros is absolutely set on having a new album out as quickly as possible, and the record, which will be released in July, ends up as a mix of the two ideas: oldies and new songs.

Disagreements within the group continue as Mike and Al insist that the album be released sooner rather than later.

Sessions for *15 Big Ones* will stretch over five months, largely as a result of incessant meetings where the group discusses at great length each song to be recorded. Some get-togethers last up to eight hours. Dr Landy is in charge of each meeting. Mike is horrified, but Dennis is pleased because, for the first time in a Beach Boys meeting, he is asked for his opinion.

March

RECORDING *15 Big Ones* **sessions** probably Brother studio *Santa Monica, CA*. Recordings resume, and started this month are a Brian/Mike original, **'It's OK'**, Brian's **'Had To Phone Ya'**, and a couple more oldies, **'Chapel Of Love'** and **'Talk To Me'**. They return to 'It's OK', which they last worked on in November 1974, a relatively successful attempt at reviving the 'fun in the sun' type of early-1960s Beach Boys sound. Saxophone is played on the song by Roy Wood, formerly of The Move, Electric Light Orchestra and Wizard. (Brian reportedly recorded 'Honeycomb' with Roy Wood and other Wizzard members around 1974.) 'Had To Phone Ya' was first recorded by Spring, and has each of the group taking turns at the lead vocal in the following order: Mike, Al, Dennis, Mike, Carl, Brian. A version of the oldie **'On Broadway'** is also recorded for the album, probably around now.

• This spring, James William Guercio is relieved of his Beach Boys managerial duties and is succeeded by Steve Love. Mike's brother becomes the group's full-time manager and will soon instigate the 'Brian is Back!' campaign, which wins favourable support from Brian's wife, Marilyn. Brian will remark to the *LA Times*: "'Brian is Back'? I still wasn't clear where I'd been."

■ Monday 15th

RECORDING *15 Big Ones* **sessions** probably Brother studio *Santa Monica, CA*. The group works today on more oldies, **'In The Still Of The Night'** and **'Mony Mony'**, the latter remaining unreleased.

■ Tuesday 16th

RECORDING *15 Big Ones* **sessions** probably Brother studio *Santa Monica, CA*. Today's session sees work begin on two more oldies, **'Rock And Roll Music'** and **'Just Once In My Life'**. Mike says on US radio: "I was over at Brian's house one afternoon, in his living room, and I said, 'You know, we did "Surfin' USA", which sort of paraphrased Chuck Berry's "Sweet Little Sixteen", so why don't we do another Chuck Berry song? Let's do "Rock And Roll Music".' And we did. We went in the studio, Brian did a great track, I sang lead on it, and we did some interesting Beach Boys backgrounds on it. It turned out to be the biggest song on the new album."

■ Wednesday 17th

RECORDING *15 Big Ones* **sessions** probably Brother studio *Santa Monica, CA*. Taping another oldie, **'A Casual Look'**, for the new LP.

■ Thursday 18th

RECORDING *15 Big Ones* **sessions** probably Brother studio *Santa Monica, CA*. A session for work on Brian's **'TM Song'**.

■ Thursday 25th

MIXING probably Brother studio *Santa Monica, CA*. A mix session is held for **'Blueberry Hill'**, **'Chapel Of Love'** and **'Palisades Park'**.

April

RECORDING *15 Big Ones* **sessions** probably Brother studio *Santa Monica, CA*. Recordings started this month include Mike's **'Everyone's In Love With You'** as well as Brian and Mike's **'That Same Song'**.

• In the UK, the Reprise-label Beach Boys single 'Susie Cincinnati' coupled with 'Child Of Winter' that at one stage was earmarked for release is now withdrawn.

• The Beach Boys cancel an appearance at Hughes Stadium in Sacramento, California, due to take place on April 26th, because of plans to tour Australia at that time. The Australian tour also fails to materialise.

• Following their recent break from James Guercio, The Beach Boys also split from Guercio's Caribou Management company.

■ Thursday 1st
MIXING Brother studio *Santa Monica, CA*. A mix session is held for **'In The Still Of The Night'**.

May

RECORDING *15 Big Ones* **sessions** probably Brother studio *Santa Monica, CA*. Recordings started this month include **'Back Home'**, by Brian and Bob Norberg, first tracked by the group (with different lyrics) back in January 1970.

■ Saturday 15th
Music Hall *Kansas City, MO*
Another in a series of one-off Beach Boys performances in preparation for the major tour scheduled to kick off on July 2nd.

■ Monday 17th
MIXING Brother studio *Santa Monica, CA*. A mix session is held today at the group's studio in Santa Monica for four songs: **'Palisades Park'** (for now without percussion), **'Chapel Of Love'**, **'Just Once In My Life'**, and **'Michael Row The Boat Ashore'** (the latter will remain unreleased).

■ Tuesday 18th
MIXING Brother studio *Santa Monica, CA*. A mix session is held for the following songs: an instrumental mix of **'TM Song'** (vocals are probably recorded tomorrow), **'Mony Mony'**, Carl's mix of **'Rock And Roll Music'** (with a verse here edited out of the final recording), an early version of **'Come Go With Me'**, **'Just Once In My Life'**, and two mixes of the inevitably unreleased **'Shake Rattle & Roll'**, one by Brian and one by Carl.

■ Wednesday 19th
The Beach Boys next single – 'Rock And Roll Music' coupled with 'TM Song' – is prepared for release. The record features a unique mix for 'Rock And Roll Music' that will not be used for the forthcoming album.

■ Monday 24th
'Rock And Roll Music' / **'TM Song'** single released in the US. It is the first new Beach Boys single for 16 months, and peaks in the Bicentennial summer chart at number 5, the band's highest singles position since 'Good Vibrations' back in late 1966.

Rock And Roll Music single

A 'Rock And Roll Music' (C. BERRY)
B 'TM Song' (B. WILSON)

US release May 24th 1976 (Brother/Reprise 1354).
UK release June 1976 (Reprise K14440).
Chart high US number 5; UK number 36.

June

'Rock And Roll Music' / 'TM Song' single released in the UK. The Reprise 45 will peak in the chart at number 36.
'Good Vibrations' / **'Wouldn't It Be Nice'** single released in the UK. Capitol's re-release of these old recordings peaks in the chart at an impressive number 18.

• News quickly spreads in the US that Brian is ready to talk to the press for the first time in a decade. (See 27th.)

■ Sunday 20th
On his 34th birthday Brian continues his comeback when he films a comedic segment at his Bel Air home for a forthcoming television special co-produced by The Beach Boys, Lorne Michaels and Above Average Productions to be called simply *The Beach Boys*. (The show becomes known affectionately but incorrectly as *It's OK!*.) The scene shot today, aptly titled 'Brian's Nightmare', sees Brian lying in his bed and arrested by *Saturday Night Live* television show regulars Dan Aykroyd and John Belushi for being unable to surf. The pair pose as the Surf Police, dressed in Highway Patrol uniforms.

Belushi: "Good afternoon, Mr Wilson. We're from the Highway Patrol, Surf Squad."
Brian: "Hello."
Aykroyd: "Brian, we have a citation for your here, sir, under Section 936A of the Californian *Catch A Wave* statute. Brian, you're in violation of paragraph 12, failing to surf, neglecting to use the state beach for surfing purposes, and otherwise avoiding surfboards, surfing and surf."
Brian (still lying in his bed): "Surfing? I don't want to go surfing. Now look, you guys, I'm not going. You get your hair wet, get sand in your shoes. OK, I'm not going."
Belushi: "Come on, Brian. Let's go surfing now."
Aykroyd: "Everybody's learning how."
Belushi and Aykroyd (in unison and dragging Brian from his bed): "Come on safari with us. Let's go."

During rehearsals for the sketch, Dr Landy is furious when he arrives to find Brian's home overrun with cigarettes, alcohol and pizzas, innocently brought in by the film crew but all no-go substances for Brian. Deprived of such luxuries for several months, Brian happily shares in the feast by downing five beers and consuming an entire pizza. When asked who brought in these items, Landy is informed that John Belushi was responsible. Immediately, Landy and Belushi stand nose to nose in a frenzied slanging match. Brian watches the rumpus whilst drinking more beer and scoffing extra pizza. Later at nearby Trancas Beach, in front of a small crowd of friends and members of the film crew, Brian is frogmarched down to the sea. Nervously and silently, and escorted by Aykroyd and Belushi, he walks out into the water, dives in, and attempts to surf whilst still wearing his bed gown. He immerses himself in the cool, cool water and the crowd cheers like crazy. Brian has made it. Inside his bath gown is a note given to him by Dr Landy and reading: "You will not drown. You will live."

Later still, back at his Bel Air house, Brian's family and friends – including Paul and Linda McCartney, taking a break from the current *Wings Over America* tour – join Brian for a 34th birthday party where he is presented with a chocolate cake adorned with the message *34 Big Ones*. The event and interviews conducted at the party also feature in *The Beach Boys* TV special, aired by NBC in the US on August 5th.

■ Thursday 24th

CNE Grandstand *Toronto, ON, Canada* with The Steve Miller Band, Pablo Cruise, Journey

■ Saturday 26th

RECORDING *15 Big Ones* **sessions** probably Brother studio *Santa Monica, CA*. **'It's OK'** is finished at today's studio session. With this, work on the new album is complete.

■ Sunday 27th

An interview with Brian by Richard Cromelin at a Beverly Hills restaurant is published in today's *Los Angeles Times* (and in Britain in *Sounds* in July). Brian was accompanied at the session by his psychiatrist, Dr Eugene Landy. Cromelin writes: "A large, amicable bear of a man, with an air of childlike vulnerability about him, Wilson is now emerging from a second collapse through an intensive program of physical and mental therapy. Three years of inactivity ended recently when Wilson, just in time to celebrate The Beach Boys' 15th anniversary, resumed control over the group's recordings. The result, *15 Big Ones*, has already yielded their biggest single in years, Chuck Berry's 'Rock And Roll Music', and next week the group – Carl, Dennis, Mike Love and long-time friend Al Jardine – will embark on a string of major stadium concerts. Brian, the non-performer, is mulling over putting in an appearance at Saturday's Anaheim Stadium show."

When asked about the longevity of The Beach Boys, Brian replies: "It's down to one simple fact: because we're a family, and the family that sings together stays together, and that's been proven by The Beach Boys a hundred times over. Absolutely! Oh my God, yeah! That's the overwhelming reason why we've had our success and why we've stayed together."

■ Monday 28th

MIXING Brother studio *Santa Monica, CA*. A mix of **'It's OK'** is made today.

July

During this month, The Beach Boys produce for US radio a six-hour documentary series about their 15-year history. Written by Ken Barnes and partly fronted by famous DJ Wolfman Jack, the show notably unveils snippets of a previously unreleased studio version of 'Good Vibrations', as well as The Beatles and assorted friends singing 'Happy Birthday Mike Love', taped by Mike in India on March 15th 1968.

■ Friday 2nd

Oakland Coliseum *Oakland, CA* with America, Elvin Bishop, John Sebastian

On the eve of a US tour, The Beach Boys headline Bill Graham's *Day On The Green Five* concert. Most notably, Brian makes his first complete concert appearance since the Whisky A Go Go concerts in November 1970 (see November 4th 1970) and his first on-stage appearance with the group since April 20th 1973. Five songs into The Beach Boys' set, Brian walks onto the stage. *Rolling Stone*: "It was the first time in 11 years [sic] that Brian Wilson had performed with the group. Sitting upright and motionless, he played throughout the rest of the boys' 90-minute set and handled lead vocals (softly) on 'In My Room'. As he left the stage, Wilson was heard to ask the group, 'Was I OK?'"

TOUR STARTS US North America (Jul 3rd-Aug 15th)

■ Saturday 3rd

Anaheim Stadium *Anaheim, CA* with Rod Stewart, Leo Sayer, Jan & Dean

Opening night of the group's first tour of 1976. After years of shying away from the idea, The Beach Boys have now become an oldies act, churning out hit after hit to the immense pleasure of the paying crowds. Mike is ecstatic at the level the group has now reached but Carl and Dennis are furious. For some time they have tried to reinvent and reintroduce themselves as a flourishing group not reliant on Brian or their past to succeed – but now they have become just that. In preparation for the tour, and in order to keep up his strenuous, highly active on-stage performance, Mike has undergone a lengthy keep-fit regime. His stage costume features a sparkly waistcoat, gold lamé jacket, and the occasional turban. (Tonight's show is professionally recorded by the group.)

As predicted in the *Los Angeles Times* a week ago, Brian rejoins the group on-stage but huddles virtually unrecognised at the piano for most of the evening. In readiness for his appearances, Brian has plugged in a bass guitar and practised for hours at Gold Star studio in LA. But unknown to the euphoric crowd, Brian has to be coaxed on-stage tonight by his psychiatrist. Moments before the concert begins, Dr Eugene Landy encourages him to take a look at what it's like on-stage.

Musically, the show marks the start of a long run where the group use 'California Girls' as the opening number, as well as the introduction of several songs from the new *15 Big Ones* album (released two days later, on the 5th). The backup band tonight includes Billy Hinsche (guitar), Ed Carter (guitar, bass), Bobby Figueroa (drums), Ron Altbach (keyboards) and Carlos Munoz (keyboards). Also tonight Al's ten-year-old son Matt is seen playing bongos (and in the 1990s Matt will become a regular touring member of the band). Scheduled support group Poco pulls out of the show and the rest of the jaunt after signing to open a tour for another act.

Portions of the concert are filmed for inclusion in the TV special *The Beach Boys*, broadcast by NBC on August 5th. Today's performance and Brian's return are witnessed by a capacity 55,000 crowd.

Richard Cromelin writes in the *Los Angeles Times*: "The show was made even more memorable by Brian Wilson's first full-length appearance in several years. Though his piano playing and occasional backing vocals weren't exactly crucial to the total sound on Saturday, his presence – greeted by the unfurling of a 'Welcome Back Brian' banner in the audience – bought an emotional edge to the proceedings. The man responsible for The Beach Boys' beginnings and development must have found it gratifying to see songs that span 15 years and which range from the engagingly primitive to the breathtakingly sophisticated being so eagerly accepted by an audience whose average age wasn't more than that of The Beach Boys' first record."

But the euphoria surrounding Brian's return is lost on some columnists. Los Angeles show business reporter Harvey Kubernik writes in *Melody Maker*: "Brian Wilson was exhibited to the throngs and the shaky figure seemed uncomfortable on stage. Apparently, performing is part of his therapy program. But he should have stayed at home. He's a friendly guy who is very hip and knows what is happening around him. He shouldn't be subjected to being propped up on stage for video purposes or group/media examination. His contributions this afternoon were nil!"

Set-list 'California Girls', 'Darlin'', 'Susie Cincinnati', ' Little Deuce Coupe', 'Catch A Wave', 'I Get Around', 'Palisades Park', 'It's OK', 'God Only Knows', 'A Casual Look', 'Surfer Girl', 'Heroes And Villains, 'Sail On Sailor' (Billy Hinsche lead vocal), 'California Saga: California', 'Be True To Your School', 'Surfin' USA', 'In My Room', 'Back Home' (Brian's only lead vocal tonight), 'Sloop John B', 'Help Me Rhonda', 'Wouldn't It Be Nice', 'Good Vibrations', 'You Are So Beautiful', 'Rock And Roll Music', ' Barbara Ann', 'Fun Fun Fun' (last four as encores).

■ Monday 5th

15 Big Ones album released in the US and UK. It is the band's first studio album since *Holland* in January 1973 and the first in ten years to bear Brian's production credit. The title refers to the group's 15th anniversary as well as the number of songs on the record. Issued as the centrepiece of the controversial yet popular 'Brian Is Back' campaign, *15 Big Ones* will peak in the US chart at number 8, making it the group's first album of new material to reach the American Top 10 since *Pet Sounds* ten years earlier, and the group's biggest commercial success in years.

Brian tells *Sounds*: "The Beach Boys are the real big group of the

1970s. There's no doubt about it. The new album is nothing too deep. We're going to do another 'Good Vibrations' next time around, another masterpiece. Material is getting harder and harder to write all the time for me. I don't know why. It just is." He continues: "This time around, we had strictly commercial stuff. If you listen to the album, you'll see that we were thinking about the public. We thought about songs that were standards and, since they were already acceptable once, we figured that they would be acceptable again, such as 'Blueberry Hill' and 'Palisades Park', songs like that. We figured it was a safe way to go."

But the album is not liked by fans – and a couple of group members. Carl and Dennis object strongly to the release of the record. Carl tells *Newsweek* that he was disappointed with *15 Big Ones*. Dennis adds: "We were heartbroken. People have waited all this time, anticipating a new Beach Boys album, and I hated to give them this. It was a great mistake to put Brian in full control. He was always the absolute producer, but little did he know that in his absence, people grew up, people became as sensitive as the next guy. Why do I relinquish my rights as an artist? The whole process was a little bruising."

20 Golden Greats compilation album released in the UK. EMI in Britain did not join their US partner Capitol in issuing the successful *Endless Summer* and *Spirit Of America* compilations of old recordings, but are now eager to cash in on The Beach Boys' resurgent popularity and issue this TV-advertised compilation LP.

Released at the time of a heatwave in Britain, the record is a great success, topping the UK album charts for a remarkable ten straight weeks. Newspaper and billboard ads for the album read: "The summers were hotter. The parties wilder. And music will never be quite the same. *The Beach Boys 20 Golden Greats*. Can you imagine summer without them?"

To help promote the release a unique 7-inch promotional single featuring an interview with Carl carried out by Tony Wilson in Los Angeles in May is issued by EMI. (The disc will be reissued in 1979 as a blue-vinyl 'limited' edition of 20,000 copies.)

• The group's happy, popular, sun-drenched music becomes a target for money-hungry advertising execs, and timeless Beach Boy melodies are soon re-peddled as soundtracks for TV commercials. A cover version of 'Good Vibrations' appears in US ads for the Sunkist soft drink, while in the UK, hot on the heels of the success of *20 Golden Greats*, a cover version of 'Wouldn't It Be Nice' with rewritten lyrics graces ads for Persil washing powder. Thanks to Murry's merciless sale of the Sea Of Tunes song catalogue back in November 1969, Brian and the other Beach Boys are powerless to do anything about these exploitations of their songs.

■ Saturday 10th

20 Golden Greats album enters UK *Melody Maker* LP chart at number 13.

■ Tuesday 13th & Thursday 15th
Pine Knob Musical Theater Independence Township, Detroit, MI
Back in the US, the group's tour rolls on.

■ Thursday 15th
MIXING Brother studio *Santa Monica, CA*. Mixes are made of three solo recordings by Dennis, **'Rainbows'**, **'River Song'** and **'Thoughts Of You'**.

■ Friday 16th – Sunday 18th
Chicago Stadium Chicago, IL 8:00pm

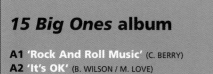

15 Big Ones album

A1 'Rock And Roll Music' (C. BERRY)
A2 'It's OK' (B. WILSON / M. LOVE)
A3 'Had To Phone Ya' (B. WILSON)
A4 'Chapel Of Love' (J. BARRY / E. GREENWICH / P. SPECTOR)
A5 'Everyone's In Love With You' (M. LOVE)
A6 'Talk To Me' (J. SENECA)
A7 'That Same Song' (B. WILSON / M. LOVE)
A8 'TM Song' (B. WILSON)
B1 'Palisades Park' (C. BARRIS)
B2 'Susie Cincinnati' (A. JARDINE)
B3 'A Casual Look' (E. WELLS)
B4 'Blueberry Hill' (A. LEWIS / L. STOCK / V. ROSE)
B5 'Back Home' (B. WILSON / B. NORBERG)
B6 'In The Still Of The Night' (F. PARRIS)
B7 'Just Once In My Life' (P. SPECTOR / G. GOFFIN / C. KING)

US release July 5th 1976 (Brother/Reprise MS 2251).
UK release July 5th 1976 (Reprise K54079).
Chart high US number 8; UK number 31.

The busy live band out on-stage again, with Mike in one of his more eye-catching outfits.

■ Monday 19th
Denver Mile High Stadium *Denver, CO*

■ Thursday 22nd
Northlands Coliseum *Edmonton, AB, Canada*

■ Friday 23rd
Arrowhead Stadium *Kansas City, MO* 5:00pm, with The Doobie Brothers, Jeff Beck, Firefall, Ozark Mountain Daredevils
The concert is attended by just under 30,000 and grosses $240,000.

■ Saturday 24th
Wisconsin State Fair *Milwaukee, WI*
• *20 Golden Greats* album peaks in UK *Melody Maker* chart at number 1, where it will remain until October 2nd before being displaced by *Abba's Greatest Hits*. Also this week, the new *15 Big Ones* album enters the listings at number 23.

■ Sunday 25th
Iowa State Fairgrounds *Des Moines, IA* with The Doobie Brothers, Jeff Beck, Firefall, Gerard
Attendance is 25,400 at this event billed as "the most famous fair in the country".

■ Thursday 29th
Avalon *Santa Catalina Island, CA*

August

■ Wednesday 4th
Masters for the group's next single – 'It's OK', which is sped up for this 45, coupled with 'Had To Phone Ya' – are prepared for release.

■ Thursday 5th
NBC TV in the US airs *The Beach Boys* (8:00-9:00pm), a Dr Pepper-sponsored show celebrating the group's 15th anniversary. The 50-minute colour film mixes concert and interview footage of the band alongside candid moments with its members, including Dennis judging the 1976 Miss California beauty pageant. Additional interview material is seen with Van Dyke Parks and the Wilson brothers' former music teacher at Hawthorne High School. The show is commonly referred to as *It's OK!* because of the title of the group's simultaneously released single. Producer Lorne Michaels tells *TV Guide* that it is "a musical documentary about the lifestyle of one of this country's most popular groups and the sounds that sprang from that lifestyle".

The film features a sketch in which Brian is dragged out of his bed and escorted to the ocean by John Belushi and Dan Aykroyd, filmed on June 20th (see entry). Three versions of 'I'm Bugged At My Ol' Man' were shot at the group's Brother studio in Santa Monica, but the one with Brian coughing is used in the show. Four versions of 'Surfer Girl' and two of Brian's 'Clangin'' (a variation of 'Ding Dang') were also filmed but not used. Live performances featured in *The Beach Boys* are from the group's Anaheim Stadium Concert of July 3rd.

Songs included in the film are: 'Fun Fun Fun' (live), 'Be True To Your School' (live), 'I'm Bugged At My Ol' Man' (Brother studio, Santa Monica; Brian, Dennis and Carl at a piano), 'God Only Knows' (live), 'I Get Around' (live and partially set to footage of The Human Fly and Mike flying his aeroplane), 'You Are So Beautiful' (live), 'That Same Song' (performed with 75-piece Double Rock Baptist Choir), 'Good Vibrations' (live and footage from a band rehearsal), 'Sloop John B' (live), 'Surfin' USA' (live), 'California Girls' (live), 'Help Me Rhonda' (live), 'It's OK' (live), 'Rock And Roll Music' (live), 'Wouldn't It Be Nice' (end-of-show credits and live performance audio only set to footage of Anaheim Stadium crowd).

Footage from this special will be regularly used in future Beach

Boys retrospective documentaries, including the 1983 Dutch TV show *Story Of The Beach Boys*, the 1984 High Ridge documentary *The Beach Boys: An American Band*, and the 1998 Delilah Films presentation *Endless Harmony*.
• In the week prior to the screening of the TV special, several FM radio stations across America have run a commercial in which The Beach Boys sing 'Drink Dr Pepper' and remind listeners about the forthcoming television show.

■ Friday 6th
Metropolitan Stadium *Minneapolis, MN* 7:00pm, with Boz Scaggs
Following a car accident involving their guitarist Terry Kath, Chicago decide to pull out of tonight's gig. Promoter Dick Shapiro, who has invested some $40,000 into the concert and shifted some 28,000 tickets, drafts in Scaggs as a replacement.

■ Saturday 7th
Milwaukee Arena *Milwaukee, WI*

■ Sunday 8th
Kiel Auditorium *St Louis, MO*

■ Monday 9th
Sports Arena *San Diego, CA*

■ Tuesday 10th & Wednesday 11th
The Spectrum *Philadelphia, PA*

■ Friday 13th
Hara Arena *Dayton, OH*

■ Saturday 14th
Three Rivers Stadium *Pittsburgh, PA* with Peter Frampton, Gary Wright

■ Sunday 15th
Veterans Memorial Auditorium *Columbus, OH*

■ Wednesday 18th – Wednesday 25th
Taking advantage of the break in tour duties, Mike heads to London where he presents *The Beach Boys* TV special recently screened in the US to prospective UK programme buyers, but is unsuccessful.

During his week-long visit, Mike gives some interviews, to the *Daily Mail* and *Daily Express* newspapers as well as to John Tobler of *Zig Zag* magazine.

Tobler's piece, headed "Mike Love: 14 Minutes With A Beach Boy", will be published in *Zig Zag* in October. Tobler asks about former Beach Boy David Marks. Mike says: "He is sorely neglected and unjustly so, for he's a fine gentleman, a nice person and he's also studied classical music at a music school in Boston. ... Now he's back on the West Coast, doing what I don't know, because I haven't talked to him for the last couple of years. When I last saw him about three years ago in Boston he was doing very well, feeling good. He'd grown up very handsomely and nicely and he wasn't the same snotty punk kid he was in the group!"

Another interview carried out during this visit is by Jan van Erp of Dutch pop magazine *Muziek Express*.

Erp will recall that he is allowed just one question for Mike, on the subject of transcendental meditation. Mike says during the interview that he does not feel like talking about The Beach Boys' new album, *15 Big Ones*.

■ Monday 23rd
People magazine in the US prints a five-page cover story about The Beach Boys entitled "Still Riding The Crest 15 Hairy Years Later".

TOUR STARTS North America (Aug 26th-Sep 5th)

■ Thursday 26th
Performing Arts Center *Saratoga Springs, NY* 7:00pm
The tour resumes.

■ Friday 27th
Rich Stadium *Buffalo, NY*

■ Saturday 28th
Roosevelt Stadium *Jersey City, NJ* 7:30pm, with The Richie Furay Band

■ Sunday 29th
Dillon Stadium *Hartford, CT*
Set-list 'California Girls', 'Catch A Wave', 'Palisades Park', 'Susie Cincinnati', 'A Casual Look', 'It's OK', 'God Only Knows', 'Sail On Sailor' (Billy Hinsche lead vocal), 'Be True To Your School', 'In My Room', 'Surfer Girl', 'California Saga: California', 'Help Me Rhonda', 'Little Deuce Coupe', 'Sloop John B', 'Wouldn't It Be Nice', 'Darlin'', 'Heroes And Villains', 'Back Home' (Al lead vocal), 'Good Vibrations', 'I Get Around', 'Surfin' USA', 'You Are So Beautiful', 'Barbara Ann', 'Rock And Roll Music', 'Fun Fun Fun' (last four as encores).

■ Monday 30th & Tuesday 31st
Capital Centre *Largo, MD* 8:00pm Mon, 8:00pm & 12midnight Tue, with Artful Dodger
Brian performs at these shows, his first concerts with The Beach Boys outside the state of California since March 22nd 1970. The *Washington Post*'s reporter writes: "'Brian Is Back!' That message, flashing on the Capital Centre telescreen on Monday night, only confirmed what 18,787 young fans knew as soon as The Beach Boys walked on-stage. For the first time in ten years [sic], Brian Wilson, leader of America's most enduring rock'n'roll band, had joined his brothers and friends for a show outside Southern California.

"It's not that Wilson had been entirely inactive the last decade, though. While Mike Love, Al Jardine and Carl and Dennis have been on the road, spreading the timeless surfer gospel, Brian Wilson has been at home, writing the songs and engineering the albums that made The Beach Boys an institution and Wilson a pop music legend. Perhaps that's why Wilson could afford not to play the dominant role on-stage during Monday's show, the first of three here.

"Sitting behind a white grand piano for most of the 90-minute performance, he was just one more voice and one more instrument to be added to the wall of sound that is The Beach Boys' trademark. So it was Carl Wilson who sang the tender lead vocal on 'God Only Knows' and Mike Love who was out front for the surfing hits that were spaced throughout the show. On these and the other numbers as many as six more voices would add harmonies to whoever was singing lead. But it was hard to pick out a flaw or sour note.

"The Beach Boys in fact seem even stronger than they did last summer or the summer before. They're leaning heavily on oldies … . But now they seem less reluctant to perform ambitious works like 'California Saga' and 'Sail On Sailor', both of which feature choir-like vocals and delicious melody lines. A horn section, stationed on board a sloop and framed by palm trees at the rear of the stage, gave familiar tunes such as 'California Girls' and 'Help Me Rhonda' a new

It's OK single

A 'It's OK' (B. WILSON / M. LOVE)
B 'Had To Phone Ya' (B. WILSON)

US release August 30th 1976 (Brother/Reprise 1368).
UK release August 1976 (Reprise K14448).
Chart high US number 29; UK none.

dimension. Other tunes such as 'It's OK' and 'Back Home' used only the five original Beach Boys. Brian Wilson summoned up enough courage to sing lead vocal on the latter.

"The crowd loved it all, of course, although it's hard to say whom they liked best. When Brian Wilson peeked out from the backstage area during the intermission, he was spotted and received a standing ovation. But during the show, the arena was rocked by the high-pitched screams of teenage girls every time that drummer Dennis Wilson was shown on the telescreen. Obviously after 15 years, The Beach Boys still have something to offer."

'It's OK' / 'Had To Phone Ya' single released in the US (30th) and around this time in the UK. This second 45 from *15 Big Ones* will peak in the US chart at number 29.

Mike is not happy with the timing of the release. "It should have been a big hit," he blasts during an interview US radio at the time. "It didn't come out until August. But it's an early summer record. My intention was that it should have been released in May or June. By the time people got hold of it, on the radio level, it was August or September and the summer was over. Who's gonna play a summer record in the fall?"

September

■ Wednesday 1st
Nassau Coliseum *Uniondale, NY*
Midway through the show Dennis introduces his mother, Audree, to the crowd.

■ Thursday 2nd
Erie Stadium *Erie, PA* with The Doobie Brothers, America, Jefferson Starship

■ Friday 3rd – Saturday 4th
Canadian National Exhibition *Toronto, ON, Canada*

■ Sunday 5th
The Forum *Montreal, PQ, Canada*
Last night of the current tour.

■ Monday 6th
RECORDING Brother studio *Santa Monica, CA*; Dennis's *Harmony* sailing boat studio *Marina Del Ray, CA*. With concert duties completed for the time being, Dennis begins recording the main bulk of work for his solo album today (some mixing, at least, was done back in July). He will work intermittently through into 1977 on the project, at present known as *Freckles*, but the record will later be renamed *Pacific Ocean Blue*. Despite earlier efforts, this will become his first proper solo studio album.

Working most days for up to 18 hours, Dennis will use the group's Brother studio for the most elaborate recordings and the equipment on his *Harmony* boat for the less demanding work. The sessions are co-produced by Dennis and long-time friend Gregg Jakobson. He will also use the skills of loyal Beach Boys producer and engineer Stephen Moffitt, plus Earl Mankey and John Hanlon as additional engineers.

Joining him on the sessions are former Beach Boys Bruce Johnston and drummer Ricky Fataar, and from the live band drummer Bobby Figueroa and guitarist Ed Carter, plus the group's erstwhile studio session drummer Hal Blaine. Carl contributes vocals to 'River Song' and 'Rainbows'. Unfortunately Dennis's once beautiful voice is now reduced to a one-octave croon, the result of constant cocaine consumption.

Songs recorded include **'River Song'**, **'What's Wrong'**, **'Moonshine'**, **'Friday Night'**, **'Dreamer'**, **'Thoughts Of You'**, **'Time'**, **'You And I'**, **'Farewell My Friend'**, **'Rainbows'** (started late 1975) and **'End Of The Show'**. The eventual title track **'Pacific Ocean Blues'** was originally recorded in 1975, and was Dennis's sole submission for The Beach Boys' *15 Big Ones* album, but it was so contrary to the feel of that album that it was rejected. *Pacific Ocean Blue* will be released in September 1977 and regarded by many critics as one of the best releases from The Beach Boys' camp during the 1970s. Surprisingly, *Pacific Ocean Blue* will be the first solo album released by anyone from the group.

TV Westinghouse Broadcasting Company, Group W Productions *Philadelphia, PA*. Syndicated *The Mike Douglas Show* live performance 'Everyone's In Love With You', 'TM Song' broadcast September 13th 5:00-6:00pm. Mike and Al sing two songs at a piano; fellow guests are Johnny Cash and June Carter Cash.

TOUR STARTS North America (Sep 16th-Oct 8th)

■ Thursday 16th
Brigham Young University *Provo, UT*

■ Friday 17th
Brian's great comeback continues as he appear as a guest presenter on the second *Don Kirshner's Annual Rock Music Awards* show at the Hollywood Palladium in Los Angeles (transmitted by CBS Television tomorrow night 10:00-11:30pm). The event is co-hosted by Diana Ross and Alice Cooper. Amid a standing ovation from the star-studded audience, Brian takes to the stage wearing a stunning new tuxedo, a trim new haircut and a less bulky figure (his weight is down from 250 to 215 pounds – from about 18 to 15 stones).

During the show he announces the winners of Best Single and Best Female Vocalist. Brian is nominated for the Hall Of Fame category alongside The Beatles (eventual winners), John Lennon, Elvis Presley, and Bob Dylan. Although The Beach Boys were announced to appear at the presentation, only brothers Carl and Dennis accompany Brian to the podium this evening.

■ Saturday 18th
Dome Stadium *Seattle, WA*

■ Sunday 19th – Monday 20th
PNE Coliseum *Vancouver, BC, Canada*

■ Tuesday 21st
Portland Coliseum *Portland, OR*

■ **Friday 24th**
San Diego Coliseum *San Diego, CA*

■ **Saturday 25th**
Hughes Stadium *Sacramento, CA*

■ **Sunday 26th**
Santa Barbara Stadium *Santa Barbara, CA*

October

RECORDING *Love You / New Album* **sessions** probably Brother studio *Santa Monica, CA*. Although dissatisfied with the tedious sessions for *15 Big Ones*, Brian returns to the studio and over the next few months records a series of essentially solo tracks that become associated with three proposed albums, only one of which will be released.

Recordings started this month include **'Let Us Go On This Way'** (co-written by Brian and Mike) and ten Brian originals: **'Mona'**, **'Johnny Carson'**, **'Honkin' Down The Highway'**, **'The Night Was So Young'**, **'I'll Bet He's Nice'**, **'Let's Put Our Hearts Together'**, **'I Wanna Pick You Up'**, **'Airplane'** and **'Love Is A Woman'**.

Other recordings made during this period include the brief **'11th Bar Blues'** with a lead vocal from Mike, a full studio take of **'Clangin''**, and a solo piano/vocal version by Brian of the *Today* song **'In The Back Of My Mind'** with a newly composed bridge.

Work is also done on **'Hey Little Tomboy'**, Van Dyke Parks's **'Come To The Sunshine'** (originally recorded October 1975; the multi-track tapes are later found to be absent from The Beach Boys' tape library), **'Michael Row The Boat Ashore'**, **'Runnin' Bear'** and **'Shake Rattle And Roll'**.

Some follow-up work is also done around this time on **'Ding Dang'** by Brian and Roger McGuinn, a piece that was originally recorded on June 9th 1974.

McGuinn, former member of The Byrds, tells Scott Keller: "I was living in Malibu, California, and by chance I looked at the monitor for the front gate of my security system and noticed an unfamiliar car pull up. The driver rang the bell. 'Who is it?' I asked because I did not recognise the man in the vehicle. 'It's Brian Wilson,' shouted the voice at the other end. 'Come on in,' I hollered, pressing the red button on the intercom box, opening the large electric gate. I was surprised and delighted. Surprised because Brian Wilson had found my house, on his own, without ever having been there before, and delighted that he wanted to see me.

"Brian parked in the driveway and approached the house. I opened the front door and invited him in. 'I just wanted to see you,' he said. 'Do you have any speed?' 'Why yes,' I replied. 'Are you sure you should be taking it?' He said, 'I'm running away from Dr Landy, so it's OK,' … with a half smile from the side of his mouth. I gave him two Biphetamine 20s [amphetamine tablets] and a glass of water and he gulped them down like someone gasping for fresh air after having been submerged for a long time. We had a beer and played pool for a while and then Brian found his way to the music room.

"He had seated himself at my upright piano and was playing a tune. 'What's that?' I asked. 'Oh nothing. Just something I came up with now,' he replied. I said, 'It sounds great! Do you want to write some words?' 'OK,' he replied. We played the tune for an hour or so but the only lyrics we had were: 'I love a girl and I love her madly / I treat her so fine but she treats me so badly,' et cetera. After about five or six hours of this, I got tired and went to bed. When I awoke

the next morning, Brian was still at the piano playing the same verse over and over. The Beach Boys later recorded the song and it only had that one verse."

The Beach Boys Love You will be the group's 28th album, and Brian says later that it is his favourite. Brian says on US radio: "The title of the album was my idea. It's telling the fans or whoever receives the album that they're admired. The Beach Boys love you; it just gives you a secure feeling. I like [it better than *15 Big Ones*]. It's bigger although it's smaller, one less song. It's a cleaner album; the tracks and the songs seem to come off cleaner. Also, there are no real oldies. They're all originals."

The big difference between *15 Big Ones* and *The Beach Boys Love You* is that Brian plays nearly all the instruments himself. His bandmates are otherwise engaged: Mike teaching Transcendental Meditation; Al and wife raising bees and horses; Dennis busy with his own studio album; and Carl producing singer Ricci Martin's first solo album. For the first time since 1967's infamous *Smile* album, Brian finds himself in sole charge of a new Beach Boys album.

His appetite for studio work has returned so much that by the close of 1976 he has completed enough music to fill an album and a half. The leftovers are earmarked for inclusion on the provisionally titled *New Album*, proposed for release in autumn 1977 with the following songs: 'My Diane' (recorded late 1976/early 1977), 'Marilyn Rovell' (recorded October 4th 1976), 'Hey Little Tomboy' (probably recorded October 1976), 'Ruby Baby' (probably recorded September 1976), 'You've Lost That Lovin' Feelin'' (autumn 1976), 'Sherry She Needs Me' (April 1965 and October 1976), 'Come Go With Me' (recorded September 1975), 'Mony Mony' (*15 Big Ones* outtake), 'On Broadway' (*15 Big Ones* outtake), 'Sea Cruise' (*15 Big Ones* outtake), 'HELP Is On The Way' (recorded 1970), 'Games Two Can Play' (1970) and 'When Girls Get Together' (November 1969).

Despite wide publicity as the next Beach Boys release, *New Album* becomes a victim of a serious group disagreement. It is also possible that Warner/Reprise rejects the master.

Of the titles recorded, 'My Diane', 'Come Go With Me' (almost entirely re-recorded) and 'Hey Little Tomboy' will be released on the group's 1978 *M.I.U. Album*. 'Sea Cruise' will appear on *Ten Years Of Harmony* in 1984 and 'Shortenin' Bread' on the 1979 *L.A. (Light Album)*, completely re-recorded, with Dennis on bass vocal. (See also January 1977.)

■ **Friday 1st**
Mid-South Coliseum *Memphis, TN*

■ **Saturday 2nd**
MIXING Brother studio *Santa Monica, CA*. A mix is made of Brian's recent version of **'Ruby Baby'**, probably recorded in September.
Arkansas State Fair *Little Rock, AR*

■ **Sunday 3rd**
Oklahoma State Fair *Tulsa, OK*

■ **Monday 4th**
MIXING probably Brother studio *Santa Monica, CA*. Mixes are made of three of Brian's recent recordings: **'Lazy Lizzie'** (a rewrite of one of the *Holland*-bonus *Fairy Tale* melodies); the autobiographical **'Marilyn Rovell'**; and a revived **'Sherry She Needs Me'**.
• Around this time *Circus* magazine's Scott Cohen visits the Brother studio and interviews Dennis in the lounge of the complex, a place Dennis affectionately calls his office.

Dennis's left foot has a heavy bandage, which naturally prompts Cohen's first question. Dennis tells him about an accident at Carl's house involving a broken bottle. "The cut was from the big toe to the little toe. ... I used to be able to wiggle each toe individually, but since the tendons on the little toe were so small, the surgeon had to sew them all together, so now they all move together."

Cohen: "Who would you want to play you in your life story?"
Dennis: "Don Knotts."
Cohen: "Is there anything you can't live without?
Dennis: "*Star Trek*."
Cohen: "What's the hardest thing about being a Beach Boy?"
Dennis: "Nothing at all. Well, maybe going on the road, leaving home, and business meetings."
Cohen: "Would you want your son to grow up to be a Beach Boy?"
Dennis: "If that's what he wanted to do."

■ Tuesday 5th
MIXING probably Brother studio *Santa Monica, CA*. Mixes are made of '**When Girls Get Together**' (the same basic recording as the 1970 version) and '**Sea Cruise**'.
Convention Center Arena *Dallas, TX* 8:00pm

■ Wednesday 6th
Hofheinz Pavilion *Houston, TX*

■ Thursday 7th
Fort Worth Dallas, TX

■ Friday 8th
Civic Auditorium *San Antonio, TX*

■ Tuesday 26th
RECORDING *Love You / New Album* **sessions** probably Brother studio *Santa Monica, CA*. Recording for Brian's '**Solar System**'.

■ Wednesday 27th
Masters for The Beach Boys' next single – 'Susie Cincinnati' coupled with 'Everyone's In Love With You' – are prepared for release.

November

■ Tuesday 2nd
RECORDING *Love You / New Album* **sessions** probably Brother studio *Santa Monica, CA*. Recording of Brian's '**Roller Skating Child**'.

■ Thursday 4th
Rolling Stone publishes a feature entitled "The Healing Of Brother Bri" which contains a lengthy interview with The Beach Boys by David Felton, illustrated with photographs by Annie Leibovitz.

■ Monday 8th
'Susie Cincinnati' / 'Everyone's In Love With You' single released in the US. It fails to chart.

■ Monday 15th
Beach Boys '69 album released in the US. Capitol Records issues the LP that was released six years ago in the UK as *Live In London*. It will peak in the US chart now at number 75.

■ Tuesday 16th
MIXING Brother studio *Santa Monica, CA*. Rough mixes are made of several of Brian's recent recordings, including: '**Airplane**'

Susie Cincinnati single

A '**Susie Cincinnati**' (A. JARDINE)
B '**Everyone's In Love With You**' (M. LOVE)

US release November 8th 1976 (Brother/Reprise 1375).
Chart high US none.

(missing some overdubs and the closing vocal tag); '**Hey There Momma**' (a backing track only at this point; in late 1977 the song will be used as the basis of '(I Saw Santa) Rockin' Around The Christmas Tree', eventually issued on 1998's *Ultimate Christmas*); '**I'll Bet He's Nice**' (lacking backing vocals and some other overdubs); '**Johnny Carson**'; '**Let Us Go On This Way**'; '**Love Is A Woman**' (with Al and Mike on lead vocals); '**Let's Put Our Hearts Together**'; '**Mona**'; '**Roller Skating Child**' (two mixes with differing vocals); '**Solar System**'; '**The Night Was So Young**'; and '**We Gotta Groove**' (fully complete, but will remain unreleased).

'**Honkin' Down The Highway**' is mixed now too, still with its rough vocal track by from Billy Hinsche, which will be replaced by Al on January 1st 1977.

Al says on US radio: "['Honkin' Down The Highway'] was like a demo. We recorded it in another studio that we built in Santa Monica. Ed Carter played bass. I co-wrote 'Good Time' with Brian; that's a typical Brian track. It was really a lot of fun doing that. But it's a shame that the [*Love You*] album cover is so crummy. Everything about that thing is home made. I think they thought it was our last album. They didn't spend a penny on the album because they knew that we weren't coming back. They used real cheap cardboard for it."

Possibly also mixed around now is '**Good Time**' (by Brian and Al); it was recorded on January 7th 1970 and is simply remixed for *Love You* using the same backing track already released by Spring in 1972.

• In the UK, BBC-2 television's late-night rock show *The Old Grey Whistle Test* transmits a pre-filmed interview with Brian by Bob Harris The 13-minute piece was recorded in the US on September 21st and contains an archive clip of The Beach Boys performing 'When I Grow Up (To Be A Man)' from the November 6th 1964 edition of *Ready Steady Go!*.

TOUR STARTS US East, Midwest (Nov 18th-29th)

■ Thursday 18th
Providence Civic Center *Providence, RI* with Eric Carmen
Six weeks after concluding their latest round of appearances the group kicks off another American tour, albeit a low-key one. Included in the backing band are Ed Carter (guitar, bass), Bobby Figueroa (drums), Billy Hinsche (guitar, bass) and Charles Lloyd (saxophone, flute). Tonight's show attracts an audience of 13,000 and grosses $91,000.

■ Monday 22nd
Cincinnati Riverfront Coliseum *Cincinnati, OH* with Dave Mason, Eric Carmen
Attendance is 15,666; gross $94,000. During the show the group is re-united with cab driver Joellyn Lambert, the heroine depicted in Al's 1969 song 'Susie Cincinnati'. Miss Lambert has been tracked

down by the local newspaper, *The Cincinnati Post*.
Set-list 'Wouldn't It Be Nice', 'Palisades Park', 'Little Deuce Coupe', 'Darlin'', 'In My Room', 'Sail On Sailor', 'California Saga: California', 'God Only Knows', 'Back Home', 'Love Is A Woman', 'Airplane', 'Catch A Wave', 'Heroes And Villains', 'Surfin' USA', 'Susie Cincinnati', 'It's OK', 'Barbara Ann', 'A Casual Look', 'Feel Flows', 'Everyone's In Love With You', 'All This Is That', 'Sloop John B', 'Be True To Your School', 'Help Me Rhonda', 'I Get Around', 'Surfer Girl', 'California Girls', 'Good Vibrations', 'You Are So Beautiful', 'Rock And Roll Music', 'Fun Fun Fun' (last three as encores).

■ Tuesday 23rd

TV Westinghouse Broadcasting Company, Group W Productions, *Philadelphia, PA*. Syndicated *The Mike Douglas Show* live performance 'Sloop John B', 'Back Home' broadcast December 8th 5:00-6:00pm. Brian plays two songs solo at a piano during his first television chat-show appearance. The performance is followed by a short but revealing interview where he discusses taking LSD and his lengthy, two-and-a-quarter-year stay in bed. "I hibernated," Brian tells Douglas. "It was like the Maharishi in the hills, hiding in his bed, snorting cocaine and meditating."

■ Wednesday 24th – Friday 26th
Madison Square Garden *New York, NY*

Three sell-out concerts at this prestigious New York venue, with Brian present at the first two.
Set-list (24th) 'Wouldn't It Be Nice', 'Darlin'', 'Sloop John B' (Brian lead vocal), 'Little Deuce Coupe', 'In My Room', 'Sail On Sailor (Billy Hinsche lead vocal), 'California Saga: California', 'God Only Knows', 'Back Home', 'Airplane', 'Love Is A Woman', 'Catch A Wave', 'Susie Cincinnati', 'It's OK', 'A Casual Look', 'Feel Flows', 'Everyone's In Love With You', 'All This Is That', 'Heroes And Villains', 'Be True To Your School', 'Help Me Rhonda', 'I Get Around', 'Surfer Girl' (Brian on solo portion), 'California Girls', 'Good Vibrations', 'Surfin' USA'. 'Wild Honey (Carl lead vocal), 'Barbara Ann', 'Rock And Roll Music', 'Fun Fun Fun' (last four as encores).

■ Friday 26th

TV NBC Television Studios *New York, NY*. NBC *Saturday Night Live* live performance 'Back Home', 'Love Is A Woman', 'Good Vibrations' broadcast November 27th 11:30pm-1:00am. Brian's comeback reaches a new high following an invitation from the show's producer Lorne Michaels when he makes an appearance as the musical guest on the top-rated NBC TV show, hosted on this occasion by actress Jodie Foster.

Backing Brian for the performances is the show's orchestra. At one point, Brian joins in the general fun atmosphere of the show by singing the songs in a sandbox.

Because of the delayed transmission of his *Mike Douglas Show* appearance, this *Saturday Night Live* presentation becomes Brian's first solo American TV appearance since CBS's *Inside Pop: The Rock Revolution* back on April 25th 1967. Other members of The Beach Boys currently in New York performing sell out shows at Madison Square Garden are angry they are not invited onto this prestigious show, but Michaels is adamant that Brian should appear alone.

■ Sunday 28th
Boston Garden *Boston, MA* **two shows**
Attendance is 27,000; the shows gross $204,000.

■ Monday 29th
Civic Center *Springfield, MA*

December

Manager Steve Love terminates the year-long service of Dr Eugene Landy who has been acting as Brian's therapist. Landy, a clinical psychologist and reputed pioneer in drug treatment, is fired after it is discovered that his fees have doubled from the initial $10,000 per month. Steve Love, Marilyn and The Beach Boys are also concerned about Landy's controversial methods of 'treatment' that require Landy to have "total therapeutic authority over the patient and the patient's environment". Under this programme, Brian has been prescribed drugs such as psychotropic tranquillisers.

Carl says: "Brian was just getting back on his feet. He had been with Dr Landy for more than a year. He was becoming a lot more productive. It was part of his therapy to make music. But [there was disagreement] about what Brian should do. [Landy] was doing it from a therapeutic angle, and Steve had business considerations. So Steve terminated [Landy]. It was really a shame, because Brian regressed pretty much after that."

Steve Schwartz becomes Brian's new therapist, but this is abruptly halted when Schwartz is killed in a freak rock-climbing accident. Stan Love is then summoned to supervise Brian, assisted by Brian's cousin Steve Korthof. Later they are joined by Rushton 'Rocky' Pamplin, a former male model and pro footballer.
Stack-o-Tracks album released in the UK. The peculiar instrumental-backing-tracks only collection is issued in Britain more than eight years since its original release in the US. It does not chart.

TOUR STARTS North America (Dec 15th-31st)

■ Wednesday 15th
Oakland Stadium *Oakland, CA*

■ Tuesday 21st
Pacific Coliseum *Vancouver, BC, Canada* 8:00pm

■ Monday 27th
San Diego Sports Arena *San Diego, CA*

■ Friday 31st
The LA Forum *Los Angeles, CA* 9:30pm–12:30am
The 15th anniversary of the group's first concert as The Beach Boys.
• At midnight, French TV channel TF2 broadcasts a special show entitled *On ne manque pas d'Air*. The one-hour-20-minute programme features excerpts from the group's August 5th US TV show plus fresh interviews carried out in Los Angeles this autumn by French reporter Pierre Lescure.
• Carl says later in *Newsweek*: "The group was really fractured at [this] time. We really went through an explosion. A lot of stuff that hadn't been acknowledged and hadn't been dealt with surfaced. That was a rough time for all of us. Relations were very strained and icy. Everyone was frightened and it came out icy. Everything was falling apart in front of us, and we didn't know how to get hold of it. What we had to do was just let everything fall apart and then realise, 'Now, wait a minute. Do I want to fight with my family and friends?' We got a chance to see if we really wanted to be a group or not. We got to choose again. It became clear that we should put it back together."
• And finally, after those 15 eventful years, a word from Dennis to the *Los Angeles Times*. "We've done everything together. Shit, eat, fart, cry, laugh. Everything. There will always be a Beach Boys. Being a Beach Boy is like being in love."

Post-1976 round-up ... *The Beach Boys Love You* album ... Dennis's solo album, *Pacific Ocean Blue* ... Australia and New Zealand tour ... first Caribou-label LP, *L.A. (Light Album)* ... *Carl Wilson* solo album ... 'Beach Boys Medley' single makes number 12 ... Mike's solo album, *Looking Back With Love* ... Dennis Wilson dies ... Beach Boys/Fat Boys single 'Wipe Out' makes number 12 ... 'Kokomo' single goes to number 1 ... *Good Vibrations* boxed set ... *Pet Sounds Sessions* boxed set ... Carl Wilson dies ... Brian's solo album, *Imagination*, and first solo tour ... *Hawthorne, CA* compilation ... Brian tours, playing *Pet Sounds* and, later, *Smile*.

1977: *The Beach Boys Love You*

Early January sees Brian back in the group's Brother studio in Santa Monica, California, to supervise the recording of seven further songs, for inclusion on an album with the working title *Adult/Child*. Reportedly, Brian is doing this on the insistence of his former doctor, Eugene Landy.

The record is due to feature a mix of new recordings and five tracks from the archive: four from *New Album* (see entry for October-through-December 1976) plus the 1973 American Spring recording of 'Shortenin' Bread' (with Brian on bass vocal) completed by a Carl lead. Of the new material, 'Life Is For The Living', 'Deep Purple', 'It's Over Now' and 'Still I Dream Of It' have Brian reunited with Dick Reynolds, the arranger who worked on the group's 1964 *Christmas Album*.

Provisional listing for *Adult/Child* has: side one 'Life Is For The Living' (by Carl and Brian; recorded early 1977), 'Hey Little Tomboy' (by Mike, Carl and Brian; *15 Big Ones* out-take), 'Deep Purple' (Brian; recorded early 1977), 'H.E.L.P. Is On The Way' (Mike; recorded 1970), 'It's Over Now' (Carl, Brian and Marilyn; early 1977), 'Everybody Wants To Live' (Carl and Brian; early 1977); side two 'Shortenin' Bread' (by Brian and Carl; recorded 1973), 'Lines' (Brian and Carl; early 1977), 'On Broadway' (Al; *15 Big Ones* out-take), 'Games Two Can Play' (Brian; 1970), 'It's Trying To Say' (Dennis; early 1977), 'Still I Dream Of It' (Brian; early 1977).

Once again, as with last year's *New Album*, this planned record will fail to appear. The Beach Boys are near the end of their contract with Warner/Reprise and perhaps decide to save material for CBS, with whom they will sign a multi-million dollar deal later in 1977. It is quite probable that the group is negotiating for a new record deal with both labels throughout the year. There is also a possibility that Warner/Reprise reject the album, or that other members of the group might not want the record released. The new recordings feature mostly Brian alongside contributions from Carl and Dennis. Mike and Al's appearances as lead vocalists are, as noted, from earlier sessions.

In March, The Beach Boys sign with Jim Guercio's CBS-affiliated label Caribou for an estimated $8million. On the 31st, Steve Love's managerial contract is not renewed. Henry Lazarus, a friend of Carl, replaces Love as the group's manager.

At the third attempt, a new Beach Boys album is released, **The Beach Boys Love You**. It's issued in April in the US (chart peak 53) with production credit to Brian, and Carl as 'mixdown producer'. Tracks are: side one 'Let Us Go On This Way' (by Brian and Mike; recorded October 1976), 'Roller Skating Child' (Brian; November 2nd 1976), 'Mona', 'Johnny Carson' (both Brian; October 1976), 'Good Time' (Brian and Al; January 7th 1970), 'Honkin' Down The Highway' (Brian; October 1976), 'Ding Dang' (Brian and Roger McGuinn; June 9th 1974); side two 'Solar System' (Brian; October 26th 1976), 'The Night Was So Young', 'I'll Bet He's Nice', 'Let's Put Our Hearts Together, 'I Wanna Pick You Up', 'Airplane', 'Love Is A Woman' (last six all Brian; October 1976). The following month sees the appearance of a single, **'Honkin' Down The Highway' / 'Solar System'**, which fails to chart.

In June a proposed tour of Europe collapses when new manager Henry Lazarus fails to complete the necessary paperwork. He resigns from his post on the 21st. The only show salvaged is the annual CBS Convention, which takes place in London on June 30th. The missed tour is believed to have cost the band near to $1million in lost revenues.

Mike and Al ask Steve Love to return as The Beach Boys' manager in August. He soon agrees. The following month, Dennis releases the first true solo Beach Boy album, **Pacific Ocean Blue**. It becomes a huge critical success. On September 1st, following a show in New York City's Central Park in front of 150,000 fans, The Beach Boys effectively split. This follows a mighty falling out between Dennis and Carl on one hand and Mike and Al on the other. Brian refuses to take sides. A meeting is arranged for the 17th at Brian's house to sort out the mess, and the split is resolved. During the meeting, Mike wins control of Brian's corporate vote, thus ensuring that he, Brian and Al can vote down Carl and Dennis on any matter.

In October, Dennis's solo single **'You And I' / 'Friday Night'** is released (fails to chart). A solo tour by Dennis is announced but swiftly cancelled. Mike, Al and Brian travel to the Maharishi's International University in Fairfield, Iowa, to record a contract-fulfilling Christmas album for Warners. Carl and Dennis make occasional visits. When the completed *Merry Christmas From The Beach Boys* is presented to Warners, the company rejects the record.

1978: from Peggy Sue to *M.I.U.*

During February and March, The Beach Boys undertake a three-week tour of Australia and New Zealand, their first visit down-under for seven years. On their return they decide to fire Steve Love again. Tom Hulett takes over managerial duties.

The single **'Almost Summer' / 'Lookin' Good'**, taken from the soundtrack of the movie *Almost Summer*, is released in April in the US by MCA (chart peak 28). It's credited to 'Celebration featuring Mike Love', a splinter band of Beach Boys touring musicians. On the 28th, Celebration make their live debut, at the University of Southern California, with special guests Brian, Carl, and Jan & Dean. Also around this time, Dennis works on his second solo project, *Bamboo*.

In July, The Beach Boys head to Florida's Criteria studio to record their first album for the Caribou label. But with Brian unable to function as the group's producer, a phone call is made to former Beach Boy Bruce Johnston, who accepts the job – and remains as a regular member of the touring Beach Boys.

The final Warners single from the group, **'Peggy Sue' / 'Hey Little Tomboy'**, is released in the US in August (chart peak 59).

The following month the group's Brother studio in Santa Monica is sold to jazz musician Tom Scott.

Following many overdubbing sessions and newly recorded pieces, the tapes from Iowa in late 1977 are finally released as the **M.I.U. Album** in October, completing the group's obligation under the Warners contract. Meanwhile, they finish their first Caribou album, announced as featuring a disco remake of a song from the 1967 album *Wild Honey*.

1979: the Caribou debut

In January, Brian and Marilyn Wilson's divorce is finalised. The following month, the much-publicised disco remake of the 1967 song **'Here Comes The Night'** is released as a 12-inch single lasting ten minutes as well as an edited-down 7-inch version (chart peak 44), backed by **'Baby Blue'**. It is co-produced by Bruce and his old friend Curt Becher.

In March the group's first Caribou record **L.A. (Light Album)** is issued, with production credits to The Beach Boys, Bruce Johnston, James William Guercio, Curt Becher and Al Jardine (chart peak 100). A month later the single **'Good Timin'' / 'Love Surrounds Me'** is released (chart peak 40), the group's first Top 40 hit for nearly three years.

In July, following an incident on stage at the Universal Amphitheater in Los Angeles, Dennis is barred from the band until he can control his substance abuse.

The group's single **'Lady Lynda' / 'Full Sail'** is released in August. Although failing to dent the US listings, it becomes a Top Ten hit in the UK and several other territories. Also this month The Beach Boys undertake a tour of Japan – their first since 1966.

1980: strolling the Walk of Fame

The group's Bruce Johnston-produced album **Keepin' The Summer Alive** is released in March (chart peak 75). Dennis missed most of the sessions. The first single from the album, **'Goin' On' / 'Endless Harmony'**, reaches number 83, and then a further single, **'Livin' With A Heartache' / 'Santa Ana Winds'**, is released in May but fails to chart.

In June the group tours Britain. Performances include an open-air show at Knebworth House in Hertfordshire on the 21st, coinciding with Brian's 38th birthday, and is filmed and recorded. It will be the last time that all six Beach Boys – Brian, Carl, Dennis, Mike, Al and Bruce – perform together on a UK stage.

The group plays an Independence Day show at The Mall in Washington DC in July, broadcast live on FM radio and transmitted in edited form on the HBO channel. On December 30th The Beach Boys are awarded a star on Hollywood's prestigious Walk Of Fame. Dennis is conspicuous by his absence.

1981: medley and *Harmony*

The solo album **Carl Wilson** is released in March (chart peak 185) and a single is lifted from the disc, **'Hold Me' / 'Hurry Love'** (fails to chart). At the same time, uneasy with the group's lack of rehearsals and their choice of new material, Carl quits The Beach Boys. To bridge the gap, the rest of the group insists on Brian returning to the fold, and UK-based Beach Boys imitator Adrian Baker is invited to fill out the sound by replicating Carl's vocals.

Beginning in Chicago on April 5th and ending in San Francisco on the 25th, Carl embarks on his first solo tour of clubs to promote his album. Later this summer he will open for acts such as The Doobie Brothers.

Dennis's boat *Harmony* is repossessed in June when he fails to maintain payments. Also this month **'Heaven'** is released, the second single from *Carl Wilson*, oddly backed once more with 'Hurry Love' (fails to chart).

In July, Capitol Records in the US takes advantage of the latest music-biz craze and assembles a sequence of eight Beach Boys classics to make a single A-side suitably called **'The Beach Boys' Medley'**. The excerpts come from 'Good Vibrations', 'Help Me Rhonda', 'I Get Around', 'Shut Down', 'Surfin' Safari', 'Barbara Ann', 'Surfin' USA' and 'Fun Fun Fun'. Backed by a complete version of 1966's 'God Only Knows', the single peaks at an impressive number 12. Also this month, the group plays their second annual Independence Day show in Washington DC, which they follow the next day with a nationally-broadcast concert from Long Beach, reportedly a poor performance.

A single featuring two tracks extracted from Mike's forthcoming solo album, **'Looking Back With Love' / 'One Good Reason'**, is released in September on the Casablanca label in the US (fails to chart). Mike is touring now with his own group, The Endless Summer Beach Band. Also this month, the album **Brian Wilson/Beach Boys Rarities** is issued only in Australia, but is later withdrawn, apparently because its liner notes mistakenly imply that The Survivors were The Beach Boys under another name. The album features the only legal release of 'What I'd Say', a track recorded live in Sydney, Australia on January 17th 1964.

Mike's album **Looking Back With Love** is released in October (fails to chart). The following month sees the release of

Ten Years of Harmony, a compilation album featuring some of the group's best work from the Warners and Caribou years. Although it includes previously unreleased material and alternate versions, it peaks no higher than number 156. A single lifted from the album, coupling **'Come Go With Me'** (1978) and **'Don't Go Near The Water'** (1971), reaches number 18. Meanwhile towards the end of the year, in December, the group tours South Africa.

1982: Carl is back

After promises that the group will reconsider their musical and rehearsal policy and will not take on Las Vegas-type engagements, Carl Wilson returns to The Beach Boys' line-up in May. He has been away for approximately 14 months, and has spent some of that time away from the group recording a second solo album.

On November 5th Brian is 'sacked' from The Beach Boys' line-up. It is part of a scheme devised by Carl, his manager Jerry Schilling, Brian's lawyer John Branca and Beach Boys manager Tom Hulett to get Brian back in the care of Dr Eugene Landy.

1983: R.I.P. Dennis Wilson

On January 16th Brian flies to Kona, Hawaii, to begin treatment with Dr Landy. The following month, Carl's second solo album, **Young Blood**, is released (fails to chart). In March, The Beach Boys' cover of the classic Mamas & The Papas recording **'California Dreamin'**" appears on Mike Love's **Rock & Roll City**, a collection of re-recordings of classic 1960s songs. Available on cassette only from branches of the US electronics store Radio Shack, it reportedly sells an impressive 100,000-plus copies. Meanwhile Brian flies back to Los Angeles, and Carl's solo single **'What You Do To Me' / 'Time'** peaks in the American chart at number 72.

The Beach Boys gain publicity and public support in July as they are effectively banned from the annual Independence Day show in Washington. James Watt, Secretary of the Interior, decrees that rock bands attract the wrong element, seemingly a personal attack on The Beach Boys. Vice-president George Bush subsequently invites the band to visit the White House in Washington DC on the 17th.

In September, Capitol Records releases **Rarities**, containing non-album A- and B-sides, alternative versions and previously unissued material, including an unreleased version of 'Good Vibrations'. It fails to chart and is soon withdrawn following a threat of legal action by the band. On the 26th at the LA County Fairgrounds, Pomona, Dennis plays what will be his last show with the band. Mike's Christmas single, **'Jingle Bell Rock' / 'Let's Party'** is released only in Britain in November.

On December 28th Dennis drowns while swimming in Marina Del Ray in Los Angeles. He is 24 days past his 39th birthday.

1984: a final farewell

On January 4th Dennis is buried at sea at 33.35N 118.38W, a point in Santa Monica Bay about 20 miles north of Santa Catalina Island. Usually civilians cannot be buried at sea, but the Reagan administration has granted an exemption.

1985: *An American Band*

In April a video documentary *The Beach Boys – An American Band* is released. It contains much previously unseen and rare footage of the band and a few snatches of previously unreleased music, most notably a snippet of the legendary 'Fire' music from the 1966 *Smile* sessions.

The following month the first new Beach Boys single for exactly five years, **'Getcha Back' / 'Male Ego'**, is released in the US (chart peak 26). The new album, ***The Beach Boys***, is also released (52), containing the first new Beach Boys material to be issued on the new Compact Disc format. Former Beatle Ringo Starr and legendary Motown recording artist Stevie Wonder are among the guests on the record. On May 12th Brian performs at a Malibu Emergency Room benefit concert.

On July 13th The Beach Boys are among the performers in Philadelphia for the American side of the groundbreaking transatlantic charity event, Live Aid. In August the group's single **'It's Gettin' Late' / 'It's OK'** is released in the US (chart peak 82). Four months later the final (unsuccessful) single from the last album, **'She Believes In Love Again' / 'It's Just A Matter Of Time'**, is released in the US.

1986: *Made In USA*

In May, Eugene Landy contacts Brian's early songwriting partner Gary Usher with a plan for producing a solo album for Brian. Over the next ten months the so-called Wilson Project will see over a dozen tracks recorded. The recordings will range from basic demos to finished masters. Very few will be given an official release.

The album *Fourth Of July – A Rockin' Celebration Of America* is released on Mike's custom Love Foundation label. Among performances by other artists it includes versions of 'Back In the USSR' with Ringo Starr on drums, 'Surfer Girl' with Julio Iglesias, and 'Barbara Ann' with Jimmy Page and friends, from 4th of July shows in Washington DC (1984) and Philadelphia (1985)

In June the Beach Boys single **'Rock & Roll To The Rescue' / 'Good Vibrations'** (recorded live in London) is released, with production by Terry Melcher (chart peak 68).

Capitol releases a 25th anniversary greatest-hits package ***Made In USA*** in July, predictably heavy on material from 1962 to 1969 (chart peak 96). On the 4th The Beach Boys perform a set at the second annual *Farm Aid* show. A reworked recording of **'California Dreamin''** is issued as a single in America in August (chart peak 57).

Brian performs a short set at an NAS tribute show on December 6th. Six days later, The Beach Boys play a 25th anniversary show on the beach in Hawaii. Special guests include Three Dog Night, former Beach Boy Glen Campbell, The Everly Brothers, and Ray Charles (who performs 'Sail On Sailor'). A highlight from the show is 'Spirit Of Rock & Roll', a solo track from the Wilson/Usher sessions that were recorded earlier this year. The event is filmed, and will be transmitted in the US on March 13th next year.

1987: Wipe Out rapping

Seymour Stein, president of Sire Records, approaches Brian on January 22nd with an offer to record a solo album. In March, his solo single **'Let's Go To Heaven In My Car' / 'Too Much Sugar'** is issued in the US to little chart action. (The version that appears on the soundtrack of *Police Academy 4 – Citizens On Patrol* later the same month is slightly different.) Working now without Gary Usher, Brian starts on his Sire solo album with producer/musician Andy Paley. But the so-called Wilson Project is effectively ended by Eugene Landy's continual interference.

ABC TV airs a Beach Boys special, *25 Years Together*, on March 13th. In May, the single **'Wipe Out'** is released in the US. It features a most unlikely collaboration between The Beach Boys and American rappers The Fat Boys (chart peak 12). Carl is absent from the video made to accompany the release.

1988: Kokomo chart-topper

On January 20th, The Beach Boys are inducted into The Rock & Roll Hall Of Fame, alongside Bob Dylan, The Drifters and The Beatles. Mike uses the occasion to make an unfortunate speech berating everyone present, notably Rolling Stones frontman Mick Jagger. Five days later The Beach Boys become the first group to receive the American Music Awards 'Award Of Merit'.

In August, Brian's first solo album ***Brian Wilson*** is released in the US. Excellent reviews follow but the disc fails to sell in great quantity (chart peak 54). Also this month **'Kokomo'** by The Beach Boys, as used in the Tom Cruise film *Cocktail*, is released on Elektra as a single and will soon go to number 1 – almost 22 years after the previous US chart topper for The Beach Boys, 'Good Vibrations'.

1989: *Still Cruisin'*...

Brian releases **'Melt Away' / 'Being With The One You Love'** in January, a second (unsuccessful) single taken from his solo album. In May he records **'Daddy's Little Girl'** for the *She's Out Of Control* movie soundtrack.

In the summer, Brian begins recording his second solo album for Sire, with a working title of *Brian* and later *Sweet Insanity*. Both versions presented to the label, in 1990 and 1991, are rejected on the grounds of Eugene Landy's lyrics and the inclusion of 'Smart Girls', Brian's attempt to do a rap song (and featuring excerpts from several Beach Boys songs). Meanwhile, The Beach Boys record a weekly television show, *Endless Summer*, at Universal Studios. Brian is among the all-star guests on 'The Spirit Of The Forest', a charity single released in June to help preserve the world's rainforests.

In August, The Beach Boys' new album ***Still Crusin'*** is released in the US. It's a curious mixture of new material and songs used in movie soundtracks (chart peak 46). The title track is released as a single (93).

Brian issues a $100million dollar lawsuit in August to recover the publishing rights that his father, Murry Wilson, signed away in November 1969, allegedly without Brian's knowledge.

1990: two LPs = one CD

Wilson Phillips release their debut album, *Wilson Phillips*. The vocal trio consists of Chynna Phillips, daughter of John and Michelle Phillips of The Mamas & The Papas, and Carnie and Wendy Wilson, daughters of Marilyn and Brian Wilson.

On April 29th ABC in the US screens the made-for-TV film *Summer Dreams*, based on *Heroes And Villains*, the controversial book about The Beach Boys by Steven Gaines.

In May, Capitol Records begins issuing The Beach Boys' 1962-1969 catalogue (except *Pet Sounds*) in a two-LPs-on-one-CD form, popularly known as a 'two-fer'. The pairings are: *Surfin' Safari–Surfin' USA*; *Surfer Girl–Shut Down Volume 2*; *Little Deuce Coupe–All Summer Long*; *Beach Boys Today!–Summer Days (And Summer Nights!!)*; *Smiley Smile–Wild Honey*; *Friends–20/20*, *(Recorded "Live" At A) Beach Boys' Party!–Stack-o-Tracks*; and *Beach Boys Concert–Live in London*. All of these Capitol two-fer CD releases feature extensive liner notes and a number of bonus tracks including B-sides, alternative takes, and a spattering of unreleased material.

On May 25th Gary Usher, Brian's original songwriting partner, dies of lung cancer at the age of 51.

The Beach Boys tour in the summer without Mike, who is in Japan fronting his Endless Summer Beach Band. Gerry Beckley of America is asked to fill in for Mike in The Beach Boys. During November CBS/Epic begin reissuing The Beach Boys' post-1985 catalogue on CD, up to and including *Keepin' The Summer Alive*. Also released on CD is Dennis Wilson's 1977 solo album *Pacific Ocean Blue*.

1991: *Wouldn't It Be Nice* in print

A compilation of the Hite Morgan recording sessions, titled ***Lost And Found (1961-1962)***, is released in February on the DCC label. The rediscovery of a cache of original session tapes, which include alternative takes, studio chatter and previously unreleased demos, enables fans of the group and audio archaeologists to hear these early Beach Boys recordings properly for the first time.

In April, The Beach Boys are honoured in Central Park, New York City, as a row of park benches is named after them. The following month Brian contributes a track to the Walt Disney charity album *For Our Children*. On May 7th Carl, Audree, Wendy and Carnie Wilson instigate a lawsuit to have Brian removed from the care of Dr Eugene Landy and to have a conservator or guardian appointed.

Roger Christian, Brian's lyricist during the early 1960s, dies at the age of 67 on July 11th after complications following liver and kidney disease.

The city of Lima, Ohio, declares August 7th 'Al Jardine Day'. The man is present at a ceremony where he is given the key to the city.

In September, Brian's revealing autobiography *Wouldn't It Be Nice – My Own Story* is published. The book will prompt lawsuits from Mike, Al, Carl, and Audree Wilson.

In October, The Beach Boys contribute a cover of **'Crocodile Rock'** to the tribute album *Two Rooms – Celebrating The Songs Of Elton John & Bernie Taupin*. Brian embarks on a marathon book-signing promotional tour of the US from October 21st to November 15th.

Following a meeting between Brian and Carl, the conservatorship case is settled out of court on December 13th. Brian's multifaceted relationship with Dr Eugene Landy is dissolved with effect from January 1st 1992, and the new arrangement is reported to have effect for three years. Brian is said to be happy with the decision. Brian's new conservator is Jerome S. Billet.

1992: *Summer In Paradise*

Brian's 1989 lawsuit to recover his 'lost' copyrights is settled out of court in April with an award to Brian of $10million. Soon afterwards, Mike announces a lawsuit against Brian to reclaim both royalties and credit for over 30 songs he claims to have contributed to. On the 5th, Mike, Al and Bruce arrive in London to attend with George Harrison a benefit concert for the Natural Law (TM) Party, an event coinciding with the UK general election. George Harrison is associated with the Natural Law Party.

The Original Beach Boys Cafe, featuring original memorabilia of the group, opens in Hermosa, California, in May. The Beach Boys and their families attend the opening.

In August the record ***Summer In Paradise*** is released on Brother Records and becomes the first Beach Boys album ever with no participation at all from Brian, and the first non-compilation Beach Boys album to fail to chart. (The band will later rework five of the recordings on the album, but the revised version is released only in Europe and Australasia in 1993.)

Eugene Landy is served with a restraining order in December following his continued interference in Brian's life. His hold over Brian is finally broken when Landy moves to Hawaii.

1993: *Good Vibrations* boxed

Steve Douglas, veteran saxophonist of many Beach Boys sessions, dies on April 19th of heart failure at the age of 55.

In June, Carl begins working with Robert Lamm of Chicago and Gerry Beckley of America on a project dubbed Trio.

The Beach Boys Cafe moves to Mission Beach, California, but shuts within a year.

A five-CD career retrospective ***Good Vibrations – 30 Years Of The Beach Boys*** is released in July to critical acclaim. Some of the tracks have been chosen by fans and collectors. Sprinkled among the first four CDs of hits and classic tracks are over 15 previously unreleased pieces, including half-an-hour of original, previously unheard *Smile* material. The fifth CD is composed entirely of collector's items and further *Smile* material. Initial pressings of the European version include a bonus sixth CD featuring European hits. To help promote the set, Capitol throws a huge 'beach party' in their parking lot and have The Beach Boys perform for the specially invited guests. On August 16th Mike is a guest on the American QVC (Quality Value Convenience) shopping channel to help promote the boxed set.

1994: song split settled

The *Good Vibrations* boxed set is certified Gold in July. On August 30th The Beach Boys appear as guests on the CBS *David Letterman Show*. Erstwhile touring Beach Boy Billy Hinsche sits in on keyboards.

At a Brian Wilson tribute concert at the Morgan-Wixon Theater in Santa Monica, California, on November 3rd Brian himself performs. He is impressed by the performance of the main group, The Wondermints.

On December 12th a federal jury decides that Mike has been unfairly deprived of his due credit on some 35 Beach Boys songs. Eight days later Mike and Brian settle the 1992 songwriting suit and Mike is awarded $5million plus future royalties on the relevant compositions.

1995: Parks & Wilson create *Crate*

During the year Capitol Records announces that it will release a *Smile* boxed set, but at the time of writing it is still to appear.

On January 25th a documentary directed by Don Was, *I Just Wasn't Made For These Times*, premieres at the Sundance Film Festival in Park City, Utah. It is a revealing programme about Brian, his life and his music. Shot in black-and-white, it includes interviews with Brian as well as performances in the studio of many classic tunes. A soundtrack CD for *I Just Wasn't Made For These Times* will be released in August, and the show debuts on The Disney Channel.

Capitol Records releases **20 Good Vibrations – The Greatest Hits** in April, a Beach Boys compilation spanning the years from 1962 to 1966 but also including the 1988 number 1 hit 'Kokomo'.

In May Brian makes a now rare live appearance with The Beach Boys at a concert in Las Vegas, Nevada. From the 14th to the 19th The Beach Boys (minus Carl) along with families and fans board the Big Red Boat Beach Boys Cruise to the Bahamas. Once the entourage arrives, The Beach Boys perform a concert for the fans on the dock, with Carl flying in specially for the show.

The **Orange Crate Art** album credited to Brian Wilson and Van Dyke Parks is released in October in the US. It features Brian's vocals on songs mostly composed by Parks.

1996: fun with Status Quo

Mike and his wife branch out into the eatery business with his trademarked Mike Love's Club Kokomo. The chain will feature a restaurant, nightclub and kids' club, and establishes a retail brand of signature merchandise.

In the UK in February **'Fun Fun Fun'** by Status Quo with The Beach Boys is released (chart peak 24) with a new verse written by Mike.

The Beach Boys perform at the Music City Country Awards with Sawyer Brown in June and sing 'I Get Around'. On the 8th, Brian and Van Dyke Parks perform at the Songwriters Symposium at the Will Geer Theater in Topanga, California. The Beach Boys perform again at Farm Aid, on October 19th.

1997: *Pet Sounds* boxed

It is announced in April that Carl has been diagnosed with lung cancer and secondary tumours in his brain. He begins chemotherapy treatment.

In May, Brian presents The Bee Gees with an award at the annual Rock & Roll Hall Of Fame event. On the 16th, Mike is one of the judges for this year's Miss Universe Pageant. Carl plays what will be his last live show with The Beach Boys in Atlantic City, New Jersey, in August.

Derek Taylor, the former Beatles PR man and The Beach Boys' publicist in 1966 and 1967, dies of cancer on September 8th at the age of 63.

To replace an ailing Carl, in October Mike asks former Beach Boy David Marks to return to the fold. On the 9th Marks plays his first show, in Las Vegas, Nevada.

Following delays lasting over a year, a four-CD boxed set **The Pet Sounds Sessions** is released in November by Capitol. It consists of the original mono version of the album, along with unreleased vocal sessions and alternative takes, as well as the first ever true stereo mix of the album.

Guitarist Tommy Tedesco, another veteran Beach Boys sessionman, dies of liver and lung cancer on November 10th.

Audree Wilson, mother of Brian, Carl and Dennis, dies at the age of 79 on December 1st of kidney failure and heart problems.

1998: R.I.P. Carl

Nik Venet, the original Beach Boys producer at Capitol Records, dies on January 2nd of Burkitt's Lymphoma.

On January 25th, Mike, Bruce, David Marks and Dean Torrence appear during the Superbowl pre-game show, billed as America's Band. The first that Al knows of this is when he sees it on TV: he has not been asked to participate in the event.

In February a CD entitled **Mike Love, Bruce Johnston & David Marks Of The Beach Boys Salute NASCAR** is made available only from Union 76 truck stops. Alongside remakes of classic Beach Boys car songs, the record also includes a previously unavailable cover of 'Little GTO'.

Carl dies of complications arising from lung and brain cancer on February 6th, just over a month past his 51st birthday. His body is later buried at the Westwood Memorial Park in Los Angeles, California.

Brian's solo single **'Your Imagination' / 'Happy Days'** is released in June on the Giant label (fails to chart). The following month, his solo album **Imagination** is released in the US, produced by Brian and Joe Thomas (chart peak 88).

The inaugural Carl Wilson Walk Against Cancer and Benefit Concert takes place in Los Angeles, California, on October 18th. Al's group Beach Boys Family & Friends headlines the event as they play their first live set. On November 23rd they make their first TV appearance, guesting on US TV show *Live With Regis & Kathie Lee*.

1999: Brian's solo Wondermints

Al's group Beach Boys Family & Friends makes their public debut on February 28th at the Strawberry Festival in Plant City, Florida, as they play two shows.

In March, Brian embarks on his first ever solo tour. He is backed by Los Angeles band The Wondermints and former Beach Boys band member Jeff Foskett.

On April 9th Brother Records sues Al Jardine for trademark infringement regarding use of the 'Beach Boys' name.

In July, Brian's contract with Giant Records is terminated. He tours Japan with The Wondermints from July 9th to the 14th. A DVD version of the 1995 documentary *I Just Wasn't Made For These Times* is released on August 17th in America.

In September **20 More Good Vibrations – The Greatest Hits Volume 2** is released by Capitol Records (chart peak 192). The label intends that together with the 1993 *Good Vibrations* boxed set, these two compilations will become the definitive Beach Boys collections and allow them to withdraw all other sets from the market.

The second annual Carl Wilson Walk Against Cancer takes place in Malibu, California on October 3rd.

All licenses issued to shareholders of Brother Records expire at midnight on December 31st. Brother votes not to renew Al's license to use the 'Beach Boys' name. Those voting are Al, Mike, Brian (via his conservator), the estate of Carl, and Brother (which acquired Dennis's vote from his estate some years earlier).

2000: *Pet Sounds* staged

During January, Brother Records wins a temporary injunction preventing Al from using the 'Beach Boys' name. He renames his group Alan Jardine's Family & Friends Beach Band and files a counter suit against Brother. On the 17th *People* magazine in the US runs an article about the ongoing lawsuit.

The compilation **Best Of The Brother Years – The Greatest Hits Volume 3** is released in February. Although it contains some previously unavailable single versions, it fails to chart.

ABC TV airs the two-part mini-series *The Beach Boys: An American Family* on February 27th and 28th. The movie is criticised for inaccuracies and distortions of history.

A preliminary injunction is granted in March against Al preventing him from using the name 'Beach Boys' in any way. The following month, the group's 1966 album *Pet Sounds* is finally acknowledged as a 'gold'-selling record.

Brian goes out on tour again in the spring and this time the centrepiece of the set is a compete performance of the *Pet Sounds* album. Although critically well received, the tour rarely plays to full houses and runs up losses of hundreds of thousands of dollars.

In the summer, Capitol Records reissues the band's albums from 1970-1985 in two-fer format (two LPs on one CD), remastered but without bonus tracks. The releases are: *Sunflower–Surf's Up, Carl & The Passions–Holland* (including the *Fairy Tale* material); *In Concert*; *15 Big Ones–The Beach Boys Love You*; *M.I.U. Album–L.A. (Light Album)*; and *Keepin' The Summer Alive–The Beach Boys*. Each CD boasts liner notes by celebrity Beach Boys fans such as Peter Buck of R.E.M. and Sir Elton John, and noted Beach Boys journalists such as *Billboard*'s Timothy White and Paul Williams.

On July 4th, Brian appears on the American QVC shopping channel to promote his new CD, **Live At The Roxy**.

Charles Dean 'Chuck' Britz, the engineer for the vast majority of Brian's classic cuts at Western studio between 1963 and 1967, dies on August 21st from brain cancer.

On October 8th the third annual Carl Wilson Walk Against Cancer takes place in Malibu, California.

2001: back to *Hawthorne, CA*

The Beach Boys receive the Grammy Lifetime Achievement Award on January 20th along with Tony Bennett, Sammy Davis Jr, Bob Marley, and The Who.

The lawsuit concerning ownership of the 'Beach Boys' name continues. Al's attempt to amend his appeal to make it more wide-ranging is denied on March 19th. Ten days later Brian is the subject of a TNT star-studded tribute held at Radio City Music Hall in New York City. The show is taped for a later airing and also appears on DVD.

Hawthorne, CA is a new two-CD 57-track compilation of Beach Boys sessions, demos, first-time stereo mixes, alternative versions and unreleased material from the years from 1961 to 1969, released on May 22nd by Capitol in the US.

On June 4th the decision to forbid Al to use the 'Beach Boys' trademark becomes final. Immediately, Al again appeals against the decision. The following day, Al and Brian carry out an internet chat on Yahoo to celebrate the release of the new *Hawthorne, CA* set.

Brian makes another appearance on David Letterman's late-night chat show on June 28th, performing 'Sail On Sailor'. On July 26th he appears on US TV show *Late Night With Conan O'Brien* and sings 'Our Prayer', 'Heroes And Villains' and 'Sloop John B'.

Long-time Beach Boys tour manager Matt Sheppard dies on September 27th from cancer. On October 14th the fourth annual Carl Wilson Walk Against Cancer takes place in Los Angeles.

2002: Brian at the Palace

On February 9th, The Beach Boys perform at the Salt Lake City Winter Olympics.

In April, Brian records vocal guest-spots on two new albums: Anton Fig's *Figments* and Nancy Sinatra's *California Girl*.

Alongside artists such as Paul McCartney, Elton John, Eric Clapton and Sting, Brian performs at the Queen's Golden Jubilee concert in the grounds of Buckingham Palace in central London on June 3rd.

In July, Al's newly revised lawsuit is once again dismissed. A proposed Beach Boys tour of Japan from August 24th to 29th is cancelled due to Mike's back problems. All Beach Boys engagements between August 11th and September 13th are also cancelled. On the 23rd, Brian is again a guest on CBS TV's *David Letterman Show* and sits in with the show's regular band.

The VH-1 channel in the US airs an end-of-summer Beach Boys marathon on September 1st, a six-hour event that includes a showing of the *Endless Harmony* documentary along with various Beach Boys videos, and a 'Listening Party' for two new releases, Brian's **Pet Sounds Live** CD, and **Beach Boys Classics Selected By Brian Wilson**, a compilation CD released the following day in the US.

Following a request by Paul McCartney, Brian performs at Adopt-A-Minefield's second annual Open Hearts Clear Mines benefit gala at the Century Plaza Hotel in Los Angeles on September 18th.

On October 6th the fifth annual Carl Wilson Walk Against Cancer takes place at Royce Hall UCLA in Los Angeles. Two days later Brian performs at a New York benefit show for Timothy White, the *Billboard* magazine editor and Beach Boys biographer who died in June.

On November 11th, **The Beach Boys Live At Knebworth 1980** CD is released in the US. In December, via his official website, Brian releases a seasonal *a cappella* version of **'White Christmas'** that fans can listen to and download. Also this month Al releases his CD single, **'PT Cruiser'**.

2003: *Sounds Of Summer*

Brian performs at an Elton John tribute concert in Anaheim, California, on January 17th. Eleven days later the US courts dismiss Al's latest appeal against the ban on him using the 'Beach Boys' name.

On March 25th in the US a DVD titled **The Beach Boys – Good Timin' Live at Knebworth England 1980** is released as

BELOW Recreating the unreleased: Brian and band on-stage in 2004 during the *Smile* tour.

a companion to last year's *The Beach Boys Live At Knebworth 1980* CD.

In April, Brother Records again sues Al for continuing to use the 'Beach Boys' name in his advertising.

At the 48th Ivor Novello Awards in London in May, Brian is presented with a special International Award to mark his outstanding contribution to popular music.

A UK tour is announced for February and March 2004, *Brian Wilson presents Smile*. While in London now Brian records a collaboration with Eric Clapton at Abbey Road studios intended for his upcoming album.

Brian is awarded an honorary doctorate from Northeastern University in Boston, Massachusetts, on June 14th.

Capitol Records in the US issues on July 22nd The Beach Boys' classic 1966 LP **Pet Sounds** on DVD-A (DVD-Audio), the first release that allows fans to hear the complete album in stereo, mono, and 5.1 surround sound. On September 30th Capitol releases in the US the two-CD compilation **Sounds Of Summer** that focuses on the group's international hits.

On October 6th the US Supreme Court justices refuse to hear Al's appeal to fight the court order which is forbidding him to use the name 'Beach Boys' when he tours.

On October 16th the sixth annual Carl Wilson Walk Against Cancer benefit concert takes place again at Royce Hall UCLA in Los Angeles, California. Brian Wilson is the headlining act. Five days later Brian releases in the US the new DVD **Brian Wilson Presents Pet Sounds Live In London**.

On November 12th Al gets the go-ahead to sue Mike over the use of the 'Beach Boys' trademark name. At the time of writing a trial date is expected in mid 2004.

The first official Dennis Wilson Bash, celebrating the life and music of The Beach Boys' drummer, is held at Chez Jay's in Santa Monica, California, on December 6th. Seven days later The Beach Boys perform at the First Flight Centennial celebration at The Wright Brothers National Memorial, Kitty Hawk, North Carolina.

The Beach Boys appear on the US TV show *Live With Regis & Kelly* on December 24th singing 'Little St Nick' while attired in their pyjamas.

2004: *Smile* staged

BriMel/Rhino released a DVD-A version of Brian Wilson's **Live At The Roxy** on January 9th. The Beach Boys appear on TNT's NBA *All-Star Saturday Night* at the Staples Center in Los Angeles on February 14th.

The *Brian Wilson Presents Smile* tour kicks off on February 20th at the Royal Festival Hall in London, England, with a live presentation by Brian and an extended band of the legendarily unreleased *Smile* album.

Jan Berry of Jan & Dean fame dies at his home on March 26th from a seizure at the age of 62.

The great jazz guitarist Barney Kessel, veteran of many Beach Boys sessions, dies on May 6th from brain cancer, aged 80.

Brian is honoured with the BMI Icon award at the Regent Beverly Wiltshire hotel in Beverly Hills, California, on May 11th. He releases his new star-studded solo album, **Gettin' In Over My Head**, on June 22nd. Paul McCartney, Eric Clapton, Van Dyke Parks and Elton John are among the musical contributors.

* At the time of writing, Brian is set to continue solo touring; a 'new' studio version of *Smile* should appear; The Beach Boys – including Mike and Bruce – have a busy ongoing schedule in the US and UK; and Al continues to tour with his band in America.

Brian Wilson solo concerts 1995-2004

1995
September 7th **Walter Reade Theater, Lincoln Center** New York, NY

1999
March 9th **Michigan Theater** Ann Arbor, MI
March 10th **Rosemont Theater** Rosemont, IL
March 12th **Pabst Theater** Milwaukee, WI
March 13th **State Theater** Minneapolis, MN
March 15th **Calvin Theater** Northampton, MA
June 17th **Tower Theater** Upper Darby, PA
June 18th **Beacon Theater** New York, NY
June 20th **Mohegan Sun Casino** Uncasville, CT
June 21st **Symphony Hall** Boston, MA
July 9th **Osaka Festival Hall** Osaka, Japan
July 13th-14th **Tokyo International Forum** Tokyo, Japan
October 15th **Moore Theatre** Seattle, WA
October 17th-18th **Aladdin Theater** Portland, OR
October 20th **The Warfield** San Francisco, CA
October 21st **The Joint** Las Vegas, NV
October 23rd **The Wiltern** Los Angeles, CA
October 24th **Sun Theatre** Anaheim, CA
October 29th **Metro Park** Jacksonville, FL
October 30th-31st **Shoreline Amphitheatre** Mountain View, CA
December 31st **Redondo Beach Performing Arts Center** Redondo Beach, CA

2000
April 7th-8th **Roxy Theatre** Hollywood, CA

PET SOUNDS SYMPHONY TOUR
July 7th **State Theater** Easton, PA
July 8th **Tropicana Casino** Atlantic City, NJ
July 9th **Meadowbrook Musical Arts Center** Gilford, NH
July 11th **Mohegan Sun Casino** Uncasville, CT
July 13th **Pier Six Concert Pavilion** Baltimore, MD
July 14th **Mann Center** Philadelphia, PA
July 18th **Fleet Boston Pavilion** Boston, MA
July 20th **Molson Amphitheatre** Toronto, ON, Canada
July 21st **Pine Knob Theater** Detroit, MI
July 22nd **Chicago Theater** Chicago, IL
July 23rd **Evans Amphitheatre at Cain Park** Cleveland Heights, OH
July 25th **Aerial Theatre** Houston, TX
July 29th **Oak Mountain Amphitheater** Birmingham, AL
July 30th **Chastain Park Amphitheater** Atlanta, GA
September 8th **Oakdale Theatre** Wallingford, CT

September 9th **PNC Arts Center** Holmdel, NJ
September 10th **Jones Beach Theater** Wantagh, NY
September 12th **Ohio Theater** Columbus, OH
September 14th **Northrop Auditorium, University of Minnesota** Minneapolis, MN
September 16th **Magness Arena, University of Denver** Denver, CO
September 20th **Villa Montalvo Winery** Saratoga, CA
September 21st **Puyallup Fair** Seattle, WA
September 22nd **County Bowl** Santa Barbara, CA
September 24th **Hollywood Bowl** Los Angeles, CA
September 26th **Humphrey's By The Bay** San Diego, CA
October 14th **Naples Philharmonic Center** Naples, FL
October 15th **King Center** Melbourne, FL
October 17th **Ruth Eckerd Hall** Clearwater, FL
October 18th **Sunrise Musical Theatre** Sunrise, FL
November 18th (two shows) **B.B. King Blues Club & Grill** New York, NY
December 14th **Ruth Eckerd Hall** Clearwater, FL
December 15th **Unknown venue** West Palm Beach, FL
December 28th-30th (two shows each day) **B.B. King Blues Club & Grill** New York, NY

2001
March 29th **Radio City Music Hall** New York, NY ("An All Star Tribute To Brian Wilson")
June 9th **The Gorge Amphitheater** Seattle, WA
June 13th **The Greek Theatre** Los Angeles, CA
June 15th **Santa Barbara Bowl** Santa Barbara, CA
June 17th **Shoreline Amphitheatre** Mountain View, CA
June 18th **Wente Brothers Winery** Livermore, CA
June 19th **Coors Amphtitheater** Chula Vista, CA
June 20th **Desert Sky Pavilion** Phoenix, AZ
June 22nd **Mandalay Bay Casino** Las Vegas, NV
June 26th **Sandstone Amphitheater** Bonner Springs, KS
June 27th **Xcel Energy Center** St. Paul, MN
June 29th **Marcus Amphitheater** Milwaukee, WI
June 30th **Tweeter Center** Tinley Park, IL
July 3rd **DTE Energy Music Center** Clarkston, MI
July 6th **Gund Arena** Cleveland, OH
July 8th **Post Gazette Pavilion at Star Lake** Burgettstown, PA
July 11th **Darien Lake PAC** Darien Center, NY
July 13th **Tweeter Center** Mansfield, MA
July 14th **Meadows Music Centre** Hartford, CT
July 18th **Tweeter Center** Camden, NJ
July 20th **PNC Arts Center** Holmdel, NJ
July 23rd **Southampton College** Southampton, NY
July 24th **Jones Beach Theater** Wantagh, NY
October 14th **El Rey Theater** Los Angeles, CA (4th Annual Carl Wilson Walk Against Cancer Benefit Concert)

October 16th **Mitchell Pavilion, The Woodlands** Houston, TX
November 3rd **Stratosphere Hotel** Las Vegas, NV
December 30th **Tropicana Casino** Atlantic City, NJ

2002
January 20th **Aanexet** Stockholm, Sweden
January 22nd **Congress Centrum** Hamburg, Germany
January 23rd **Internationales Congress Centrum** Berlin, Germany
January 25th **Armadillo** Glasgow, Scotland
January 27th-30th **Royal Festival Hall** London, England
February 1st **The Point** Dublin, Ireland
February 21st-22nd **Tokyo International Forum A** Tokyo, Japan
February 25th **Aichi Gaijyustu Hall** Nagoya, Japan
February 26th **Sun Palace Hall** Fukuoka, Japan
February 27th **NHK Hall** Osaka, Japan
May 11th (two shows) **Roxy Theatre** Los Angeles, CA
June 3rd **Buckingham Palace** London, England. (Queen's Golden Jubilee Concert. Brian shares the bill with stars such as Paul McCartney, Elton John, Eric Clapton, Ozzy Osbourne, and Sting)
June 5th **Centre** Brighton, England
June 6th **Colston Hall** Bristol, England
June 7th **Royal Centre** Nottingham, England
June 9th-10th **Royal Festival Hall** London, England
June 12th-13th **Apollo Theatre** Manchester, England
June 14th **Symphony Hall** Birmingham, England
August 14th **House of Blues** Chicago, IL
August 16th **Avalon Ballroom** Boston, MA
August 18th **Theater of Living Arts** Philadelphia, PA
August 19th (two shows) **B.B. King Blues Club & Grill** New York, NY
October 6th **Royce Hall** Los Angeles, CA (5th Annual Carl Wilson Benefit Concert)
December 6th **Kakaako Park Waikiki Shell** Honolulu, HI
December 10th **Entertainment Centre** Brisbane, Australia
December 12th-14th **State Theatre** Sydney, Australia
December 16th **Canberra Theatre** Canberra, Australia
December 17th-**18th Melbourne Concert Hall** Melbourne, Australia

2003
June 16th **Beacon Theater** New York, NY
October 16th **University Of California** Los Angeles, CA ("An Evening With Brian Wilson And Friends" –

6th annual benefit concert for the Carl Wilson Foundation, CWF)

2004

January 30th **Shaw Conference Centre** *Edmonton, AB, Canada* (dress rehearsal for *Smile* tour)
BRIAN WILSON PRESENTS SMILE
February 20th-22nd, 24th, 26th-27th **Royal Festival Hall** *London, England*
March 1st **The Pavilion** *Bournemouth, England*

March 2nd **Colston Hall** *Bristol, England*
March 4th **Clyde Auditorium** *Glasgow, Scotland*
March 6th **City Hall** *Newcastle Upon Tyne, England*
March 7th **Empire Theatre** *Liverpool, England*
March 8th **Symphony Hall** *Birmingham, England*
March 10th **Alter Oper** *Frankfurt, Germany*
March 11th **Queen Elizabeth Hall** *Antwerp, Belgium*
March 13th **Pepsi Stage** *Amsterdam, Netherlands*
March 14th **Olympia Theatre** *Paris, France*
July 13th **Congresscentre** *The Hague, Netherlands**

July 16th **Eden Project** *St. Austell , England**
July 17th **Apollo Theatre** *Oxford, England**
July 19th **Guildhall** *Portsmouth, England**
July 20th **Regent Theatre** *Ipswich, England**
July 22nd **Apollo Theatre** *Manchester, England**
July 24th-25th, 27th-28th **Royal Festival Hall** *London, England**
August 5th-8th **Benicassim Festival** *Benicassim, Spain**

* Still to play at the time of writing.

Selected US/UK discography
Official original releases, 1961 to 1976

SELECTED ALBUMS

Before *Smiley Smile*'s release in 1967, Beach Boys albums were released in a different order in the UK compared to the US, as noted.

Surfin' Safari
US October 1st 1962 (Capitol T1808).
UK April 1963 (Capitol T1808).

Surfin' USA
US March 25th 1963 (Capitol T1980).
UK August 1965 (Capitol T1980).

Surfer Girl
US September 16th 1963 (Capitol T1981).
UK April 1967 (Capitol T1981).

Little Deuce Coupe
US October 7th 1963 (Capitol T1998).
UK October 1965 (Capitol T1998).

Shut Down Volume 2
US March 2nd 1964 (Capitol T2027).
UK July 1964 (Capitol T2027).

All Summer Long
US July 13th 1964 (Capitol T2110).
UK June 1965 (Capitol T2110).

Beach Boys Concert
US October 19th 1964 (Capitol TAO2198).
UK February 1965 (Capitol T2198).

The Beach Boys Christmas Album
US November 9th 1964 (Capitol T2164).
UK November 1964 (Capitol T2164).

Beach Boys Today!
US March 8th 1965 (Capitol T2269).
UK April 1966 (Capitol T2269).

Summer Days (And Summer Nights!!)
US July 5th 1965 (Capitol T2354).
UK June 1966 (Capitol T2354).

(Recorded "Live" At A) Beach Boys' Party!
US November 8th 1965 (Capitol MAS2398).
UK February 1966 (Capitol T2398).

Pet Sounds
US May 16th 1966 (Capitol T2458).
UK June 27th 1966 (Capitol T2458).

Smiley Smile
US September 18th 1967 (Brother 9001).
UK November 1967 (Capitol T9001).

Wild Honey
US December 18th 1967 (Capitol T2859).
UK March 1968 (Capitol T2859).

Friends
US June 24th 1968 (Capitol ST2895).
UK September 1968 (Capitol ST2895).

Stack-o-Tracks
US August 19th 1968 (Capitol DKAO2893).
UK December 1976 (Capitol EAST24009).

20/20
US February 10th 1969 (Capitol SKA O133).
UK March 1969 (Capitol EST133).

Live In London / Beach Boys '69
US November 15th 1976 (Capitol ST11584).
UK May 1970 (Capitol ST21715).

Sunflower
US August 31st 1970 (Brother/Reprise 6382).
UK November 1970 (Stateside SSLA8251).

Surf's Up
US August 30th 1971 (Brother/Reprise 6453).
UK October 1971 (Stateside SSL10313).

Carl And The Passions – "So Tough"
US May 15th 1972 (Brother/Reprise 2MS 2083; released in gatefold package with the group's 1966 album, *Pet Sounds*).
UK May 15th 1972 (Reprise K44184).

Holland
US January 8th 1973 (Brother/Reprise MS 2118).
UK January 1973 (Reprise K54008).

The Beach Boys In Concert
US November 19th 1973 (Brother/Reprise 2MS 6484).
UK November 1973 (Reprise K84001).

15 Big Ones
US July 5th 1976 (Brother/Reprise MS 2251).
UK July 5th 1976 (Reprise K54079).

SELECTED COMPILATIONS

Endless Summer
US June 24th 1974 (Capitol SVBB 11307).
UK November 1974 (Capitol EAST11037).
'Surfin' Safari', 'Surfer Girl', 'Catch A Wave', 'The Warmth Of The Sun', 'Surfin' USA', 'Be True To Your School', 'Little Deuce Coupe', 'In My Room', 'Shut Down', 'Fun Fun Fun', 'I Get Around', 'The Girls On The Beach', 'Wendy', 'Let Him Run Wild', 'Don't Worry Baby', 'California Girls', 'Girl Don't Tell Me', 'Help Me

Ronda', 'You're So Good To Me', 'All Summer Long', 'Good Vibrations'.

Spirit Of America
US April 14th 1975 (Capitol SVBB 11384).
UK September 1975 (Capitol VMP1007).
'Dance Dance Dance', 'Break Away', 'A Young Man Is Gone', '409', 'The Little Girl I Once Knew', 'Spirit Of America', 'Little Honda', 'Hushabye', 'Hawaii', 'Drive-In', 'Good To My Baby', 'Tell Me Why', 'Do You Remember', 'This Car Of Mine', 'Please Let Me Wonder', 'Why Do Fools Fall In Love', 'Custom Machine', 'Barbara Ann', 'Salt Lake City', 'Don't Back Down', 'When I Grow Up (To Be A Man)', 'Do You Wanna Dance', 'Graduation Day'.

20 Golden Greats
UK July 5th 1976 (EMI EMTV1).
'Surfin' USA', 'Fun Fun Fun', 'I Get Around', 'Don't Worry Baby', 'Little Deuce Coupe', 'When I Grow Up (To Be A Man)', 'Help Me Rhonda', 'California Girls', 'Barbara Ann', 'Sloop John B', 'You're So Good To Me', 'God Only Knows', 'Wouldn't It Be Nice', 'Good Vibrations', 'Then I Kissed Her', 'Heroes And Villains', 'Darlin', 'Do It Again', 'I Can Hear Music', 'Break Away'.

SELECTED US SINGLES & EPs

A-side/B-side, release date, label and catalogue number

'Surfin'' / 'Luau' December 8th 1961 (Candix 331; shortly thereafter as X 301 and then Candix 301).

'409' / 'Surfin' Safari' June 4th 1962 (Capitol 4777).
'Ten Little Indians' / 'County Fair' November 26th 1962 (Capitol 4880).

'Surfin' USA' / 'Shut Down' March 4th 1963 (Capitol 4932).
'Surfer Girl' / 'Little Deuce Coupe' July 22nd 1963 (Capitol 5009).
'Be True To Your School' / 'In My Room' October 28th 1963 (Capitol 5069).
'Little St. Nick' / 'The Lord's Prayer' December 9th 1963 (Capitol 5096).

'Fun Fun Fun' / 'Why Do Fools Fall In Love' February 3rd 1964 (Capitol 5118).
'I Get Around' / 'Don't Worry Baby' May 11th 1964 (Capitol 5174).
'When I Grow Up (To Be A Man)' / 'She Knows Me Too Well' August 24th 1964 (Capitol 5245).
4 By The Beach Boys ('Wendy', 'Don't Back Down', 'Little Honda', 'Hushabye') September 21st 1964 (Capitol R5267).
'Dance Dance Dance' / 'The Warmth Of The Sun' October 26th 1964 (Capitol 5306).
'The Man With All The Toys' / 'Blue Christmas' November 9th 1964 (Capitol 5312).
'Do You Wanna Dance' / 'Please Let Me Wonder'

February 15th 1965 (Capitol 5372).
'Help Me Rhonda' / 'Kiss Me Baby' April 5th 1965 (Capitol 5395).
'California Girls' / 'Let Him Run Wild' July 12th 1965 (Capitol 5464).
'The Little Girl I Once Knew' / 'There's No Other (Like My Baby)' November 27th 1965 (Capitol 5540).
'Barbara Ann' / 'Girl Don't Tell Me' December 20th 1965 (Capitol 5561).

'Caroline No' / 'Summer Means New Love' (credited to Brian Wilson) March 7th 1966 (Capitol 5610).
'Sloop John B' / 'You're So Good To Me' March 21st 1966 (Capitol 5602).
'Wouldn't It Be Nice' / 'God Only Knows' July 18th 1966 (Capitol 5706).
'Good Vibrations' / 'Let's Go Away For Awhile' October 10th 1966 (Capitol 5676).

'Heroes And Villains' / 'You're Welcome' July 31st 1967 (Brother 1001).
'Gettin' Hungry' / 'Devoted To You' (credited to Brian & Mike) August 28th 1967 (Brother 1002).
'Wild Honey' / 'Wind Chimes' October 23rd 1967 (Capitol 2028).
'Darlin'' / 'Here Today' December 18th 1967 (Capitol 2068).

'Friends' / 'Little Bird' April 8th 1968 (Capitol 2160).
'Do It Again' / 'Wake The World' July 8th 1968 (Capitol 2239).
'Bluebirds Over The Mountain' / 'Never Learn Not To Love' December 2nd 1968 (Capitol 2360).

'I Can Hear Music' / 'All I Want To Do' March 3rd 1969 (Capitol 2432).
'Break Away' / 'Celebrate The News' June 16th 1969 (Capitol 2530).

'Add Some Music To Your Day' / 'Susie Cincinnati' February 23rd 1970 (Brother/Reprise 0894).
'Cotton Fields' / 'The Nearest Faraway Place' April 20th 1970 (Capitol 2765).
'Slip On Through' / 'This Whole World' June 29th 1970 (Brother/Reprise 0929).
'Tears In The Morning' / 'It's About Time' October 12th 1970 (Brother/Reprise 0957).

'Cool Cool Water' / 'Forever' March 1971 (Brother/Reprise 0998).
'Wouldn't It Be Nice' (live) /other artist B side April 23rd 1971 (Ode 66016).
'Long Promised Road' / 'Deirdre' May 24th 1971 (Brother/Reprise 1015).
'Long Promised Road' / ''Til I Die' October 11th 1971 (Brother/Reprise 1047).
'Surf's Up' / 'Don't Go Near The Water' November 1971 (Brother/Reprise 1058).

'You Need A Mess Of Help To Stand Alone' /

'Cuddle Up' May 15th 1972 (Brother/Reprise 1091).
'Marcella' / 'Hold On Dear Brother' June 26th 1972 (Brother/Reprise 1101).

'Sail On Sailor' / 'Only With You' February 1973 (Brother/Reprise 1138).
'California: On My Way To Sunny Californ-i-a' / 'Funky Pretty' May 1973 (Brother/Reprise 1156).
'Child Of Winter' / 'Susie Cincinnati' December 23rd 1974 (Brother/Reprise 1321).

'Sail On Sailor' / 'Only With You' March 10th 1975 reissue (Brother/Reprise 1325).

'Rock And Roll Music' / 'TM Song' May 24th 1976 (Brother/Reprise 1354).
'It's OK' / 'Had To Phone Ya' August 30th 1976 (Brother/Reprise 1368).
'Susie Cincinnati' / 'Everyone's In Love With You' November 8th 1976 (Brother/Reprise 1375).

SELECTED UK SINGLES & EPs

A-side/B-side, release date, label and catalogue number

'Surfin' Safari' / '409' October 5th 1962 (Capitol CL 15273).

'Ten Little Indians' / 'County Fair' January 1963 (Capitol CL 15285).
'Surfin' USA' / 'Shut Down' June 1963 (Capitol CL 15305).
Surfin' USA ('Surfin' USA', 'Shut Down', 'Surfer Girl', 'Surfin' Safari') July 1963 (Capitol EAP1-20540).

'Fun Fun Fun' / 'Why Do Fools Fall In Love?' March 1964 (Capitol CL 15339).
'I Get Around' / 'Don't Worry Baby' June 1964 (Capitol CL 15350).
Fun Fun Fun ('Fun Fun Fun', 'In My Room', 'Little Deuce Coupe', 'Why Do Fools Fall In Love?') June 1964 (Capitol EAP1-20603).
'When I Grow Up (To Be A Man)' / 'She Knows Me Too Well' Oct 23rd 1964 (Capitol CL 15361).
Four By The Beach Boys ('Wendy', 'Don't Back Down', 'Little Honda', 'Hushabye') November 1964 (Capitol EAP1-5267).

'Dance Dance Dance' / 'The Warmth Of The Sun' January 1965 (Capitol CL 15370).
Beach Boys Concert ('The Little Old Lady From Pasadena', 'Papa-Oom-Mow-Mow', 'Johnny B. Goode', 'Let's Go Trippin') February 1965 (Capitol EAP-1 2198).
'All Summer Long' / 'Do You Wanna Dance' March 1965 (Capitol CL 15384).
'Help Me Rhonda' / 'Kiss Me Baby' May 1965 (Capitol CL 15392).
'California Girls' / 'Let Him Run Wild' August 1965 (Capitol CL 15409).

'The Little Girl I Once Knew' / 'There's No Other (Like My Baby)' December 1965 (Capitol CL 15425).

'Barbara Ann' / 'Girl Don't Tell Me' February 1966 (Capitol CL 15432).

'Caroline No' / 'Summer Means New Love' (credited to Brian Wilson) April 1966 (Capitol CL 15438).

'Sloop John B' / 'You're So Good To Me' April 1966 (Capitol CL 15441).

Beach Boys' Hits ('Help Me Rhonda', 'California Girls', 'The Little Girl I Once Knew', 'Barbara Ann') May 1966 (Capitol EAP1-20781).

'God Only Knows' / 'Wouldn't It Be Nice' July 22nd 1966 (Capitol CL 15459).

'Good Vibrations' / 'Wendy' October 28th 1966 (Capitol CL 15475).

God Only Knows ('God Only Knows', 'Here Today', 'Sloop John B', 'Wouldn't It Be Nice') November 1966 (Capitol EAP1-2458).

'Then I Kissed Her' / 'Mountain Of Love' April 28th 1967 (Capitol CL 15502).

'Heroes And Villains' / 'You're Welcome' August 18th 1967 (Capitol CL 15510).

'Gettin' Hungry' / 'Devoted To You' (credited to Brian & Mike) September 1967 (Capitol CL 15513).

'Wild Honey' / 'Wind Chimes' November 1967 (Capitol CL 15521).

'Darlin'' / 'Country Air' Jan 1968 (Capitol CL 15527).

'Friends' / 'Little Bird' May 1968 (Capitol CL 15545).

'Do It Again' / 'Wake The World July 19th 1968 (Capitol CL 15554).

'Bluebirds Over The Mountain' / 'Never Learn Not To Love' November 29th 1968 (Capitol CL 15572).

'I Can Hear Music' / 'All I Want To Do' February 14th 1969 (Capitol CL 15584).

'Break Away' / 'Celebrate The News' June 1969 (Capitol CL 15598).

'Cotton Fields' / 'The Nearest Faraway Place' May 1970 (Capitol CL 15640).

'Tears In The Morning' / 'It's About Time' November 1970 (Stateside SS 2181).

'Sound Of Free' / 'Lady' December 4th 1970 (Dennis Wilson & Rumbo) (Stateside SS 2184).

'Long Promised Road' / 'Deirdre' June 1971 (Stateside SS 2190).

'Don't Go Near The Water' / 'Student Demonstration Time' November 1971 (Stateside SS 2194).

'You Need A Mess Of Help To Stand Alone' / 'Cuddle Up' May 1972 (Reprise K14173).

'California Saga (California)' / 'Sail On Sailor' February 1973 (Reprise K14232).

'Little St. Nick' / 'The Lord's Prayer' November 1973 (Capitol CL 15572).

California Saga ('California Saga : California', 'Sail On Sailor', 'Marcella', 'I'm The Pied Piper') August 1974 (Reprise K14346).

'Sail On Sailor' / 'Only With You' June 1975 (Reprise K14394).

'Child Of Winter' / 'Good Vibrations' December 1975 (Reprise K14411; pressed but unreleased).

'Rock And Roll Music' / 'TM Song' June 1976 (Reprise K14440).

'It's OK' / 'Had To Phone Ya' August 1976 (Reprise K14448).

Song recording index

Selected Beach Boys songs recorded by the group 1961-1976 and officially released. Listings show song title; (composers); album, single or CD location; recording dates.

'Add Some Music To Your Day'
(Brian Wilson / Joe Knott / Mike Love) *Sunflower*
October 1969

'All Dressed Up For School'
(Brian Wilson / Roger Christian)
Little Deuce Coupe–All Summer Long CD
September 16th 1964

'All I Wanna Do'
(Brian Wilson / Mike Love) *Sunflower*
March 19th 1969
July 1969

'All I Want To Do'
(Dennis Wilson) *20/20*
May 24th 1968
November 12th, 21st 1968

'All Summer Long'
(Brian Wilson / Mike Love) *All Summer Long*

May 6th, 7th 1964

'All This Is That'
(Al Jardine / Carl Wilson / Mike Love)
Carl And The Passions
December 4th-10th 1971
April 3rd-April 13th 1972

'Alley Oop'
(Dallas Frazier) *Party!*
From sessions September 8th, 14th, 15th and 23rd 1965

'Amusement Parks USA'
(Brian Wilson / Mike Love) *Summer Days*
April 14th 1965
May 5th 1964

'And Your Dream Comes True'
(Brian Wilson / Mike Love) *Summer Days*
May 24th 1965

'Anna Lee The Healer'
(Mike Love / Brian Wilson) *Friends*
April 2nd 1968

'Aren't You Glad'
(Brian Wilson / Mike Love) *Wild Honey*

October 4th 1967
November 8th-15th 1967

'At My Window'
(Al Jardine / Brian Wilson) *Sunflower*
July 1969
November 11th 1969

'Auld Lang Syne'
(trad arr Brian Wilson) *Christmas Album*
June 25th 1964

'Back Home'
(Brian Wilson / Bob Norberg) *15 Big Ones*
January 1970
May 1976

'The Baker Man'
(Brian Wilson) *Surfin' Safari–Surfin' USA* CD
March 7th 1963

'Ballad Of Ole' Betsy'
(Brian Wilson / Roger Christian) *Little Deuce Coupe*
September 2nd 1963
November 4th 1963

'Barbara Ann'
(Fred Fassert) *Party*, single
September 23rd 1965

'Beach Boys Stomp' aka 'Karate'
(Carl Wilson) *Studio Sessions 61/62* CD
February 8th 1962

'Be Here In The Mornin''
(Brian Wilson / Carl Wilson / Mike Love / Dennis
Wilson / Al Jardine) *Friends*
March 6th 1968
March 29th 1968
March 31st 1968

'Be Still'
(Dennis Wilson / Stephen Kalinich) *Friends*
April 13th 1968

'Be True To Your School'
(Brian Wilson / Mike Love) *Little Deuce Coupe*
September 2nd 1963

'Be True To Your School'
(Brian Wilson / Mike Love) single version
Late September 1963

'Be With Me'
(Dennis Wilson) *20/20*
November 2nd 1968

'Better Get Back In Bed'
(Brian Wilson)
Mount Vernon & Fairway, bonus EP with *Holland*
June 3rd-22nd 1972
June 28th-August 2nd 1972
September/October 1972

'Blue Christmas'
(B. Hayes / J. Johnson) *Christmas Album*
June 18th 1964
June 28th 1964

'Blueberry Hill'
(Lewis / Stock / Rose) *15 Big Ones*
January 30th 1976
January 31st 1976

'Bluebirds Over The Mountain'
(Ersel Hickey) *20/20*
September 29th 1967
November 14th 1968

'Boogie Woodie'
(Rimsky-Korsakov arr by Brian Wilson) *Surfer Girl*
July 16th 1963

'Break Away'
(Brian Wilson / 'Reggie Dunbar' [Murry Wilson])
single, *Spirit Of America, Friends–20/20* CD
March 31st 1969
April 23rd 1969

'Bull Session With "Big Daddy"'
(Brian Wilson / Carl Wilson / Dennis Wilson / Mike
Love / Al Jardine) *Today!*
January 13th 1965

'Busy Doin' Nothin''
(Brian Wilson) *Friends*
March 26th 1968 (as 'Even Steven')
April 11th 1968

'Cabinessence'
(Brian Wilson / Van Dyke Parks) *20/20*
Sessions in full: October 3rd 1966
October 11th 1966
October 12th 1966
December 6th 1966
December 27th 1966
November 20th 1968

'California Girls'
(Brian Wilson / Mike Love) *Summer Days*
April 6th 1965
June 4th 1965

'California Saga: Big Sur'
(Mike Love) *Holland*
August 15th 1970 (first version)
August 1st 1972
August 2nd 1972
September / October 1972
December 2nd 1972
March 6th 1973

'California Saga: California'
(Al Jardine) *Holland*
August 1st 1972
August 2nd 1972
September / October 1972
December 2nd 1972
March 6th 1973

'California Saga: The Beaks Of Eagles'
(Robinson Jeffers / Al Jardine) *Holland*
August 1st 1972
August 2nd 1972
September / October 1972
December 2nd 1972
March 6th 1973

**'Can't Wait Too Long'
aka 'Been Way Too Long'**
(Brian Wilson) *Smiley Smile–Wild Honey* CD
October 28th 1967
November 1st 1967
July 25th 1968
July 26th 1968
July 30th 1968

'Car Crazy Cutie'
(Brian Wilson / Roger Christian) *Little Deuce Coupe*
September 2nd 1963

'Carl's Big Chance' aka 'Memphis Beach'
(Chuck Berry / Brian Wilson / Carl Wilson)
All Summer Long
April 29th 1964

'Caroline No'
(Brian Wilson / Tony Asher) *Pet Sounds*
January 31st 1966
February 2nd/3rd 1966

'"Cassius" Love Vs. "Sonny" Wilson'
(Mike Love / Brian Wilson) *Shut Down Volume 2*
February 20th 1964

'A Casual Look'
(Edward Wells) *15 Big Ones*
March 17th 1976

'Catch A Wave'
(Brian Wilson / Mike Love) *Surfer Girl*
July 14th 1963
July 16th 1963

'Celebrate The News'
(Dennis Wilson / Greg Jakobson)
Rarities, Friends–20/20 CD
February 24th 1969

'Chapel Of Love'
(Jeff Barry / Ellie Greenwich / Phil Spector)
15 Big Ones
March 1976

'Cherry Cherry Coupe'
(Brian Wilson / Roger Christian) *Little Deuce Coupe*
September 2nd 1963

'Child Of Winter (Christmas Song)'
(Brian Wilson / Steve Kalinich)
rejected singles, *Ultimate Christmas*
November 5th 1974
November 18th 1974

'Christmas Day'
(Brian Wilson) *Christmas Album*
June 25th 1964
June 27th 1964

'Chug-A-Lug'
(Brian Wilson / Mike Love / Gary Usher) *Surfin' Safari*
August 8th 1962

'Cindy Oh Cindy'
(Bob Barron / Burt Long) *Surfin' Safari–Surfin' USA* CD
September 13th 1962

'Cool Cool Water'
(Brian Wilson / Mike Love) *Sunflower*
June 7th 1967
October 26th 1967
October 29th-November 3rd 1967
January 1970

July 1st-6th 1970
July 21st 1970

'Cotton Fields (The Cotton Song)'
(Huddie Ledbetter) *20/20*
November 18th, 19th 1968

'Cotton Fields (The Cotton Song)'
(Huddie Ledbetter) single version
August 15th 1969

'County Fair'
(Brian Wilson / Gary Usher) *Surfin' Safari*
August 5th 1962

'Country Air'
(Brian Wilson / Mike Love) *Wild Honey*
November 14th 1967

'Cuckoo Clock'
(Brian Wilson / Gary Usher) *Surfin' Safari*
August 5th 1962

'Cuddle Up'
(Dennis Wilson / Daryl Dragon) *Carl And The Passions*
April 3rd-13th 1972

'Custom Machine'
(Brian Wilson / Mike Love) *Little Deuce Coupe*
September 2nd 1963

'Dance Dance Dance'
(Brian Wilson / Carl Wilson / Mike Love) *Today!*
September 22nd 1964
October 9th 1964

'Darlin''
(Brian Wilson / Mike Love) *Wild Honey*
October 27th 1967

'A Day in The Life Of A Tree'
(Brian Wilson / Jack Rieley) *Surf's Up*
April 1971

'Deirdre'
(Bruce Johnston) *Sunflower*
March 21st 1969
August 18th 1969
January 9th 1970

'Denny's Drums'
(Dennis Wilson) *Shut Down Volume 2*
February 20th 1964

'Devoted To You'
(Boudleaux Bryant) *Party!*
From sessions September 8th, 14th, 15th and 23rd 1965

'Diamond Head'
(Albert Vescozo / Lyle Ritz / James Ackley / Brian Wilson) *Friends*
April 12th 1968

'Disney Girls (1957)'
(Bruce Johnston) *Surf's Up*
June 3rd 1971

'Do It Again'
(Brian Wilson / Mike Love) *20/20*
May 26th 1968
June 6th, 12th 1968

'Do You Remember'
(Brian Wilson / Mike Love) *All Summer Long*
May 6th 1964
May 18th 1964

'Do You Wanna Dance'
(Bobby Freeman) *Today!*
January 11th 1965

'Don't Back Down'
(Brian Wilson / Mike Love) *All Summer Long*
April 29th 1964

'Don't Go Near The Water'
(Al Jardine / Mike Love) *Surf's Up*
April 3rd 1971

'Don't Hurt My Little Sister'
(Brian Wilson / Mike Love) *Today!*
June 22nd 1964
January 18th 1965

**'Don't Talk
(Put Your Head On My Shoulder)'**
(Brian Wilson / Tony Asher) *Pet Sounds*
October 13th 1965
February 11th 1966
April 3rd 1966

'Don't Worry Baby'
(Brian Wilson / Roger Christian) *Shut Down Volume 2*
February 20th 1964

'Drive-In'
(Brian Wilson / Mike Love) *All Summer Long*
October 18th 1963
April 29th 1964

'Everyone's In Love With You'
(Mike Love) *15 Big Ones*
April 1976

**'Fall Breaks And Back To Winter
(Woody Woodpecker Symphony)'**
(Brian Wilson) *Smiley Smile*
June 29th 1967

'Farmer's Daughter'
(Brian Wilson / Mike Love) *Surfin' USA*
January 5th 1963
January 16th 1963
January 31st 1963
February 11th 1963

'Feel Flows'
(Carl Wilson / Jack Rieley) *Surf's Up*
January-April 1971

'Finders Keepers'
(Brian Wilson / Mike Love) *Surfin' USA*
February 12th 1963

'Forever'
(Dennis Wilson / Greg Jakobson) *Sunflower*
January 9th 1969
March 17th 1969

'409'
(Brian Wilson/ Mike Love / Gary Usher) *Surfin' Safari, Little Deuce Coupe*
April 19th 1962

'Friends'
(Brian Wilson / Carl Wilson / Dennis Wilson / Al Jardine) *Friends*
March 13th 1968

'Frosty The Snowman'
(Steve Nelson / Walter Rollins) *Christmas Album*
June 24th 1964
June 29th 1964

'Fun Fun Fun'
(Brian Wilson / Mike Love) *Shut Down Volume 2*
January 1st 1964

'Funky Pretty'
(Brian Wilson / Mike Love / Jack Rieley) *Holland*
January 21st 1972
June 3rd-June 22nd 1972
June 28th-August 2nd 1972

'Gettin' Hungry'
(Brian Wilson / Mike Love) *Smiley Smile*
July 14th 1967

'Girl Don't Tell Me'
(Brian Wilson) *Summer Days*
April 30th 1965

'The Girl From New York City'
(Brian Wilson / Mike Love) *Summer Days*
May 24th 1965

'Girls On The Beach'
(Brian Wilson) *All Summer Long*
May 19th 1964

'God Only Knows'
(Brian Wilson / Tony Asher) *Pet Sounds*
March 8th, 9th, 10th 1966
April 11th 1966

'Good To My Baby'
(Brian Wilson / Mike Love) *Today!*
January 13th, 19th 1965

'Good Vibrations'
(Brian Wilson/ Mike Love) *Smiley Smile*
Sessions in full:
February 17th 1966
February 18th 1966
February 23rd 1966
March 24th 1966
April 9th 1966
May 4th 1966
May 24th 1966
May 25th 1966
May 27th 1966
June 2nd 1966 (as 'Inspiration')
June 12th 1966 (as 'Inspiration')
June 13th 1966
June 16th 1966
June 18th 1966
August 24th 1966
August 25th 1966
September 1st 1966
September 12th 1966
September 21st 1966

'Got To Know The Woman'
(Dennis Wilson) *Sunflower*
February 13th 1969
July 1969

'Graduation Day'
(Joe Sherman / Noel Sherman)
Today!–Summer Days CD
May 5th 1965

'Had To Phone Ya'
(Brian Wilson) *15 Big Ones*
March 1976

'Hawaii'
(Brian Wilson / Mike Love) *Surfer Girl*
July 16th 1963

'He Come Down'
(Al Jardine / Carl Wilson / Mike Love)
Carl And The Passions
December 4th-10th 1971
April 3rd-13th 1972

'Heads You Win Tails I Lose'
(Brian Wilson / Gary Usher) *Surfin' Safari*
August 5th 1962

'Help Me Rhonda'
(Brian Wilson / Mike Love)
single version, *Summer Days*
February 24th 1965
March 3rd 1965
March 4th 1965
March 21st 1965
March 22nd 1965

'Help Me Ronda'
(Brian Wilson / Mike Love) album version *Today!*

January 8th 1965
January 19th 1965

'Here Comes The Night'
(Brian Wilson / Mike Love) *Wild Honey*
October 26th 1967

'Here She Comes'
(Ricky Fataar / Blondie Chaplin) *Carl And The Passions*
December 4th-10th 1971
April 3rd-13th 1972

'Here Today'
(Brian Wilson / Tony Asher) *Pet Sounds*
March 11th 1966 (as 'Good Good Good Vibrations')
March 12th 1966
March 25th 1966

'Heroes And Villains'
(Brian Wilson / Van Dyke Parks) *Smiley Smile*
Session dates in full: May 11th 1966
October 20th 1966
October 27th 1966
December 13th 1966
December 19th 1966
December 22nd 1966
December 28th 1966
January 3rd 1967
January 5th 1967
January 6th 1967
January 20th 1967
January 27th 1967
January 31st 1967
February 3rd 1967
February 7th 1967
February 9th 1967
February 10th 1967
February 15th 1967
February 18th 1967
February 20th 1967
February 21st 1967
February 24th 1967
February 26th 1967
February 27th 1967
February 28th 1967
March 1st 1967
March 2nd 1967
May 11th 1967
June 12th 1967
June 13th 1967
June 14th 1967

'Hold On Dear Brother'
(Ricky Fataar / Blondie Chaplin) *Carl And The Passions*
April 3rd-13th 1972

'Honky Tonk'
(Bill Doggett / Clifford Scott / Billy Butler / Shep Shepherd / Henry Glover) *Surfin' USA*
February 11th 1963

'How She Boogalooed It'
(Mike Love / Bruce Johnston / Al Jardine / Carl Wilson)
Wild Honey
November 15th 1967

'Hully Gully'
(Fred Smith / Clifford Goldsmith) *Party!*
From sessions September 8th, 14th, 15th and 23rd 1965

'Hushabye'
(Doc Pomus / Mort Shuman) *All Summer Long*)
April 29th 1964

'I Can Hear Music'
(Jeff Barry / Ellie Greenwich / Phil Spector) *20/20*
October 1st 1968

'I Do'
(Brian Wilson / Roger Christian)
Surfer Girl–Shut Down Volume 2 CD
November 4th 1963
November 7th 1963

'I Get Around'
(Brian Wilson / Mike Love) single, *Little Deuce Coupe*
April 2nd 1964

'I Get Around'
(Brian Wilson / Mike Love) *Party!* version
From sessions September 8th, 14th, 15th and 23rd 1965

'I Just Wasn't Made For These Times'
(Brian Wilson / Tony Asher) *Pet Sounds*
February 14th 1966
March 10th 1966
April 13th 1966

'I Know There's An Answer'
(Brian Wilson / Terry Sachen) *Pet Sounds*)
February 7th 1966 (as 'Hang On To Your Ego')
February 9th 1966

'I Should Have Known Better'
(John Lennon / Paul McCartney) *Party!*
From sessions September 8th, 14th, 15th and 23rd 1965

'I Was Made To Love Her'
(Henry Cosby / Lula Mae Hardaway / Sylvia Moy / Stevie Wonder) *Wild Honey*
October 28th 1967

'I Went To Sleep'
(Brian Wilson / Carl Wilson) *20/20*
June 5th 1968
November 18th 1968

'I'd Love Just Once To See You'
(Brian Wilson / Mike Love) *Wild Honey*
November 13th 1967

'I'll Be Home For Christmas'
(Walter Kent / Kim Gannon / Buck Ram)
Christmas Album
June 24th 1964
June 30th 1964

'I'm Bugged At My Ol' Man'
(Brian Wilson) *Summer Days*
May 24th 1965

'I'm So Young'
(William Tyus) *Today!*
January 18th 1965
January 19th 1965

'I'm So Young'
(William Tyus)
alternative take *Today–Summer Days* CD
September 9th 1964

'I'm The Pied Piper'
(Brian Wilson)
Mount Vernon & Fairway bonus EP with *Holland*
June 3rd-22nd 1972
June 28th-August 2nd 1972
September / October 1972

'I'm Waiting For The Day'
(Brian Wilson / Mike Love) *Pet Sounds*
March 1st 1966
March 6th 1966
March 10th 1966

'In My Room'
(Brian Wilson / Gary Usher) *Surfer Girl*
July 16th 1963

'In My Room'
(Brian Wilson / Gary Usher)
German version 'Ganz Allein' *Surfer Girl–Shut Down Volume 2* CD, *Rarities*
March 3rd 1964

'In The Back Of My Mind'
(Brian Wilson / Mike Love) *Today!*
January 13th 1965
January 19th 1965

'In The Parkin' Lot'
(Brian Wilson / Roger Christian) *Shut Down Volume 2*
February 20th 1964

'In The Still Of The Night (I'll Remember)'
(Frederick Parris) *15 Big Ones*
March 15th 1976

'It's About Time'
(Dennis Wilson / Bob Burchman / Al Jardine)
Sunflower
First week July 1970

'It's OK'
(Brian Wilson / Mike Love) *15 Big Ones*
November 5th 1974
March 1976
June 26th 1976

'Johnny B Goode'
(Chuck Berry) *Concert* album and EP
August 1st 1964

'Judy'
(Brian Wilson) *Studio Sessions 61/62* CD
February 8th 1962

'Judy'
(Brian Wilson) Gary Usher session
April 19th 1962

'Just Once In My Life'
(Gerry Goffin / Carole King / Phil Spector) *15 Big Ones*
March 16th 1976

'Keep An Eye On Summer'
(Brian Wilson / Bob Norman) *Shut Down Volume 2*
February 19th 1964

'Kiss Me Baby'
(Brian Wilson / Mike Love) *Today!*
December 16th 1964
January 15th 1965

'Lana'
(Brian Wilson) *Surfin' USA*
January 5th 1963
January 16th 1963
January 31st 1963
February 11th 1963

'Land Ahoy'
(Brian Wilson) *Surfin' Safari–Surfin' USA* CD, *Rarities*
August 6th 1962

'Lavender'
(Dorinda Morgan) *Studio Sessions 61/62* CD
September 15th 1961
October 3rd 1961

'Leaving This Town'
(Ricky Fataar / Carl Wilson / Blondie Chaplin / Mike Love) *Holland*
June 3rd-22nd 1972
June 28th-August 2nd 1972
September / October 1972

'Let Him Run Wild'
(Brian Wilson / Mike Love) *Summer Days*
March 16th, 30th 1965
April 28th 1965

'Let The Wind Blow'
(Brian Wilson / Mike Love) *Wild Honey*
October 29th-November 3rd 1967

'Let's Go Away For Awhile'
(Brian Wilson) *Pet Sounds*
January 18th 1966
January 19th 1966

'Let's Go Trippin''
(Dick Dale) *Surfin' USA*
February 11th 1963

'Little Bird'
(Dennis Wilson / Stephen Kalinich) *Friends*
February 29th 1968

'Little Deuce Coupe'
(Brian Wilson / Roger Christian) *Little Deuce Coupe*
June 12th 1963

'Little Deuce Coupe'
(Brian Wilson / Roger Christian) *Party!* version
From sessions September 8th, 14th, 15th and 23rd 1965

'The Little Girl I Once Knew'
(Brian Wilson) single
October 13th 1965
October 24th 1965

'Little Girl (You're My Miss America)'
(Vincent Catalano / Herb Alpert) *Surfin' Safari*
August 6th 1962

'Little Honda'
(Brian Wilson / Mike Love) *All Summer Long*
April 2nd 1964

'Little Honda'
(Brian Wilson / Mike Love)
alternative take *Little Deuce Coupe–All Summer Long* CD
June 23rd 1964

'The Little Old Lady From Pasadena'
(Donald Altfeld / Roger Christian) *Concert* album & EP
August 1st 1964

'Little Pad'
(Brian Wilson) *Smiley Smile*
June 19th 1967 (as 'The Hawaiian Song')
June 20th 1967
June 21st 1967
June 28th 1967

'Little Saint Nick'
(Brian Wilson) single version
October 18th 1963
October 20th 1963

'Little Saint Nick'
(Brian Wilson) *Christmas Album* version
June 18th 1964

'Lonely Sea'
(Gary Usher / Brian Wilson) *Surfin' USA*
April 19th 1962

'Long Promised Road'
(Carl Wilson / Jack Rieley) *Surf's Up*
July 8th 1970
August 14th 1970
April 3rd 1971

'Long Tall Texan'
(Henry Strzelecki) *Concert*
August 1st 1964

'Lookin' At Tomorrow (A Welfare Song)'
(Al Jardine / Gary Winfrey) *Surf's Up*
August 14th 1970

'Loop De Loop'
(Brian Wilson / Carl Wilson / Al Jardine)
Endless Harmony soundtrack
June 8th 1968 (as a demo entitled 'Sail Plane Song')
March 5th 1969
March 6th 1969
Late March 1969
(July 3rd 1998)
(July 4th 1998)

'The Lord's Prayer'
hymn, single B-side
November 1963

'Louie Louie'
(Richard Berry) *Shut Down Volume 2*
February 20th 1964

'Luau'
(Bruce Morgan) *Studio Sessions 61/62* CD
September 15th 1961
October 3rd 1961

'Magic Transistor Radio'
(Brian Wilson)
Mount Vernon & Fairway bonus EP with *Holland*
June 3rd-22nd 1972
June 28th-August 2nd 1972
September / October 1972

'Make It Good'
(Dennis Wilson / Daryl Dragon) *Carl And The Passions*
April 3rd-13th 1972

'Mama Says'
(Brian Wilson / Mike Love) *Wild Honey*
November 8th-15th 1967

'The Man With All The Toys'
(Brian Wilson) *Christmas Album*
June 25th 1964
June 27th 1964

'Marcella'
(Carl Wilson / Jack Rieley) *Carl And The Passions*
December 4th-10th 1971

'Meant For You'
(Brian Wilson / Mike Love) *Friends*
April 1st 1968

'Merry Christmas Baby'
(Brian Wilson) *Christmas Album*
June 25th 1964
June 30th 1964

'Misirlou'
(Nicholas Roubanis / Fred Wise / Milton Leeds / S.K. Russell) *Surfin' USA*
February 11th 1963

'The Monkey's Uncle'
(*Walt Disney* soundtrack with Annette Funicello)
June 16th 1964

'Monster Mash'
(Bobby Pickett / Leonard Capizzi) *Concert*
August 1st 1964

'Moon Dawg'
(Derry Weaver) *Surfin' Safari*
August 5th 1962

'Mount Vernon And Fairway – Theme'
(Brian Wilson)
Mount Vernon & Fairway bonus EP with *Holland*
June 3rd-22nd 1972
June 28th-August 2nd 1972
September / October 1972

'Mountain Of Love'
(Harold Dorman) *Party!*
From sessions September 8th, 14th, 15th and 23rd 1965

'The Nearest Faraway Place'
(Bruce Johnston) *20/20*
June 20th 1968
November 16th 1968

'Never Learn Not To Love'
(Dennis Wilson) *20/20*
September 11th 1968
September 17th 1968

'No-Go Showboat'
(Brian Wilson / Roger Christian) *Little Deuce Coupe*
September 2nd 1963

'Noble Surfer'
(Brian Wilson / Mike Love) *Surfin' USA*
February 11th 1963

'Old Folks At Home / Ol' Man River'
(Stephen Foster) *Friends–20/20* CD
June 10th 1968

'Only With You'
(Dennis Wilson / Mike Love) *Holland*

June 3rd-22nd 1972
June 28th-August 2nd 1972
September / October 1972

'Our Car Club'
(Brian Wilson / Mike Love) *Surfer Girl*
July 16th 1963

'Our Favorite Recording Sessions'
(Brian Wilson / Carl Wilson / Dennis Wilson / Mike Love / Al Jardine) *All Summer Long*
May 6th 1964

'Our Prayer'
(Brian Wilson) *20/20*
September 19th 1966
October 4th 1966
November 17th 1968

'Our Sweet Love'
(Brian Wilson / Carl Wilson / Al Jardine) *Sunflower*
November 1969
January 26th 1970

'Palisades Park'
(Charles Barris) *15 Big Ones*
January 30th 1976
January 31st 1976

'Papa-Oom-Mow-Mow'
(Alfred Frazier / Carl White / John Harris / Turner Wilson Jr) *Party!)*
From sessions September 8th, 14th, 15th and 23rd 1965

'Passing By'
(Brian Wilson) *Friends*
March 22nd 1968

'Pet Sounds'
(Brian Wilson) *Pet Sounds*
November 17th 1965 (as 'Run James Run')

'Please Let Me Wonder'
(Brian Wilson / Mike Love) *Today!*
January 7th 1965
January 9th 1965
January 18th 1965

'Pom-Pom Play Girl'
(Brian Wilson / Gary Usher) *Shut Down Volume 2*
February 19th 1964

'Radio King Dom'
(Brian Wilson)
Mount Vernon & Fairway bonus EP with *Holland*
June 3rd-22nd 1972
June 28th-August 2nd 1972
September / October 1972

'Rock And Roll Music'
(Chuck Berry) *15 Big Ones*
March 16th 1976

'The Rocking Surfer'
(trad arr Brian Wilson) *Surfer Girl*
July 16th 1963

'Sail On Sailor'
(Brian Wilson / Tandyn Almer / Van Dyke Parks / Jack
Rieley / Raymond Kennedy) *Holland*
November 28th 1972
November 29th 1972
November 30th 1972

'Salt Lake City'
(Brian Wilson / Mike Love) *Summer Days*
March 30th 1965

'Santa Claus Is Comin' To Town'
Fred Coots / Haven Gillespie) *Christmas Album*
June 18th 1964
June 28th 1964

'Santa's Beard'
(Brian Wilson) *Christmas Album*
June 25th 1964
June 27th 1964

'She Knows Me Too Well'
(Brian Wilson / Mike Love) *Today!*
June 8th 1964
August 5th 1964
August 8th 1964

'She's Goin' Bald'
(Brian Wilson / Mike Love / Van Dyke Parks)
Smiley Smile
July 5th 1967

'The Shift'
(Brian Wilson / Mike Love) *Surfin' Safari*
August 8th 1962

'Shut Down'
(Brian Wilson / Roger Christian)
Surfin' USA, *Little Deuce Coupe*
January 5th 1963
January 31st 1963

'Shut Down Part II'
(Carl Wilson) *Shut Down Volume 2*
February 20th 1964

'Slip On Through'
(Dennis Wilson) *Sunflower*
July 8th 1969
October 6th 1969

'Sloop John B'
(Trad arr Brian Wilson) *Pet Sounds*
July 12th 1965
December 22nd 1965
December 29th 1965

'Soulful Old Man Sunshine'
(Brian Wilson / Rick Henn) *Endless Harmony*
November 6th, 9th 1969

'South Bay Surfer'
(Brian Wilson / Dennis Wilson / Al Jardine) *Surfer Girl*)
July 14th 1963

'Spirit Of America'
(Brian Wilson / Roger Christian) *Little Deuce Coupe*
September 2nd 1963

'Steamboat'
(Dennis Wilson / Jack Rieley) *Holland*
June 3rd-22nd 1972
June 28th-August 2nd 1972
September / October 1972

'Stoked'
(Brian Wilson) *Surfin' USA*
February 12th 1963

'Student Demonstration Time'
(based on 'Riot In Cell Block #9' Jerry Leiber / Mike
Stoller, new lyrics Mike Love) *Surf's Up*
October 1970
January-April 1971

'Summer Means New Love'
(Brian Wilson) *Summer Days*
May 12th 1965
June 1st 1965

'Summertime Blues'
(Eddie Cochran / Jerry Capehart) *Surfin' Safari*
August 6th 1962

'Surf Jam'
(Carl Wilson) *Surfin' USA*
February 12th 1963

'Surf's Up'
(Brian Wilson / Van Dyke Parks) *Surf's Up*
(Sessions in full)
November 4th 1966
November 7th/8th 1966
December 5th 1966
December 15th 1966 (*Inside Pop: The Rock
Revolution* session 1)
December 17th 1966 (*Inside Pop: The Rock
Revolution* session 2, transmitted version)
January 23rd 1967
February 8th 1967
(Mid) June-(early) July 1971

'Surfer Girl'
(Brian Wilson) *Studio Sessions 61/62* CD
February 8th 1962

'Surfer Girl'
(Brian Wilson) *Surfer Girl*
June 12th 1963

'The Surfer Moon'
(Brian Wilson) *Surfer Girl*
September 13th 1962
May 9th 1963

'Surfers Rule'
(Brian Wilson / Mike Love) *Surfer Girl*
July 16th 1963

'Surfin''
(Brian Wilson / Mike Love) *Studio Sessions 61/62* CD,
Surfin' Safari
September 15th 1961
October 3rd 1961

'Surfin' Safari'
(Brian Wilson / Mike Love) *Studio Sessions 61/62* CD
February 8th 1962

'Surfin' Safari'
(Brian Wilson / Mike Love) *Surfin' Safari*
April 19th 1962
June 12th 1962

'Surfin' USA'
(Chuck Berry) *Surfin' USA*
January 5th 1963
January 31st 1963

'Susie Cincinnati'
(Al Jardine) *15 Big Ones*
December 1969
January 7th 1970
From sessions January 30th-May 1976

'Take A Load Off Your Feet (Pete)'
(Al Jardine / Gary Winfrey) *Surf's Up*
January 1970
January 26th 1970
January-April 1971

'Talk To Me'
(Joe Seneca) *15 Big Ones*
March 1976

'Tears In The Morning'
(Bruce Johnston) *Sunflower*
November 18th 1969
January 26th 1970
January 28th 1970

'Tell Me Why'
(John Lennon / Paul McCartney) *Party!*
From sessions September 8th, 14th, 15th and 23rd 1965

'Ten Little Indians'
(Brian Wilson / Gary Usher) *Surfin' Safari*
August 8th 1962

'That Same Song'
(Brian Wilson / Mike Love) *15 Big Ones*
April 1976

'That's Not Me'
(Brian Wilson / Tony Asher) *Pet Sounds*
February 15th 1966

'Their Hearts Were Full Of Spring'
(Bobby Troup) *Live In London*
December 8th 1968

'Then I Kissed Her'
(Phil Spector / Ellie Greenwich / Jeff Barry)
Summer Days
May 3rd 1965

'There's No Other Like My Baby'
(Phil Spector / Leroy Bates) *Party!*
From sessions September 8th, 14th, 15th and
23rd 1965

'A Thing Or Two'
(Brian Wilson / Mike Love) *Wild Honey*
October 27th 1967

'This Car Of Mine'
(Brian Wilson / Mike Love) *Shut Down Volume 2*
February 20th 1964

'This Whole World'
(Brian Wilson) *Sunflower*
November 13th 1969

''Til I Die'
(Brian Wilson) *Surf's Up*
August 15th 1969
November 1969
January-April 1971

'Time To Get Alone'
(Brian Wilson) *20/20*
October 14th 1967
October 15th 1967
November 13th 1967
October 2nd 1968
October 4th 1968
November 21st 1968

'The Times They Are A-Changing'
(Bob Dylan) *Party!*
From sessions September 8th, 14th, 15th and 23rd
1965

'TM Song'
(Brian Wilson) *15 Big Ones*
March 18th 1976
May 19th 1976 (approx)

'The Trader'
(Carl Wilson / Jack Rieley) *Holland*
June 3rd-22nd 1972
June 28th-August 2nd 1972
September / October 1972

'Transcendental Meditation'
(Brian Wilson / Mike Love / Al Jardine) *Friends*
April 4th 1968

'Trombone Dixie'
Pet Sounds bonus track
November 1st 1965

'Vegetables'
(Brian Wilson / Van Dyke Parks) *Smiley Smile*
Sessions in full: November 11th 1966
November 16th 1966
(as 'Vegetables Arguments' piece)
April 4th 1967
April 5th 1967
April 6th 1967
April 7th 1967
April 10th 167
April 11th 1967
April 12th 1967
April 13th 1967
April 14th 1967
June 3rd 1967
June 5th 1967
June 6th 1967
June 7th 1967
June 15th 1967

'Wake The World'
(Brian Wilson / Al Jardine) *Friends*
March 28th 1968
March 30th 1968

'Walk On By'
(Burt Bacharach / Hal David) *Friends–20/20* CD
May 26th 1968

'The Wanderer'
(Ernest Maresca) *Concert*
August 1st 1964

'The Warmth Of The Sun'
(Brian Wilson / Mike Love) *Shut Down Volume 2*
January 1st 1964

'We Got Love'
(Ricky Fataar / Blondie Chaplin / Mike Love)
In Concert
From recordings November 1972, April, August,
September 1973

'We Three Kings Of Orient Are'
(John Hopkins) *Christmas Album*
June 18th 1964
June 29th 1964

'We'll Run Away'
(Brian Wilson / Gary Usher) *All Summer Long*
April 29th 1964
April 30th 1964
May 18th 1964

'Wendy'
(Brian Wilson / Mike Love) *All Summer Long*
April 29th 1964

'We're Together Again'
(Brian Wilson / Ron Wilson) *Friends–20/20* CD
May 27th 1968
May 29th 1968
September 3rd 1968
September 5th 1968
September 6th 1968
September 11th 1968

'When A Man Needs A Woman'
(Brian Wilson / Carl Wilson / Dennis Wilson / Al
Jardine / Steve Korthof / Van Dyke Parks) *Friends*
February 1968
March 18th 1968

'When I Grow Up (To Be A Man)'
(Brian Wilson / Mike Love) *Today!*
August 5th 1964
August 10th 1964

'Whistle In'
(Brian Wilson) *Smiley Smile*
July 13th 1967

'White Christmas'
(Irving Berlin) *Christmas Album*
June 18th 1964
June 28th 1964

'Why Do Fools Fall In Love'
(Frankie Lymon / Morris Levy) *Shut Down Volume 2*
January 7th 1964
January 8th 1964

'Wild Honey'
(Brian Wilson / Mike Love) *Wild Honey*
September 26th 1967
September 27th 1967

'Wind Chimes'
(Brian Wilson) *Smiley Smile*
Sessions in full: August 3rd 1966
October 3rd 1966
October 5th 1966
October 10th 1966
July 10th 1967
July 11th 1967

'With Me Tonight'
(Brian Wilson) *Smiley Smile*
June 30th 1967

'Wonderful'
(Brian Wilson / Van Dyke Parks) *Smiley Smile*
July 12th 1967

'Wouldn't It Be Nice'
(Brian Wilson / Tony Asher) *Pet Sounds*
January 22nd 1966
March 10th 1966
April 11th 1966

'You Need A Mess Of Help To Stand Alone'
(Brian Wilson / Jack Rieley) *Carl And The Passions*
December 4th-10th 1971
April 3rd-13th 1972

'You Still Believe In Me'
(Brian Wilson / Tony Asher) *Pet Sounds*
November 1st 1965 (as 'In My Childhood')
January 24th 1966

'A Young Man Is Gone'
(Bobby Troup) *Little Deuce Coupe*
September 2nd 1963

'Your Summer Dream'
(Brian Wilson / Bob Norberg) *Surfer Girl*
July 16th 1963

'You're So Good To Me'
(Brian Wilson / Mike Love) *Summer Days*
May 24th 1965

'You're Welcome'
(Brian Wilson) *Smiley Smile–Wild Honey* CD, *Rarities*
December 13th 1966
December 16th 1966

'You've Got To Hide Your Love Away'
(John Lennon / Paul McCartney) *Party!*
From sessions Sept 8th, 14th, 15th and 23rd 1965

Smile recording index

Songs recorded for the album variously known as *Dumb Angel* and *Smile*, which was never released at the time. Some are working titles only.

'Barnyard Suite'
October 20th 1966

'Cabinessence'
see main Song Recording Index

'Child Is Father Of The Man'
October 7th 1966
October 12th 1966
December 2nd 1966
December 6th 1966

'Do You Like Worms'
October 18th 1966
October 21st 1966
December 21st 1966

'The Elements'
November 28th 1966
December 5th 1966

'Fire'
see 'Mrs O'Leary's Cow', 'The Elements'

'Friday Night'
November 29th 1966

'George Fell Into His French Horn'
November 7th 1966

'Good Vibrations'
see main Song Recording Index

'Grand Coulee Dam'
see 'Cabinessence'

'He Gives Speeches'
September 1st 1966

'Heroes And Villains'
see main Song Recording Index

'Holidays'
September 8th 1966

'Home On The Range'
see 'Cabinessence'

'I Love To Say Da Da'
May 16th/17th 1966
May 18th 1966

'I Ran'
August 12th 1966
October 13th 1966

'I Wanna Be Around'
November 29th 1966

'I'm In Great Shape'
November 29th 1966

'Jazz'
November 29th 1966

'Look'
see 'I Ran'

'Mrs O'Leary's Cow'
November 28th 1966

'My Little Red Book'
February 14th 1967

'My Only Sunshine'
see 'You Are My Sunshine'

'Prayer'
September 19th 1966
October 4th 1966

'Surf's Up'
see main Song Recording Index

'Tones – Part 3'
March 3rd 1966
March 13th 1966
March 15th 1966
March 31st 1966
April 11th 1966

'Tune X'
see 'Tones – Part 3'

'Vegetables'
see main Song Recording Index

'Who Ran The Iron Horse'
see 'Cabinessence'

'Wind Chimes'
see main Song Recording Index

'Wonderful'
August 25th 1966
October 6th 1966
December 15th 1966
December 27th 1966
January 9th 1967
January 23rd 1967

'You Are My Sunshine'
November 14th 1966
November 30th 1966

'You're Welcome'
see main Song Recording Index

Session musicians

A comprehensive listing of session musicians who have contributed to Beach Boys recordings.

A

James Ackley (probably keyboards)
Michael Anthony (guitar)
John Audino (trumpet)

B

Israel Baker (violin)
Robert Barene (violin)
Gary Barone (trumpet)
Mike Barone (trombone)
Arnold Belnick (violin)
Harold Bemko (cello)
Ron Benson (guitar)
Charles Berghofer (upright bass),
Harry Betts (trombone)
Allan Beutler (saxophone)
Louis Blackburn (trombone)
Hal Blaine (drums, percussion)
Harry Bluestone (violin)
Jimmy Bond Jr, (upright bass)
Norm Botnick (viola)
Allen Breneman (drums)
Russell Bridges (piano, organ)
Arthur Briegleb (French horn)
Marvin Brown (trumpet)
James Burton (guitar)

C

George Callender (tuba)
Glen Campbell (guitar, banjo)
Frankie Capp (percussion, drums)
Ed Carter (guitar)
Dwight Carver (mellophonium, French horn)
Al Casey (guitar)
Roy Caton (trumpet)
Marion Childers (trumpet)
Peter Christ (English horn)
Gene Cipriano (saxophone)
David Cohen (guitar)
Jerry Cole (guitar)
Gary Coleman (timpani, bongos)
Michel Colombier (keyboards)
John Conrad (bass)
Sonny Curtis (guitar)

D

Henry David (instrument unknown)
Douglas Davis (cello)
Mike Deasy (guitar)
Al de Lory (piano, harpsichord, organ),
Frank De Vito (percussion, drums)
Joe Difiore (viola)
Eugene DiNovi (piano)
Alvin Dinkin (viola)
Joseph DiTullio (cello)
Justin DiTullio (cello)
Bonnie Douglas (violin)
Steve Douglas (saxophone, flute, percussion)
Daryl Dragon (keyboards)
Dennis Dragon (drums)
David Duke (French horn)
Steve Dweck (vibes)

E

Bob Edmondson (trombone)
Jesse Ehrlich (cello)
Alan Estes (percussion)
Gene Estes (guitar, percussion, vibes, bells, piano)
Virgil Evans (trumpet)

F

David Filerman (cello)
Chuck Findley (trombone)
Dick Forrest (trumpet, flugelhorn)
Carl Fortina (accordion)
Sam Freed (violin)
David Frisina (violin)
Sal Frohman (instrument unknown)
Ritchie Frost (drums)

G

David Gates (guitar, bass guitar)
Jim Getzoff (violin)
Joseph Gibbons (guitar),
Sam Glenn (clarinet, flute, woodwind)
Anne Goodman (cello)
Jim Gordon (drums, percussion),
Billy Green (alto sax, flute, bass flute, woodwind, piccolo, whistle)
Urban Green (trombone)
John Guerin (drums)
Frank Guerrero (percussion)

H

Allan Harshman (viola)
Len Hartman (English horn, saxophone)
Michael Henderson (saxophone)
Arthur 'Skeets' Herfurt (saxophone)
Jay Higliori (saxophone)
Clifford Hils (upright bass)
Jim Hilton (flute)
Billy Hinsche (guitar)
Bill Hinshaw (French horn)
Jim Horn (saxophone)
Paul Horn (saxophone, woodwind)
Igor Horoshevsky (cello)
Dayton Howe (percussion)
Steve Huffsteter (trumpet)
Larry Hulley (guitar)
Harry Hyams (viola)
George Hyde (French horn)
Richard Hyde (trombone)

J

Jules Jacob (flute, oboe)
Norm Jeffries (drums)
Plas Johnson (saxophone)
Robert Jung (saxophone)

K

Alexander Kaminsky (violin leader)
Armand Kaproff (cello)
Nathan Kaproff (violin)
George Kast (violin)
Carol Kaye (bass guitar)
Jan Kelley (cello)
Ray Kelley (cello)
Barney Kessel (guitar)
Jerome Kessler (cello)
Robert Klein (tenor saxophone)
Larry Knechtel (organ, bass guitar)
Bernard Kundell (violin)
William Kurasch (violin)

L

Henry Laubach (trumpet)
Marvin Limonick (violin)
Irving Lipschultz (violin, cello)
Randall A Locroft (trombone)
Abe Luboff (upright bass)
Alfred Lustgarten (violin)
Edgar Lustgarten (cello)

M

Arthur Maebe (French horn)
Virginia Majewski (viola)
Lenny Malarsky (violin)
Frank Marocco (clarinet)
Gail Martin (trombone)
Nicholas Martinis (drums)
Lew McCreary (trombone, bass trombone)
Terry Melcher (tambourine)
Michael Melvoin (harpsichord)
Frank Messina (horn)
Jay Migliori (saxophone, flute, piccolo, whistle, clarinet)
Oliver Mitchell (trumpet, viola)
Tommy Morgan (bass harmonica)
Abe Most (clarinet)

N

Richard Nash (trombone)
Alexander Neiman (viola)
Jack Nimitz (saxophone),
Wilbert Nuttycombe (violin)

O

Robert Ostrowsky (viola)

P

Earl Palmer (drums)
Van Dyke Parks (harmonium)
Don Peake (probably guitar)
Nick Pellico (percussion)
Gene Pello (drums)
Richard Perissi (French horn)

Bill Pitman (guitar)
Ray Pohlman (bass guitar, guitar)
Melvin Pollan (upright bass)
Al Porcino (trumpet)

R

Lou Raderman (violin)
Emil Radocchia (percussion),
Don Randi (piano, harpsichord, organ)
Jerry Reisler (violin)
Dorothy Remsen (harp)
Chester Ricord (percussion)
Billy Lee Riley (harmonica)
Lyle Ritz (upright bass, ukulele, guitar, cello)
Howard Roberts (guitar)
Alan Robinson (French horn)
Jay Rosen (violin)
Karl Rossner (cello)
Henry Roth (violin)
Mike Rubini (keyboards)
Leon Russell (piano)

S

Joe Saxon (cello)
Ralph Schaeffer (violin)
Wilbur Schwartz (saxophone)
Tom Scott (woodwind)
Leonard Selic (viola)
Emmet Sergeant (violin, cello)
Frederick Seykora (cello)
Sidney Sharp (violin)
David Sherr (woodwind)
Claude Sherry (French horn)
Paul Shure (violin)
Arthur C. Smith (possibly flute)
Marshall Sossen (violin)
Billy Strange (guitar)

T

Ernie Tack (trombone)
Paul Tanner (theremin).
Tommy Tedesco (guitar)
Tony Terran (trumpet)
Darrel Terwilliger (violin, viola)
George Tyler (instrument unknown)

V

Al Vescovo (guitar)
Dorothy Victor (harp)
John Vidor (violin)
Al Viola (guitar)

W

Dorothy Wade (violin)
Eirik Wangberg (instrument unknown)
Julius Wechter (timpani, vibes, bicycle bell, finger cymbals, tambourine, percussion)
Alan Weight (trumpet)
Walter Wiemeyer (violin)
Jerry Williams (percussion)
Artie Wright (probably saxophone)

Y

David York (instrument unknown)

Z

Tibor Zelig (violin)

TV listings

Listed in alphabetical order, with show
title (plus in brackets the production
company and/or network), country, and
the recording or air date. The main text
in this book includes only musical
appearances; some additional non-
musical features are also listed here.

A

Age Tendre Et Tete De Bois (TF2) France
Nov 18 '64
American Bandstand (ABC) US Mar 14 '64
The Andy Williams Show (NBC) US Nov 2 '65
Au Dela De I Ecran (TF1) France Nov 18 '64

B

Bandstand (Channel 9) Australia Jan 13 '64
The Beach Boys (Beach Boys / Above Average) US
Aug 5 '76
Beat Club (Radio Bremen) Germany Dec 12 '68,
Jun 3 '69
The Beat Room (BBC) UK Nov 5 '64
The Bob Hope Special (NBC) US Dec 18 '64
The Bob Rogers Show (ATN7) Australia Apr 27 '70
Bratislava Song Festival (InterVision / WZT)
Czechoslovakia Jun 18 '69

C

Chicago's New Year's Rockin' Eve (ABC) US
Nov 1 '74

D

The David Frost Show (Westinghouse Group) US
Jul 30 '69, Feb 25 '71, May 7 '71
The Dick Cavett Show (ABC) US Aug 12 '68
Discs A Go Go (TWW) UK Nov 4 '64
Don Kirschner's Rock Music Awards (CBS) US
Sep 17 '76 (Brian Dennis & Carl)

E

The Ed Sullivan Show (CBS) US Sep 27 '64,
May 16 '65, Oct 13 '68
Eddie Ready Go! (NCR) Netherlands Jun 7 '72
Edisons Voor De Vuist Weg (AVRO) Netherlands
Mar 9 '73 (Carl)

F

Fanclub (VARA) Netherlands May 14 '67
4-3-2-1 Hot And Sweet (ZDF) Germany Dec 13 '68

G

Get It Together (ABC) US Mar 9 '70
Good Vibrations From Central Park (NBC) Jul 2 '71
Good Vibrations From London (NBC) US Jun 3 '72
Grand Gala Du Disque Populaire '72 (AVRO)
Netherlands Feb 25 '72

H

Happening (ABC) US Aug 12 '68, Aug 19 '69

I

Inside Pop: The Rock Revolution (CBS News) US
Dec 17 '66 (Brian)

J

Jack Benny Hour (NBC) US Nov 3 '65
The Joey Bishop Show (ABC) US Nov 1 '68
Juke Box Jury (BBC) UK Aug 12 '67 (Bruce)

K

Kraft Music Hall (NBC) US Feb 16 '69

L

The Les Crane Show (ABC) US Jun 4 '68

M

Midi Premiere (TFI) France Jun 16 '69
The Mike Douglas Show (Westinghouse Group) US
May 10 '68, Aug 26 '68, Jul 8 '69, Aug 16 '69, Sep
13 '76 (Mike & Al), Nov 23 '76 (Brian)
The Mike Walsh Show (HSV7) US Apr 23 '70

N

NBC News (NBC) US Jun 27 '74 (Mike)
Noel Des Enfants Du Monde (TF1) / *UNICEF Gala*
Variety From Paris (BBC) France/UK Dec 15 '67

O

The Old Grey Whistle Test (BBC) UK May 16 '72,
May 1 '74 (Carl), Dec 27 '74 (Bruce),
Nov 16 '76 (Brian)
On Ne Manque Pas d'Air (TF2) France Dec 31 '76
Open House (BBC) UK Nov 7 '64

P

Pop2 (TF2) France Dec 8 '70

R

De Raiders En De Beach Boys (NCR) Netherlands
Jun 30 '69
Ready Steady Go! (Associated Rediffusion) UK
Nov 6 '64, May 20 '66 (Bruce)
The Red Skelton Show (CBS) US Sep 24 '63,
May 12 '64

S

Saturday Night Live (NBC) US Nov 26 '76 (Brian)
Shindig! (ABC) US Dec 17 '64, Apr 21 '65
Something Else (Robert E. Petersen) US May 28 '70
The Steve Allen Show (KFMB) US Mar 2 '63,
Mar 12 '64
Surf Sound (ATN7) Australia Jan 24 '64

T

Thank Your Lucky Stars (ABC) UK Nov 8 '64
Tilt Magazine (TF1) France Oct 26 '66
The Tommy Leonetti Show (ATN7) Australia
May 14 '70
The Tonight Show (NBC) US Aug 13 '68
Tonight With Barry Ion (ADS7) Australia
Apr 24 '70
Top Of The Pops (BBC) UK Nov 30 '68, Nov 18 '70,
May 31 '72
Toppop (AVRO) Netherlands Dec 15 '70 (Bruce),
Feb 24 '72
Twien (NCR) Netherlands Dec 14 '68

W

Where The Action Is (ABC) US Sep 24 '66 (Carl)

Concert location index 1961–1976

AUSTRALIA

Adelaide Apollo Stadium Apr 25 '70; Centennial Hall Jan 20 '64
Brisbane Festival Hall Jan 13 '64, Apr 30 '70
Canberra Theatre Apr 26 '70
Hobart Town Hall Jan 23 '64
Melbourne Festival Hall Jan 21-22 '64, Apr 23 '70
Newcastle Century Theatre Apr 29 '70
Perth Perry Lakes Stadium Apr 24 '70
Surfers Paradise Beachcomber Tiki Village Motel May 2 '70
Sydney Silver Spade, Chevron Hotel May 4-13 '70; Stadium Jan 17-18 '64, Apr 27 '70
Wollongong Capitol Hall Apr 28 '70

AUSTRIA

Stadthalle May 14 '72

BELGIUM

Antwerp Pop Festival Jun 21 '69; Queen Elizabeth Hall May 15 '72
Brussels Amerikaans Theater Jun 24 '69

CANADA

Calgary (Alberta) Jubilee Auditorium Aug 22 '68
Edmonton (Alberta) Jubilee Auditorium Dec 2 '69; Kinsmen Field House Aug 21 '68; Northlands Coliseum Jul 22 '76
Halifax (Nova Scotia) Metro Center Aug 5 '68
Hamilton (Ontario) Wentworth Curling Club Aug 14 '69
Kitchener (Ontario) Memorial Auditorium Nov 21 '66
Montreal (Quebec) Forum Feb 19 '65, Sep 6 '65, Nov 22 '66, Aug 4 '68, Aug 31 '75, Sep 5 '76
Ottawa (Ontario) Capital Theatre Feb 20 '65; Coliseum Sep 4 '65; New Civic Center Aug 2 '68
Regina (Saskatchewan) Agridome At Exhibition Park Aug 20 '68; Centre Of The Arts Dec 5 '69
Toronto (Ontario) Borough of York Stadium Jun 26 '72; Canadian National Exhibition (CNE) Jun 24 '76, Sep 3-4 '76; Maple Leaf Gardens Feb 21 '65, Sep 5 '65, Nov 20 '66, Aug 28 '74; Massey Hall Aug 18 '68, Sep 2 '73; O'Keefe Center Jun 24 '72; Varsity Stadium, University of Toronto Jun 26 '70
Vancouver (British Columbia) Agrodome Feb 3 '68, Jan 18 '69, Nov 4 '72; Empire Stadium Jan 29 '65, Sep 24 '65, Aug 17 '66; National Exhibition Grandstand Aug 30 '75; Pacific Coliseum; Pacific (PNE) Coliseum Aug 23-24 '68, Mar 11 '73, Dec 14 '74, Dec 14 '75, Sep 19-20 '76, Dec 21 '76;

Queen Elizabeth Theatre Aug 18 '66, Jan 15 '69, Mar 20 '70, Dec 15 '71
Victoria (British Columbia) Memorial Arena Jul 23 '68, Jan 16 '69, Mar 10 '73
Winnipeg (Manitoba) Arena Aug 19 '68; Centennial Concert Hall Aug 14 '66, Aug 13 '69

CZECHOSLOVAKIA

Bratislava Song Festival Jun 18 '69
Brno Hala Rondo Jun 18 '69
Prague Lucerna Hall Jun 17 '69

DENMARK

Copenhagen KB Hallen Nov 14 '64
Torsdagm Falkoner Centret Nov 3 '66

ENGLAND

See also Scotland, Northern Ireland, Wales
Bardney *see* Lincoln
Birmingham Kinetic Circus May 18 '72; Odeon Theatre May 6 '67, Dec 6 '68, Jun 6 '69, Nov 25 '70; Theatre Nov 13 '66
Bournemouth Winter Gardens Dec 12 '70
Brighton Dome May 30 '69, May 24 '72
Bristol Colston Hall Dec 2 '68; Top Rank Ballroom May 23 '72
Coventry Theatre Nov 22 '70
Leeds King Edward Nurses Home, Leeds General Infirmary Jun 8 '69; Odeon Theatre Nov 10 '66
Leicester De Montfort Hall Nov 9 '66, May 21 '72
Lincoln Tupholme Hall, Bardney May 28 '72
Liverpool Empire Jun 7 '69, Dec 13 '70, May 20 '72
London Astoria Theatre, Finsbury Park Nov 6 '66, May 5 '67, Dec 8 '68, Jun 10 '69, Dec 11 '70; Crystal Palace Sports Stadium Jun 3 '72; Empire Pool, Wembley May 7 '67; Granada Theatre, Tooting Nov 8 '66; Odeon, Hammersmith Nov 14 '66, May 4 '67, May 31 '69, Nov 20 '70; Palladium Dec 1 '68; Royal Albert Hall Dec 17 '70; Royal Festival Hall May 27 '72; Wembley Stadium Jun 21 '75
Manchester Free Trade Hall Jun 8 '69; Kings Hall May 19 '72; Odeon Theatre Nov 11 '66, May 8 '67, Dec 5 '68; Palace Nov 21 '70
Newcastle Upon Tyne City Hall May 16 '72
Oxford New Theatre Nov 19 '70
Reading Top Rank Ballroom May 22 '72
Sheffield City Hall Dec 4 '68; Fiesta Night Club Nov 30-Dec 6 '70
Southampton Gaumont Theatre Nov 23 '70

FINLAND

Helsinki Finlandia Hall May 13 '67; Jaahalli Jun 20 '69

FRANCE

Lyon Palais D'Hiver Dec 9 '70
Paris Gaumont Palace Dec 8 '70; Olympia Theatre Nov 18 '64, Oct 25 '66, Dec 16 '68, Jun 4 '69, Jun 16 '69

GERMANY

Berlin Deutchlandhalle Oct 27 '66, Jun 14 '69; Sportspalast May 19 '67; Stadthalle Dec 12 '68
Cologne Sportshalle May 17 '67
Dusseldorf Kongresshalle Dec 13 '68
Essen Grugahalle Oct 29 '66, May 7 '72
Frankfurt Festhalle Nov 12 '64, Jun 13 '69, May 8 '72
Hamburg Ernst Merck Halle Nov 13 '64, Oct 28 '66
Hanover Messe Sportpalast Oct 31 '66
Munich Circus Krone Nov 2 '66, May 9 '72
Munster Halle Munsterland Oct 30 '66

HOLLAND

See Netherlands

HUNGARY

Budapest Sporthall Jun 11 '69

IRELAND

See also Northern Ireland
Dublin Adelphi Theatre May 2 '67; National Boxing Stadium Nov 8 '64

ITALY

Milan Piper Club Nov 11 '64

JAPAN

Fukuoka Kyuden Taikukan Jan 14 '66
Kobe Kokusai Kaikan Jan 12 '66
Kyoto Kaikan Hall Jan 10 '66
Nagoya Nagoya-shi Koukaido Jan 8 '66

Osaka Sankei Hall Jan 9 '66, Jan 13 '66
Sendai Miyagi Kenmin Kaikan Jan 18 '66
Shizuoka Sumpu Kaikan Jan 20 '66
Tokyo Otemachi Sankei Hall Jan 15 '66; Ootaku Taikukan Jan 23 '66; Shibuya Koukaido Jan 7 '66; Shinjuku Kousei Nenkin Hall Jan 16 '66, Jan 22 '66, Jan 23 '66
Yokohama Bunka Taikukan Jan 21 '66

THE NETHERLANDS

Amsterdam Concertgebouw Dec 14 '68, Jun 1 '69, Dec 18 '70, Dec 20 '70
Groningen Martinihall May 11 '72
Rotterdam Ahoy Halle Dec 10 '70; De Doelen Jun 1 '69, Dec 19 '70; Sportpaleis Ahoy May 13 '72

NEW ZEALAND

Auckland Town Hall Jan 31-Feb 1 '64, Apr 18 '70
Christchurch Majestic Theatre Apr 21 '70
Dunedin Town Hall Apr 22 '70
Hamilton Founders Hall Jan 30 '64
Wellington Town Hall Jan 29 '64, Apr 20 '70

NORTHERN IRELAND

See also Ireland; England, Scotland, Wales
Belfast ABC Theatre May 3 '67

NORWAY

Oslo Njordhallen Nov 15 '64

PUERTO RICO

San Juan Hiram Bithorn Stadium Nov 21 '71

SCOTLAND

See also England, Northern Ireland, Wales
Edinburgh ABC Theatre May 10 '67
Glasgow Green's Playhouse Nov 26 '70; Odeon Theatre May 9 '67, Dec 10 '68, Jun 9 '69

SWEDEN

Gothenburg Scandinavium May 6 '72
Stockholm Konserthuset Nov 16 '64, Nov 4 '66, May 20 '67, May 5 '72

UNITED KINGDOM

See England, Northern Ireland, Scotland, Wales

UNITED STATES OF AMERICA

Albany (New York) New York State University, State University Plaza Mar 16 '72; Palace Theater Nov 14 '72; Theater May 11 '73
Albuquerque (New Mexico) Civic Auditorium Dec 4 '65, Jul 15 '68
Alexandria (Virginia) Roller Rink Sep 23 '64
Allentown (Pennsylvania) Fairgrounds Aug 19 '72, Aug 24 '75; Muhlenberg College Mar 26 '72
Ames (Iowa) Iowa State University Jul 10 '68
Amherst (Massachusetts) University Of Massachusetts Nov 23 '65
Anaheim (California) Convention Center Nov 16 '73; Melodyland Theatre Apr 5 '65; Stadium May 23 '75, Jul 3 '76
Anchorage (Alaska) West High Auditorium Jul 20 '68
Ann Arbor (Michigan) University of Michigan Apr 23 '74
Asbury Park (New Jersey) Convention Center/Hall Jul 10 '65, Jul 8 '66, Jul 23 '66, Aug 17 '68
Ashland (Oregon) McNeal Gymnasium, Southern Oregon State College Mar 6 '66
Athens (Georgia) Convocation Center Nov 22 '75; University of Georgia Nov 6 '72
Atlanta (Georgia) Alexander Memorial Coliseum, Georgia Tech Mar 30 '72; Auditorium Apr 11 '65, Jul 18 '65, Apr 10 '69, Apr 11 '74; Omni Coliseum Apr 11 '73, Apr 3 '75; Stadium Sep 20 '64; University Nov 1 '72
Atlantic City (New Jersey) Steel Pier Jul 30 '66, Jul 24-26 '68, Aug 9-11 '68, Jul 24-26 '69
Auburn (Alabama) College Fieldhouse Apr 11 '74
Austin (Texas) Masonic Auditorium Mar 18 '67; Municipal Auditorium Apr 5 '66, Mar 23 '67, Apr 24 '67, Feb 11 '69
Azuza (California) Azuza Canteen, Azuza Teen Club Jul 28 '62

Bakersfield (California) Civic Auditorium/Center Dec 20 '62, Dec 19 '74
Baltimore (Maryland) Civic Centre Apr 23 '65, Nov 23-24 '66, Nov 26 '67, May 34 '68, Jul 23 '69, Nov 22 '74; Ocean City Sep 3 '72
Bangor (Maine) Auditorium Jul 14 '65
Baton Rouge (Louisiana) Louisiana State University Nov 30 '73
Beverly Hills (California) Beverly Hilton Hotel Apr 18 '69
Birmingham (Alabama) Alabama Theater Sep 19 '64; Boutwell Auditorium Oct 1 '65, Nov 27 '75; Municipal Auditorium Apr 19 '68, Dec 12 '75; Legion Field May 7 '65
Blacksburg (Virginia) Polytechnic Institute Oct 25 '68
Bloomington (Indiana) Assembly Hall, Indiana University Sep 1 '74
Boise (Idaho) County Fairgrounds Dec 7 '74; High School Auditorium Sep 13 '64; Mountain Home Oct 18 '64; Pavilion Sep 12 '64
Boston (Massachusetts) Back Bay Theatre Apr 28 '67, Nov 23 '67; College Apr 29 '66, Mar 24 '72;

Common Aug 23-24 '72; Garden Sep 6 '64, Nov 26 '65, Nov 17 '66, Nov 19 '75, Nov 28 '76; Music Hall Nov 27 '68, Sep 23 '71, Dec 8 '73, Nov 23 '74; Symphony Hall Feb 23 '71
Bridgeport (Connecticut) University May 7 '71
Bristol (Rhode Island) Roger Williams College Sep 22 '71
Bronx see New York
Brooklyn see New York
Buffalo (New York) Century Theater Sep 1 '73; Peace Bridge Center Jul 6 '66; Kleinhans Music Hall Apr 23 '72; Memorial Auditorium Sep 3 '64, Jul 21 '66, Nov 18 '67; Rich Stadium Aug 27 '76
Burlington (Vermont) University of Vermont Nov 20 '75, Nov 25 '75; Vermont Memorial Hall Nov 20 '74

Calgary (Alabama) Jubilee Auditorium Aug 16 '66
Canton (Ohio) Memorial Auditorium May 19 '65, Nov 24 '68
Cedar Rapids (Iowa) Danceland Ballroom Apr 27 '63
Champaign (Illinois) RKO Orpheum Theater Jul 14 '64; University of Illinois Oct 28 '75
Chapel Hill (North Carolina) University Of North Carolina Apr 10 '73
Charleston (Illinois) Eastern Illinois University Dec 6 '73
Charleston (West Virginia) Civic Center Aug 16 '68, Oct 26 '68
Charlotte (North Carolina) Coliseum Dec 31 '64, Apr c.25-29 '65, Apr 4 '75, Apr 6 '75
Chicago (Illinois) Aragon Ballroom Nov 28 '69; Arie Crown Theater Jul 24 '64, Mar 26 '65, Aug 28-29 '65, Jul 16-18 '66, Aug 17 '72, Mar 30 '73; Auditorium Theater Aug 11 '63, Jul 5 '68, Aug 14-16 '73; Civic Opera House Oct 8 '67; Comiskey Park Jul 5 '66; International Ampitheater Jan 7 '65; North Gym, Chicago State College Nov 20 '73; Stadium Aug 17 '74, Jun 1-5 & 7 '75, Jul 16-18 '75; Unknown venue Aug 30 '63
Cincinnati (Ohio) Football Field, University of Cincinnati Aug 12 '73; Gardens Aug 27 '65, Apr 23 '67, Apr 2 '68; Riverfront Coliseum Nov 23 '75, Nov 22 '76; Taft Auditorium Sep 29 '71
Clarkston (Michigan) Pine Knob Theatre Aug 22 '75
Cleveland (Ohio) Auditorium Aug 21 '64, May 31 '75; Music Hall Mar 11 '66, Oct 7 '67, Nov 20 '71, Dec 7 '73; Stadium Sep 26 '65, Jun 23 '74
College Park (Maryland) University of Maryland, Cole Field House Arena Mar 28 '72
Colorado Springs (Colorado) Gymnasium, Airforce Academy Feb 18 '74
Columbia (Maryland) Merriweather Post Pavilion Jul 28 '69, Aug 30 '72, Aug 30 '73
Columbia (South Carolina) University of South Carolina Nov 28 '75
Columbus (Ohio) Memorial Auditorium Feb 18 '67; Apr 1 '68, Nov 23 '68, Aug 15 '76; St John's Arena, Ohio State University Apr 19 '74; State Fair Aug 29 '74
Commack (New York) Long Island Arena Apr 26 '67, Jul 19 '69

Cranston (Rhode Island) Rhodes Ballroom Feb 17 '65; Pawtuxet Ballroom Feb 17 '68

Dallas (Texas) Bronco Bowl Apr 22 '73; Convention Center Apr 27 '68, Oct 5 '76; Cotton Bowl Stadium May 3 '75; Fort Worth Oct 7 '76; Market Hall Apr 20 '68; Memorial Auditorium Dec 26 '64, Feb 10 '65, Apr 1 '66, Mar 24 '67, Feb 13 '69; Texas Stadium Jul 31 '74

Danbury (Connecticut) Prison Aug 23 '73

Dania (Florida) Pirate's World Arena Mar 23 '73, Apr 14 '73

Davenport (Iowa) Capital Theater Apr 19 '67; Colonial Ballroom Mar 21 '67; RKO Orpheum Jul 2 '68

Dayton (Ohio) Hara Arena May 21 '65, Sep 17 '65, Aug 13 '76; Memorial Hall Feb 18 '67; UP Fieldhouse, University of Dayton Mar 17 '66

Daytona Beach (Florida) Peabody Auditorium Apr 7 '69, Mar 28 '75

Denver (Colorado) Civic Auditorium Jul 7 '64, May 30 '65; Convention Center Nov 14 '73, Dec 5 '74; Mile High Stadium Aug 9 '66, Jul 19 '76; Red Rocks Jul 28 '64, Apr 26 '73, Jul 25 '74

Des Moines (Iowa) Ice Arena Jul 11 '68; State Fairgrounds Aug 21 '75, Jul 25 '76; Veterans Memorial Auditorium Jul 13 '64, Jul 20 '64

Detroit (Michigan) Cobo Hall Nov 21 '64, May 23 '65; Masonic Temple Auditorium Feb 19 '67, Nov 17 '67; Olympia Stadium Nov 16 '75

Duluth (Minnesota) Arena Auditorium Aug 13 '66; Jul 7 '68

Durham (New Hampshire) University Of New Hampshire Dec 10 '73

Edinboro (Pennsylvania) State University Apr 15 '74

Edwardsville (Illinois) Mississippi River Festival, Southern Illinois University Aug 16 '72

Erie (Pennsylvania) Penn State University Sep 30 '71; Stadium Sep 2 '76

Everett (Washington) Rainer Hall, College Gym, Everett Community College Feb 1 '68

Excelsior (Minnesota) Amusement Park May 3 '63

Fairbanks (Alaska) University of Alaska Jul 19 '68

Fairfield (Connecticut) University Gym Nov 20 '67

Fargo (North Dakota) Civic Memorial Auditorium Aug 11 '66, Jul 8 '68

Farmington see Salt Lake City

Fort Collins (Colorado) Colorado State Stadium Jul 6 '75; Colorado State University Feb 19 '74

Fort Myers (Florida) Mann Theater Mar 29 '75

Fort Wayne (Indiana) Coliseum Sep 23 '65; Quimby Auditorium Nov 28 '65

Fort Worth (Texas) Will Rogers Coliseum Apr 2 '66, Apr 20 '68; Tarrant County Convention Center Feb 15 '69

Foxboro (Massachusetts) Schaeffer Stadium Aug 20 '73, Jun 29-30 '75, Jul 3 '75

Fresno (California) Convention Hall, Ratcliffe Stadium Jul 3 '66; Exhibition Hall Dec 22 '62; Selland Arena Jul 11 '65; Warner Theatre Dec 18 '74

Gainesville (Florida) University of Florida Apr 12 '73

Galveston (Texas) Moody Civic Center Apr 21 '68

Grand Rapids (Michigan) Calvin College Apr 20 '74

Greensboro (North Carolina) Coliseum Jul 13 '65, Apr 23 '68, Oct 20 '68, Apr 5 '75; War Memorial Auditorium Jan 5 '65; University of North Carolina Apr c.25-29 '65, Apr 25 '68

Greenvale (New York) CW Post College May 4 '71

Greenville (South Carolina) Memorial Auditorium Jul 17 '65

Grove City (Ohio) College Aug 9 '73

Grove City (Pennsylvania) College May 9 '73

Hampton Beach (New Hampshire) Casino Jul 7 '65

Hampton Rhodes (Virginia) Coliseum Aug 25 '72, Aug 26 '73

Harrington (Delaware) Delaware State Fair Grounds Aug 2 '69

Harrisburg (Pennsylvania) State Farm Show Building Aug 14 '68

Hartford (Connecticut) Bushnell Auditorium May 15 '66, Nov 20 '67, May 5 '68, Nov 25 '68; Civic Center Sep 12 '75; Dillon Stadium Sep 10 '64, Jun 25 '65, Oct 7 '65, Aug 18 '72, Aug 24 '73, Aug 29 '76; Trinity College May 2 '71

Hawthorne (California) Presbyterian Church Jan 25 '62

Hermosa Beach (California) Hermosa Beach High School Feb 14 '63; Hermosa Biltmore Nov 21 '62

Highland Hills (New York) South Auditorium, West Point Military Academy Nov 24 '67

Hollywood (California) see Los Angeles

Hollywood (Florida) Sportatorium Apr 13 '74, Mar 30 '75

Honolulu (Hawaii) Civic Auditorium Jun 15 '63; Honolulu International Center (HIC) Arena Jul 3-4 '64, Jan 29 '66, Aug 25-26 '67, Jan 31 '75; Waikiki Shell Aug 5-6 '65

Houston (Texas) Civic Center Apr 21 '73; Hofheinz Pavilion Oct 6 '76; Jefferson Stadium May 2 '75; Jeppesen Stadium Jul 28 '74; McDonald Gym, Lamar Technical College Apr 21 '68; Music Hall Dec 23 '64, Apr 3 '66, Mar 25 '67; Sam Houston Coliseum Dec 24 '64, Apr 21 '68, Feb 14 '69

Independence (Michigan) Pine Knob Musical Theater Sep 4 '72, Sep 3 '73, Sep 3 '74, Jul 13 & 15 '76

Indiana (Pennsylvania) University of Pennsylvania Sep 13 '71

Indianapolis (Indiana) Clowes Hall, Butler University Oct 1 '71; Indiana Beach Jul 17 '64; Fairgrounds Coliseum Jul 18 '64, Nov 18 '66, Jul 6 '68; Market Square Arena Oct 27 '75; Theater Apr 3 '68

Inglewood (California) Inglewood Women's Club Apr 4 '62, May 4 '62

Ithaca (New York) Cornell University Apr 29 '66

Jacksonville (Florida) Civic Auditorium Jul 23 '65, Apr 7 '66, Feb 12 '67, Apr 9 '69; Coliseum Feb 13 '67, Apr 12 '68, Nov 29 '75; University of Florida, Florida Field Apr 10 '68

Jamaica (New York) St. John's University Alumni Hall Nov 19 '66, Nov 25 '67

Jersey City (New Jersey) Roosevelt Stadium Aug 19 '72, Aug 25 '73, Aug 23 '74, Aug 28 '76; Stanley-Warner Theatre Nov 26 '68 **Johnstown** (Pennsylvania) War Memorial Auditorium Apr 16 '67

Joliet (Illinois) Memorial Stadium May 19 '74

Jonesboro (Arkansas) Arkansas State University Apr 17 '68

Kalamazoo (Michigan) Wings Stadium Sep 5 '75

Kansas City (Missouri) Arrowhead Stadium May 17 '75, Jul 23 '76; KS Memorial Hall Jul 14 '68; Municipal Auditorium Jul 12 '64, Nov 20 '65, Apr 17 '67, May 15 '74; Music Hall May 15 '76; Royals Stadium Jul 19 '74

Keene (New Hampshire) Colonial Theatre Apr 21 '65

Kingsport (Kentucky) Civic Center, Bobyns Bennett High School Oct 24 '68

Kingston (Rhode Island) University Of Rhode Island Sep 28 '71, Dec 9 '73

Knoxville (Tennessee) Civic Auditorium Sep 21 '64, Dec 2 '73; Civic Coliseum May 8 '66; Stokely Athletic Center Apr 2 '75

Lacey (Washington) St Martin's College, Capital Pavilion Feb 4 '68

LaCrosse (Wisconsin) Avalon Ballroom Aug 29 '63; Mary E Sawyer Auditorium Jul 25 '64

Lake Geneva (Wisconsin) Majestic Hills Jul 4 '68

Landover (Maryland) Capital Center Jun 24-28 '75

Lansing (Michigan) Civic Center May 12 '66; University Oct 22 '66, Dec 10 '66, Apr 4 '74, May 18 '74

Largo (Maryland) Capital Center Aug 24 '74, Aug 30-31 '76

Las Vegas (Nevada) Convention Center Jul 1 '66; International Ice Palace Feb 11 '68

Lawrence (Kansas) Hoch Auditorium Apr 28 '73; University, Allen Field House Nov 1 '75

Lincoln (Nebraska) Pershing Municipal Auditorium Jul 13 '68

Little Rock (Arkansas) Civic Auditorium Apr 22 '68; State Fair Oct 2 '76

Long Beach (California) Arena Oct 17 '64, Dec 3 '71, Dec 31 '73, Dec 29-31 '74; Municipal Auditorium Dec 31 '61

Long Pond (Pennsylvania) Pocono International Raceway Aug 31 '74

Los Angeles (California) Cinnamon Cinder Feb 23-24 '62; Civic Arena Apr 17 '73; Forum Dec 27 '74, Dec 31 '76; Hollywood Bowl Nov 1 '63, Jul 3 '65, Jun 25 '66; Hollywood Palladium Nov 12 '62, Mar 16 '73, Apr 20 '73; Newport High School Mar 24 '62; Ontario National Guard Armory, John Gavin Park Mar 31 '62; Pandora's Box Oct 28 '62, Nov 4 '62, Nov 11 '62, Aug 3-6 '63; Rainbow Gardens Feb 16-17 '62; Sports Arena Feb 17 '63; Aug 31'63; Whisky A Go Go Nov 4-7 '70, Jan 19 '71, Apr 13-14 '71

Louisville (Kentucky) Fairgrounds Jul 16 '64, Aug 26

'65, Oct 22 '68; Freedom Hall Apr 1 '75

Lowell (Massachusetts) Auditorium Apr 28 '71

Lubbock (Texas) Municipal Coliseum Apr 22 '68

Macomb (Illinois) Western Illinois University Apr 21 '67, May 14 '74; UBB Western Hall Mar 17 '67

Macon (Georgia) College Oct 27 '68

Madison (Wisconsin) Capitol Theater Jul 23 '64; Dane County Memorial Coliseum Nov 9 '72, Dec 5 '73

Manchester (New Hampshire) John F Kennedy Coliseum Stadium Apr 22 '71

Marysville (California) Memorial Auditorium Nov 22 '63

Massillon (Ohio) Tiger Stadium Aug 17 '73

McAlester (Oklahoma) Oklahoma State Penitentiary Apr 13 '69

Memphis (Tennessee) Ellis Auditorium Amphitheatre Apr 10 '65; Apr 6 '66, Dec 1 '73; Mid-South Coliseum Mar 22 '67, Apr 24 '68, Apr 11 '69, Nov 26 '75, Oct 1 '76

Merced (California) County Fairgrounds Auditorium Dec 28 '62

Miami (Florida) Cameo Theater Sep 17 '64; Convention Center/Hall Apr 15 '65, Apr 9 '66, Feb 10 '67, Apr 14 '68, Apr 5 '69, Apr 1 '72; Newport Hotel Feb 2-8 '71

Milwaukee (Wisconsin) Arena Aug 7 '76; Auditorium Jul 19 '64; County Stadium (Milwaukee Baseball Stadium) Jul 21 '74; Marcus Amphitheater Jul 12 '75; Performing Arts Center Nov 22 '71; State Fair Jul 24 '76

Minneapolis (Minnesota) Civic Center Coliseum Jul 23 '74; Guthrie Theater Nov 19 '65; Metropolitan Stadium Aug 6 '76

Minot (North Dakota) Municipal Auditorium Aug 15 '66; State University Nov 29 '69

Mitchell (South Dakota) Corn Palace Nov 27 '69

Modesto (California) Memorial Auditorium Jun 5 '63

Montclair (New Jersey) State College Mar 18 '72

Monterey (California) Big Sur Folk Festival, Pattee Arena Oct 3 '70

Montgomery (Alabama) Alabama State Coliseum Sep 18 '64, Sep 30 '66; Coliseum Jul 23 '65

Morgantown (West Virginia) University of West Virginia Coliseum Apr 18 '74

Nashville (Tennessee) Municipal Auditorium Jul 19 '65, Apr 12 '69

New Haven (Connecticut) Arena May 5 '65, Aug 8 '68; Coliseum Nov 21 '72, Aug 25 '75, Sep 13 '75

New Orleans (Louisiana) Loyola Field House, Loyola University Apr 18 '68; Municipal Auditorium Apr 9 '65, Apr 10 '74

New Paltz (New York) State University College May 6 '71

New Rochelle (New York) Iona College Jul 24 '66, May 4 '68

New York (New York) Academy Of Music Feb 13 '65; Brooklyn College Dec 18 '73; Carnegie Hall Feb 24 '71, Sep 24 '71, Mar 20-22 '72, Nov 23 '72; Fillmore East Oct 11 '68, Apr 27 '71, Jun 27 '71;

Fordham College Mar 18 '66; Gaelic Park Jul 22 '69; Kingsbridge Armory Jun 29 '71; Madison Square Garden Nov 14 '65, Dec 19 '73, Nov 21 '74, Jan 2 '75, May 10 '75, Jun 12-15 '75, Nov 24-26 '76; Wollman Skating Rink, Central Park Aug 1 '69, Jul 2 '71; Yankee Stadium Jun 10 '65, May 10 '66

Newark (New Jersey) Mosque Theatre Apr 29 '67

Newport Beach (California) Rendezvous Ballroom Dec 23 '61

Niagara Falls (New York) Convention Center Nov 21 '75

Norfolk (Virginia) Scope Arena Apr 7 '73

North Andover (Massachusetts) Merrimack College Apr 28 '71

Notre Dame (Indiana) University Apr 26 '71, Sep 9 '72, May 28 '73

Oakland (California) Coliseum Jun 8 '74, May 24 '75, Jul 2 '76; Civic Auditorium Jul 31 '64, Dec 30 '65; Stadium Dec 15 '76

Oklahoma City (Oklahoma) Municipal Auditorium May 31 '65; Music Hall Nov 11 '72; Myriad Arena May 11 '75; Springlake Park Aug 28-29 '64

Omaha (Nebraska) Civic Auditorium Jul 11 '64, Dec 27 '64, Aug 10 '66, Apr 29 '73, Nov 2 '75

Orlando (Florida) Municipal Auditorium Apr 8 '69; Sports Stadium Apr 14 '74, Nov 30 '75; Tinker Field Stadium Apr 19 '65

Owings Mills (Maryland) Painters Mill Music Fair Apr 30 '71

Oxford (Mississippi) University Of Mississippi Apr 9 '74

Oxford (Ohio) Millett Hall, Miami University May 11 '74

Paramus (New Jersey) Fairleigh Dickinson University May 12 '73

Passaic (New Jersey) Capitol Theater Nov 19 '72, Dec 13 '72

Peoria (Illinois) Bradley University Fieldhouse Feb 17 '67

Philadelphia (Pennsylvania) Convention Hall Feb 12 '65; Spectrum May 4 '68, May 7 '71, Mar 17 '72, Apr 6 '73, Dec 14 '73, Nov 14 '74, Jul 1 '75, Aug 10-11 '76

Phoenix (Arizona) Celebrity Theater Apr 25 '73, Nov 15 '73

Pittsburgh (California) Civic Arena Sep 1 '65

Pittsburgh (Pennsylvania) Civic Arena Apr 17 '74, Sep 6 '75, Jan 19 '76; Penn Theater Apr 16 '67, Nov 22 '67; Syria Mosque Aug 22 '64, Mar 13 '66, Aug 31 '73; Three Rivers Stadium Aug 14 '76

Pittsfield (Massachusetts) Armory Aug 7 '68; Boys Club Aug 8 '68

Plattsburg (New York) New York State University May 9 '71

Pointe Coupee (Louisiana) Celebration Island Jun 24 '71

Pomona (California) Californian Polytechnic, State University Mar 24 '73

Portland (Maine) Ballpark At Old Orchard Beach Jul

15 '65; Civic Auditorium Aug 6 '68

Portland (Oregon) Civic Auditorium Mar 21 '70; Coliseum Jan 27 '65, Sep 25 '65, Aug 19 '66; Feb 4 '68, Dec 13 '74, Sep 20 '75, Dec 15 '75, Sep 21 '76; Paramount Theater Mar 1 '70, Dec 18 '71

Princeton (New Jersey) University Feb 13 '71, Nov 11 '71

Providence (Rhode Island) Alumni Hall, Providence College May 7 '66; Arena May 5 '68; Auditorium Nov 24 '65, Nov 16 '66, Nov 24 '67; Civic Center Nov 18 '75, Nov 18 '76; Loew's State Theater Sep 24 '64, Apr 29 '71

Provo (Utah) Brigham Young University Sep 16 '76

Raleigh (North Carolina) Dorton Arena Jul 12 '65, Apr 23 '68; Pier Apr c.25-29 '65

Redondo Beach (California) Redondo High School Auditorium Apr 21 '62

Reno (Nevada) Arena May 28 '65; State Building Auditorium Jul 30 '64

Richmond (Virginia) Arena Nov 19 '67; Mosque Jan 3 '65, Aug 18 '73

Riverside (California) Haze Feb 18 '73

Rochester (New York) Mayo Civic Center Nov 18 '65; War Memorial Theater/Auditorium Nov 20 '64, Aug 23 '75

Sacramento (California) Hughes Stadium Sep 25 '76; Memorial Auditorium May 24 '63, Sep 14 '63, Nov 23 '63, Dec 19 '63, May 9 '64, Aug 1 '64, Feb 27 '65, Nov 21 '73, Apr 25 '74; National Exhibition Hall Dec 21 '74

St. Louis (Missouri) Arena May 18 '75; Kiel Opera House/Auditorium Jul 15 '64, Nov 21 '65, Mar 20 '67, Apr 27 '73, May 17 '73, Dec 3 '73, Aug 8 '76; University of Missouri Oct 30 '75 **St. Paul** (Minnesota) Civic Center Arena Jul 22 '74, Oct 31 '75; Minneapolis Auditorium Sep 28 '65, Jul 9 '68

St. Petersburg (Florida) Bayfront Center Arena Apr 8 '66; Bayfront Civic Center Auditorium Feb 11 '67

Salem (New Hampshire) Canobie Lake Park Ballroom Jul 6 '65

Salem (Oregon) Armory Dec 16 '71

Salem (Virginia) Civic Center, Salem-Roanoke Valley Oct 25 '68

Salina (Kansas) Bicentennial Center Arena Jul 12 '68

Salt Lake City (Utah) Lagoon Sep 7 '63, Sep 11 '64, May 29 '65; Terrace Ballroom Jul 29 '64, Dec 6 '74

San Antonio (Texas) Auditorium Apr 4 '66, Apr 15 '68, Oct 8 '76

San Bernardino (California) Ralph Swing Auditorium Dec 29 '73, Dec 28 '74, Feb 5 '75

San Carlos (California) Circle Star Theater Dec 29 '65, Apr 28 '66

San Diego (California) Balboa Stadium Jul 8 '65, Aug 9 '75; Coliseum Sep 24 '76; Community Concourse Arena Jul 2 '65; Community Concourse Exhibit Hall Jul 4 '66; Convention Hall Jul 17 '68; Russ Auditorium Aug 8 '64; Sports Arena Feb 26 '65, May 26 '65, Dec 4th '71, Aug 9 '76, Dec 27 '76

San Francisco (California) Civic Auditorium Dec 28 '66, Dec 20 '74; Cow Palace Sep 28 '63, Jul 4 '65,

Jun 24 '66, Feb 19 '73, Jun 13 '74; Winterland Dec 10-11 '71, Dec 10-11 '72, Apr 19 '73, Nov 17-18 '73

San Jose (California) Civic Auditorium Oct 16 '64; Santa Clara County Fairgrounds Feb 28 '64

Sandusky (Ohio) Cedar Point May 2 '74

Santa Barbara (California) Earl Warren Showgrounds/Center Dec 17 '62, Aug 4 '64, Jul 2 '66, Dec 22 '74; University of California, Campus Stadium Mar 23 '75, Sep 26 '76

Santa Catalina Island (California) Avalon Jul 29 '76

Santa Maria (California) Veterans Memorial Stadium Jul 6 '63

Santa Monica (California) Civic Auditorium Dec 27-28 '62, Oct 28 '64, Jan 23-24 '71, Feb 20 '71; Monica Hotel Mar 16-18 '62

Saratoga Springs (New York) Arts Festival Aug 27 '73; Performing Arts Center Aug 26 '76

Schenectady (New York) Municipal Auditorium Apr 29 '67

Scranton (Pennsylvania) University Apr 16 '74

Seattle (Washington) Center/Coliseum Jan 30 '65, Jan 1 '66, Dec 27 '66, Jan 17 '69, Feb 28 '70, Mar 22 '70, Dec 10 '74; Jul 9 '74, Sep 19 '75, Dec 16-17 '75; Dome Stadium Dec 18 '76; Hoquiam Hi-School Gymnasium Feb 21 '64; Opera House Sep 29 '63, Feb 22 '64, Sep 4-5 '64; Paramount Theater Dec 17 '71, Nov 2 '72, Nov 2 '74; Sports Arena Feb 2 '68

Sioux City (South Dakota) Auditorium Nov 26 '69

Sioux Falls (South Dakota) Arena Jul 3 '68, Nov 25 '69

Slippery Rock (Pennsylvania) State College Apr 21 '74

South Bend (Indiana) Notre Dame University Oct 2 '71

South Orange (New Jersey) Seton Hall University Nov 26 '67, Dec 16 '73

Spokane (Washington) Coliseum Aug 19 '66, Jul 22 '68, Dec 9 '74; Kennedy Pavilion Dec 19 '71

Springfield (Illinois) Illinois State Fair Aug 12 '66; Western Illinois University Hall Apr 22 '67

Springfield (Massachusetts) Civic Center Nov 29

'76; College May 1 '71; Shrine Mosque Apr 3 '71

Starkville (Mississippi) Animal Husbandry Service Building, State University Apr 13 '67

Stockton (California) Civic Memorial Auditorium Dec 20 '63; Gold Rush Festival Auditorium Dec 31 '62

Stony Brook (New York) State University Of New York Sep 26 '71

Syracuse (New York) Le Moyne College Athletic Center Nov 18 '67; Manley Field House, Syracuse University May 11 '71; Onondaga County War Memorial Jul 22 '66; State Fairgrounds Sep 2 '75; War Memorial Hall/Auditorium Jul 7 '66, Nov 16 '72

Tacoma (Washington) Pacific Lutheran University Mar 16 '74; UPS Field House Dec 31 '65

Tampa (Florida) Curtis-Hixon Hall Apr 4 '69, Apr 12 '74; Ft Hesterly Hall Apr 2 '72

Teaneck (New Jersey) Fairleigh Dickinson College/University Nov 19 '66, May 6 '73

Tempe (Arizona) Arizona Hall Mar 22 '75

Toledo (Ohio) Sports Arena May 20 '65

Tucson (Arizona) Hi-Corbett Field Jul 16 '68; University of Arizona Auditorium Jul 6 '64

Tulsa (Oklahoma) Assembly Center Jul 10 '64, Dec 19 '64, Mar 19 '67; Bradley Theater Apr 20 '67; State Fair Oct 3 '76

Tuscaloosa (Alabama) University of Alabama Apr 13 '73

Union (New Jersey) Newark State College Theater For The Performing Arts Dec 13 '73

Uniondale (New York) Nassau Coliseum Aug 8 '72, Aug 21 '72, Aug 19 '73, Jun 14 '74, Aug 7 '75, Aug 28 '75, Sep 1 '75, Sep 1 '76

Villanova (Pennsylvania) University Sep 25 '71

Virginia Beach (Virginia) Alan B Shepard Convention Center Jan 2 '65; Dome Apr 3 '69; High School Stadium Jul 29 '66

Waco (Texas) Heart O' Texas Coliseum Feb 12 '69

Wallingford (Connecticut) Oakdale Theater Jul 27 '69

Washington (DC) Coliseum Apr 24 '65, May 3 '68; Daughters Of The American Revolution (DAR) Constitution Hall Nov 19 '67, Nov 22 '72, Dec 12 '73; Georgetown University Nov 7 '71, Dec 12 '72; Monument May 1 '71; National Guard Armory Sep 19 '65

Waterville (Maine) Colby College Mar 7 '73, May 13 '73

Waynesboro (Virginia) Alexandria Roller Rink Aug 27 '72

West Point (New York) US Military Academy Fieldhouse Nov 25 '67

Westbury (New York) Roosevelt Raceway Sep 8 '74

Westchester (California) Loyola Carnival, Loyola University Oct 31 '63

Wheeling (West Virginia) Capital Music Hall Aug 15 '68; West Virginia Fair Aug 22 '63

White Plains (New York) Westchester Community Center Nov 21 '67; Westchester County Center Apr 25 '67

Whittier (California) High School Auditorium Apr 3 '64

Wichita (Kansas) Kemper Arena Feb 6 '65

Wildwood (New Jersey) Convention Hall Sep 1 '72

Williamsburg (Virginia) William & Mary Hall, College of William & Mary Apr 7 '75

Wilmington (Delaware) State Armory Jan 6 '65, Apr 20 '65

Worcester (Massachusetts) Memorial Auditorium Sep 30 '64, May 1 '66; Paris Cinema May 2 '71

Youngstown (Ohio) Bedley Auditorium, State College Apr 21 '74

Ypsilanti (Michigan) Bowens Fieldhouse, Eastern Michigan University Oct 29 '75

Yuba City see Marysville

WALES

See also England, Scotland, Northern Ireland

Cardiff Capitol Theatre Nov 12 '66, Dec 7 '68, Nov 24 '70

Acknowledgements

AUTHOR'S THANKS

In no special order, a roll-call of some of the world's finest rock researchers: Joe McMichael, Doug Hinman, Richard Groothuizen, Rory Fuller, Simon Smith, Alan Smith, Bob Boyer, and The Commander.

Thanks also to...

David Leaf, Mark Linett, Alan Boyd, Tony Rivers, Bob Embrey, Scott Keller, Brad Elliot, Ben Chaput (Rock Video 60s Project), Kingsley Abbott, Earl Leaf, Bob Harris, Mark Lamaar, Tracy Bryant, Michel (Mustomax), Gerard Hubert, Gino Francesconi (Museum Director & Archivist at New York's Carnegie Hall), Andrew G. Doe, Stephanie Bennett, Paul J. MacArthur, George (Geedog), Patrick MacDonald (*Seattle Post-Intelligencer*), Pete & Fenella Walkling, Monica Nåhls (Swedish radio archives), Rolf B. Tiesler, Annette Basse, Michael Kleff, Ken Higa (Japan), Peter Ciraolo, Kim Simmons, Simon Rogers, Tom Koehlert, Neville Stannard, Mike Dalton, Mike Grant, John Hellier, Paul Wayne (Tracks), Andy Neill, Peter Lewry, Steve Holmes, Terry Rawlings, Lois Wilson (*Mojo*), Sylvie Simmons (*Mojo*), Steve Marinucci, Juan Carty, James Fielding, Spencer Pete, Dave Carter, Stephen Rouse, Chris Charlesworth, Ken Sharp, Pete Nash, Laurence Moore, Helen Donlan, Carl Stickley, Carol-Anne Lennie, Anne Marie Trace; my friends and colleagues at *Record*

Collector magazine: Alan Lewis, Joel McIver, Jake Kennedy and Tim Jones; and the wonderful Frederick Vail for sharing with me his absorbing stories about his time with The Beach Boys.

Fan-clubs, websites, fanzines

http://members.tripod.com/~fun_fun_fun/setlists.html (Eric Anniversario's Setlist Archive)
www.aljardine.com (Al's official site)
www.angelfire.com/la/Beachboysbritain (Val Johnson-Howe's UK-oriented site)
www.beachboysfanclub.com (Alice's official fan organisation)
www.brianwilson.com (Brian's official site)
www.cabinessence.net (marvellous Brian web page)
www.carlwilsonfoundation.org (official Carl memorial)
www.esquarterly.com (*Endless Summer Quarterly*)
www.mountvernonandfairway.de (Matthias Hechler's tribute to The Beach Boys)
www.sonic.net/~dsktracy/bbstuff/bbstuff.html (Disk Tracy's Beach Boys Memorabilia site)
www.thesmileshop.net (dedicated to the *Smile* album)
www.thebeachboys.com (official current Beach Boys site)
www.bbstomp.co.uk (Mike Grant's *Beach Boys Stomp* fanzine)
Kie Miskelly & Linda Ranger's *Blueboarders Newsletter*

Books

Brad Elliott *Surf's Up: The Beach Boys On Record 1961-1981* (Helter Skelter 2003)
Steven S. Gaines *Heroes & Villains: The True Story Of The Beach Boys* (Da Capo 1995)
David Leaf *The Beach Boys* (Courage 1985)
Stephen J. McParland *Our Favourite Recording Sessions: In The Studio With Brian Wilson And The Beach Boys* (Cmusic 2000)
Byron Preiss *The Beach Boys: The Authorised Illustrated Biography* (Ballantine 1979)
Domenic Priore *Look! Listen! Vibrate! Smile!* (Last Gasp 1998)
Brian Wilson *Wouldn't It Be Nice: My Own Story* (Bloomsbury 1991)

Newspapers and magazines

Amusement Business (US), *Billboard* (US), *Cheetah* (US), *Creem* (US), *Disc & Music Echo* (UK), *Goldmine* (US), *Melody Maker* (UK), *Mojo* (UK), *Music Now* (UK), *New Musical Express* (UK), *Record Collector* (UK), *Record Mirror* (UK), *Rolling Stone* (US), *Sounds* (UK), *Teen Beat* (US), *Tiger Beat* (US), *Trouser Press* (US), *Variety* (US).

Libraries

BBC Written Archives, Colindale Newspaper Library (special thanks to Jane Walsh and Victor Bristoll), Oxnard Public Library (special thanks to Jo Ann Van Reenan), Slough Public Library, Westminster Reference Library.

TV and radio programmes

Art That Shook The World: Pet Sounds (BBC-2 TV 2003)

The Beach Boys (Vic Kettle's unreleased 1968 European tour documentary)
The Beach Boys: An American Band (High Ridge Productions 1984)
The Beach Boys Story (BBC Radio-1 1974)
Brian Wilson – A Beach Boy's Tale (A&E 1999)
Endless Harmony (Delilah Films 1998)
Smile (BBC Radio-2 1995)
The Story Of The Beach Boys (Veronica TV 1983)

Film, video and tape archives

I have consulted many, many stations worldwide, including ABC Television, BBC Worldwide, BVL Enterprises, Capitol Records, CBS Television, Dave Clark, Dick Clark Productions, E! Network, Radio Bremen (Germany), Westinghouse Productions, ZDF (Germany).

Inspirational thanks must go to Arsene Wenger, still the finest manager in the world and a man who has turned my beloved Arsenal into the greatest football club in the world.

Last and by no means least a very special thanks go to Sheila, Pauline, Michael, Tas, my mother Kathleen (a Beach Boys fan for over 30 years), my agent Lanning Aldrich, to Tony Bacon and Nigel Osborne at Backbeat UK for commissioning this book and sharing my enthusiasm on the project, and to Mark Brend, John Ryall, Phil Richardson, Paul Cooper and Kim Devlin at Backbeat UK. Additional praise must go to Tony Bacon for his wonderful editing of my text and making sense of my thousands of pieces of Beach Boys trivia (and he does love his sources).

PUBLISHER'S THANKS

Paul Cooper (Cleveland Street Sandbox), Kim Devlin, Mark Easter, Debra Geddes (EMI Music London), David Leaf, Mark Linett, Mark London, John Morrish, Odile Noel, Jim Roberts, Jean Sievers (The Lippin Group), Dave Simons, Kim Simmons, Jaap van Eik, and The Commander.

PICTURE CREDITS

The photographs reproduced come from a variety of sources, listed here by page number followed by photographer and/or agency and/or collection. In a few cases, despite our efforts, we could not trace the original photographer, and would welcome any further information. **Jacket**: all Michael Ochs Archives/Redfern's. **2** Michael Ochs Archives/Redfern's. **9** Los Angeles Jazz Institute/CTS Images. **12/13** Ray Avery/CTS Images. **19** Los Angeles Jazz Institute/CTS Images. **20** Pictorial Press. **25** Michael Ochs Archives/Redfern's. **26** Michael Ochs Archives/Redfern's. **27** Michael Ochs Archives/Redfern's. **28** Michael Ochs Archives/Redfern's. **31** Frank Driggs Collection. **43** Michael Ochs Archives/Redfern's. **44** Redfern's. **47** Rex Features. **56** Redfern's. **58** Pictorial Press. **60/61** Michael Ochs Archives/Redfern's. **64/65** Michael Ochs Archives/Redfern's. **68** Retna. **69** Rex Features. **70**

Redfern's. **76/77** Michael Ochs Archives/Redfern's. **78** Michael Ochs Archives/Redfern's. **81** Ray Avery/CTS Images. **87** Michael Ochs Archives/Redfern's. **88** Pictorial Press. **94** Record Collector. **95** Michael Ochs Archives/Redfern's. **107** Michael Ochs Archives/Redfern's. **112/113** Michael Ochs Archives/Redfern's. **117-137** all Michael Ochs Archives/Redfern's. **138** Pictorial Press. **140** Pictorial Press. **141** Michael Ochs Archives/Redfern's. **143** Pictorial Press. **154** Michael Ochs Archives/Redfern's. **158** Jan Persson. **159** Record Collector. **171** Pictorial Press. **176** Jasper Dailey/© David Leaf Productions. **177** Jasper Dailey/© David Leaf Productions. **183** London Features International. **184** Pictorial Press. **185** Pictorial Press. **186** Pictorial Press. **191** Frank Driggs Collection. **196** Michael Ochs Archives/Redfern's. **198** Michael Ochs Archives/Redfern's. **209** Pictorial Press. **211** Private Collection. **213** Redfern's. **226/227** Retna. **228** Pictorial Press. **233** Record Collector. **235** SKR/Record Collector. **237** Alec Byrne/Record Collector. **239** Rex Features. **245** London Features International. **246/247** Rex Features. **249** Rex Features. **254/255** Pictorial Press. **261** Record Collector. **263** Private Collection. **265** Private Collection. **267** Private Collection. **269** Private Collection. **271** Private Collection. **276** Pictorial Press. **280/281** Emerson-Loew. **282** Barry Plummer. **283** Pictorial Press. **284** Pictorial Press. **285** Pictorial Press. **286** Amalie R. Rothschild. **291** Amalie R. Rothschild. **292** Bob Jenkins. **293** Bob Jenkins. **294/295** Bob Jenkins. **302/303** Record Collector. **305** AVRO. **307** Bob Jenkins. **309** London Features International. **310** Record Collector. **311** Record Collector. **312** SKR/Record Collector. **314/315** Redfern's. **317** Michael Ochs Archives/Redfern's. **318** London Features International. **319** Record Collector. **325** Pictorial Press. **335** London Features International. **337** London Features International. **341** Michael Ochs Archives/Redfern's. **345** London Features International. **349** Record Collector. **352/353** Redfern's. **354** Redfern's. **357** Pictorial Press. **359** Pictorial Press. **360/361** Michael Ochs Archives/Redfern's. **365** Redfern's. **372** Michael Ochs Archives/Redfern's. **378** Redfern's.

UPDATES

If you have any additions or corrections to the material in this book, the author would be pleased to hear from you. He may be contacted by email:
beachboy@backbeatuk.com
or you can write to him:
Keith Badman, c/o Backbeat Books, 2A Union Court, 20-22 Union Road, London SW4 6JP, England.

"The harmonies we were able to produce gave us a uniqueness, which is really the only important thing you can put into records: some quality no one else has got into."
Brian Wilson *Melody Maker* 1964